CIVIL DISPUTE RESOLUTION

BALANCING THEMES AND THEORY

Understanding how to resolve conflicts between private parties is essential for Australian lawyers. *Civil Dispute Resolution: Balancing Themes and Theory* presents a comprehensive framework within which both civil procedure and alternative dispute resolution are addressed. This framework, based on balancing competing objectives of dispute resolution, simplifies and explains the many aspects of resolving disagreements between private parties.

This book guides readers through every aspect of civil dispute resolution, including the interaction between negotiation, mediation, arbitration and litigation as means to resolve civil disputes and the many stages of litigation — from the commencement of proceedings through to judgment and enforcement. The 'balancing' themes are applied to demystify the resolution of civil disputes, including the role of specialist courts and tribunals, alternatives to court proceedings, pleadings, gathering documentary and witness evidence, legal costs, and trial preparation and attendance.

Civil Dispute Resolution uses clear definitions and examples from every Australian state and territory to provide an engaging and thorough analysis of resolving civil disputes.

Sonya Willis is a Senior Lecturer researching and teaching in civil procedure and professional skills and practice at the Macquarie University Law School.

CIVIL DISPUTE RESOLUTION

BALANCING THEMES AND THEORY

Sonya Willis

CAMBRIDGE
UNIVERSITY PRESS

CAMBRIDGE
UNIVERSITY PRESS

University Printing House, Cambridge CB2 8BS, United Kingdom

One Liberty Plaza, 20th Floor, New York, NY 10006, USA

477 Williamstown Road, Port Melbourne, VIC 3207, Australia

314–321, 3rd Floor, Plot 3, Splendor Forum, Jasola District Centre, New Delhi – 110025, India

103 Penang Road, #05–06/07, Visioncrest Commercial, Singapore 238467

Cambridge University Press is part of the University of Cambridge.

It furthers the University's mission by disseminating knowledge in the pursuit of education, learning and research at the highest international levels of excellence.

www.cambridge.org
Information on this title: www.cambridge.org/9781316606346

First published by Palgrave Macmillan as *Civil Procedure* in 2012
First published by Cambridge University Press in 2022

Cover designed by Carolina Kerr
Typeset by Integra Software Services Pvt. Ltd
Printed in China by C & C Offset Printing Co., Ltd, October 2021

A catalogue record for this publication is available from the British Library

A catalogue record for this book is available from the National Library of Australia

ISBN 978-1-316-60634-6 Paperback

Additional resources for this publication at
https://www.cambridge.org/highereducation/isbn/9781316606346/resources

Please be aware that this publication may contain several variations of Aboriginal and Torres Strait Islander terms and spellings; no disrespect is intended. Please note that the terms 'Indigenous Australians' and 'Aboriginal and Torres Strait Islander peoples' may be used interchangeably in this publication.

FOREWORD

This work is a comprehensive thematic analysis of the current state of civil dispute resolution in Australia and an impressive display of many decades of work in practice and academia.

It is both an important and timely reminder of the fundamentally human and social nature of legal disputes, that is, that they inescapably arise out of and impact upon human relationships and emotions. In both content and form, this work reflects the author's appreciation that established rules and procedures in civil dispute resolution, whilst serving some utility in and of themselves, are first and foremost developed to manage the confluence and necessary conflict of social and moral objectives which arise when the justice system is engaged. Those social and moral objectives include efficiency, fair procedure, careful reasoned decision-making, predictability, flexibility and access to and open justice. A resolute focus on taxonomy and minutiae, not uncommon amongst some practitioners, fails to appreciate the context within which words and rules operate. With an appreciation of the human context, practitioners may engage in civil dispute resolution in a more flexible, cooperative and pragmatic way in fulfilling their duties to the Court and client.

This thematic focus comes at a particularly relevant moment of reflection as the COVID-19 pandemic accelerated civil practice into online spaces. In order to ensure the good and proper integration of technology into court and alternative dispute resolution processes, we, that is judges, the profession and broader community, must understand and converse about the overarching and underlying driving themes and theories of litigation and civil dispute resolution so that we may engage in what Dr Willis calls "contemplation of realistic reform". Technology has and will continue to go some way towards reducing costs and increasing access to and open justice, however, that cannot be taken as given, nor does it say anything about the impact on other objectives. It is only with the benefit of a broader lens that we can critically assess whether and how any reforms further or detract from the aims of the justice system.

Dr Willis points out that courts have and perhaps always will have an intractable image problem. Whilst improvements certainly can and must be made, this thematic analysis recognises that litigation will almost always be unsatisfactory to someone at some stage. Whilst delivery of perfect justice through the court system may be a noble aspiration, it may also be a fool's errand. The courts are places where these competing objectives collide most acutely. As "caretakers" (a label coined by Dr Willis which neatly encompasses this role) courts must grapple with these conflicts and competitions day-to-day and at all levels. Active case management ensures a focus on the real issues and an appreciation of the human elements, as well as providing the space for ongoing reflection and nuanced problem-solving. This is an imperfect balancing act, but one which we must continue to perform and strive to improve because it is trust in the courts' ability to manage competently and fairly these competing moral and social objectives by which justice is measured.

One of the most important insights of this valuable and rewarding work is that dispute resolution is about legal and human problem-solving, which requires a legal culture dedicated to problem-solving and the necessary co-operation involved, and not just to process and rules. Problem-solving (with a necessary degree of co-operation between litigants and their lawyers) is at the heart of the variously expressed overarching purposes of different courts which emphasise the not always reconcilable requirements of justice, speed and efficiency, and reasonable and proportionate expense.

Dr Willis is to be congratulated on the work, which deserves to be widely read.

The Honourable James Allsop
Chief Justice of the Federal Court of Australia

CONTENTS

PREFACE

This book is the culmination of several decades of practice, research and teaching in civil dispute resolution (CDR). What began as a hunch became increasingly concrete: that there were a very small number of very challenging balancing acts which pervaded, shaped, defined and explained the resolution of civil disputes. This book employs these balancing themes to explain the resolution of civil disputes in Australia, why CDR is such a vexed and criticised area of law, why there are so many conflicts which can never be resolved, why CDR will remain expensive, time-consuming and unpleasant and why, paradoxically, all this makes perfect logical sense and is rarely evidence of any systemic failure.

Australian states and territories are not uniform, and their idiosyncrasies sometimes display themselves in their differing dispute resolution procedures, and the Acts and rules regulating them. This book attempts to identify and, where possible, explain these differences while simultaneously demonstrating the strong thread of uniformity throughout Australia which is caused as much by shared legal history, a single High Court and common underlying principles as by recent explicit efforts to increase uniformity. In the current environment, where legislation changes frequently and cases and legislation are freely and readily available on the internet, there is little benefit to setting out detailed procedural provisions or lengthy case extracts. However, brief extracts from cases and, occasionally, legislation have been incorporated into this book where these demonstrate the principles and concepts of CDR. I owe a huge debt of gratitude to the Australian judiciary for so frequently providing such succinct and wonderful analyses of key legal principles.

The law discussed in this book is up to date to the best of my knowledge as at February 2021.

Dr Sonya Willis
February 2021

ACKNOWLEDGEMENTS AND DEDICATION

I would like to acknowledge the incredible patience and positivity of the editorial team at Cambridge University Press whose assistance and encouragement have been invaluable. I would also like to thank my colleagues, particularly Keith Williams, Teresa Somes, Shireen Daft, Holly Doel-Mackaway, Zara Bending and Yi Wong and the many people who have fuelled my interest in civil dispute resolution, including the Civil Justice Research Group and my many inspiring students who have written CDR theses. I would also like to thank Austlii, Jade and First Point for always being there with cases and legislation.

Most importantly, I would like to thank my family for their tolerance and support without which I simply could not have found the time necessary to research and write this book. I dedicate this book to James, Jonathan, Felicity, Anastasia and Genevieve.

Dr Sonya Willis
February 2021

Permissions acknowledgements

The author and Cambridge University Press would like to thank the following for permission to reproduce material in this book.

Figure 14.1: © Federal Register of Legislation. Reproduced under Creative Commons Attribution 4.0 International. For the latest information on Australian Government law please go to https://www.legislation.gov.au.

Extracts from *Report on the Statutory Review of the Tribunals Amalgamation Act 2015*; *Report on the Statutory Review of the Tribunals Amalgamation Act 2016*; *2014 Access to Justice Report*: © Commonwealth of Australia. Source reproduced under Creative Commons Attribution 3.0 Australia Licence (https://creativecommons.org/licenses/by/3.0/au/).

Extracts from the High Court of Australia: Reproduced with permission of the High Court of Australia.

Extracts from New South Wales Court of Appeal; New South Wales Supreme Court; New South Wales state legislation; New South Wales Land and Environment Court: © State of New South Wales (Department of Justice). For current information go to www.justice.nsw.gov.au. Reproduced under CC BY 4.0 licence.

Extracts from *Australian Law Journal Reports*; *Commonwealth Law Reports*: Reproduced with permission of Thomson Reuters (Professional) Australia Limited, legal.thomsonreuters.com.au.

Extracts from Supreme Court of Victoria: © Supreme Court of Victoria.

Extracts from Federal Court of Australia: © Federal Court of Australia. Reproduced under Creative Commons Attribution 3.0 Australia Licence (https://creativecommons.org/licenses/by/3.0/au/).

Extracts from Commonwealth legislation: Sourced from the Federal Register of Legislation. Reproduced under Creative Commons Attribution 4.0 International. For the latest information on Australian Government law please go to https://www.legislation.gov.au.

Extracts from Supreme Court of Tasmania: Reproduced with permission from the Council of Law Reporting for Tasmania.

Extracts from South Australia Supreme Court: © South Australia Supreme Court.

Extracts from ACT Civil and Administrative Tribunal: © Government of the Australian Capital Territory.

Extracts from South Australian state legislation: © State of South Australia. Reproduced under Creative Commons Attribution 4.0 International (CC BY 4.0). Sourced from the South Australian Legislation website at January 2019. For the latest information on South Australian Government legislation, please go to www.legislation.sa.gov.au/.

Extracts from Victorian Court of Appeal: © Victorian Court of Appeal.

Extracts from *New South Wales Law Reports*: © Council of Law Reporting for New South Wales. Reproduced with permission of the Council of Law Reporting for NSW.

Every effort has been made to trace and acknowledge copyright. The publisher apologises for any accidental infringement and welcomes information that would redress this situation.

ABBREVIATIONS

AAT	Administrative Appeals Tribunal
ACAT	ACT Civil and Administrative Tribunal
ACCS	Accident Compensation Conciliation Service (Vic)
ACICA	Australian Centre for International Commercial Arbitration
ADC	Australian Disputes Centre
ADR	alternative dispute resolution
AHRC	Australian Human Rights Commission
ANZOA	Australian and New Zealand Ombudsman Association
ASIO	Australian Security Intelligence Organisation
CAG	Council of Attorneys-General
CDR	civil dispute resolution
CLP	client professional privilege
COAT	Council of Australasian Tribunals
EDR	external dispute resolution
FOI	Freedom of Information
LCCSC	Law, Crime and Community Safety Council
LPP	legal professional privilege
LPUL	*Legal Profession Uniform Law*
NADRAC	National Alternative Dispute Resolution Advisory Council
NCAT	New South Wales Civil and Administrative Tribunal
NMAS	National Mediator Accreditation System
NST	National Sports Tribunal
NTCAT	Northern Territory Civil and Administrative Tribunal
QCAT	Queensland Civil and Administrative Tribunal
RI	Resolution Institute
RMAB	Recognised Mediator Accreditation Boards
RMPAT	Resource Management and Planning Appeal Tribunal (Tas)

SACAT	South Australian Civil and Administrative Tribunal
SAT	State Administrative Tribunal (WA)
SCAG	Standing Committee of Attorneys-General
TasCAT	Tasmanian Civil and Administrative Tribunal
UEL	Uniform Evidence Law
VCAT	Victorian Civil and Administrative Tribunal

TABLE OF CASES

TABLE OF STATUTES

Australia

Australian Capital Territory

New South Wales

Northern Territory

Queensland

South Australia

Tasmania

Victoria

Western Australia

International instruments

PART 1

CIVIL DISPUTES AND THEIR MEANS OF RESOLUTION

1 INTRODUCTION TO CIVIL DISPUTE RESOLUTION

1.1 Overview

A civil dispute is one which arises between private parties (including governments acting in their private capacity) and excludes criminal prosecutions.

This chapter will introduce the themes and theory of civil dispute resolution (CDR) and explain the structure and limitations of this book to assist readers in navigating through the chapters. This chapter will also introduce the procedures for resolving civil disputes, each of which will be canvassed in more detail in subsequent chapters. While this book need not be read cover to cover, it is recommended that Chapters 1, 2 and 3 be read first as they are fundamental to understanding the remainder of the book.

1.1.1 The theory and themes in civil dispute resolution

The theory underpinning this book is that the complexities, strengths and flaws of Australia's dispute resolution processes can all be explained and rationalised through a relatively small number of key themes. The themes running through CDR each concern the balancing of competing objectives. These objectives are procedural fairness, procedural efficiency, open justice and judicial discretion. Chapter 2 explores how these competing objectives explain and influence the operation of CDR and how their conflicting nature explains the difficulties which plague procedures designed to resolve disputes. Chapter 3 continues the thematic analysis of CDR, focusing on the desirable but impossible aim of courts to provide access to justice and open justice, and how these justice-based objectives interact with non-court-based dispute resolution. These key themes and theories inform all CDR procedures discussed throughout this book.

Australia, as a federation of states, in many ways operates as nine separate jurisdictions (six states, two territories and the federal jurisdiction). Formal methods of CDR — civil procedure — varies between different states and territories but there is significant and increasing uniformity between different jurisdictions within Australia due, in large part, to the key CDR themes which this book argues are central to CDR. This book will outline dispute resolution practices federally and in each state and territory; however, cases and legislation will be used by way of example rather than as exhaustive statement of the law each jurisdiction.

This book argues that key underlying themes apply to all aspects of Australian CDR enabling comprehension of its mechanics as a rational cohesive system rather than as a series of disparate rules and regulations.

1.1.2 Structure of the book

In most instances, this book uses one or two examples of statutory provisions or cases from one or two sample jurisdictions to explain concepts and principles. The examples are selected from all states and territories as well as the federal jurisdiction in Australia. Where useful, the legislative framework for each state commands a separate subheading; however, the key themes, which form the focus of this book, apply in all Australian jurisdictions.

This book is divided into two parts. Part 1, comprising Chapters 1 to 7, introduces CDR, its core themes and theory and their application to the resolution of disputes. Part 1 also considers how different aspects and players in CDR interact with each other. Chapters 1 to 3 explain the key themes of CDR. Chapters 4 to 7 apply these themes to the resolution of disputes outside the formal court system and through interactions with the formal court system. Part 2, comprising Chapters 8 to 17, explores how the themes and theories of CDR play out in litigation. Litigation is the last resort for CDR but also plays a critical role as the formal legislative and institutional backdrop against which all civil disputes are resolved. Litigation, and the shadow it casts over all aspects of CDR, defines and motivates all the key themes of dispute resolution, justifying the dedication of so many chapters to it.

1.1.3 Legislative and case examples

This book contains short extracts from cases and occasional statutory provisions. These extracts have been chosen because they summarise the relevant principles concisely and authoritatively. Readers should pay close attention to the jurisdiction of extracted cases to assist in placing the material and identifying the relevant legal background of the extract. Case extracts are generally selected to provide excellent summaries of High Court authority on a principle. The criteria for choosing examples of statutory provisions and cases throughout this book is as follows:

- **Authoritative**: All case examples will be from the High Court, Federal Court or Supreme Courts (particularly appellate division) to ensure the examples have the maximum precedent value.
- **Recent**: Recent cases and legislation will be preferred for examples. In relation to case law, newer cases have a higher precedent value and routinely refer to prior authoritative

decisions, including those from different states and territories. In relation to legislation, the movement towards uniformity both within states and nationally means that the more recent statutes are most likely to be reflective of CDR trends expected to apply in the next 10 years throughout Australia.

- **Representative**: This book will endeavour to provide examples of legislation and cases from all jurisdictions while taking into consideration that populous states and litigious states produce a larger percentage of recent authoritative examples.

Cases have been cited using the most authoritative report available at the time of publication. For all case extracts and references to specific points within cases, pinpoint citations are generally to the relevant paragraph numbers within cases. Use of paragraph pinpoints means readers can easily locate the referenced material using any report of a case, as well as unreported versions published freely through services such as Austlii and Jade. However, readers referring to cases in their research should note that, where compliance with *Australian Guide to Legal Citation* 4th Edition (AGLC4) is required, authorised report page references should be used in place of (or in addition to) paragraph references for pinpoint citations."[1]

1.1.4 Limitations in scope for jurisdictional variations

It is beyond the scope of this book to exhaustively list the legislation and rules governing civil procedure in each court in each state and territory. Where civil procedure legislation is not uniform in a particular state or territory, only the procedure governing the Supreme Court of that state or territory will be discussed.

Even where civil procedure legislation is uniform throughout a state, such as in New South Wales, the uniform legislation is not an exhaustive statement of all procedure for any given court. Differentiation between courts persists and individual courts can and will continue to issue practice notes and other directions specific to users of that court and, in many instances, specific to certain types of litigation.

1.1.5 Limitations on currency

Civil procedure law is in a constant state of flux. Most Australian jurisdictions have substantially amended their civil procedure and evidence legislation in the past decade. Even where rules and acts may appear from their enactment dates to be old, it is likely they have undergone significant and recent amendment. The various law reform bodies are constantly reviewing aspects of civil procedure and the practice of law and dispute resolution is fluid so future legislative change is inevitable. This book endeavours to capture the state of CDR as at mid-2020.

1.1.6 Linguistic note

The issue as to use of gender specific language arises in this book, as in any other. CDR commonly involves corporations as well as individuals. Therefore, a "party" to a dispute may

1 Use of authorised report page numbers for pinpoint references is specified in AGLC4 Paragraph 2.2.5 for authorised reports of cases.

properly be "he", "she" or "it." To preserve gender neutrality and enable linguistic simplicity, wherever pronouns are required "it" is the preferred pronoun for generic references to parties.

Similarly, this book requires constant reference to the different states and territories in Australia. In some instances, the term "states" has been used to mean "states and territories" to simplify the sentence. It is hoped that readers from the Northern Territory and the Australian Capital Territory will forgive this ellipsis.

1.1.7 Using this book as a resource

This book is a single work designed to flow from start to finish. In order to properly understand this theory of CDR, it is necessary to read Chapters 1, 2 and 3. However, each chapter (and even sub-chapter) should be also accessible to a researcher seeking the answer to a specific question.

1.2 Terminology of civil dispute resolution

CDR encompasses all the means by which disputes between private parties may be resolved. These means of dispute resolution are commonly separated into civil procedure and alternative dispute resolution (ADR) and this book will also separate them in this way. However, it is critical to appreciate that civil procedure and ADR are inextricably intertwined and that the operation of both are relevant to the resolution of most civil disputes.

1.2.1 Defining civil procedure

Civil procedure, as opposed to criminal procedure, might be described as the body of law governing litigation undertaken by private parties who are mostly individuals and corporations. Litigation means court proceedings where the outcome is determinative and is made by an independent decision-maker.

Civil procedure can also involve government organisations but excludes criminal litigation — cases where the Crown prosecutes an individual or corporation for offences or breaches of legislation. Hence, a litigation between the State of Queensland and a developer in relation to a contract for development, such as occurred in the High Court case of *Queensland v JL Holdings Pty Ltd*,[2] is a civil litigation governed by civil procedure.

1.2.2 Defining alternative dispute resolution

Alternative dispute resolution (ADR), sometimes described as appropriate dispute resolution, refers to means of resolving civil disputes outside of court proceedings.[3] The most common forms of ADR used to resolve civil disputes are negotiation, mediation, conciliation and arbitration. The only common feature of ADR is the resolution of a dispute outside the court setting and this is the basis for the term "alternative".

2 *Queensland v JL Holdings Pty Ltd* (1997) 189 CLR 146.

3 Jeffrey Scott Wolfe, 'Across the Ripple of Time: The Future of Alternative (Or, is it "Appropriate?") Dispute Resolution' (2001) 36(4) *Tulsa Law Journal* 785.

The difficulty with such a broad definition of ADR is that, arguably, any form of CDR not involving a court determination is ADR. However, this book will limit its analysis of ADR to appropriate and legal forms of ADR and will thus exclude improper and illegal means of resolving disputes between private parties such as violence, blackmail, extortion and undue influence.

1.2.3 Defining procedure

Essentially, the law governing dispute resolution can be divided into substantive law and procedural law. The substantive law relates to the substance of the claim, being the issues in dispute. The procedural law governs where and how the claim is to be heard.

The division between substantive and procedural law is not always simple and the division can have significant consequences. The grey area between substance and procedure revolves around questions of when a claim can be made and in what circumstances. Disputes arise where there is a conflict between the applicable substantive law and the applicable procedural law on questions such as the time limit or preconditions required for making a claim. Such conflicts are relatively rare but can occur in circumstances where the substantive law is governed by a different jurisdiction from the procedural law or where the law has changed between the time of the dispute arising and the time of the hearing.

For example, in the Queensland case of *Taylor v Queensland Law Society Inc*,[4] Mrs Taylor had claimed from the Queensland Legal Practitioners Fidelity Guarantee Fund in respect of money allegedly misappropriated by her solicitor in breach of his trust money obligations. There was a dispute as to whether the statutory limitations on the claim were governed by the old *Legal Profession Act 2004* (Qld) or the new *Legal Profession Act 2007* (Qld) as the alleged breach occurred in August 2003 but the claim was made in August 2008. It was held that the claim was not a nullity and that s 24(3) of the *Queensland Law Society Acts Amendment Act of 1952* (Qld) was the law governing the liability of the Fund in respect of the appellant's claim by virtue of s 742(2)(b) of the *Legal Profession Act 2007* (Qld) (ie the new Act).

In *Taylor's* case, extracted below, Daubney J cites the two leading High Court cases on the distinction between procedure and substance: *John Pfeiffer Pty Ltd v Rogerson*[5] and *McKain v RW Miller & Co (South Australia) Pty Ltd*.[6] Unlike *Taylor's* case, both *Rogerson* and *McKain* involved disputes where the applicable substantive law was governed by a different jurisdiction to the relevant procedural law:

> [41] Issues concerning procedural provisions and substantive provisions commonly arise when considering the retrospective operation of legislation.
>
> [42] The distinction between procedural and substantive issues was explained in the joint judgment of Gleeson CJ, Gaudron, McHugh, Gummow and Hayne JJ in *John Pfeiffer Pty Ltd v Rogerson*, in which their Honours said (omitting citations):
>
> > 97 As already indicated, the choice of law rules traditionally distinguish between questions of substance and questions of procedure. There is much history that lies behind the distinction, but search as one may, it is very hard, if not impossible, to identify some unifying principle which would assist in making the distinction in a particular case. But, as the majority said in *McKain*:

4 *Taylor v Queensland Law Society Inc* [2011] QSC 8.
5 *John Pfeiffer Pty Ltd v Rogerson* (2000) 203 CLR 503.
6 *McKain v RW Miller & Co (South Australia) Pty Ltd* (1992) 174 CLR 1.

> Though the dividing line is sometimes doubtful or even artificial, the need to distinguish between substantive law and procedural law is clearly recognised for a number of forensic purposes.
>
> Some statutes of limitation have traditionally been held to be procedural on the basis that they bar the remedy not the right; other limitation provisions have been held to be substantive. But all limitation provisions can affect whether a plaintiff recovers. Questions of what heads of damage are allowable have been held to be substantive; but questions of quantification of damages have been held to be procedural. But all questions about damages can affect how much a plaintiff recovers and, thus, statutes such as the NSW Compensation Act, which is in issue in this case, alter the rights of plaintiffs and, also, the obligations of defendant.
>
> Two guiding principles should be seen as lying behind the need to distinguish between substantive and procedural issues. First, litigants who resort to a court to obtain relief must take the court as they find it. A plaintiff cannot ask that a tribunal which does not exist in the forum (but does in the place where a wrong was committed) should be established to deal, in the forum, with the claim that the plaintiff makes. Similarly, the plaintiff cannot ask that the courts of the forum adopt procedures or give remedies of a kind which their constituting statutes do not contemplate any more than the plaintiff can ask that the court apply any adjectival law other than the laws of the forum. Secondly, matters that affect the existence, extent or enforceability of the rights or duties of the parties to an action are matters that, on their face, appear to be concerned with issues of substance, not with issues of procedure. Or to adopt the formulation put forward by Mason CJ in *McKain*, "rules which are directed to governing or regulating the mode or conduct of court proceedings" are procedural and all other provisions or rules are to be classified as substantive.
>
> These principles may require further elucidation in subsequent decisions but it should be noted that giving effect to them has significant consequences for the kinds of case in which the distinction between substance and procedure has previously been applied. First, the application of any limitation period, whether barring the remedy or extinguishing the right, would be taken to be a question of substance not procedure (which is the result arrived at by the statutes previously referred to). The application of any limitation period would, therefore, continue to be governed (as that legislation requires) by the *lex loci delicti*. Secondly, all questions about the kinds of damage, or amount of damages that may be recovered, would likewise be treated as substantive issues governed by the *lex loci delicti*.
>
> [43] In my view, s 24(3) of the QLSA is not merely procedural. By its terms, it clearly goes to the substance of a person's entitlement to make a claim on the Fund....[7]

1.3 Means of civil dispute resolution

There are, arguably, infinite means of resolving civil disputes. However, in practice, most CDR methods[8] can be summarised into the two broad sub-categories of ADR and litigation

7 *Taylor v Queensland Law Society Inc* [2011] QSC 8, [41]–[43]. See also *Rowe v Electoral Commissioner* (2010) 243 CLR 1, [152].

8 This analysis excludes illegal means of resolving disputes, such as violence.

Figure 1.1 Substance v procedure Venn diagram

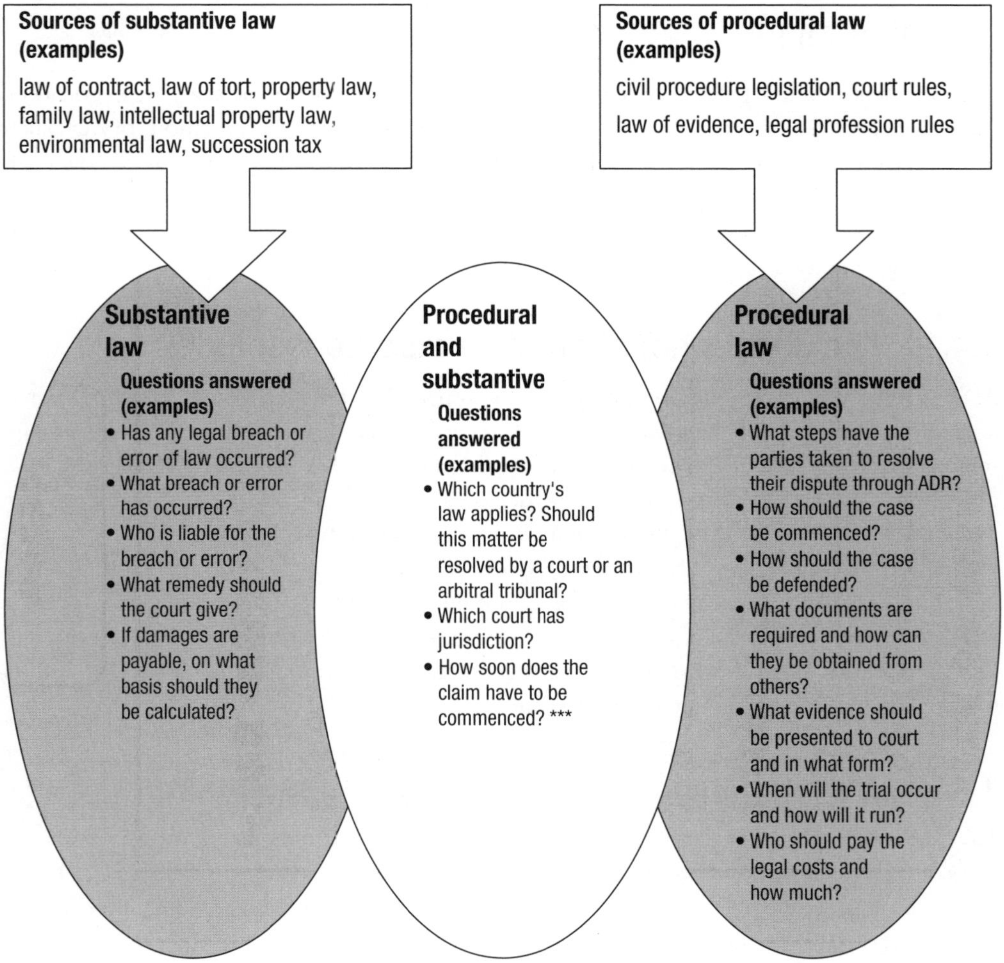

*** In some instances, inherently procedural questions are held to be substantive because their answers fundamentally affect the substantive entitlements of the parties.

identified above. Any course of action parties take which successfully resolves their dispute qualifies as CDR and this may include using ADR processes to enter into new contracts, agreeing to forgive and forget and numerous other options which do not directly involve money changing hands. Parties do not always realise they are engaged in CDR and may not even appreciate that they are in dispute. It is also common for disputes to be resolved through the combination of multiple forms of CDR. For example, parties may negotiate some issues to resolution, mediate their way through other complexities, commence litigation and then, through pre-trial litigation processes such as discovery, realise the real issues in dispute and negotiate a final settlement before any hearing. There is also increasing recognition of the role of ADR in CDR by courts and civil procedure legislation which will often direct parties to ADR prior to and during proceedings.[9]

9 See Chapter 5 for further detail.

1.4 Alternatives to court for dispute resolution

The four most common types of ADR in Australia in ascending order of formality are negotiation, mediation, conciliation and arbitration. There are also a variety of hybrid methods of ADR such as med-arb (combining mediation with arbitration). There are endless variations of how each of these forms of ADR can proceed and it is possible for parties to undertake multiple forms of ADR in a single day or to undertake a hybrid of two types of ADR. ADR will be discussed in detail in Chapter 4 once the key themes of CDR have been explored in Chapters 2 and 3.

1.4.1 The concept of alternative dispute resolution

ADR involves skills we begin learning as children and is practiced daily in school yards and family homes. ADR has been around forever because humans have been informally negotiating resolutions to their disputes for centuries before courts ever existed, let alone practitioners in the business of selling ADR services. ADR should not be construed narrowly, as to do so is to understate its importance to the proper functioning of society and its interaction with litigation. ADR varies between cultures and legal systems but is strongly based in societal concepts of cooperation and mutual benefit. Many lawyers who specialise in litigation routinely write offers of settlement, agree to compromises on scope of evidence and otherwise engage in ADR. This work recognises the enormous breadth of ADR and its fundamental interconnectedness with litigation.

1.4.2 Theory behind alternative dispute resolution

The philosophy of ADR can essentially be summarised as doing everything possible to resolve a dispute without needing a judge in a court to hand down judgment. The bases for desiring alternatives to judicial determination intertwine with the key theories of dispute resolution. Parties seek efficiency by way of reduced cost and reduced time, and to maximise party autonomy for party privacy, to protect party reputation and for other aims which relate to retention of party control of the dispute resolution process. Litigation represents relinquishing control of the decision and the decision-making process to a higher authority and is, therefore, rightly viewed as a last resort by most disputants.

1.4.3 Introducing negotiation

Negotiation is by far the most common and versatile means of CDR and occurs in every dispute with varying degrees of success. Negotiation can occur many times in different contexts during the resolution of a single civil dispute. Negotiation itself varies considerably but is the only form of ADR that rarely involves any third party. Most negotiation involves only the parties and/or their legal representatives. Conferences, correspondence (particularly settlement offers), informal meetings and telephone calls are all common means by which parties negotiate. Some negotiation can occur within the context of litigation and may even be imposed on parties as a requirement by courts. Negotiation can be aimed at completely settling a dispute or at smaller goals such as coming to agreement on one step in another dispute resolution process; for example, agreeing the parameters for discovery in litigation (see Chapter 11). Negotiation can be through formal offers to settle disputes and agreement to settle can then be verified by a Deed of Settlement where the negotiation is successful. Negotiation is discussed in more detail in Chapter 4.

1.4.4 Introducing mediation

Mediation is widely used in Australia. It involves the parties, sometimes their lawyers, and a third-party independent mediator who may be accredited as a mediator. Mediation is confidential, non-binding, flexible and can be relatively inexpensive although this depends somewhat on the mediator and other factors. The mediator facilitates communications between the parties in an attempt to bring the parties to agreement. It is common for courts to order parties litigating to attend mediation and for court rules and civil procedure legislation to encourage or require litigating parties to attempt mediation. Mediation is discussed in more detail in Chapter 4 and court-ordered mediation in Chapter 5.

1.4.5 Introducing conciliation

Conciliation is similar to mediation in many respects. In fact, it is difficult to accurately differentiate mediation and conciliation as neither term is consistently defined or applied in legal literature or common parlance. However, the most important distinction is that conciliators will often have expertise in the substance area of the dispute and are allowed to advise the parties including advice as to possible settlement agreements.[10] Like mediation, conciliation varies considerably depending on the circumstances of the conciliation, the nature of the dispute, the administration of the conciliation and the personal style of the conciliator. Conciliation is discussed in more detail in Chapter 4.

1.4.6 Introducing arbitration

Arbitration is the most formal means of ADR. Arbitration is similar to litigation because it is determinative. Parties agree to allow someone else, the arbitrator, to determine their dispute. The decision of the arbitrator (or tribunal of arbitrators) is final and binding on the parties. The most significant difference between arbitration and litigation is that the parties must choose to go to arbitration, whereas only the plaintiff must choose litigation with the defendant being forced into the process by the court's processes and enforcement mechanisms.

The other significant difference between arbitration and litigation is the rules of evidence and procedure employed by arbitral tribunals which are generally less formal and costly than their court equivalents. Arbitration will be discussed in Chapter 4.

Compulsory statutory tribunals are not a form of ADR because they are the only litigation path available to disputants with disputes encompassed by the relevant statutes. Statutory tribunals will be considered in Chapter 7.

10 National Alternative Dispute Resolution Advisory Council, *A Fair Say: Managing Differences in Mediation and Conciliation: A Guide for All Involved* (Commonwealth of Australia, 1999).

1.5 Alternative dispute resolution bodies

Although ADR has existed informally since before litigation was invented, ADR has become far more formalised in recent decades. This increased profile and legitimacy is reflected through the creation of bodies administering ADR processes and the formalisation of ADR standards. From 1985 to 2013, the Australian Attorney General's Department was advised by a government-funded body called the National Alternative Dispute Resolution Advisory Council (NADRAC). NADRAC published discussion papers, issues papers, statements of principle and reports on ADR for the public, ADR practitioners and the government.

There are also a number of private associations which advise or assist in ADR processes. The Mediators Standards Board is a public company limited by guarantee owned by its members responsible for administering the National Mediator Accreditation System (NMAS) which was introduced in 2008. Other private institutions include the Resolution Institute (RI), the Australian Centre for International Commercial Arbitration (ACICA) and the Australian Disputes Centre (ADC).

There are also a large number of government-run ADR bodies which deal with disputes individuals have with government and quasi-government bodies, and with essential services such as power, telecommunications, water, banking, aged care and privacy (even where such services are privatised). These bodies are sometimes described as external dispute resolution (EDR). The dispute resolution process will usually be managed through a commission (sometimes called a complaints commission) or an ombudsman. These bodies commonly only operate in one direction, so a consumer of the service may bring a complaint against the provider, but providers cannot bring complaints against consumers. These government-run dispute resolution bodies are not always determinative and generally do not preclude subsequent litigation against the relevant service provider.

1.6 Litigation and statutory alternatives

Litigation remains the most important aspect of CDR. It is determinative, binding, final and enforceable. Court-based litigation has always been the most formal and final form of CDR. However, it also tends to be the most costly and time-consuming way to resolve a dispute, and the one which leaves the litigant with the least control over the dispute resolution process. The hierarchy of civil courts in Australia varies across jurisdictions as set out below. In addition to courts, there are statutory tribunals with legislated authority to resolve a wide range of civil and administrative disputes.

1.6.1 The role of the courts

The certainty offered by courts is critical to the success of all forms of dispute resolution because it motivates, or forces, parties to engage in resolving their disputes. Without the courts, there would be no incentive for powerful parties to equitably settle disputes with non-powerful parties. Courts, theoretically, create a level playing field where each litigant's view is of equal value. In reality, differing levels of litigant resources can adversely influence outcomes in litigation, with the ability (or lack thereof) to afford legal representation being the most obvious source of inequality (see Chapter 6).

Judges are trained to be impartial and independent arbiters of justice. Courts are designed to provide final and binding determinations with enforcement mechanisms to ensure compliance (see Chapter 16).

1.6.2 Specialist tribunals

A significant portion of Australian civil disputes are resolved through statutory tribunals. Every Australian state and territory, other than Tasmania, now has a Civil and Administrative Tribunal. These "super tribunals" have jurisdiction over a wide range of civil disputes which were previously determined by large numbers of smaller tribunals. Tasmania still retains at least eight separate tribunals to handle areas such as motor accidents, anti-discrimination and asbestos compensation. The Civil and Administrative Tribunals in each state and territory (other than Tasmania) cover wide varieties of dispute. For example, in New South Wales, the New South Wales Civil and Administrative Tribunal (NCAT) commenced in 2014, replaced 22 existing tribunals and currently boasts 4 divisions: Administrative and Equal Opportunity, Consumer and Commercial, Guardianship, and Occupational. NCAT now caters for over 30 different types of disputes ranging from discrimination to consumer claims to guardianship appointment to disputes about professionals, including legal practitioners. In the ACT and the Northern Territory all civil disputes below $25,000 must be settled in the ACT Civil and Administrative Tribunal and the Northern Territory Civil and Administrative Tribunal respectively. These tribunals have, therefore, assumed part of the courts' jurisdiction. The role of specialist tribunals will be considered in more detail in Chapter 7.

1.6.3 Advantages of litigation

Litigation provides parties with known processes based on requirements of procedural fairness. Most of these processes focus on access to and delivery of evidence. This can be of critical importance in matters where parties have unequal access to relevant evidence or where there are power imbalances between parties. The ability of litigation to compel a reluctant party to engage in dispute resolution, the finality of judicial determination and the ability to enforce that decision are all key advantages of litigation. In Australia, the rule of law is strongly adhered to and, therefore, parties have very strong prospects of recovering favourable judgments.[11]

11 World Justice Project, *Rule of Law Index 2019* (Web Page, 2019) 39 <https://worldjusticeproject.org/sites/default/files/documents/ROLI-2019-Reduced.pdf>. The World Justice Project, based in the United States, "[m]easures how the rule of law is experienced and perceived worldwide" by the general public and legal practitioners in 126 countries and jurisdictions, based on more than 120,000 household and 3,800 expert surveys: see World Justice Project, *Rule of Law Index 2019* (Web Page, 2019) <https://worldjusticeproject.org/our-work/research-and-data/wjp-rule-law-index-2019>. Australia's ranking in Civil Justice in the *Rule of Law Index 2019* is 14 of 126 states

1.7 Court-based dispute resolution: litigation steps

The steps involved in CDR vary from case to case, but the steps set out below are a good guide to how disputes can proceed through litigation, particularly disputes in higher courts (such as Supreme and Federal Courts). ADR processes commonly occur prior to any litigation process commencing and, where not initially successful, at any step during the litigation process. Accordingly, disputes can be (and frequently are) resolved at any stage of litigation proceedings. It is important to note that some courts have abbreviated processes for certain types of litigation or may have special procedures, particularly specialist tribunals. Finally, the court may determine, and sometimes the parties may agree without the need for a court order, that one or more of the steps below is not necessary for the case in question. Accordingly, only a very small percentage of cases actually involve all the steps set out below.

In relation to each of the steps set out below, the heading indicates which chapter of this book addresses that step in more detail.

1.7.1 A dispute arises

The substance of this dispute could be contractual, tortious, employment-related, equitable, corporate, familial or a combination of these or many other possibilities. Many commercial parties will contact their existing lawyers or hire lawyers at this point in time.

1.7.2 Parties negotiate (Chapter 4)

Many parties will have meetings or correspondence (with or without lawyers) prior to even considering litigation. Some parties will engage in alternative dispute resolution (ADR) at this time. ADR will be discussed in more detail in Chapter 14. Large commercial contracts often have detailed dispute resolutions clauses requiring parties to proceed with several phases of dispute resolution with each phase becoming more formal and legalistic in nature prior to commencing litigation.

1.7.3 Precursors to litigation (Chapter 8)

There are many types of civil litigation and not all involve steps prior to commencing litigation. However, there are numerous circumstances in which steps must be taken prior to starting proceedings. For a liquidated claim,[12] the potential plaintiff must send a letter of demand giving the other party a reasonable time to comply prior to commencing any litigation. Federal Court litigants must undertake genuine steps to resolve a dispute prior to commencing proceedings pursuant to the *Federal Court Rules 2011* (Cth). Most sensible parties will warn of an intention to litigate before commencing proceedings, but it can be a breach of legal profession obligations to threaten litigation if the party does not intend to commence proceedings.

12 A liquidated claim is one where the plaintiff can quantify a monetary amount of damage suffered.

1.7.4 The plaintiff commences proceedings (Chapter 8)

Proceedings are generally commenced by filing a statement of claim or summons in court. If the claim and/or the remedies sought are complicated, it can take some time to commence proceedings. Any action should be commenced within the applicable limitation period. Limitation periods are discussed in more detail in Chapter 2.

1.7.5 The claim is served on defendant (Chapter 9)

Service in most commercial cases is straightforward but can be very difficult with individuals or family businesses and this is where it may be necessary to hire a process server or even obtain substituted service.

1.7.6 The defendant appears (Chapter 9)

The defendant notifies the court that it intends to defend the claim. This is to prevent a summary judgment against it (summary judgment is discussed in Chapter 12). An alternative, available in some jurisdictions, is simply to file a defence, usually within two weeks, but this time frame may be too short to properly understand the claim and prepare a proper defence in many cases.

1.7.7 Court directions hearing (Chapter 10)

Often at this time, the parties (having now been identified) will appear before the court for directions. This hearing may be called a directions hearing, a status conference or a status hearing, depending on the court. The directions are usually a timetable for what the parties need to do in the matter and the last direction is when the parties should next appear before court having (hopefully) done what has been ordered by the court. In many cases, the timetable will contain all the steps required to have the matter ready for trial.

1.7.8 Defendant requests further particulars (Chapter 9)

If the statement of claim is complex or poorly worded or unclear, the defendant is likely to seek further and better particulars of the claim. In complex matters, a request for further and better particulars is almost inevitable. Obtaining particulars can be a time-consuming and frustrating process involving months of increasingly unpleasant correspondence in some large commercial matters.

1.7.9 Plaintiff provides further particulars (Chapter 9)

Hopefully, having received further particulars of the claim, the defendant now has a proper understanding of the case it has to meet.

1.7.10 Defendant files defence (Chapter 9)

Having now understood the claim, the defendant prepares and files its defence. The defence must traverse[13] each matter pleaded in the claim. If an aspect of a claim is not traversed, it is taken as an admission by the defendant.

1.7.11 Further pleadings and amended pleadings (Chapters 5, 9 and 10)

In a complex matter, the defence may well be filed with one or more cross claims. A cross claim may be a claim against the plaintiff or a claim against a third party which relates to the original claim.[14] A party cross claimed against will then file a cross defence. It is not uncommon, in large matters, for there to be 20 or more parties involved and resulting in parties with titles such as "cross-defendant to the third cross-claim and cross-claimant on the eighth cross-claim". Pleadings, other than originating processes, are discussed in Chapter 9.

There are often attempts to strike out all or part of statements of claim or the realisation by the plaintiff, upon receiving the defence, that the claim as pleaded is defective. Interlocutory motions, including those in relation to pleadings, are discussed in more detail in Chapter 10. Summary disposition, strike outs and other non-consensual ways in which pleadings can result in matters being disposed of prior to judgment are discussed in Chapter 5. In large commercial disputes, it is not uncommon to see the third, fourth or even tenth amended statement of claim which is likely to have been reached after many months or even years of correspondence, interlocutory applications and requests for further and better particulars.

1.7.12 Pleadings close (Chapter 9)

When the claim, the defence and any cross-claims have all been filed (with or without numerous amendments), the parties should be at the point where they understand and agree as to the issues remaining in dispute between them. At this point, the pleadings are considered closed and it is time for the parties to start preparing their evidence for trial.

1.7.13 Parties undertake discovery (Chapter 11)

When parties prepare their evidence, discovery is commonly the first and most significant task. Discovery is the process whereby each party discloses to the other parties, in a list, the documents they possess which are relevant to the litigation and makes those documents available for inspection by any other party. Many civil cases include a court order requiring

13 The defendant responds to each statement in the claim by either admitting, not admitting or denying the statement.

14 Sometimes described as a "third-party claim".

the parties to serve lists of discovered documents on each other. Reviewing the documents which might potentially be relevant to any litigation and working out which ones are discoverable can be time-consuming and expensive. Due to the high monetary and time cost associated with discovery, it is one of the steps most commonly excluded by Court Practice Notes and legislation.[15]

1.7.14 Parties determine privilege claims (Chapter 13)

Once the discoverable documents have been located by a party, that party must consider whether any of the discoverable documents might attract privilege. Privilege is the substantive right not to disclose information of a privileged nature. There are several types of privilege but legal professional privilege (now called client legal privilege in many jurisdictions) is perhaps the most commonly occurring privilege. Privileged documents are discoverable but are listed separately on each party's discovery list and are allowed to be described in a way which is sufficiently limited so as not to disclose the privileged information contained in the document. Unlike unprivileged documents, parties are not required to make privileged documents available for inspection by the other side thus preserving their privilege.

1.7.15 Parties serve lists of discovered documents (Chapter 11)

The parties exchange lists of discovered documents and make the documents on the list available for inspections by the other side (other than those over which privilege is claimed). Usually, it is lawyers who inspect the other party's documents. Increasingly, documents are being made available electronically and virtual discovery rooms now exist for many complex commercial matters.

1.7.16 Interlocutory motions on discovery and privilege (Chapters 10, 11 and 13)

Discovery is a common area in which interlocutory disputes arise between parties. Parties in dispute often don't trust each other so they question whether the other parties have honestly discovered everything and are often suspicious about claims of privilege. This often means the parties arrive back at court for another argument where sometimes allegedly privileged documents are handed up in sealed envelopes for judges to review and determine whether the documents are privileged. For example, the High Court decision of *Expense Reduction Analysis Group Pty Ltd v Armstrong Strategic Management and Marketing Pty Ltd*,[16] which is one of the key High Court case management decisions, is a case concerning inadvertent disclosure of privileged documents which began as an interlocutory motion.

15 See, eg, Supreme Court of New South Wales, *Practice Note SC EQ 11: Disclosure in the Equity Division*, 22 March 2012 <http://www.lawlink.nsw.gov.au/practice_notes/nswsc_pc.nsf/a15f50afb1aa22a9ca2570ed000a2b08/180b8c6777403534ca2579c9000c11a4?OpenDocument> discussed further in Chapter 11.

16 *Expense Reduction Analysis Group Pty Ltd v Armstrong Strategic Management and Marketing Pty Ltd* (2013) 250 CLR 303.

1.7.17 Notices to produce and subpoenas (Chapter 12)

Notices to produce and subpoenas are litigation procedures which can occur earlier or later in the evidence preparation phase and can occur several times in a single litigation. Sometimes, especially after discovery, when parties have a better idea about what important documents might exist, parties realise that there are corporations or individuals who are not a party to the litigation who might possess relevant documents. Those documents may be able to be subpoenaed. A subpoena is a formal order by the court requiring an individual or corporation to produce documents to the court. The same issues of privilege and relevance relating to discovery also arise for other forms of document production such as subpoenas and notices to produce.

1.7.18 Parties serve witness evidence including expert reports (Chapter 14)

Once all the documentary evidence has been reviewed by all the parties, it is time to prepare witness evidence. Traditionally, the plaintiff prepared and served its witness evidence first and the defendant then served its witness evidence in reply. However, it is increasingly common for both parties to be directed to serve their witness evidence simultaneously. Witness evidence is a crucial aspect of civil procedure but involves specific and complex evidentiary law that cannot be comprehensively addressed within the core themes and theory of CDR. The procedural aspects of evidence will, however, be discussed in some detail in Chapter 14.

There are two common types of witness evidence: lay evidence and expert evidence. Lay witnesses are, in general, the people who were involved in the dispute. For example, in a personal injury claim, the person who saw the plaintiff slip over in the supermarket on a squished grape may be a key lay witness to a claim against the supermarket. Individual plaintiffs and defendants are usually key lay witnesses and, where the parties are corporations, senior executives are often key lay witnesses.

Expert witnesses differ from lay witnesses in that they are allowed, under the various Commonwealth and state *Uniform Evidence Acts* and the common law, to give an opinion. Unlike lay witnesses, experts have rarely had direct involvement in the events leading to the dispute being litigated. Common types of expert witnesses include medical experts, accounting experts, forensic handwriting and computer experts. It is increasingly common for courts to appoint expert witnesses to report to the court rather than each party serving conflicting expert reports which the court must then assess and choose between. Other collaborative processes such as expert "hot tubbing" and joint conferences are ways for courts to reduce the burden on the judge in deciding between conflicting expert evidence.[17] Court rules and practice notes may contain codes of conduct directing experts in the giving of their evidence.

17 Adam Butt and Hugh Stowe, 'Playing in the Hot Tub: A Guide to Concurrent Expert Evidence in New South Wales' (2018) (Spring) *Bar News: Journal of the NSW Bar Association* 66.

1.7.19 Parties prepare and serve evidence in reply (Chapter 14)

After both sides have served their witness evidence, the parties have the opportunity to serve further witness evidence which is responsive to an issue raised by another party. Such affidavits in reply are usually very short and often consist of further affidavits from existing witnesses. However, there is sometimes the need to introduce new witnesses and new experts (if another party raises new factual matters) which may then necessitate another round of replies.

1.7.20 Matter set down for trial (Chapter 15)

Finally, all the evidence for both parties has been prepared, served and reviewed by all parties and the parties then typically return to court and are given a hearing date. The hearing may be months away if the expected trial time is lengthy and the court is busy. The longer the trial requires, the harder it is to find a judge with a long enough block of time to hear the case all at once. For example, the Western Australian case of *Bell Group Ltd (in liq) v Westpac Banking Corporation (No 9)* ('*Bell Group*'),[18] where the judge sat for over 400 hearing days, was not able to be heard without breaks and required an enormous investment of time for the sitting judge.

1.7.21 Trial preparation (Chapter 15)

Once a trial date has been allocated, the parties must prepare for the hearing. It is advisable to subpoena all witnesses on whose evidence you wish to rely (unless you can reach agreement between parties to rely solely on the written evidence of one or more witnesses — see Chapter 12). Many courts also seek written submissions to the court. In addition, parties need to prepare a court book or tender bundle (which may be electronic) containing all the documents it actually intends to rely on in the trial. It is also sensible to have readily available all documents you consider the other parties are likely to refer to during the trial. This is not the same as discovery because the documents relied on in trial will come from different discovery lists and the parties will probably only refer to a small percentage of the documents actually discovered. This may still be thousands of documents.

1.7.22 Trial (Chapter 15)

The trial process itself can vary significantly depending on the court and the nature of the proceedings. A common structure for trial consists of opening submissions, followed by presentation of evidence including examination and cross examination of witnesses, followed by closing submissions. There are many rules governing the process of trial and different judges have different styles which impact how they run their courts. In addition to the formal rules set out in civil procedure legislation, court rules, legal profession legislation and court practice notes, there are rules of etiquette which guide lawyers' behaviour in court.

18 *Bell Group Ltd (in liq) v Westpac Banking Corporation (No 9)* (2008) 39 WAR 1.

1.7.23 Judgment (Chapter 16)

Sometime after the hearing finishes, the court hands down its judgment. Sometimes, especially in smaller claims in lower courts, the judgment is delivered *ex tempore* in an oral judgment.[19] Urgent interlocutory hearings, such as freezing order and search order hearings (which are discussed further in Chapter 8), almost always require *ex tempore* judgments. In complex cases, however, it can take months to hand down lengthy written judgments.

1.7.24 Appeal (Chapter 16)

Only a small percentage of cases are appealed. The laws governing the circumstances in which cases can be appealed are complex. The appeal process attempts to balance the need of parties for finality against the need for there to be mechanisms to ensure the court system runs as it should, that more important cases are heard by the best judges and that instances of injustice are minimised. In very important or hard-fought cases, an appeal from the original hearing court is virtually inevitable. For example, in *Bell Group*, the novelty and complexity of legal issues to be determined and the enormous amounts at stake made it almost inevitable that the losing party (if not both parties) would appeal the trial court judgment.

1.7.25 Enforcement (Chapter 16)

Many parties accept the decision of the court and comply willingly with all court orders. However, where a party fails to comply with a court's order, courts have enforcement mechanisms to force compliance including through police and sheriffs. Courts also have powers to enforce the decisions of other courts, including overseas courts, to enable access to Australian assets for payment of foreign judgments.

1.8 Civil dispute resolution's state of flux

In 2007, the then Chief Justice of the High Court, Murray Gleeson, in his State of the Judicature Address, stated:

> Modern civil trials before judges sitting without juries rely much more on written presentation of evidence and argument. This does not mean that civil procedure is speeding up. On the contrary, most forms of trial seem to be lengthening. Trial judges place much emphasis on case management, both before and during hearings, but over-vigorous intervention can expose them to complaints of unfairness. Litigation is a perfect example of Parkinson's law: work expands to fill the available time. A capacity to exert firm control of counsel and witnesses without sacrificing fairness is necessary for a modern judge.[20]

---

19 An *ex tempore* judgment is a judgment delivered at the time of the hearing so that the parties do not have to wait for a later judgment.

20 Murray Gleeson, 'The State of the Judicature' (Speech, 35th Australian Legal Convention, 25 March 2007) 8 <https://cdn.hcourt.gov.au/assets/publications/speeches/former-justices/gleesoncj/cj_25mar07.pdf>.

Litigation and its alternatives change and develop with changes in technology and changes in the agreements that people enter, the ways people interact and the novel disputes arising from those new interactions. The challenge inherent in civil procedure is to balance the competing needs of society for speedy, cheap and efficient litigation, allowing justice to be accessible to everyone against the equally important need for the law to be developed carefully and thoughtfully with parties having sufficient time to prepare their cases properly. ADR interacts with this balance in complex ways as people endeavour to counter the natural tendency of dispute resolution to become ever more complex and time-consuming in response to the increasing complexity of modern life. The balance between efficiency and fair procedure is always uneasy and, as disputes within society change constantly, so must the procedures for best dealing with those disputes. Although Australian civil procedure has been more stable in the past decade, future change is inevitable.

1.9 Court hierarchy and legislative framework for civil procedure

As noted above, Australia is not a single uniform jurisdiction. In the High Court case of *McKain v RW Miller & Co (South Australia) Pty Ltd*, the joint judgment of Brennan, Dawson, Toohey and McHugh JJ stated:

> To describe the States, as Windeyer J. once described them, *Pedersen v. Young* (1964) 110 CLR at p 170, as 'separate countries in private international law' may sound anachronistic. Yet it is of the nature of the federation created by the Constitution that the States be distinct law areas whose laws may govern any subject matter subject to constitutional restrictions and qualifications. The laws of the States, though recognized throughout Australia, are therefore capable of creating disparities in the legal consequences attached in the respective States to the same set of facts unless a valid law of the Commonwealth overrides the relevant State laws and prescribes a uniform legal consequence.[21]

When it comes to civil litigation, the applicable law depends very much on where you are litigating and what you are litigating. For example, a court in New South Wales will apply different procedural rules to a court in Victoria. Each state or territory in Australia has its own jurisdiction with its own civil litigation laws and procedures, and matters which attract federal jurisdiction are different again. To further complicate matters, in some jurisdictions, the applicable rules vary between courts within a single state or territory. In addition, there has been significant legislative reform in civil litigation in many Australian jurisdictions in the last two decade such that few Australian courts are administering the same rules they were using at the turn of the century. The most significant reforms, which will be discussed in detail in Chapter 2, concern the increased focus on case management with most jurisdictions introducing overarching judicial obligations relating to justice and efficiency. In addition to major reform, the rules and procedures in most courts change regularly to accommodate the ever-changing nature of modern life as reflected in litigation. Some of the more obvious recent changes in Australian courts relate to the adoption of technology by courts and lawyers.

21 *McKain v RW Miller & Co (South Australia) Pty Ltd* (1992) 174 CLR 1, 36.

Although the plethora of legislative regimes and court rules may seem daunting, there is, in practice, a high level of common ground between all jurisdictions in Australia. All Australian courts have essentially evolved from the English court system and all Australian jurisdictions share the same ultimate court of appeal, being the High Court of Australia. There have been several attempts to reach uniform civil procedure legislation which have had varying success. For example, the rules adopted by the Victorian and Northern Territory Supreme Courts are essentially uniform. In addition, current intention to nationalise the legal profession will renew pressure on court systems to become more uniform.

The following sub-headings set out the Supreme Court legislative regime for each state and territory as well as the relevant federal civil procedure legislation.

Table 1.1 Civil procedure legislation for the High Court, the Federal Court, and every state and territory

Court/state	Civil procedure legislation
High Court	*High Court of Australia Act 1979* (Cth)
	High Court of Australia Rules 2004 (Cth)
Federal Court	*Federal Court of Australia Act 1976* (Cth)
	Federal Court of Australia Rules 2011 (Cth)
	Federal Circuit Court of Australia Act 1999 (Cth)
	Family Law Rules 2004 (Cth)
	Federal Circuit Court Rules 2001 (Cth)
	Federal Circuit Court (Bankruptcy) Rules 2016 (Cth)
Australian Capital Territory	*Court Procedures Act 2004* (ACT)
	Court Procedures Rules 2006 (ACT)
Northern Territory	*Supreme Court Act 1979* (NT)
	Supreme Court Rules 1987 (NT)
	Local Court Act 2015 (NT)
New South Wales	*Civil Procedure Act 2005* (NSW)
	Uniform Civil Procedure Rules 2005 (NSW)
Queensland	*Civil Proceedings Act 2011* (Qld)
	Supreme Court of Queensland Act 1991 (Qld)
	Uniform Civil Procedure Rules 1999 (Qld)
South Australia	*Supreme Court Act 1935* (SA)
	District Court Act 1991 (SA)
	Magistrates Court Act 1991 (SA)
	Uniform Civil Rules 2020 (SA)
Tasmania	*Supreme Court Civil Procedure Act 1932* (Tas)
	Supreme Court Rules 2000 (Tas)
Victoria	*Civil Procedure Act 2010* (Vic)
	Supreme Court Act 1986 (Vic)
	Supreme Court (General Civil Procedure) Rules 2015 (Vic)
Western Australia	*Supreme Court Act 1935* (WA)
	Rules of the Supreme Court 1971 (WA)
	Magistrates Court (Civil Proceedings) Rules 2005 (WA)

Table 1.2 Court hierarchy for the Federal Court and every state and territory

Court/State	Court Hierarchy
Federal Court	*Federal Circuit Court*: shared jurisdiction with Family and Federal court and no exclusive jurisdiction; jurisdiction up to $750,000 for general federal matters
	Federal Circuit and Family Court of Australia: unlimited jurisdiction for family law matters
	Federal Court of Australia: unlimited jurisdiction for federal matters
Australian Capital Territory	*ACT Civil and Administrative Tribunal*: matters up to $25,000
	ACT Magistrates Court: matters up to $250,000
	ACT Supreme Court: matters above $250,000
Northern Territory	*NT Civil and Administrative Tribunal*: matters up to $25,000
	NT Local Court: matters from $25,000–$250,000
	NT Supreme Court: matters over $250,000
New South Wales	*NSW Local Court*: matters up to $100,000 (small claims division up to $20,000)
	NSW District Court: matters between $100,000 and $750,000
	NSW Supreme Court: matters over $750,000
Queensland	*QLD Civil and Administrative Tribunal (QCAT)*: debt disputes up to $25,000 (non-exclusive jurisdiction)
	QLD Magistrates Court: matters up to $150,000 (matters below $25,000 may be commenced in QCAT).
	QLD District Court: matters between $150,000 and $750,000
	QLD Supreme Court: matters over $750,000
South Australia	*SA Local Court*: matters up to $100,000 (Minor Claims Division up to $12,000)
	SA District Court: matters over $100,000
	SA Supreme Court: complex matters over $100,000
Tasmania	*Tasmanian Magistrates Court*: matters up to $50,000 (or by agreement)
	Tasmanian Supreme Court: matters over $50,000
Victoria	*Victoria Local Court*: matters up to $100,000
	Victoria County Court: matters over $100,000 (unlimited monetary jurisdiction)
	Victoria Supreme Court: complex matters over $100,000
Western Australia	*WA Magistrates Court*: matters up to $75,000 (minor claims $10,000)
	WA District Court: matters between $75,000 and $750,000 (unlimited for personal injury)
	WA Supreme Court: matters over $750,000

It is important to recall that the Supreme Court for each jurisdiction, and the Federal Court, also contain an appellate jurisdiction where decisions from those courts, and sometimes lower courts, can be appealed. The appellate courts (Court of Appeal for Supreme Courts and Full Federal Court for the Federal Court) are solely for appealing cases already heard and such appeals are usually heard by three or more judges rather than a single judge as is the case for most original trials.

1.9.1 Civil procedure in the federal jurisdiction

Where matters are governed by federal law, disputes will attract federal jurisdiction. The most well-known federal courts are the High Court of Australia, the Federal Court of Australia, the Family Court of Australia and the Federal Circuit Court. Some of the most common areas of law attracting federal jurisdiction are family law, competition and consumer law, corporations law, bankruptcy/insolvency law, migration law and constitutional law matters. Federal Courts have jurisdiction over any dispute arising in relation to a Commonwealth law; for example, the *Marriage Act 1961* (Cth), *Competition and Consumer Act 2010* (Cth), *Corporations Act 2001* (Cth) and the *Income Tax Assessment Act 1997* (Cth).

1.9.1.1 High Court

The High Court of Australia is unique in that it is the final court of appeal for all Australian states and territories. The High Court is also a court of original jurisdiction for certain matters such as disputes on the interpretation of the *Commonwealth Constitution*.

1.9.1.2 Federal Court

As with the High Court rules, the Federal Court has significant discretion in relation to its rules pursuant to ch 1 pt 1 div 1.3 *Federal Court Rules 2011* (Cth), which provides; for example, at r 1.32 that "The Court may make any order that the Court considers appropriate in the interests of justice."

1.9.1.3 Other federal courts and tribunals

In addition to the High Court and the Federal Court, there are numerous other federal courts and tribunals, some of which will be considered further in Chapter 7. Examples of federal courts and tribunals include the Federal Circuit and Family Court of Australia, the Administrative Appeals Tribunal, the Australian Competition Tribunal and the National Sports Tribunal.

1.9.2 Australian Capital Territory

The Australian Capital Territory has Magistrates Courts and a Supreme Court. It is one of many Australian states and territories to have introduced civil procedure rules which are uniform throughout the territory.

In addition, the ACT Civil and Administrative Tribunal (ACAT) resolves a wide variety of disputes through statutory authority.

1.9.3 New South Wales

New South Wales has a three-tier hierarchy with the Local Courts, District Courts and the Supreme Court and all levels all governed by essentially uniform civil procedure rules. However, New South Wales has retained its *Supreme Court Act 1970* (NSW), *Supreme Court Rules 1970* (NSW), *District Court Act 1973* (NSW), *District Court Rules 1973* (NSW), *Local Court Act 1982* (NSW) and *Local Court Rules 1982* (NSW) as well as practice notes and directions for individual courts and court lists.

In addition, there are numerous specialised tribunal functions housed under the New South Wales Civil and Administrative Tribunal (NCAT).

1.9.4 Northern Territory

The Northern Territory does not have uniform civil procedure rules within its jurisdiction but its Supreme Court rules are essentially uniform with Victoria's Supreme Court rules. Matters commenced in the Supreme Court of the Northern Territory are governed by the *Supreme Court Act 1979* (NT) and the *Supreme Court Rules 1987* (NT). The Northern Territory Supreme Court has broad discretion set out in r 1.10 of the *Supreme Court Rules 1987* (NT) to ensure proceedings are "effectively, completely, promptly and economically determined" (r 1.10(1)(a)).

In addition to the Supreme Court, the Northern Territory has a Local Court which is one of the Northern Territory Magistrates Courts and is governed by the *Local Court Act 1989* (NT) and the *Local Court Rules 1998* (NT). Other Northern Territory Magistrates Courts relevant to civil disputes include the Family Matters Court which makes orders concerning the welfare and custody of children considered to be in need of care, and the Work Health Court which handles workers compensation claims. Victoria and the Northern Territory have essentially the same Supreme Court Rules.

1.9.5 Queensland

Queensland has a hierarchy of courts similar to New South Wales, comprising a Supreme Court, District Courts and Magistrates Courts. The *Uniform Civil Procedure Rules 1999* (Qld) apply to all three tiers of the Queensland courts. The *Supreme Court of Queensland Act 1991* (Qld) relates to the Supreme Court but also governs the District Court and Magistrates Courts as regards enforcement of orders and rules of court. The *Supreme Court Act 1995* (Qld) also operates and covers some issues relevant to civil proceedings.

1.9.6 South Australia

In South Australia, there is a three-tier court hierarchy with Magistrates Courts, District Courts and a Supreme Court. South Australia introduced uniform civil procedure rules in 2020.

1.9.7 Tasmania

The *Supreme Court Rules 2000* (Tas) are authorised by s 195 of the *Supreme Court Civil Procedure Act 1932* (Tas). Tasmania has separate rules for corporations law matters entitled the *Supreme Court (Corporations) Rules 2008* (Tas). In addition to the *Supreme Court Rules 2000* (Tas), Tasmania also has the *Supreme Court Forms Rules 2000* (Tas), sch 1 of which sets out a table of the forms required in civil proceedings. The *Supreme Court Rules 2000* (Tas) are lengthy, running to 978 rules including many sub-rules and subsequent additions.

The Tasmanian court hierarchy consists of the Supreme Court and Magistrates Courts but does not have a middle tier court (similar to the Northern Territory and the Australian Capital Territory). Civil proceedings in Tasmania's Magistrates Court are governed by the *Magistrates Court (Civil Division) Act 1992* (Tas) and the *Magistrates Court (Civil Division) Rules 1998* (Tas).

1.9.8 Victoria

Similar to New South Wales, Victoria has three court tiers governed by a uniform *Civil Procedure Act 2010* (Vic).

However, unlike New South Wales, the Victorian *Civil Procedure Act* does not purport to comprehensively govern civil procedure in Victoria. In Victoria, each court continues to be primarily governed by its own Act and rules. Accordingly, the Supreme Court of Victoria is governed by the *Supreme Court Act 1986* and the *Supreme Court (General Civil Procedure) Rules 2005* (Vic). The County Courts are governed by the *County Court Act 1958* (Vic) and the *County Court Civil Procedure Rules 2018* (Vic) and the Magistrates' Courts by the *Magistrates' Court Act 1989* (Vic) and the *Magistrates' Court General Civil Procedure Rules 2010* (Vic).

Underlying these different rules, however, is essential uniformity including consistency in the numbering of all three sets of court rules and this is explicitly stated in the preliminary introduction to the *Magistrates' Court General Civil Procedure Rules 2010* (Vic).

In addition to the uniformity within the Victorian courts, there is also consistency between the Victorian Supreme Court rules and the Northern Territory Supreme Court rules.

1.9.9 Western Australia

In Western Australia, civil claims are heard in the Supreme Court of Western Australia, the District Court or the Magistrates Court. Civil Procedure is not uniform in Western Australia. The Supreme Court of Western Australia is governed by the *Supreme Court Act 1935* (WA) and the *Rules of the Supreme Court 1971* (WA). The District Courts of Western Australia are governed by the *District Court Rules 2005* (WA) and the Magistrates Courts are governed by the *Magistrates Court (General) Rules 2005* (WA). In addition, as with all jurisdictions, there are numerous practice notes and directions which further govern civil procedure in each court.

1.10 Conclusion

Civil disputes arise in an enormous variety of contexts, involving a wide range of substantive law and can be resolved in an infinite number of ways. However, all CDR invokes the same core conflicts between efficiency and fair procedure, between discretion and certainty, and between formality and informality. The rules governing civil litigation vary between different Australian state jurisdictions and sometimes between courts within a jurisdiction, but there is underlying consistency in the themes which shape Australian CDR. Despite significant recent attempts to standardise civil litigation in Australia, there remains a large array of relevant legislation and a complex hierarchy of courts and tribunals in which civil litigation may be commenced. The complexities and consequent barriers to entry for litigation influence the decisions of parties to engage with ADR mechanisms and the likely success of such mechanisms. The interaction between ADR and litigation varies but both are relevant to every civil dispute. Litigation almost invariably involves aspects of ADR and ADR is always influenced by the shadow of litigation as the best alternative to a negotiated agreement. This book will demonstrate how every aspect of CDR is explained and shaped by conflicting imperatives, particularly those of efficiency and procedural fairness which drive the processes of both ADR and litigation.

2 BALANCING COMPETING OBJECTIVES: THE KEY THEMES OF CIVIL DISPUTE RESOLUTION

2.1 Introduction

The theory underlying this book is that civil dispute resolution (CDR) can be explained by the need to balance four key themes which pervade the resolution of civil disputes. The key themes of CDR themselves involve balancing conflicting objectives and, hence, it is the conflicts within the conflict resolution process which drive that process. This chapter will explain each of these key balancing acts and how they are managed by courts and outside courts. The key themes of CDR are based upon fundamental moral and societal imperatives. Viewed through this thematic lens, current CDR practices, including the rules of civil procedure, are both logical and explicable and their apparent conflicts are shown to be necessary rather than nonsensical.

These key themes are both causative and symptomatic of the rules of civil procedure and the operation of ADR. Understanding this chapter is, therefore, essential to understanding CDR. Comprehending the themes of CDR leads to an appreciation of the strengths of our current system and the challenges it faces.

2.2 The overarching theory of civil dispute resolution: balancing competing objectives

CDR revolves around balancing competing objectives. It is the competing nature of the requirements for CDR which dictate the rules of civil procedure and the scope and operation of alternatives to dispute resolution. Civil procedure rules, such as the case management rules discussed below, demonstrate these conflicts. For example, s 56 of the *Civil Procedure Act 2005* (NSW) provides an "overriding purpose" that the resolution of disputes be "just, quick and cheap". While all three aims are undeniably desirable in civil procedure, they are also fundamentally in conflict and in surprisingly complex ways. When litigants seek justice from a judge, they want that judge to carefully assess the merits of their case, apply the relevant laws and come to a just and fair solution. This requires time on behalf of the litigants preparing and presenting their cases and the judge deciding. Such preparations are rarely quick or cheap. The more complex the facts and law involved in the dispute, the more its resolution is likely to be both time consuming and costly. This conflicts with the "quick" and "cheap" overriding requirements of civil procedure.[1]

Even the above analysis is an oversimplification of the conflict between justice and efficiency because inefficiency is itself unjust, making the concepts of justice and efficiency thoroughly intertwined. It is indisputable and frequently stated that "justice delayed is justice denied."[2] This is true in several ways. First, the longer parties must wait for justice, the longer they are wronged by the injustice they seek to resolve. Second, witness memories fade over time, documents are lost, destroyed or corrupted and the quality of most evidence declines as time passes such that judicial prospects of locating an objective truth decline with time. Third, litigants run out of funds and energy resulting in a survival of the fittest, or richest, in many disputes. Thus, justice is unlikely to be achieved with highly expensive and time-consuming processes.

On the other hand, a judge who can tell just by looking at a party that they should lose the case, is unlikely to be a just judge because the procedures he or she has followed are not fair. Parties desire fairness of procedure because procedural fairness is a strong indicator of substantive fairness.[3] Most civil disputes involve parties who all believe they should win. There is usually evidence supporting each party's position and many disputes entail genuine legal questions with uncertain answers. As the complexity of human interaction increases,

1 See, eg, *Civil Procedure Act 2005* (NSW) s 56 with its overriding requirement to be "just, quick and cheap".

2 This statement is commonly attributed to the 19th century British politician William Gladstone; see, eg, *Hodgson v Amcor Ltd* (2011) 32 VR 495, [11] which also refers to earlier expressions in the Magna Carta and states that "Ulpian, a Roman jurist who wrote between AD 211 and 222, expressed the idea in similar terms: '*Justitiae dilatio est quaedam negatio*'." It is also well recognised in civil law jurisdictions and internationally. French jurists say "*Justice rétive, justice fautive*", and the *European Convention on Human Rights* provides by art 6 that "everyone is entitled to a fair and public hearing within a reasonable time". The exact statement has also been made by many judges and politicians: see Laurence J Peter, *Peter's Quotations: Ideas for Our Times* (Morrow, 1992) 276; see also Naomi Burstyner and Tania Sourdin, 'Justice Delayed is Justice Denied' (2014) 4(1) *Victoria University Law and Justice Journal* 46, 46.

3 Hazel Genn, *Judging Civil Justice* (Cambridge University Press, 2010) 13; Tom R Tyler, *Why People Obey the Law* (Princeton University Press, 2006) 104–105.

the factual complexity of disputes and the laws applicable to such disputes also increase. Resolving such disputes inside and outside courts takes time and effort on behalf of the parties, those assisting them, and those facilitating or determining the disputes. It is simply impossible in most disputes to reach a fair resolution quickly or cheaply.

The difficulty inherent in balancing carefully reasoned decision-making with desirable efficiency is the most significant example of intractable conflict in CDR. However, as this chapter will demonstrate, all the key themes of CDR require complex balancing acts and the interaction of these themes is similarly complex. Thus, the overarching theory of CDR could be described as the delicate balancing of conflicting justice related objectives.

2.3 The key themes in civil dispute resolution

CDR is about balancing competing parties, competing objectives and competing problems. The key balancing themes of dispute resolution can be summarised as: balancing efficiency with due consideration, balancing certainty with flexibility, balancing privacy with openness, and balancing autonomy with constraint. Each of these themes require a balancing of conflicting objectives. The themes also interact with each other, sometimes in conflicting ways.

2.3.1 Balancing efficiency with due consideration

The theme of balancing efficiency with due consideration is perhaps the most important theme in CDR. Sometimes this conflict is described as balancing efficiency with truth. This is problematic, however, because the existence of the "truth" or the "right answer" is not universally agreed on.[4] However, it is undisputed that carefully considered evidence and a carefully reasoned decision are more likely to be just than their hasty equivalents. There are two simple aphorisms which nicely sum up the complexity of balancing efficiency with attention to detail: "justice delayed is justice denied" and "rough justice is no justice".[5]

Both sayings are difficult to dispute and yet they are in conflict. As discussed in Chapter 2.2, there are numerous strong arguments in favour of the idea that expensive and time-consuming CDR reduces justice. However, hasty determination without careful consideration of evidence or law, so called "rough justice", is unlikely to satisfy either party or to result in faith in the administration of justice.[6]

---

4 Some jurisprudential scholars believe in the existence of a right answer. See, eg, Ronald Dworkin, 'Hard Cases' (1975) 88(6) *Harvard Law Review* 1057, 1083. See also Ronald Dworkin, *Law's Empire* (Belknap Press, 1986) 240–266. Other scholars believe that not all cases have right answers and that legal correctness does not always equate to justice. See, eg, HLA Hart, 'Legal Positivism' *Stanford Encyclopedia of Philosophy* (Web Page, 3 January 2003) <https://plato.stanford.edu/archives/fall2009/entries/legal-positivism/>; Lawrence Solum, 'On the Indeterminacy Crisis: Critiquing Critical Dogma' (1987) 54(2) *University of Chicago Law Review*, 462; Leslie Green, 'Positivism and the Inseparability of Law and Morals' (2008) 83(4) *New York University Law Review* 1035, 1050.

5 See Chapter 2.5; Neil Andrews, 'Affordable and Accurate Civil Justice — Challenges Facing the English and Other Modern Systems' (2014) 25(4) *European Business Law Review* 545, 563.

6 Neil Andrews, 'Affordable and Accurate Civil Justice — Challenges Facing the English and Other Modern Systems' (2014) 25(4) *European Business Law Review* 545, 563.

Efficiency is also a court imperative due to the recognition, since *Aon Risk Services Australia Ltd v Australian National University* ('*Aon*', discussed below),[7] that court resources are limited and that case management involves managing the allocation of these scarce resources between current and potential future litigants. In *Trevor Roller Shutter Service Pty Ltd v Crowe*,[8] the Victorian Court of Appeal suggested that "more generally, *Aon* may be thought to have re-invigorated the procedural paradigm, to some extent and for some time diminished by JL Holdings, that time, costs and limited judicial resources are relevant considerations ... ".[9] Courts, in duly considering one case, must consider how the time spent hearing that case might affect the time available for future cases. This raises issues of whether future litigants will benefit more from increased availability of judges (due to high judicial speed in existing cases) or from the, perhaps superior, precedent created by a more carefully considered decision.[10]

The balance between efficiency and due consideration is similarly critical in the context of ADR, particularly referral to ADR by courts. Referral will save time and cost where a matter settles. However, ADR does not create judicial precedent because ADR is almost invariably confidential (see Chapter 3). The lack of precedent then reduces the potential for parties to resolve disputes without recourse to ADR or the courts through following the precedent.

Understanding this fundamental conflict provides a logical explanation for many of the complexities and criticisms levied at CDR by the media and members of the public. It explains why litigation is invariably expensive and time-consuming and why the alternatives to dispute resolution contain risks of injustice.

2.3.2 Balancing certainty with flexibility

The second key thematic conflict in CDR is the conflict between certainty and flexibility. The desire for certainty of procedure is a key motivator for parties to choose litigation rather than ADR to resolve their disputes. Conversely, parties seeking flexible procedures are far more likely to choose ADR. ADR encompasses an almost limitless range of possible procedures, including remedial processes which may contribute to a dispute's resolution.[11] By contrast, litigation procedures are more rigid and limited, although case management, discussed at Chapter 2.4, has increased the potential for flexibility in litigation procedures.

The conflict between flexibility and certainty of process is evident in civil procedure statutes and case law. Litigants desire certainty of process for numerous reasons. First, it is easier to predict the costs of dispute resolution if the process is consistent and well understood. Second, it can appear fairer for all parties to be faced with the same process leaving less scope for judicial bias. Third, parties are more likely to follow procedures correctly where these are well understood and consistently applied. Flexibility of procedure requires communication between parties and the court to establish agreed procedures (which takes time and money). Fourth, it

7 *Aon Risk Services Australia Ltd v Australian National University* (2009) 239 CLR 175.
8 *Trevor Roller Shutter Service Pty Ltd v Crowe* (2011) 31 VR 249.
9 Ibid [42] cited with apparent approval in *Hodgson v Amcor Ltd* (2011) 32 VR 495, [20].
10 Genn (n 3).
11 For example, an apology can be a remedial process which forms part of the resolution of a dispute particularly in cases involving negligence, inadvertent contractual breach or family disputes.

is comforting to parties, where the outcome of their claim is unknown, to at least know what procedures will be applied to reach that outcome.

Conversely, there are several reasons why flexible procedures are desirable for courts and parties. First, each case is different and judicial discretion as to procedure can enable greater fairness by tailoring procedures to the actual needs of the parties. Second, flexibility as to procedure enables courts and parties to skip procedures (such as discovery) which are not essential to a particular case, thereby saving considerable time and money for the court and the litigants.

It is impossible to be both flexible and certain simultaneously, so it becomes the task for the courts and litigants to find an optimal balance. This is an optimal balance which changes over time influenced by factors such as levels of litigant access to procedural information, the ease with which parties can communicate with each other and the court, and the rate of change of litigation with which procedure must maintain pace.

Greater levels of specificity in rules and procedures increase certainty but reduce flexibility. The current case management legislation in Australia opts for overarching provisions of justice and efficiency which override the more detailed and specific rules of procedure.[12] In this way, the parliament is attempting to grant the courts broad discretion while retaining specific guidelines as to common procedures.

This balancing act explains the significant focus of modern civil procedure legislation on case management, because case management is a tool which balances prescriptive rules (certainty) with judicial discretion (flexibility).

2.3.3 Balancing privacy with openness

The third key thematic conflict in CDR is the conflicting desirability of confidentiality and openness. This theme is dealt with in more detail in Chapter 3 which focuses on open justice. It is also the underlying conflict discussed in Chapter 13 concerning privilege and confidentiality, and a significant motivator for many forms of ADR discussed in Chapter 4.

There are important incentives in favour of confidentiality. Disputants would almost always prefer that details of their dispute remained private and this is a common reason for parties to resort to ADR rather than litigation to resolve their disputes.[13] Confidentiality encourages full and frank disclosure between disputants and in interactions between disputants and their lawyers which increase the chances of fully understanding the basis of a dispute and reaching an agreed resolution.[14]

Conversely, there are critical motivations for open justice (discussed in detail in Chapter 3). The public nature of litigation encourages societal engagement with justice and the rule of law. Open justice provides a public check on the independence of the judiciary and reduces the potential for judicial bias and fraud. Strong faith in legal institutions which

12 See, eg, the general case management provisions in ss 7–9 of the *Civil Procedure Act 2010* (Vic) or ss 56–60 of the *Civil Procedure Act 2005* (NSW), discussed in Chapter 2.4.3.2, which impose justice and efficiency imperatives which overlay the detailed procedures of the civil procedure rules in those jurisdictions.

13 *Rinehart v Hancock Prospecting Pty Ltd* (2019) 366 ALR 198, [32]–[49].

14 See Chapter 4 for analysis of ADR and to Chapter 13 for analysis of privilege and confidentiality.

results from public engagement is a critical aspect of democracy.[15] As a common law jurisdiction, judicial precedent forms a significant part of Australian law. Disputes which are resolved through ADR do not contribute to the growth of common law.[16] Where disputes are routinely resolved through arbitration or other confidential means of dispute resolution, there is a dearth of precedent to direct future disputants. This lack of judicial guidance on legal interpretation may result in higher volumes of disputes and significant economic costs associated with market uncertainty. So, for example, if all disputes concerning responsibility for non-combustible cladding in commercial buildings were settled without litigation, this may result in problematic uncertainty for future construction contracts which could, in turn, dampen the construction market and adversely affect all stakeholders.

The conflicting motivations for both privacy and openness particularly influences, and is influenced by, whether disputes are resolved through ADR or litigation.

2.3.4 Balancing autonomy with control

The final thematic conflict is between party autonomy and non-party control of CDR processes. The Australian legal system, like all common law systems, is founded on the idea of party autonomy. Parties should be free to resolve their disputes as they see fit within the constraints of the law. There are obvious constraints in the form of our criminal law system which prevents parties from resolving their disputes through violence or other illegal means.[17] However, there are also numerous procedural constraints on how parties resolve disputes particularly once they engage with the court system. Parties must fill in forms, comply with timetables, cooperate with each other and the courts and follow rules of evidence. In addition, case management obligations (discussed below) can restrict parties' ability to choose how to litigate.[18] These procedural constraints of litigation are a key motivator for parties to resolve disputes using ADR as ADR maximises retention of party autonomy. Even within the ADR sphere, the involvement of third parties decreases party autonomy.

However, party autonomy is not always desirable as it brings significant risks and, often, costs. Where parties have unequal bargaining power, party autonomy can result in bullying and undue influence. Where parties have low legal literacy, party autonomy leads to inefficiency because parties fail to bring their cases effectively and may waste time on legal irrelevancies. The decision to engage with third parties, such as courts or ADR practitioners, represents an acknowledgement by at least one party that the dispute cannot be resolved without external assistance. It is then a delicate balancing exercise for the external party — commonly courts, arbitrators, mediators and conciliators — to determine the balance between taking full control of the process and allowing the parties to retain autonomy.

CDR procedures impose obligations on parties which reduce their autonomy but promise procedural fairness and justice as the reward for relinquishing party control. Many litigation procedures, such as discovery (Chapter 11) and preparation of witness evidence

15 World Justice Project, *Rule of Law Index 2019* (Web Page, 2019) <https://worldjusticeproject.org/our-work/research-and-data/wjp-rule-lawindex-2019>.

16 Genn (n 3).

17 *Crimes Acts* in every Australian state and territory make physical assault an offence punishable by imprisonment. See, eg, *Crimes Act 1900* (NSW) ss 33, 35, 59, 61.

18 *UBS AG v Tyne* (2018) 265 CLR 77; see Chapter 2.2.5.

(Chapter 14), are designed to increase judicial ability to determine a just outcome. Without these procedures, there is an increased risk of an unfair outcome. Where ADR is used in cases of significant power imbalance, the reduced procedural protections for parties available in ADR can result in unjust dispute resolution. The challenge for the courts or ADR institutions is balancing parties' need for external intervention through fair processes against the ongoing desire of parties to have maximum autonomy and control over the dispute resolution process.

Even within a litigation context, there is a constant balancing exercise for the courts between controlling parties and processes and allowing parties autonomy to run their case as they see fit. Inquisitorial systems in other jurisdictions, such as France and Germany, allow greater judicial control of processes and less party autonomy in proceedings. The common law system has always allowed parties to choose how to present their case through pleadings (Chapter 8) and to select which evidence they choose to present (Chapters 14 and 15).[19] This level of autonomy is attractive to many parties but may be problematic for self-represented litigants who may struggle to properly plead their case and fail to raise key issues or engage properly with processes such as discovery (Chapter 11).

2.4 Managing cases in and out of court

"Case management" is the term generally used to describe the role of the courts in administering and intervening in the preparation of a case for trial. However, case management also arises in all forms of ADR which involve a third-party decision-maker or facilitator. This sub-chapter will focus predominantly on case management in the judicial context with the management of ADR discussed in Chapter 4 and the interaction between ADR and litigation discussed in Chapter 5.

Australian courts began taking a more active role in managing litigation following 21st century statutory reforms, such as the *Civil Procedure Act 2005* in New South Wales and the *Civil Procedure Act 2010* in Victoria. Australian courts now almost invariably give directions as to the timing and nature of the steps parties undertake to prepare a case for court, including the extent of document discovery, the volume of oral and written evidence and submissions, and even the issues in dispute. Courts are increasingly guided by overarching principles concerning justice and fairness.

Relevant aspects of case management will be discussed throughout Chapters 8 to 16 in relation to each of the stages of litigation. In addition, Chapter 10 will discuss the role of courts in directions hearings and Chapter 5 will discuss court powers to manage cases through summary procedures.

2.4.1 What is case management?

The term "case management" in the litigation context can be used to refer to both how courts manage their workload of cases and what a court does in the context of a particular case to manage that case. At its broadest, case management could be defined as every action

19 *Timbercorp Finance Pty Ltd (in liq) v Collins* (2016) 259 CLR 212, [38], [68].

by all interested stakeholders in relation to every litigation. Every judicial order, instruction or suggestion would thereby form part of case management, including the court's final determination and consequent orders. Although not every aspect of every judicial order is procedural, there is, arguably, a procedural aspect to every judicial order and every court requirement. However, in practice, more narrow definitions of case management are usually envisaged and there is considerable inconsistency in the literature on case management.

Some academics and judges draw distinctions between the rules put in place by courts to manage their resources and the management by courts of individual cases. Either or both may be considered case management. For example, Michael Legg defines case management by dividing it into "structural case management" and "managerial judging".[20] Legg defines "structural case management", which he also terms "case flow management", as the use of special court lists and tracks supported by practice notes to manage cases.[21] Legg then defines "managerial judging" as how each judge tailors procedures in individual cases.[22] Legg's dichotomy is useful but downplays the level of interaction between structural case managing (eg practice notes, docket systems) and managerial judging (individual judicial case management decisions). In addition, Legg's definition potentially understates the influence of legislation, lawyers and parties on how the courts and individual judges manage cases. Similarly, in 2009, then Chief Justice of the New South Wales Supreme Court, Spigelman CJ, differentiated between rules for case management and individual case management, stating:

> I should, at the outset, distinguish between individual case management and caseload or caseflow management. The latter does not focus on particular cases. Its concern is the overall caseload encompassing delays in the system for cases generally as well as costs which the system imposes on the parties to particular proceedings. Managing individual cases efficiently is a necessary, but not a sufficient condition, for effective management of the caseload.[23]

Some law reports and papers do not explicitly define case management but most, at least impliedly, focus on case management as the actions of judges in relation to individual cases rather than the content of practice notes, civil procedure legislation or other documents which direct how cases are run.[24] The 2008 Victorian Law Reform Commission Civil Justice Review Report 14 devoted its chapter 5 to case management, including defining "active judicial case management" as:

> The proactive judicial management by individual judges of individual cases is one aspect of this process. Another equally important aspect is the systems used by the

20 Michael Legg, *Case Management and Complex Civil Litigation* (Federation Press, 2011).

21 Ibid 3–4.

22 Ibid 5. Legg's text focuses predominantly on managerial judging.

23 JJ Spigelman, 'Case Management in New South Wales' (Speech, Judicial Delegation from India, 21 September 2009) 3–4 <https://www.supremecourt.justice.nsw.gov.au/Documents/Publications/Speeches/Pre-2015%20Speeches/Spigelman/spigelman_speeches_2009.pdf>.

24 Ross Cranston et al., *Delays and Efficiency in Civil Litigation* (Australian Institute of Judicial Administration, 1985) 6, 170; Australian Law Reform Commission, *Managing Justice: A Review of the Federal Justice System* (Report No 89, February 2000) 18; Australian Law Reform Commission, *Managing Discovery: Discovery of Documents in Federal Courts* (Report No 115, May 2011) 14, 16, 18, 22, 197–208; Attorney-General's Department, Access to Justice Taskforce, *A Strategic Framework for Access to Justice in the Federal Civil Justice System* (2009) 70, 97, 106–110.

> courts for the control of the overall caseload of the court. Such systems encompass not only the mechanisms for the assignment and control of cases by judges, but also computerised and other methods of tracking the status and progress of cases.[25]

The perceived importance of case management has varied over time depending on High Court precedent and legislative support. The last decade has seen considerable strengthening in case management obligations on the court and litigating parties. Parties to litigation are no longer left to negotiate timetables for case preparation without judicial input. This increases judicial ability to manage cost and delay.

2.4.2 Managing cases through alternative dispute resolution

Although case management is usually discussed in the context of litigation, it plays important roles in ADR.[26] ADR engages in case management and is, itself, used as a form of case management. Any form of ADR which involves a third party introduces case management issues, as the third party must make decisions on how to facilitate interactions between the parties. Third parties in dispute resolution are, therefore, inevitably, involved in the management of disputes although the nature of the case management varies depending on the form of ADR and the role of the third party. For example, the case management actions of an arbitrator may closely mirror those of a judge in a litigation. In arbitration, a key role of the arbitrator or arbitral tribunal is to prescribe procedures for the management of the case, including timing, pre-hearing processes and evidentiary processes. Arbitration processes will be discussed further in Chapter 4, but it is worth noting here that arbitral case management is highly variable because it does not have legislative provisions and case precedent guiding it the way litigation does. Mediators, conciliators and negotiators case manage in a more facilitative and less directive manner than arbitrators. Their aim is to case manage through facilitation not determination and they may take a more active role in managing processes and parties although, often, over a shorter timeframe. These processes are also discussed in Chapter 4.

ADR is also used as a case management tool by judges. Case management aims to reduce the cost and delay associated with civil litigation and ADR can be a cheap and efficient way to resolve disputes. Therefore, judges will direct parties to different forms of ADR, such as mediation, as an important aspect of judicial case management. Engaging with ADR is often an important aspect of litigation which makes it common for cases to be simultaneously managed by courts and ADR practitioners. This will be discussed further in Chapter 5.

Finally, judicial case management is a consideration for cases where litigation is yet to commence. Parties attempting to resolve their dispute through ADR must necessarily consider how the courts are likely to manage the case if it is not resolved by ADR and this can be a motivation to settle.

Therefore, although discussion of case management is usually confined to litigation, it also affects ADR because of the close interrelationship between ADR and litigation.

25 Victorian Law Reform Commission, *Civil Justice Review* (Report No 14, March 2008) 297.
26 Different forms of ADR are discussed in detail in Chapter 4.

2.4.3 The legislative strengthening of courts' case management obligations

The role of case management has been changing in Australia due to a combination of legislative changes and judicial precedent.[27] Modern civil procedure statutes are centred on overarching obligations of justice, speed and efficiency. In practice, such statutory obligations potentially increase the discretion of courts because the overriding obligations are relatively abstract and undefined concepts such as "justice" and "efficiency". These general concepts then become the most important obligation of the courts to comply with; overriding more certain requirements, such as having a set period to undertake a certain process.

The insertion of overriding obligations in civil procedure legislation increases the uniformity of civil procedure across state boundaries. Allowing courts to override more detailed pedestrian rules, in order to ensure justice and efficiency, not only simplifies the process for courts, lawyers and parties but simultaneously increases the likelihood of uniformity between different court systems which are all required to follow the same High Court precedents such as *Aon*.[28]

In the 21st century, parliaments have exercised significant influence over civil procedure through the introduction or amendment of civil procedure legislation across Australian jurisdictions. Most Australian civil procedure systems now impose active case management obligations on courts.

In the 20th century, case management was driven by courts on an ad hoc basis and was commonly articulated in cases and practice notes which were authored and entirely controlled by courts.[29] The central concepts of justice and efficiency have, arguably, been embodied in court rules for several decades.[30] New South Wales judges certainly recognise the prior existence of active case management as well as the value of the active case management provisions. In *McMahon v John Fairfax Publications Pty Ltd*, President Allsop of the New South Wales Court of Appeal (as he then was), stated:

> The operation of the Civil Procedure Act, ss 56–60 has brought about important changes to the conduct of civil litigation in this State. To a significant degree those provisions enshrined many of the developments in case management and the approach to litigation over the previous 20–30 years in this country. They now have statutory form. They are, however, a clear statutory watershed.[31]

There are at least two relevant differences in recent civil procedure legislation compared with historical Australian civil procedure systems. The first is a very deliberate move towards

27 Key judicial case management decisions are discussed in Chapters 2.2.4 and 2.2.5.

28 *Aon Risk Services Australia Ltd v Australian National University* (2009) 239 CLR 175, discussed in detail in Chapter 2.2.4.

29 Productivity Commission, *Access to Justice Arrangements* (2014) vol 1, 387 (Sackville J); Ronald Sackville, 'Civil Justice Reform: The Third Phase' in Miiko Kumar and Michael Legg (eds), *Ten Years of the Civil Procedure Act 2005 (NSW)* (Thomson Reuters, 2015) 209. See, eg, Brennan, Deane and Mchugh JJ in *Sali v SPC Ltd* (1993) 67 ALJR 841, 844; Allsop J in *White v Overland* [2001] FCA 1333, [4].

30 John Basten, 'Civil Procedure Act 2005 (NSW): The Overriding Purpose Provisions' in Kumar and Legg (eds) (n 29) 63, 69.

31 *McMahon v John Fairfax Publications Pty Ltd* [2010] NSWCA 308, [26].

uniformity across courts within state civil procedure systems. In the 20th century, most Australian courts had court-specific procedures which varied from other courts in the same state hierarchy as well as from interstate courts.[32] Conversely, modern civil procedure legislation in several Australian states has substantially unified procedures throughout the state legislation.[33] This has reduced the administrative complexity for lawyers and litigants and increased the ease with which matters may be transferred between courts. It is possible that eventually there will be unified civil procedure throughout Australia.[34]

The second relevant difference in recent civil procedure legislation, discussed in detail below, is the introduction in many Australian jurisdictions of central overriding or overarching purpose provisions. The insertion of overriding or overarching obligations in civil procedure legislation potentially increases the uniformity of civil procedure across state boundaries. Allowing courts to override detailed rules in order to ensure justice and efficiency not only simplifies the process for courts, lawyers and parties but may simultaneously increase the likelihood of uniformity between different court systems which are all required to follow the same High Court precedents such as *Aon*.[35] However, while the uniformity between jurisdictions increases through the common adoption of central purpose justice and efficiency provisions, the potential for justice to vary between judges within a court increases as a reflection of the increased discretion allowed to each judicial member in fulfilling his/her obligation to proceed however appropriate to maximise justice and efficiency.

Whilst the exact terminology varies throughout Australia, in all jurisdictions the attainment of justice is identified as a key aim of active case management. In addition, the need for efficient process is a dominant feature of this central purpose, commonly worded as a need to minimise cost and time taken for civil litigation. For example, in New South Wales, the terminology is an "overriding purpose" to ensure "just, quick and cheap" civil procedure. [36]

2.4.3.1 Various legislative approaches apply

The ways in which governments have introduced central purpose active case management provisions varies between Australian jurisdictions and is set out in more detail below. Arguably, the strongest adoption of the central purpose is primary legislation applying across all courts in a particular jurisdiction. This is the form adopted by New South Wales, Victoria and, more

32 For example, in New South Wales, before the *Civil Procedure Act 2005* (NSW) and *Uniform Civil Procedure Rules 2005* (NSW), civil procedure in the Supreme Court was governed by the *Supreme Court Act 1970*, the *Supreme Court Rules 1970* and Supreme Court practice notes; while District Court civil procedure was governed by the *District Court Act 1973*, the *District Court Rules 1973* and District Court practice notes; and the Local Court civil procedure was governed by the *Local Court (Civil Claims) Act 1970*, the *Local Court Act 1982*, the *Local Court (Civil Claims) Rules 1988* and the Local Court practice notes.

33 New South Wales, Victoria, Queensland and the Australian Capital Territory have uniform civil procedure case management provisions discussed in further detail below.

34 Arguably, a recent step towards unification of procedure has been the Council of Australian Governments (COAG) drafting legislation for a national legal profession; known as *Legal Profession National Law 2011 (draft)*. This law was passed in Victoria pursuant to the *Legal Profession Uniform Law Application Act 2014* (Vic) and then in New South Wales pursuant to the *Legal Profession Uniform Law Application Act 2014* (NSW) and is known as the *Legal Profession Uniform Law* (NSW) or (Vic).

35 *Aon Risk Services Australia Ltd v Australian National University* (2009) 239 CLR 175.

36 *Civil Procedure Act 2005* (NSW) s 56.

recently, the Australian Capital Territory. The other parliamentary approaches include primary legislation applicable solely to a particular court, which is the Federal Court approach; uniform subsidiary legislation (rules), which is the approach taken in the Queensland; and court-specific subsidiary legislation, as applies in Western Australia, Tasmania, South Australia and the Northern Territory. This chapter will consider the New South Wales provisions in the most detail as they are, arguably, the most longstanding of the jurisdictions with extensive active case management provisions in Australia, and New South Wales is Australia's most litigious state.[37]

2.4.3.2 Uniform Acts: New South Wales, Victoria and the Australian Capital Territory

One approach to increasing active case management is to enact legislation containing active case management provisions or amend existing legislation to incorporate provisions on case management. New South Wales and Victoria have gone the furthest in this regard, introducing civil procedure acts centred on overarching or overriding case management objectives. These acts differ from traditional legislation governing court procedure because they do not blend civil and criminal law requirements and are uniform across all courts in the states they govern. The ACT recently elevated its case management provision from its rules to s 5A of its *Court Procedures Act 2004* (ACT).

The *Civil Procedure Act 2005* (NSW) and the *Uniform Civil Procedure Rules 2005* (NSW) apply to all New South Wales Supreme Court, District Court and Local Court disputes.[38] Consideration of the *Civil Procedure Act 2005* (NSW) demonstrates how comprehensively the active case management provisions affect civil procedure and the breadth of discretion they provide the New South Wales judiciary.

The *Civil Procedure Act 2005* (NSW) is divided into nine parts, of which pt 6 (comprising six divisions) is most critical to case management, particularly ss 56–61, 64 and 84. Part 6 div 1 is the case management centrepiece and commences with s 56 which relevantly provides that:

> (1) The overriding purpose of this Act and of rules of court, in their application to civil proceedings, is to facilitate the just, quick and cheap resolution of the real issues in the proceedings.
>
> (2) The court must seek to give effect to the overriding purpose when it exercises any power given to it by this Act or by rules of court and when it interprets any provision of this Act or of any such rule.
>
> (3) A party to civil proceedings is under a duty to assist the court to further the overriding purpose and, to that effect, to participate in the processes of the court and to comply with directions and orders of the court.
>
> ...

37 See, eg, Productivity Commission (n 29) 712, 7.17 which notes that New South Wales spent $178.3 million on civil disputes (Table 7.1) and had 162,900 total civil lodgements (Table 7.3) in 2013–2014 compared to the next highest expenditure by Victoria of $132.4 million, with 113,000 total civil lodgements. The *Civil Procedure Act 2005* (NSW) commenced 15 August 2005.

38 *Civil Procedure Act 2005* (NSW) s 4, sch 1. This Act and the *Uniform Civil Procedure Rules 2005* (NSW) do not apply to Federal Court or High Court matters which are governed by the *Federal Court of Australia Act 1976* (Cth), the *Federal Court Rules 2011* (Cth), *Federal Court (Corporations) Rules 2000* (Cth), *High Court of Australia Act 1979* (Cth), and the *High Court Rules 2004* (Cth).

(4) Each of the following persons must not, by their conduct, cause a party to civil proceedings to be put in breach of a duty identified in subsection (3):
(a) any solicitor or barrister representing the party in the proceedings,
(b) any person with a relevant interest in the proceedings commenced by the party.
(5) The court may take into account any failure to comply with subsection (3) or (4) in exercising a discretion with respect to costs.
(6) For the purposes of this section, a person has a relevant interest in civil proceedings if the person:
(a) provides financial assistance or other assistance to any party to the proceedings, and
(b) exercises any direct or indirect control, or any influence, over the conduct of the proceedings or the conduct of a party in respect of the proceedings.

Note. Examples of persons who may have a relevant interest are insurers and persons who fund litigation.[39]

Section 56(1), setting out the "overriding purpose", is the most cited New South Wales case management sub-provision but the remaining s 56 sub-provisions are also important as they establish the far-reaching nature of the overriding purpose and the responsibilities of the courts, parties, solicitors and even litigation funders to ensure that the proceedings are as "just, quick and cheap" as possible.

Section 57 of the *Civil Procedure Act 2005* (NSW) is headed "Objects of case management" and is essentially a statutory interpretation provision. In theory, it directs how the overriding purpose is to be attained. However, in practice, it adds little to s 56 because the objects of s 57(1) are essentially the same "just, quick and cheap" purposes reworded. Summarised, the objects of case management are:

- s 57(1)(a) just
- s 57(1)(b) quick for the court
- s 57(1)(c) cheap for the court; and
- s 57(1)(d) quick and cheap for parties and efficient for other proceedings.

What s 57(1) adds to s 56 is clarification that the relevant speed and cost to be considered include those expended by the court, not simply the parties. Section 57 does not, however, instruct the court as to the weight to apply to the different (and potentially competing) interests of the court, the parties to a case, and litigants in general. Section 57(2) provides that all other rules and practice are to be interpreted with s 57(1) in mind.

Section 58 of the *Civil Procedure Act 2005* (NSW) is headed "Court to follow dictates of justice" but its definition of justice in s 58(2)(a) simply requires the court to have regard to ss 56 and 57. Section 58(2)(b) provides possible considerations which encourage the court to differentiate between necessary and unnecessary time incurred in order to punish parties for perceived delaying tactics without inadvertently punishing all parties in complex or difficult cases.[40]

39 s 56 *Civil Procedure Act 2005* NSW.

40 *Civil Procedure Act 2005* (NSW) s 58(2)(b) achieves this by enabling courts to take account of difficulties and complexities in the case (s 58(2)(b)(i)) and lack of expedition beyond the parties' control (s 58(2)(b)(iii)) while also allowing the courts to consider whether the parties have made the best of their opportunities and fulfilled their obligations (ss 55(2)(b)(ii), (iv), (v)).

Section 59 requires the courts to implement any procedure to reduce the time of proceedings to what is reasonably required for preparation of the case for trial and for "the interlocutory activities necessary for the fair and just determination of the issues in dispute between the parties". Essentially, s 59 reiterates the speed requirement already set out in ss 56, 57 and 58.

Section 60 requires the court to ensure costs are proportional to the "importance and complexity of the subject matter in dispute". This differs from the requirements of ss 56 and 57 concerning affordability for the parties and general cheapness. Rather, s 60 is aimed at curbing litigation where the costs are out of proportion to the dispute regardless of absolute cost or the capacity of the parties to pay. Although s 60 refers to the "costs to the parties" it also, arguably, demonstrates the government's commitment to a society-based approach to managing justice by empowering the court to limit party expenditure thereby protecting the limited resources of the court. Case management, as envisaged by ss 56–60, encompasses the entire proceedings from commencement and not merely final hearings.

Other relevant provisions include s 61(1), which entitles a court to give whatever directions it thinks fit even if inconsistent with the rules of court. This is reinforced by s 61(3) which sets out the punishments the court can impose on defaulters including striking out pleadings, dismissing proceedings and anything else the court considers appropriate. Although s 61 overrides the rules of court, it remains subject to s 56, such that all directions or punishments for failure to follow directions must still "facilitate the just, quick and cheap resolution of proceedings".[41]

Section 64(1) of the *Civil Procedure Act 2005* (NSW) entitles courts to make any amendment to any document without any restriction as to circumstances. This statutory power may have its origins in the court's inherent jurisdiction to prevent abuse of its process but is statutorily extended in both its scope and its application beyond the Supreme Court to lower courts.[42] Conversely, s 64(2) appears to impose a positive obligation on the Courts. Section 64(2) states:

> Subject to section 58, all necessary amendments are to be made for the purpose of determining the real questions raised by or otherwise depending on the proceedings, correcting any defect or error in the proceedings and avoiding multiplicity of proceedings.

While in no way purporting to define case management, s 64(2) clarifies that case management is not simply administrative but imposes a positive judicial obligation to substantively alter cases where justice requires. Subsection 64(3) allows for new causes of action via amendment where the new action arose after commencement of proceedings but stipulates that the date of commencement of any new cause of action is the date of amendment. The power of s 64 is starting to become evident from cases such as *Expense Reduction Analysis Group Pty*

41 As set out in s 56(1). This analysis is consistent with the Court of Appeal findings in *Halpin v Lumley General Insurance Ltd* (2009) 78 NSWLR 265 and in *Hans Pet Constructions Pty Ltd v Cassar* [2009] NSWCA 230.

42 Inherent jurisdiction only applies to courts of unlimited jurisdiction such as the New South Wales Supreme Court; *Grassby v The Queen* (1989) 168 CLR 1, 16 [21] (Dawson J (with Mason CJ, Brennan J and Toohey J agreeing)).

Ltd v Armstrong Strategic Management and Marketing Pty Ltd (*Expense Reduction Analysis Group*)[43] in which the High Court held that the Supreme Court of New South Wales should simply have used s 64 to order amendment to the list of discovered documents to correct the privilege errors and thence to require the return of documents over which privilege had been inadvertently waived.

Two other case management-related provisions in the *Civil Procedure Act 2005* (NSW) are ss 86 and 14. Section 86 gives the court the right to make an order (and withdraw such order)[44] by leave or by direction on whatever terms it thinks fit and to do so by application or of its own motion.[45] Section 14 provides the court discretion to dispense with any rules where appropriate. This gives New South Wales courts extensive discretion.

The more recent *Civil Procedure Act 2010* (Vic) commenced on 1 January 2011 and contains many similarities to the *Civil Procedure Act 2005* (NSW). The two key provisions are set out in ch 2 of the Act. Part 2.1 of the *Civil Procedure Act 2010* (Vic) sets out the overarching purpose of the legislation while the remaining subdivisions of pt 2 set out the overarching obligations and who they apply to.

Part 2.1 of the *Civil Procedure Act 2010* (Vic) contains the overarching purpose in ss 7 and 9. Section 7(1) states that the "overarching purpose … to facilitate the just, efficient, timely and cost effective resolution of the real issues in dispute". This provision is very similar to the key s 56 overriding purpose provision in the *Civil Procedure Act 2005* (NSW).

Part 2.2 of the *Civil Procedure Act 2010* (Vic) sets out the application of the overarching obligations. In essence, pursuant to s 10, the obligations apply to parties, their lawyers, litigation funders, insurers (running litigation in the name of their clients) and expert witnesses (but not lay witnesses). This focus on the obligations of litigation participants other than the judiciary is an important element of the *Civil Procedure Act 2010* (Vic) aimed at improving civil procedure through changing legal culture.[46]

Part 2.3 of the *Civil Procedure Act 2010* (Vic) sets out the overarching obligations themselves. In essence (and some of the obligations are qualified by exceptions), the overarching obligations may be summarised as follows:

First, there is a "paramount duty to the court to further the administration of justice in relation to any civil proceeding in which that person is involved" (s 16).

In addition, there are overarching obligations to:

- act honestly (s 17)
- for claims to have a proper basis such that they are not "frivolous, vexatious or an abuse of process" (s 18)
- only take steps "necessary to facilitate resolution or determination" of a dispute (s 19)
- cooperate with court and parties in the conduct of civil proceedings (s 20)

43 *Expense Reduction Analysis Group Pty Ltd v Armstrong Strategic Management and Marketing Pty Ltd* (2013) 250 CLR 303, 323 [58].

44 The right to undo any order is enshrined in s 43 of the *Interpretation Act 1987* (NSW) which is explicitly preserved by s 86(4) of the *Civil Procedure Act 2005* (NSW).

45 The other provisions in div 6 are of limited application and not relevant to the courts' general case management practices.

46 Based on recommendations from the Victorian Law Reform Commission (n 25) 17–20, 148–205.

- "not to mislead or deceive" (s 21)
- "use reasonable endeavours to resolve dispute" (s 22)
- "narrow the issues in dispute" if unable to resolve the dispute (s 23)
- "ensure costs are reasonable and proportionate" given the complexity and amount in dispute (s 24)
- "minimise delay" (s 25)
- "disclose existence of documents" (s 26).

Part 2.4 of the *Civil Procedure Act 2010* (Vic) then sets out the sanctions for contravening the overarching obligations. Many of the sanctions, set out in s 29(1), involve costs penalties, although the courts' power is extensive. For example, ss 29(1)(d), (e) and (f) give the court broad powers including rectification and preventing a party from taking steps in the litigation. The *Civil Procedure Act 2010* (Vic) also contains s 49(1) which further demonstrates the elevation of judicial discretion through the overarching provisions by providing:

> In addition to any other power a court may have, a court may give any direction or make any order it considers appropriate to further the overarching purpose in relation to the conduct of the hearing in a civil proceeding.[47]

It should be noted that, despite its *Civil Procedure Act 2010* (Vic), Victoria does not have uniform court rules throughout its court systems, the way New South Wales does.[48]

The Australian Capital Territory *Court Procedures Act 2004* (ACT) was amended in 2015 to include s 5A, which states that: "The main purpose of the civil procedure provisions is to facilitate the just resolution of disputes (a) according to the law; and (b) as quickly, inexpensively and efficiently as possible."[49] Section 5A of the *Court Procedures Act 2004* (ACT) replaced r 21 of the *Court Procedures Rules 2006* (ACT) which was the provision relied on by the High Court in *Aon* and stated that the rules are "to facilitate the just resolution of the real issues in civil proceedings with minimum delay and expense".[50] Rules 501 and 502 of the *Court Procedures Rules 2006* (ACT) also contain statements regarding the circumstances and purpose for amendment of documents and these provisions were also referred to in *Aon*.[51]

2.4.3.3 Court-based Acts: Federal Court

The *Federal Court of Australia Act 1976* (Cth) was amended in 2009, via the *Access to Justice (Civil Litigation Reforms) Amendment Act 2009* (Cth), which inserted s 37M. Section 37M

47 *Civil Procedure Act 2010* (Vic) s 49(1).

48 In Victoria, the Supreme Court is governed by the *Supreme Court (General Civil Procedure) Rules 2015* (Vic) which replaced the *Supreme Court (General Civil Procedure) Rules 2005* (Vic) while the County Court is governed by the *County Court Civil Procedure Rules 2008* (Vic).

49 *Court Procedures Act 2004* (ACT) s 5A.

50 *Court Procedures Rules 2006* (ACT) r 21. The *Courts Legislation Amendment Act 2015 (No 2)* (ACT) (ss 16 and 22 respectively) introduced s 5A of the *Court Procedures Act 2004* (ACT) and omitted r 21 of the *Court Procedures Rules 2006* (ACT). The ACT Court of Appeal equated s 5A with its predecessor r 21 in *Ryan v Vizovitis* [2017] ACTCA 3.

51 *Court Procedures Rules 2006* (ACT) and *Aon Risk Services Australia Ltd v Australian National University* (2009) 239 CLR 175.

creates an "overarching" purpose "to facilitate the just resolution of disputes" according to law and as efficiently as possible. Section 37N of the *Federal Court of Australia Act 1976* (Cth) extends the obligation to parties to act consistently with the overarching purpose. Section 37M(2) has a list of objectives of overarching purposes, which include:

(a) just determination of all proceedings
(b) efficient use of judicial and administrative resources
(c) efficient disposal of the Court's caseload
(d) timely disposal of proceedings
(e) costs proportionate to importance and complexity.

Unlike s 37M(1), which envisages just as including inexpensive and efficient, in s 37M(2) "just" is described as a separate objective to cheap and quick, similar to s 56 *Civil Procedure Act 2005* (NSW). Section 37P clarifies the types of directions court can make. Other federal courts are governed by different legislation which does not contain the overarching purpose provision.[52]

It is noteworthy that, significantly prior to the 2009 introduction of the "overarching" principle in the *Federal Court of Australia Act 1976* (Cth), in 1997 the Federal Court introduced an individual docket system to promote case management which allocated each case to a judge for case management of the entire case including pre-trial preparation and trial. This system was designed to improve case management. A preliminary review in 2002 considered it to be effective in relation to the Federal Court's workload, which is relatively low compared with many courts except for some high-volume areas such as migration cases and very complex areas such as native title.[53] The Federal Court then introduced the "Fast Track List" initially in its Victorian Registry in May 2007, commonly known as the "the rocket-docket," which was also designed to increase efficiency in civil procedure through case management.[54] Due to the contemporaneous nature of the changes, it is difficult to determine to what extent changes in Federal Court case management were a result of the introduction of the central overarching principle as opposed to the docketing case management initiatives.

More recently, at a court-based case management level, the Federal Court introduced a National Court Framework late in 2016 which contains a series of practice notes directed towards case management and other issues to improve consistency throughout the Federal Court system.[55] This framework divides Federal Court cases into nine national practice areas and aims to foster consistency, simplify practice and procedure, facilitate ADR and improve efficiency.[56]

52 See, eg, *Federal Circuit Court of Australia Act 1999* (Cth) governing the Federal Circuit Court which does not contain an equivalent provision to s 37M of the *Federal Court of Australia Act 1976* (Cth) nor does the *Family Law Act 1975* (Cth) governing the Family Court.

53 Caroline Sage, Ted Wright and Carolyn Morris, *Case Management Reform: A Study of the Federal Court's Individual Docket System* (Law and Justice Foundation of New South Wales, 2002) 3.

54 Stephen Rares, 'The Significance of the Commercial Jurisdiction of the Federal Court of Australia' (Speech, Commercial Law Association's Leading Edge Seminar, 5 September 2008) 17.

55 Federal Court of Australia, *Central Practice Note CPN-1: National Court Framework and Case Management,* 25 October 2016.

56 Federal Court of Australia, 'National Court Framework' (Web Page) <http://www.fedcourt.gov.au/about/national-court-framework>.

2.4.3.4 Uniform court procedure rules: Queensland

The first central purpose case management provision was legislated by Queensland, with its *Uniform Civil Procedure Rules 1999* (Qld), r 5 of which provides the "Philosophy – overriding obligations of parties and court" including:

> The purpose of these rules is to facilitate the just and expeditious resolution of the real issues in civil proceedings at a minimum of expense.

Rule 5(2) then imposes obligations on the court and r 5(3) on the parties, but these sub-rules focus on efficiency rather than justice.[57]

2.4.3.5 Non-uniform court-based rules: South Australia, Western Australia, Tasmania and the Northern Territory

Other states have imported case management objectives, or overarching provisions enabling case management, through their court-based civil procedure rules.

For example, the provisions in order 1 r 4A on elimination of delays and r 4B headed "case management" of the *Rules of the Supreme Court 1971* (WA) are similar to the Victorian and New South Wales case management rules. Rule 4A confines the lapse of time to what is reasonable for "just determination" of "issues bona fide in contention." Order 1 r 4B of the *Rules of the Supreme Court 1971* (WA), amended in 2010, on use and objects of case flow management states:

> (1) Actions, causes and matters in the Court will, to the extent that the resources of the Court permit, be managed and supervised in accordance with a system of positive case flow management with the objects of —
> (a) promoting the just determination of litigation; and
> (b) disposing efficiently of the business of the Court; and
> (c) maximising the efficient use of available judicial and administrative resources; and
> (d) facilitating the timely disposal of business; and
> (e) ensuring the procedure applicable, and the costs of the procedure to the parties and the State, are proportionate to the value, importance and complexity of the subject matter in dispute; and
> (f) that the procedure applicable, and the costs of the procedure to the parties, are proportionate to the financial position of each party.
>
> (2) These rules are to be construed and applied and the processes and procedures of the Court conducted so as best to ensure the attainment of the objects referred to in subrule (1).[58]

The justice and efficiency aims in the *Rules of the Supreme Court 1971* (WA) are similar to the *Civil Procedure Act 2005* (NSW) and *Civil Procedure Act 2010* (Vic) case management

57 *Uniform Civil Procedure Rules 1999* (Qld).
58 *Rules of the Supreme Court 1971* (WA) r 4B.

provisions but, unlike New South Wales and Victoria, Western Australia does not have uniform procedure legislation.[59] Order 1 r 4B has a "pervasive impact" on interlocutory judicial decision-making in Western Australia, as noted by Martin CJ of the Supreme Court of Appeal (WA):

> It is difficult to overstate the importance of the principle of proportionality embodied in O 1 r 4B of the Rules of the Supreme Court 1971 (WA).[60]

In Tasmania, pt 14 (Pre-Trial Directions) div 1 (Case Management) r 414A was inserted into the *Supreme Court Rules 2000* (Tas) in April 2011 and provides:

> The overarching purpose of case management is to ensure that proceedings are conducted and resolved justly and efficiently.[61]

Rule 414A is also very similar to the *Civil Procedure Act 2005 (NSW)* and *Civil Procedure Act 2010 (Vic)* general case management provisions.

Rule 3 of the *Supreme Court Civil Rules 2006* (SA) provides that the purpose of the legislation includes the achievement of similar central justice and efficiency aims as those of Victoria and New South Wales, stating at r 3:

> 3. The objects of these rules are —
> (a) to establish orderly procedures for the just resolution of civil disputes; and
> (b) to facilitate and encourage the resolution of civil disputes by agreement between the parties; and
> (c) to avoid all unnecessary delay in the resolution of civil disputes; and
> (d) to promote efficiency in dispute resolution so far as that object is consistent with the paramount claims of justice; and
> (e) to minimise the cost of civil litigation to the litigants and to the State.[62]

The Northern Territory has probably taken the least steps of any Australian jurisdiction towards a central case management provision. There is no overriding or overarching central purpose and no discussion of case management. Order 48 of the *Supreme Court Rules 1987* (NT), which applies to proceedings commenced by writ, or at the Court's discretion, is titled "Case flow management and setting down for trial" and provides for directions hearings and what is, in essence, a case management process. In addition, pt 3 r 1.10 in ch 1 of the *Supreme Court Rules 1987* (NT), which applies to all matters unless excluded by other rules,[63] states:

> (1) In exercising a power under this Chapter the Court:
> (a) shall endeavour to ensure that all questions in the proceeding are effectively, completely, promptly and economically determined; and

59 *Magistrates Court (Civil Proceedings) Act 2004* (WA) and *Magistrates Court (Civil Proceedings) Rules 2005* (WA) apply to proceedings in the Western Australian Magistrates Court and do not contain equivalent case management provisions to their Supreme Court equivalents.

60 *Kelbush Pty Ltd v Australia and New Zealand Banking Group Ltd* (2016) 49 WAR 374, 376 [2]–[3].

61 *Supreme Court Rules 2000* (Tas) r 414A was inserted by the *Supreme Court Amendment (Miscellaneous) Rules 2011* (Tas) and came in force on 8 April 2011. The *Supreme Court Civil Procedure Act 1932* (Tas) contains no references to case management and no overriding or overarching justice or efficiency measures although the Act describes itself as relating to the "better administration of justice".

62 *Supreme Court Civil Rules 2006* (SA).

63 *Supreme Court Rules 1987* (NT) r 1.02(1), qualified by r 1.02(3).

(b) may give any direction or impose any term or condition it thinks fit.

(2) The Court may exercise a power under this Chapter of its own motion or on the application of a party or of a person who has a sufficient interest.[64]

Rule 1.11 then provides a broad procedural discretion for the judiciary in any circumstance where there is no explicit procedure or the procedure is in doubt. There are, however, no relevant references to any general obligation for justice in the *Supreme Court Rules 1987* (NT) equivalent to the New South Wales or Victorian provisions.[65]

2.4.4 The High Court resurrection of case management

High Court decisions on case management are extremely influential, mostly because they are so rare.[66] Appeals to the High Court on issues of case management are rare because it is difficult to appeal exercises of judicial discretion.[67] The leading High Court decision on case management remains *Aon*.[68] The central messages of *Aon* have been reinforced in subsequent High Court case management decisions such as *Expense Reduction Analysis Group*, *Rozenblit v Vainer*[69] and *UBS AG v Tyne* ('*UBS*')[70].

The power of High Court precedent to influence the meaning of case management is evident from the two earlier High Court cases, *Queensland v JL Holdings Pty Ltd* ('*JL Holdings*')[71] and *Sali v SPC Ltd*,[72] which preceded the enactment of the active case management provisions (see Chapter 2.2.3). It is probable the active case management

64 *Supreme Court Rules 1987* (NT) r 1.10.

65 There are also no general justice obligations in the *Supreme Court Act 1961* (NT).

66 For example, the High Court's decision in *UBS AG v Tyne* (2018) 265 CLR 77, discussed in Chapter 2.2.5, was cited in over 60 cases in the first year after being handed down.

67 This limitation on appellate review is caused by the rule in *House v The King* (1936) 55 CLR 499, [504]–[505] which restricts appeals of discretionary decisions of trial judges to circumstances where "the judge acts upon a wrong principle, … allows extraneous or irrelevant matters to guide or affect him, … mistakes the facts [or] … does not take into account some material consideration". This limitation has been accepted by the courts in numerous case management cases, such as *McMahon v John Fairfax Publications Pty Ltd* [2010] NSWCA 308, [34] (Allsop P), [42] (Giles JA). See also *Karl Suleman Enterprizes Pty Ltd (in liq) v Pham* [2013] NSWCA 93, [11] (Meagher and Barrett JJ); *Hans Pet Constructions Pty Ltd v Cassar* [2009] NSWCA 230, [31]; *Newton v Ellis* [2012] NSWCA 106, [17]; *Menzies v Paccar Financial Pty Ltd (No 4)* (2014) 101 ACSR 25, 36 [57], 37 [64] (Emmett JA, Leeming JA, Sackville AJA) and *Littore v Rabobank Australia Ltd* [2016] VSCA 258, [32] (Maxwell P and Weinberg JA).

68 *Aon Risk Services Australia Ltd v Australian National University* (2009) 239 CLR 175 has been cited in well over 2,000 decisions, including over 1,000 Supreme Court and Federal Court level decisions and across every Australian jurisdiction. Some decisions expressly discuss its application beyond the ACT, such as *Tamaya Resources Ltd (in liq) v Deloitte Touche Tohmatsu* (2016) 332 ALR 199, [121] for the federal jurisdiction and *Expense Reduction Analysis Group Pty Ltd v Armstrong Strategic Management and Marketing Pty Ltd* (2013) 250 CLR 303 for New South Wales. *Aon* has even been cited in over 20 overseas decisions ranging from New Zealand to Namibia. See also Peta Spender, 'Wavering Alternations of Valour and Caution: Commercial and Regulatory Litigation in the French CJ High Court' (2013) 2(3) *Journal of Civil Litigation and Practice* 118; Sonya Willis, 'Courting Incompetence: Should the High Court More Carefully Consider its Influence on Legal Culture?' (2016) 35(2) *Civil Justice Quarterly* 129.

69 *Rozenblit v Vainer* (2018) 262 CLR 478.

70 *UBS AG v Tyne* (2018) 265 CLR 77; see Chapter 2.2.5.

71 *Queensland v JL Holdings Pty Ltd* (1997) 189 CLR 146.

72 *Sali v SPC Ltd* (1993) 67 ALJR 841.

provisions were themselves designed to counter inefficiencies which resulted from the High Court's decision in *JL Holdings*.[73] Most significantly, the High Court, in *Aon*,[74] utilised the Australian Capital Territory's then recent, central purpose justice and efficiency legislation to overrule the longstanding anti-efficiency decision in *JL Holdings*.[75]

Aon was an insurance dispute where the insured party, the Australian National University (ANU), eventually settled its claim against the insurer but wished to proceed with its claim against its insurance broker, Aon. ANU sought to amend its pleadings to plead matters which would have been damaging to its, now settled, claim against the insurers, but which strengthened its claim against the insurance broker. The High Court overruled the decisions in the courts below, holding that ANU could not amend its pleadings at such a late stage, due to active case management considerations.

In the words of French CJ, *Aon* concerned:

> an application which was made late in the day, was inadequately explained, necessitated the vacation or adjournment of the dates set down for trial, and raised new claims not previously agitated apparently because of a deliberate tactical decision not to do so.[76]

Based on this description, it is perhaps unsurprising that the High Court ruled that the application should not have been allowed. The lower courts, though, had allowed ANU's application to be made following the previous authority of *JL Holdings*.[77]

In *Aon*, the High Court considered the importance of case management. Chief Justice French, discussing *JL Holdings*, stated:

> However, to the extent that statements about the exercise of the discretion to amend pleadings in that case suggest that case management considerations and questions of proper use of court resources are to be discounted or given little weight, it should not be regarded as authoritative.[78]

The above statement resurrects the importance of case management. It also suggests that there are well understood "case management considerations".[79]

Aon was an Australian Capital Territory case; however, as a High Court authority on case management, *Aon's* application to all Australian jurisdictions is unquestionable.[80] Accordingly, the Australian judicial conception of case management now extends to broad consideration of management of the court's business and the public's conception of justice, rather than a narrow consideration simply of the interests of parties within a case. The High Court's case management strategy even extends beyond some modern civil procedure legislation because it contemplates hypothetical future cases and the need to

73 See, eg, Gummow, Hayne, Crennan, Kiefel and Bell JJ in *Aon Risk Services Australia Ltd v Australian National University* (2009) 239 CLR 175 [97]; *Trevor Roller Shutter Service Pty Ltd v Crowe* (2011) 31 VR 249 [42].

74 *Aon Risk Services Australia Ltd v Australian National University* (2009) 239 CLR 175.

75 *Queensland v JL Holdings Pty Ltd* (1997) 189 CLR 146.

76 *Aon Risk Services Australia Ltd v Australian National University* (2009) 239 CLR 175, 181–182 [4] (French CJ).

77 *Queensland v JL Holdings Pty Ltd* (1997) 189 CLR 146.

78 *Aon Risk Services Australia Ltd v Australian National University* (2009) 239 CLR 175, 182 [6].

79 Ibid 211 [92] (Gummow, Hayne, Crennan, Kiefel and Bell JJ).

80 See Chapter 2.2.4.

ensure the business of courts supports the rule of law and public confidence by managing present and future judicial workload. *Aon* enabled the High Court to "buttress reforms to the civil justice system".[81]

2.4.5 Utilising legislation and precedent for case management

The combination of the High Court's resurrection of case management in *Aon* (discussed in Chapter 2.2.4) and the modern active case management legislation (discussed in Chapter 2.2.3) provides courts with ample support for emphasising case management imperatives in judicial decision-making. This is demonstrated by recent High Court decisions which utilise *Aon* and active case management provisions.[82]

One significant High Court active case management decision is *Expense Reduction Analysis Group,* which reiterated the case management findings in *Aon. Expense Reduction Analysis Group* concerned the inadvertent waiver of client legal privilege in the pre-trial discovery process. There were 60,000 documents involved in Expense Reduction Analysis Group's (ERA) discovery process (at that time) and an electronic database was used which had a privilege field. Numerous documents were not marked as privileged which should have been marked privileged, including the 13 documents which were the subject of the High Court litigation. In overruling the decision of the New South Wales Court of Appeal, the High Court found that documents, which had been disclosed by Expense Reduction Analysis Group's lawyers through being listed and made available for inspection by the Armstrong parties, should be destroyed by the Armstrong parties or returned. The basis for the decision was that the ERA parties had intended to claim privilege but had inadvertently failed to identify the relevant documents as privileged on their list of discovered documents.

It is evident, from many statements by the High Court in *Expense Reduction Analysis Group,* that the Court's intention was to improve efficiency within the court system and the litigation process by discouraging parties from engaging in lengthy interlocutory skirmishes. However, in so doing, it approached case management in a way which effectively discouraged judicial engagement with case management issues and encouraged parties to manage their cases without reference to the court.[83] The High Court has, arguably, recently confined its findings in *Expense Reduction Analysis Group* as regards the influence of case management on privilege in *Glencore International AG v Commissioner of Taxation,*[84] but this decision does not affect the *Expense Reduction Analysis Group* disincentive for parties to engage with the Court on interlocutory matters.[85]

The decision in *Expense Reduction Analysis Group* did not seek to redefine case management to include the activities of the parties and their lawyers.[86] However, the High

81 Spender (n 68) 130.

82 For the reasons set out in Chapter 2.2.4, there remain very few procedural cases which reach the High Court and so each of the cases discussed in this section are influential.

83 *Expense Reduction Analysis Group Pty Ltd v Armstrong Strategic Management and Marketing Pty Ltd* (2013) 250 CLR 303, 325 [64]. For a more detailed discussion, see Willis (n 68).

84 *Glencore International AG v Commissioner of Taxation* (2019) 265 CLR 646.

85 Ibid [36].

86 *Expense Reduction Analysis Group Pty Ltd v Armstrong Strategic Management and Marketing Pty Ltd* (2013) 250 CLR 303, 308 [3], 318 [39], 321 [51].

Court did expressly recognise the obligations on lawyers and players to assist the Court imposed by the *Civil Procedure Act 2005* (NSW).[87]

The *Expense Reduction Analysis Group* decision explicitly relied on the decision in *Aon*. The ACT Supreme Court of Appeal in *Aon* referred to case management principles, "including" the availability of court resources, yet still allowed ANU's late pleading amendment.[88] By contrast, in the High Court, French CJ discussed the positive obligation judges may have to initiate, by judicial motion, amendment of parties' pleadings in order to determine the real questions in dispute.[89] This positive obligation was explicitly accepted by the High Court in *Expense Reduction Analysis Group*.[90] The High Court's analysis was made in the context of the Court's power to amend pleadings, which falls within the scope of case management. Accordingly, the High Court has effectively directed the judiciary to look beyond the interests of the disputing parties in undertaking case management.

Another High Court decision subsequent to *Aon* which briefly discusses case management is the decision of Nettle J in *Construction Forestry Mining and Energy Union v Director of the Fair Work Building Industry Inspectorate*[91] ('*CFMEU*'). In this case, Nettle J concluded that the CFMEU should not have sought administrative writs of prohibition, mandamus or certiorari from the High Court because it had not exhausted its constitutional right of appeal to the Full Federal Court.[92] This was because the Federal Court decision was a judicial decision and not an administrative decision.[93] The CFMEU was refused leave by the Federal Court to withdraw evidence and amend pleadings after the hearing closed, as such leave would have necessitated a rehearing.

CFMEU was an appeal from Federal Court trial judge, Collier J, who relied on *Aon*, *Expense Reduction Analysis Group* and s 37M of the *Federal Court of Australia Act 1976* (Cth), in finding that the need for timely and efficient disposition of court business and limited court resources were factors which militated against granting leave.[94] Justice Nettle found that Collier J had not denied the CFMEU procedural fairness because her Honour had considered its application and detailed submissions and had decided the matter on multiple bases as expressed in her reasons.[95] This case demonstrates the increasing power of case management considerations as a justification for interlocutory decisions to limit or deny further hearing of a matter.

Rozenblit v Vainer concerned an order for immediate payment of interlocutory costs which had not been met due to the impecuniosity of the plaintiff. The High Court found that the proceedings should not have been stayed purely due to the non-payment, thereby overriding the decision of the Victorian Court of Appeal. The trial judge had noted that the

87 Ibid 321 [52].

88 *Aon Risk Services Australia Ltd v Australian National University* (2009) 239 CLR 175, 181 [4] and footnote 40 referring to the decision of *Aon Risk Services Australia Ltd v Australian National University* (2008) 227 FLR 388, 390 [10] per Higgins CJ; at 395 [54] per Penfold J; at 416–417 [196] per Lander J.

89 *Aon Risk Services Australia Limited v Australian National University* (2009) 239 CLR 175, 185 [14].

90 *Expense Reduction Analysis Group Pty Ltd v Armstrong Strategic Management and Marketing Pty Ltd* (2013) 250 CLR 303.

91 *Construction Forestry Mining and Energy Union v Director of the Fair Work Building Industry Inspectorate* (2016) 338 ALR 360.

92 Ibid [22], [27], [32], [35].

93 Ibid [27].

94 Ibid [12]–[14].

95 Ibid [30].

behaviour of the plaintiff leading to the adverse interlocutory costs order was not vexatious. It was also a significant factor in the High Court's decision that requiring payment would result in the plaintiff being unable to pursue his case.[96]

The High Court relied on *Aon*[97] and discussed the "overarching" purpose of the *Civil Procedure Act 2010* (Vic) in some detail, concluding that "overarching obligations do not displace the need for the court to safeguard the administration of justice in the context of ordering a stay for abuse of process."[98]

Another recent High Court case management decision is *UBS AG v Tyne* (*UBS AG*). *UBS AG* is a complicated private international law dispute involving multiple jurisdictions, several corporate and individual parties essentially controlled by an individual, Scott Tyne, in a dispute against UBS bank in relation to a disastrous 2007 investment in Kazakhstan bonds.[99] Mr Tyne tried to hold UBS responsible for advising his investment in Kazakhstan bonds which resulted in his debt to UBS when the bond price collapsed during the Global Financial Crisis (GFC) of 2008. The 2008 GFC resulted in margin call in excess of US$28 million and defaults leading to a complex unwinding of the transaction with significant losses to the interests of Mr Tyne. A battle between UBS and Mr Tyne as to the appropriate jurisdiction saw UBS strategically outmanoeuvring Mr Tyne, resulting in a Singapore-based decision where consumer law protection was not available to Mr Tyne. This Singapore decision resulted in a chain of New South Wales Supreme Court and Australian Federal Court cases being struck out to avoid breaches of the finality doctrines or abuse of process (see Chapter 5 and Chapter 16), as well as proceedings to enforce the Singapore decision in Australia. The Federal Court claim was based on the rights of a private trust which had been excluded from the Supreme Court proceedings. The dispute in the High Court was about whether Mr Tyne was entitled to have the trust's case heard in the Federal Court or whether he should not have removed this aspect of his claim from earlier New South Wales Supreme Court proceedings.

The High Court, in a rare 4:3 split decision, rejected Mr Tyne's Federal Court proceedings using case management arguments. The majority found that Mr Tyne should not have removed the Trust from the Supreme Court proceedings and was, therefore, not now entitled to bring that Trust's claim in the Federal Court. Kiefel CJ, Bell and Keane JJ (with whom Gageler J agreed to form the majority) referred to the overriding case management provision in the *Civil Procedure Act 2005* (NSW), s 56 as earlier proceedings had been run in the New South Wales Supreme Court:

> Mr Tyne perceived a forensic advantage to the Tyne-related parties in holding back the Trust's claim. This was a decision that, were Telesto's claim to be stayed, would lead to duplication of resources and increased cost, and would delay the resolution of the dispute between the Tyne-related parties and UBS. Hiving off the Trust's claim, with a view to bringing it in another court after the determination of the SCNSW proceedings,

96 *Rozenblit v Vainer* (2018) 262 CLR 478 at [113].

97 Ibid [11], [31], [41].

98 Ibid [75].

99 Some of the key decisions in the dispute include: *UBS AG v Telesto Investments Ltd* (2011) 4 SLR 503; *Telesto Investments Ltd v UBS AG* (2012) 262 FLR 119; *Telesto Investments Ltd v UBS AG* (2013) 94 ACSR 29; *Australia and New Zealand Banking Group Ltd v Marks* [2013] QSC 186; *Tyne v UBS AG* (2014) 102 ACSR 403; *Tyne v UBS AG (No 2)* [2014] FCA 1228; *Marks v Australia and New Zealand Banking Group Ltd* [2014] QCA 102; *Tyne v UBS AG (No 4)* [2017] FCA 374; *Tyne (Trustee) v UBS AG (No 2)* (2017) 250 FCR 341; *UBS AG v Tyne* (2018) 265 CLR 77.

> was the antithesis of the discharge of the duty imposed on parties to civil litigation in the Supreme Court of New South Wales [CPA, s 56(3] and in the Federal Court [FCA, s 37N(1).] That duty is to conduct the proceedings in a way that is consistent with the overriding/overarching purpose.[100]

Unfortunately, the above analysis by the majority of the High Court ignores the circumstances of how Mr Tyne came to hive off the Trust claim in the New South Wales Supreme Court proceedings and completely ignores the strategic nature of UBS's original commencement of proceedings in Singapore (which were triggered by Mr Tyne notifying his intention to litigate in Australia).

Interestingly, the minority of the High Court also relied on case management principles to come to the opposite conclusion that, in fact, Mr Tyne had never actually had his case properly heard and had not breached any obligations in New South Wales by removing the Trust's claim with Nettle and Edelman JJ (with whom Gordon J agreed), finding that the discontinuance of the Trust's claim in New South Wales was not inconsistent with s 37M of the *Federal Court of Australia Act 1976* (Cth):

> The previous trustee did not stand back and allow the Supreme Court proceedings to proceed to a 'final judicial determination'. It stood back after the proceedings had been temporarily stayed to see whether they would be permanently stayed, with the reasonable expectation that they would not be permanently stayed, and thus that it would not be necessary to prosecute the previous trustee's claims. As has been observed, that was not an unreasonable course to adopt in the circumstances of this case. And it was not inconsistent with the statutory shibboleth of making litigation as quick, inexpensive and efficient as possible. As Mr Tyne deposed, he was looking to limit the boundaries of the litigation.[101]

The Tyne litigation saga shows the extent to which case management principles can influence the substantive outcome of litigation. *UBS AG* also demonstrates how complex and uncertain the application of seemingly straightforward objectives of justice and efficiency can be in a real-life dispute. The High Court's decision in *UBS AG* is a particularly disappointing one as it enabled the desirable aims of case management efficiency to be effectively subverted by a strategic litigator, UBS, to prevent Mr Tyne obtaining a substantive hearing of his case in Australia.

2.5 Litigation deterrents

There are several significant deterrents to litigating: cost, time, and emotional stress. These deterrents are well known and are some of the key factors which encourage parties to resolve their disputes through ADR, which tends to be somewhat cheaper, quicker and less stressful. The deterrents to litigation are often listed as key reasons why case management reforms are required.[102] Despite recent case management reform, it is well recognised by the judiciary that litigation should remain a last resort. It is very rare that litigants do not find litigation to be expensive, time-consuming and stressful. Only very frequent litigators (such

100 *UBS AG v Tyne* (2018) 265 CLR 77, [55].
101 *UBS AG v Tyne* (2018) 265 CLR 77, [108].
102 Productivity Commission (n 29).

as insurance companies) are likely to be pleasantly surprised by the achievements of case management reform in improving the efficiency of civil litigation in Australia.

The Victorian Supreme Court case of *Hodgson v Amcor Ltd*[103] concerned an application for proceedings to be struck out for disregard of court orders and consequent prejudice caused by delay in a dispute about sale of businesses.[104] The number of judgments, mostly interlocutory, in the *Hodgson v Amcor Ltd* litigation demonstrate how time-consuming, costly and stressful a hard-fought litigation can be.[105] In the following extract from the first 2011 judgment, Vickery J engages with the history and development of case management while discussing the endless battle of the judiciary with delay and costs, citing others in support of his analysis. The deterrents to litigation are made abundantly clear in this extract.

Justice delayed is justice denied

7 Central to Mr Hodgson's application is the prejudice he claims has arisen from the delay in commencing his trial caused by Amcor's failure to deliver its witness statements in accordance with the orders of the Court.

8 French CJ in *Aon Risk Services Australia Limited v Australian National University* said:

> The impetus for civil procedure reform in the 19th century was provided by critics of the system in place at the beginning of that century, which was described by Jeremy Bentham as one of 'exquisitely contrived chicanery which maximises delay and denial of justice'.

9 Civil procedure has developed markedly since the dark days described by Bentham. In most cases the rules of the superior courts in Australia state in various ways that the overriding purpose behind the administration of court processes is to facilitate the just resolution of the real issues in civil proceedings with minimum delay and expense. In Victoria this objective has received statutory momentum by the recent introduction of the *Civil Procedure Act 2010*, which commenced operation on 1 January 2011.

10 Nevertheless, and in spite of these reforms, the present applications before the Court starkly illustrate that our legal system continues to be challenged by the ancient maladies which have always confronted it — delay and cost.

11 Delay is a natural enemy of justice. The maxim attributed to William Gladstone 'justice delayed is justice denied' is uncontroversial. The concept is of ancient origin. The Magna Carta pronounced in definitive terms: 'To no one will we deny or delay right or justice', and earlier, Ulpian, a Roman jurist who wrote between AD 211 and 222, expressed the idea in similar terms: '*Justitiae dilatio est quaedam negatio*'. It is also well recognised in civil law jurisdictions and internationally. French jurists say '*Justice rétive, justice fautive*, and the European Convention on Human Rights provides by Article 6

103 *Hodgson v Amcor Ltd* (2011) 32 VR 495.

104 Ibid [7]–[17].

105 This dispute was lengthy with many related decisions, counterclaims, cross-claims, numerous parties, costs disputes, allegations of collusion and complicated facts. See, eg, *Amcor Ltd v Barnes (Ruling No 3)* [2019] VSC 393; *Amcor Ltd v Barnes (Ruling No 2)* [2018] VSC 137; *Amcor Ltd v Barnes (Ruling No 1)* [2018] VSC 21; *Amcor Ltd v Barnes* [2016] VSC 707; *Hodgson v Amcor Ltd* [2015] VSC 90, *Amcor Ltd v Barnes (No 11)* [2013] VSC 739; *Amcor Ltd v Barnes* [2012] VSC 434; *Holihan v Amcor Ltd* [2011] VSCA 225; *Hodgson v Amcor Ltd (No 6)* [2011] VSC 294.

provides that 'everyone is entitled to a fair and public hearing within a reasonable time' in the determination of a person's civil rights and obligations.

12 Lord Denning MR, in *Allen v Sir Alfred McAlpine and Sons Ltd* lamented of the need to put this wrong right with potent allusions to Shakespeare's *Hamlet* and Dickens' *Bleak House*:

> All through the years men have protested at the law's delay and counted it as a grievous wrong, hard to bear. Shakespeare ranks it among the whips and scorns of time. Dickens tells how it exhausts finances, patience, courage, hope.

13 Delay may have a direct impact on the quality of the justice able to be administered. Indeed, it has been said that the longer the delay in commencing proceedings, the more likely it is that the case will be decided on less evidence than was available to the parties at the time that the cause of action arose. As McHugh said in *Brisbane South Regional Health Authority v Taylor*:

> The enactment of time limitations has been driven by the general perception that '[w]here there is delay the whole quality of justice deteriorates.' Sometimes the deterioration in quality is palpable, as in the case where a crucial witness is dead or an important document has been destroyed. But sometimes, perhaps more often than we realise, the deterioration in quality is not recognisable even by the parties. Prejudice may exist without the parties or anybody else realising that it exists. As the United States Supreme Court pointed out in *Barker v Wingo*, 'what has been forgotten can rarely be shown'. So, it must often happen that important, perhaps decisive, evidence has disappeared without anybody now "knowing" that it ever existed. Similarly, it must often happen that time will diminish the significance of a known fact or circumstance because its relationship to the cause of action is no longer as apparent as it was when the cause of action arose. A verdict may appear well based on the evidence given in the proceedings, but, if the tribunal of fact had all the evidence concerning the matter, an opposite result may have ensued.

14 Delay in litigation gives rise to increased costs for the parties. In recognition of the problem of costs in civil litigation, in November 2008 Jackson LJ was appointed to lead a fundamental review of the rules and principles governing the costs of civil litigation in the United Kingdom and to make recommendations in order to promote access to justice at proportionate cost. The final report, known as the Jackson Report, was published to the then Master of the Rolls, Lord Neuberger, on 14 January 2010. It sets out a coherent package of reforms which are designed to reduce costs in civil litigation and by this means to promote access to justice.

15 Of no less import are the insidious social and indirect commercial costs which arise from delay in litigation. The Hon. Michael Black AC, at the 18th Pacific Judicial Conference, Papeete, Polynésie Français (Tahiti), said the following in his paper '*The role of the judge in attacking endemic delays*':

> Delay does more than deny justice. It has multiple cost implications, some more apparent than others. In commercial enterprise, for example, the unnecessary resulting from delay has both direct and incidental costs. Some of these will be measurable, and some not. In either case they may have a substantial impact upon an enterprise and the lives of those involved in it.

> In the private lives of people engaged in litigation the uncertainty associated with delay also has a social cost. Moreover, in all litigation — although most obvious in commercial litigation — there is the cost attributable to the time of those involved in the litigation as parties and witnesses.
>
> There is a broader point about the role of courts with a commercial jurisdiction as part of what may be seen as the commercial infrastructure of a county. If courts are to perform that role — as well as their fundamental constitutional roles — commercial dispute resolution should function on a commercial timescale. Corporations see many courts as operating on a timescale foreign to commercial thinking. The timelines for a commercial enterprise are quarterly, six-monthly and yearly — so that matters that take more than a year to resolve are outside normal operational timelines for commercial decision-making. As well, in some cases the principal remedy sought becomes redundant when a case is drawn out too long, such as where a party seeks corrective advertising as the most effective remedy for a misleading statement.
>
> I should also note that while delay is difficult enough for large scale corporations, for smaller corporations it may be life imperilling and can impose great personal cost on the owners of the enterprise. Large corporations can, and do, take advantage of this imbalance by using delay as a tactic to force resolution in litigation against smaller players. If competitive markets are to be maintained we should not allow this imbalance.
>
> In short, the need to reduce delay in litigation, and the uncertainties and costs associated with delay, is incontrovertible.

> 16 Since the delivery of Black's paper, two things have occurred which are of significance to the present case.
>
> 17 The first was the handing down of the decision of the High Court in *Aon Risk Services Australia v Australian National University* on 5 August 2009. This decision affirmed the importance, not only to the parties, but to the Court and other litigants, of a 'just but timely and cost-effective resolution of a dispute between the parties to a proceeding'. French CJ noted there is 'an irreparable element of unfair prejudice in unnecessarily delaying proceedings'. In particular, the Chief Justice drew attention to 'the waste of public resources', the 'strain and uncertainty imposed on litigants' and 'the potential for loss of public confidence in the legal system' arising from adjournment of trials without adequate justification. Similarly, in *Aon*, Gummow, Hayne, Crennan, Kiefel and Bell JJ referred to the 'ill-effects of delay' upon employees and officers of corporations, as well as upon defendant corporations whose ability to plan financially may be affected by a contingent liability.[106]

Due to the conflicts discussed in Chapter 2.3, the reforms to case management explored in Chapter 2.4 cannot ever hope to eradicate the issues Justice Vickery addressed in *Hodgson v Amcor Ltd*.[107] The best that can ever hope to be achieved is some amelioration of these concerns by careful judicial management and ethical legal practice.

106 *Hodgson v Amcor Ltd* (2011) 32 VR 495, [7]–[17].
107 Ibid.

2.5.1 Emotional stress

Although the bulk of legislation focuses on reducing the cost and time associated with litigating, it is also undisputed that litigation is very emotionally stressful, particularly for the litigants. There is the significant risk of losing the case, the strain caused from the cost and time involved in litigating, the unfamiliarity and complexity of legal process and, often, pre-existing levels of animosity which can be exacerbated by the adversarial system.

Richards v Cornford (No 3)[108] was a New South Wales Court of Appeal case management decision of Allsop P, McColl JA and Basten JA appealing from the District Court of New South Wales. The Court of Appeal upheld the district court decision denying the right of the second defendant, an insurer, QBE, to commence a late cross appeal.

President Allsop, with whom McColl and Basten JJA agreed, found that the case raised important issues regarding the approach to litigation in New South Wales and operation of ss 56–60 of the *Civil Procedure Act 2005* (NSW). President Allsop discussed the need for efficiency as a requirement of justice due to the recognised stressfulness of litigation to the litigants:

> 42. The litigious process is inherently stressful for any party, in particular an individual. Ms Richards embarked upon a time-consuming, stressful and potentially very expensive process. ... That stress includes the uncertainty and concern as to the effects of legal costs that can lead to bankruptcy and financial ruin. The reality of the personal strain of litigation is now clearly recognised by the Courts: *Ketteman v Hansel Properties Ltd* [1987] AC 189 at 220; *Berowra Holdings Pty Ltd v Gordon* [2006] HCA 32; 225 CLR 364 at [37]; *GSA Industries Pty Ltd v NT Gas Ltd* (1990) 24 NSWLR 710 at 715–716; *Aon Risk Services Australia Ltd v Australian National University* [2009] HCA 27; 239 CLR 175 at [100].
>
> ...
>
> 44. To put the matter simply and bluntly, parties are entitled to expect that the costly and stressful, though necessary evil that is litigation be resolved with reasonable despatch so as to minimise, where reasonably possible, the time during which people are subjected to its rigours and strains.[109]

Richards v Cornford noted the loss of "justice" inherent in delay and concluded that denying a party, the second defendant (QBE) the right to be heard was the less unjust outcome in the circumstances of the case. This case is an excellent example of the injustice which may result from delay because allowing the appeal would have involved requiring Ms Richards to hand back compensation money, some of which was already spent, or earmarked for spending, on important necessities including transport and accommodation.[110]

2.5.2 Costs

The cost of litigation is a never-ending topic of discussion for law reform bodies, politicians, judges, lawyers and litigants.[111] The Australian Law Reform Commission and the Productivity

108 *Richards v Cornford (No 3)* [2010] NSWCA 134.

109 Ibid [42].

110 *Richards v Cornford* was expressly approved in *Sung v Malaxos (No 2)* [2015] NSWSC 290, [12]–[14], in the context of a family provision claim where it was noted that disputes can entirely dissipate an estate. See also *Olsen v Olsen* [2019] NSWSC 217, [48].

111 Costs are addressed more comprehensively in Chapter 6 of this book.

Commission, which are Federal reform bodies, have spent significant resources on attempts to reduce the cost of litigation. Similar efforts have also been undertaken by state law reform bodies, such as the Victorian Law Reform Commission which produced an extensive report in 2008 titled *Civil Justice Review: Report* in which reducing litigation costs was a major focus. Some examples of Commonwealth law reform reports focussed on reducing litigation costs include:

- Senate Standing Committee on Legal and Constitution Affairs, *The Cost of Justice: First Report: Foundations for Reform* (1993)
- Senate Standing Committee on Legal and Constitutional Affairs, *The Cost of Justice: Second Report: Checks and Imbalances* (1993)
- Access to Justice Advisory Committee, *Access to Justice: An Action Plan* (2014) Chairman: Justice R Sackville
- Australian Law Reform Commission, *Managing Justice: A Review of the Federal Justice System* (Report No 89, February 2000)
- Access to Justice Taskforce, *A Strategic Framework for Access to Justice in the Federal Civil Justice System* (2009)
- Productivity Commission, *Access to Justice Arrangements* (2014)
- Australian Law Reform Commission, *Integrity, Fairness and Efficiency: An Inquiry into Class Action Proceedings and Third-Party Litigation Funders* (Report No 134, January 2019).

There have also been Commonwealth reports on specific areas of law which have had a strong focus on reducing dispute resolution costs, such as the Australian Law Reform Commission's 2019 report *Family Law for the Future*.[112]

Disputes are often complex, and parties almost invariably disagree on the relevant facts. Despite this, each party believes the court should decide in its favour and each party wants to spend as little time and money as possible in the process. This is, of course, impossible. Almost invariably one or more party will lose each case and the more complex and disputed the facts are, the more cost and time is likely to be incurred in determining which party should prevail.

The obligations for lawyers to disclose and manage their costs is a significant area of law in itself relevant to all areas of legal practice but with particular challenges for civil litigators and raising issues regarding ethics and trust accounting, not all of which can be covered. Professional requirements for lawyers to estimate costs are particularly problematic in CDR where the level of interlocutory disagreements and the complexity and volume of relevant evidence are impossible to predict at the commencement of the litigation.

The common requirement for unsuccessful parties in litigation to pay the costs of their successful litigants increases the costs and risks associated with litigating and provides a strong incentive to resolve disputes through ADR where each party usually bears its own costs. In practice, the amount of the successful party's costs payable by the opposing party is usually less than the full cost but it adds significantly to the risk of litigation for parties that they may be liable in the future for an undisclosed sum being incurred by their opposite party. The calculation of the amount payable may also be a complex, time-consuming and disputed process.

112 Australian Law Reform Commission, *Family Law for the Future: An Inquiry into the Family Law System* (Report No 135, April 2019).

It is not difficult to find examples of cases where legal costs became a matter for considerable concern to the parties and the judge.[113] One infamous example is the litigation between Seven Network Limited and News Limited concerning rights to air sport on cable television (commonly known as the '*C7* litigation) decided by Sackville J in *Seven Network Ltd v News Ltd*[114] and upheld on appeal in *Seven Network Ltd v News Ltd*[115] by Mansfield, Dowsett and Lander JJ. In addition to his main judgment, Sackville J delivered two separate judgments on the issue of who should pay the extraordinary costs involved in the *C7* litigation; *Seven Network Ltd v News Ltd*[116] and *Seven Network Ltd v News Ltd.*[117] Paragraphs 1 to 12 of the substantive decision, *Seven Network Ltd v News Ltd,*[118] set out Sackville J's concerns with the costs of the "mega-litigation", noting the extraordinary volume of materials and concluding:

> Electronic trials have many advantages, but reducing the amount of documentation produced or relied on by the parties is not one of them.
>
> ...
>
> It is difficult to understand how the costs incurred by the parties can be said to be proportionate to what is truly at stake, measured in financial terms. In my view, the expenditure of $200 million (and counting) on a single piece of litigation is not only extraordinarily wasteful, but borders on the scandalous.[119]

2.5.3 Time

Litigation is time-consuming, especially for complex commercial cases. The duration of many commercial cases is measured in years, rather than months or weeks. The Western Australian case of *Bell Group Ltd (in liq) v Westpac Banking Corporation (No 9)* ('*Bell Group*')[120] is an example of a case which has been running for decades and is, arguably, the pinnacle of time-consuming litigation in modern Australia.

Bell Group involved 20 defendant banks who had established securities over the Bell Group in 1990 which they then realised as it descended into liquidation in 1991. As a result of the banks' actions, other creditors were faced with very poor recovery prospects and the liquidators for Bell took action against the banks, claiming the securities were established improperly at a time when the banks knew the Bell Group would not survive. Proceedings were finally commenced in the Supreme Court of Western Australia by the liquidator in 1995, some four years after the Bell Group went into liquidation. After numerous preliminary disputes occurring over 13 years of case preparation, the matter was heard before Owen J in the Supreme Court of Western Australia over 404 days between 2003 and 2006. In an interlocutory hearing in relation to the appeal, Wheeler J noted that

113 See also the *Bell* litigation, discussed at Chapter 2.4.3 in relation to time, which also incurred over $500,000 in lawyers' costs.
114 *Seven Network News Ltd v News Ltd* [2007] FCA 1062.
115 *Seven Network Ltd v News Ltd* (2009) 182 FCR 160.
116 *Seven Network Ltd v News Ltd* (2007) 244 ALR 374.
117 *Seven Network Ltd v News Ltd* [2007] FCA 2059.
118 *Seven Network News Ltd v News Ltd* [2007] FCA 1062.
119 Ibid [4], [10].
120 *Bell Group Ltd (in liq) v Westpac Banking Corporation (No 9)* (2008) 39 WAR 1.

the litigation involved 166 witnesses, of whom 155 were called and cross-examined, that over 86,000 pages of documents were tendered in evidence and that the total number of pages of written closing submissions was 36,932.[121] The resulting judgment of Owen J is a staggering 2643 pages long. The catchwords relevant to the case alone run for five pages and Owen J expressly justifies and apologises for the length of the decision.[122]

Justice Owen's decision was immediately appealed and, in an early preliminary hearing on the appeal, the ambit nature of the appeal papers caused Wheeler JA to order, at paragraph 47 of his judgment, that the parties limit their reasons in support of appeal to an extraordinary 700 pages.[123] The main *Bell Group* litigation eventually settled in September 2013 prior to its scheduled High Court hearing, but proceedings in relation to costs, related state legislation and other issues have continued for many years.[124] A brief history of proceedings is set out in the more recent interlocutory proceeding of *Woodings (as Liquidator of Bell Group Ltd and Bell Group Finance Pty Ltd) v WA Glendinning & Associates Pty Ltd*.[125]

The deterrents to litigation of cost, time and stress explain why prospective litigants and their lawyers should not rush into litigation without first considering the alternatives.

2.6 Balancing desires and deterrents in dispute resolution

Given the strong disincentives to litigate discussed above, it is perhaps surprising that more matters are not resolved through ADR. However, there are opposing strong incentives to litigate such that the decision whether to litigate or resolve a dispute by alternate means becomes yet another balancing act of CDR.

Some key factors which encourage parties toward litigation are:

- the desire to be heard fully and fairly
- the desire for objectively determined justice
- the desire to win without compromise
- the desire to punish the other party
- the need for processes and procedural protections to equalise inequality between parties
- party relations so adversarial that a third party with recognised authority is an essential intermediary to resolve the dispute.

121 *Westpac Banking Corporation v Bell Group Ltd (No 2)* [2009] WASCA 223.

122 *Bell Group Ltd (in liq) v Westpac Banking Corporation (No 9)* (2008) 39 WAR 1, [4], [5], [19], [20], [21].

123 *Westpac Banking Corporation v Bell Group Ltd (No 2)* [2009] WASCA 223, [47].

124 See, eg, *Westpac Banking Corporation v Bell Group Ltd (in liq) (No 3)* (2012) 44 WAR 1; *Westpac Banking Corporation v Bell Group Ltd* [2013] HCATrans 85; *Re Bell Group Ltd (in liq); Ex Parte Woodings (as Liquidator of Bell Group Ltd (in liq))* (2013) 97 ACSR 117; *Bell Group NV (in liq) v Western Australia* [2016] HCATrans 11; *Westpac Banking Corporation v Official Liquidator of Bell Group Ltd (in liq) (No 5)* [2017] WASC 77; *Bell Group NV (in liq) v Insurance Commission of Western Australia* [2017] WASCA 229; *Bell Group NV (in liq) v Insurance Commission of Western Australia* [2018] WASCA 179; *Insurance Commission of Western Australia v Woodings as Liquidator of Bell Group Ltd (in liq) (No 3)* [2018] WASC 44.

125 *Woodings (as Liquidator of Bell Group Ltd and Bell Group Finance Pty Ltd) v WA Glendinning & Associates Pty Ltd* [2019] WASC 54.

When parties feel personally and morally wronged by each other's actions, it can be difficult to contemplate compromising in order to come to a mutually acceptable resolution. In such cases, a decision by an accepted authority, such as a court, may seem the only possible option for resolving the dispute. Even arbitration, which has a third-party decision-maker, requires a level of party cooperation in agreeing to arbitration which some parties are unable to achieve. All other forms of ADR, besides arbitration, require cooperation and a willingness to reach a common consensus position. This level of cooperation may seem impossible where relations are significantly strained (as is often the case in family law disputes) or where there is a desire to punish the other party for perceived wrongs which the litigant hopes, or assumes, the court will deliver by way of a favourable judgment at significant cost to the opposing party.

Truth and the moral high ground associated with a public and independent vindication of correctness can also strongly motivate some parties towards litigation rather than ADR.[126] Even a commercial party may see reputational value from a court decision in its favour, where it is confident of winning, which cannot be achieved by a confidential settlement. Parties to litigation commonly want to prove that they were right and the other party was wrong. This may not be satisfactorily achieved through a negotiated or mediated settlement or even a confidential arbitration award. In such cases, litigation may seem the only avenue for a party to vindicate its claim.

Thus, the decision regarding how to resolve a civil dispute will often involve the weighing of complex emotional factors as well as more concrete resources such as time and money. Due to the emotional and moral factors in deciding how to resolve a dispute, this balancing act may not always result in an objectively rational decision.

2.7 Conclusion

This chapter could be viewed as presenting a negative view of CDR as an area of law doomed to unsatisfactory outcomes and perennial dissatisfaction. The need to constantly compromise between conflicting obligations and desires means perfect dispute resolution is an impossibility. However, there is also room for significant optimism. Understanding the inherent conflicts within CDR leads to a recognition that Australia's current CDR systems are generally praiseworthy despite their imperfections. The theory of CDR and its inevitable conflicts also enables contemplation of realistic reform. While perfection may be impossible, improvements can be made to optimise civil procedure and the interaction between civil procedure and ADR. Identifying the competing factors enables focus on optimally balancing the competing objectives of efficiency and procedural fairness, discretion and certainty, openness and confidentiality, and formality and informality of process. The many processes and procedures considered throughout this book are all influenced by the key conflicts identified in this chapter. Considering how these conflicts play out in relation to the public and the social and moral underpinnings of CDR are the subject of Chapter 3 which explores the underlying CDR motivations of access to justice and open justice.

126 Genn (n 3) 11, describing a litigant's "right of action".

3 ACCESS TO JUSTICE AND OPEN JUSTICE

3.1 Introduction

This chapter continues the analysis begun in Chapter 2 regarding the theory of civil dispute resolution (CDR). Chapter 2 focused on the many conflicts which must be balanced by governments, courts, alternative dispute resolution (ADR) practitioners and parties engaging with CDR, and how those conflicts define and explain CDR. This chapter will consider two key principles: access to justice and open justice, which underlie our dispute resolution system and how these principles play out through policy, legal reform and practice. These principles interact in sometimes complex ways with the balancing acts discussed in Chapter 2. The ability of every member of society to access justice and the openness of the justice system are two of the most important requirements of the civil justice system but they are simultaneously complex and impossible to achieve.

Access to justice is critical to a fair society. If the justice system fails some or all of society, particularly where it fails people who are already vulnerable to injustice, these failures significantly reduce societal faith in the justice system. Similarly, if the justice system is opaque or not accountable to the public, this significantly reduces faith in the justice system. For CDR to work effectively, justice needs to be open and accessible. This chapter will consider the challenges and complexities of achieving these critical aims.

3.2 Access to justice: the theory behind civil procedure

CDR in Australia is inherently about justice and fairness. Disputes arise because parties feel an injustice has occurred and they turn to ADR and/or litigation to resolve that injustice. Access to justice is an issue which spans both the criminal and civil justice systems. Although this book will focus on the civil justice aspect, the two overlap because civil law difficulties can result in criminal penalties and interaction with the criminal law system often results in civil law difficulties in areas such as housing, employment and family law. Access to justice is intimately related to legal costs as unaffordability of legal representation is a key barrier to accessing the justice system.[1]

3.2.1 Identifying the gaps in accessing justice

Access to justice is one of the most studied areas of CDR. Numerous studies and reports at a state, national and international level have explored the significance of access to justice and the barriers to its achievement. However, there remain significant gaps in the statistical evidence demonstrating access to justice issues, partly because many who struggle to access justice have so little visibility in the legal system that they do not even register in the statistics of justice failures.[2] This chapter will focus on civil access to justice problems and the ability of CDR mechanisms to reduce the access to justice gap in Australia.

3.2.1.1 International comparison

Access to justice is a global issue. Consideration of the international prevalence of barriers to accessing justice demonstrates the complexity of the issue and the relative position of advantage in Australia.

The OECD emphasises the high cost to society caused by lack of access to justice and the inability to resolve legal problems which then become civil disputes:

> The failure to resolve legal problems can contribute to a 'cycle of decline' … in which one problem leads to another with escalating individual and social costs. Inability to resolve legal problems and limited access to justice may diminish access to economic opportunity, reinforce the poverty trap, and undermine human potential …[3]

---

1 Many of the issues raised in this chapter are also relevant to Chapter 6 which considers lawyers and legal costs.

2 Australian Government Productivity Commission, 'Access to Justice Arrangements' (Report No 72, 2014) <http://www.pc.gov.au/inquiries/completed/access-justice/report>, 879–91 references concerns expressed by the Law Council of Australia, the Commonwealth Attorney General's Department and the Queensland Public Interest Law Clearing House; Australian Centre for Justice Innovation, 'Timeliness in the Justice System: Ideas and Innovations' (Paper 27, 2015) 9; Justice Ronald Sackville, 'Civil Justice Reform: The Third Phase' in Miiko Kumar and Michael Legg (eds), *Ten Years of the Civil Procedure Act 2005 (NSW)* (Thomson Reuters, 2015) 209, 211; Robyn Sheen and Penny Gregory, 'Building an evidence-base for the Civil Justice System: Civil justice system framework and literature review Report' (Australian Government's Attorney-General's Department, 2012) http://www.ag.gov.au 61; Peter Cashman, 'Civil Procedure, Politics and the Process of Reform' in Miiko Kumar and Michael Legg (eds), *Ten Years of the Civil Procedure Act 2005 (NSW)* (Thomson Reuters, 2015) 259–260.

3 Organisation for Economic Co-operation and Development and Open Society Foundation, 'Workshop Background Paper' (Understanding Effective Access to Justice Workshop, 3–4 November 2016) 12 <http://www.oecd.org/gov/Understanding-effective-access-justice-workshop-paper-final.pdf>.

The 2019 international analysis by the New York-based Task Force on Justice suggested that 5.1 billion of the 7.7 billion comprising the world's population suffered from a "justice gap".[4] The gaps in access to justice were categorised by the Task Force as follows:

1. **Extreme conditions of injustice**: 253 million people: stateless people (12 million), those living in countries with no rule of law (203 million) and those living in modern slavery (40 million).[5]
2. **Unable to resolve justice problems**: 1.5 billion people: including 1.4 billion people with unmet civil and administrative justice needs.[6]
3. **Lacking access to legal infrastructure**: 4.5 billion people: including 1.1 billion lacking legal identity (eg having no certification of their birth), 2.3 billion lacking evidence of tenure or ownership of where they live and 2.1 billion employed by the informal economy without legal protection against exploitation.[7]

The extreme conditions of injustice are useful reminders of the severity of legal problems that most Australians do not suffer from. However, even in Australia, there have been instances of serious denials of justice, including recent cases of modern slavery which have led to the introduction of legislation such as the *Modern Slavery Act 2018* (Cth) and the *Modern Slavery Act 2018* (NSW).[8] There are also instances of Australians without legal identity and workers exploited by their employers even when they are within the formal economy let alone when they are outside it, particularly temporary migrant workers who are routinely underpaid and exploited.[9] Many of these injustices arise due to lack of knowledge of rights but they are compounded by lack of access to CDR mechanisms.

The Task Force on Justice surveys indicated that, internationally, people are about nine times more likely to have a civil and administrative justice problem than a criminal justice issue, and most people do not turn to lawyers or courts due to ignorance, cost and other barriers.[10] Barriers to accessing justice in relation to civil disputes are both symptomatic and causative of societal collapse. Those jurisdictions with poor access to justice tend to be the more disadvantaged and inequitable jurisdictions with lower-than-average standards of living.

4 Task Force on Justice, *Justice for All: Final Report* (Centre on International Cooperation, 2019) 6: "The Task Force on Justice is an initiative of the Pathfinders for Peaceful, Just and Inclusive Societies — a multi-stakeholder partnership that brings together UN member states, international organizations, civil society, and the private sector to accelerate delivery of the Sustainable Development Goal targetsfor peace, justice and inclusion."

5 Ibid 34.

6 Ibid 36.

7 Ibid 38.

8 *R v Tang* (2008) 237 CLR 1 was a criminal law case involving modern slavery.

9 Australian Government, *Report of the Migrant Workers' Taskforce* (Commonwealth of Australia, 2019) <https://www.ag.gov.au/industrial-relations/industrial-relations-publications/Pages/report-migrant-workers-taskforce.aspx> confirmed that the underpayment of wages has become more entrenched and widespread with up to 50% of temporary migrant workers being underpaid. Litigation has been launched against Woolworths, Caltex, 7 Eleven, Dominos and numerous employers in the hospitality industry in relation to underpayment of Australian workers in the past decade.

10 Task Force on Justice (n 4) 37.

3.2.1.2 Australian access to justice issues

Australia's access to justice issues are less severe than those of many jurisdictions because of our relatively well-resourced legal institutions, stable government and high levels of societal compliance with the law. However, barriers in access to justice remain a serious problem in Australia. The difficulties experienced in some other countries emphasise the importance of continuing to monitor access to justice and to take all available steps to improve access to justice or, at least, protect against its decline.

In August 2018, the Law Council of Australia concluded its Justice Project with the publication of a lengthy final report which was the culmination of hundreds of consultations with a wide range of stakeholders, including consideration of 129 written submissions.[11] The Ex-President of the Law Council, Fiona McLeod SC, stated:

> This Project was inspired by the realisation of a simple truth — that despite our lofty commitment to equality before the law, for many tens of thousands of Australians, equality, and justice, remain out of reach.[12]

The Law Council of Australia report made significant findings in relation to the difficulties faced by many Australians in accessing justice and set out numerous priorities and recommendations, including:

- building legal capacity through education
- improving the provision of Government funded legal services
- expanding and improving the equity of ADR
- improving court resources and judicial training, increased support for early intervention in legal issues
- building capacity of government services with links to the justice system such as social security, immigration, housing, and child protection services
- adopting "justice impact tests" and "Aboriginal Justice Impact Assessments" for government policy and legislative proposals to reduce unintended downstream justice implications particularly on disadvantaged communities.[13]

The Law Council Report concluded Legal Aid funding in Australia is inadequate, noting that only 2.3% of Legal Aid funding went to civil disputes and recommending that a minimum of $390 million per annum extra funding was required across all Legal Aid.[14] The Report found that 9% of the Legal Australia-Wide survey[15] respondents accounted for 65% of legal problems with homeless and disabled people likely to have multiple substantial legal problems.[16] The Report considered 13 groups who experience significant disadvantage in accessing justice in Australia:

- people with disability
- people experiencing economic disadvantage

11 Law Council of Australia, *The Justice Project: Final Report* (2018) <https://www.lawcouncil.asn.au/justice-project/final-report>, Introduction and Overview, 10–11.
12 Ibid 6.
13 Ibid 26
14 Ibid Recommendations and Group Priorities 4, Overarching Themes 10.
15 Law and Justice Foundation of New South Wales, *Legal Australia-Wide Survey: Legal Need in Australia 2008* (2012).
16 Ibid Overarching Themes 6.

- LGBTI+ people
- prisoners and detainees
- Aboriginal and Torres Strait Islander people
- people who experience family violence
- people who have been trafficked and exploited
- recent arrivals to Australia
- children and young people
- RRR (Rural, Regional and Remote) Australians
- asylum-seekers
- older persons
- people who are homeless.[17]

The above listed disadvantaged groups often suffer from both civil and criminal justice problems, with civil law problems often spiralling into criminal law issues. The current low level of Legal Aid allocated for civil disputes means that many disadvantaged disputants fail to engage with the civil dispute processes entirely or engage poorly as self-represented litigants. There have been numerous earlier studies into access to justice in Australia which have made similar findings in terms of barriers to access and areas of need, including: *Access to Justice: An Action Plan*;[18] *A Strategic Framework for Access to Justice in the Federal Civil Justice System*;[19] and *Access to Justice Arrangements*.[20] The persistence of these problems is reflective of their complexity, including their budgetary complexity. Government funding for legal resources and legal welfare have benefits which are difficult, or impossible, to measure because they are indirectly improving productivity, societal wellbeing and faith in democracy and the rule of law. The United Kingdom has introduced a "Justice Impact Model" which includes accountability for downstream justice costs which the Law Council of Australia has suggested Australia should adopt.[21]

In the absence of adequate Legal Aid, civil disputants often rely on pro bono assistance from the private sector. Many solicitors (particularly in large law firms) and barristers provide significant free assistance to civil litigants who are unable to afford legal services but are not eligible for Legal Aid. In 2019, the Australian Pro Bono Centre reported that 473,379.4 pro bono hours were performed by signatories of the Centre in 12 months, averaging 35.83 hours per annum for each lawyer member (or per full-time equivalent lawyer for multi-lawyer member firms).[22] Many law firms work closely with not-for-profit community legal centres, such as the Public Interest Advocacy Centre, LawRight (Qld), the North Australian Aboriginal Justice Agency (NT) and the Aboriginal Legal Service (NSW/ACT/VIC/WA) to

17 Ibid Introduction and Overview, Part 1.

18 Access to Justice Advisory Committee, *Access to Justice: An Action Plan* (Australian Government Publishing Service, 1994) (also known as the Sackville Report).

19 Attorney-General's Department, Access to Justice Taskforce, *A Strategic Framework for Access to Justice in the Federal Civil Justice System* (2009) <https://www.ag.gov.au/LegalSystem/Pages/Accesstojustice.aspx>.

20 Productivity Commission, *Access to Justice Arrangements* (Report No 72, 2014).

21 Law Council of Australia (n 11), Recommendation and Group Priorities 13.

22 Australian Pro Bono Centre, *Annual Report 2018-2019* (Report, 2019) 6 <https://www.probonocentre.org.au/wp-content/uploads/2019/11/2019.11.04_Annual-Report-FINAL.pdf>.

assist in meeting the significant demand for legal services for those who would otherwise be ineligible for Legal Aid and unable to afford legal representation.

The inequality in access to justice which persists in Australia has significant ramifications for CDR with relevance to all the remaining chapters of this book. The lack of access to Legal Aid for civil disputants and the inability of many Australians to pay for legal assistance negatively affects the ability of many litigants to engage in litigation processes and the complexity of those processes contributes to their unaffordability for disadvantaged Australians.[23] The unaffordability of litigation encourages the use of ADR and, commonly, results in summary disposition of litigation.[24] The inability of many civil disputants to afford legal representation is central to issues concerning legal costs[25] and is a policy driver for the creation of specialist tribunals and courts.[26]

3.2.2 Maximising access to justice: the vexed role of alternative dispute resolution

It is the aim of all justice systems to maximise access to justice and the delivery of just outcomes. Conflicting requirements for delivering just outcomes make optimising justice complex.[27] Improving access to justice, conversely, can be achieved simply through increased government funding of Legal Aid. In the absence of additional government financial support for legal processes, ADR can be a way to maximise access to justice with the existing limited resources.

ADR can be an excellent way to reduce the costs of CDR and thereby make justice more accessible. ADR is more flexible and often significantly quicker and cheaper than litigation and has an increased range of possible resolutions including the potential for win/win resolutions where all parties perceive benefits from their CDR.[28]

ADR can also assist access to justice by providing cultural and linguistic accessibility to parties whose cultural or linguistic background may limit their access to Australian courts. All Australian court cases are conducted in English (this is partially to meet requirements of open justice),[29] but ADR can be conducted in any language which suits the parties. For example, a dispute between Mandarin-speaking parties could be mediated in Mandarin by a mediator fluent in Mandarin. Using Mandarin as the language of the mediation would facilitate access to justice for all parties by overcoming linguistic barriers to accessing justice.[30]

Similarly, Australian courts are procedurally and substantively based on the English legal system which may interpret disputed agreements between some civil disputants in ways which do not reflect the intentions of either party in entering the agreement due to the cultural or religious background of the disputing parties. Conversely, the flexibility of ADR can resolve disputes using dispute resolution systems specific to the culture of the

23 Litigation processes are considered in detail in Chapters 8 to 16 of this book.
24 Summary disposition is a term used to describe procedural processes whereby courts dispose of cases without hearing the substantive merits of the case. Summary disposition and its interaction with ADR are discussed in detail in Chapter 5.
25 See Chapter 6.
26 See Chapter 7.
27 See Chapter 2.
28 Chapters 4 and 5 discuss this in more detail.
29 See Chapter 3.3.
30 Chapter 4 discusses mediation in more detail.

disputants, provided all parties agree. For example, if all parties to a dispute agreed that Sharia law should apply to govern the dispute, those parties could agree on the selection of an expert in Sharia law to determine their dispute in accordance with Sharia law and the parties would then be bound by that determination as a form of ad hoc arbitration.[31] Courts will generally enforce such ad hoc arbitrated agreements through contract law provided the arbitrated determination is not itself illegal or unenforceable.

Indigenous Australians have their own diverse dispute resolution systems and the need for such systems to be understood, recognised and respected has been increasingly appreciated but, due to the complexity of Indigenous society and the lack of prior research, requires significant further work before Indigenous Australians are able to optimally utilise their own legal systems to resolve civil disputes.[32] There are significant variations across Indigenous nations in methods of dispute resolution and Indigenous CDR practitioners may describe their practice as "peacemaking" or using Indigenous terms which focus on management rather than resolution of disputes and on healing and the renewal of relationships.[33] Sometimes Indigenous dispute resolution concepts can be integrated within Western Court processes, such as the Care Circle Pilot Program in Nowra, New South Wales, which involved Aboriginal Elders in developing care arrangements for Aboriginal children.[34] However, there are risks to Indigenous people, particularly from ADR which can exacerbate power imbalances where those forms of ADR are not consistent with Indigenous values and culture.[35]

ADR does not always provide access to justice because its lack of procedural protections can result in injustice when ADR is undertaken by vulnerable disputants. ADR does not

---

31 Arbitration is discussed in more detail in Chapter 4. See Ann Black and Kerri Sadiq, 'Good and Bad Sharia: Australia's Mixed Response to Islamic Law' (2011) 34(1) *University of New South Wales Law Journal* 383, 384: "Shari'a, Shariah, syariah, Shariat are transliterations from the Arabic script. Whilst there are debates about whether Sharia precisely equates with the 'Islamic law', the terms are often used interchangeably when English is used. Sharia refers to the divinely ordained law embodied in the Qur'an (the actual word of God as revealed to the Prophet Mohammad), Sunnah (practices and traditions of the Prophet) and fiqh (jurisprudence). The fiqh is the means by which jurists can extend principles contained in the Qur'an and Sunnah to deal with new situations. There are a range of approved juristic techniques including ijma (consensus of scholars) and qiyas (analogical deduction and application) with maslaha (in the public interest) playing an increasing role.".

32 Australian Law Reform Commission, *Recognition of Aboriginal Customary Laws* (Report No 31, June 1986) [692]-[720] is one early attempt at understanding Indigenous dispute resolution which acknowledges the need for further research. See also National Alternative Dispute Resolution Advisory Council, *Indigenous Dispute Resolution and Conflict Management* (2006); Australian Mediation Association, 'Indigenous Dispute Resolution' (Web Page) <https://ama.asn.au/indigenous-dispute-resolution/> states: "The AMA recognises that Indigenous people at the local level need to be involved in the design and delivery of dispute resolution and conflict management services directed to them, and services need to take into account Indigenous perspectives on disputes and their resolution."

33 Federal Court of Australia, Indigenous Dispute Resolution & Conflict Management Case Study Project, *Solid Work You Mob are Doing: Case Studies in Indigenous Dispute Resolution & Conflict Management in Australia* (National Alternative Dispute Resolution Advisory Council, 2009) xiii, 6, 25–8, 102. See also Larissa Behrendt, *Aboriginal Dispute Resolution: A Step Towards Self-Determination and Community Autonomy* (Federation Press, 1995).

34 Sarah Ciftci and Deirdre Howard-Wagner, 'Integrating Indigenous Justice into Alternative Dispute Resolution Practices: A Case Study of the Aboriginal Care Circle Pilot Program in Nowra' (2012) 16(2) *Australian Indigenous Law Review* 81.

35 Larissa Behrendt and Loretta Kelly, *Resolving Indigenous Disputes: Land Conflict and Beyond* (Federation Press, 2008) vii-viii.

provide the same procedural and evidentiary protections as litigation, which means that it can result in injustice where parties have unequal bargaining power or unequal knowledge.[36] Many of the factors which make litigation slower and more expensive than arbitration are processes designed to protect procedural fairness and reduce inequality caused by power imbalance and uneven ownership of vital evidence. These protections are largely absent from ADR meaning it can exacerbate injustice instead of improving access to justice.

3.2.3 The role of summary disposition in civil procedure theory

Summary disposition requires special consideration in this chapter because of its effect on access to justice.[37] Summary disposition describes a range of procedures whereby courts dispose of cases without hearing the substantive case, including default judgment, summary judgment, and summary dismissal. Summary disposition engages with the first competing objectives discussed in Chapter 2 of juggling efficiency with due consideration. Summary disposition is an efficient way to dispose of improper proceedings but it increases the risk of denying access to justice where proceedings have underlying merit which is not apparent due to lack of legal representation and poorly resourced litigants. The potential for complexity and competing interests in summary disposition cases was evident in *Robert Carl Klewer v Sydney Children's Hospital Specialty Network*.[38] Justice Campbell struck out the proceedings for want of prosecution, whilst acknowledging the potential for recommencement and expressing sympathy for the disabled plaintiff who was unable to secure a tutor and whose mother was unable to perform the role due to an order under the *Vexatious Proceedings Act 2008* (NSW).[39] Some courts have processes to intervene and manage cases which are not progressing which reduce the chances of unfair summary disposition.[40]

3.2.3.1 Summary dismissal can increase access to justice by limiting unmeritorious proceedings

Maximising access to justice involves balancing the desirability of easy access to courts with the undesirability of forcing parties to engage with unmeritorious litigation. One cause of court backlogs is unmeritorious litigation. Court time which could be used in solving genuine civil disputes is, instead, wasted on strategic, incompetent and vexatious litigants who use an improper and disproportionate amount of limited judicial resources.[41] Summarily dismissing disputes which should not be before the court is an important way to manage the court's workload to ensure that backlogs and delays do not prevent effective access to justice.

36 See Chapters 4–5 and 8–14 for further detail.

37 Summary disposition is considered in more detail in Chapter 5.

38 *Robert Carl Klewer v Sydney Children's Hospital Specialty Network* [2017] NSWSC 88.

39 Ibid [6]–[8].

40 See, eg, Supreme Court of Queensland, *Practice Direction No 4 of 2020: Case Flow Management — Civil Jurisdiction*, 3 March 2020 which uses case flow management processes based on the overriding case management provision at r 5 of the *Uniform Civil Procedure Rules 1999* (Qld) to assist parties towards compliance with trial preparation procedures.

41 *Aon Risk Services Australia Ltd v Australian National University* (2009) 239 CLR 175 (discussed in Chapter 2) is an example of strategic litigation which the High Court found improperly squandered limited court resources.

Sometimes, courts go further than summary disposition to prevent unmeritorious litigation. Vexatious litigants are rare but can be incredibly time-consuming for courts, making it important to have a means of limiting their impact and discouraging others from following their example so that courts are not clogged with vexatious litigation.[42] Legislation enables courts to prevent a vexatious party from commencing litigation without permission. The prevention order can prevent the vexatious litigant from commencing any litigation or purely restrict litigation against a particular defendant or in relation to a particular matter without prior permission of the court. Australian jurisdictions each have legislation to declare litigants vexatious either through a dedicated Act, such as the *Vexatious Proceedings Restriction Act 2002* (WA), the *Vexatious Proceedings Act 2005* (Qld), the *Vexatious Proceedings Act 2008* (NSW), the *Vexatious Proceedings Act 2011* (Tas) and the *Vexatious Proceedings Act 2014* (Vic) or through provisions within a court procedure Act such as the *Federal Court of Australia Act 1976* (Cth) s 37AO or the *Supreme Court Act 1935* (SA) s 39.

3.2.3.2 Summary dismissal can decrease access to justice by dismissing meritorious proceedings

Judicial decisions to summarily dispose of proceedings raise obvious issues of procedural fairness because of the restrictions they impose on parties' right to be heard. These issues are exacerbated by the limitations on appealing summary disposition. The core rationale for summary disposition is the lack of a proper underlying case or significant procedural irregularity such that the case constitutes an abuse of process. From an efficiency perspective, it is, therefore, beneficial to dispose of such unmeritorious cases. However, where summary disposition may have denied access to justice, it is problematic that those unfairly dismissed must also overcome judicial reluctance to overturn a discretionary decision, making their appeals less likely to succeed than those appealing after a full hearing.[43]

The justification for the interlocutory nature of summary dispositions originates from the underlying failure of the original claim. In *Macatangay v New South Wales (No 2)*,[44] the Court relied on the High Court's statement in *Re: Luck*[45] as its key justification, quoting:

> An order is an interlocutory order, therefore, when it stays or dismisses an action or refuses leave to commence or proceed with an action because the action is frivolous vexatious, an abuse of the process of the court or does not disclose a reasonable cause of action.[46]

The discussion in *Macatangay* also included the need for consistency in the approach of summary disposition cases, including the treatment of such decisions as interlocutory since the 19th century.[47] At the same time, however, summary disposition decisions have the

42 See Chapter 5 for a more detailed discussion.

43 *D v Australian Financial Security Authority formerly known as Insolvency & Trustee Service Australia* [2017] NSWCA 50, [49].

44 *Macatangay v New South Wales (No 2)* [2009] NSWCA 272.

45 *Re Luck* [2003] 78 ALJR 177.

46 *Macatangay v New South Wales (No 2)* [2009] NSWCA 272, [11] (Allsop P, Tobias JA and Handley AJA) purporting to be from the High Court in the case of *Re Luck* [2003] 78 ALJR 177, 179 but is actually found in the headnote at 177[E], although the High Court's analysis (McHugh ACJ, Gummow and Heydon JJ) at 179 is consistent with the headnote and is consistent with the Court's analysis in *Macatangay*.

47 *Macatangay v New South Wales (No 2)* [2009] NSWCA 272, [11].

potential to deny access to justice particularly where the procedural failures which resulted in the disposition were caused due to the vulnerability of the litigant.[48] Decisions where procedural unfairness was found upon appeal against summary disposition demonstrate the risks of summative processes. Summary disposition is difficult to appeal, yet there are sufficient appellate decisions overturning summary disposition decisions to indicate that summary disposition may be a significant inadvertent means of limiting access to justice.[49]

3.2.4 Costs as a barrier to accessing justice

It is important to note here the effect of legal costs on access to justice.[50] The unaffordability of legal representation in civil disputes is possibly the greatest barrier to access to justice, making legal costs an important aspect of CDR. In 2002, the New South Wales Law and Justice Foundation described the dissatisfaction with cost and delay as "so apparently deep and widespread" that remarking on access to justice concerns was "practically a cliché".[51]

While access to justice is served best by free legal services, lawyers are entitled to be properly paid.[52] Law is complex and challenging, requiring many years of study and then continued learning after qualifying. Therefore, it is unsurprising that lawyers expect to be well remunerated for their services. Many lawyers specialising in CDR rely on litigation to earn their living.[53] This causes an immediate and obvious conflict of interest with their clients.[54] Many clients would prefer to avoid litigation and, if they must litigate, they usually wish it to be brief and cheap.[55] Conversely, the larger, longer and more complex a civil dispute is, the better, at least financially, for the lawyer.[56]

48 *D v Australian Financial Security Authority formerly known as Insolvency & Trustee Service Australia* [2017] NSWCA 50, [49] discussing the limitation of appeals for interlocutory matters. See Sonya Willis, 'Could Civil Case Management Benefit from a Litigant Vulnerability Assessment Scheme?' (2018) 7(2) *Journal of Civil Litigation and Practice* 94 for a discussion of litigant vulnerability.

49 See, eg, *Spencer v Commonwealth* (2010) 241 CLR 118; *Sutton Investments Pty Ltd v Realistic Investments Pty Ltd* [2017] WASCA 14, *Hilton v Gidley* [2014] NSWSC 874, *Goater v Commonwealth Bank of Australia* (2014) 88 NSWLR 362, *Lysaght Building Solutions Pty Ltd v Blanalko Pty Ltd* (2013) 42 VR 27, *Feldman v Frontlink Pty Ltd* [2014] VSCA 27, [42], *Manderson M & F Consulting v Incitec Pivot Ltd* (2011) 35 VR 98.

50 See Chapter 6 for a detailed analysis of legal costs in CDR.

51 Caroline Sage, Ted Wright and Carolyn Morris, *Case Management Reform: A Study of the Federal Court's Individual Docket System* (Law and Justice Foundation of NSW, 2002) 13.

52 Affordability of legal costs presents similar conflicts to those raised in Chapter 2.

53 Gergely Czoboly, 'Deterring Dilatory Tactics in Civil Litigation' (2013) 151 *Studia Iuridica Auctoritate Universitatis Pecs Publicata* 9, 18; Melissa Weresh, 'The Chicken or the Egg? Public Service Orientation and Lawyer Well-Being' (2013) 36(3) *University of Arkansas at Little Rock Law Review* 463, 467–8. See also *Doyles* (Web Page) <http://doylesguide.com/leading-commercial-litigation-dispute-resolution-lawyers-australia-2015/>; *The Legal 500* (Web Page) <http://www.legal500.com/c/australia/dispute-resolution> and other websites which demonstrate the concentration of litigators in large commercial law firms.

54 Michael Legg, *Case Management and Complex Civil Litigation* (Federation Press, 2011) 20.

55 See Mark J Rankin, 'Settlement at all Cost: The High Price of an Inexpensive Resolution?' (2009) 20 *Alternative Dispute Resolution Journal* 153 for discussion of the benefits of settlement and a counter argument of the benefits of adjudication. Another counter example to the benefits of settlement is strategic litigation run for commercial purposes (eg to disrupt a competitor). Legal practitioners knowingly running such litigation are in breach of legal professional obligations to the court.

56 See *Seven Network News Ltd v News Ltd* [2007] FCA 1062, [2]–[8] for Sackville J's illustrative discussion of "mega-litigation" and its costs.

In addition, lawyers tend to love justice, truth and "answers".[57] Terms like "hardball", "aggressive", "competitive", "persistent", and "determined" tend to be applied to successful litigators; rather than labels like "compromising", "reasonable" or "empathic".[58] Therefore, aside from their commercial interests in not settling large civil disputes, lawyers can develop an intellectual interest in not settling: being a desire to have the "truth" determined by the judge. Lawyers' desire for "the truth" or "justice" is often shared by clients and is a commonality of interest which operates against settlement in litigation. Chief Justice Murray Gleeson stated: "Litigation is a perfect example of Parkinson's law: work expands to fill the available time."[59] Civil litigators are often perfectionists who will, therefore, spend as long as they are allowed in trying to improve their clients' cases.[60] Both the commercial and intellectual factors influencing lawyers to increase their legal costs operate in stark contrast to the desirability of low-cost legal services to improve access to justice.

3.2.5 Class actions as a tool for access to justice

Class actions, also called "representative actions", are a somewhat controversial CDR tool designed to increase access to justice. Class actions are designed to increase access to justice by allowing people with substantially the same dispute to make a single claim as a class rather than each commencing separate actions.[61] Class actions are common in areas such as product liability where a faulty product may be purchased by thousands of people. The value of each product purchased may make it impractical for any single plaintiff to make a claim but, by bringing an action as a group, the cost is more viable. Some large class actions which have been commenced in Australia (some of which have settled) include:

- Product liability claims against manufacturers in relation to faulty products (particularly medical and pharmaceutical) including: car airbags (*BMW Australia Ltd v Brewster*);[62] vaginal mesh (*Gill v Ethicon Sarl (No 5)*);[63] silicone breast implants (*Bates v Dow Corning (Australia) Pty Ltd*)[64], *Re Application by Rowell*);[65] tobacco (*Nixon v Phillip Morris (Australia) Ltd*);[66] pacemakers (*Courtney v Medtel Pty Ltd (No 5)*);[67] knee replacement surgery (*Casey v DePuy International Ltd (No 2)*);[68] sterilisation clips (*Bright v Femcare*);[69] and arthritis medication (*Peterson v Merck Sharp & Dohme (Australia) Pty Ltd*).[70]

57 Robert P Burns, 'A Lawyer's Truth: Notes for a Moral Philosophy of Litigation Practice' (1985) 3(2) *Journal of Law and Religion* 229, although Burns notes at 253 that these desires can be subverted through practice.

58 Robert N Sayler, 'Rambo Litigation Why Hardball Tactics Don't Work' (1988) 74(3) *American Bar Association Journal* 78, 78–79; Melissa Weresh (n 53) 468.

59 Murray Gleeson, 'The State of the Judicature' (Speech, 35th Australian Legal Convention Sydney, 25 March 2007) <http://www.hcourt.gov.au/speeches/cj/cj_25mar07.pdf> 8.

60 Steven Keeva, 'Problematic Perfectionism' (2006) 92(4) *American Bar Association Journal* 80, 80; Weresh (n 52) 470–1.

61 Class actions are discussed further in Chapter 8.4.2.

62 *BMW Australia Ltd v Brewster* (2019) 374 ALR 627.

63 *Gill v Ethicon Sarl (No 5)* [2019] FCA 1905.

64 *Bates v Dow Corning (Australia) Pty Ltd* [2005] FCA 927.

65 *Re Application by Rowell* [2002] VSC 63.

66 *Nixon v Phillip Morris (Australia) Pty Ltd* (1999) 95 FCR 453.

67 *Courtney v Medtel Pty Ltd (No 5)* (2004) 212 ALR 311.

68 *Casey v DePuy International (No 2)* [2012] FCA 1370.

69 *Bright v Femcare Ltd* (2002) 195 ALR 574.

70 *Peterson v Merk Sharpe & Dohme (Australia) Pty Ltd* (2010) 184 FCR 1.

- Mass tort claims such as claims in relation to bushfire damage (Kilmore East and Murrindindi: *Andrew Watson as Trustee for the Murrindindi Bushfire Class Action Settlement Fund v Commissioner of Taxation*;[71] and claims from personal injury from food contamination: oysters (*Ryan v Great Lakes Council*)[72]; pork rolls (*Lopez v Star World Enterprises Pty Ltd (in liq)*);[73] cruise ship food (*Neil v P & O Cruises Australia Ltd*).[74]
- Claims against service providers for poor service, including claims against banks for fees charged for no services and cruise lines for drought-affected cruises (*Moore v Scenic Tours Pty Ltd*;[75] *Kelly v Scenic Tours Pty Ltd*).[76]
- Claims by shareholders and investors in relation to deceptive conduct, shareholder oppression and failures to disclose, including *King v AG Australia Holdings Ltd*;[77] *Dorajay Pty Ltd v Aristocrat Leisure Ltd*;[78] *Kirby v Centro Properties Ltd (No 6)*;[79] *Pathway Investments Pty Ltd v National Australia Bank Ltd (No 3)*;[80] *Earglow Pty Ltd v Newcrest Mining Ltd*;[81] *Money Max Int Pty Ltd v QBE Insurance Group Ltd*;[82] *Kelly v Willmott Forests Ltd (in liq) (No 4)*;[83] *TPT Patrol Pty Ltd as trustee for Amies Superannuation Fund v Myer Holdings Ltd*;[84] *Timbercorp Finance Pty Ltd (in liq) v Collins*;[85] *Endeavour River Pty Ltd v MG Responsible Entity Ltd*[86].
- Industrial claims against employers such as for underpayment and exploitation of workers (*Gall v Domino's Pizza Enterprises Ltd* (ongoing)).[87]

Unfortunately, there are still difficulties for members of class actions (many of whom may have no ability to pay lawyers) to fund their disputes. More importantly, most individuals are not prepared to be personally liable for the costs of the other side if they lose the case and have an adverse costs order awarded against them. This has led to the growth of litigation funders who professionally fund class action disputes and accept the risks of adverse costs orders on behalf of the plaintiff class. Litigation funders enable class action litigants to pursue their claim in the courts and through ADR without having to pay for the process. Litigation funders, therefore, solve many of the access to justice issues for class action plaintiffs but they also create problems of their own, as follows:

- Litigation funding has become big business but is not a well-regulated industry because it is new. Litigation funders are not governed by the same professional and ethical rules

71 *Watson as Trustee for Murrindini Bushfire Class Action Settlement Fund v Commissioner of Taxation* [2019] FCA 228.
72 *Ryan v Great Lakes Council* (1999) ATPR 46–191.
73 *Lopez v Star Enterprises Pty Ltd (in liq)* (1999) ATPR 41–678.
74 *Neil v P & O Cruises Australia Ltd* [2002] FCA 1325.
75 *Moore v Scenic Tours Pty Ltd* [2018] NSWSC 1777.
76 *Kelly v Scenic Tours Pty Ltd* [2019] NSWSC 1266.
77 *King v AG Holdings Ltd* [2003] FCA 980.
78 *Dorajay Pty Ltd v Aristocrat Leisure Ltd* [2009] FCA 19.
79 *Kirby v Centro Properties Ltd (No 6)* [2012] FCA 650.
80 *Pathway Investments Pty Ltd v National Australia Bank Ltd (No 3)* [2012] VSC 625.
81 *Earglow Pty Ltd v Newcrest Mining Ltd* [2016] FCA 1433.
82 *Money Max Int Pty Ltd v QBE Insurance Group Ltd* (2016) 245 FCR 191.
83 *Kelly v Wilmott Forests Ltd (in liq) (No 4)* (2016) 335 ALR 439.
84 *TPT Patrol Pty Ltd as trustee for Ames Superannuation Fund v Myer Holdings Ltd* (2019) 140 ACSR 38.
85 *Timbercorp Finance Pty Ltd (in liq) v Collins* (2016) 259 CLR 212.
86 *Endeavour River Pty Ltd v MG Responsible Entity Ltd* [2009] FCA 1719.
87 *Gall v Domino's Pizza Enterprises Ltd* [2019] FCA 1799.

as lawyers. Many class action plaintiffs feel that they pay too high a percentage of their payout to litigation funders and lawyers.

- Litigation funders only take on matters where there is a very high chance of success as they are wearing the costs and risks of the litigation or ADR processes. This means that many cases involving high risks and vulnerable disputants are simply not run because the litigation funders are not motivated by the precedential value nor the societal value of running an action.
- Litigation funders have an added incentive to settle disputes through ADR rather than pursuing a precedent creating judgment. Some litigants sue to prove a principle specifically intending to create a precedent for society. Many litigants are indifferent to precedent they create for future disputants. However, litigation funders have a disincentive to create precedent because precedent is likely to reduce the incidence of future disputes. This makes litigation funders preternaturally disposed to ADR resolution, despite the difficulty of getting class agreement, to ensure continued legal uncertainty results in maximum future disputes. Unlike other litigation, class action settlements require court approval and are complex to administer.
- Litigation funders struggle with what is known as the "free rider" problem. Litigation funders need litigants to agree to pay a portion of their payout to the funder for it to be financially worthwhile to run the action. Free riders are people who seek to benefit from the decision without paying the litigation funder. The ability to prevent free riders was recently reduced by the High Court in the case of *BMW Australia Ltd v Brewster*[88] which found that the New South Wales Supreme Court and the Federal Court could not make orders requiring all members of a class to pay to contribute to a common fund to pay the litigation funder unless those litigants had signed a funding agreement.
- As litigation funding becomes a more developed industry, competition for claims can lead to multiple litigation funders backing different representatives for what should be a single class action (*Perera v Getswift Ltd*).[89]

3.2.6 The role of technology in improving access to justice

The role of technology in the law is increasing.[90] However, the ability of technology, including artificial intelligence, to improve access to justice is less certain.[91] While technology is, increasingly, replacing tasks formerly performed manually by lawyers, such as the review of documents,[92] technology does not always improve access to justice due to the cost of technology, low digital literacy among many vulnerable populations, and psychological barriers to managing legal issues without expert human assistance.[93] It is inevitable that

88 *BMW Australia Ltd v Brewster* (2019) 374 ALR 627.
89 *Perera v Getswift Ltd* (2018) 263 FCR 92.
90 See Chapter 10.6.
91 Emily S Taylor Poppe, 'The Future Is Complicated: AI, Apps & Access to Justice' (2019) 72(1) *Oklahoma Law Review* 185.
92 John Armour and Mari Sako, 'AI-enabled Business Models in Legal Services: From Traditional Law Firms to Next-generation Law Companies?' (2020) 7(1) *Journal of Professions and Organization* 27.
93 Sonya Willis, 'Could Civil Case Management Benefit from a Litigant Vulnerability Assessment Scheme?' (2018) 7(2) *Journal of Civil Litigation and Practice* 94; Poppe (n 91) 201–4.

more court processes and ADR options will move online and this can remove barriers to access such as for people living in remote or regional areas where there are no nearby courts while, simultaneously, increasing barriers to justice for those with poor digital literacy such as many elderly people and those with limited English.[94] The complexity of law and the emotional distress which frequently accompanies civil disputes make CDR a challenging area to develop technological solutions which improve access to justice.[95]

3.3 Open justice: community and accountability in dispute resolution

Open justice is a key aim of Australia's CDR system which requires a delicate balancing act between the strong motivations in favour of open justice and the strong motivations in favour of privacy. In the New South Wales case of *John Fairfax Publications Pty Ltd v District Court of NSW*, Spigelman J stated: "It is well established that open justice is one of the most fundamental aspects of the system of justice in Australia. The conduct of proceedings in public … is an essential quality of an Australian court of justice."[96]

The competing interests of open justice and confidentiality are one of the key distinctions between ADR and litigation because ADR is usually confidential while litigation is usually public. The contrast between the common desire of parties for confidentiality and the open nature of litigation provides a key incentive for parties to engage in ADR in order to resolve their disputes confidentially. There are also limited circumstances where courts will be closed to the public, such as family law cases involving custody of children. Orders to suppress information or close courts are most commonly made in criminal law cases. Unfortunately for privacy-conscious litigants, suppression and non-publication orders are only allowed in extremely limited circumstances, such as where the material suppressed would pose a threat to national security or where the suppression is required to protect the administration of justice. The principle of open justice is a common law principle of litigation that has also been embodied in statutes and which applies across both civil and criminal disputes.

3.3.1 Weighing public policy objectives

Open justice is considered a key requirement for the proper administration of justice. Therefore, it is usually only brought into issue in cases where one or more parties seek to suppress material or identities from being heard and published, usually for the protection of a competing principle or societal interest which is more essential to the administration of justice. There are strong public policy objectives which favour open justice, including the engagement of the public with the courts, judicial process and the assurance of the honesty and independence of the judiciary. Open justice cases often involve competing public policy issues and the task of the court in balancing the competing benefits of open justice and protection of confidentiality.

94 Richard E Susskind, *Online Courts and the Future of Justice* (Oxford University Press, 2019); Law Council of Australia (n 11) Part 1.

95 See Chapter 2.5 regarding litigation deterrents.

96 *John Fairfax Publications Pty Ltd v District Court of New South Wales* (2004) 61 NSWLR 344, [18].

Open justice was considered by the High Court in the case of *Hogan v Hinch*,[97] in the context of determining that s 42 of the *Serious Sex Offenders Monitoring Act 2005* (Vic) was not invalid on the grounds of jurisdiction, the obligation to maintain open justice or the implied freedom of political communication. *Hogan v Hinch* concerned the identification, on a website and at a rally, by Derryn Hinch, then a radio broadcaster, of persons convicted of sex offences in breach of suppression orders preventing their identification. Hinch's High Court claim was an unsuccessful attempt to defend his breach by arguing that the law was invalid. Chief Justice French (who agreed with his fellow judges in rejecting Hinch's claim of invalidity) gave an excellent summary of the circumstances in which open justice has been outweighed by competing requirements for the administration of justice:

> It has long been accepted at common law that the application of the open justice principle may be limited in the exercise of a superior court's inherent jurisdiction or an inferior court's implied powers. This may be done where it is necessary to secure the proper administration of justice. In a proceeding involving a secret technical process, a public hearing of evidence of the secret process could "cause an entire destruction of the whole matter in dispute". Similar considerations inform restrictions on the disclosure in open court of evidence in an action for injunctive relief against an anticipated breach of confidence. In the prosecution of a blackmailer, the name of the blackmailer's victim, called as a prosecution witness, may be suppressed because of the 'keen public interest in getting blackmailers convicted and sentenced' and the difficulties that may be encountered in getting complainants to come forward 'unless they are given this kind of protection'. So too, in particular circumstances, may the name of a police informant or the identity of an undercover police officer. The categories of case are not closed, although they will not lightly be extended. Where 'exceptional and compelling considerations going to national security' require that the confidentiality of certain materials be preserved, a departure from the ordinary open justice principle may be justified. The character of the proceedings and the nature of the function conferred upon the court may also qualify the application of the open-court principle. The jurisdiction of courts in relation to wards of the State and mentally ill people was historically an exception to the general rule that proceedings should be held in public because the jurisdiction exercised in such cases was 'parental and administrative, and the disposal of controverted questions ... an incident only in the jurisdiction'. Proceedings not 'in the ordinary course of litigation', such as applications for leave to appeal, can also be determined without a public hearing.[98]

Even "the mere protection of commercial-in-confidence information" can be an appropriate basis for making a suppression or non-publication order as confirmed by Perram J in the Federal Court case of *Motorola Solutions, Inc v Hytera Communications Corporation Ltd (No 2)*.[99]

The requirement for open justice also extends to interlocutory proceedings (i.e. any court hearings regarding the process of CDR) as well as trials and judgments. This is because

97 *Hogan v Hinch* (2011) 243 CLR 506.

98 Ibid [21]. The footnotes within this quotation have not been included but provide an excellent list of authorities in support of each of the exceptions to open justice listed by French CJ for those interested in delving further.

99 *Motorola Solutions, Inc v Hytera Communications Corporation Ltd (No 2)* [2018] FCA 17, [8]

it is important for public faith in the administration of justice to extend to all aspects of the dispute resolution process. This was confirmed in the high-profile defamation dispute between actor Geoffrey Rush and Nationwide News in relation to reports of indecent behaviour by Rush against a co-star in the Sydney Theatre Company performances of the play *King Lear* where Wigney J stated:

> The principle of open justice demands and requires that the public be able to follow and understand all stages of a proceeding, including interlocutory steps such as the striking out of part of a defence. It is difficult to see how such a step could be fully understood, or fairly reported on, if the parts of the defence that are struck out are suppressed.[100]

3.3.2 Exceptions: suppression, non-publication and closed court orders

Although open justice is a common law concept, the circumstances in which courts should make suppression orders or close courts is now governed by statute in numerous Australian jurisdictions. Many recent cases, therefore, involve interpretation of state-based or Federal legislation regulating closed court, suppression and non-publication orders. This legislation sets out in what circumstances jurisdictions should suppress information but is founded on the importance of open justice and its maximisation.

An increase in suppression and non-publication orders in most Australian jurisdictions led to a project by the Standing Committee of Attorneys-General (SCAG) (now the Council of Attorneys-General (CAG))[101] in 2010 to create national model rules for suppression and non-publication orders and to create a national register.[102] Concerns as to the overuse of suppression orders led the Commonwealth Government to introduce s 102PD of the *Access to Justice (Federal Jurisdiction) Amendment Act 2012* (Cth) aimed at reducing the application of suppression orders in Federal cases which is now embodied in multiple statutes:[103]

> **Safeguarding public interest in open justice**
> In deciding whether to make a suppression order or non-publication order, the court concerned must take into account that a primary objective of the administration of justice is to safeguard the public interest in open justice.[104]

For example, the Commonwealth *Judiciary Act 1903*, since 2012, includes pt XAA Suppression and Non-Publication Orders (ss 77RA–77RK) governing High Court suppression and non-publication orders, including the above quoted open justice provision at s 77RD. Similarly, the *Federal Court of Australia Act 1976* (Cth) now contains pt VAA Suppression

100 *Rush v Nationwide News Pty Ltd* (2018) 359 ALR 473, [195].

101 CAG met for the first time in December 2017, having been created from the division of the Law, Crime and Community Safety Council (LCCSC) with separate councils for Attorneys-General and Ministers for Police and Emergency Management. The LCCSC replaced SCAG in 2013. Suppression orders are not on the current CAG agenda.

102 In 2013, the Commonwealth Director of Public Prosecutions developed a National Register of Suppression Orders for Commonwealth criminal prosecutions.

103 *Access to Justice (Federal Jurisdiction) Amendment Act 2012* (Cth) s 102PD.

104 *Judiciary Act 1913* (Cth) s 77RD.

and Non-Publication Orders (ss 37AA–37AL) but is based upon open justice pursuant to s 37AE created pursuant to s 102PD above.

In New South Wales, suppression and non-publication orders are governed by the *Court Suppression and Non-Publication Orders Act 2010* (NSW) (pt 2) and includes s 6 which protects open justice in identical terms to s 102PD above. There have been hundreds of New South Wales cases discussing suppression and non-publication including issues such as the meaning of "necessary" as a "strong word" requiring "exceptional circumstances" in s 8(1) of the *Court Suppression and Non-Publication Orders Act 2010* (NSW) discussed in *New South Wales v Wilmot* in overturning an interim suppression order.[105]

In Victoria, the *Open Courts Act 2013* (Vic), governs suppression orders (pts 2–4) and closed court orders (pt 5).[106] However, the entire *Open Courts Act 2013* (Vic) is based on a presumption in favour of open justice, set out in s 4:

> **Presumption in favour of disclosure of information**
> To strengthen and promote the principles of open justice and free communication of information, there is a presumption in favour of disclosure of information to which a court or tribunal must have regard in determining whether to make a suppression order.[107]

Other Australian jurisdictions do not have dedicated suppression and non-publication legislation but have capacity to restrict publication in limited circumstances while also upholding the principle of open justice through statutory provisions and common law:

- Queensland: the *Supreme Court of Queensland Act 1991* (Qld) at s 8(1)(b) requires the conduct of the Court to be conducted "in open court" but, at s 8(2), empowers the Court to limit the extent to which its business is open to the public where "the public interest or the interests of justice require"[108]
- South Australia: the *Evidence Act 1929* (SA) at s 69A provides for the granting of suppression orders in South Australia, noting the primary objective of safeguarding open justice at s 69A(2)(a)[109]
- Tasmania: there is no statutory provision for suppression or non-publication orders in Tasmania but statutory cases have been referred to as analogous to the inherent common law power[110]

105 *New South Wales v Wilmot* [2019] NSWSC 1002, [16]-[20]. See also *Capilano Honey Ltd v Dowling (No 2)* [2018] NSWCA 217 as an example of interlocutory suppression orders.

106 For further analysis of the Victorian position, see Jason Bosland, 'Two Years of Suppression under the *Open Courts Act 2013* (Vic)' (2017) 39(1) *Sydney Law Review* 25; Frank Vincent, *Open Courts Act Review* (2017) <https://s3.ap-southeast-2.amazonaws.com/hdp.au.prod.app.vic-engage.files/9215/2211/1859/Review_of_the_Open_Courts_Act_2013_-_March_2018.pdf> for further analysis of the Victorian position.

107 *Open Courts Act 2013* (Vic) s 4. See also *AB v CD and EF* [2019] VSCA 28 which considered the *Open Courts Act 2013* (Vic) and were commenced in parallel with the High Court proceedings *AB v CD* (2019) 364 ALR 202 discussed below.

108 See *Velocity Frequent Flyer Pty Ltd v BP Australia Pty Ltd* [2019] QSC 29 for a discussion of open justice in Queensland by Jackson J.

109 See *D v Director of Public Prosecutions (Cth)* (2018) 131 SASR 1 for a discussion of open justice in the criminal law context in South Australia. See *Dang Pharmacy Pty Ltd v Dang* [2016] SADC 106 for the civil dispute context.

110 *Brooks v Easther* [2017] TASSC 44, [7], [15].

- Western Australia: there is no statutory provision for suppression or non-publication orders in Western Australia but cases have confirmed the fundamental common law principle of open justice and its limited exceptions[111]
- Australian Capital Territory: there is no specific Act concerning open justice but the Court in *R v Meegan*[112] notes there are specific provisions protecting evidence from publication and the common law principle of open justice
- Northern Territory: there is no specific Act concerning open justice but cases recognises the principle and its exceptions, including for NTCAT, in s 60 of the *Northern Territory Civil and Administrative Tribunal Act*.[113]

Courts can also close hearings, including excluding parties to the proceedings from the hearing in a variety of circumstances, such as where the presence of the public would damage the proper administration of justice.[114] Closed courts, also known as "in camera proceedings", are also required in certain types of disputes such as cases concerning the status of children.[115] In the High Court case of *HT v The Queen,*[116] Gordon J explained the difference between closed court and suppression or non-publication orders as follows:

> What is described as an '*in camera* order', or a closed court order, which excludes the public from proceedings, is a different kind of order. By itself, it does not restrain the publication or disclosure of evidence in the proceedings by persons permitted to attend the hearing. A suppression or non-publication order may stand without an *in camera* order. The distinction between the two types of order is important. Unlike an *in camera* order, a suppression or non-publication order binds persons in the courtroom and, depending on its terms, third parties, who may be found to be in contempt if they intentionally interfere with the proper administration of justice by deliberately frustrating the effect of the order[117].

However, there is an (unsurprising) overlap between cases involving closure of courts and orders for suppression or non-publication. For example, in *Jasem v Presmist Formwork Contractors Pty Ltd,*[118] the Supreme Court of New South Wales heard an application ex parte and in closed court, pursuant to s 71 of the *Civil Procedure Act 2005* (NSW). The closed court application granted a request by the defendant to prevent the plaintiff's access to surveillance material until cross-examination of the plaintiff as the plaintiff's credit was a key issue in the case and showing the surveillance footage sooner might result in an unfair trial.[119]

The following High Court cases demonstrate that a number of factors will be considered by courts when overriding the principle of open justice and these will include the policy

111 See, eg, *Medical Board of Western Australia v A Medical Practitioner* [2011] WASCA 151 (S); *Collard v Western Australia (No 3)* [2013] WASC 70.

112 *R v Meegan* [2014] ACTSC 263.

113 See *Nationwide News Pty Ltd v Binsaris* (2019) 170 NTR 69; *Kapser v Psychology Board of Australia and News Corporation Australia* [2018] NTCAT 338.

114 See, eg, ss 28–32 of the *Open Courts Act 2013* (Vic) which includes criminal penalties for contravening closed court orders; s 71(b) of the *Civil Procedure Act 2005* (NSW).

115 See, eg, s 17 *Status of Children Act 1978* (NT); s 32 *Status of Children Act 1974* (Vic); s 24 *Status of Children Act 1996* (NSW).

116 *HT v the Queen* (2019) 374 ALR 216

117 Ibid 239 [85].

118 *Jasem v Presmist Formwork Contractors Pty Ltd* [2020] NSWSC 859.

119 Ibid [17].

arguments in favour of suppression but also the value of the suppressed information in understanding the work of the court and the value to the public of knowing the material sought to be suppressed.

The recent High Court case of *Northern Territory v Griffiths (No 2)* ('*Griffiths*') provides an excellent example of where the objective of open justice was overshadowed by a variety of factors which favoured continued suppression of information. In *Griffiths,* the restricted information for which a suppression order was sought was evidence provided by Aboriginal Elder men. Justice Nettle found that:

> Such matters (gender restricted knowledge, which includes performance, song, narrative and objects) are a fundamental component of Aboriginal religious belief and practice. The integrity of their restricted domain is sustained through a structured system where knowledge is controlled by some and allocated to others according to customary rules for its dissemination. Failure to comply with those rules is believed to result in exposure to harmful and potentially fatal spirituality.[120]

As a result, Nettle J extended an earlier suppression order in relation to gender restricted materials for a period of 10 years, despite noting the importance of open justice:

> I take into account, as is mentioned in s 77RD of the *Judiciary Act*, that a primary objective of the administration of justice is to safeguard the public interest in open justice. I also bear in mind, as is required by s 77RI of the Judiciary Act, that, in deciding the period for which an order is to operate, the Court is to ensure that the order operates for no longer than is reasonably necessary to achieve the purpose for which it is made. Other things being equal, I should be disinclined therefore to make the orders sought or at least to make orders of the duration of ten years that is proposed.[121]

In making the requested 10-year suppression order, Nettle J considered the following factors in favour of suppression outweighed the open justice incentives:

1. The extension of the suppression order was uncontested with none of the interested parties wishing to be heard on the matter.
2. The Court's reasons for judgment in the underlying decision could be fully understood without reference to the restricted materials.
3. "[F]ailure to make orders of the kind sought would risk subjecting the men who gave evidence to serious fears and other substantial adverse psychological consequences, and, I infer, would have the potential to inhibit other Aboriginal men in giving evidence regarding gender restricted knowledge in future compensation proceedings."[122]
4. The length of the order was necessary to achieve the purpose of the order given the life expectancy of the men.[123]

---

120 *Northern Territory v Griffiths (No 2)* (2019) 368 ALR 77, [3].
121 Ibid [6].
122 Ibid [7].
123 Ibid [6].

Similarly, the case of *AB v CD*, which concerned a suppression order sought in relation to the names and images of the two young children of a Victorian police informant, involved several competing considerations.[124] The Court agreed to suppress the names and images of the police informant's children for a period of not less than 15 years after the publication of the final report of the Royal Commission into the Management of Police Informants. This order was despite Nettle J noting that: "It is also essential to bear in mind that a primary objective of the administration of justice is to safeguard the public interest in open justice."[125] The interest in open justice was outweighed by the following circumstances favouring suppression:

1. The risk to safety of the children was "acute" and would increase upon disclosure of the informant's name in March 2019 according to a senior experienced police officer whose evidence was uncontested.
2. The children were young and in no way involved in any of the proceedings.
3. "It is not suggested that the interests or administration of justice would be at all compromised by non-publication of their names and images. There is no evident basis to suppose that public understanding of the judgments of the trial court or the Court of Appeal, or of this Court, would be affected. Nor is there any legitimate public interest in the publication of the details of EF's children in connection with the subject matter of the Supreme Court proceedings or these proceedings."[126]
4. The suppression order was not opposed by the Royal Commission, the Commonwealth Department of Public Prosecution (CDPP) or most of the media.[127]

Some concerns regarding open justice cannot be discerned from the cases precisely due to their lack of reporting. Journalists argue that legislation such as the *Court Suppression and Non-Publication Orders Act 2010* (NSW) have led to an explosion of suppression orders, particularly in New South Wales and Victoria, which prevent journalists gaining sufficient access to court documents to report effectively to the public on cases of interest.[128] Journalists have also raised concerns about secret trials, such as the cases of Witness J and Witness K, which have been completely suppressed on the basis of national security risks.[129]

3.3.3 The role of open justice in precedents and freedom of reporting

Open justice is critical for Australian law and democracy because it enables the creation of precedent and the freedom to report on court decisions to the public. As a common

124 *AB v CD* (2019) 364 ALR 202
125 Ibid [21].
126 Ibid [20].
127 Ibid.
128 Amy Dale, 'Access Denied: The "Right-to-Know" Act that was Never Enacted' (2019) *Law Society Journal* 62 (December), 36–39. See also *Rinehart v Welker* (2011) 93 NSWLR 311; *X v Sydney Children's Hospital* [2011] NSWSC 1272.
129 Jack Snape, 'Witness J: How to Hide a Criminal Trial from the Public Despite Australia's Principle of Open Justice', *ABC News* (Web Page, 5 December 2019) <http://www.abc.net.au/news/2019-12-05/witness-j-how-can-a-trial-be-kept-secret/11739288>.

law jurisdiction, we rely on case precedent for much of our law.[130] Closed court rooms and suppressed decisions limit the creation of precedent for future decisions because they cannot be referred to or relied on. Precedent is important for the cases which follow and even more important for the cases which do not eventuate as a result of the precedent. In CDR, disputants will often face problems which have been resolved in previous cases. If those cases were open and reported, the new disputants can resolve their dispute purely by reference to the law as developed through case precedent without any need to commence their own proceedings. Thus, many disputes settle with minimal engagement in legal processes because they can rely on reported precedents. Decisions not available to the public restrict the development of precedent in the common law system.

The suppression of case information and the closing of courts can also negatively impact freedom of reporting. In *Hogan v Hinch*, French CJ discussed the interaction between open justice and reporting:

> It is a common law corollary of the open-court principle that, absent any restriction ordered by the court, anybody may publish a fair and accurate report of the proceedings, including the names of the parties and witnesses, and the evidence, testimonial, documentary or physical, that has been given in the proceedings (165).
>
> The existence and nature of the common law or implied power in a court to make orders restricting the publication of proceedings in open court has been the subject of considerable judicial exegesis. The question whether the power extends to orders purporting to bind the world at large is contentious. As the Law Reform Commission of New South Wales said in 2000 (166): 'the common law regarding suppression orders is relatively unclear and unsettled'.
>
> ...
>
> In my opinion the better view is that there is inherent jurisdiction or implied power in limited circumstances to restrict the publication of proceedings conducted in open court. The exercise of the power must be justified by reference to the necessity of such orders in the interests of the administration of justice. Such an order may be made to and bind the parties, witnesses, counsel, solicitors and, if relevant, jurors and media representatives, or other persons present in court when the order is made, or to whom the order is specifically directed. It is not necessary for present purposes to reach a concluded view on the full extent of the power in relation to the general public.
>
> ...
>
> The open hearing is an essential characteristic of courts, which supports the reality and appearance of independence and impartiality. Its corollary is the freedom to make a fair and accurate report of what transpires in court proceedings, including the orders made by the court. However, at common law the open justice principle has, consistently with the judicial function, long been subject to qualifications reflected in the inherent jurisdiction of courts or their implied incidental power to hear part of their proceedings in camera and to restrict the publication of evidence or the names of witnesses. Chapter III does not impose on federal courts or the courts of the States a

130 See Chapter 2.3.

more stringent application of the open justice principle than that described above. The extent at common law of a power to prohibit publication of evidence or information disclosed in proceedings in open court may be contentious. The existence of a power to make such orders to bind the world at large is doubtful. Debate on that issue goes to the common law and implied powers of courts.[131]

3.3.4 Alternative dispute resolution: trading open justice for accessibility

The importance of open justice is significant to evaluating ADR because one of the most commonly cited advantages of ADR is its confidentiality. The value of open justice and the value of precedent, referred to above, helps to define the role of ADR in Australia's legal system because ADR is not open to the public and does not create precedent for future disputants. However, as discussed in Chapter 3.2.2, ADR can significantly increase access to justice and its confidentiality can be a positive factor in making it accessible where parties desire confidentiality in the resolution of their disputes. In addition to the circumstances discussed above in relation to closed courts and suppressed proceedings where confidentiality is essential, there are many other circumstances where confidentiality is highly desirable, including disputes involving families and many commercial and trade related legal disputes. For these disputes, the desire for confidentiality is not sufficient to close court and ADR becomes a very desirable alternative.

Australian billionaire Georgina Rinehart's ongoing dispute with her children as to distribution of the family fortune provides an excellent example of the battle between open justice and confidentiality. The Rinehart family's affairs are of considerable interest to the media and the public due to her extreme wealth and ownership power in Australia. However, Georgina Rinehart would, understandably, prefer to keep her affairs confidential. In order to preserve confidentiality, the Rinehart family entered various deeds which required any disputes to be resolved through arbitration. However, arbitration agreements (as discussed in Chapter 4) are consensual so disputes can be brought before courts as to the validity of arbitration agreements and this has happened in the Rinehart dispute. Litigation as to the effectiveness of the arbitration agreements in the Rinehart dispute ended up before the High Court in 2019, following many years of litigation in other courts. The High Court stayed the litigation in favour of arbitration in accordance with the disputed deed which aimed to protect the confidentiality of the parties.[132] In an earlier interlocutory dispute in 2014, Georgina Rinehart's failed bid for suppression of the dispute led to a detailed discussion of the requirements of open justice wherein the judge refused to suppress the decision despite the embarrassment to Georgina Rinehart from its publication and the fact that this was not consistent with the confidentiality aims of

131 *Hogan v Hinch* (2011) 243 CLR 506, [22]–[23], [26], [46]. The footnotes within this quotation have not been included. The remaining judges (with whose orders French CJ agreed), Gummow, Hayne, Heydon, Crennan, Kiefel and Bell JJ, in a joint judgment held that it was not necessary to consider inherent jurisdiction to restrict publication of open court proceedings because the issue concerned statutory authority to grant courts powers: [88].

132 *Rinehart v Hancock Prospecting Pty Ltd* (2019) 366 ALR 635.

the underlying disputed arbitration agreement.[133] The Federal Court decided the dispute regarding the arbitration clause should not be struck out as an abuse of process for the following reasons:

1. A suppression order must be "necessary" to prevent prejudice to administration of justice.
2. Open justice fundamental principle of justice system which generally operates from the commencement of proceedings.
3. The court must consider primary objective is to safeguard public interest in open justice (suppression order legislation supports this).
4. The need to do justice is part of "necessity" principle.
5. Media reporting is corollary of "open justice" because public access to the conduct and deliberations of the court is a "human right".
6. Possible embarrassment, loss of reputation, consequential loss is generally price parties must pay to litigate.
7. There are recognised exceptions including where openness would destroy justice such as by vindicating a blackmailer or seriously reducing the commercial value of the dispute's subject matter.[134]

Therefore, the substantive dispute between the Rineharts will be decided by confidential arbitration but the interlocutory proceedings in relation to the validity of the arbitration agreement are open to the public to read and to the media to report.

The balance between the value of open justice and the right to confidentiality can be particularly complex in disputes with broader public relevance. For example, *Jenkings v Northern Territory of Australia (No 4)*,[135] determined that the Court would not suppress the details of a settlement order in a class action against the Northern Territory government involving approximately 1,200 (95% Indigenous) youth incarcerated in Northern Territory youth detention centres, such as Don Dale and Holtze Youth Detention Centres. The Court relied on the principle of open justice as an element of the rule of law in refusing the Northern Territory Government's request to suppress the amount of the settlement stating:

> Putting to one side the disclosure of the settlement sum in the settlement notices as being in the interests of group members, it is also the case, in my opinion, that members of the Australian community are entitled to know and understand the core components of the settlement reached by the parties, including the amount the Territory has agreed (with a denial of liability) to pay for compensation and legal costs. The Territory is expending public funds on making that payment, and in defending this proceeding. The Court expends public funds in approving the settlement, and performs a supervisory role given to it by Parliament, because the settlement of a Part IVA proceeding affects the rights and interests of all those within the class as defined. Here, those individuals were mostly Aboriginal, were minors, and were deprived of their

133 *Rinehart v Rinehart* (2014) 320 ALR 195.
134 Ibid [23]–[31] (Jacobson J).
135 *Jenkings v Northern Territory of Australia (No 4)* [2021] FCA 839.

liberty, when the impugned conduct occurred. In a civil society governed by the rule of law, those are additional reasons for a high level of transparency about how such a proceeding is proposed to be resolved. There should be informed public scrutiny of what has occurred, so that there may be informed public discussion of it – these are some of the proper consequences of open justice.[136]

3.4 Conclusion

It would be easy to conclude that Australian CDR is neither open nor accessible given the problems identified in this chapter. The Australian legal system is far from perfect and, as the law reform reports, investigations and cases discussed above have demonstrated, there is significant room for improvement. However, to take such a negative view of our legal system would be to ignore the challenges and balancing acts discussed in Chapter 2. In fact, Australian CDR is among the most accessible and open systems in the world. It is evident from the cases discussed in this chapter (and Chapter 2) that Australian judges are well aware of the value of both open and accessible justice and that they carefully balance competing interests to achieve these key aims to the greatest extent possible. The fact that so much work has been undertaken by law reform bodies, courts, and legal institutions into improving access to justice and preserving open justice, underscores the commitment of the Australian government and the Australian legal profession to optimising Australia's CDR system.

136 Ibid, [93]. The settlement sum was disclosed to be $35,000,000 in Schedule 2 of the Federal Court's 27 July 2021 order.

4 ALTERNATIVES TO COURT: ALTERNATIVE DISPUTE RESOLUTION

4.1 Introduction

This chapter introduces the key types and uses of alternative dispute resolution (ADR) and their role in civil dispute resolution (CDR). ADR refers to the alternatives to litigation which individuals may wish to pursue instead of, before, or during, litigation. ADR is usually less formal than litigation — the procedures tend to be more flexible and more variable so the procedures discussed in this chapter are, of necessity, simply examples of how various forms of ADR can occur.

ADR is almost certainly the most common method of resolving civil disputes. However, due to its confidential nature, it is less easy to measure, analyse or research than litigation.[1] ADR improves the efficiency of CDR but at a cost to procedural fairness.[2] ADR resolution frequently has little or nothing to do with justice or underlying legal or factual issues in dispute, and more to do with the broader interests, bargaining power, and relationships of the parties. Therefore, ADR has complex advantages and disadvantages compared with litigation. Court-ordered and compulsory ADR are increasingly common in Australia but this important aspect of ADR will be discussed in Chapter 5 which considers the interaction between ADR and litigation. This chapter will focus on the many ways civil disputes can be resolved outside the courtroom.

4.2 Defining alternative dispute resolution

ADR is a term used to describe any means of resolving a dispute other than litigation (which is covered in detail in Chapters 8–16). Accordingly, it encompasses a wide range of actions. Although ADR is generally considered to be an acronym for "alternative dispute resolution", it is also sometimes referred to as appropriate dispute resolution, additional dispute resolution or even attractive dispute resolution.[3] Therefore, "alternative" is no longer the only possible descriptor used for the "A" in ADR. This chapter will focus on negotiation, mediation, conciliation, case appraisal and arbitration although there are numerous hybrids and variations to these key forms of ADR. Different types of ADR have different levels of formality and procedure and the only real limit to format for ADR is the imagination of the parties engaging in it.

4.2.1 Types and circumstances of alternative dispute resolution

The four most common types of ADR in Australia in ascending order of formality are negotiation, mediation/conciliation, and arbitration. There are countless variations of how each of these forms of ADR can proceed and it is possible for parties to undertake multiple forms of ADR in a single day or to undertake a hybrid of two types of ADR.[4]

1 The effect of ADR on open justice was discussed in Chapter 3.3.

2 The balance between efficiency and procedural fairness was discussed in Chapter 2.3.

3 See Jeffrey Scott Wolfe, 'Across the Ripple of Time: The Future of Alternative (Or, Is It Appropriate) Dispute Resolution' (2000) 36(4) *Tulsa Law Journal* 785 for an early US example. See also the entire issue of this journal: (2012) 35(3) *University of New South Wales Law Journal* which was a special edition dedicated to a Forum on Appropriate Dispute Resolution for a more recent Australian view. See also Mavis Maclean, 'Family mediation: alternative or additional dispute resolution?' (2010) 32(2) *Journal of Social Welfare and Family Law* 105.

4 An example of hybrid ADR is med-arb which combines mediation and arbitration. The mediator becomes an arbitrator and makes a final determination binding on the parties if the initial mediation fails.

Figure 4.1 The four most common types of ADR in Australia

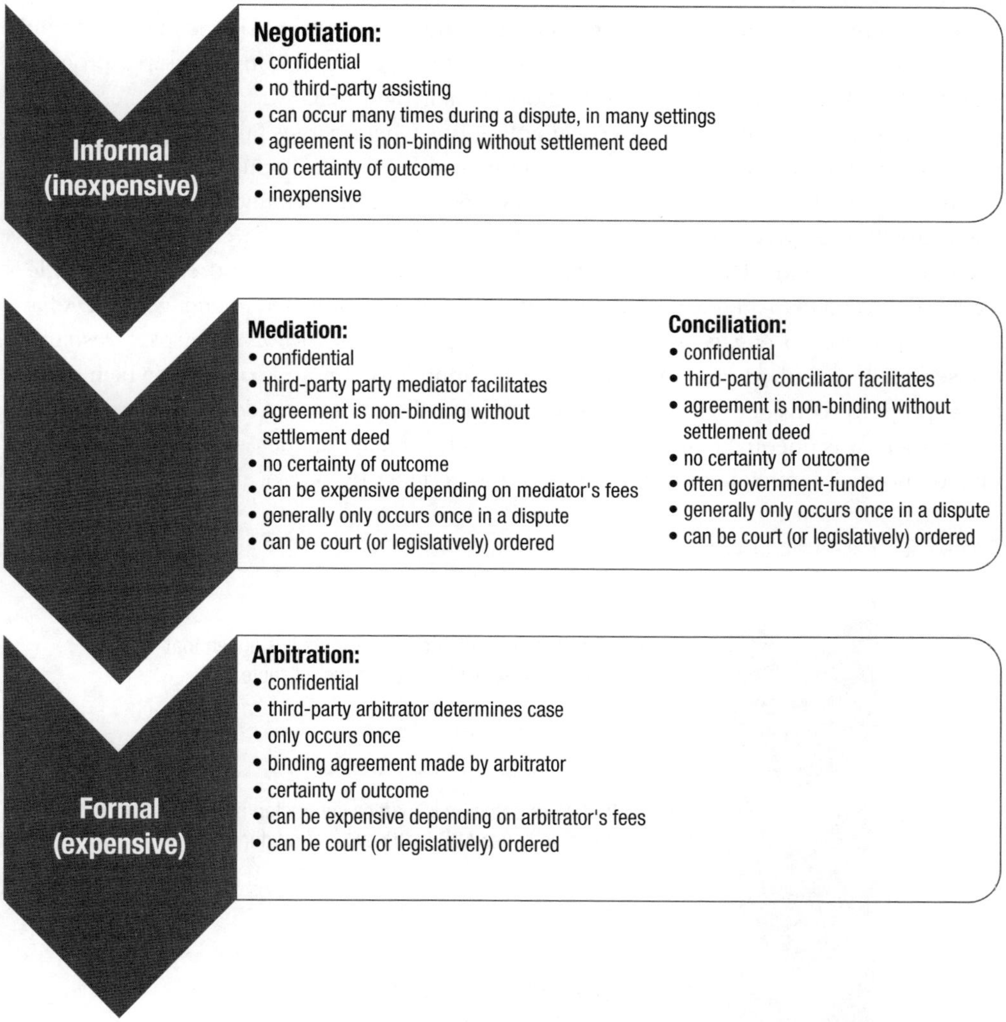

ADR occurs in a wide range of circumstances which can be broadly categorised as ad hoc ADR, contracted ADR, court-ordered ADR and legislated ADR.[5]

The circumstances in which ADR is undertaken significantly impact its prospects of success. Where parties agree, at any stage of a dispute, that they may be able to settle that dispute through ADR (whether negotiation, conciliation, mediation or arbitration) that process has high prospects of success. Parties motivated to settle are very likely to succeed. At the other end of the spectrum, where parties are forced by legislation, with no regard

5 "Ad hoc" is a Latin phrase meaning "for this purpose specially". It is a term used in ADR, particularly arbitration, to describe ADR procedures which are not pre-agreed, ordered or required. In relation to arbitration, however, "ad hoc" can also be used to describe the nature of the arbitration process itself rather than the circumstances of its occurrence. Hence, a contractually agreed arbitration can sometimes be described as "ad hoc" because the contracted procedures do not follow a publicly available set of rules or procedures (eg the ACICA rules) but are instead uniquely defined in the contract.

whatsoever to the nature of their dispute, to attempt ADR, the prospects for success are reduced. This is not to say that many cases will not settle through compulsory ADR.[6] Rather, there are certain intractable, highly adversarial disputes, for which ADR is almost certainly a waste of time because parties cannot be forced to engage in a non-adversarial process if they loathe each other and seek vindication of their own perceived righteousness from a court. There are often also adverse costs implications where parties fail to engage with ADR processes and these can provide a significant incentive to settle disputes.[7]

In between the motivated ad hoc ADR and the compulsorily legislated ADR lies contractually pre-agreed ADR and court-ordered ADR. ADR in these circumstances is less likely than legislated ADR to prove a farcical waste of time, money and energy but is less likely to succeed than ad hoc arbitration. Parties who have contracted to engage in ADR have a pre-disposition to engage properly when a dispute arises. However, dispute resolution clauses can be standard provisions in contracts running to hundreds of pages which neither party properly considered at the time of entering the contract. Additionally, particularly where there was unequal bargaining power when the initial contract was entered into, there may be no real commitment to the terms of the contract by one or more parties once the

Figure 4.2 The circumstances that ADR occurs in

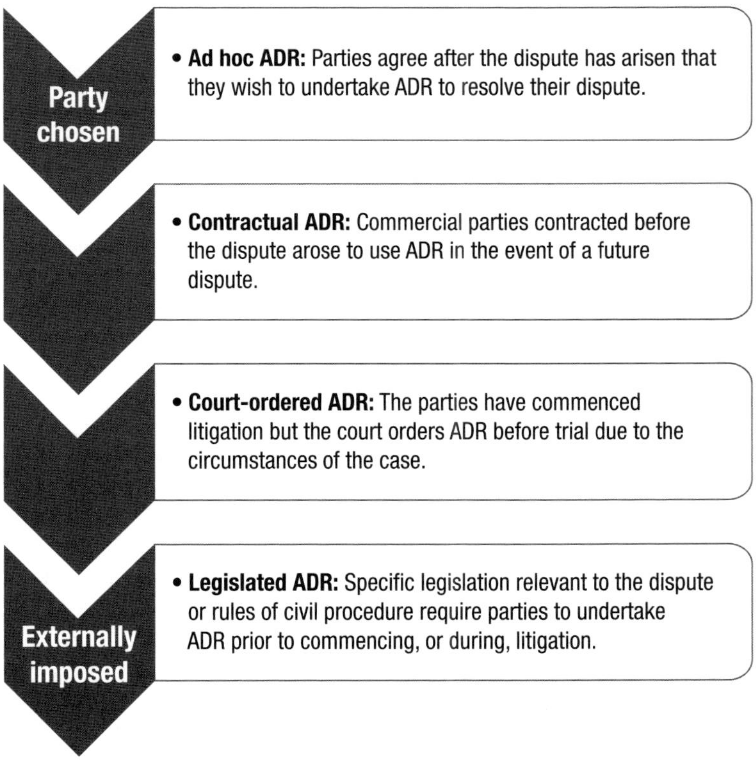

6 See Chapter 5.2 for discussion of compulsory ADR.

7 See Chapter 4.2.4 and Chapter 6.8 regarding adverse costs orders relating to rejected settlement offers.

dispute arises. In such cases, contractually agreed ADR may suffer the same problems as compulsory ADR for highly adversarial parties.

Court-ordered ADR can have very good prospects of success where cases are tightly managed by a judge with a good understanding of the parties and their dispute. For example, many parties ordered by a court to mediate in good faith at a point in proceedings where each other's cases are becoming well understood are likely to engage well in the process, with high prospects of success. Conversely, judges who routinely send all parties to mediation or conciliation with little knowledge of the parties or their dispute are likely to encounter the same problems discussed above in relation to legislated ADR.

4.2.2 External dispute resolution

In addition to entirely private forms of ADR, there are also government-run complaints and ombudsman schemes, sometimes called external dispute resolution (EDR), and these are another significant form of ADR. EDR is useful where the civil dispute is with a government or quasi-government organisation or with a heavily government-regulated industry where the government has established EDR. EDR is designed to protect consumers in relation to the provision of essential services such as energy and communications. A list of relevant ombudsmen can be found at the Australian and New Zealand Ombudsman Association (ANZOA)[8] including the Commonwealth Ombudsman, various state-based energy and water ombudsmen, public transport, telecommunications and financial ombudsmen.

There can be significant advantages to EDR over other forms of ADR and litigation. Complaining to an ombudsman is generally free, does not require any legal representation, and is designed to be efficient, impartial and independent. Another advantage is that EDR enables a concentration of similar disputes because there can be thousands of people reporting the same service flaw. Ombudsmen can also have the power to improve services where a common flaw is identified. However, EDR, because it is free, requires significant government funding and is, therefore, only common in relation to necessities and government services. As for most forms of ADR (other than arbitration), EDR proceedings do not usually prevent subsequent litigation.

4.2.3 Regulation of alternative dispute resolution

There are numerous sources of ADR law ranging from dedicated Acts to minor provisions within Acts. Major sources of ADR regulation include:

- Acts dedicated to a particular type of ADR, such as the *Mediation Act 1997* (ACT) and the *Commercial Arbitration Act 2010* (NSW)
- Acts dedicated to ensuring parties undertake ADR, such as the *Civil Dispute Resolution Act 2011* (Cth)
- Provisions in civil procedure legislation and court rules containing ADR requirements, such as the *Federal Court Rules 2011* (Cth) (especially pt 28: Alternative Dispute Resolution).

8 Australian and New Zealand Ombudsman Association, *Making Complaints* (Web Page) <http://www.anzoa.com.au/for-complaints.html>.

These many sources of law combine with practice notes and judicial directions to direct civil disputants towards ADR at every stage possible of the dispute and are discussed further in this chapter and Chapter 5.

In addition to laws regulating ADR, there are numerous institutions, organisations and bodies engaged in the ADR industry which often impose obligations on their members and may provide systems of accreditation such as Recognised Mediator Accreditation Bodies (RMABs) which provide training and accreditation as part of the Mediator Standards Board's national scheme to accredit mediators.[9] However, there is no longer a Commonwealth Government agency dedicated to ADR following the abolition of NADRAC (National Alternative Dispute Resolution Advisory Council) in November 2013.[10]

4.2.4 Confidentiality of alternative dispute resolution

A key feature of ADR is confidentiality. Most parties do not like the fact that their personal business becomes public when it is taken to court, despite the important societal benefits of open justice discussed in Chapter 3. ADR is usually confidential including arbitration with the decision and reasoning in arbitral awards usually known only to the parties. ADR offers parties a chance to discuss their dispute "off the record." Generally, matters disclosed in mediation or settlement conferences are confidential from both the public and any court proceedings. Accordingly, parties may talk fully and frankly about the options available to them during ADR. Confidentiality is discussed further in relation to negotiation at Chapter 4.3.5 and in Chapter 13, particularly at Chapter 13.6 concerning negotiations privilege.

The exception to the confidentiality of ADR is the use of offers of settlement for the purposes of determining costs orders in subsequent court proceedings where the attempted ADR is unsuccessful. When a court is determining the allocation of costs in a litigation, the attempts made by the parties to settle can be very relevant. Where a party is partially successful in court but had previously rejected a settlement offer for a greater amount of money than the court awarded, the rejected settlement offer will generally prevent the partially successful party from recovering their costs incurred after rejecting the offer.[11]

9 Mediator Standards Board (Web Page) <https://msb.org.au/about-msb>. The Mediator Standards Board coordinates the National Mediator Accreditation System (NMAS) to enable approved members to provide training and accreditation and maintains a register of accredited mediators and member organisations to improve the level of regulation in the mediation industry: Mediator Standards Board, 'Register of Nationally Accredited Mediators' (Web Page) <https://msb.org.au/mediators>; Mediator Standards Board, 'MSB Member List' (Web Page) <https://msb.org.au/msb-member-list>.

10 The National Alternative Dispute Resolution Advisory Council (NADRAC) was established by charter in 1985, and concluded in 2013 due to a government decision to abolish or rationalise non-statutory government bodies in order to streamline business. Fortunately, many NADRAC publications, including those from 1997 to 2013, remain available through National Library of Australia, Trove, <https://webarchive.nla.gov.au/awa/20191107002234/https://www.ag.gov.au/LegalSystem/AlternateDisputeResolution/Pages/NADRACpublications.aspx>. Unfortunately, there do not appear to have been any substantive Commonwealth Attorney-General's Department publications on ADR since the abolition of NADRAC in 2013.

11 See Chapter 6.8.

4.2.5 Advantages of alternative dispute resolution

ADR has numerous potential advantages for parties over litigation. Most obviously, it tends to be cheaper, quicker and less stressful than litigation. As time, expense and emotional cost are the most significant detrimental factors in litigation (see Chapter 2.5 for detailed analysis), these savings constitute a major attraction for ADR. The extent of time, cost and stress saved by using ADR instead of litigation varies dramatically across different forms of ADR. Less formal modes of ADR, such as informal negotiation, tend to be quicker and less costly and bear little or no resemblance to litigation compared to more formal ADR methods, such as arbitration.

In addition to the general cost advantages of ADR, there are some important additional potential ADR advantages which litigation cannot hope to offer — however efficient it may become. Mediation, conciliation and negotiation offer significant potential for preservation of party relationships and the creation of resolutions to disputes which are not limited by the terms of the original relationship and are uniquely beneficial to both parties because they extend beyond the scope of the original dispute. For example, commercial parties to a negotiation or mediation may agree on a future contract with terms which recognise and resolve a dispute in relation to a prior contract where the new contracts terms are attractive to both parties. This sort of dispute resolution is not available to courts. Arbitration also generally has significantly less scope for flexible solutions but has its own potentially significant advantages to parties by enabling party control over forum and arbitrator selection.

4.2.6 Problems with alternative dispute resolution

As with litigation, the problems with ADR also generally relate to the time, cost and stress involved in undertaking it (see Chapter 2.5). While ADR is generally cheaper, faster and less stressful (due to its informality) than litigation, it is by no means a perfect alternative. The more formal the method of ADR, the more it tends to resemble litigation in terms of expense, delay and emotional cost. Hence, arbitration is perhaps the most criticised form of ADR as it most closely resembles litigation.

ADR has the additional problem that it is often in addition to litigation rather than instead of it. Hence the costs, time and stress involved in ADR may be on top of the cost, time and stress of litigation rather than instead of it. The added burden of unsuccessful ADR is evident in the comment of Stone J in the Federal Court case of *Transpacific Pty Ltd v Prudential Retirement Insurance and Annuity Co (No 2)*:

> The procedural history of this matter is not straightforward. The parties have been distracted in their preparation for trial by efforts to settle the dispute either directly between the parties or with the assistance of an independent mediator. These efforts may have been admirable but they were wholly unsuccessful.[12]

ADR can also combine with litigation to add costs through unsuccessful litigation designed to prevent ADR, as occurred in *Rinehart v Hancock Prospecting Pty Ltd*

12 *Transpacific Pty Ltd v Prudential Retirement Insurance and Annuity Co (No 2)* [2011] FCA 1215, [14].

discussed in Chapter 3.3.[13] Parties who are contractually bound to undertake ADR — usually arbitration — may commence unsuccessful court proceedings disputing their ADR obligation resulting in additional wasted court costs in addition to the costs of ADR.[14] In an earlier decision in relation to this dispute, *Hancock Prospecting Pty Ltd v Rinehart (No 2)*, the New South Wales Court of Appeal noted:

> The costs will be large. That is a result of how both sides have treated the applications. With some exception in oral address, no stone has been left unturned, no opportunity for opposition passed up, and no proposition in writing expressed otherwise than to the fullest.[15]

4.2.7 Formalities of alternative dispute resolution

Regardless of how informal ADR may be, the process of settling a dispute (particularly one for which litigation has commenced) is best accompanied by formal procedures to validate the settlement and, where proceedings exist, to terminate those proceedings. Agreed settlements should be documented in writing, preferably by a deed of settlement.[16] In the absence of formal evidence of agreement, settlements can unravel leaving parties back where they started prior to commencing ADR.

4.3 Negotiation

Negotiation is undertaken by almost every party to a civil dispute, often many times, including before and during litigation, and often in conjunction with other forms of ADR. Negotiation itself varies considerably but usually involves only the parties and their legal representatives. Unlike other forms of CDR negotiation need not involve any third party and may be so informal that the disputants may not even be aware they are undertaking ADR when they engage in negotiation. Negotiation is required in some civil litigation where offers of settlement, Offers of Compromise or attendance at settlement conferences are legislatively imposed procedures forming part of the litigation.

4.3.1 Types and circumstances of negotiation

Parties often negotiate with each other about many aspects of their dispute including negotiations regarding civil procedure which can occur throughout trial preparation and trial (discussed in Part II of this book). However, negotiation as a type of ADR concerns negotiations aimed at settling the dispute itself. There are a variety of ways in which parties attempt to negotiate settlement, including:

- ***Conferences***: These can range in formality and location. Many settlement conferences take place in the offices of legal representatives of one or other of the parties, but it is not necessary for parties to even have legal representatives to arrange a settlement conference.

13 *Rinehart v Hancock Prospecting Pty Ltd* (2019) 366 ALR 635.
14 Ibid.
15 *Hancock Prospecting Pty Ltd v Rinehart (No 2)* [2017] FCAFC 208, [6]
16 Settlement deeds and termination of proceedings following settlement are discussed in Chapter 5.5.

It is almost never too late to negotiate, and a negotiated settlement can even be reached in a conference during an adjournment in a court hearing. It is also possible for settlement conferences to take place by telephone or video link up and such conferences can be both formal and effective despite the parties not meeting face-to-face.

- ***Formal correspondence***: Correspondence to negotiate settlement ranges in formality and can occur at any time in a dispute, including after commencement of litigation. Offers of Compromise are the most formal offer of settlement and are made during litigation. These offers must comply with certain court rules which give rejected offers protective cost consequences.[17] Calderbank offers are less formal than Offers of Compromise, but are usually formal letters written by legal representatives. Calderbank offers can be made at any time in a dispute but are recognised by courts, in the event of litigation, as providing protection for parties in relation to costs orders. Calderbank offers are more flexible than Offers of Compromise. Some settlement offers may be neither an Offer of Compromise nor a Calderbank offer, but may still be capable of acceptance and consequent settlement. See Chapters 4.3.2 and 4.3.3 for more detail.
- ***Informal discussion***: It is also possible for parties to have an informal but highly effective settlement negotiation on the street, in a corridor, or a lift, or over the telephone. Informal negotiations can occur during court hearings, in the course of other forms of ADR such as mediations, and at any other time before or during proceedings. Most parties will have undertaken some form of negotiation to attempt to resolve their differences prior to commencing litigation proceedings.
- ***Electronic communications***: The rise of the internet and smart phones has resulted in an increase in informal written settlement negotiations. Significant percentages of formal legal correspondence now takes place through email and other electronic means.[18] While email correspondence from lawyers is often identical to the formal letters lawyers have written for centuries, there is also an increase in less formal email communication including communication between parties and the courts (see Chapters 10.6, 10.7). There is an increasing volume of informal negotiation between disputants which occurs through email, SMS and social media, including Twitter, Facebook, Instagram and Snapchat. Informal electronic negotiations are particularly common where the underlying disputes concern transactions, such as online purchasing, where the parties have no pre-existing relationship other than the online transaction leading to the dispute.

The forms of negotiation discussed above are neither exhaustive, nor capable of rigid definition. For example, a brief meeting in a corridor might be described as an informal settlement conference, a meeting or a conversation. In addition, it is common for a range of negotiation techniques to be utilised simultaneously. The South Australian Supreme Court case of *Southern Waste Resourceco Pty Ltd v Adelaide Hills Region Waste Management Authority (No 3)* provides an excellent and detailed case study of the complexity, extent and variety of dispute settlement negotiations which can occur over time in a single dispute. This case concerned a privately owned landfill site, a waste disposal company (SWM) and a waste management authority established by four local councils. The dispute negotiations

17 See Chapter 6.8 regarding the potential costs ramifications of offers of settlement.

18 See, eg, *Tom Kerr (Subaru) Pty Ltd v Hanks* [2018] NSWSC 1871; *Southern Waste Resourceco Pty Ltd v Adelaide Hills Region Waste Management Authority (No 3)* [2019] SASC 192.

went for many years and included new contracts, deeds, meetings, conferences, emails and conversations. The litigation by SWM, which alleged misleading conduct by the waste management authority in the course of the negotiations, was unsuccessful but the court refused to find that it amounted to an abuse of process and, therefore, did not award indemnity costs against SWM.[19]

Negotiation is often an entirely voluntary undertaking by the parties but there are also circumstances where courts direct parties to negotiate and where parties are required by statute to negotiate. The case of *FMG Pilbara Pty Ltd v Cox* in the Full Federal Court concerned whether the parties had met legislative obligations pursuant to s 31 of the *Native Title Act 1993* (Cth) to "*negotiate in good faith with a view to obtaining the agreement of each of the native title parties*" (emphasis added). Matters not settled by good faith negotiation are then referred to arbitration by s 31 of the *Native Title Act 1993* (Cth). Justices Spender, Sundberg and Mckerracher overruled the Native Title Tribunal by holding that the applicant mining company had negotiated in good faith with the native title holders in accordance with s 31 of the *Native Title Act 1993* (Cth) stating:

> 18 ... Correctly, PKKP argue that the right to negotiate regime is an element of the protection of native title which is one of the main objects of the Act and that it is not to be narrowly construed (*Smith on behalf of the Gnaala Karla Booja People v State of Western Australia* (2001) 108 FCR 442 at [23]). ...
>
> ...
>
> 20. It has been repeatedly recognised that the requirement for good faith is directed to the quality of a party's conduct. It is to be assessed by reference to what a party has done or failed to do in the course of negotiations and is directed to and is concerned with a party's state of mind as manifested by its conduct in the negotiations: see, for example, *Brownley v Western Australia (No 1)* [1999] FCA 1139; (1999) 95 FCR 152 at [24]-[25] per Lee J, Strickland [1998] FCA 868; 85 FCR 303 at 319–320 and *Western Australia/Thomas on behalf of the Walgen People/Anaconda Nickel Ltd* [1998] NNTTA 8 at [7]-[18].
>
> ...
>
> 38. The Act does not dictate the content and manner of negotiations by compelling parties to negotiate in a particular way or over specified matters. Providing what was discussed and proposed was conducted in good faith and was with a view to obtaining agreement about the doing of the future act, then the requirement under s 31(1)(b) will be satisfied.[20]

The Full Federal Court (North and Griffiths JJ with White J dissenting) confirmed, in *Charles v Sheffield Resources Ltd*,[21] that s 31 of the *Native Title Act 1993* (Cth) obligation to negotiate in good faith, for non-native title parties, also extended to voluntary negotiations occurring after a dispute had been referred to arbitration pursuant to s 35 of the *Native Title Act 1993*.[22]

19 *Southern Waste ResourceCo Pty Ltd v Adelaide Hills Region Waste Management Authority (No 3)* SASC 192, [1538]-[1542].

20 *FMG Pilbara Pty Ltd v Cox* (2009) 175 FCR 141, [18], [20], [38].

21 *Charles v Sheffield Resources Ltd* (2017) 257 FCR 29.

22 Ibid [56]-[71]. The importance of s 31 of the *Native Title Act 1993* has recently been confirmed by the High Court in *Northern Territory v Griffiths* (2019) 364 ALR 208 although only Gageler J discussed the obligation to negotiate in good faith: [248]-[249].

4.3.2 Offers of Compromise and Calderbank offers

Some written settlement offers have additional advantages which only become apparent where the offer is not accepted and the matter proceeds in court to a final judgment. Offers of Compromise are offers to settle disputes which comply with specific legislative guidelines. They are a form of negotiation in their own right and may also be made at the culmination of a settlement conference as a written statement of the parties' final offers at the conference. The guidelines for Offers of Compromise vary between jurisdictions but relate to the determination of responsibility for costs in cases where the offer is not accepted and the matter proceeds to litigation with a final judgment. Where an offer is accepted resulting in settlement, it is of little relevance whether the offer is a formal Offer of Compromise, a Calderbank offer or an informal offer. The costs implications of Offers of Compromise are more complex and are discussed in detail in Chapter 6.8.

Calderbank offers (also known as Calderbank letters), named after the English case of *Calderbank v Calderbank*,[23] are another type of written settlement offer which can be a negotiation tool in their own right and a follow up to a settlement conference. A Calderbank offer is essentially a letter offering to settle a case for a certain amount, and the offer must remain open for a reasonable amount of time. The importance of a Calderbank offer concerns the allocation of legal costs where such an offer is rejected. This principle is discussed in more detail in Chapter 6.

From an ADR perspective, a Calderbank offer is essentially the same as any written letter of offer but, from a costs perspective, the differing legislation and case law in each state can affect the operation of Calderbank offers.

4.3.3 Advantages of negotiation

Negotiation is fast, cheap, flexible and confidential. Each of these advantages can be significant:

1. **Speed**: A brief telephone call offering the right amount of money, or other goods or services, can resolve a dispute which might otherwise have required thousands of hours of work and taken years to resolve.
2. **Cost**: Negotiation can occur between parties with no involvement from third parties and even, sometimes, without legal representation. Minimal facilities are required to write offers of settlement or negotiate over the telephone or through email or text messages. The earlier in the dispute negotiations occur, the less money parties have invested in resolving the dispute. As each party spends more on litigation, the gap between what the plaintiff is asking for and what the defendant was originally offering to pay tends to widen as each party builds their legal costs into the equation. The more costs each party incurs, the more money the plaintiff wants to settle and the less the defendant has in available funds to offer. Hence, early inexpensive negotiation can improve the likelihood of settlement.
3. **Flexibility**: Negotiation is very flexible. Particularly for disputing parties who had a good relationship prior to the dispute, a negotiated settlement is more likely to

23 *Calderbank v Calderbank* [1975] 3 WLR 586.

enable preservation of that relationship than litigation. Family law cases, commercial cases and neighbourhood disputes are all matters where it is strongly beneficial for the parties to preserve their relationship as much as possible. This is difficult to achieve in the win/lose litigation arena but much more possible in most forms of ADR, particularly negotiation.

Divorcing parents may be able to negotiate compromises in financial and carer obligations which exceed the flexibility possible in an adversarial family litigation. For example, parties might agree that the children can stay with one parent for a whole month if their grandparents on that side of the family happen to visit from overseas.

Commercial parties frequently negotiate settlements predominantly to preserve their relationships and minimise losses. For example, if a delivery of perishable goods to a retail purchaser was late, the wholesale supplier might offer to provide free extra produce the following month provided the late delivery is accepted without imposing any penalty or terminating the contract. The litigated alternative to settlement might involve rejection and spoilage of the produce leaving the purchaser with a substantial claim for damages due to loss of business and complaints from its retail customers while the supplier has incurred the full cost of delivery with zero payment. Both parties have then suffered a substantial loss which a court can only attempt to apportion as justly as possible. By settling in early negotiation, the loss of both parties is minimised and the ongoing relationship is preserved.

4. **Confidentiality**: Negotiation is usually confidential. Most parties when commencing a negotiation (whether in person, by telephone or in writing) agree that the negotiation is confidential and "without prejudice". Without prejudice means that the discussion cannot prejudice any litigation because whatever occurred in the negotiation cannot be raised in the litigation. Hence, a defendant being sued for $1 million might offer $800,000 in settlement on a without prejudice basis. The plaintiff cannot then argue in court that the defendant effectively admitted liability because it would not otherwise have offered such a high percentage of the claim in settlement. Without prejudice privilege is discussed in Chapter 13.6.

4.3.4 Problems with negotiation

The most significant flaw with negotiation as a means of CDR is that it is the least final and binding form of ADR. Parties may attend a settlement conference in person or by telephone, reach agreement and even sign heads of agreement then have the settlement fail because details critical to the settlement cannot be agreed or preconditions of settlement are not met. In negotiation run by lawyers, it is likely that heads of agreement will be drafted where parties reach in principle agreement but subject to certain pre-conditions being met and/or to final terms being negotiated. Heads of agreement are signed by all parties to the negotiation and set out the terms of settlement to the extent agreed but are not deeds and are not automatically binding on the parties. The only way to ensure a negotiated settlement is binding on parties is by executing a deed of settlement (discussed in Chapter 5.3.1). The non-binding nature of negotiated settlement applies similarly in mediated agreements, but the presence of a neutral third party (the mediator) may increase the chances that a deed of settlement will be prepared and signed at the mediation.[24]

However, it should be noted that heads of agreement can be held to constitute a binding agreement between the parties depending on the terms of the agreement and the conduct of the parties.[25] The recent New South Wales Supreme Court case of *Re Leslie Muir Holdings Pty Ltd*[26] concerned heads of agreement signed at a mediation to resolve a family dispute regarding the management of the family estate trust. The case discussed the principles for when a heads of agreement to resolve a civil dispute can be held to be binding on parties finding that, despite an intention to be bound, the heads of agreement was too uncertain to be enforceable:

> … For the reasons set out below, I accept that a binding agreement was formed between the parties, but that agreement is so uncertain, in essential respects, that it is not enforceable.
>
> Not surprisingly, Counsel referred to *Masters v Cameron* [1954] HCA 72; (1954) 91 CLR 353 at 360–362, where the High Court identified three categories of case which may exist where parties which have been in negotiation reach agreement upon terms of a contractual nature. The first category of case is one where the parties have reached finality and intend to be immediately bound to the performance of the relevant terms, but propose to have the terms restated in a form which will be fuller or more precise, but not different in effect. A second case is where the parties have reached complete agreement, but nevertheless have made performance of one or more of the terms conditional upon the execution of a formal document. A third case is one in which the intention of the parties is not to make a concluded bargain unless and until they execute a formal contract. …
>
> Whether a contract has been formed in this situation depends on the objective intention of the parties ascertained from the terms of the relevant document, read in light of the surrounding circumstances, and, if the terms of that document indicate that the parties intended to be bound immediately, then effect must be given to that intention irrespective of the subject matter, magnitude or complexity of the transaction: *GR Securities Pty Ltd v Baulkham Hills Private Hospital Pty Ltd* (1986) 40 NSWLR 631 at 634, 636; *Australian Broadcasting Corporation v XIVth Commonwealth Games Ltd* (1988) 18 NSWLR 540 at 548–9; *Sagacious Procurement Pty Ltd v Symbion Health Ltd* [2008] NSWCA 149 at [66]. …
>
> In *Pavlovic v Universal Music Australia Pty Limited* [2015] NSWCA 313; (2015) 90 NSWLR 605, Beazley P (with whom Bathurst CJ generally agreed and Meagher JA agreed) observed (at [64]-[65]) that whether parties intend to be immediately bound, where they have reached agreement as to the terms of a contract but have also agreed that a further, formal agreement is to be executed, is to be determined objectively, having regard to the 'outward manifestations' of their intentions. Her Honour also observed (at [65]) that the question was 'what each party by words and conduct would have led a reasonable person in the position of the other party to believe'. Beazley P also observed (at [69]) that the three classes of case in *Masters v Cameron* above no longer

24 See Chapter 4.4.4 for other problems facing mediation.

25 *Darzi Group Pty Ltd v Nolde Pty Ltd* (2019) 100 NSWLR 394.

26 *Re Leslie Muir Holdings Pty Ltd* [2019] NSWSC 1519.

applied, if they ever were, as strict categories into which cases must fall. Her Honour noted (at [72]) that it was relevant to consider the commercial context and surrounding circumstances of the parties' dealings in determining whether a binding agreement had come into existence. The Court of Appeal also noted (per Bathurst CJ at [15] and per Beazley P at [118] (with whom Meagher JA agreed)), and consistently with the case law to which I referred above, that the Court may have regard to subsequent conduct of the parties in determining whether, at an earlier juncture, the parties intended to enter into a binding agreement.

In *Nurisvan Investment Ltd v Anyoption Holdings Limited* [2017] VSCA 141 at [106], the Court of Appeal of the Supreme Court of Victoria similarly observed that:

> In determining whether the Heads of Agreement constituted a binding contract to enter into a Share Sale Agreement, the critical issue concerns the intention of the parties which must be ascertained objectively from the terms of the document, construed in the context of the surrounding circumstances. In that respect, it is relevant to take into account the commercial context and surrounding circumstances of the parties' dealings. [citations omitted]

The fact that the parties might negotiate further, additional terms, that were not included in the first agreement, is not necessarily inconsistent with a conclusion that the first agreement constituted a binding contract between them: *Nurisvan Investment Ltd* above at [107]. The Court may have regard to the conduct of the parties after the date of entry into the alleged contract to determine whether they entered a binding contract: *Sagacious Procurement Pty Ltd* above at [105]; *Nurisvan Investment Ltd* above at [77]ff, [82]-[83]. In setting out these principles, I have also drawn on my summary of them in *The Owners – Strata Plan No 58087 v Matthews* [2015] NSWSC 1906 and *ADG United Pty Ltd v EG Enterprises Pty Ltd* [2019] NSWSC 745.[27]

Another key difficulty with negotiation is the lack of procedural protection it offers parties. The informal nature of negotiation allows more scope for unequal bargaining power between parties to result in injustice as, in most negotiations, there is no independent third party to protect a party with less bargaining power. A negotiated settlement which has been agreed to under duress is not enforceable but vulnerable parties may agree to, formally document, and comply with inadvisable settlements with no knowledge that the agreement disadvantages them compared to what a court would likely have decided.

4.4 Mediation

Mediation is widely used in Australia as a means for resolving civil disputes. As confirmed by the High Court in *Waller v Hargraves Secured Investments Ltd*: "The function of mediation is to explore the means for settling a dispute."[28] It involves the parties, sometimes their lawyers, and a third-party independent mediator who may be accredited as a mediator. Mediation is confidential, non-binding, flexible and can be relatively inexpensive, although this can depend somewhat on the mediator. It is increasingly common for courts to order mediation and for court rules and civil procedure legislation to encourage or require parties to attempt mediation.

27 Ibid [26]-[31].
28 *Waller v Hargraves Secured Investments Ltd* (2012) 245 CLR 311, [53] (Heydon J).

4.4.1 Mediation circumstances and process

As for negotiation, mediation can be court ordered, legislatively required, contracted between parties or voluntarily entered into. Mediation commonly takes place within court buildings, in purpose-built rooms provided by specialist organisations such as the Resolution Institute (RI) and the Australian Disputes Centre (ADC), or at law firms or other specially hired venues.

There are no absolute rules as to how mediation should be run and there are a huge range of possibilities. Mediation held prior to the commencement of litigation may run differently to mediation held during the course of a litigation because the level of documentation and the parties' understanding of the issues in dispute is likely to be significantly higher where litigation has already commenced and parties are likely to have filed pleadings and possibly even undertaken some discovery (the information likely to result from Pleadings and Discovery are discussed in Chapters 8, 9 and 10). One possible structure for mediation occurring in a matter where litigation has commenced is as follows:

1. **Parties agree to mediate**. This can occur at any time in a dispute and may be following court rules or a court order or be a private agreement. The mediation is likely to be noted on the court timetable in disputes where proceedings are already commenced.
2. **Parties correspond regarding a suitable date, location and mediator**. This may be a quick discussion at court or over the telephone or may involve considerable correspondence and, occasionally, dispute. Different mediators have different personalities. Some mediators push parties hard to settle and are focussed on finding a monetary compromise with little interest in the underlying dispute. Others are more interested in unravelling the dispute to try to reach points of commonality with monetary haggling left until the end. Mediation is more likely to succeed if parties select a mediator who suits the nature of their dispute. The timing of the mediation can also be disputed with some parties wanting to mediate early while others consider completion of discovery or service of evidence would benefit the mediation. For example, in the Victorian Supreme Court case of *Matthews v SPI Electricity Pty Ltd (Ruling No 4)*, Forrest J determined that the mediation would be more beneficial if held after the expert conclave.[29]
3. **Parties brief the mediator**. Once selected, the mediator is briefed by the parties. This may be simply receiving a copy of court proceeding documents but will more commonly involve parties preparing position papers setting out relevant facts and law. Position papers, or at least an oral briefing, are more necessary where there are no litigation proceedings on foot.
4. **Parties arrive at mediation**. There should, ideally, be at least three rooms available for a mediation: one for the parties (with their lawyers) to meet with the mediator and break-out rooms that each party can go to on their own. The mediator will usually spend time in each room. For multi-party disputes numerous rooms may be necessary to accommodate all the parties separately.

29 *Matthews v SPI Electricity Pty Ltd (Ruling No 4)* [2011] VSC 613.

5. **Mediator addresses parties**. Generally, the mediator will commence the mediation with all parties present in the main mediation room and will explain his or her credentials and how the mediation will operate. However, the address can be made to the parties separately and a party is not required to attend a joint session if he or she does not wish to as confirmed by Beach J in the Supreme Court of Victoria case of *Case v Woolworths Ltd*.[30]
6. **Parties address mediation**. Commonly each party (or its lawyers) will have an initial opportunity to explain their position and their grievances, although this does not always occur.
7. **Parties break out**. The parties (with their lawyers) then break out into their separate rooms to discuss what they have heard and to consider whether they are ready to make a settlement offer. The mediator will usually visit each of the parties in turn and discuss what has been heard and raise concerns if parties are holding to untenable positions. The mediator will also try to encourage parties to make an offer. Sometimes the parties will spend the rest of the mediation in their break-out rooms with the mediator coming back and forwards between them with offers and counteroffers.
8. **Further meetings**. During the course of the mediation, the parties may reassemble in the main mediation room several times or not at all. The mediator may call just the lawyers for both sides into the mediation room if he or she feels the parties are acting unreasonably and need their lawyers to talk sense to them. Alternatively, the mediator may send the lawyers out and call just the parties into the mediation room if it seems the parties are ready to talk and might be more likely to reach settlement without their lawyers present.
9. **Settlement deed**. If the mediation leads to a successful settlement, this must be documented to become binding on the parties. It is, therefore, advisable to prepare, and have all parties sign, a deed of settlement at the mediation, if possible. Alternatively, if there are details of the settlement which are unable to be resolved in the mediation, the parties may sign heads of agreement but, as discussed in Chapter 4.3.4, such documents are not always binding on the parties.

4.4.2 Sources of mediation regulation

Mediation is often provided for in civil procedure legislation and regulations; for example, pt 4 (ss 25–34) of the *Civil Procedure Act 2005* (NSW) and pt 4 div 3 of the *Uniform Civil Procedure Rules 1999* (Qld). In addition, some states have more specialised legislation, such as the *Mediation Act 1997* (ACT) and the *Alternative Dispute Resolution Act 2001* (Tas). However, such legislation often only regulates the circumstances in which courts can order parties to mediate during the course of litigation.

In addition to legislation, a national system of accreditation now exists for mediators. Although mediation had historically been unregulated, in 2008 a National Mediator Accreditation System (NMAS) was introduced which is administered by the Mediator Standards Board (MSB) to improve the regulation of mediators, including through maintenance of a national

30 *Case v Woolworths Ltd* [2011] VSC 635.

register of accredited mediators.[31] The previous lack of accreditation was not necessarily problematic, provided all parties agreed on the choice of mediator. It was common for complex commercial litigation to be mediated by retired judges or senior barristers who often had extensive relevant expertise regardless of mediator accreditation. The Australian National Mediator Accreditation System sets out Accreditation Standards and Practice Standards. The Standards were updated in July 2015, and include training and education requirements and practice obligations such as confidentiality, procedural fairness and impartiality, competency and ethics, understanding power imbalances and when to terminate proceedings.

4.4.3 Advantages of mediation

Mediation can be an inexpensive, fast and flexible way to settle a dispute. There is significant scope for parties to discuss what they need from their relationship with the other party and to negotiate a settlement which meets both parties' needs and which delivers solutions well beyond the scope of what a court could order. For example, commercial parties can agree on future contracts as part of mediated settlement and disputing neighbours can reach a compromise position without requiring either party to relinquish potential rights.

Mediation can be beneficial even in circumstances where it does not result in immediate settlement. Mediation usually gives parties an opportunity to discuss their differences face-to-face with a neutral third party — the mediator — present to diffuse tensions and to indicate where one or more party is behaving unreasonably. It is not uncommon for matters to settle shortly after mediation or for parties to agree at mediation not to pursue less reasonable aspects of their dispute. In this way, mediation can be a catalyst for settlement or a means of improving the efficiency of subsequent determinative means of dispute resolution, such as arbitration or litigation.

4.4.4 Problems with mediation

Like negotiation, discussed in Chapter 4.3.4, a mediated agreement is not binding unless accompanied by a formal agreement, such as a deed of settlement. In addition, mediation is not suitable for all disputes. The Australian National Mediator Standards Practice Standard 6 notes that mediators must recognise power imbalance issues and indicates that mediation may be inappropriate where there is intimidation or safety issues.[32] Accredited mediators are trained to recognise and neutralise such issues to a limited extent. Certainly, in cases of significant power imbalance, mediation is preferable to negotiation where there is no third party to neutralise the power imbalance, but, in such situations, a court or arbitration may be the fairest option.

Mediation may also be expensive and time-consuming. Where parties are unable to immediately agree on a suitable mediator, undertaking mediation may be delayed and the process hijacked by disputes as to suitable mediators. Mediation takes time to prepare for and often requires parties and their lawyers to attend. In complex matters, several days of lawyers' time may be spent preparing for mediation, including writing position papers and discussing settlement options with clients. Mediators who are retired judges or senior counsel

31 See Mediator Standards Board (n 9).

32 Mediation Standards Board, *National Mediator Accreditation Standards* (2016) Practice Standard 6 <https://msb.org.au/themes/msb/assets/documents/practice-standards.pdf>.

may be expensive, with such costs usually shared equally by the parties. Accordingly, the costs of running mediation in a complex matter may be substantial. This is a worthwhile cost if the parties reach settlement or reduce the issues in dispute. However, if the mediation is undertaken on court orders or following court rules, in circumstances where one or more parties may have no real intention of settling, then the mediation costs may be largely wasted. The comment of Lander J in the Federal Court case of *Smart Co Pty Ltd (in liq) v Clipsal Australia Pty Ltd (No 7)*, relating to indemnity costs, highlights the difficulty faced by judges when deciding whether to order compulsory mediation:

> On 13 November 2008 the respondent's counsel sought an order that the matter be referred to mediation. That application was opposed by the applicant, but I made an order that the proceeding be referred to mediation and, in due course, appointed the Hon J W von Doussa QC as mediator. The mediation failed. If I had known of the differences in the two offers made by the parties to each other in December 2004 I would not have ordered that the matter be referred to mediation. That is not meant to be a criticism of the parties because, of course, they could not make known the offers made. I merely note by way of hindsight that the parties were so far apart that a mediation was of no assistance.[33]

4.5 Conciliation

Conciliation is similar to mediation in many respects, so most of the analysis for mediation can be equally applied to conciliation. In fact, it is difficult to accurately differentiate mediation and conciliation, as neither term is consistently defined or applied in legal literature or common parlance. Like mediation, conciliation varies considerably depending on the circumstances of the conciliation, the nature of the dispute, the body administering the conciliation and the personal style of the conciliator.

4.5.1 Similarities and differences between mediation and conciliation

Like mediation, conciliation is confidential, non-binding, flexible and involves the disputing parties attempting to resolve their dispute with the assistance of an independent third party — the conciliator. It is somewhat less common for conciliation to involve lawyers than mediation, and conciliation is more likely than mediation to be administered by courts, tribunals or other government-funded institutions. Conciliation is also more likely than mediation to focus on the parties having an opportunity to discuss their issues and explore mutually satisfactory resolution rather than bargaining to reach a monetary compromise. However, like mediation, this varies depending on the dispute, the intentions of the parties and the style of the conciliator.

The Commonwealth Attorney-General's Department suggests that the role of conciliators "may be more directive and advisory" than that of arbitrators.[34] This distinction was noted by

33 *Smart Co Pty Ltd (in liq) v Clipsal Australia Pty Ltd (No 7)* [2011] FCA 1359, [23].

34 See Attorney-General's Department, *Your Guide to Dispute Resolution* (2012) 18 <https://www.ag.gov.au/legal-system/publications/your-guide-dispute-resolution>.

the Administrative Appeals Tribunal in *Re Mumbler and Registrar of Aboriginal and Torres Strait Islander Corporations* in deciding to order conciliation in a case where a mediation had already been held unsuccessfully:

> The main advantage of conciliation over mediation in the present circumstances is that conciliation contemplates that the conciliators may make suggestions for terms of settlement and may actively encourage the participants to reach an agreement that accords with legal requirements.[35]

However, in *Mumbler's* case, the AAT also placed significant weight on the expertise and experience of senior AAT staff who would be running the proposed conciliation rather than any inherent difference between mediation and conciliation.[36]

In practice, therefore, any distinction between conciliation and mediation is of limited utility as the nature of the ADR industry is such that mediations do sometimes involve mediators advising parties, while conciliators may not have the necessary expertise to advise parties on all conciliations and some conciliations do not allow conciliators to advise parties. Many conciliation services run by government agencies may not accord with the standard definition of conciliation. Despite the variable nature of both mediation and conciliation, many conciliation conferences will follow steps similar to points 4 to 9 set out in Chapter 4.4.1 concerning mediation.

4.5.2 Types of conciliation

Conciliation is compulsory for certain types of disputes and is typical in certain areas of law, including human rights and family law. Conciliation is often very structured but the structure varies depending on the nature of the dispute and the body administering the conciliation. In some types of conciliation, the parties do not meet each other at all in the course of the conciliation, while other conciliations are predominantly about the parties having an opportunity to discuss their views and grievances face-to-face with each other. Three different types of government-run conciliation are discussed briefly below.

One example of conciliation is the Australian Human Right Commission (AHRC) conciliation service for victims of discrimination — including sexual, racial, disability and age discrimination, human rights discrimination — by the Commonwealth and discrimination in employment. The AHRC maintains a conciliation register which provides de-identified summaries of recent conciliations in different areas of discrimination, including age discrimination, sex discrimination, disability discrimination and race discrimination.[37] Some conciliations cover multiple areas of dispute. For example, a 2017 case involving a claim by a female car detailer whose shifts had been cancelled after she had needed to leave early on multiple occasions to collect sick children, argued discrimination on numerous grounds including age, disability, family responsibility and gender under the *Age Discrimination Act 2004* (Cth), *Disability Discrimination Act 1992* (Cth) and the *Sex Discrimination Act 1984* (Cth). The conciliation resulted in cessation of the employment relationship by agreement,

35 *Re Mumbler and Registrar of Aboriginal and Torres Strait Islander Corporations* (2009) 49 AAR 448, [40].

36 Ibid [43].

37 Australian Human Rights Commission, 'Conciliation Register' (Web Page) <https://humanrights.gov.au/complaints/conciliation-register>.

$2,000 compensation to the employee, a statement of regret by the employer and provision of a statement of service by the employer. An early report based on five years of client surveys of the AHRC conciliation process found that almost half of AHRC conciliations were attended by legal representatives and around 30–40% of initial complaints were successfully conciliated with another 40–60% being declined, terminated or withdrawn and only 10–20% unable to be conciliated.[38]

In Family Court conciliations, contrary to the common role of conciliators, Family Court registrars (the conciliators) are not allowed to give the parties legal advice, although they can discuss legal principles. The parties are encouraged to meet face-to-face in the conciliation but can be accommodated in separate rooms. Parties who have representation will usually have their lawyers attend the conciliation.[39] However, the Family Court has reduced its focus on conciliation in favour of mediation with parties now required to demonstrate a genuine attempt to resolve their disputes before attending court and the government directing parties to engage with Family Dispute Resolution, which is specialised mediation that can be paid for or subsidised by the government depending on the party's financial circumstances.[40]

The Victorian Accident Compensation Conciliation Service (ACCS), funded and run by the Victorian State Government, is a free conciliation service for workers compensation claims. The ACCS is a statutory authority established under the *Accident Compensation Act 1985* (Vic). It gives parties considerable detail on what is required in attending the conciliation conference,[41] strongly encourages face-to-face meeting and results in a recommendation by the conciliator which, if accepted, is reflected in an outcome certificate prepared by the conciliator and binding on all parties.[42]

4.6 Arbitration

Arbitration is the most formal means of resolving a civil dispute other than litigation. Arbitration is final and binding. Some arbitration procedures closely resemble civil procedure in litigation. Some large statutory tribunals such as the Victorian Civil and Administrative Tribunal (VCAT) would be indistinguishable from a court to most unrepresented litigants.[43] The only obvious difference between some quasi-judicial tribunals and a court is the rules of evidence and civil procedure employed by tribunals and even these may closely resemble court procedure for some tribunals. However, there may be less obvious differences in

38 Australian Human Rights Commission, *Five Years On: An Update on the Complaint Handling Work of the Human Rights Commission* (2005) <https://humanrights.gov.au/our-work/complaint-information-service/publications/five-years-update-complaint-handling-work>.

39 Family Court of Australia, 'Conciliation Conference' (Web Page, 3 May 2016) <http://www.familycourt.gov.au/wps/wcm/connect/fcoaweb/family-law-matters/about-going-to-court-and-court-processes/if-your-case-is-in-the-family-court-of-australia/conciliation-conference>.

40 See Family Relationships Online (Web Page) <https://www.familyrelationships.gov.au/>.

41 Accident Compensation Conciliation Service, 'Guide to Conciliation – Video' (Web Page) <https://www.conciliation.vic.gov.au/conciliation-process/preparing-for-conciliation>.

42 Accident Compensation Conciliation Service, 'Potential Outcomes' (Web Page) <https://www.conciliation.vic.gov.au/conciliation-process/outcomes/potential-outcomes>.

43 Chapter 7 discusses some of the statutorily-created tribunals which resolve the majority of certain types of dispute.

relation to enforcement of decisions where parties do not comply with the tribunal's decision. Accordingly, statutory tribunals will not be discussed further in this chapter but will be, instead, considered in detail in Chapter 7.

This chapter will focus on arbitral tribunals appointed by the agreement of parties. These tribunals may be formed with the assistance of arbitral institutions or on an entirely ad hoc basis. Most tribunals do not adhere to the rules of evidence discussed in Chapters 13, 14 and 15, unless both the parties and the tribunal decide it would be beneficial to do so. Tribunals are also likely to have somewhat less formal commencement and case exposition processes than court pleadings[44] and most tribunals will not order parties to provide discovery.[45]

4.6.1 Types and circumstances of arbitration

Arbitration tends to concentrate in specific areas of law where there are individuals appointed as arbitrators who have specialist knowledge or skills and are uniquely qualified to resolve disputes to the satisfaction of all parties. Parties with disputes of great technical depth or involving extensive technical jargon, parties with disputes requiring a cultural or religious understanding, and international parties all commonly prefer arbitration to litigation because of the ability to choose arbitrators with pre-existing expertise, understanding, and/or neutrality to resolve their disputes. Some common types of arbitration are discussed further in Chapters 4.6.6 to 4.6.8.

There are also numerous tribunals created by governments pursuant to statutes to determine cases in particular areas of law governed predominantly by statute, including administrative appeals, motor vehicle accidents, workers compensation claims, industrial disputes, dust diseases, and migration. These tribunals are quasi-judicial bodies and operate more like courts. Due to their compulsory nature, these tribunals cannot be considered ADR and will be discussed separately in Chapter 7.

4.6.2 Sources of arbitral law

Unlike negotiation, mediation and conciliation, arbitration is binding on the parties who enter it. To ensure parties comply with binding arbitral awards, such awards are enforceable by courts. It is perhaps unsurprising, therefore, that arbitration tends to be more legislated than the other forms of ADR discussed above. There is a plethora of Acts which invoke arbitration, including many of the Acts concerning the quasi-judicial tribunals discussed in Chapter 7.

Private international arbitration is governed by the *International Arbitration Act 1974* (Cth) which incorporates into Australian law the *UNCITRAL Model Law on International Arbitration* (originally 1985 and amended in 2006). In addition, Australia has now adopted uniform domestic arbitration also based on the *UNCITRAL Model Law* bringing private domestic arbitration into line with private international arbitration. The uniform state arbitration Acts for domestic arbitration resulted from proposals from the Standing Committees of Attorney Generals (SCAG) in the form of the Model Commercial Arbitration Bill 2010 and the Model Provision of the Commercial Arbitration Bill Amendment 2011.

44 See Chapters 8 and 9.
45 See Chapter 11.

The *Uniform Commercial Arbitration Acts* were designed to reinvigorate private domestic arbitration in Australia which had otherwise been significantly declining for many years. The Model Law led to the following state legislation:

- *Commercial Arbitration Act 2010* (NSW)
- *Commercial Arbitration Act 2011* (SA)
- *Commercial Arbitration Act 2011* (Tas)
- *Commercial Arbitration Act 2011* (Vic)
- *Commercial Arbitration (National Uniform Legislation) Act 2011* (NT)
- *Commercial Arbitration Act 2013* (WA)
- *Commercial Arbitration Act 2013* (Qld)
- *Commercial Arbitration Act 2017* (ACT)

The *Uniform Commercial Arbitration Act* states at s 1C(1):

> The paramount object of this Act is to facilitate the fair and final resolution of commercial disputes by impartial arbitral tribunals without unnecessary delay or expense.

4.6.3 Advantages of arbitration

The newly improved uniformity of domestic commercial arbitration between Australian states and between domestic and international arbitration improve the attractiveness of private arbitration. When effectively run, arbitration can offer the advantages of litigation in terms of finality, enforceability and the opportunity to be heard while simultaneously providing a faster, cheaper, less formal and more specialised environment tailored to the particular needs of disputing parties.

Arbitration also has unique benefits which result from the fact that it is more like litigation than other forms of ADR. Arbitration has the advantage of being the only dispute resolution process which is both determinative and confidential. This makes it ideal for certain types of disputes. Complex commercial disputes involving confidential matters, such as terms of trade, are good candidates for arbitration because they can employ court-like evidentiary processes, provided parties agree such is necessary and they result in a binding reasoned decision while still protecting parties' confidential trading information, which is often highly valuable and the disclosure of which may be ruinous to businesses.

Another type of dispute where the confidential but determinative nature of arbitration can be desirable is disputes where one or more parties are very high profile, such that the media is likely to take an intense interest in any litigation involving those parties. The recent Rinehart family dispute, discussed at length in Chapter 3.3.4, provides an excellent example of the extent to which high-profile parties may value confidentiality.[46] Unfortunately, the Rinehart court cases disputing the validity of the arbitration agreement also demonstrate the risk ADR brings to civil disputants due to the limitation of all ADR: that it is only as binding as the level of respect the parties pay to their ADR agreements, combined with the power of the courts to rectify any failures to do so.[47]

46 *Rinehart v Hancock Prospecting Pty Ltd* (2019) 366 ALR 635.
47 *Rinehart v Rinehart* (2014) 320 ALR 195; *Hancock Prospecting Pty Ltd v Rinehart (No 2)* [2017] FCAFC 208; *Rinehart v Hancock Prospecting Pty Ltd* (2019) 366 ALR 635.

4.6.4 Problems with arbitration

The most common criticism of arbitration is that it is too expensive and time-consuming. Essentially, arbitration can be too much like litigation and, therefore, suffer the same drawbacks discussed in relation to litigation in Chapter 2.5. In private arbitration, parties are responsible for paying the arbitrators and for the facilities used in the arbitration. These are additional costs not generally born by litigants, where court fees are often little more than a token amount compared to the cost of operating the courts. Consequently, arbitration can prove more costly than litigation.

Another difficulty with arbitration is the risk of parties disputing their agreement to arbitrate when a dispute arises. Ensuing litigation or arbitration as to the jurisdiction of the arbitral tribunal result in additional cost or time spent in litigation (or arbitral hearings) where courts (or tribunals) are purely determining whether the tribunal has jurisdiction to hear the dispute before any consideration can be given to the substance of the dispute. See, for example, the High Court case of *Neilson v Overseas Projects Corporation of Victoria Ltd*.[48]

Arbitral awards are final and binding but, similar to court decisions, this is subject to possible rights to appeal (see Chapter 16 regarding appeals from court decisions). Arbitration appeal rights are very limited in accordance with the applicable arbitral legislation, the rules governing the arbitration and any contractual agreement between the parties relating to appeal rights. In the High Court case of *Westport Insurance Corporation v Gordian Runoff Ltd*, French CJ, Gummow, Crennan and Bell JJ (with Heydon and Kiefel agreeing in separate judgments) set aside an arbitral award thereby reinstating the primary New South Wales Supreme Court decision of Einstein J, which had been set aside by the New South Wales Court of Appeal. The appeal concerned the inadequacy of reasons provided by the arbitrators in an insurance arbitration and the requirement for there to be a manifest error of law to appeal an arbitral award under the *Commercial Arbitration Act 1984* (NSW) (now replaced by the uniform *Commercial Arbitration Act 2010* (NSW)). In relation to the limited appeal rights, Kiefel J noted:

> [163.] I agree with French CJ, Gummow, Crennan and Bell JJ that manifest error of law requires that the error appear on the face of the Award, which includes the reasons for it, and that the error be apparent to the understanding of the reader. Such is the case here. It does not require that the error be of a particular quality or that errors involving complex questions be disqualified.
>
> ...
>
> [168.] The *Commercial Arbitration Act* does not bind the parties to an arbitration to the outcome of the arbitration they have agreed will take place. It allows for an appeal, albeit one limited to a question of law and one subject to conditions for the grant of leave to appeal. The Act therefore comprehends something of a public, as well as a private, element in the making of an award of arbitration. It is in this context that an arbitrator's 'reasons for making the award' are required, by s 29(1)(c).[49]

48 *Neilson v Overseas Projects Corporation of Victoria Ltd* (2005) 223 CLR 331.
49 *Westport Insurance Corporation v Gordian Runoff Ltd* (2011) 244 CLR 239, [163], [168].

4.6.5 Arbitration in specialist areas of law

There are certain areas of law which have commonly used arbitration because specialist knowledge of matters other than law is critical to fair resolution of the dispute. Some specialist disputes are resolved by quasi-judicial tribunals, such as VCAT, NCAT and ACAT. These tribunals employ arbitrators to sit on their panels who have specialist knowledge of areas, such as medicine, which can be critical to fairly determine appropriate damages and are discussed in more detail in Chapter 7. However, there are other areas of civil dispute which attract entirely private arbitration, sometimes through general arbitral bodies such as RI (Resolution Institute). These areas include building and construction disputes and engineering disputes, which commonly contain very few legal issues but complex technical issues. Such disputes may be suited better to an arbitrator who is a structural engineer or an architect than someone with purely legal training. Often, specialist arbitrators hold qualifications in both law and their area of technical specialty, making them ideal to resolve technical disputes in their area of expertise. Choosing arbitrators with specialist expertise can prevent the need to hire expensive expert witnesses to provide opinions on complex technical issues (see Chapter 14).

4.6.6 Arbitration to accommodate culture or religion

Arbitration can also be a way for parties who have cultural or religious objections to the Australian court system to resolve their disputes in a binding and enforceable way within the Australian legal system but applying their own rules. For example, two Muslims might contract with each other and agree that they would like their dispute to be resolved by an imam using sharia law. The contract could therefore contain a provision that the decision of the imam is binding on the parties. Essentially, the provisions in the contract concerning dispute resolution by an imam constitute an agreement to arbitrate. In the event of a dispute, the decision of the imam would be binding on the parties pursuant to the terms of the contract and could, therefore, be enforced by an Australian court provided the contract was not illegal or otherwise unenforceable. Arbitration can, thereby, increase access to justice for certain cultural or religious groups.[50]

4.6.7 International commercial arbitration

One area in which arbitration is commonly considered preferable to litigation is for international commercial disputes. There is a significant body of literature in relation to international commercial arbitration and its merits, but probably the strongest advantages of arbitration for international disputes are neutrality of forum, flexibility and neutrality of procedure and enforceability.[51]

As there is currently no widely accepted international civil court hearing private disputes, civil litigation between parties of differing nationalities must, inevitably, be heard by the court of a particular country with which the dispute has a connection. Most parties wish to litigate in their home state and do not wish to appear before a foreign court, particularly if

50 See Chapter 3.2.2.

51 See *United Nations Commission on International Trade Law* (Web Page) <https://uncitral.un.org/>.

that foreign court is the home court of the other party. To avoid disputes about jurisdiction, parties seek a neutral forum which has jurisdiction to hear their dispute. International arbitration enables parties to choose such a neutral forum and, provided the relevant countries are parties to the *Convention on the Recognition and Enforcement of Foreign Arbitral Awards 1958*,[52] it is a fairly routine process to enforce the award wherever the assets of the losing party are held in through the courts of that country.

An international arbitral award is often the most enforceable determination international parties can obtain and, therefore, parties' best hope of justice. As at March 2021, 168 countries were party to the *New York Convention* with Malawi and Belize both having ratified in March 2021. This means that an arbitral award can be enforced by the winning party in any of those 168 countries in which the losing party holds assets sufficient to meet the payment. In addition, pursuant to the *New York Convention*, the process of recognition of foreign awards is generally straightforward, involving registration of the international arbitral award in the jurisdiction where enforcement is sought. Australia is a party to the *New York Convention* and its consequent international rights and obligations are legislated through the *International Arbitration Act 1974* (Cth). In addition, all of Australia's key trading partners and developed countries are party to the *New York Convention*, such as China, USA, New Zealand, India, and the European Union.[53]

In the Supreme Court of Victoria Court of Appeal case of *IMC Aviation Solutions Pty Ltd v Altain Khuder LLC*, Warren CJ (in agreement with Hansen and Kyrou JJ) allowed an appeal against enforcement of a Mongolian arbitral award on the basis that the party seeking to enforce the arbitral award bore the onus of proving to the Court whether the other party was actually a party to the arbitration agreement.[54] However, Warren CJ stated in his introduction:

> [2] The appeal concerns the interpretation of the International Arbitration Act 1974 (Cth) (the 'Act'), which provides a mechanism for enforcing foreign arbitral awards. The critical issue is how the Act applies in a situation where the alleged award debtor is not expressly named as a party to the arbitration agreement pursuant to which the award was made.
>
> [3] This matter is unusual. It required this Court to decide an issue which is ordinarily uncontroversial in enforcement proceedings. The unique circumstances of this case have made a complex investigation into that issue unavoidable. However, as I will explain in my reasons, in all but the most unusual cases, applications to enforce foreign arbitral awards should involve only a summary procedure.[55]

Many parties involved in international trade place arbitration clauses in their contracts to ensure that any future disputes which arise can be resolved by arbitration rather than

52 *Convention on the Recognition and Enforcement of Foreign Arbitral Awards*, opened for signature 10 June 1958, 330 UNTS 3 (entered into force 7 June 1959) (*New York Convention*).

53 The non-members of the *New York Convention* include Iraq, Libya, Chad, Ethiopia, Yemen, South Sudan, Somalia, Somaliland, Eritrea, Guinea Bissau, Sierra Leone, Gambia, Turkmenistan, Namibia, Taiwan, North Korea, East Timor Belize, Suriname, Puerto Rico.

54 *IMC Aviation Solutions Pty Ltd v Altain Khuder LLC* (2011) 38 VR 303. This case has since been cited in numerous decisions in other Australian jurisdictions, including *Sino Dragon Trading Ltd v Noble Resources International Pte Ltd (No 2)* (2015) 246 FCR 498; *Colin Joss & Co Pty Ltd v Cube Furniture Pty Ltd* [2015] NSWSC 829.

55 *IMC Aviation Solutions Pty Ltd v Altain Khuder LLC* (2011) 38 VR 303, [2]-[3].

becoming the subject of litigation. Arbitration clauses in contracts will usually specify the rules of the arbitration and the governing law to ensure any future dispute is resolved using procedures acceptable to all the parties. There are numerous arbitral bodies which assist international parties to arbitration by providing pro forma rules, support for appointing arbitrators and facilities, including, in Australia, the Australian Centre for International Commercial Arbitration (ACICA).

International commercial arbitration is not without its difficulties and sometimes parties agree to arbitration but then, when a dispute arises, commence proceedings in court because they consider their dispute outside the scope of the arbitration agreement. Sometimes, multiple actions are commenced in multiple jurisdictions increasing costs contrary to the efficiency supposedly associated with arbitration. The High Court case of *Michael Wilson & Partners Ltd v Nicholls* concerned such a jurisdictional dispute in relation to London arbitration proceedings running simultaneously with New South Wales Supreme Court proceedings. In this case, concerning abuse of process, (discussed further in Chapter 5), Heydon J commented, in conclusion, that the abuse of process aspect of the appeal was "… yet a further reminder of the unwisdom of consenting to arbitration … ."[56]

However, there is a strong trend in Australia for courts to honour international arbitration agreements wherever possible, as evidenced by cases such as *Warner Brothers Feature Productions Pty Ltd v Kennedy Miller Mitchell Films Pty Ltd*.[57] In this case, the New South Wales Supreme Court stayed its proceedings in favour of international arbitration in a dispute regarding a bonus payment of the directors of the *Mad Max: Fury Road* movie even though one defendant in the litigation was not a party to the arbitration agreement.

Not all jurisdictional disputes regarding arbitration are heard before a court. Tribunals have the power to determine their own jurisdiction pursuant to the international principle of *kompetenz-kompetenz*, the application of which was confirmed in the recent High Court decision of *Rinehart v Hancock Prospecting Pty Ltd*:

> [13.] It is also necessary to mention certain principles stated in the NSW Act in connection with the arbitral clauses. There is no dispute that the NSW Act applies to the clauses even though the Deeds pre-date the Act. The Act is part of an integrated statutory framework for international and domestic arbitration which implements the UNCITRAL Model Law on International Commercial Arbitration. The Act adopts principles such as that which recognises an arbitration agreement as distinct and limits attacks upon its validity (the separability principle) and the related principle by which an arbitral tribunal is competent to rule on its jurisdiction (kompetenz-kompetenz).[58]

However, even where a tribunal determines its own jurisdiction, this decision can be appealed to a court. In *Lin Tiger Plastering Pty Ltd v Platinum Construction (Vic) Pty Ltd*, the Victorian Supreme Court analysed art 16(9) of the *Commercial Arbitration Act 2011* (Vic) to determine that, where a court is required to reconsider a decision on competence, the court

56 *Michael Wilson & Partners Ltd v Nicholls* (2011) 244 CLR 427, [119].

57 *Warner Brothers Feature Productions Pty Ltd v Kennedy Miller Mitchell Films Pty Ltd* (2018) 130 IPR 527.

58 *Rinehart v Hancock Prospecting Pty Ltd* (2019) 366 ALR 635, [13]. This case was discussed in more detail in Chapter 3 in relation to the principle of open justice.

is entitled to consider the tribunal's jurisdiction de novo (from the beginning) rather than simply reviewing the decision of the Tribunal:

> 40. On the basis of these authorities and commentaries, the position is, in my view, that a hearing de novo is the correct standard of review to be applied under section 16(9) of the CAA. Deference should duly be given to the cogent reasoning of the arbitral tribunal but the Court is the final 'arbiter' on the question of jurisdiction. As has been observed, this is an aspect of court assistance and support of arbitral processes and is not at odds with the policy of minimal court intervention or 'interference'.[59]

Lin Tiger Plastering Pty Ltd v Platinum Construction (Vic) Pty Ltd was a domestic arbitration case but, because the uniform *Commercial Arbitration Acts* including the *Commercial Arbitration Act 2011*(Vic) are based on the *UNCITRAL Model Law on International Arbitration*, the Victorian Supreme Court considered international commercial arbitration decisions from a range of jurisdictions in coming to its conclusion.

4.7 Case appraisal

Another form of ADR which has become increasingly popular, particularly in Queensland, is case appraisal.[60] Case appraisal operates similarly to court-ordered arbitration. It is court-, or tribunal-, ordered and the case appraiser hears both parties' evidence and submission and makes a decision.[61] Unlike arbitration, however, the decision is not binding and the parties can proceed to litigation if they do not accept the case appraiser's decision.[62] Given the ease with which some arbitral decisions can be appealed (eg in NSW), case appraisal bears strong resemblance to New South Wales court-ordered arbitration.[63]

Case appraisal involves the case appraiser meeting with the parties to agree an appropriate process which may include delivery of witness statements and submissions.[64] After conducting the hearing, the case appraiser assesses the merits of the case and provides a written decision and certificate to the court (or tribunal) which the parties may choose to accept in order to complete the proceedings.

4.8 Conclusion

ADR is central to CDR. It pervades the resolution of civil disputes because it almost invariably occurs in one or more forms in the course of resolving all disputes, ranging from the most trivial to the most complex and acrimonious. Parties commonly engage in negotiation, the most informal mode of ADR, sometimes before even recognising that they are in a dispute and without realising they are negotiating. For most civil disputes, whatever form

59 *Lin Tiger Plastering Pty Ltd v Platinum Construction (Vic) Pty Ltd* (2018) 57 VR 576, [40].
60 *Uniform Civil Procedure Rules 1999* (Qld) rr 334–345; *Civil Proceedings Act 2011* (Qld) s 45.
61 ADR embedded in court processes is discussed in more detail in Chapter 5.2.
62 Although it should be noted that there can be adverse costs consequences for failing to accept a case appraisal decision (*Uniform Civil Procedure Rules 1999* (Qld) r 344).
63 See Chapter 5.2.2.
64 *Civil Proceedings Act 2011* (Qld) s 45.

of ADR works to resolve a dispute is usually worthwhile, particularly where such resolution can be achieved more efficiently than through litigation.[65] However, as this chapter has demonstrated, there are important limitations on the resolution that can be obtained through ADR which may disadvantage vulnerable parties (due to lack of procedural protections) and prevent future parties from learning from past mistakes (due to confidentiality and the consequent lack of precedent). In addition, most forms of ADR are non-determinative and, therefore, sometimes fail to resolve a dispute. In such cases, ADR constitutes more time, effort, and money in addition to that spent on litigation.

ADR encompasses a wide range of methods for resolving disputes, many of which are flexible and informal. In some respects, grouping these diverse methods of CDR under the single heading of ADR implies a level of uniformity which does not exist. As will be explored further in Chapter 5, the only true unifying factor in ADR is its relationship to litigation. Litigation remains the common counterpoint to all ADR by providing the non-consensual, determinative and binding solution for parties unable to resolve their disputes through ADR.

65 See Chapters 2 and 3 for detailed analysis of the balancing act between efficiency and fairness in CDR and how they affect access to justice and open justice.

5 MANAGING COURT RESOURCES THROUGH ALTERNATIVE DISPUTE RESOLUTION AND SUMMARY DISPOSITION

5.1 Introduction

This is the first chapter in this book to focus predominantly on the role of the courts and litigation in civil dispute resolution (CDR). Part II of this book focuses predominantly on civil procedure in the courts; however, this chapter concerns the interaction between courts and alternative dispute resolution (ADR) and the management of court resources which is central to the themes and theory of CDR. Much of the analysis in Chapters 2 and 3, including balancing competing objectives, managing cases, access to justice and open justice, are strongly influenced by limitations on court resources and the management of those limitations. ADR and summary disposition are the key tools available to the courts to limit exploitation of court resources. Matters resolved through ADR can then be consensually dismissed by the courts. While ADR is the preferred way to limit party use of court time, some parties do not respect the scarcity of the court's resources or the rights of their opposing parties, and non-consensual summary disposition then becomes the court's key tool for managing parties and the structure of their disputes. Therefore, this chapter will focus on ADR run in conjunction with litigation. As noted in Chapter 4, this is not the most common form of ADR, as the majority of civil disputes are resolved through ADR without litigation ever commencing. However, the interaction between litigation and ADR is relevant to the resolution of all civil disputes because the right to litigation (and the limitations of that right) influences party behaviour in all forms of CDR.

In part, this chapter endeavours to further explain the symbiotic relationship between litigation and ADR in the resolution of civil disputes. Most civil disputes involve some form of ADR — even those which proceed to litigation — and that ADR invariably influences the course of the litigation. Similarly, the civil disputes resolved without litigation (which is the vast majority) are influenced by the possibility of litigation, the threat of which is a constant motivator to engage meaningfully with ADR. This chapter begins with an analysis of the first aspect of this mutualism, exploring how courts summarily dispose of matters consensually which have entered the court system and then been resolved through ADR.

However, a significant percentage of matters are summarily dismissed non-consensually by courts as unmeritorious litigation. This chapter will, therefore, also consider the cases which are struck out, set aside or otherwise summarily dismissed by court, including management of litigants who bring multiple vexatious proceedings. The powers of a court to dismiss unmeritorious litigation, suppress hearings and deter vexatious litigants must be finely balanced against the underlying concepts of our legal system discussed in Chapters 2 and 3, particularly the entitlement to due consideration, access to justice and an open hearing. Summary disposition cases are a key source of judicial analysis on CDR theory, particularly civil procedure. Accordingly, many of the cases discussed in this chapter are also relevant to Part II of this book that focusses on litigation and civil procedure.

5.2 Court-ordered and compulsorily legislated alternative dispute resolution

Australian courts recognise the importance of ADR in resolving civil disputes and often play an active role in encouraging, or even requiring, parties to use ADR. Court-ordered ADR is one of the less voluntary forms of ADR (see Chapter 4). However, court-ordered ADR can be very successful, particularly where the judge ordering the ADR does so with a genuine understanding of the nature and needs of the parties. Compulsorily legislated ADR is unable to give consideration to the particular circumstances of the parties which increases the chances of it not succeeding due to party reluctance to engage in good faith with a process forced upon them. However, even legislated ADR often leads to positive outcomes where parties take advantage of the forced opportunity to reach amicable resolution.

5.2.1 The distinction between private and court-ordered alternative dispute resolution

The distinction between party selected ADR (considered in Chapter 4) and court-ordered ADR can be blurry because of the role directions hearings and court timetables play in much litigation (see Chapter 10.6). It can be relevant whether or not ADR is court-ordered because some provisions regarding settlement costs (discussed in Chapter 6) and timing of proceedings apply only to court-ordered ADR.

Some ADR is definitely court-ordered; such as where a judge, often in accordance with recommended court practices, requires the parties to attend mediation. More informally, judges will sometimes adjourn a litigation briefly for the parties to discuss settlement if they feel this is likely to settle the matter, and this is also court-ordered ADR. Conversely, some ADR is definitely private; for example, cases where the parties have held settlement conferences or mediations prior to commencement of litigation or without informing the court. This private ADR can be contractually required or through party agreement.

However, there are cases where privately agreed ADR becomes court-ordered because it is included in a consensually drafted court timetable or set of directions (see Chapter 10.6). For example, if parties to litigation privately agree they should mediate at some point after the commencement of proceedings, they are likely to include a date for mediation in any court timetable provided to the judge at a directions hearing. When the judge approves the consensual directions, attending the mediation then becomes a direction made by the court. At this point, the mediation becomes a court-ordered mediation even though the decision to mediate was privately made between the parties in all other respects.

5.2.2 Court power to order alternative dispute resolution

Australian courts now generally have legislated power to send parties to ADR even without the consent of those parties as discussed in Chapter 4 in relation to various forms of ADR. The source of this power varies from specific ADR legislation, such as the *Alternative Dispute Resolution Act 2001* (Tas); to court rules, such as the *Uniform Civil Procedure Rules 1999* (Qld) (ch 9 pt 4);[1] and civil procedure legislation, such as the *Civil Procedure Act 2010* (Vic) s 66 (which relates only to binding appropriate dispute resolution including arbitration and referral to referees). It is increasingly common for ADR to be considered a requirement of litigation, such as the *Federal Court Rules 2011* (Cth) which contains pt 28 on ADR. Part 28 of the *Federal Court Rules 2011* (Cth) is additional to the *Civil Dispute Resolution Act 2011* (Cth) discussed below, requiring parties to file a genuine steps statement prior to commencing proceedings. Part 28 of the *Federal Court Rules 2011* (Cth) deals with ADR; in particular, mediation (pt 28.3), arbitration (pt 28.2), international arbitration (pt 28.5) and refereeing (pt 28.6).

Mediation is the most common form of ADR ordered by courts.[2] Although mediation takes time and incurs costs, it fits well within the aims of civil procedure where the court considers they have a significant prospect of successfully resolving the dispute or reducing

1 *Uniform Civil Procedure Rules 1999* (Qld) ch 9 pt 4. Queensland has additional authority pursuant to the *Civil Proceedings Act 2011* (Qld) pt 6 s 43 to refer parties to ADR.

2 See Chapter 4.4 for information on how mediation operates.

the issues in concern. The Tasmanian Supreme Court Case of *Coad v Dimmick* held that a court-ordered mediation was "a step in the proceeding," such that a litigation should not be stayed for inaction because the parties had undertaken the relevant step of court-ordered mediation during the relevant time period.[3] The analysis of Porter J in *Coad v Dimmick* nicely summarises the role of court-ordered mediation in litigation as follows:

> Ordinarily, the effect of an activity said to amount to a step in a proceeding is readily ascertainable. That is not so with mediations which, assuming the action is not settled, may not have the obvious effect of having moved the action forward, and what may have been achieved is not capable of being assessed … .
>
> Mediations may fail to resolve the action or differences between the parties, but the parties may gain a better understanding of their strengths and weaknesses, and respond in some way in the progression of the litigation. Differences which are resolved may not be formally reflected in the subsequent shape of the proceedings, as would occur with, for instance, the resolution of liability. The difficulty arises in the form of s10(4) of the *Alternative Dispute Resolution Act* [*2001* (Tas)] which makes inadmissible evidence of anything said or of any admission made in a mediation. What was resolved or achieved at a mediation may not [be] ascertainable. …
>
> In my view there is clear room for the proposition that an activity may be a step even though it has not in fact carried the action forward, provided that it is done with that intention. Obviously, at the very least, an activity must have the capacity to carry the action forward. …
>
> …
>
> Mediation may cause changes in the way the parties approach the case. It has the potential to formally resolve such things as liability or quantum, and evidentiary points or similar matters which might be said to impact on a party's case. …[4]

Arbitration is an area where interaction with the court is particularly complex because arbitration is a determinative process which does not require parties to reach agreement and is final and binding (see Chapter 4.6). Court-ordered arbitration is, therefore, particularly problematic because the aim of such arbitration must be to replace the litigation process rather than to supplement it. An arbitration award which is appealed to a court defeats the intention of arbitration to be final and binding. In addition, the decision to arbitrate itself is fundamentally intended to be a consensual process and this key aspect of arbitration is missing in compulsorily-ordered arbitration. In some jurisdictions, such as the Federal Court and Victoria, the court is unable to refer parties to arbitration without their consent.[5] In jurisdictions such as New South Wales, where parties can be compulsorily referred to arbitration, such referrals are virtually unheard of.[6] In New South Wales, dissatisfied parties have 28 days to apply for a rehearing by the court which then entirely disregards the

3 *Coad v Dimmick* [2013] 22 Tas R 351, [57].

4 Ibid [30]-[31], [32], [49].

5 *Federal Court of Australia Act 1976* (Cth) s 53A. *Civil Procedure Act 2010* (Vic) s 66 requires parties to consent to arbitration.

6 New South Wales, South Australia and the Northern Territory allow compulsory referral: *Civil Procedure Act 2005* (NSW) pt 5 s 38; *District Court Civil Rules 2006* (SA) s 221; *Supreme Court Act 1935* (SA) s 66; *Local Court (Civil Procedure) Act 1989* (NT) s 16.

tribunal's findings.[7] Although limited right to rehearing is, arguably, necessary to protect the parties' right to be heard, the current unlimited right to rehearing effectively destroys the final and binding nature of arbitration, such that New South Wales courts are sensibly reluctant to compulsorily refer any matters to arbitration.[8]

In Queensland, parties are only referred to arbitration where there is an existing arbitration agreement. This may be either an international arbitration agreement pursuant to the *International Arbitration Act 1974* (Cth) s 7,[9] or a domestic arbitration agreement pursuant to the *Commercial Arbitration Act 2013* s 8.[10] However, in Queensland, the courts have the option to compulsorily refer the parties to case appraisal. Case appraisal operates similarly to arbitration, except that there is no suggestion that the case appraiser's decision should be final or binding.[11] Instead, the parties can choose whether to accept the case appraisal decision or proceed to litigation, but with negative cost ramifications applying where a party rejects case appraisal and ends up worse off from the judicial decision than had they accepted the arbitration.[12]

5.2.3 Court referral to referees

Another way in which courts employ ADR to assist in the resolution of litigation is the use of referees. Courts may refer a disputed issue to an expert referee, thereby potentially obviating the need for competing experts and judicial analysis of an area of the dispute. Referring matters to referees can be an effective way to reduce the time and cost of court proceedings without removing the final judicial decision.

Complications with referee reports can arise in relation to the extent to which the court and parties must accept the report provided by the referee. For example, in New South Wales, referee reports are now governed by the *Uniform Civil Procedure Rules 2005* (NSW) pt 20 div 3. New South Wales courts also rely on case-based guidelines for the use of referee reports, established in *Chocolate Factory Apartments Ltd v Westpoint Finance Pty Ltd*,[13] which set out 15 points that have since been applied in many cases including, recently, *Depofo Pty Ltd v Barnes*[14] and *Dean v Zeene*[15] and which importantly include:

> (5) Where a report shows a thorough, analytical and scientific approach to the assessment of the subject matter of the reference, the Court would have a disposition towards acceptance of the report, for to do otherwise would be to negate both the

7 *Civil Procedure Act 2005* (NSW) s 44.

8 Before the introduction of the *Civil Procedure Act 2005* (NSW), hundreds of matters were compulsorily referred to arbitration each year by the New South Wales District Court, but those referrals dropped to zero within four years of the introduction of the *Civil Procedure Act 2005* (NSW). This is almost certainly due to the removal of the *Arbitration (Civil Actions) Act 1983* (NSW) which previously governed arbitration in New South Wales courts and required a party seeking rehearing to substantially improve their position under the original arbitral award, or become liable for the costs that the other party incurred in connection with the rehearing: *Arbitration (Civil Actions) Act 1983* (NSW) s 18(c).

9 *Uniform Civil Procedure Rules 1999* (Qld) r 365C.

10 Ibid r 365M.

11 *Uniform Civil Procedure Rules 1999* (Qld) rr 334–45.

12 Ibid r 344.

13 *Chocolate Factory Apartments Ltd v Westpoint Finance Pty Ltd* [2005] NSWSC 784.

14 *Depofo Pty Ltd v Barnes* [2019] NSWSC 949, [34].

15 *Dean v Zeene* [2019] NSWSC 1481.

purpose and the facility of referring complex technical issues to independent experts for enquiry and report.

...

(11) Referees should give reasons for their opinion so as to enable the parties, the Court and the disinterested observer to know that the conclusion is not arbitrary, or influenced by improper considerations; but that it is the result of a process of logic and the application of a considered mind to the factual circumstances proved. The reasoning process must be sufficiently disclosed so that the Court can be satisfied that the conclusions are based upon such an intellectual exercise.

(12) The right to be heard does not involve the right to be heard twice.

...

(15) Where the court decides that the reasons are flawed, either on their face or because they have been shown not to deal with important matters, the court has a choice. It may decline to adopt the report. Or it may itself look at the detail of the evidence to decide whether or not the expense of further proceedings before the referee (which would be the consequence of non-adoption) is justified.[16]

5.2.4 Compulsorily legislated alternative dispute resolution: pre-litigation protocols

In addition to court-ordered ADR, some jurisdictions also contain legislation requiring parties to attempt ADR without even requiring a court order. These courts require parties to undertake ADR prior to commencing litigation through pre-litigation protocols which are designed to encourage parties to settle without recourse to court proceedings (see also Chapter 8.1.3). The *Civil Dispute Resolution Act 2011* (Cth) is a short Act dedicated to implementing the Federal Court (and Federal Magistrates Court) requirements for parties to undertake genuine steps to resolve a matter prior to commencing proceedings. There are also provisions in the *Federal Court Rules 2011* (Cth), rr 8.02 and 5.03, implementing the *Civil Dispute Resolution Act 2011* (Cth) genuine steps provisions.

For example, the Federal Court of Australia requires parties commencing litigation to demonstrate that they have undertaken "genuine steps" to resolve their dispute, pursuant to s 6 of the *Civil Dispute Resolution Act 2011* (Cth). The federal pre-litigation protocol effectively requires parties to undertake ADR before commencing proceedings by requiring applicants to file a statement setting out the "genuine steps" they have undertaken to resolve the dispute at the time they commence proceedings and respondents to file a similar statement in response. Parties which fail to comply with their "genuine steps" obligations can be held to have abused the court's process, although, in practice, the courts appear reluctant to make such findings. Statements of genuine steps were considered in some detail in *Ashby v Slipper*, which concerned a claim by political staffer James Ashby against the then Speaker of the House, Peter Slipper. The Full Federal Court in *Ashby v Slipper* overruled the trial judge's finding of abuse of process, including rejecting the trial judge's

16 *Caska v Leigh* [2018] NSWSC 466, [37] cited in *Dean v Zeene* [2019] NSWSC 1481, [69].

finding that the "genuine steps" statement was incorrect as the lawyer and litigant had not been given sufficient opportunity to explain their evidence.[17] Failure to properly undertake genuine steps is also a factor which can count against an award of costs where that failure had significant consequences.[18]

Care must be taken by parties, and their lawyers, when undertaking pre-litigation ADR to ensure they are genuinely attempting to resolve the dispute and not merely paying lip-service to the process or, worse, making improper threats of litigation under the guise of genuine steps to resolve a dispute. For example, in *CQMS Pty Ltd v Bradken Resources Pty Ltd*, the Federal Court was required to closely consider a range of pre-litigation correspondence concerning a claim for patent infringement.[19] The Court concluded that some of the correspondence by the prospective plaintiff represented genuine steps to resolve the dispute while other correspondence constituted improper threats of litigation.

New South Wales provides a strong counter-example to the federal position on compulsory ADR measures. In New South Wales, there are no legislated pre-litigation protocols, despite provisions being drafted and enacted in 2011. Part 2A of the *Civil Procedure Act 2005* (NSW) containing pre-litigation protocols was introduced in September 2011, but placed on hold for 18 months to assess the success of the new federal system. Part 2A was repealed in February 2013 without ever becoming operational, reflecting the concerns of the judiciary and the legal profession concerning pre-litigation protocols. Pre-litigation protocols can be seen as a threat to the role of courts, or as a sensible process complementary to court procedures.[20] The value of pre-litigation protocols is contested because of the conflict inherent in rules requiring parties to engage in a process which is designed to be consensual.

In addition to pre-litigation protocols, there are specific legislative provisions in some Acts requiring parties to undertake ADR, such as the *Native Title Act 1993* (Cth) s 86B, which requires the Federal Court to refer matters to mediation, subject to limited exceptions. In the Federal Court case of *Jones v South Australia*, Mansfield J refused to agree to a general restriction on s 86B *Native Title Act 1993* (Cth) mediations in South Australia, holding:

> For these reasons I have given, I do not propose to accede to the present motion upon the basis upon which it is presented. That is, I do not accept that the Court should order that there be only limited mediation in this matter (and in all other matters in which there are claims for the determination of native title) as a matter of principle because of the Statewide ILUA Strategy. I think it is necessary to consider in each case, including the present, whether the Court should follow s 86B(1) either generally or by referring

---

17 *Ashby v Slipper* (2014) 219 FCR 322, [207]-[218] (Mansfield and Gilmour JJ with Siopis J dissenting). It should be noted that Ashby later discontinued his proceedings against Slipper and also lost an appeal to benefit from an interlocutory indemnity costs order in his favour which was vacated: *Ashby v Slipper* (2016) 241 FCR 55.

18 *Umoona Tjutagku Health Service Aboriginal Corporation v Walsh* (2019) 268 FCR 401, [72].

19 *CQMS Pty Ltd v Bradken Resources Pty Ltd* (2016) 120 IPR 44.

20 Tania Sourdin, 'Civil Dispute Resolution Obligations: What is Reasonable?' (2012) 35(3) *University of New South Wales Law Journal* 889.

> part only of the matter: see s 86B(4) to mediation by the NNTT. The consideration should be given to the individual circumstances of the case. The status or progress of the Statewide ILUA Strategy, the nature of the issues, the extent of any private negotiations between the parties and the prospects of resolution of those negotiations, the existence of overlapping claims, the resources of the parties, and a range of other matters may be relevant to such consideration. Ultimately, it must be borne in mind that the purpose of mediation is to assist the parties to reach agreement on some or all of the issues which arise in the proceeding.[21]

There are also entire Acts dedicated to requiring ADR in specific circumstances, such as the *Farm Debt Mediation Act 1994* (NSW), described by Heydon J in the High Court Case of *Waller v Hargraves Secured Investments Ltd* as "difficult legislation", subject to criticism and borne out of political compromise.[22] The rationale and operation of the *Farm Debt Mediation Act 1994* (NSW) is succinctly explained by Heydon J (with whom the rest of the High Court agreed) in *Waller v Hargraves* as:

> The background to the Act lies in the notorious problems which face Australian farmers. They include harsh climatic conditions; the vulnerability of crops and animals to disease; unpredictable volatility in prices on world markets; the tendency of farmers to be asset-rich but cash-poor; their dependence on loans; the risk of speedy ejection from their land if there is entire freedom for creditors to enforce their general law rights, despite the possibility of remedying defaults if climatic and market conditions change; and the expense of and often delay in litigation as a method of keeping creditors within their rights. In contrast, some perceive in mediation a capacity to produce much cheaper and speedier outcomes.
>
> In outline the legislative scheme is that if a farmer incurs a 'farm debt' that is secured by a 'farm mortgage', the 'creditor' is unable to take 'enforcement action' under the farm mortgage until, inter alia, a certificate is issued that the Act does not apply because satisfactory mediation has taken place. The question which the appeal raises is how far that scheme works if a certificate is issued in respect of one farm debt but the creditor later wishes to take enforcement action in relation to another.[23]

In *Waller v Hargraves Secured Investments Ltd,* the High Court held that a certificate confirming a farm debt mediation had been held in 2005 did not apply to the current dispute between the parties, as the mediation related to the first loan agreement between the parties, while the dispute concerned the third loan agreement which was a subsequent refinancing of the first loan agreement. Therefore, the creditor, Hargraves, was not entitled to repossess Ms Waller's farm.

Although ADR can be an efficient means of resolving disputes, legislative or industrially required ADR is, arguably, the type least likely to result in settlement because parties who are determined to fight are less likely to properly engage in the ADR process. Hence, it is arguable that the value of compulsory ADR may be outweighed by the risk of increased costs and delay from imposing an additional costly unsuccessful process.

21 *Jones v South Australia* [2003] FCA 538, [48].

22 *Waller v Hargraves Secured Investments Ltd* (2012) 245 CLR 311, [27].

23 Ibid [28]-[29].

5.3 Formal aspects of settlement following successful alternative dispute resolution

Whichever means of ADR parties use, if settlement is successfully reached, it should be properly documented and any active proceedings should be terminated. This formal aspect enables enforcement of ADR settlements and is critical to making a binding resolution of a civil dispute and, where litigation has commenced, for the successful completion of proceedings. In some court-ordered ADR proceedings, such as compulsory conciliation, the formal aspects of settlement following successful ADR will be managed by the court. In all other cases, the parties should use a deed of settlement to ensure their civil dispute is properly terminated.

5.3.1 Deeds of settlement

Particularly where parties have been in an adversarial position and where trust has been lost due to the dispute between the parties, a deed of settlement ensures that parties are bound by the terms of their agreement to settle. A deed is a formal document executed by each party signing in front of a witness which, unlike a contract, does not require each signatory party to provide consideration for what they receive pursuant to the deed. Parties commonly file the settlement deed as part of the process of discontinuing settled proceedings. A deed of settlement is then enforceable in court in the event a party fails to comply voluntarily with its settlement obligations under the deed. Defendants, in particular, need to ensure that the deed of settlement includes a requirement for plaintiffs to discontinue any existing litigation proceedings and not to commence any future litigation proceedings in relation to the previously disputed matters. Deeds of settlement should also specify how parties will pay for legal costs incurred prior to settlement.[24]

Deeds of settlement must be drafted carefully, or they can, themselves, be the subject of further disputes. The Supreme Court of Victoria, Court of Appeal case of *John Holland Group Pty Ltd v Automotive, Food, Metals, Engineering, Printing and Kindred Industries Union* concerned the enforceability and interpretation of a deed of settlement resolving an industrial relations dispute between John Holland Group and five unions.[25] The decision of Neave J (with Nettle and Judd JJ agreeing) dismissing the appeal demonstrates how complex the drafting of settlement deeds may be, particularly in this case where industrial relations legislation postdating the deed had potentially affected its operation. Settlement deeds can be particularly complex and difficult to draft in class action disputes, which typically involve large numbers of plaintiffs, many of whom are not active in the dispute.[26] Class action settlements require court approval to ensure all interested parties are dealt with fairly pursuant to the settlement deed. However, as the case of *Dimitrov v Supreme Court of Victoria* demonstrates,

24 See Chapter 6 for more detailed discussion of legal costs.

25 *John Holland Group Pty Ltd v Automotive, Food, Metals, Engineering, Printing and Kindred Industries Union* (2011) 34 VR 635.

26 See Chapter 3.2 and Chapter 8.4.2 for discussion of class actions.

even such approval can create difficulties for the court where one of more members of a plaintiff class is unhappy with the court's approval of the settlement deed. Although Dimitrov was unsuccessful in his appeal to the High Court, the time and cost associated with proceedings in relation to the settlement deed were time-consuming and expensive.[27]

5.3.2 Termination of court proceedings

As discussed in Chapter 2, courts are increasingly active in managing cases. Accordingly, modern courts are often aware of much of the ADR undertaken in relation to matters where litigation has commenced and some courts even facilitate ADR processes. However, it is the responsibility of parties to litigation to inform the court when matters settle through ADR and to take the necessary steps to terminate proceedings once settlement is reached. Generally, this will include filing a motion to discontinue the proceedings and handing up a sealed copy of the deed of settlement to the court. The court will then make consent orders discontinuing the proceedings in accordance with the terms of the settlement.

5.4 The role of summary disposition in civil procedure theory

Summary disposition plays a critical role in civil procedure. The most obvious forms of summary disposition are the award of summary judgment or default judgment and an order for summary dismissal. The first favours plaintiffs and the second defendants.

Summary judgment for the plaintiff or default judgment is where a court gives judgment in favour of the plaintiff without hearing the matter. This most commonly occurs where the defendant fails to defend the proceedings (default judgment). Once summary judgment or default judgment is ordered, the plaintiff can commence enforcement proceedings against the problem defendant.

Summary judgment for the defendant (also called summary dismissal) is where a court dismisses the plaintiff's claim without hearing the matter. This most commonly occurs where a problem plaintiff has instigated proceedings which are an abuse of process or ill conceived. Vexatious litigants constitute an extreme example of a problem plaintiff.[28]

Balancing competing factors is at the heart of CDR as discussed in Chapter 2, and judicial consideration of abuse of process is an example of the courts applying judicial discretion in balancing litigants' right to be heard against the courts' need have fair and efficient processes which protect litigants and scarce resources from abuse. It is obviously in courts' interests for everyone to comply with the rules of civil procedure. Actions taken in breach of civil procedure rules will often be labelled an "abuse of process of the court" and courts may penalise parties for such abuses. The power to dispose summarily of unmeritorious litigation is arguably the strongest tool available to judges to maximise access to justice. Without the threat of summary dismissal, the temptation for parties to run litigation poorly would increase

27 *Dimitrov v Supreme Court of Victoria* (2017) 263 CLR 130.
28 See Chapter 5.5.4 for more detail.

as would the likelihood of the courts being overrun with frivolous and vexatious litigation. At the same time, the summary dismissal of proceedings can result in a denial of access to justice if a party's claim or defence is dismissed unfairly without a proper hearing. Any award of summary judgment creates a risk that access to justice has been denied because the court has failed to allow a "fair hearing." Hence, it is critical that summary disposition be used cautiously and fairly by the judiciary as a tool for managing civil procedure. Hence, summary disposition is an area where the balancing obligations discussed in Chapter 2, particularly those of efficiency and due consideration are most evident.

5.4.1 Limiting unmeritorious proceedings and procedures

Unmeritorious litigation prevents access to justice. Unmeritorious cases and poorly run cases clog the courts, increase the public cost of the justice system and impose unnecessary costs of litigation (discussed in Chapter 2) on other parties. Hence, it is critical that courts identify unmeritorious litigation, improper litigation tactics and poor adherence to procedures as soon as possible and limit them so as to maximise access to justice.

Civil procedure is designed to maximise access to justice by enabling everyone within the litigation system, including litigants, lawyers, judges and court workers, to operate as efficiently as possible. Sometimes, this is best achieved by disposing of a matter without hearing where, for example, that matter is an abuse of the court's process and an unfair burden upon other parties.

5.4.2 Preventing abuse of process

Abuse of process is a concept employed by courts to ensure that the administration of justice runs smoothly and fairly. There are several ways parties can be found to have abused the courts' processes, including by commencing unmeritorious litigation or by running litigation using improper tactics. Sometimes, a court will conclude a party has abused the courts' processes, despite having no intention to do so, purely through legal incompetence or strategic misfortune.[29] Parties which have abused the courts' processes are likely to have their matter summarily dismissed and/or be subject to significant adverse costs consequences.[30] Abuse of process is a common basis for courts striking out claims, defences or parts of pleadings or permanently staying proceedings. Abuse of process of the court can be established against any party to litigation.

The term "abuse of process" is incapable of exhaustive categorisation as the High Court confirmed in the 2011 case of *Michael Wilson & Partners Ltd v Nicholls*.[31] This case concerned the alleged breaches of employment terms by ex-employees and conflicts of jurisdiction where arbitration and litigation proceedings were running simultaneously in

---

29 See, eg, *National Australia Bank Ltd v McCann (No 2)* [2010] NSWSC 1032, where Ms McCann's lack of legal expertise and self-represented status resulted in a finding she had abused the Court's process. In *UBS AG v Tyne* (2018) 265 CLR 77, the High Court reinstated the primary judge's finding of abuse of process in a complex strategic private international law dispute where Mr Tyne was outmanoeuvred by UBS. *Tyne* is discussed in more detail below.

30 See Chapter 6.

31 *Michael Wilson & Partners Ltd v Nicholls* (2011) 244 CLR 427.

multiple jurisdictions. In relation to "abuse of process" generally, Gummow, Hayne, Crennan and Bell JJ (with Heydon J agreeing) held:

> 88. It has long been recognised that the term 'abuse of the process of the court' may be used in different senses. ....
>
> 89. As the majority pointed out in *Batistatos v Roads and Traffic Authority (NSW)*, '[w]hat amounts to abuse of court process is insusceptible of a formulation comprising closed categories'. In *Ridgeway v The Queen*, Gaudron J noted that the concept extended to proceedings 'instituted for an improper purpose', and to proceedings that are 'seriously and unfairly burdensome, prejudicial or damaging' or 'productive of serious and unjustified trouble and harassment'. In *Rogers v The Queen*, McHugh J concluded that, although the categories of abuse of process are not closed, many cases of abuse can be identified as falling into one of three categories: '(1) the court's procedures are invoked for an illegitimate purpose; (2) the use of the court's procedures is unjustifiably oppressive to one of the parties; or (3) the use of the court's procedures would bring the administration of justice into disrepute.'
>
> 90. One recognised class of abuse of process is where proceedings are instituted against a party in a second forum when there are proceedings against that party pending in another and the continuance of the second would be an abuse of the process of the first. ....[32]

In *Michael Wilson & Partners Ltd v Nicholls,* the High Court concluded that there was no abuse of process because the Supreme Court of New South Wales proceedings were not limited by the nature and extent of relief sought in the London arbitration.[33] Hence, the multiplicity of proceedings was not, in this instance, an abuse of process but would be subject to the equity that the respondents would have to prevent double recovery.

The dispute between UBS and Mr Tyne and his companies is a complex multijurisdictional dispute involving forum shopping and strategic litigating.[34] It is also a High Court example of summary disposition. Mr Tyne tried, unsuccessfully, to hold UBS responsible for a disastrous 2007 investment in Kazakhstan bonds: first, in the New South Wales Supreme Court, and then in the Federal Court, culminating in the High Court's decision in *UBS AG v Tyne* that Tyne's proceedings were an abuse of process.[35] The High Court's conclusion against Tyne focussed on the importance of efficiency and the importance of case management to prevent abuse of process although, perhaps unfortunately, it overlooked the earlier strategic litigating by UBS AG. UBS commenced proceedings in Singapore upon being notified of an intention by Tyne to commence New South Wales Supreme Court proceedings.[36] The earlier timing of the Singapore proceedings and the existence of a negotiated agreement led to the New South

32 Ibid [88]-[90].

33 *Michael Wilson & Partners Ltd v Nicholls* (20110) 244 CLR 427.

34 "Forum shopping" is a term used to describe cases where multiple courts potentially have jurisdiction over the same dispute and there are different strategic advantages to commencing in a particular court for a particular party. Forum shopping is commonly associated with international disputes, but can also arise in interstate disputes or even in the decision of whether to proceed to court or a tribunal.

35 *UBS AG v Tyne* (2018) 265 CLR 77.

36 *Telesto Investments Ltd v UBS AG* (2013) 94 ACSR 29, [26], [29]. On 8 October 2010, Mr Tyne notified his intention to commence New South Wales proceedings on 16 October or as soon as practicable thereafter. On 15 October 2010, UBS commenced proceedings against Mr Tyne in Singapore.

Wales Supreme Court rejecting Tyne's New South Wales' proceedings.[37] Tyne then brought proceedings in the Federal Court, which were held to be an abuse of process by the High Court (in a split decision of 4:3). The High Court held that Tyne, or the entities managed by him, had abused the Federal Court's process in commencing proceedings which involved the same issues which other Tyne entities had attempted to litigate in the New South Wales Supreme Court.[38] Chief Justice Kiefel with Bell and Keane JJ (whose decision combined with Gageler J to form the majority finding) held:

> The courts must be astute to protect litigants and the system of justice itself against abuse of process. It is to hark back to a time before this Court's decisions in Aon and Tomlinson and the enactment of s 37M of the FCA to expect that the courts will indulge parties who engage in tactical manoeuvring that impedes the 'just, quick and efficient' resolution of litigation. To insist, for example, on 'inexcusable delay' as a precondition of the exercise of the power to stay proceedings as an abuse of process is to fail to appreciate that any substantial delay is apt to occasion an increase in the cost of justice and a decrease in the quality of justice. And other litigants are left in the queue awaiting justice. Further, there is no reason why the courts should tolerate attempts to manipulate other parties and the courts themselves by the deployment, by a single directing mind and will, of different legal entities under common control for such a purpose. The concern is as to whether the processes of the court are being abused. Given that this is the central concern, the circumstance that the abuse is effected by the use of multiple entities orchestrated by a single mind and will is no reason to tolerate it.
>
> Nor does the undue vexation which a stay of proceedings is concerned to prevent arise only when proceedings in respect of the same issue have been concluded by a judgment on the merits. Serial proceedings discontinued prior to judgment would be an obvious example of an abuse of process. The pursuit of substantially the same claim by serial proceedings conducted by different entities under common control is no less obviously an abuse of process.[39]

The courts must continue to expand the definition of abuse of process as new abuses arise. *Melbourne City Investments Pty Ltd v Myer Holdings Ltd* concerned a company (MCI) which purchased small parcels of shares in many major companies in the hope that the shares would lose value attributable to a corporate breach, enabling MCI to become the lead plaintiff in a class action employing lawyers and litigation funders connected to MCI for profit. The Victorian Supreme Court of Appeal concluded that:

> 56 The judge correctly stayed the proceeding brought by MCI against Myer. MCI commenced the proceeding with the predominant purpose of generating income from the proceeding itself. Its predominant purpose was not to seek compensation for any wrong done to it, nor to assist the group members by acting as lead plaintiff. It instituted the proceeding not for the purpose for which class actions are designed but instead to gain a collateral advantage. That constitutes an abuse of process.[40]

37 *Telesto Investments Ltd v UBS AG* (2013) 94 ACSR 29, [286].
38 *UBS AG v Tyne* (2018) 265 CLR 77, [55] (Kiefel CJ, Bell and Keane JJ), [80] (Gageler J).
39 Ibid [45]-[46] (Kiefel CJ, Bell and Keane JJ).
40 *Melbourne City Investments Pty Ltd v Myer Holdings Ltd* (2017) 53 VR 709, [56] (Osborn and Ferguson JJ, with Whelan J agreeing in a separate judgment).

However, courts must also ensure that conduct is not improperly found to be abuse of process as this, itself, causes injustice. In *Rozenblit v Vainer*, the High Court overruled the Victorian Court of Appeal which had stayed proceedings until interlocutory costs orders were paid in circumstances where it was not in dispute that the plaintiff was unable to pay the costs orders.[41] The High Court held that there were insufficient grounds for the grant of a stay which would effectively prevent the plaintiff's claim where his actions were inefficient but not vexatious or significantly prejudicial to the defendant. Justices Gordon and Edelman noted that "overarching obligations do not displace the need for the court to safeguard the administration of justice in the context of ordering a stay for abuse of process", highlighting the need for the court to balance the competing obligations of efficiency, cost and the right to be heard.[42]

5.5 Summary disposition: disposal of problem plaintiffs

As discussed in Chapter 3, it is important to protect access to the court system. However, there also needs to be protection of the court system and other litigants from those who abuse their court access. Plaintiffs most commonly pose difficulties for courts and defendants in one or more of the following ways:

- commence proceedings which are an abuse of process
- excessively and vexatiously commence proceedings
- fail to comply with requirements for originating process or service (see Chapter 8)
- delay or fail to comply with court directions in preparation of their case
- fail to appear at directions hearings, interlocutory hearings or the final hearing
- initiate excessive, unnecessary interlocutory disputes (see Chapter 10)
- fail to engage in dispute resolution mechanisms (see Chapter 4 and above)
- fail to pay an adverse costs order made by the court (see Chapter 6).

In dealing with the above failings, courts must balance the plaintiff's right to seek justice with the need to prevent injustice to the defendants and ensure the efficiency of the court system. For most plaintiff failings, courts will allow plaintiffs second chances including opportunities to amend their case and comply with court procedures. However, sometimes extreme solutions are required and courts then resort to summary dismissal or even a vexatious litigant declaration.

5.5.1 Summary dismissal

The most straightforward way for a judge to dispose of unmeritorious litigation is by summary dismissal of a case. Summary dismissal is where a court dismisses the claim made by the plaintiff without hearing the case. A court may summarily dismiss litigation on application

41 *Rozenblit v Vainer* (2018) 262 CLR 478. The decision contained three separate judgments (Kiefel CJ with Bell J, Keane J, and Gordon with Edelman JJ) but was unanimous with all judges agreeing to the orders proposed by Gordon and Edelman JJ.

42 Ibid [76]. See Chapter 2.3.1 for further discussion of the key theme of balancing efficiency with due process.

from a defendant (or putative defendant) or by its own motion. There are specific legislated circumstances in which matters may be summarily dismissed and courts generally have broad discretion pursuant to the applicable court rules to dismiss cases summarily where appropriate.

One example of a legislative provision empowering summary disposition is s 31A of the *Federal Court Act 1976* (Cth). Section 31A enables a judge to grant summary judgment in favour of either party where the other party's case "has no reasonable prospects of success."[43] A proceeding or part of a proceeding need not be "hopeless" or "bound to fail" to have "no reasonable prospect of success."[44]

The application of s 31A was discussed by the Full Court of the Federal Court in the case of *Kowalski v MMAL Staff Superannuation Fund Pty Ltd*.[45] The dispute between Kowalski and Mitsubishi at the heart of this litigation will be discussed further in relation to vexatious litigants below. In this case, the Full Court of the Federal Court (Spender, Graham and Gilmore JJ), dismissed the appeal by Kowalski as incompetent and refused to overrule the application of s 31A by the primary judge. In its judgment, the Full Court considered, in detail, the pursuit of the interests of justice including the role of case management elucidated in cases such as *Aon Risk Services Australia Ltd v Australian National University*[46] (discussed in Chapter 2).

The power of s 31A and similar state-based abuse of process provisions remain difficult to define. As noted by the High Court case of *Spencer v Commonwealth*: "Section 31A(2) requires a practical judgment by the Federal Court as to whether the applicant has more than a 'fanciful' prospect of success."[47] The Full Court in *Kowalski v MMAL Staff Superannuation Fund Pty Ltd* noted that s 31A *Federal Court of Australia Act 1976* (Cth) was designed to "soften the test for a successful application" established by the High Court common law for summary judgment in *Theseus Exploration NL v Foyster*[48] and for summary dismissal in *Dey v Victorian Railways Commissioners*.[49]

In *Spencer v Commonwealth*, confirming the analysis in *Kowalski v MMAL Staff Superannuation Fund Pty Ltd*,[50] the full High Court (French CJ, Gummow, Hayne, Heydon, Crennan, Kiefel and Bell JJ, in three separate judgments) determined that s 31A should not have been applied to summarily dismiss Mr Spencer's case.[51] The majority, Hayne, Crennan, Kiefel and Bell JJ, analysed the term "no reasonable prospect of success", noting the issues with defining the term as follows:

> 58. How then should the expression 'no reasonable prospect' be understood? No paraphrase of the expression can be adopted as a sufficient explanation of its operation, let alone definition of its content. Nor can the expression usefully be understood by

---

43 *Federal Court Act 1976* (Cth) ss 31A(1), 31A(2).

44 *Federal Court Act 1976* (Cth) s 31A(3).

45 *Kowalski v MMAL Staff Superannuation Fund Pty Ltd* (2009) 178 FCR 401.

46 *Aon Risk Services Australia Ltd v Australian National University* (2009) 239 CLR 175.

47 *Spencer v Commonwealth* (2010) 241 CLR 118, [25].

48 *Theseus Exploration NL v Foyster* (1972) 126 CLR 507.

49 *Dey v Victorian Railways Commissioners* (1949) 78 CLR 62.

50 *Kowalski v MMAL Staff Superannuation Fund Pty Ltd* (2009) 178 FLR 301.

51 It is interesting to note that, having succeeded in the High Court in having the summary dismissal application against him dismissed, Mr Spencer was eventually unsuccessful on the hearing of the merits of his case in *Spencer v Commonwealth* (2015) 240 FCR 282 and on appeal in *Spencer v Commonwealth* (2018) 262 FCR 344.

> the creation of some antinomy intended to capture most or all of the cases in which it cannot be said that there is 'no reasonable prospect'. The judicial creation of a lexicon of words or phrases intended to capture the operation of a particular statutory phrase like 'no reasonable prospect' is to be avoided. Consideration of the difficulties that bedevilled the proviso to common form criminal appeal statutes, as a result of judicial glossing of the relevant statutory expression, provides the clearest example of the dangers that attend any such attempt.
>
> 59. In many cases where a plaintiff has no reasonable prospect of prosecuting a proceeding, the proceeding could be described (with or without the addition of intensifying epithets like 'clearly', 'manifestly' or 'obviously') as 'frivolous', 'untenable', 'groundless' or 'faulty'. But none of those expressions (alone or in combination) should be understood as providing a sufficient chart of the metes and bounds of the power given by s 31A. Nor can the content of the word 'reasonable', in the phrase 'no reasonable prospect', be sufficiently, let alone completely, illuminated by drawing some contrast with what would be a 'frivolous', 'untenable', 'groundless' or 'faulty' claim.
>
> 60. Rather, full weight must be given to the expression as a whole. The Federal Court may exercise power under s 31A if, and only if, satisfied that there is 'no reasonable prospect' of success. Of course, it may readily be accepted that the power to dismiss an action summarily is not to be exercised lightly. But the elucidation of what amounts to 'no reasonable prospect' can best proceed in the same way as content has been given, through a succession of decided cases, to other generally expressed statutory phrases, such as the phrase 'just and equitable' when it is used to identify a ground for winding up a company. At this point in the development of the understanding of the expression and its application, it is sufficient, but important, to emphasise that the evident legislative purpose revealed by the text of the provision will be defeated if its application is read as confined to cases of a kind which fell within earlier, different, procedural regimes.[52]

The High Court case of *Trkulja v Google LLC* concerned an appeal from an application to set aside defamation proceedings brought by Mr Trkulja against Google because of search engine results which incorrectly associated Mr Trkulja with notorious Melbourne underworld figures. *Trkulja*'s case again required consideration of the test for summary dismissal, with the High Court holding that the primary judge had been correct in refusing to summarily dismiss the case pursuant to ss 62 and 63 of the *Civil Procedure Act 2010* (Vic). The High Court, in a unanimous (five judge) decision, compared the s 31A *Federal Court of Australia Act 1976* (Cth) test with the *Civil Procedure Act 2010* (Vic) and found them to be similar and both less stringent than the old common law tests, stating:

> In Victoria, the test for summary judgment is prescribed by s 62 of the *Civil Procedure Act*: whether the plaintiff's claim has 'no real prospect of success'. Consistently with Spencer, the view taken in Victoria is that the power to dismiss an action summarily is not lightly to be exercised but that, like the test applicable to s 31A of the *Federal Court of Australia Act*, the 'no real prospect of success' test is to some degree more liberal than Dey and General Steel. It permits of the possibility of cases in which, although the plaintiff's case is not 'hopeless' or 'bound to fail', it does not have a real prospect of succeeding.[53]

52 *Spencer v Commonwealth* (2010) 241 CLR 118, [58]-[60].
53 *Trkulja v Google LLC* (2018) 263 CLR 149, [22]-[23].

5.5.2 Dismissal for want of prosecution

Where a plaintiff commences proceedings but then fails to take necessary steps in the proceedings, the proceedings may be dismissed for want of prosecution. In the New South Wales Supreme Court case of *Re SCW (Express Detailing) Pty Ltd*,[54] White J summarily dismissed a case for want of prosecution pursuant to r 12.7 of the *Uniform Civil Procedure Rules 2005* (NSW) only four months after the last action by the plaintiff. In that case, however, the plaintiff was not resident in New South Wales, the plaintiff's New South Wales solicitor had ceased to act, and the only address for the plaintiff provided by his former solicitor was a Hong Kong address which proved no longer valid. The failure to have an address for service in New South Wales was in breach of the *Civil Procedure Act 2005* (NSW) and the Court determined the plaintiff had no intention of proceeding with the case. In dismissing the proceedings for want of prosecution, White J noted:

> [24]. … The power to dismiss an action for want of prosecution is not defined or confined by rigid guidelines, but given the drastic nature of summary dismissal it is a power to be exercised with caution, and I think only in a clear case, where justice so requires. In exercising the power under that rule, the court is required to have regard to the matters in ss 56, 57 and 58 of the *Civil Procedure Act 2005*. The essential requirement is that the court seek to act in accordance with the dictates of justice.[55]

However, summary dismissal for want of prosecution can be more complex as was the case in the Full Court of the Supreme Court of South Australia's majority decision not to grant summary dismissal for want of prosecution in the case of *Beverage Bottlers (SA) Ltd (in liq) v Abode Enterprises Pty Ltd*. In this case, Vanstone and Kourakis JJ held, on appeal (with Layton J dissenting), that summary judgment for want of prosecution should not have been awarded despite no correspondence or action by the plaintiff for 5 years and the matter having run for 11 years at the time of the summary dismissal hearing. Had the matter been summarily dismissed, the plaintiff would have been entitled to reinstitute proceedings, except for the contract aspect of its claim which would have become statute barred.[56]

The Northern Territory Supreme Court case of *Booth v An Assessor* concerned summary dismissal for want of prosecution due to the failure of a self-represented litigant with an arm injury, who was ineligible for Legal Aid, to provide relevant written notice to the court regarding which documents he sought to rely on. Despite his difficulties, the task was straightforward. The Court denied leave to appeal due to the absence of any error of law. The Court explained the connection between procedural fairness (the right to be heard) and the right to summarily dismiss for want of prosecution:

> [41] I turn first to deal with the contention that the applicant was denied procedural fairness. As the courts have frequently observed, natural justice and procedural fairness lie at the heart of the judicial process. That process involves the ultimate standard of procedural fairness, which includes notice to the parties of the issues to be dealt with; adequate notice of time and place of hearing; the right to call evidence; the right to

54 *Re SCW (Express Detailing) Pty Ltd* [2011] NSWSC 688.

55 Ibid [24].

56 *Beverage Bottlers (SA) Ltd (in liq) v Abode Enterprises Pty Ltd* [2009] SASC 272.

legal representation; a decision based on evidence presented at the hearing; and the giving of reasons for decisions. Even in the application of that high standard, the law recognises that a prosecuting party may forego the right to a hearing if it does not comply with the orders and processes of the court. That is recognised by the power to dismiss for want of prosecution, be that power inherent, implied or statutory in nature.[57]

5.5.3 Automatic summary dismissal

It is worth noting that issues of efficiency are more critical in lower courts which experience higher volumes of cases for less significant amounts of money. For example, in the Local Courts of New South Wales, *Practice Note Civ 1: The Case Management of Civil Proceedings in the Local Court*, authorised by s 15 of the *Civil Procedure Act 2005* (NSW) and s 27 of the *Local Court Act 2007* (NSW), automatically dismisses any proceedings which remain inactive after commencement for nine months.[58] Such provisions indicate how easily parties can lose their right to a hearing if they do not comply with procedures and proceed with efficiency in lower courts.

5.5.4 Vexatious litigants

Summary judgment is sufficient to deter most plaintiffs, but there are a small number of plaintiffs who become obsessed with their claim or claims and bring endless proceedings against one or more parties. Vexatious litigants are commonly self-represented and frequently suffer from mental illnesses such as paranoia. As a means of preventing vexatious litigation, some jurisdictions have introduced legislation to specifically deter or prevent vexatious litigation, such as the *Vexatious Proceedings Act 2008* (NSW), the *Vexatious Proceedings Restriction Act 2002* (WA), and the *Vexatious Proceedings Act 2005* (Qld). Other jurisdictions have specific provisions in their court procedure rules and civil procedure legislation, such as s 39 of the *Supreme Court Act 1935* (SA) and rr 6.01 to 6.03 of the *Federal Court Rules 2011* (Cth). The *Federal Court Rules 2011* (Cth) are further supported by the *Federal Court Act 1976* (Cth) which contains s 59(2)(1), empowering the court to make rules for "the prevention or termination of vexatious proceedings". Even the High Court can make an order prohibiting a vexatious litigant from instituting proceedings pursuant to the *Judiciary Act 1903* (Cth) s 77RN, as occurred in the case of *Conomy v Maden*.[59]

The seemingly endless claims brought by South Australian litigant, Mr Kazimir Kowalski, provide an excellent example of vexatious litigation. Mr Kowalski made a workers' compensation claim against his former employer, Mitsubishi, who employed him as a tooling analysist, following an eye injury and a back injury at work in May 1989. After receiving weekly payments and medical expenses paid by Mitsubishi, Mr Kowalski commenced common law proceedings against his employer which were unsuccessful although payment

57 *Booth v An Assessor* [2019] NTSC 89, [41].

58 Local Court New South Wales, *Practice Note Civ 1: Case Management of Civil Proceedings in the Local Court*, 15 March 2019, [7].

59 *Conomy v Maden* [2019] HCA Trans 49.

of $200,000 was subsequently made by Mitsubishi under a settlement agreement in 1998.[60] After a very large number of failed proceedings, including against his lawyers, Mr Kowalski was declared a vexatious litigant by the Supreme Court of South Australia in *Mitsubishi Motors Australia Ltd v Kowalski*[61] and then again in January 2014 by Blue J.[62] Mr Kowalski also commenced numerous Federal Court proceedings and was declared a vexatious litigant in the Federal Court in the 2011 decision of *Soden v Kowalski*.[63] Mr Kowalski did not limit his claims to his former employer. He has also made claims against Veterans Affairs, his own lawyers, and numerous court and tribunal personnel arguing bias.[64] His Veterans Affairs proceedings resulted in him also being declared a vexatious litigant in the Administrative Appeals Tribunal in 2014 and banned from making applications under the *Veterans' Entitlements Act 1986* (Cth) or the *Military Rehabilitation and Compensation Act 2004* (Cth) after his unsuccessful claims for veteran's affairs compensation had resulted in 20 written judgments with reasons in the tribunal and courts.[65]

Soden v Kowalski listed just the Federal Court cases commenced by Kowalski against his former employer, Mitsubishi, and its staff superannuation fund, MMAL Staff Superannuation Fund Pty Ltd, up until 2011, as follows:

> *Kowalski v Mitsubishi Motors Australia Ltd* (1998) FCR 55;
> *Kowalski v Mitsubishi Motors Australia Ltd Staff Superannuation Fund Pty Ltd* [2002] FCA 1153;
> *Kowalski v Trustee of Mitsubishi Motors Australia Limited Staff Superannuation Fund Pty Ltd* [2003] FCA 14;
> *Kowalski v Trustee, Mitsubishi Motors Australia Limited Staff Superannuation Fund Pty Ltd* [2003] FCAFC 18;
> *Kowalski v MMAL Staff Superannuation Fund Pty Ltd* [2007] FCA 1069, (2000) 242 ALR 370;
> *Kowalski v MMAL Staff Superannuation Fund Pty Ltd (No 2)* [2008] FCA 691;
> *Kowalski v Mitsubishi Motors Australia Ltd* [2008] FCA 1873;
> *Kowalski v Repatriation Commission* [2008] FCA 1970;
> *Kowalski v Repatriation Commission* [2009] FCA 47;
> *Kowalski v Mitsubishi Motors Australia Ltd* [2009] FCA 48;
> *Kowalski v Repatriation Commission* [2009] FCA 153;
> *Kowalski v Repatriation Commission* [2009] FCA 794;
> *Kowalski v Repatriation Commission* [2009] FCAFC 107, (2009) 259 ALR 444;
> *Kowalski v Mitsubishi Motors Australia Ltd* [2009] FCA 991;
> *Kowalski v MMAL Staff Superannuation Fund Pty Ltd* [2009] FCAFC 117, (2009) 259 ALR 319;

60 *Mitsubishi Motors Australia Ltd v Kowalski* (2019) 134 SASR 1.
61 *Mitsubishi Motors Australia Ltd v Kowalski* [2005] SASC 154.
62 *Attorney-General v Kowalski* [2014] SASC 1. The second declaration of vexatious litigant was discussed in *Attorney-General v Kowalski (No 6)* [2017] SASC 122, [103].
63 *Soden v Kowalski* [2011] FCA 318.
64 See, eg, *Kowalski and Repatriation Commission* (2014) 62 AAR 495 (against the Repatriation Commission); *Kowalski v Sim* [2019] SASCFC 96 (against his former lawyers); and *Soden v Kowalski* [2011] FCA 318 (against the Registrar of the Federal Court).
65 *Kowalski and Repatriation Commission* (2014) 62 AAR 495, [119]-[122]. A list of Mr Kowalski's proceedings against the Veteran's Affairs Commission is set out in a lengthy table at [27].

> *Kowalski v Military Rehabilitation and Compensation Commission* [2009] FCA 1044;
> *Kowalski v Chief Executive Officer of Medicare Australia* [2009] FCA 1072;
> *Kowalski v Mitsubishi Motors Australia Ltd* [2009] FCA 1289;
> *Kowalski v Chief Executive Officer of Medicare Australia* [2009] FCA 1420;
> *Kowalski v Superannuation Complaints Tribunal* [2009] FCA 1466;
> *Kowalski v Military Rehabilitation and Compensation Commission* [2010] FCA 5;
> *Kowalski v Superannuation Complaints Tribunal* [2010] FCA 104;
> *Kowalski v Military Rehabilitation and Compensation Commission* [2010] FCAFC 10, (2010) 114 ALD 8;
> *Kowalski v Repatriation Commission* [2010] FCAFC 19;
> *Kowalski v Complete Exhaust Specialists* [2010] FCA 222;
> *Kowalski v Chief Executive Officer of Medicare Australia* [2010] FCA 265;
> *Kowalski v Military Rehabilitation and Compensation Commission* [2010] FCA 408;
> *Kowalski v Repatriation Commission* [2010] FCA 409;
> *Kowalski v Cole, Sim and RJ Cole Partners* [2010] FCA 410;
> *Kowalski v Chief Executive Officer of Medicare Australia* [2010] FCA 411;
> *Kowalski v Complete Exhaust Specialists* [2010] FCA 412;
> *Kowalski v Chief Executive Officer of Medicare Australia* [2010] FCA 413, (2010) 185 FCR 42;
> *Kowalski v Superannuation Complaints Tribunal* [2010] FCA 473;
> *Kowalski v AMP Superannuation Limited* [2010] FCA 1170;
> *Evidence of applicants in SAD 96 of 2010.*[66]

The frustration and concern of the judiciary with Mr Kowalski is frequently palpable despite the fact that every judgment is carefully and respectfully reasoned and Mr Kowalski is invariably treated with politeness and respect. A 2019 South Australian Full Federal Court decision indicates the high cost of such civility as well as the limited effectiveness of vexatious litigant declarations:

> 106 To be blunt, during the subject 16 year period Kowalski continually harassed the respondents with proceedings designed to set aside the judgment of Judge Anderson and with numerous proceedings designed to recover the same sum of $18,634.66 as is now sought here. All of those proceedings failed but they no doubt were of great expense, worry and inconvenience to the respondents. They have also been of great expense to the public when one considers the true cost of an hour, or a day, in Court having regard to the cost of time of Judges, numerous support staff and other expenses — and hence the reference to broader public policy considerations.[67]

As is common with vexatious litigants, Mr Kowalski suffers from mental illnesses which apparently impair his ability to comprehend views other than his own.[68] Unfortunately, while the vexatious litigant declarations against Mr Kowalski may have reduced the length of the many proceedings commenced by him, these declarations have not decreased

66 *Soden v Kowalski* [2011] FCA 318, [19], [35]-[36].

67 *Kowalski v Sim* [2019] SASCFC 96, [106].

68 *Kowalski and Repatriation Commission* (2014) 62 AAR 495. Mr Kowalski openly claims to be suffering from depression, anxiety and other mental illness but appears to have little insight that his mental health may affect his understanding of his litigation losses.

the frequency of proceedings brought as Mr Kowalski relentlessly seeks permission to commence new proceedings or reinvigorate old ones. As demonstrated by examples of more recent Kowalski proceedings, from 2017 to 2019, Mr Kowalski continues to commence extraordinary numbers of proceeding including High Court applications for special leave predominantly against his former employer, Mitsubishi, and his former lawyers, RJ Cole:

- *Kowalski and Repatriation Commission* (2014) 62 AAR 495
- *Kowalski v Bourne* [2017] SASCFC 24
- *Kowalski v Cole* [2017] SASCFC 23
- *Kowalski v Mitsubishi Motors Aust Staff Superannuation Fund Pty Ltd* [2017] SADC 57
- *Attorney-General v Kowalski (No 5)* [2017] SASC 120
- *Attorney-General v Kowalski (No 6)* [2017] SASC 122
- *Kowalski v Cole* [2017] HCASL 194
- *Kowalski v Mitsubishi Motors Australia Staff Superannuation Pty Ltd* [2017] SASCFC 175
- *Attorney-General (SA) v Kowalski (No 7)* [2018] SASC 62
- *Kowalski v Mitsubishi Motors Australia Staff Superannuation Fund Pty Ltd* [2018] SASCFC 44
- *Mitsubishi Motors Australia Ltd v Kowalski* [2018] SASCFC 63
- *Kowalski v Mitsubishi Motors Australia Staff Superannuation* [2018] HCASL 86
- *Kowalski v Mitsubishi Motors Australia Staff Superannuation Pty Ltd* [2018] HCASL 325
- *Kowalski v Mitsubishi Motors Australia Ltd* [2018] HCASL 326
- *Mitsubishi Motors Australia Ltd v Kowalski* [2019] SASCFC 95
- *Kowalski v Sim* [2019] SASCFC 96
- *Kowalski v Stanley & Partners* [2019] HCASL 167
- *Kowalski v Mitsubishi Motors Australia Staff Superannuation Pty Ltd* [2019] HCASL 277
- *Kowalski v Mitsubishi Motors Australia Ltd* [2019] HCASL 390
- *Kowalski v Sim* [2019] HCASL 391.

The extraordinary number of proceedings brought by Mr Kowalski gives an indication of the sort of extreme litigant behaviour which leads courts to declare a litigant vexatious. Due to the nature of the South Australian and Commonwealth provisions for vexatious litigants, the declarations made against Mr Kowalski are still limited in their application. Conversely, the New South Wales case of *Attorney-General (NSW) v Chan* decided according to the *Vexatious Proceedings Act 2008* (NSW) ss 8(7)(a) and 8(7)(b) prohibited Mr Chan from commencing any proceedings in New South Wales without leave of the court and all actions currently instigated by him were permanently stayed. Justice Adamson considered the principles of vexatious litigation including:

> 35. The purpose of an order is not to impose punishment for past litigious misdeeds, but to shield both the public and the Court itself: *Official Trustee in Bankruptcy v Gargan (No 2)* [2009] FCA 398 at [3], cited with approval in *Attorney General v Gargan* at [8].
>
> 36. It is a serious thing to deprive litigants of their access to the courts: Wilson at [11].[69]

69 *Attorney-General (NSW) v Chan* [2011] NSWSC 1315, [35]-[36].

In making vexatious proceedings orders against Mr Chan, Adamson J concluded:

> 177. … The right to bring proceedings in a court or tribunal is a right that ought not be abused. The Defendant has repeatedly, as referred to above, used the processes of courts and tribunals to assert rights and grievances for which he has no reasonable ground. He has abused the processes of the Court by re-litigating issues which he has lost, and selected new defendants against whom to vent his complaints. He has also made several damaging allegations of reprehensible conduct against individuals, including judicial officers, who have no practical right of redress. He has taken up the time of judges, court staff, litigants and solicitors in a wholly unproductive way. He has sought adjournments on unsubstantiated grounds, in circumstances where it appears that he is toying with the Court, albeit that he may not intend to do so.[70]

Chan's case also touches on the lack of insight and potential paranoia of vexatious litigants who often believe any failure in court results from conspiracies against them, rather than the shortcomings in their claims. Such delusions frequently result in litigation by vexatious litigants against the courts or court employees, government and other authorities.

In New South Wales, limited vexatious litigant rulings, preventing a party from commencing proceedings in relation to a limited issue, also occur in cases such as the New South Wales Court of Appeal decision of *Quach v New South Wales Civil and Administrative Tribunal (No 2)*, where the Court held:

> 51 The problem which confronts this Court and the respondents is that Mr Quach will not or cannot accept that his claims for judicial review of the Stage One and Stage Two decisions of NCAT have been determined by this Court and that further attempts to re-litigate those claims are both futile and an abuse of process.[71]

In 2019, in *Mohareb v Fairfax Media Publications Pty Ltd,* the New South Wales Supreme Court employed security for costs orders against a vexatious plaintiff, as a means of limiting litigation by requiring the plaintiff to pay money into court to cover a potential future adverse costs order without which payment the proceedings would be stayed.[72] Security of costs are discussed further in Chapter 6.

5.6 Summary disposition: disposal of problem defendants

Plaintiffs are not the only parties to litigation capable of behaving unreasonably. Defendants can, essentially, make life difficult for plaintiffs in the following ways:

- avoid service of originating process (see Chapter 8)
- fail to appear in court (in writing or in person) (see Chapter 9)
- fail to file a defence (see Chapter 9)

70 Ibid [177].
71 *Quach v New South Wales Civil and Administrative Tribunal (No 2)* [2017] NSWCA 182, [51].
72 *Mohareb v Fairfax Media Publications Pty Ltd* [2019] NSWSC 1685.

- file an improper or inadequate defence (see Chapter 9)
- delay or fail to comply with court directions in preparing the matter (see Chapter 10)
- initiate excessive, unnecessary interlocutory disputes (see Chapter 10)
- fail to engage in alternative dispute resolution mechanisms (see Chapter 4)
- fail to pay on a judgment ordered against them by court (see Chapter 16).

Most procedural breaches by defendants will result in nothing more than an adverse costs order (see Chapter 6). Serious or repeated procedural breaches by a defendant can result in summary judgment in favour of the plaintiff.

5.6.1 Summary judgment against defendants

Much of the discussion regarding summary disposition in relation to problem plaintiffs in Chapter 5.5 is equally applicable for problem defendants. Whereas innocent defendants obtain summary dismissal against unmeritorious plaintiffs, genuine plaintiffs generally obtain default judgment or summary judgment against problem defendants. The main difference between the two types of summary disposition relates to the enforcement or reversal of such judgments. In summary dismissal cases, the claims of the problem plaintiff are dismissed and can only be reinvigorated by the plaintiff reinstating proceedings (where it is not statute barred from so doing). The only enforcement proceedings in summary dismissal cases generally concern costs orders in favour of the defendant. Conversely, in summary judgment cases against defendants, the outcome is an enforceable judgment of the court which the plaintiff may seek to immediately enforce unless the defendant makes a successful application to have the default judgment set aside.

As with all forms of summary disposition, parties may apply to have a summary judgment set aside and most authoritative appellate level decisions on summary judgment therefore concern applications to set summary judgment aside. The Federal Court case of *Commissioner of Taxation v Bosanac (No 5)* held that a summary judgment in relation to a tax assessment of over $9 million was final in nature and should not be set aside even when there were errors in the underlying assessment. The summary judgment obtained by the plaintiff Commissioner against the defendant taxpayer was final in nature because there had been argument and evidence adduced and there was no policy or legal basis for setting it aside given the revised assessment required payment by Bosanac of an even greater sum than the summary judgment.[73]

The Full Federal Court decision of *Mogilevsky v Leroy (Trustee)* was an appeal from a Federal Circuit Court case and, therefore, concerned the *Federal Circuit Court of Australia Act 1999* (Cth) s 17A, which the Court noted is equivalent to s 31A of the *Federal Court of Australia Act 1976* (Cth) and therefore required the same analysis as *Spencer v Commonwealth* (discussed above).[74] However, Mr Mogilevsky was successful in the Full Federal Court in setting aside the Federal Circuit Court's summary judgment against his defence to bankruptcy despite the reduced requirement for granting summary disposition

---

73 *Commissioner of Taxation v Bosanac (No 5)* [2019] FCA 2126, [34], [40]-[41]. See Chapter 16 for detailed discussion on finality of decisions.

74 *Spencer v Commonwealth* (2010) 241 CLR 118.

and the difficulty inherent in his wife's having transferred assets to him in exchange for "natural love and affection". The Full Federal Court held:

> … [I]t seems to us that too great an onus was put on Mr Mogilevsky to prove all the facts on which he would rely in his defence if the matter went to trial. Notably, the terms of documents that he may well be required to subpoena and expert evidence he may be required to call as to the valuation of interests in property fall into this category. …
>
> It is not at all difficult to understand the scepticism which attaches to a transfer which is merely for "natural love and affection" in this context, but in this instance, with the considerable complexity of the multiple transactions, in our view, Mr Mogilevsky should have had the opportunity to put his position at trial or at least have the benefit of a further interlocutory process, including discovery. While the bar has been lowered in moving for summary judgment, in our view it has not been lowered to the point of rejecting summarily a case which may be arguable even though it appears to have substantial difficulties. …[75]

5.6.2 Default judgment

Many summary judgments, particularly in lower courts, against defendants are default judgments, which are findings for the plaintiff as a result of the defendant failing to defend the proceedings. Default judgments are easily made and relatively easy to set aside if the defendant subsequently realises that it has a good defence which should have been heard. The originating process of the plaintiff and supporting affidavits are usually sufficient to establish a prima facie case and, in the absence of any defence, the court is at liberty to conclude that the plaintiff should succeed. If it then becomes apparent that there is a proper defence to the claim, the court will generally wish to hear both parties to ensure compliance with the right to procedural fairness through due consideration of their case (see Chapter 2).

Although default judgment is easier to set aside than summary judgment, once default judgement has been entered, it will not be set aside simply because the defendant now wishes to file a defence. In order to set aside default judgment, the onus is on the defendant to explain the basis for the delay and establish the merits of its defence through an application to set aside the default judgment. In *National Australia Bank Ltd v McCann (No 2)*, Davies J in the Supreme Court of New South Wales dismissed Mrs McCann's third application to set aside default judgment on the basis that it was an abuse of process or, in the alternative, that Mrs McCann had failed to show that she had a defence on the merits. Justice Davies held that "no real effort has been made to deal with the issues clearly pointed out in the earlier judgment that resulted in the earlier application failing".[76] Davies J's decision was a tough decision to make against an unrepresented litigant who was in difficult financial circumstances, poor health and facing eviction from her home as a result of the proceedings which concerned mortgage documents with NAB.

The extraordinary case of *Attorney-General (SA) v Marmanidis* provides an excellent example of the procedural complexities which can arise from default judgment and attempts

75 *Mogilevsky v Leroy (Trustee)* [2017] FCAFC 52, [80]-[81] (McKerracher, Farrell and Markovic JJ).
76 *National Australia Bank Ltd v McCann (No 2)* [2010] NSWSC 1032, [56].

to set it aside. It also demonstrates the high volume of minor claims in lower courts and that approximately 50% of those claims result in default judgments which then result in applications to set aside in relation to approximately one-third of those default judgments.[77] A minor claim by Mr Germein, an IT specialist, against Dr Marmanidis, a psychiatrist, for $2,080 for damage to his car in a traffic incident, resulted in a default judgment in August 2013, eventually followed by enforcement action by the Sherriff's office changing the locks and advertising to auction Dr Marmanidis' Adelaide mansion in 2016 to pay the judgment debt. The day before the auction, Dr Marmanidis sought to set aside the default judgment and the judgment was stayed on condition that Dr Marmanidis paid into court $14,769 for the judgment, costs and interest (including the Sheriff's costs). The magistrate refused to set aside the default judgment and Dr Marmanidis then appealed to the Supreme Court which quashed the default judgment.[78] The Attorney-General then appealed the Supreme Court decision to the Full Court of the South Australian Supreme Court, which allowed the appeal and set aside the decision to quash the default judgment. The Full Court found numerous errors but also held that, given the small amount of the original dispute, finality was essential and reinstated the default judgment. The Court held:

> 213 To reiterate, the following conclusions are drawn from the above analysis:
>
> 1 liability judgment was properly entered by the Registrar pursuant to r 60(1) of the *Magistrates Court (Civil) Rules*;
>
> 2 judgment was properly entered by the Registrar with respect to the liquidated sum for property damage of $1,589.40, but not for the costs of the hire car of $490.91; this error was capable of correction under r 104 of the *Magistrates Court (Civil) Rules*;
>
> 3 the Magistrate was correct in declining to set aside the liability judgment, but incorrect in failing to set aside the unproven judgment for the hire car fees; the latter error was amenable to correction on both appellate and judicial review;
>
> 4 the review Judge erred in concluding that jurisdictional error resulted by reason of the Registrar's entry of liability judgment and in determining to grant orders for judicial review by failing to alert the parties to the issue and by failing to afford them the opportunity to be heard upon it as well as the extension of time required;
>
> 5 although the Magistrate's and the review Judge's conclusions that Dr Marmanidis did not have an arguable case on the merits were otherwise susceptible to correction on appellate (but not judicial review), there are findings that should not be disturbed.
>
> 214 It must be steadily borne in mind that the underlying proceedings involve a relatively minor claim resulting from a minor traffic accident and that such matters form a significant portion of the 'bread and butter' jurisdiction of the small claims jurisdiction in the Magistrates Court. Evidence submitted to the review Judge demonstrates that for the financial year 2013–2014, 21,549 minor civil claims were lodged in the Magistrates

77 See below *Attorney-General (SA) v Marmanidis* (2019) 132 SASR 320, [214]. These statistics are for South Australia but default judgments and applications to set them aside are also high in other states.

78 Dr Marmanidis' appeal was not competent but the Supreme Court allowed her to convert her appeal to an application for judicial review, which both parties agreed to do.

> Court, of which 11,762 became default judgments, of which 424 applications to set aside were lodged. For the financial year 2014–2015, there were 19,602 such claims of which 10,240 judgments were entered in default, 398 of which attracted applications set aside. For the financial year 2015–2016, there were 17,615 such claims, of which 9,413 were entered in default, of which there were 323 applications filed to set aside the default judgment.[79]

The *Marmanidis* dispute is also a reminder to litigants of the importance of not ignoring court correspondence and proceedings.[80]

5.6.3 Striking out defences

A default judgment is appropriate where there has been a failure to defend the case but, where a defence has been filed, summary judgment generally requires that defence to be struck out in order to award summary judgment. Accordingly, applications to strike out defences are not limited to cases where the defence itself is manifestly defective or an abuse of process. Courts may strike out a defence in order to dispose of that defence, in any circumstances where the actions (or inaction) of the defendant warrant summary judgment in favour of the plaintiff.

The Victorian Supreme Court case of *Hodgson v Amcor Ltd* before Vickery J (discussed in Chapter 2.5 in the context of litigation deterrents) concerned an application by Mr Hodgson to strike out the defence and counterclaim of Amcor "for its repeated and contumelious failure to comply with" directions to serve witness statements and the claim fixed for a trial as to damages only. Hodgson relied on the *Civil Procedure Act 2010* (Vic) which was introduced after the commencement of the original proceedings. Justice Vickery declined to strike out the defence or counterclaim of Amcor, accepting that the time taken to prepare the statements was inordinate because the delay had not caused any further interlocutory proceedings, or consequential delay and loss and was far from rendering a fair trial impossible.

Hodgson v Amcor confirmed the Court's power to strike out a defence because of delays in compliance with court orders rather than because the action could not possibly succeed. Justice Vickery set out the legal principles of summary dismissal for breaches of compliance, noting that the Victorian Supreme Court Rules empowered a court to strike out a defence for failure to comply with directions. Justice Vickery also discussed the Court's inherent power to summarily dispose of proceedings and discussed the scope of that power and the multiplicity of potential abuses of process concluding:

> Given the gravity and effect of a striking out order, it should only be made in a clear case where the exercise of the discretion properly calls for this to occur and when the sanction ordered is the least that is necessary to achieve the ends of appropriate case management. ...[81]

79 *Attorney-General (SA) v Marmanidis* (2019) 132 SASR 320, [213]-[214].

80 In the subsequent costs dispute, Dr Marmanidis was ordered to pay 50% of the appeal costs of both the Attorney General and Mr Germein: *Attorney-General (SA) v Marmanidis (No 2)* [2019] SASCFC 77, [22].

81 *Hodgson v Amcor Ltd* (2011) 32 VR 495, [68]-[100].

Summary judgment cases can be even more complex for plaintiffs where defendants have filed counterclaims, as the court must then consider whether to strike out the counter claim as well as the defence in awarding summary judgment for the plaintiff. The complexity this can engender is demonstrated in the Victorian Supreme Court of Appeal case of *De Saram v Brown* where the summary judgment for the plaintiff was upheld but defendant's counterclaim was reinstated on appeal having been initially struck out with the summary judgment application.[82]

5.7 Conclusion

Courts play an important role in managing CDR. As well as being final decision-makers, courts are also significant facilitators of ADR and important managers of disputant behaviour. The finite nature of court resources and the need to protect members of the public from unnecessary litigation mean courts must always look to ensure efficient use of court time, by maximising the appropriate use of ADR and summarily disposing of unmeritorious disputes. Summary disposition cases require judges to balance access to justice with protection of court processes, protection of litigants and public interest. Whether courts are attempting to control vexatious litigants or simply ensuring the rapid movement of straightforward default judgments through the court, summary disposition is an essential tool to ensure civil procedure remains fair and efficient. Summary disposition is also the way courts authoritatively and enforceably finalise court disputes which have been settled through ADR.

However, summary disposition cases also frequently involve difficult exercises of discretion in emotionally charged cases where one or more party almost inevitably leaves the litigation feeling somewhat dissatisfied with civil procedure. Whilst some degree of dissatisfaction may be inevitable, the care and skill which judges exercise in summary disposition cases is critical to ensuring public respect for the litigation system and the rule of law in Australia. Courts are ultimately the caretakers of Australia's CDR system and summary disposition cases demonstrate the importance of this role as well as the high level of interconnection between ADR and litigation.

82 *De Saram v Brown* [2015] VSCA 142, [150]-[152] (Digby AJA with Ashley and Tate JA agreeing).

6 LAWYERS, LEGAL COSTS AND THEIR ROLE IN CIVIL DISPUTE RESOLUTION

6.1 Introduction

Lawyers play a central role in civil dispute resolution (CDR). Due to the complexity and importance of law and legal process, it is strongly advisable for those involved in civil disputes to engage lawyers. However, the cost of resolving civil disputes is one of the most variable aspects of CDR. When disputants are represented by lawyers, legal costs can mount very quickly, making costs one of the most significant incentives to resolve disputes promptly and one of the largest deterrents to litigating. For an example of how expensive complex commercial litigation can become, it is estimated the Bell Litigation, accrued legal costs for the Western Australian government (and its taxpayers) of $328 million, representing almost half of its final settlement payout of $670 million. The final order of Master Sanderson, in the Supreme Court of Western Australia, was accompanied by the following extraordinary words:

> 1. These reasons are not so much a judgment as a requiem.
> 2. This was an application to terminate the winding up by Bell Group (UK) Holdings Ltd (In liq) (the company) of Western Interstate Pty Ltd. This was one of a group of companies around which what is known as the 'Bell litigation' swirled for 25 years.
> 3. Thousands of people worked on this case. Most have put the experience behind them and moved on; many, shattered by the experience, have retired; more than a few have gone mad. …
> 4. The trial involving this company, and others, lasted for 404 days between July 2003 and September 2006. The judgment took two years and ran to 2,643 pages. …
>
> …
>
> 8. It was tempting to drive a wooden stake through the heart of the company to ensure it does not rise zombie-like from the grave.[1]

Due to the complexity of law and legal process, self-represented litigants tend to do poorly and it remains advisable for disputants to hire lawyers where possible.[2] The question of who should pay legal costs and how much is therefore a significant aspect of CDR and a significant influencer as to whether to litigate or use ADR (see Chapter 2.5.2 for analysis of the impact of costs on litigation). This chapter will explore the role of lawyers in resolving legal disputes, focusing particularly on how their costs are dealt with by courts.

The laws and rules governing the professional obligations of lawyers, including the allocation of legal costs, vary between different Australian jurisdictions. This chapter will explain the different types of legal costs and discuss generally how courts deal with costs disputes between lawyers and their clients (solicitor-client costs). This chapter will also consider how courts allocate costs between parties in litigation (party-party costs and indemnity costs), including the important impact of settlement offers on costs consequences and the growing role of litigation funders. This chapter will also consider the use of costs

1 *Re Bell Group (UK) Holdings Ltd (in liq)* [2020] WASC 347. See *Bell Group Ltd (in liq) v Westpac Banking Corporation (No 9)* (2008) 39 WAR 1 for the original 2008 judgment of Owen J.

2 See Chapter 3.2 for analysis of the access to justice issues that prevent many disputants from obtaining representation. Refer to Chapter 5.5.4 (vexatious litigants) for extreme examples of the difficulties self-represented litigants can face when engaging with the courts.

as both a compensatory and deterrent mechanism, including in the context of interlocutory skirmishes and personal liability of legal practitioners for costs.

6.2 The role of lawyers and professional responsibility

Many civil disputants resent hiring lawyers to resolve their disputes. This is understandable given it is generally assumed that all members of society must understand the law sufficiently to abide by it and interact with it in their day-to-day activities. Ignorance of the law is rarely an acceptable excuse for wrongdoing and knowledge is assumed in our daily interactions with the law, such as the contracts we enter for our grocery shopping and our use of public transport. Needing a lawyer can, therefore, be a frustrating experience for disputants because it requires acknowledgment that the disputant's understanding of the law is inadequate to resolve their dispute. However, such frustration involves a false understanding of the law and its operation in society. For example, we all use plumbing in our daily lives by turning taps on and off, yet most of us do not hesitate to call a plumber when our plumbing fails. Just as plumbers are well paid for their expertise, so too lawyers deserve payment for the work they undertake in assisting clients in resolving civil disputes.

However, in recognition of the importance of law in society, law is a profession which demands particularly high standards from its participants and imposes fiduciary obligations on their interactions with clients. For the reasons discussed in Chapters 2 and 3, civil disputants are often particularly stressed and vulnerable in relation to their disputes and this complicates the relationship they have with their lawyers. Lawyers' professional obligations, including charging for services, are now largely governed by specific legislation. Additional obligations regarding dispute resolution and legal costs are imposed through civil procedure legislation, including express costs provisions.

This section will provide an overview of the obligations of lawyers to civil disputants focusing on legal costs, using the new *Legal Profession Uniform Law* (*LPUL*) as an example. *LPUL* currently only applies in New South Wales and Victoria but may, hopefully, be adopted in other Australian states in the future.

6.2.1 Legal profession legislation

Regulation of the legal profession in Australia is governed by state-based legislation, including the charging and documentation of legal costs. Until the turn of the 21st century, lawyers admitted to practice in one Australian state were not even entitled to practice in another state without undertaking an additional qualification process. Australian states now allow lawyers from other Australian states to practice pursuant to mutual recognition legislation, such as the *Legal Profession Uniform Law* (NSW) div 2 (ss 16–25) and the *Mutual Recognition (Western Australia) Act 2010* (WA).[3] Legislation governing legal professionals requires updating fairly frequently, as the needs of society and the nature of the profession change over time. All

3 This Act replaced the *Mutual Recognition (Western Australia) Act 2001* (WA).

Australian states currently have at least some legal profession legislation that is less than 20 years old and much Australian legal profession legislation is less than 10 years old.

There have been considerable attempts in the past decade to introduce uniform legal profession obligations throughout Australia, including the introduction of the *LPUL* by Victoria and New South Wales in 2014–15. Unfortunately, despite encouragement from New South Wales and Victoria for other states to adopt the *LPUL*, other states are yet to join.[4] However, in 2011, attempts to unify the legal profession have been much more successful in relation to solicitors' conduct and have resulted in the Australian Solicitors' Conduct Rules being adopted in South Australia, Queensland, Victoria, New South Wales and the Australian Capital Territory.[5]

6.2.1.1 Victoria and New South Wales: *Legal Profession Uniform Law*

The *Legal Profession Uniform Law* (*LPUL*) is hosted by Victoria and governs the legal profession in Victoria and New South Wales (which are the two most populous and dispute-ridden states in Australia).[6] The *LPUL* commenced on 1 July 2015 in New South Wales and Victoria and regulates all aspects of legal professional conduct including the charging of legal costs.

The *LPUL* created the Legal Services Council and the Office of the Commissioner for Uniform Legal Services Regulation (who is also CEO of the Legal Services Council) as additional regulatory bodies to oversee the uniform scheme. The *LPUL* is supported by Uniform Rules, created by the Legal Services Council, which provide operational details for the legislation. These Rules include General Rules, Legal Practice Rules and Conduct Rules, all of which impact the way in which legal costs are handled. The *LPUL* also allows complaints relating to costs to be submitted to the Commissioner for Uniform Legal Services Regulation. The Legal Services Council also oversees amendments to *LPUL*, such as through its *Consultation Paper On Proposed Amendments To The Legal Profession Uniform Law* in January 2020 which makes numerous recommendations for amendments to improve *LPUL*.

In New South Wales, lawyers' conduct is regulated through the *LPUL*, embodied in the following legislation:

- *Legal Profession Uniform Law (NSW)* (created pursuant to the *Legal Profession Uniform Law Application Act 2014* (NSW))
- *Legal Profession Uniform General Rules 2015* (NSW)
- *Legal Profession Uniform Law Australian Solicitors' Conduct Rules 2015* (NSW)
- *Legal Profession Uniform Continuing Professional Development (Solicitors) Rules 2015* (NSW)

4 Victoria, *Parliamentary Debates*, Legislative Assembly, 12 December 2013, 4662 (Robert Clarke); New South Wales, *Parliamentary Debates*, Legislative Assembly, 27 March 2014, 1458 (Greg Smith). It is noteworthy that the Law Society of Western Australia, after undertaking an extensive review, in 2014 recommended Western Australia should adopt the *LPUL*.

5 Agreement was reached in 2011 and amended in 2015 with the *LPUL* resulting in rules such as: *Australian Solicitors Conduct Rules 2012* (Qld); *Legal Profession Uniform Law Australian Solicitors' Conduct Rules 2015* (NSW); *Legal Profession (Solicitors) Conduct Rules 2015* (ACT). The Northern Territory has given consideration to joining, as has Tasmania: see, eg, Law Society Northern Territory, 'Review of the Australian Solicitors Conduct Rules' (Web Page, 9 February 2018) <https://lawsocietynt.asn.au/about-lsnt/news/765-review-of-the-australian-solicitors-conduct-rules.html>.

6 *LPUL* s 5(2).

- *Legal Profession Uniform Conduct (Barristers) Rules 2015* (NSW)
- *Legal Profession Uniform Continuing Professional Development (Barristers) Rules 2015* (NSW).

In Victoria, the legal profession is regulated through the following equivalent *LPUL* legislation:

- *Legal Profession Uniform Law (Vic)* (set out in sch 1 of the *Legal Profession Uniform Law Application Act 2014* (Vic))
- *Legal Profession Uniform General Rules 2015* (Vic)
- *Legal Profession Uniform Law Australian Solicitors' Conduct Rules 2015* (Vic)
- *Legal Profession Uniform Continuing Professional Development (Solicitors) Rules 2015* (Vic)
- *Legal Profession Uniform Conduct (Barristers) Rules 2015* (Vic)
- *Legal Profession Uniform Continuing Professional Development (Barristers) Rules 2015* (Vic).

The *LPUL* governs legal costs through ch 4 (Business Practice and Professional Conduct) pt 4.3 (Legal Costs). The fundamental legal costs obligation, in s 172 of the *LPUL*, provides that legal costs charged must be "no more than fair and reasonable in all the circumstances". Pursuant to s 172(2) of the *LPUL*, numerous factors are taken into account in assessing reasonableness including: the lawyers' skill, experience, specialisation and seniority, the complexity of the matter, the amount of work involved, the matter's specific circumstances (e.g. urgency), the quality of the work performed, the existence and contents of the retainer and the instructions provided.[7] Further matters a costs assessor may apply in determining what is "fair and reasonable", pursuant to s 200 of the *LPUL*, include compliance with the *LPUL* and interactions with the client such as disclosure and advertising. The New South Wales Supreme Court Case of *Arenas v Fica (No 3)* confirmed that the requirement for fairness and reasonableness overrides any contractual provision to the contrary.[8] In addition to fairness and reasonableness, s 173 of the *LPUL* also stipulates that law practices must not take unnecessary action or cause unnecessary delay that results in increased legal costs.

Other jurisdictions have similar requirements preventing lawyers from excessive charging. For example, ss 319 and 341 of the *Legal Profession Act 2007* (Qld) require cost assessors to consider fairness and reasonableness when assessing costs, and s 46 of sch 3 of the *Legal Practitioners Act 1981* (SA) requires the Supreme Court to consider fairness and reasonableness of costs in the context of costs recovery disputes.

6.2.1.2 Australian Capital Territory

In the Australian Capital Territory, the legal profession is governed by the following legislation:

- *Legal Profession Act 2006* (ACT)
- *Legal Profession Regulation 2007* (ACT)
- *Legal Profession (Solicitors) Conduct Rules 2015* (ACT).

Part 3.2 of the *Legal Profession Act 2006* (ACT) relates to cost disclosure and assessment.

7 *LPUL* s 200.

8 *Arenas v Fica (No 3)* [2018] NSWSC 385, [23]; *Legal Profession Uniform Law Application Act 2014* (NSW) s 184. See also *Johnston v Dimos Lawyers* (2019) 59 VR 16.

6.2.1.3 Queensland

In Queensland, the legal profession is governed by the following legislation:

- *Legal Profession Act 2007* (Qld)
- *Legal Profession Regulation 2017* (Qld)
- *Legal Profession (Society) Rules 2007* (Qld)
- *Australian Solicitors Conduct Rules 2012* (Qld)
- *Queensland Law Society Indemnity Rule 2005* (Qld)
- *Supreme Court (Admission) Rules 2004* (Qld)
- *Queensland Law Society Administration Rule 2005* (Qld).

Part 3.4 of the *Legal Profession Act 2007* (Qld) regulates costs disclosure and assessment.

6.2.1.4 Northern Territory

In the Northern Territory, the legal profession is governed by the following legislation:

- *Legal Profession Act 2006* (NT)
- *Rules of Professional Conduct and Practice 2005* (NT).

Part 3.3 of the *Legal Profession Act 2006* (NT) relates to costs, with s 341 detailing the criteria cost assessors must follow when conducting an assessment.

6.2.1.5 South Australia

In South Australia, the legal profession is governed by the following legislation:

- *Legal Practitioners Act 1981* (SA)
- *Legal Practitioners Disciplinary Tribunal Rules* (SA)
- *Legal Practitioners Regulations 2014* (SA)
- *Legal Practitioners Education and Administration Council Rules 2018* (SA)
- *Rules of Court (Legal Practitioners Act – Trust Accounts) 1939* (SA)
- *Australian Solicitors' Conduct Rules 2015* (SA).

6.2.1.6 Tasmania

In Tasmania, the legal profession is principally governed by the *Legal Profession Act 2007* (Tas), supported by rules and regulations as follows:

- *Legal Profession Act 2007* (Tas)
- *Legal Profession Regulations 2018* (Tas)
- *Legal Profession (Prescribed Authorities) Regulations 2018* (Tas)
- *Rules of Practice 1994* (Tas)
- *Law Society By-Laws 2010* (Tas)
- *Legal Profession Barrister Rules 2016*
- *Legal Profession Uniform Conduct (Barristers) Rules 2015*.

The *Legal Profession Act 2007* (Tas) sets out cost assessment criteria in s 327, with further provisions for costs disclosure and assessment in the Act and the *Legal Profession Regulations 2018* (Tas).

6.2.1.7 Western Australia

In Western Australia, the legal profession remains governed by the *Legal Profession Act 2008* (WA) despite the efforts of its law society to join the *LPUL*. The legislation governing Western Australian lawyers is:

- *Legal Profession Act 2008* (WA)
- *Legal Profession Regulations 2009* (WA)
- *Legal Profession Rules 2009* (WA)
- *Legal Profession (Admission) Rules 2009* (WA)
- *Legal Profession Conduct Rules 2009* (WA).

The charging of legal costs is principally addressed in pt 10 of the *Legal Profession Act 2008* (WA) ss 251–326, which regulates costs disclosures, costs agreements, the billing of costs and mechanisms for assessment and setting aside of costs.

6.2.1.8 Federal jurisdiction

All practicing lawyers must be admitted in one of the above states or territories and their professional obligations are governed by those states rather than by any federal legislation. However, costs orders awarded between parties are governed by Commonwealth legislation; for example, under s 43 *Federal Court of Australia Act 1976* (Cth). The Federal Court must grapple with the same issues regarding the appropriateness of costs as the state and territory courts.

However, the obligations on lawyers regarding charging costs do not necessarily prevent high legal costs. In the Federal Court case of *Money Max Int Pty Ltd (Trustee) v QBE Insurance Group Ltd*, the judge expressed concern as to the high costs, noting:

> Large, complex and strenuously defended class action litigation is notoriously expensive, but the $22,514,715.33 million estimate Maurice Blackburn provided for its costs and disbursements (costs) incurred and to be incurred in the proceeding was unusually high.[9]

However, following the report by an independent referrer, it was held that, despite the unusually high legal costs charged by Maurice Blackburn, the amount was fair and reasonable given the size and complexity of the class action matter. In a subsequent decision concerning settlement administration costs — *Money Max Int Pty Ltd (Trustee) v QBE Insurance Group Ltd (No 4)* — the Federal Court thanked Maurice Blackburn for voluntarily agreeing to charge only 45% of their actual costs.[10]

6.2.2 Reasonable prospects of success in litigation

Lawyers have obligations to both their clients and the courts not to pursue litigation, interlocutory applications or appeals where such proceedings do not have reasonable prospects of success. These obligations are often embodied in civil procedure legislation

9 *Money Max Int Pty Ltd (Trustee) v QBE Insurance Group Ltd* (2018) 358 ALR 382, [5].
10 *Money Max Int Pty Ltd (Trustee) v QBE Insurance Group Ltd (No 4)* [2018] FCA 2107, [11]–[13].

and/or legal profession legislation and are supported by judicial decision-making. This does not mean that lawyers must be persuaded that they will win in order to take a step in a court.

In some circumstances, the requirements for reasonable prospects of success are very low. For example, in New South Wales, a lawyer must not file a statement of claim or defence for a client if it does not reasonably believe the pleading has reasonable prospects of success.[11] In the New South Wales Court of Appeal decision of *Newell; Muriniti v De Costi*, the Court approved the earlier test:

> … 'without reasonable prospects of success' … equates its meaning with 'so lacking in merit or substance as to be not fairly arguable'. The concept is one that falls appreciably short of 'likely to succeed'.[12]

However, despite the relatively minimal requirements for reasonable prospects of success, the Court still found the solicitor, Mr Muriniti, to have breached this requirement resulting in a personal costs order against him. Consequent upon Mr Muriniti's repeated appeals and refusal to accept the costs order and the decision of his insurer, Law Cover, to pay the personal costs order on his behalf and not to appeal the decision, the New South Wales Court of Appeal directed the Registrar to forward the papers to the Legal Services Commissioner to investigate whether Mr Muriniti's conduct amounted to unsatisfactory professional conduct or professional misconduct.[13]

Requirements for reasonable prospects of success can also appear in specific legislation such as s 486I in pt 8B of the *Migration Act 1958* (Cth) which prevents a lawyer from commencing migration proceedings without certifying there are "reasonable grounds for believing that the migration litigation has a reasonable prospect of success" with the potential for adverse costs orders for failure in s 486F.[14] In *SZTOG v Minister for Immigration and Border Protection*, in dismissing the appellants appeal due to a complete absence of grounds for appeal, the Federal Court analyses the complex balance of public interest involved in pt 8B of the *Migration Act 1958* (Cth). There are competing public interests in pt 8B of the *Migration Act 1958* (Cth) because the court wishes to ensure lawyers do not commence unmeritorious litigation without unduly discouraging lawyers from representing clients, thereby increasing the, already high, numbers of self-represented migration litigants who pose an even greater drain on the courts' resources.[15]

Appeals must also have reasonable prospects of success and applications for leave to appeal, or for extensions of time to appeal, will fail if it is shown the underlying appeal does not have reasonable prospects of success. For example, in *Cleret v Rago*, the Supreme Court (Court of Appeal) of Queensland rejected an application for extension of time to appeal in a de facto separation property dispute, despite there being no prejudice from the

---

11 *Legal Profession Uniform Law Application Act 2014* (NSW) s 62, sch 2 cls 2, 4.

12 *Newell; Muriniti v De Costi* (2018) 97 NSWLR 398, [57] (Beazley P with Gleeson and White JJA agreeing). It should be noted that this case concerns the predecessor legislation to *Legal Profession Uniform Law Application Act 2014* (NSW) s 62 — the *Legal Profession Act 2004* (NSW) s 348 — but the relevant wording is identical as demonstrated by subsequent cases applying *Muriniti* to the new law, such as *Isobella Madeline Szczerbanik v Carnival plc* [2019] NSWDC 197, [12].

13 *Muriniti v King* [2019] NSWCA 232, [43] (Payne JA with McCallum JA and Simpson AJA agreeing).

14 *Migration Act 1958* (Cth) ss 486I(1), 486F.

15 *SZTOG v Minister for Immigration and Border Protection* [2018] FCA 112, [11]–[21].

delay, because the underlying appeal had no prospects of success.[16] In Western Australia, the Supreme Court (Court of Appeal) has jurisdiction to strike out a ground of appeal that has no reasonable prospects of success and dismiss an appeal where no grounds have reasonable prospects of success, pursuant to rr 43(2)(f) and 43(2)(g)(i) of the *Supreme Court (Court of Appeal) Rules 2005* (WA) respectively.[17]

6.2.3 Balancing competing interests for legal practitioners

Legal practitioners owe obligations to numerous people and, in CDR, it is not uncommon for these obligations to conflict. Just as the courts are faced with difficult balancing acts, discussed in Chapter 2, lawyers practicing CDR can have conflicts between their own best interests and those of their clients, and between their clients' best interests and those of the court (see also Chapter 2.5.2). In theory, these conflicts are easily solved: lawyers should put their clients' interests before their own, and the courts' interests before their clients' interest.[18] However, in practice, this is more difficult to achieve because sometimes conflicts are difficult for lawyers to appreciate. For example, it is easy for a lawyer to focus on how strong their client's case is and how much money the client would win by litigating rather than focusing on the legal costs (which the lawyer personally benefits from) and the emotional and time costs of the litigation for their client (see Chapter 2.5) which would be saved through ADR. This may lead a lawyer to undersell the benefits of ADR to their clients, thereby subconsciously placing their personal interests above those of their client by persuading their client to litigate.

It can also be challenging for lawyers to balance their obligations to the court and their clients and surprisingly easy to breach the paramount obligations to the court. For example, in the New South Wales Supreme Court of Appeal case of *Wollongong City Council v Papadopoulos*,[19] counsel for Wollongong Council failed to provide dates in response to an emailed court invitation to specify available dates to attend a further hearing and, instead, made short written submissions without leave. While there was no sanction against counsel, the Court found counsel effectively declined the opportunity to appear, meaning the City Council had not been denied procedural fairness, holding:

> It may be assumed that the view of the Council was that the hearing contemplated by the primary judge was inappropriate. But the occasion to make that submission was in open court, in the presence of the other side, not by unilateral written submission made without leave.

16 *Cleret v Rago* [2014] QCA 158, [14], [46].

17 It should be noted that the requirement for reasonable prospects of success is not limited to legally represented actions and unmeritorious appeals are more commenced by self-represented litigants; see, eg, *Stewart v Hames* [2020] WASCA 9.

18 The Australian Solicitors' Conduct Rules (introduced in Chapter 6.2.1) govern the obligations of most Australian solicitors and include r 3.1: "A solicitor's duty to the court and the administration of justice is paramount and prevails to the extent of inconsistency with any other duty"; and r 4.1: "A solicitor must also: 4.1.1 act in the best interests of a client in any matter in which the solicitor represents the client, 4.1.2 be honest and courteous in all dealings in the course of legal practice, 4.1.3 deliver legal services competently, diligently and as promptly as reasonably possible, 4.1.4 avoid any compromise to their integrity and professional independence, and 4.1.5 comply with these Rules and the law.": *Legal Profession Uniform Law Australian Solicitors' Conduct Rules 2015* (NSW). See also *D'Orta-Ekenaike v Victoria Legal Aid* (2005) 223 CLR 1, [26], [111].

19 *Wollongong City Council v Papadopoulos* [2019] NSWCA 178.

> Further, counsel's primary obligation was to assist the Court. That duty has long been described as 'paramount' or 'overriding'. In *Rondel v Worsley* [1969] 1 AC 191 at 227, Lord Reid said:
>
> > [Counsel] has an overriding duty to the court, to the standards of his profession, and to the public, which may and often does lead to a conflict with his client's wishes or with what the client thinks are his personal interests.
>
> The same principles are stated in *Giannarelli v Wraith* (1988) 165 CLR 543 at 555–556, 572; [1988] HCA 52, and *D'Orta-Ekenaike v Victoria Legal Aid* (2015) 223 CLR 1; [2005] HCA 12 at [111]. The same principles are reflected in the *Legal Profession Uniform Conduct (Barristers) Rules 2015*: see r 23, 'A barrister has an overriding duty to the court to act with independence in the interests of the administration of justice' and r 4(a), 'barristers owe their paramount duty to the administration of justice'.
>
> Counsel had an obligation to respond to the primary judge, and to do so promptly. He was required to do so even if he considered, or was instructed, that it was contrary to the interests of his client. ...[20]

A legal practitioner's paramount duty to the court can often involve acting contrary to the client's interests, as demonstrated by the examples set out by McHugh J in the much cited[21] High Court decision of *D'Orta-Ekenaike v Victoria Legal Aid*:

> The adversarial system of justice has its critics, many of whom claim that it hampers rather than helps the achievement of justice. But when all the consequences of the adversarial system are taken into account, the fact remains that the administration of justice, as now known, would be greatly impaired without the assistance of an independent Bar. Despite being in a relationship of confidence with a lay client, the first duty of the barrister is not to the client but to the court in which the barrister appears. The duty to the instructing solicitor or the lay client is secondary. Where the respective duties conflict, the duty to the court is paramount. That duty to the court imposes obligations on the barrister with which the barrister must comply even though to do so is contrary to the interests or wishes of the client. Thus, the barrister can do nothing that would obstruct the administration of justice by:
>
> - deceiving the court;
> - withholding information or documents that are required to be disclosed or produced under the rules concerned with discovery, interrogatories and subpoenas;
> - abusing the process of the court by preparing or arguing unmeritorious applications;
> - wasting the court's time by prolix or irrelevant arguments;
> - coaching clients or their witnesses as to the evidence they should give;
> - using dishonest or unfair means or tactics to hinder an opponent in the conduct of his or her case.
>
> Moreover, the advocate owes a duty to the court to inform it of legal authorities that 'bear one way or the other upon matters under debate'. The duty applies 'quite irrespective of whether or not the particular authority assists the party which is so aware of it'.

20 Ibid [52]–[54] (Leeming JA with Basten and McCallum JJA agreeing).
21 See, eg, *Clone Pty Ltd v Players Pty Ltd (in liq)* (2016) 127 SASR 1, [642] (Debelle JA).

> Thus, in many situations arising in the conduct of litigation, the common law requires an advocate to act contrary to the interests of his or her client. I doubt if there is any other profession where the common law requires a member of another profession to act contrary to the interests of that person's client. In some professions and callings, statutes now impose specific obligations on members to disclose information against the interests of the client. But advocacy is probably unique in imposing common law obligations on a professional person to act contrary to the interests of a lay client. This factor alone is probably sufficient to preclude reasoning by analogy from the liability of other professions and occupations for negligent conduct. But however that may be, two other factors show conclusively that it is in the public interest to give advocates an immunity from liability for in-court conduct and conduct intimately connected with in-court conduct. They are the difficulties of proof concerned with showing that, but for the advocate's carelessness, a different result would have ensued and the undermining of public confidence that would flow from inconsistent verdicts. It will be necessary at a later stage of this judgment to return to those matters.[22]

This extract demonstrates the variety and extent of the conflicts of interest in CDR between a lawyer's duty to court and their duty to the client. These conflicts are so common that it is a rare litigation where there is not some element of conflict between the interests of the court, the client, and the lawyer.[23]

6.2.4 Advocates' immunity from suit

Although the obligations of legal practitioners to the court and their clients are high, it is difficult for disgruntled CDR clients to sue their lawyers for professional negligence. This is due to the principle of advocate immunity which protects lawyers from being found negligent for errors made in court but not in relation to ADR processes. Disgruntled clients may, however, complain to the Legal Services Commission (as discussed in Chapter 6.2.6) where their lawyer has engaged in unprofessional conduct or professional misconduct.

Lawyers who make errors in the *course* of litigation generally cannot be sued for negligence pursuant to *D'Orta-Ekenaike v Victoria Legal Aid*.[24] However, in *Attwells v Jackson Lalic Lawyers Pty Ltd*[25] and *Kendirjian v Lepore*,[26] the High Court confirmed that advocate immunity does not extend to lawyer negligence in advising on settlement proceedings. However, the High Court refused the invitation in *Attwells v Jackson Lalic Lawyers Pty Ltd* to reconsider whether that immunity applied in decisions which influence judicial decision-making, effectively reinforcing the decision in *D'Orta-Ekenaike* that advocates could not be sued for their work in court.[27]

22 *D'Orta-Ekenaike v Victoria Legal Aid* (2005) 223 CLR 1, [111]–[113].

23 See Chapter 11, which focuses on providing discovery, is an area where it is particularly common for the interests of the client to conflict with the interests of the court. The obligations of the client and their lawyers is to provide documents to the opposing side some of which are likely to be deleterious to their own case, but which may be provided to court by their opponent to assist the court.

24 *D'Orta-Ekenaike v Victoria Legal Aid* (2005) 223 CLR 1, [111]–[113].

25 *Attwells v Jackson Lalic Lawyers Pty Ltd* (2016) 259 CLR 1.

26 *Kendirjian v Lepore* (2017) 259 CLR 275.

27 *Attwells v Jackson Lalic Lawyers Pty Ltd* (2016) 259 CLR 1; *D'Orta-Ekenaike v Victoria Legal Aid* (2005) 223 CLR 1.

The most recent High Court case on advocate immunity, *Kendirjian v Lepore*, concerned a claim by Mr Kendirjian against his solicitor, Mr Lepore, and barrister, Mr Conomos, in relation to the rejection of an offer of $600,000 plus costs to settle a motor vehicle accident claim where the Court only awarded $308,432.75 plus costs when the matter eventually proceeded to trial and judgment. The High Court held, in favour of Mr Kendirjian, that the primary judge had erred in summarily dismissing Mr Kendirjian's claim on the basis of advocates' immunity. Justice Edelman (with the rest of the High Court agreeing) held:

> Subsequent to the decisions of the primary judge and the Court of Appeal, this Court decided *Attwells v Jackson Lalic Lawyers Pty Ltd*. In *Attwells*, a majority of this Court held that the advocates' immunity from suit did not extend to negligent advice which leads to a compromise of litigation by agreement between the parties. As the majority joint judgment explained, by the same reasoning it is difficult to envisage how the immunity could ever extend to advice not to settle a case.[28]

It is worth noting that, when the matter finally returned to the District Court for a full hearing, nearly 20 years after the original injury, Mr Kendirjian's action against his lawyers failed. The Court preferred the evidence of the lawyers to that of Mr Kendirjian's finding that Mr Kendirjian had been informed of the $600,000 settlement offer and had chosen to reject it.[29]

However, the reasoning behind advocates immunity is important and logical. The immunity of advocates from suit is to protect the administration of justice not the negligent advocates. The basis for advocates' immunity resides in the principle of *res judicata* (discussed in Chapter 16) that a court should not redetermine a matter which is already finally determined. Were a litigator's actions to be reviewed for negligence causing loss, it would be necessary, in order to establish and quantify that loss, to determine how the previous substantive decision of the court would have differed but for the lawyer's negligence, thus proving the final substantive decision between the original disputants to be incorrect.[30] Such a finding would reopen the dispute between the original disputants (at least one of whom was not even party to the subsequent legal negligence litigation), bringing the administration of justice into disrepute.

However, although the basis for advocates' immunity is indisputable, the immunity does not encourage professionalism in litigators and can appear, to lay people, as unmerited favouritism towards lawyers compared to their clients and to other professionals who do not have any comparable immunity from being sued for negligence. Another unfortunate result of the current state of advocate immunity is that it, inadvertently, provides a disincentive for lawyers to engage to the fullest extent possible with ADR processes. However, this disadvantage is arguably outweighed by the importance of protecting the administration of justice from the disrepute and confusion by effectively relitigating aspects of finally resolved civil disputes.

6.2.5 Alternative dispute resolution incentives: case management obligations and pre-litigation protocols

The obligations of lawyers to their civil disputant clients include advising in relation to the most appropriate means of dispute resolution and running disputes efficiently. Where

28 *Kendirjian v Lepore* (2017) 259 CLR 275, [18].
29 *Kendirjian v Lepore* [2019] NSWDC 43, [66].
30 *Attwells v Jackson Lalic Lawyers Pty Ltd* (2016) 259 CLR 1, [32]–[37].

litigation has been commenced, poor advice (such as recommending a client dismiss a generous offer to settle) can result in adverse costs orders against clients and even against lawyers personally.[31] Adverse costs orders are an important tool through which courts can penalise litigation parties for failing to sufficiently engage with ADR.

In federal cases, where civil disputants have an obligation, through pre-litigation protocols,[32] to engage with ADR prior to commencing litigation, failing to do so can also result in adverse costs orders pursuant to s 12 of the *Civil Dispute Resolution Act 2011* (Cth).[33] However, even where there is legislated requirement for parties to engage with ADR, legal costs are strongly influenced by engagement with ADR. Parties who resolve their disputes through ADR generally incur significantly less costs than those who proceed to litigation. However, parties who succeed in litigation can commonly expect an order for the losing party to pay their costs (or a portion of them — see Chapter 6.5).

Case management provisions in civil procedure legislation have increased obligations on lawyers both to engage with ADR and to run litigation efficiently (see Chapter 2.4). Courts may order lawyers to bear the other side's legal costs or may disallow costs billed by a practitioner to their client (see Chapter 6.9).

The Victorian Supreme Court of Appeal case of *Yara Australia Pty Ltd v Oswal* held that the case management obligations imposed upon lawyers in Victoria overrode their duty to their clients and their obligation to comply with client instructions.[34] The solicitors for the applicant in *Yara* failed to comply with their overarching obligation to ensure costs are reasonable and proportionate by filing over 2700 pages of unnecessary or peripheral information and were ordered to indemnify their client for 50% of the costs owing to the other side and had 50% of their own costs relating to the application books disallowed.[35] Similarly, in *Harris v Villacare Pty Ltd*, the New South Wales Supreme Court ordered a solicitor to pay his client's costs, pursuant to s 99 of the *Civil Procedure Act*, for preparing an affidavit where Hulme J determined, the "vast bulk — of the order of 90% — of Mr Myles' affidavit was a waste of paper".[36]

6.2.6 Penalties for poor practice

Legal practitioners who breach their professional obligations to the court or their clients can be found guilty of unsatisfactory professional conduct or professional misconduct and may even be struck off the roll of practitioners. Professional misconduct is more serious than unsatisfactory professional conduct and can include repeated instances of unsatisfactory

31 See Chapter 6.8 and Chapter 5.2.

32 See Chapter 5.2.4.

33 It should be noted, however, that it is difficult to succeed in obtaining costs orders for failing to take necessary steps against solicitors as demonstrated by *Shape Shopfitters Pty Ltd v Shape Australia Pty Ltd (No 4)* [2017] FCA 1277, where indemnity costs were not ordered; and *Auss Metals Pty Ltd v Express Mobile Services Australia Pty Ltd* [2015] FCA 745, where the solicitors were protected by a settlement agreement between the parties because they were agents of a party.

34 *Yara Australia Pty Ltd v Oswal* (2013) 41 VR 302, [36].

35 Ibid [40], [61]. *Yara* has been cited in over 100 cases, including the Federal Court decision of *Petersen Superannuation Fund Pty Ltd v Bank of Queensland Ltd (No 3)* (2018) 132 ACSR 258, [132]; and Victorian Court of Appeal decisions such as *Trailer Trash Franchise Systems Pty Ltd v GM Fascia & Gutter Pty Ltd* [2017] VSCA 293.

36 *Harris v Villacare Pty Ltd* [2012] NSWSC 452, [31].

professional conduct. As occurred in several cases referred to above, solicitors can also be made personally liable to pay adverse costs orders or have their own costs disallowed and this is discussed in Chapter 6.9.3.

The Australian Capital Territory Supreme Court of Appeal decision in *Legal Practitioner v Council of the Law Society (ACT)* provides excellent examples of professional misconduct and unsatisfactory professional conduct as well as the circumstances in which a solicitor may be struck off the roll of practitioners.[37] The Legal Practitioner, who was the unsuccessful appellant, had failed to properly effect a sale of property for his client, failed to promptly reply to correspondence, mistakenly sent the wrong documentation, misrepresented the events, and then essentially threatened to blackmail his client as a means of discouraging the client reporting the matter to the Law Society. His failures in relation to complying with his correspondence obligations and failing to produce the correct documentation were unsatisfactory professional conduct. He was also found to have engaged in misleading conduct by misrepresenting to his client the correspondence he had received from the other party, and threatening and intimidating conduct by threatening to inform his client's employer that his client had been working on the sale during work hours.[38] It was the misrepresentations and the threatening conduct which constituted the more serious breach of professional misconduct.

6.3 Nature of legal costs orders

For the vast majority of civil disputes not involving litigation, the parties bear their own costs of the dispute and there are no discussions or disputes as to costs. In the rare varieties of ADR where costs disputes do arise, such as international commercial arbitration, costs decisions are usually made by the arbitrator in much the same way as courts make costs decisions. Accordingly, cost dispute cases almost invariably focus on litigation costs. However, as discussed in Chapter 6.8, costs decisions are, themselves, often influenced by the ADR undertaken by the parties where rejected settlement offers are taken into consideration when awarding costs.

Orders by courts in relation to legal costs in litigation are discretionary and there is a wide range of factors the courts may consider. However, the factors for consideration relate to the dispute itself, how successful each disputant was, and the running of the dispute. The court's discretion to order costs does not focus on the external circumstances of the litigant, such as their capacity to pay or their comprehension of court processes when commencing litigation.

In the High Court decision of *Foots v Southern Cross Mine Management Pty Ltd*, the joint majority judgment of Gleeson CJ, Gummow, Hayne and Crennan JJ (with Kirby J dissenting) held that an indemnity costs order made after a declaration of bankruptcy was not a provable

37 *Legal Practitioner v Council of the Law Society (ACT)* (2018) 335 FLR 116. It should be noted that this case was decided pursuant to the previous Solicitors Rules (*Legal Profession (Solicitors) Rules 2006* (ACT)) rather than the current, more uniform, *ACT Legal Profession (Solicitors) Conduct Rules 2015* (ACT) discussed in Chapter 6.2.1.

38 *Legal Practitioner v Council of the Law Society (ACT)* (2018) 335 FLR 116, [21]. The ACAT findings of professional misconduct and unsatisfactory professional conduct were upheld by the primary judge and the Court of Appeal upheld the primary judge's findings.

debt at the time of bankruptcy and, accordingly, the bankrupt party was still liable for the debt. *Foots* case was an appeal from the Queensland Supreme Court of Appeal. The High Court also relied on its own decision in *Oshlack v Richmond River Council*,[39] which was an appeal from the New South Wales Supreme Court of Appeal and remains a leading authority in the role of judicial discretion in awarding costs. In defining the nature of costs orders, the High Court emphasised the discretionary nature of the Court's power to award costs, and the fact that the monetary value of a costs order, while capable of estimation, cannot be finally determined without assessment or taxation.[40]

What is meant by the term "legal costs" or "costs" varies depending on the context in which the term is used. There are two main contexts in which the term "costs" is used. The first is the costs payable by clients to their lawyers, known as "solicitor-client costs" (discussed at Chapter 6.4). The second, and more common, context is where one party is ordered to pay another's costs, *inter partes* (meaning between parties), known as "party-party costs" (discussed at Chapter 6.5). Litigation regarding costs is usually either a dispute between clients and their solicitors as to how much is payable for services rendered or a dispute between parties as to which party should be responsible for payment of the other's legal costs or, most commonly, in what amount.

In *Northern Territory v Sangare*, the High Court held impecuniosity did not protect against an adverse costs order in the context of an impecunious appellant running a wholly unsuccessful defamation case. Kiefel CJ, Bell, Gageler, Keane and Nettle JJ discussed the parameters of the Court's costs discretion in party-party disputes, holding:

> It is well established that the power to award costs is a discretionary power, but that it is a power that must be exercised judicially, by reference only to considerations relevant to its exercise and upon facts connected with or leading up to the litigation. While the width of the discretion 'cannot be narrowed by a legal rule devised by the court to control its exercise', the formulation of principles according to which the discretion should be exercised does not 'constitute a fetter upon the discretion not intended by the legislature'. Rather, the formulation of principles to guide the exercise of the discretion avoids arbitrariness and serves the need for consistency that is an essential aspect of the exercise of judicial power.
>
> A guiding principle by reference to which the discretion is to be exercised — indeed, 'one of the most, if not the most, important' principle — is that the successful party is generally entitled to his or her costs by way of indemnity against the expense of litigation that should not, in justice, have been visited upon that party. The application of that principle may be modified or displaced where there is conduct on the part of the successful party in relation to the conduct of the litigation that would justify a different outcome. For example, a successful defendant may be refused its costs on the ground that its conduct induced the plaintiff to believe that he or she had a good cause of action. But in the present case, there was nothing of this kind in the conduct of the appellant in relation to the litigation that might have weighed against

39 *Oshlack v Richmond River Council* (1998) 193 CLR 72.

40 *Foots v Southern Cross Mine Management Pty Ltd* (2007) 234 CLR 52, [25]–[28]. The analysis in *Foots* has been endorsed in many subsequent cases, such as the Full Federal Court in *Central Queensland Development Corporation Pty Ltd v Sunstruct Pty Ltd* (2015) 231 FCR 17, [66]–[67].

the exercise of the discretion in its favour. There was no suggestion of any conduct on the part of the appellant, whether by unreasonable delay or a want of the cooperation required of litigants to ensure the 'just resolution of the real issues in civil proceedings with minimum delay and expense', that might have been taken into account to justify refusing the appellant an order for its costs.[41]

6.4 Solicitor-client costs

The relationship between lawyers and their clients is complicated and involves contract law, trust law and the law of professional obligations. Beneath this complexity, lawyers essentially provide a service to clients in exchange for money. When clients retain solicitors, they enter into a contract whereby they agree to pay fees in consideration for services rendered. In most cases, lawyers will send their clients an invoice which the clients then pay. If clients are unhappy with the amount of the invoice, a dispute arises which may eventually reach a court. It is the costs charged by a lawyer to their client which are described by courts as solicitor-client costs.

Traditionally, solicitor-client costs were based on common law but there are now statutory provisions restricting how much and for what solicitors are entitled to charge in a growing variety of circumstances. The fee rate and method of determining the fees payable is agreed upfront in a contract, usually in writing, between the lawyer and the client. There are numerous methods by which lawyers calculate fees discussed further below. Fees may also be incurred using a mixture of the methods below as agreed between lawyers and their clients.

Solicitor-client costs are, themselves, frequently a source of civil disputes for a number of reasons:

1. CDR is inherently costly and time-consuming for the reasons discussed in Chapter 2.
2. Clients, except for those very experienced in CDR, almost invariably believe that dispute resolution should be quicker and cheaper than it is. This is commonly because their comprehension of the processes discussed throughout this book is, understandably, insufficient for them to realise how much they do not know about what may be involved in resolving their dispute.
3. As this book demonstrates, the variety of possible procedures necessary to resolve a civil dispute is considerable and it is impossible for lawyers to accurately foretell the future so as to predict how most civil disputes will progress and what each future aspect of the dispute will cost. Some of the most unpredictable features of CDR for lawyers drafting costs agreements are:
   - whether (and at what point) parties will settle the dispute and how many types of ADR might be engaged to achieve settlement (see Chapters 4 and 5)
   - if the matter proceeds to litigation, how many interlocutory disputes might be raised, what might be the behaviour of opposing parties, what role might technology play, might any aspect of the case be summarily disposed of and will parties accept judgment or seek to appeal (see Chapters 5, 10 and 16)

41 *Northern Territory v Sangare* (2019) 265 CLR 164, [24]–[25].

- how much relevant evidence each party possesses and how long it might take to extract that evidence and to provide it to other parties/ADR practitioners/ court including determining issues of privilege (see Chapters 11, 12, 13, 14 and 15).

The above uncertainties and common client misconceptions make entering costs agreements and invoicing clients some of the most challenging and unpleasant tasks CDR lawyers undertake.

6.4.1 Time-based costing

In Australia, probably the most common method of calculating legal fees, particularly for CDR services, remains time-based costing. Time-based costing involves charging for time incurred multiplied by an agreed rate for that time. For example, a lawyer may charge an hourly rate (disclosed to the client in advance) with each time unit charged equating to six minutes, representing one-tenth of an hour. Time-based costing means the more time lawyers spend running a case, the higher the fees payable by the clients for that case.

There are several disadvantages for clients of time-based costing. Essentially, the clients, rather than their lawyers, bear the risk of the case proving complex and expensive to run although this is something over which they may have little control. Time-based costing gives lawyers a disincentive to be efficient in their work, as they are paid more for inefficient work than efficient work. It should be noted, however, that clients have the right to dispute the number of hours spent on tasks and agreed time discounts are common in the CDR industry.

One strong advantage of time-based costing is that it encourages clients to use ADR which is quicker and cheaper.[42] Another advantage of time-based costing is that, provided lawyers comply with their professional obligations to their clients, including obligations of efficiency and acting in the clients' best interests (see Chapter 6.2), time-based costing should minimise the costs charged to clients.

6.4.2 Task-based and fixed-fee costing

Lawyers may also charge a set amount per task, with total fees varying depending on what tasks the dispute calls for. Task-based costing is more common in high volume disputes where lawyers manage large numbers of files, requiring similar tasks many of which may be semi-automated or performed by non-legally qualified or junior staff.

An increasingly popular method of calculating costs is a fixed-fee method where the clients and lawyers agree on a fixed amount for a matter or stages in a matter. A key advantage to clients of this method of charging costs is that the lawyers bear the risk of the case proving complex and expensive to run. The key disadvantage is that the clients bear the risk that the lawyers will cut corners or overlook tasks to improve profits or to prevent losses where a matter has proved more complex than predicted.

42 Subject to their lawyers persuading them otherwise due to the disincentives for the lawyer discussed above.

6.4.3 Costs scales

Some courts and tribunals require solicitors to charge costs in accordance with a published scale for litigation. Scale-based costing is essentially a form of task-based or fixed-fee costing whereby solicitors are expected to charge only a particular amount for a given task or step in the proceedings. Scale-based costing assists with the affordability of litigation and increases litigant knowledge as to likely future costs. Unfortunately, unless the scale is updated frequently and rigorously, scaled costs tend to fall below market rates for equivalent legal services. This increases the risk of solicitors taking shortcuts with the work they undertake and tends to reduce the number of the solicitors who are interested in undertaking scale-based work. Courts can also award less than 100% of an agreed scale, such as occurred in *Champions Lawyers v Rohrt* where the Court awarded 65% of the Victorian Supreme Court Scale.[43]

6.4.4 No-win no-fee

In some circumstances, it is acceptable for solicitors to contract only to charge clients in the event their cases are successful. Such no-win no-fee costs arrangements are most commonly offered in high volume civil dispute areas affecting individuals, such as transport accident and workplace injury. Personal injury victims often have no money to pay lawyers and little or no dispute resolution experience, making no-win no-fee costs arrangements often their only feasible means of obtaining legal representation. In such cases, legal fees are usually charged at a premium (eg a 25% uplift on normal rates: see *Batrouney v Forster*[44] discussed at Chapter 6.9.1) for the cases which succeed to compensate the lawyers for carrying the risk of receiving no payment for loss cases and to compensate for the delay between the time the lawyers commence work and the time they receive payment (which may be many months or even years) later.[45] No-win no-fee costs agreements do not usually protect clients from potential adverse costs orders (see Chapter 6.5.1) and the clients are also likely to be required to pay disbursements (see Chapter 6.4.5). Representative actions (class actions) are another area where no-win no-fee arrangements are common, with litigation funders usually prepared to cover adverse costs orders as well as only charging litigants where they are successful (see Chapter 6.10).

6.4.5 Disbursements

Most legal invoices will also include a component for disbursements. Disbursements are expenses which have been incurred by the lawyers in undertaking work for their clients and for which the lawyers seek to be reimbursed. Where the client is on a fixed-fee arrangement, disbursements may fall within the fixed fee and therefore not be separately itemised. Expenses incurred by solicitors on behalf of their clients can be very substantial.

43 *Champions Lawyers v Rohrt* [2018] VSC 400.
44 *Batrouney v Forster* [2016] VSCA 80.
45 See, eg, *Legal Profession Act 2007* (Qld) s 324 which provides a maximum 25% uplift, and s 325 which confirms that the fees charged must not be calculated by reference to the amount of the award for the dispute.

The highest cost expenses on legal invoices are often third-party services, such as barrister fees, expert witness fees and mediator fees, which can amount to hundreds of thousands of dollars in complex litigation. Where possible, lawyers contract to pass these third-party expenses directly to their clients, rather than paying them personally and seeking reimbursement. Court filing fees, printing, copying and technology services can also amount to considerable sums.

6.4.6 Trust accounts

Another important responsibility lawyers have in relation to costs involves holding client money on trust. Lawyers have very high professional responsibilities in relation to the management of their trust accounts and must ensure they keep trust account money separate from general funds and only spend such funds in accordance with client instructions. In *Legal Services Board v Gillespie-Jones*,[46] the High Court held that money paid by a client to his solicitor for legal costs, including barristers' costs which the solicitor had misappropriated, had not been held on trust for the barrister because the barrister was a debtor of the solicitor not the client due to the contractual arrangements between the parties. This case demonstrates the complexity of the laws surrounding trust moneys, which are generally held on trust for the client but may also be held on trust to pay third parties where that is the client's instruction.

6.4.7 Interest on costs

Lawyers are entitled to charge interest on unpaid legal costs but the rates at which they are allowed to charge are regulated by legislation; for example, in New South Wales, s 195 of the *Legal Profession Uniform Law 2014* (NSW) and r 75 of the *Legal Profession Uniform General Rules 2015* (NSW) govern the charging of interest on unpaid costs by solicitors.[47]

6.5 Party-party costs

When a court makes an award for one party to pay another party's costs, these are known as *inter partes* costs or party-party costs. Party-party costs are statute-based and, as discussed above, often involve significant court discretion. Legal costs of litigation can exceed the value of the dispute and, in such cases, the allocation of costs can be more significant than the outcome of the litigation.

Party-party costs are usually assessed on an "ordinary basis" or "standard basis" which amounts to less than the total solicitor-client costs charged.[48] When a lawyer renders an invoice for costs to his client, the amount payable is often significantly more than the amount a court is prepared award against the other party to litigation pursuant to a costs

46 *Legal Services Board v Gillespie-Jones* (2013) 249 CLR 493.

47 *Legal Profession Uniform Law Application Act 2014 (NSW)* s 195; *Legal Profession Uniform General Rules 2015* (NSW) r 75. The Victorian law is uniform with New South Wales. Similarly, Queensland regulates the charging of interest through s 321 of the *Legal Profession Act 2007* (Qld).

48 See, eg, *Uniform Civil Procedure Rules 1999* (Qld) r 702 for "standard basis".

order following judgment; that is, a party ordered to pay another party's costs does not usually pay 100% of that other party's legal costs. Party-party costs assessed on an ordinary basis are most commonly 60–70% of the total legal costs incurred by a party.

Courts can, however, make adverse costs orders between parties calculated on an indemnity basis (see Chapter 6.5.3), a solicitor-client basis, or in accordance with a published scale of costs. Hence, cases concerning allocation of costs between parties can also involve calculations of "solicitor-client" costs.

Determining who should pay the legal costs of running litigation and how much is a matter in which judges often have considerable discretion. Costs are most commonly awarded at judgment or following judgment, although interlocutory costs orders are increasingly common. The most common costs award is costs in the cause (the losers pay their own costs and also pay the winner's costs). The amount of party-party costs payable is generally agreed between the parties or assessed by a costs assessor.

6.5.1 Adverse costs orders

An adverse costs order is an order requiring a party or lawyer to pay the costs of another party. "Costs in the cause" (discussed at Chapter 6.5.2) is the most common example of an adverse costs order which requires the losing party to pay the legal costs of the winning party. "Adverse costs orders" include those against lawyers (discussed at Chapter 6.9.3). Courts generally have broad discretion concerning the award of costs and can allocate costs in the way they consider most fair. The most common factors which effect costs awards are:

- which party succeeds in the substantive dispute
- the circumstances and amount of any settlement offers (discussed in Chapter 6.8)
- the behaviour of the parties and their legal representatives during the dispute.

In *Council of the Law Society of New South Wales v Hislop*,[49] the New South Wales Court of Appeal discussed which discretionary factors New South Wales courts should consider when awarding adverse costs orders and confirmed that these factors only extend to matters connected with the dispute. In this matter, both parties agreed that a solicitor convicted of aggravated robbery should have his name removed from the roll but the solicitor's lawyers argued that the Court should not make an adverse cost order against him given the tragic events of the lawyer's life, the lack of an alternative to the proceedings and the solicitor's cooperativeness throughout the trial. The judges acknowledged that an adverse cost order would serve as an impediment to the solicitor's rehabilitation. Despite these factors, however, Bell ACJ and Barrett AJA (Brereton JA dissenting) awarded costs against Mr Hislop, noting:

> As much as one may sympathise with Mr Hislop and hope that he may in due course rehabilitate himself, those considerations do not provide any secure basis for departing from the prima facie course laid down by r 42.1 of the Uniform Civil Procedure Rules 2005 (NSW). Departure is, in general, warranted only if matters connected with the litigation itself and the course it has taken provide good reason to deprive the

49 *Council of the Law Society of New South Wales v Hislop* [2019] NSWCA 302.

> successful party of the whole or some part of that party's costs. It is well established that impecuniosity of an unsuccessful party and inability to pay do not, of themselves, provide any sound basis for departing from the general rule. Neither, in my opinion, does the fact that life has dealt harshly with the unsuccessful party and that he may be thought deserving of an opportunity to attempt to make a fresh start.[50]

6.5.2 Costs in the cause

The most common award of costs is "cost in the cause," also commonly called "costs follow the event". Costs in the cause means the loser pays the legal costs of the winner. The justification behind costs in the cause is hypothetical assumption that all parties knew, or ought to have known, from the outset of the litigation what the court would eventually decide. The loss of the case demonstrates that party should not have proceeded with the case and should therefore be required to pay all the legal costs. If a plaintiff's claim fails, then the court is saying its claim was not meritorious, hence the plaintiff should not have brought the claim and should bear the costs. If a plaintiff's claim succeeds, then the defendant should have acceded to the plaintiff's claim rather than defending the matter, so it should pay costs. In reality, cases often involve errors by multiple parties, issues which all parties wish the court to determine, and sometimes monetary awards which represent a compromise between the positions of the parties. The allocation of costs becomes more complex, for example, where the plaintiff succeeds but for a significantly lesser sum than claimed.

The Western Australian Supreme Court costs decision of *Computer Accounting and Tax Pty Ltd v Professional Services of Australia Pty Ltd*, and the subsequent appellate costs decision of *Professional Services of Australia Pty Ltd v Computer Accounting & Tax Pty Ltd (No 2)* demonstrate the level of complexity that can arise in costs allocations including, sometimes, issues in dispute needing to be separated for the purposes of allocating costs.[51] These costs decisions led to further appeals where the Court then had to decide on cost orders for the costs hearings, as well as for freezing and ancillary orders that were subsequently made (to enable enforcement of the costs orders) and an application for indemnity costs.[52]

Similarly, the New South Wales Supreme Court decision in *Owners of Strata Plan 17719 v Arcidiacono (No 2)* involved numerous issues which can cause courts to alter the general rule of costs in the cause, including a partially successful plaintiff, a new cause of action introduced after the trial's commencement being the basis upon which the plaintiff succeeded, questions as to the necessity of expert evidence, and peremptory party behaviour. The Court ordered the defendants to pay 50% of the plaintiff's costs assessed on an ordinary basis calculated "as a matter of discretion and in a broad-brushed and impressionistic manner".[53] The Court

50 *Council of the Law Society of New South Wales v Hislop* [2019] NSWCA 302, [66].

51 *Computer Accounting and Tax Pty Ltd v Professional Services of Australia Pty Ltd* [2008] WASC 133; *Professional Services of Australia Pty Ltd v Computer Accounting and Tax Pty Ltd (No 2)* [2009] WASCA 183.

52 See, eg, *Frigger v Professional Services of Australia Pty Ltd (No 3)* [2014] WASCA 69; *Frigger v Kitay (No 2)* [2017] WASCA 139.

53 *Owners of Strata Plan 17719 v Arcidiacono (No 2)* [2019] NSWSC 1800, [51].

analysed the New South Wales position as follows, relying on key High Court and New South Wales Court of Appeal authorities:

> 17 The power to award costs is a matter within the discretion of the Court. That discretion is a broad one which must be exercised judicially having regard to the circumstances of the case: *Civil Procedure Act 2005* (NSW), s 98(1)(a); *Oshlack v Richmond River Council* (1998) 193 CLR 72; [1998] HCA 11 (Oshlack), at [134].
>
> 18 The usual rule is that costs follow the event, unless it appears that some other order should be made: Uniform Civil Procedure Rules 2005 (NSW), r 42.1.
>
> 19 While an unsuccessful party typically bears the liability for costs, there is no absolute rule with respect to the exercise of the Court's discretion. A successful party has no right to an order for costs and there may be special circumstances, such as the conduct of the successful party, which justify not making a costs order in accordance with the usual rule: *Oshlack*, at [67], [69] and [134].
>
> 20 Generally, the Court will award costs to a successful party without seeking to apportion costs between the issues on which it has been successful and those on which it has failed, although it may be appropriate to do so if a particular issue or group of issues is 'clearly dominant or separable': *Doppstadt Australia Pty Ltd v Lovick & Son Developments Pty Ltd (No 2)* [2014] NSWCA 219 at [14]–[19]; *Bostik Australia Pty Ltd v Liddiard (No 2)* [2009] NSWCA 304 at [38].
>
> 21 The question of apportionment of costs is very much a matter of discretion, and mathematical precision is illusory. The exercise of the discretion depends on matters of impression and evaluation: *James v Surf Road Nominees Pty Ltd (No 2)* [2005] NSWCA 296 at [36], citing *Dodds Family Investments Pty Ltd v Lane Industries Pty Ltd* (1993) 26 IPR 261; *Macquarie International Health Clinic Pty Ltd v Sydney South West Area Health Service (No 2)* [2011] NSWCA 171 at [22].[54]

6.5.3 *Inter partes* costs assessed on indemnity or solicitor-client basis

Costs awarded between parties are not always awarded on the ordinary party-party costs basis, as this still results in a significant shortfall for the successful party between costs incurred and costs reimbursed by the losing party. Indemnity costs may be awarded against a party who has behaved inappropriately to compensate the party inconvenienced or prejudiced by another's inappropriate actions and to punish and deter against the inappropriate conduct. Indemnity costs are usually close to the entire invoiced legal costs (the solicitor-client costs) of the other party.

In the Western Australian Supreme Court case of *Currie v Currie (No 3)*, Le Miere J recognised that an indemnity cost order may be made if a party persists in a defence when they know or ought to have known it was hopeless (see also Chapter 5.4), where they engage in misconduct in connection with litigation that results in unnecessary costs (eg if a party is unable to explain a failure to discover an important document) as well as where a party unreasonably rejects a settlement offer (see Chapter 6.8).[55]

54 *Owners of Strata Plan 17719 v Arcidiacono (No 2)* [2019] NSWSC 1800, [17]–[21].
55 *Currie v Currie (No 3)* [2018] WASC 306, [6]–[9].

Indemnity costs should roughly equate to the actual costs paid by the party in whose favour costs order is made. In *Macquarie International Health Clinic Pty Ltd v Sydney South West Area Health Service (No 2)*, Hodgson J, with whom Allsop P and Macfarlan J agreed, stated:

> 36. In my opinion, solicitor and own client costs are not identical with indemnity costs: in some respects, they could be somewhat more generous and in other respects possibly somewhat less so. However, in my opinion they closely approximate indemnity costs, rather than party and party costs. ...[56]

6.5.4 Costs assessment (taxation of costs)

Party-party costs must generally be agreed between the parties or assessed, whether on an ordinary party-party, indemnity or other basis. In order to ensure that opposing parties are not liable for unreasonable costs, courts will often order that costs are payable as assessed. Cost assessment is undertaken by costs assessors who are usually themselves lawyers and can be court employees such as registrars. The process of assessing costs involves reviewing itemised solicitors' invoices and determining which costs are properly payable and in what amount. Costs assessment is also commonly referred to as "taxation". A taxed bill of costs is the bill of costs rendered by the costs assessor. Parties do not always agree with the costs assessment and this can result in further litigation regarding the costs payable, such as occurred in the Full Federal Court case of *Cassimatis v Australian Securities and Investments Commission* which involved a costs dispute following proceedings by ASIC in relation to the Storm Financial Limited collapse.[57]

6.5.5 Parties bear their own costs

A common alternative to an award of costs in the cause is a determination that each party should bear its own costs. Where this award is made, there is no complex process of assessing and allocating costs. Rather, each party pays their own lawyers, and no one is responsible for anyone else's costs. There may, in such cases, be some shared costs, such as mediator expenses, but these are usually pre-determined and agreed so do not cause distress. In many of the tribunals discussed in Chapter 7.2, and in an increasing number of specialist courts and lower courts, the default position is for parties to bear their own costs unless the court or tribunal determines otherwise due to specific circumstances. An order for parties to bear their own costs is essentially the same as making no order in relation to costs. Courts also sometimes specifically state that they make "no order as to costs".

6.5.6 Costs orders do not cover self-represented litigants' time

Self-represented litigant may have costs awarded in their favour but, unfortunately, this only covers their out-of-pocket expenses and not the value of their time spent acting on their own behalf. Until recently, there was an exception to this rule for lawyers who represented

56 *Macquarie International Health Clinic Pty Ltd v Sydney South West Area Health Service (No 2)* [2011] NSWCA 171, [36].

57 *Cassimnatis v Australian Securities and Investments Commission* (2016) 334 ALR 350.

themselves: the *Chorley* exception.[58] However, following the High Court decision in *Bell Lawyers Pty Ltd v Pentelow*,[59] in which a barrister sought costs for representing herself in a costs recovery action against a solicitor's firm, the *Chorley* exception is no longer part of the Australian common law and all lawyers incurring costs on their own behalf are now unable to recover those costs when acting as self-represented litigants. The plurality (Kiefel CJ, Bell, Keane and Gordon JJ) in *Pentelow* stated:

> As a general rule, a self-represented litigant may not obtain any recompense for the value of his or her time spent in litigation. ...
>
> ... the Chorley exception is not only anomalous, it is an affront to the fundamental value of equality of all persons before the law. It cannot be justified by the considerations of policy said to support it. Accordingly, it should not be recognised as part of the common law of Australia.[60]

The Queensland Supreme Court decision of *Equititrust Ltd (recs and mgrs apptd) (in liq) v Tucker* confirmed that *Pentelow* extended to solicitors (not merely barristers) and that there was nothing in the relevant Queensland civil procedure legislation which would provide any solicitor with a positive right to costs such as might enable payment despite the removal of the common law *Chorley* entitlement. The Queensland Supreme Court in *Equititrust* stated:

> [22] The High Court has decided the *Chorley* exception is not part of the common law of Australia. It follows that the exception — which might have entitled a solicitor acting for himself or herself to recover costs of their own attendances — is not part of the law. The interpretation of the relevant statutory provisions and rules proceeds without any such exception. This puts Mr Tucker in the same position as any other self-represented litigant. The decision did not affect the making of costs orders, but did affect the assessment of costs the subject of such orders.[61]

6.5.7 Evaluating costs orders

Consideration of costs orders raises many of the key themes of CDR raised in Chapter 2. Costs orders raise issues regarding balancing certainty with judicial discretion because costs are one of the most discretionary areas of judicial reasoning. Costs order also raise important considerations for the balance between efficiency and fairness. An award of costs in the cause (costs follow the event) is more complex than parties bearing their own costs. Costs in the cause has greater potential to cause dispute between the parties. Where parties bear their own costs, significant time and effort in agreeing or assessing costs may be saved by both parties. Where there is a presumption, in a particular court or tribunal, that parties will bear their own costs, this increases the certainty and reduces the potential costs exposure for all litigants and increases the efficiency of the costs determination process.

58 Named after the 1884 United Kingdom decision: *London Scottish Benefit Society v Chorley* (1884) 13 QBD 872.

59 *Bell Lawyers Pty Ltd v Pentelow* (2019) 372 ALR 555.

60 Ibid [1], [3].

61 *Equititrust Ltd (recs and mgrs apptd) (in liq) v Tucker* [2019] QSC 308, [22].

Figure 6.1 Costs decision tree

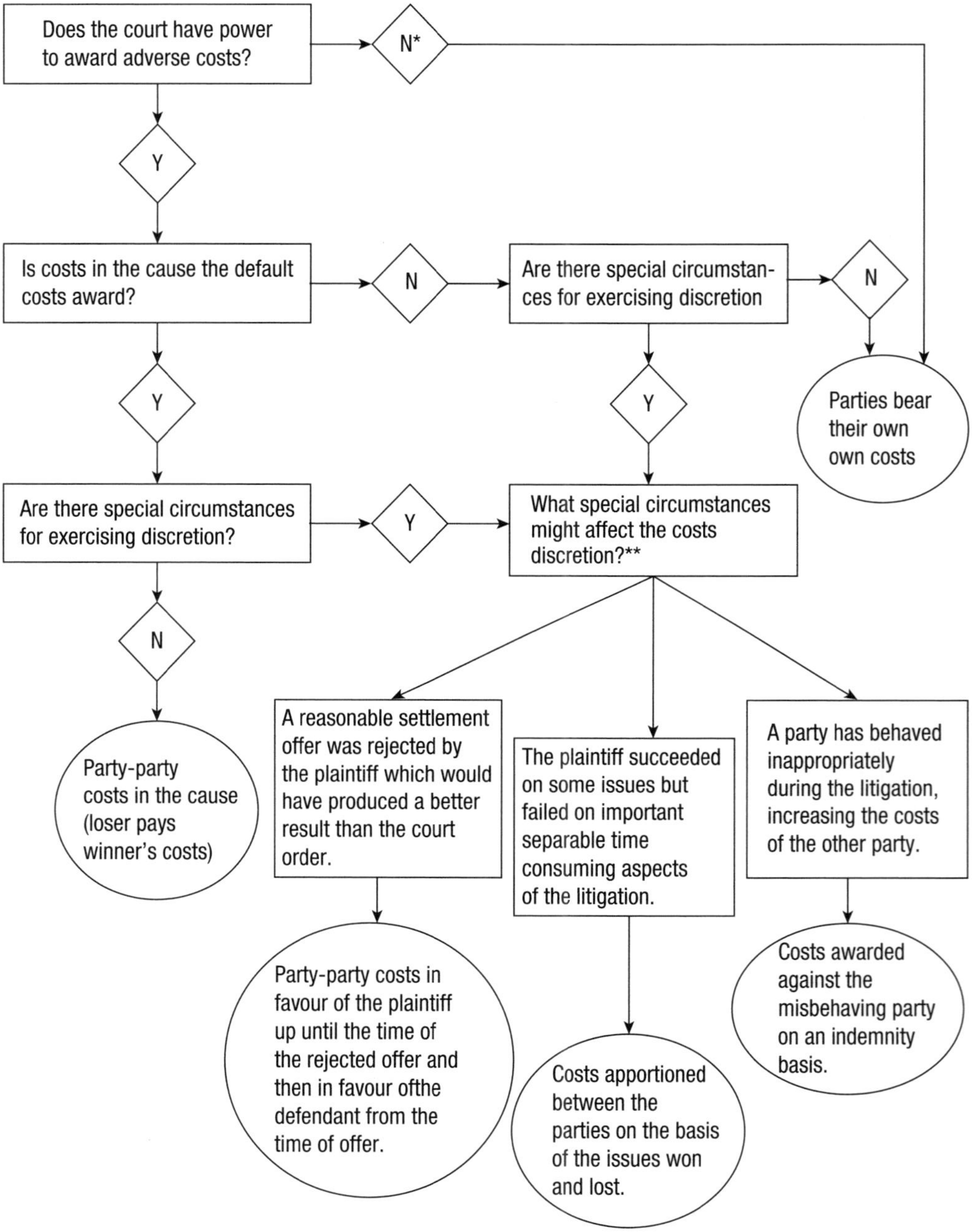

*This is rare. Courts almost always have some discretion as to awarding costs.

**The examples above are by no means exhaustive of the special circumstances which may affect judges' discretion or the ways in which judges may exercise their discretion in attempting to fairly allocate costs.

On the other hand, the ability to make adverse costs orders enables courts to use costs orders and the threat of costs orders as a tool to encourage parties, and their legal counsel, to comply with overarching civil procedure obligations to run matters properly and efficiently. Adverse costs orders can be the only compliance tool for courts other than the summary dismissal procedures discussed in Chapters 5.4 to 5.6. In addition, there is considerable logic behind the theory that it is more equitable for losers to be required to pay the costs of the winning party and adverse costs orders are a significant deterrent against commencing unmeritorious or purely tactical litigation. The risk of protracted costs disputes may be outweighed by the value of encouraging model litigant behaviour through the threat of adverse costs orders.

6.6 Costs for interlocutory proceedings

When judgment is given on an interlocutory dispute, costs are often reserved until judgment on the substantive dispute. Judges will, however, sometimes award costs in relation to an interlocutory application immediately, particularly where the interlocutory application was in some way inappropriate. Costs awarded in interlocutory decisions are a means for the court to impose control over the behaviour of the parties and encourage compliance with case management objectives of efficiency and justice.[62] Where judges feel parties have engaged in inappropriate practices, adverse interlocutory costs orders provide a disincentive to continue such behaviour without jeopardising the substantive rights of the parties the way summary disposition does.[63]

When adverse costs are awarded in interlocutory proceedings, they will sometimes be payable forthwith (immediately). However, it is more common for interlocutory costs orders to be reserved for assessment upon completion of the dispute. In this way, if there are numerous interlocutory skirmishes, with costs going in both directions, these can be offset against each other and the final costs award upon completion of the dispute. In *Young v Cooke (No 2)*,[64] which concerned forthwith orders and security for costs (see Chapter 6.7), the New South Wales Supreme Court set out in detail the general principles of costs orders and held, in relation to their timing:

> [28] Costs orders in relation to interlocutory applications are generally not to be paid until the conclusion of the proceedings 'unless the court orders otherwise': r 42.7 of the UCPR. However, the court may order that interlocutory costs be payable forthwith: *Solarus Products v Vero Insurance (No 4)* [2013] NSWSC 1012; *Fiduciary Ltd v Morningstar Research Pty Ltd* (2004) 208 ALR 564 ('Fiduciary No 1') at [171]–[173]; *Australian Securities and Investments Commission v Rich* [2003] NSWSC 297. The question is one of time of enforcement of the costs order. The court must take into account whether the costs in question should be determined prior to the conclusion of litigation, or whether one occasion of enforcement of costs orders at the end of a case, with costs orders going different ways being set off, is preferable: *Richards v Kadian (No 2)* [2005] NSWCA 373 at [7].
>
> . . .

62 See Chapter 2.
63 See Chapter 5.
64 *Young v Cooke (No 2)* [2018] NSWSC 1787.

> [31] The decision in Fiduciary No 2 also concerned the jurisdiction of the Court to order that costs be payable forthwith and the relevant factors to be considered. Barrett J identified three relevant factors, which may be summarised as:
>
> (1) the subject matter of the interlocutory application is discrete and self-contained making it a suitable vehicle for a separate order for costs;
>
> (2) whether some of the conduct of the unsuccessful party to the motion may be seen as being unreasonable; and
>
> (3) that there is still some considerable distance to go in the litigation so that it may be appropriate that the successful party obtain the fruits of its costs order now.[65]

Sometimes reserved interlocutory costs orders are subsequently vacated as it becomes apparent to the court that the costs order is no longer appropriate. Reserved interlocutory costs orders can, however, create difficulties for parties where proceedings are discontinued. In *Ashby v Slipper*[66], Mr Ashby had discontinued proceedings without a formal agreement as to what should happen with an earlier interlocutory indemnity costs order. Mr Slipper successfully sought to have the earlier costs order vacated and Mr Ashby unsuccessfully appealed the court's decision. The Full Federal Court (Mansfield, Siopis and Gilmour JJ) held that:

> The fact of the proposed discontinuance of the principal proceeding is not of itself a reason why, or a premise upon which, the discontinuing party should normally not be entitled to retain the benefit of prior interlocutory costs orders, as Jessup J decided in *Fastlane*. It is neither appropriate nor useful to endeavour to stipulate the circumstances in which that might be the case. Clearly, *O'Neill* was one such case. Equally, we do not consider that there should be a predisposition by the operation of the Rules themselves that existing interlocutory orders for costs should be preserved when leave to discontinue the proceeding is sought by their beneficiary, and the Court is required to fix the terms on which leave to discontinue is given.
>
> The proper approach is to address the justice of the case in the particular circumstances.
>
> The primary judge at [27], has in fact considered how he should exercise his discretion in accordance with "basic notions of fairness". That is an unexceptionable approach.[67]

However, *Rozenblit v Vainer* ('*Rozenblit*')[68] confirms that courts should be very careful when making interlocutory costs orders immediately payable if such orders will prevent the proceedings continuing. In *Rozenblit*, the High Court held that proceedings should not have been stayed purely on the basis that an order for immediate payment of interlocutory costs had not been met due to the impecuniosity of the plaintiff. The behaviour of the plaintiff leading to the adverse interlocutory costs orders was not vexatious in *Rozenblit* and the trial judge was aware that the stay until payment would result in the plaintiff being unable to pursue his case. Therefore, Gordon and Edelman JJ held:

65 Ibid [28], [31].

66 *Ashby v Slipper* (2016) 241 FCR 55. This case is discussed in Chapter 5.4.2.

67 Ibid [84]–[86].

68 *Rozenblit v Vainer* (2018) 262 CLR 478.

> In this case, the grant of the stay has prevented Mr Rozenblit from pursuing a claim honestly made. There were insufficient grounds for such an order. The result was not the only fair and practical way to ensure justice between the parties.[69]

6.7 Security for costs

Security for costs is a statutory mechanism whereby a plaintiff is required to provide the court with security (commonly money paid into the court's trust account) against a possible adverse costs order. This protects the defendant from spending funds in successfully defending a claim but then failing to recover these funds even where there is a costs order in their favour but the plaintiff is impecunious. The main purpose of security for costs is to prevent plaintiff companies with limited liability from divesting their assets and then being unable to pay an adverse costs order. All Australian states have security for costs provisions in their civil procedure Acts or Supreme Court rules; however, the terms of the provisions vary. In addition, s 1335 of the *Corporations Act 2001* (Cth) empowers courts to order security for costs from corporations.

Security for costs is, however, difficult to obtain, particularly against individual plaintiffs, because it has the potential to limit access to justice by stultifying the claim (preventing the plaintiff from continuing due to lack of funds). Parties with excellent claims should not be prevented from obtaining justice from the court simply because they would not be able to pay the other side's costs if they lost due to impecuniosity (lack of money). Therefore, requiring plaintiffs to pay in advance when they are known not to have the means to do so is a denial of access to justice.[70] As the cases discussed below demonstrate, determining security for costs applications is a discretionary exercise dependent on the individual circumstances of the case and requiring judges to balance numerous competing factors.

For example, although courts try to protect impecunious plaintiffs from security for costs orders to enable access to justice, courts will make security for costs orders against impecunious individual plaintiffs in appeal cases with no reasonable prospects of success, particularly where the impecuniosity is not caused by the subject of the litigation. For example, in *Michos v Eastbrooke Medical Centre Pty Ltd,*[71] Mr Michos sought to appeal a VCAT decision in relation to his unsuccessful complaint against the Transport Accident Commission (TAC) for not making it easier for him to obtain the report of a psychiatrist in a TAC claim.[72] The Victorian Court of Appeal held:

> 76 In the light of the above considerations, in particular, the impecuniosity of the applicant and the low prospects of success on appeal, an order for security is justified. We are fortified in this view when consideration is given to the overarching purpose in the CPA. The applicant has not only had his 'day' in court, he has consumed an entirely disproportionate amount of private funds and public resources, particularly

69 Ibid [113]. The remaining High Court judges (Kiefel and Bell JJ, [35] and Keane J, [50]) agreed with the orders proposed by Gordon and Edelman JJ.

70 See Chapter 3.

71 *Michos v Eastbrooke Medical Centre Pty Ltd* [2019] VSC 282.

72 VCAT is the Victorian Civil and Administrative Tribunal, discussed in Chapter 16.

> when weighed against any prejudice he might have suffered having obtained his report on the very same day he requested it.[73]

Applications for security for costs orders must be made on a timely basis but the relevance of delay will depend on demonstrating prejudice as a result of that delay and such prejudice cannot be automatically assumed. Recent cases have, arguably, weakened the power of delay as a basis for refusing security for costs orders in both the New South Wales Supreme Court of Appeal and the Victorian Supreme Court of Appeal. In *United Commercial Projects Pty Ltd v PHHH Investments No 2 Pty Ltd*, the appeal was allowed to enable a security for costs application as it was held that the primary judge had erred in not allowing a late application for security for costs because there was no evidence of prejudice to the other party from the delay, and the Victorian Court of Appeal cited its New South Wales counterpart:

> In our opinion, delay will invariably be a relevant discretionary factor in any application for security for costs, but the degree or extent of its relevance will vary according to the circumstances of any given case along a spectrum from the slight to the extreme.[74]

In *PPK Willoughby Pty Ltd v Baird*, leave to appeal against an order in favour of security for costs was refused by the New South Wales Court of Appeal which also discussed other key considerations for courts exercising security for costs orders, including the potential for such orders to stultify proceedings and whether impecuniosity preventing payment of security was caused by the defendant's actions:

> In this latter context, the Applicant has not established that it would suffer any substantial injustice if leave were not granted: *CBX2 Pty Ltd v National Australia Bank Ltd* [2016] NSWCA 79 at [29]. Indeed, we see no injustice whatsoever in the grant of security for costs in the present case. Neither at first instance nor on this application was there any suggestion that the orders for security for costs would stultify or stifle the litigation, and even if that were the effect of the orders, that would not be determinative: *Live Board Holdings Ltd v Cody Live Pty Ltd* [2017] NSWCA 302 at [91]–[96].
>
> Nor is this a case where there is any suggestion that the conduct impugned in the principal proceedings was in any way causative of the impecuniosity of the Applicant for leave to appeal. The impecuniosity was caused by what the primary judge referred to as the Plaintiff's 'business model', namely withdrawing the proceeds of sale of various properties that had been developed from the company's accounts over time. That was the prerogative of the Plaintiff's directors but it does not generate an injustice that should result in either the Plaintiff being free to conduct expensive commercial litigation insulated from the risks of an adverse costs order or the Defendants being deprived of the security which the primary judge, in the exercise of his discretion, saw fit to order.[75]

73 *Michos v Eastbrooke Medical Centre Pty Ltd* [2019] VSCA 282, [76]. See also *Faris v Savage* [2019] ACTSC 94, [13]; *Hughes v Janrule Pty Ltd* (2011) 252 FLR 397. The lack of underlying merit of an appeal is an important factor in determining security for costs where a plaintiff has already had the opportunity to be heard in court and lost that initial hearing.

74 *PPK Willoughby Pty Ltd v Baird* [2019] NSWCA 48, 11] (Bell P and Simpson AJA). Cited with approval by Whelan JA in *United Commercial Projects Pty Ltd v PHHH Investments No 2 Pty Ltd* [2019] VSCA 192, [37], [39].

75 *PPK Willoughby Pty Ltd v Baird* [2019] NSWCA 48, [20]–[21] (Bell P and Simpson AJA).

Once a security for costs order has been made, it must also be complied with in a timely fashion but, in the case of *Bodycorp Repairers Pty Ltd v Maisano*, the Victorian Supreme Court of Appeal granted an extension of time to provide security of costs of nearly a year where the parties had been negotiating to settle and, had negotiations succeeded, the security for costs would have been rendered unnecessary.[76]

6.8 Effect of settlement offers on costs

Settlement offers are almost invariably expressed to be "without prejudice except as to costs."[77] This means that courts cannot see or be influenced by them when determining the substantive dispute but can consider them when exercising their discretion to award costs.[78] Settlement offers most commonly take the form of a formal Offer of Compromise in accordance with statutory rules or an informal Calderbank offer (named after the case of *Calderbank v Calderbank*).[79] The law regarding the requirements and effect of settlement offers on costs varies somewhat between different Australian jurisdictions.

The existence and quantum of settlement offers can have a significant impact on the allocation of costs. This is a logical extension of the principle that the unsuccessful party is proved wrong by the court and should therefore pay costs. Where a party has success in court but remains worse off than it would have been had it accepted a settlement offer, the existence of that settlement offer will adversely affect the costs awarded to that party for its success in court. This is because it can no longer be suggested that the offeror was in the wrong in continuing with the proceedings. Instead, the recipient of the offer was unreasonable in not accepting the offeror's generous offer. Had the offeree accepted the settlement offer, it would have been better off than under the court's award. Hence, from the time the offeree refused (or failed to accept) the offer which, in hindsight, it should have accepted, it will be liable for the costs of proceedings commonly at an indemnity level.

The Federal Court case of *Harcourts WA Pty Ltd v Roy Weston Nominees Pty Ltd (No 6)* was a costs dispute arising from a trademark case which discussed the impact of settlement offers on costs including Offers of Compromise and Calderbank offers culminating in the following costs order:

> Save for the costs order dated 6 December 2012, the Respondent/Cross-Claimant pay to the Applicant/Cross-Respondent costs of the action:
> (a) up to and including 30 June 2014 on a party-party basis, and
> (b) from and after 1 July 2014 on an indemnity basis but so that such costs not include costs of an unreasonable amount or costs which have been unreasonably incurred.
> ...

76 *Bodycorp Repairers Pty Ltd v Maisano* [2019] VSCA 187, [51].
77 See, eg, *Smith v Gould* [2014] VSCA 138, [156]; *Saba v Plumb* [2017] NSWSC 622; *Fordyce v Fordham (No 2)* [2006] NSWCA 362; *Linville Holdings Pty Ltd v Fraser Coast Regional Council (No 2)* [2018] QSC 62.
78 See Chapter 13.6 for further information regarding settlement privilege.
79 *Calderbank v Calderbank* [1975] 3 WLR 586.

> The Applicant pay to the Respondent costs of the action:
> (a) up to and including 30 June 2014 on a party-party basis, and
> (b) from and after 1 July 2014 90% of the Respondent's costs on an indemnity basis but so that such costs not include costs of an unreasonable amount or costs which have been unreasonably incurred.
> Note: Entry of orders is dealt with in Rule 39.32 of the Federal Court Rules 2011.[80]

The Federal Court in *Harcourts* analysed the admissibility of evidence regarding the settlement offers, concluding all the settlement offers were admissible including an offer which reiterated an offer made at mediation.[81] The Court also considered the circumstances in which indemnity cost can be ordered as a result of rejected settlement offers including differentiating between formal Offers of Compromise under the *Federal Court of Australia Act 1976* (Cth) and Calderbank letters as follows:

> Whether there has been an imprudent refusal of an offer to compromise is relevant to the question of indemnity costs: *Colgate Palmolive Co v Cussons Pty Ltd* [1993] FCA 536; (1993) 46 FCR 225 (at 233) per Sheppard J, cited more recently in *Finishing Services Pty Ltd v Lactos Fresh Pty Ltd* [2007] FCAFC 15 per Kiefel, Sundberg and Edmonds JJ (at [4]). It is well established that parties may make offers pursuant to the Federal Court Rules 2011 (Cth) or pursuant to common law principles in relation to Calderbank letters: *Australian Postal Corporation v Digital Post Australia Pty Ltd (No 3)* [2012] FCA 1049 per Marshall J (at [16]).
>
> The considerations relevant to an application for indemnity costs following a Calderbank offer were recently summarised in *Veda Advantage Limited v Malouf Group Enterprises Pty Limited (No 2)* [2016] FCA 470 per Katzmann J (at [31]):
>
> In contrast, however, to an offer of compromise made under r 25.01, refusal to accept an offer not made in compliance with the rules (a Calderbank offer, see *Calderbank v Calderbank* [1975] 3 All ER 333) does not give rise to any presumption in favour of the offeror. The offeror needs to show that there was a genuine offer of compromise, and that it was unreasonable for the offeree not to accept it: *Black v Lipovac* at [217]–[218]. In deciding whether it is unreasonable for an offer to be rejected, the following matters should ordinarily be considered:
>
> - the stage of the proceeding when the offer was made;
> - the time afforded to the offeree to consider the offer;
> - the extent of compromise involved;
> - the offeree's prospects of success, assessed as at the date of the offer;
> - the clarity with which the terms of the offer were expressed;
> - whether the offer foreshadowed an application for indemnity costs in the event of refusal.
>
> See *Hazeldene's Chicken Farm Pty Ltd v Victorian WorkCover Authority (No 2)* [2005] VSCA 298; (2005) 13 VR 435 at [25].[82]

The Federal Court case of *Bayer Pharma Aktiengesellschaft v Generic Health Pty Ltd*[83] provides a straightforward example where the rejection of a genuine, reasonable Offer

80 *Harcourts WA Pty Ltd v Roy Weston Nominees Pty Ltd (No 6)* [2016] FCA 1492, [1].
81 Ibid [62]–[66].
82 Ibid [17]–[18].
83 *Bayer Pharma Aktiengesellschaft v Generic Health Pty Ltd* [2017] FCA 428.

of Compromise by Bayer to accept payment of $19 million in damages was better for the defendant than the $25 million awarded to Bayer by the Court, leading to an indemnity costs award for Bayer against Generic for costs incurred after the offer.

The law concerning the impact of settlement offers on costs can also be influenced by specific legislation, such as s 40 the *Defamation Act 2005* (Qld) (and its counterparts in other states) which impose a positive obligation on a defendant to attempt to settle. Following a defamation dispute, in which Senator Hanson-Young was found to have been defamed by Senator Leyonhjelm, the Federal Court awarded indemnity costs in favour of Senator Hanson-Young. In *Hanson-Young v Leyonhjelm (No 5)*, the Federal Court noted the need to consider all relevant circumstances in finding that Senator Leyonhjelm had sought "complete capitulation" rather than making any offer, thus unreasonably failing to make a settlement offer.[84]

6.9 Lawyers' rights and obligations regarding costs

The complexity of costs and the difficulties they create for civil disputants have led to complex and significant obligations for lawyers when charging fees, recovering those fees, and managing their role in disputes so as to prevent any party incurring unnecessary costs. There are obligations imposed on lawyers regarding notification, charging, and recovery of legal costs, particularly when a client changes lawyers in the middle of a dispute. The ability of courts to award costs against lawyers personally is a powerful incentive for lawyers to comply efficiently with CDR procedures.

The relationship between lawyers and their clients is a fiduciary relationship meaning that lawyers have special obligations to their clients beyond ordinary contractual obligations due to the trust placed in lawyers by their clients. Lawyers have three types of obligations towards clients which affect how they charge and recover costs:

1. Contractual obligations
2. Fiduciary obligations
3. Professional obligations.

These three areas of obligation overlap significantly. For example, a lawyer's professional obligations may require the lawyer to fully disclose their fiduciary obligations to clients in their costs agreement and may require them to contract with their client in a way which ensures protection of the client's best interests in satisfaction of the lawyers' professional obligations (see also Chapter 6.2).

6.9.1 Lawyers' costs disclosure obligations

Lawyers have significant professional and legislative obligations to inform clients regarding legal costs. These obligations are particularly onerous in CDR due to its uncertain nature. At the commencement of a dispute, it is usually impossible for a lawyer to predict how complex the dispute will be, whether it is likely to settle through ADR or require a court trial,

84 *Hanson-Young v Leyonhjelm (No 5)* [2020] FCA 34, [42], [57], [72].

how the other side will behave, how many interlocutory proceedings might be involved if the dispute proceeds to court, or even the likely scope of litigation steps such as discovery.

In addition, civil dispute lawyers should attempt to estimate the costs of other parties for which their client may become liable if unsuccessful. This is even more uncertain given the actions of the other parties' and their lawyers are often largely unknown.

To ensure compliance with regulations, it is increasingly necessary for civil dispute lawyers to repeatedly revise estimates, with such revisions proving time-consuming and unable to be charged to clients. Courts, legislators and lawyers are engaged in an uneasy balancing act between trying to maximise client understanding of legal costs exposure without overburdening the legal profession by requiring the preparation of endless useless guesstimates of future costs.

Even in no-win no-fee arrangements, where no estimates are required, the costs agreement obligations are significant, as demonstrated in the *Batroumeny v Forster* dispute. Litigation in relation to the receivership of Mr Forster's law firm provides a detailed analysis of Victorian costs disclosure obligations and evidence of their use in *Batrouney v Forster*.[85] In the late 1990s, Mr Forster acted on a no-win no-fee with a 25% uplift basis for victims of the collision between the HMAS Voyager and the HMAS Melbourne in 1964, but had issues with managing disbursements from his trust accounts consistently with his costs agreements, such that his practice was put into receivership. *Batrouney v Forster* was successfully appealed by the receivers in the Victorian Court of Appeal, in *Batrouney v Forster* in 2016,[86] but there was no attempt to appeal the trial judge's finding that Mr Forster had likely properly provided all clients with costs agreements as was his practice.[87] The *Batrouney v Forster* cases demonstrate the complex balancing act for the Court, weighing up evidence of Mr Forster's costs agreements and allocations as compared to the required professional standards.

6.9.2 Solicitors' liens

There are also laws which assist lawyers to recover costs from clients, such as the possessory lien, known as the "solicitor's lien", which operates over client files, or money held in the solicitor's trust account, where clients have unpaid invoices. The solicitor's lien over client files becomes significant where a client changes solicitor mid-dispute and instructs its former solicitor to transfer files to a new solicitor. The solicitor may refuse to hand the files over until all outstanding fees have been paid. Where a dispute has reached litigation, courts seek to facilitate continuation of existing litigation while simultaneously protecting the former solicitor's lien. This can sometimes be achieved by agreement or by security arrangements involving the court.

In the Supreme Court of New South Wales case of *Great Wall Resources Pty Ltd (in liq) v Davidovic Pty Ltd*,[88] Macready AJ held that security paid into Court by a plaintiff in exchange for a former solicitor handing files to a new solicitor did not amount to a secured judgment

85 *Batrouney v Forster* [2015] VSC 230, [458]–[757].

86 *Batrouney v Forster* [2016] VSCA 80.

87 It was noted in a subsequent costs appeal that Mr Forster had succeeded on that aspect of his defence: *Batrouney and Lyle v Forster (No 2)* [2016] VSCA 131, [13]–[14].

88 *Great Wall Resources Pty Ltd (in liq) v Davidovic Pty Ltd* (2011) 255 FLR 422.

debt for the former solicitors. In considering the nature of solicitor's liens, Macready AsJ stated:

> 25. … In characterising the nature of the interest which Lewis & McKinnon had, it is necessary to recognise that the authorities recognise two distinct classes of solicitors' lien:
>
> (a) First, the 'retaining lien', also known as the 'general' or 'possessory' lien, enabling a solicitor to retain all papers or other chattels of the client that have come into his or her possession as his or her client's solicitor until all costs and expenses as solicitor are paid; and
>
> (b) Second, the 'fruits of the action' lien, also known as the 'non-possessory' or 'particular' lien, over property recovered or preserved, or any judgment obtained, for the client by the solicitor's exertions in litigation: *Colour Point Pty Limited v Markby's Communication Group Pty Limited* [1998] FCA 1516 per Weinberg J.[89]

In *Rusca Brothers Services Pty Ltd v DLaw Pty Ltd*, the Federal Court declined to find a "fruits of the action" equitable lien for the lawyer in relation to an ADR settlement deed effectively limiting the lien to settlement of litigation.[90]

6.9.3 Lawyers' personal liability for costs

Lawyers are increasingly likely to be made personally responsible for legal costs where a court finds that the actions or inaction of lawyers is responsible for increasing the costs of litigation. Statutory provisions assist in making lawyers personally responsible, such as s 43(3)(f) of the *Federal Court of Australia Act 1976* (Cth) that outlines where solicitors may be liable for costs in the Federal Court.[91]

Similarly, in Victoria, r 63.23 of the *Supreme Court (General Civil Procedure) Rules 2015* (Vic) (formerly r 63.23 of the 2005 rules) states that a Victorian solicitor may be made personally liable for costs improperly incurred or failure to act with competence and expedition. In *Gippsreal Ltd v Kenny*, the Victorian Court of Appeal considered both r 63.23 (the 2005 version) and s 29 of the *Civil Procedure Act 2010* (Vic) which provides personal costs orders can be ordered against any person who breaches any overarching obligation (discussed in Chapter 2.4.3). The Victorian Court of Appeal found that a lawyer must act expeditiously in seeking an order under r 63.23, such that it was inappropriate for the applicant to delay proceedings for two years against the opposing party's solicitors personally while it explored the possibility of obtaining costs against its opposing party, stating:

> Although the power falls within the Court's supervisory jurisdiction over legal practitioners, it is essentially compensatory and for the benefit of parties to litigation, and it should be exercised as simply and as expeditiously as the requirements of procedural fairness permit.[92]

89 Ibid [25].

90 *Rusca Brothers Services Pty Ltd v DLaw Pty Ltd* [2019] FCA 562, [15].

91 See, eg, *Ryan v Primesafe* (2015) 323 ALR 107; *Re Kuek* (2012) 291 ALR 443; *Kuek v Honourable Justice Gray* [2012] HCATrans 273.

92 *Gippsreal Ltd v Kenny* (2016) 52 VR 149, [95], [102].

Section 99 of the *Civil Procedure Act 2005* (NSW) also imposes liability on solicitors for unnecessary costs. For example, in *Walton v Walton*,[93] the solicitor, Mr Neagle, who had defended a costs application inappropriately and unsuccessfully, was ordered, pursuant to s 99 of the *Civil Procedure Act 2005* (NSW), to personally pay to the other side 90% of the costs order made by the Court against his client, as well as having his own costs charged to his client disallowed and having the matter referred to the New South Wales Law Society for further consideration.

The New South Wales Court of Appeal case of *McCrohon v Harith*[94] concerned the liability of New South Wales solicitors for costs in a Queensland matter which had been adjourned immediately prior to trial due to insufficient funds to proceed. *McCrohon v Harith* demonstrates the circumstances in which lawyers can be made personally responsible for costs, the complexity of cost allocation, the effect of impecuniosity on enforceability of costs orders, and the differences between state practices within Australia. demonstrating the ongoing obstacles to nationalisation of the Australian legal profession. McCrohon were New South Wales solicitors acting for Harith in Queensland litigation. The solicitors failed to advise their clients that they could receive more expert and cheaper legal advice from Queensland-based solicitors and that they might suffer an adverse costs order by seeking to adjourn a hearing on the hearing date. In this appeal, the solicitors accepted the trial court findings as to their negligence but disputed the impact of a costs settlement between the original litigating parties and the effect of the defendant's impecuniosity.[95] The appellant solicitors succeeded in their appeal, resulting in a significant reduction in their liability to their clients for negligence. In essence, the appellants successfully argued that the original defendant's impecuniosity was such that costs order against the original defendant (which was lost as a result of the adverse adjournment costs order caused by the appellant's negligence) would never have been recovered by the plaintiffs and should not, therefore, be payable by the appellants.[96]

6.10 Litigation funding

It is increasingly common for non-parties to be involved in the funding of litigation. Litigation funders typically pay the costs of running litigation in exchange for a success fee. Litigation funding is particularly useful in representative actions where a large number of potential plaintiffs collectively have a significant potential legal entitlement, but where each individual's claim is too small to warrant the costs of litigating. Litigation funding can, however, apply in any litigation where a potential litigant has insufficient funds to proceed with litigation, but a non-party is prepared to pay legal costs on behalf of the potential litigant. Litigation funding brings its own complications to the process of determining costs.

Funding of litigation used to be illegal in Australia pursuant to the now obsolete common law torts of maintenance (improperly enlivening litigation) and champerty (profiteering from litigation). These torts were specifically statutorily abolished in the Australian Capital

93 *Walton v Walton* [2015] NSWSC 409.

94 *McCrohon v Harith* [2010] NSWCA 67.

95 *Harith & Kanuth v McCrohon* [2009] NSWSC 111, [126]–[134] sets out in detail the solicitors' breaches of duty. This aspect of the trial case was not appealed.

96 *McCrohon v Harith* [2010] NSWCA 67, [64]–[69]. Note that, in Queensland, personal costs orders may also be made pursuant to r 690 of *the Uniform Civil Procedure Rules 1999* (Qld) for delay or neglect.

Territory, New South Wales, South Australia and Victoria.[97] Litigation funding is now supported as it assists the crucial public policy objective of improving access to justice.

The important but complex High Court decision in *Campbells Cash & Carry* concerned whether representative proceedings commenced by Firmstones, a proactive litigation funder which sought out potential litigants, were properly constituted representative proceedings and whether the funding arrangements constituted an abuse of process. The proceedings, controlled by Firmstones, were to enable tobacco retailers to recover refunded tobacco licence fees paid to tobacco wholesalers pursuant to legislation which had been subsequently found to be constitutionally invalid, resulting in refunds to the wholesalers.

In *Campbells Cash & Carry*, the majority (Gummow, Hayne, Crennan, Callinan and Heydon JJ) allowed the appeal against the litigation funder on the basis that the proceedings were not properly constituted representative proceedings. The findings of the Court on the litigation funding issue were, therefore, obiter dicta.[98] In relation to litigation funding, the joint judgment of Gummow, Hayne and Crennan JJ and the separate judgments of Gleeson CJ and Kirby J all found the litigation funding arrangement was valid and not an abuse of process. The judgment of Gummow, Hayne and Crennan JJ (cited with approval in the subsequent High Court case of *Jeffery & Katauskas Pty Ltd v SST Consulting Pty Ltd*)[99] held:

> 89. As Mason P rightly pointed out in the Court of Appeal, many people seek profit from assisting the processes of litigation. That a person who hazards funds in litigation wishes to control the litigation is hardly surprising. That someone seeks out those who may have a claim and excites litigation where otherwise there would be none could be condemned as contrary to public policy only if a general rule against the maintenance of actions were to be adopted. But that approach has long since been abandoned and the qualification of that rule (by reference to criteria of common interest) proved unsuccessful. …[100]

Litigation funding is particularly complex in jurisdictions, such as Queensland, where the torts of maintenance and champerty have not been repealed. The Queensland Court of Appeal decision in *Gladstone Ports Corporation Ltd v Murphy Operator Pty Ltd* discussed the limited modern relevance of maintenance and champerty in relation to the enforceability of contractual agreements between a litigation funder and plaintiffs to a class action, pursuant to pt 13A of the *Civil Proceedings Act 2011* (Qld), for the purposes of providing security for costs to the defendant.[101] The Court, in dismissing the defendant's (appellant's) appeal, confined the operation of maintenance and champerty and found that the champertous

97 Pursuant to the *Civil Law (Wrongs) Act 2002* (ACT) s 221; *Criminal Law Consolidation Act 1935* (SA) sch 11 s 1(3); *Wrongs Act 1958* (Vic) s 32; *Maintenance, Champerty and Barratry Abolition Act 1993* (NSW) (this last Act has since been repealed; however, the High Court case of *Campbell's Cash & Carry Pty Ltd v Fostif Pty Ltd* (2006) 229 CLR 386 confirmed that litigation funding is permitted within New South Wales.

98 The term "obiter dicta" means things said by the way or on the side and contrasts to "ratio decidendi" which are the reasons for the decision. Things said obiter dicta do not form binding precedent but are extremely persuasive, particularly when said by the High Court.

99 *Jeffery & Katauskas Pty Ltd v SST Consulting Pty Ltd* (2009) 239 CLR 75.

100 *Campbell's Cash & Carry Pty Ltd v Fostif Pty Ltd* (2006) 229 CLR 386, [89].

101 *Gladstone Ports Corporation Ltd v Murphy Operator Pty Ltd* (2020) 384 ALR 725. Part 13A of the *Civil Proceedings Act 2011* (Qld) commenced in March 2017.

litigation funding arrangements of the plaintiffs (respondents) were not a breach of public policy and were very unlikely to lead to misbehaviour by the litigation funder given its interest in remaining in business.[102]

An important issue for funded litigation is the arrangements for the payment of adverse costs orders. The High Court case of *Jeffery & Katauskas Pty Ltd v SST Consulting Pty Ltd* concerned the ability of the Court to make an award of costs against a non-party litigation funder.[103] The case was based on the *Civil Procedure Act 2005* (NSW) and the *Uniform Civil Procedure Rules 2005* (NSW). Section 98(1) of the *Civil Procedure Act 2005* (NSW) gave the court discretion as to costs orders, subject to the *Uniform Civil Procedure Rules 2005* (NSW). Rule 42.3 provided that costs could not be awarded against a non-party except where such costs were occasioned by contempt of court or abuse of process by that non-party (note that r 42.3 has since been repealed). The case concerned a construction litigation funded on behalf of an impecunious company. The alleged abuse of process was that the non-party funder had not indemnified the impecunious company against an adverse costs order. The majority, French CJ, Gummow, Hayne and Crennan JJ (with Heydon J in dissent), held that *Jeffery & Katauskas'* case did not warrant an award of costs against the litigation funder for contempt or abuse (see Chapter 5.4 regarding abuse of process). In making their decision, the High Court majority placed considerable reliance on the earlier High Court reasoning in *Campbell's Cash & Carry*. The majority in *Jeffery & Katauskas* stated:

> 43. The proposition that those who fund another's litigation must put the party funded in a position to meet any adverse costs order is too broad a proposition to be accepted. As stated, the proposition would apply to shareholders who support a company's claim, relatives who support an individual plaintiff's claim and banks who extend overdraft accommodation to a corporate plaintiff. ...[104]

International Litigation Partners Pte Ltd v Chameleon Mining NL raised questions around whether additional regulatory burdens should be placed upon litigation funders.[105] This case involved ILP, a Singaporean corporation, which agreed to fund a litigation an agreement which was terminated triggering payment of an early termination fee. The High Court held that litigation funding arrangement constituted a credit facility. As a result, the *Corporations Amendment Regulation 2012 (No 6)* (Cth) was enacted, exempting litigation funders provided they conduct reviews and maintain procedures in identifying and managing conflicts of interest.

In late 2019, the High Court handed down *BMW Australia Ltd v Brewster*,[106] determining that courts are not able to make common fund orders under the existing s 33ZF of the *Federal Court Act 1976* (Cth) or s 183 of the *Civil Procedure Act 2005* (NSW). The BMW class action concerned the recall of dangerous Takata air bags, while the Westpac action

102 *Gladstone Ports Corporation Ltd v Murphy Operator Pty Ltd* (2020) 384 ALR 725, [102]–[106]. This case provides a delightful history of maintenance and champerty for those interested to know more.

103 *Jeffery & Katauskas Pty Ltd v SST Consulting Pty Ltd* (2009) 239 CLR 75.

104 Ibid [43].

105 *International Litigation Partners Pte Ltd v Chameleon Mining NL (recrs and mgrs apptd)* (2012) 246 CLR 455.

106 *BMW Australia Ltd v Brewster* (2019) 374 ALR 627.

concerned Westpac financial advisors recommending clients purchase their own products despite the availability of superior products.

Common fund orders have enabled courts to prevent the "free rider" problem in Australia's "opt out" class action system. The opt-out system means that an individual may benefit from a class action simply by not opting out of it, regardless of whether that individual has reached agreement with the funder of the litigation. In class action matters, common fund orders allowed litigation funders to charge fees to all individuals who sought to benefit from a class action, regardless of whether they had individually signed up to an agreement with the litigation funder — thereby preventing "free riders" who seek to benefit from the class action without paying the funder. In *BMW Australia Ltd v Brewster*, the appeal was allowed by Kiefel CJ, Bell and Keane JJ (with Nettle and Gordon JJ both agreeing in separate judgments, and Gageler J and Edelman J both dissenting in separate judgments). The plurality (Kiefel CJ, Bell and Keane JJ) conceded the value of common fund orders (CFOs) but still determined they were not within the Court's power to order:

> But while access to justice may be expected to be improved in a general way by the availability of litigation funding, it does not follow that the making of a CFO is necessary or appropriate to ensure that justice is done in a particular proceeding in accordance with Pt IVA of the FCA or Pt 10 of the CPA.[107]

The removal of CFOs means that litigation funders will once again be required to "build books" of all possible litigants and sign up such litigants within funding agreements to make it viable for them to fund the litigation.

As the litigation funding market in Australia has grown, it has created new challenges for courts where multiple class actions are commenced in relation to the same dispute. Efficiency strongly favours only a single class action being allowed to continue, but this presents the courts with the unenviable task of choosing between competing class actions. In *Wigmans v AMP Ltd*, five competing class actions were commenced in quick succession acting for AMP shareholders who lost money when the AMP share price plummeted due to revelations of misleading conduct relating to charging fees for no service.[108] The High Court majority, in dismissing the appeal by Ms Wigman, who filed first out of the five groups, upheld the multifactorial approach of the primary judge in assessing the competing plaintiff actions holding that:

> The task undertaken by the primary judge was not a judgment regarding a matter of 'mere' case management but a larger task of ensuring that justice is done in the competing representative proceedings which have been commenced under Pt 10 of the CPA where all courts must be astute to protect the best interests of group members.[109]

This area will continue to develop as the High Court canvassed a variety of possibilities for deciding between competing plaintiff class actions in future cases depending on the interests of the potential plaintiffs.[110]

107 Ibid [93].
108 *Wigmans v AMP Ltd* (2021) 388 ALR 272.
109 Ibid [116] (Gageler, Gordon and Edelman JJ in the majority with Kiefel CJ and Keane J in dissent).
110 Ibid [116]–[123].

6.11 Conclusion

Lawyers, their responsibilities to their clients, and the costs they charge are a complex and important aspect of CDR. As discussed in Chapter 2.5.2 and Chapter 3.2.4, legal costs are a major deterrent to litigation and a significant bar to the accessibility of justice which can sometimes force disputants to represent themselves despite the suboptimal nature of such arrangements. However, the nature of CDR makes the work of dispute resolution lawyer inherently costly, time-consuming and potentially riskier, from a remuneration perspective, than other legal work.

The high level of legal costs and the uncertainty of legal costs associated with litigation provide a powerful incentive for disputants to engage with ADR to reduce legal costs. Bona fide engagement with ADR also reduces the exposure of parties to adverse costs orders where matters don't settle, providing a significant further incentive to undertake ADR. Some tribunals (see Chapter 7) discourage legal representation and this can significantly reduce costs for parties but can also increase stress, where parties feel inadequate to self-represent, and lack of representation can result in inefficient hearings due to high levels of party ignorance.

Questions of legal costs impose on the judiciary unenviable, simultaneous and often conflicting obligations to:

- fairly allocate legal costs between parties
- protect litigants from unreasonable costs and poor legal representation
- ensure litigants obtain the benefits of favourable costs orders without compromising access to justice
- protect the rights of solicitors to receive fair payment for services rendered
- use judicial discretion regarding costs orders to assist the efficiency of court procedures.

The conflicting nature of these obligations explains why the use of lawyers and the legal costs they charge frequently become an additional matter for civil disputation.

7 MANAGING RESOURCES THROUGH SPECIALIST COURTS AND TRIBUNALS

7.1 Introduction

Civil dispute resolution (CDR) does not only occur through ADR and mainstream courts; there is also a significant volume of civil litigation heard by specialist courts and tribunals that have been created by statutes with specific and limited jurisdictions. Many specialist areas of law are dealt with by "super tribunals" run by every state and territory except Tasmania, which is committed to introducing a super tribunal in 2021. The super tribunals are commonly described as: ACAT (ACT), NCAT (NSW), NTCAT (NT), QCAT (Qld), SACAT (SA), SAT (WA) and VCAT (Vic). The state-based super tribunals are relatively recent and each deal with a number of different types of disputes which were previously dealt with by smaller, more specialised tribunals.[1] Many statutory tribunals resolve disputes relating to administrative decisions by government, and government-related institutions and organisations. However, there is a wide variation in the jurisdiction of these super tribunals, with some replacing only a portion of statutory tribunals and others comprehensively replacing statutory tribunals. In addition, in some jurisdictions, the super tribunal can hear all civil disputes up to a certain threshold and effectively acts as a small claims court. In the federal sphere, there are statutory tribunals such as the Administrative Appeals Tribunal (AAT), as well as specialist courts such as the Land and Environment Court and the Family Court.

This chapter will briefly discuss some of the specialist courts and tribunals operating in Australia and the types of matters they hear. The significant variation between different tribunals, including the different state-based super tribunals, exists because the powers of each are determined by the underlying statute empowering the tribunal itself and, in many cases, the underlying acts which govern the different disputes within the tribunal's jurisdiction which are often unique to each state. In addition, the jurisdiction of each super tribunal is influenced by the previously existing tribunals which that super tribunal replaced.

There are important differences in procedure which apply to statutory tribunals and specialist courts, most significantly that tribunals tend to be faster, less formal, and, often, more flexible in terms of their procedures. Tribunals and, to a lesser extent, specialist courts commonly dispense with evidentiary rules and other procedures which increase the cost, time and complexity associated with resolving civil disputes through mainstream courts. In some cases, parties are even forbidden or discouraged from using legal representation. As Basten JA stated in relation to NCAT in *Attorney-General (NSW) v Gatsby*:

> Nor is this a matter of mere semantics; the objects of the Civil and Administrative Tribunal Act demonstrate that, as was the case with many of the 22 tribunals and other bodies which were combined to create NCAT, a significant purpose of the creation of NCAT was to provide an alternative mechanism for dispute resolution, allowing persons with disputes in particular categories to obtain a resolution outside the formal court structure.[2]

However, like mainstream courts, statutory courts and tribunals render enforceable decisions and are managed and funded by governments rather than by the parties to the disputes. In most respects, statutory tribunals and specialist courts far more closely resemble mainstream courts than they do ADR.

The role of statutory tribunals and courts raises many of the key themes of CDR introduced in Chapters 2 and 3. By reducing the formality of procedures and, in some instances, removing the use of lawyers, statutory tribunals engage directly with access to justice issues. Reduced cost and formality increase the range of potential disputants who can afford to engage with dispute resolution. Simultaneously, reduced procedures can increase

1 See, eg, the commencement of NCAT, the New South Wales Civil and Administrative Tribunal, in 2014, which subsumed the work of over 20 individual New South Wales tribunals, including a significant number of health-related tribunals.

2 *Attorney-General (NSW) v Gatsby* (2018) 99 NSWLR 1, [224] noting that Basten JA agreed with the majority on the issue that NCAT was not a court, while disagreeing on some matters in the case.

the risk of procedural unfairness and lack of legal representation can disproportionately disadvantage disputants who have the greatest barriers to comprehending legal process.[3]

This chapter does not attempt to consider the procedures of every tribunal in each jurisdiction, particularly as different parts of super tribunals often have differing procedures suited to the particular nature of the disputes they resolve. Rather, this chapter seeks to demonstrate how certain disputes may be legislatively directed to, or better suited to, a tribunal hearing or a specialist court which may result in the application of procedures substantially different to the litigation procedures discussed in the remaining chapters of the book.

7.2 Role of statutory tribunals

Tribunals have an increasing role in the Australian civil justice system. Each tribunal, specialist court or special area of law has its own unique procedures which may vary significantly from the Supreme and Federal Court procedures discussed in preceding chapters. Tribunals are established by statutes and, accordingly, their jurisdiction and procedures may be tailored by statute as well as by procedural guidelines released by tribunals and case precedent.

7.2.1 The jurisdiction of statutory tribunals: closer to courts than arbitration

Chapter 4 discussed ADR including arbitration. Arbitrators sitting to determine a dispute constitute a tribunal, but an arbitral tribunal must be distinguished from the statutory tribunals which form the subject of this chapter. The term "tribunal" is also used to define numerous government-run institutions which have legislated power to compulsorily determine disputes in much the same way as courts. Some of these statutory tribunals have been found to be courts and all of them have many of the characteristics of courts.

In the New South Wales Supreme Court of Appeal decision of *Attorney-General (NSW) v Gatsby*, the majority of a bench of five judges determined, in four separate judgments, that NCAT had been acting judicially in determining two termination of tenancy cases involving parties from different states but were not the "court of a state" for the purposes of Chapter III of the *Commonwealth Constitution*.[4] In considering this issue, Bathurst CJ (in the majority) concluded that NCAT was not a Chapter III "court of a state" and discussed at length the requirements of a court,[5] stating:

> 184. Applying these principles to the present case, I am of the view that, although the Tribunal has many of the features of a 'court' and can, in a number of areas, exercise State judicial power, it is not a 'court of a State' for the purpose of Chapter III of the

3 See Sonya Willis, 'Could Civil Case Management Benefit from a Litigant Vulnerability Assessment Scheme?' (2018) 7(2) *Journal of Civil Litigation and Practice* 94.

4 *Attorney-General (NSW) v Gatsby* (2018) 99 NSWLR 1 is a complex decision with Bathurst CJ delivering the lead decision with substantial agreement from Beazley JA, McColl JA and Leeming JA and partial agreement from Basten JA.

5 Ibid [172]-[192].

Constitution. My reasons are set out below. While none of these may be decisive individually, in combination, they lead to the clear conclusion that the Tribunal is not a 'court of a State'.

185. First, the Tribunal is not designated as a 'court of record'. I do not think that the existence of the limited contempt power in s 73 of the NCAT Act detracts from the force of this consideration, particularly having regard to the terms of s 73(2), which provides that a person is 'guilty of contempt of the Tribunal if the person does or omits to do any thing' which would constitute a contempt 'if the Tribunal were a court of law' (emphasis added). That provision clearly draws a distinction between the Tribunal and a 'court of law'.

186. More importantly, it could not be said that the Tribunal is composed 'predominantly' of judges. As the applicant submitted, the members of the Tribunal included a considerable number of non-lawyers, and many of the members, including the lawyers, were part-time appointments. The fact that, from time to time, the members of the Tribunal may exercise judicial powers and might colloquially be described in those circumstances as 'judges in substance', does not alter the fact that the Tribunal is not 'predominantly' composed of judges in the sense described in the authorities.

187. Of equal, if not greater, importance, as pointed out in Skiwing, Sudi, Lustig and Tasmanian Anti-Discrimination Tribunal, is the absence of security of tenure for members of the Tribunal comparable to that held by judges under the *Act of Settlement 1701* (UK) and its statutory or constitutional equivalents. Apart from the President, members of the Tribunal are appointed by the Minister. The term of appointment cannot exceed five years, but a member is eligible for reappointment. There are no restrictions on the other activities which can be undertaken by a part-time member, which presumably could include employment by a government department or agency. That does not seem to me to be ameliorated by the regulation-making power relating to disclosure of pecuniary or other material interests in cl 13(a) of Schedule 2 to the NCAT Act, or the power contained in cl 13(b) to make regulations dealing with the participation by members in proceedings where there is a conflict of interest. Indeed, regulation of the latter matter by the Executive seems to me to be contrary to the necessary requirement of independence for a body to be a 'court of a State'.

188. In addition, the appointment of general members under s 13(6) of the NCAT Act on the basis that they are 'capable of representing' a 'group of persons' in respect of 'any one or more classes of matters in respect of which the Tribunal has jurisdiction' appears to me to be contrary to the basis on which appointments of judges to a court are made and directly raises questions of impartiality.

189. Finally, members other than the President can be removed from office by the Governor for 'incapacity, incompetence or misbehaviour' under cl 7(2) of Schedule 2 to the NCAT Act. This can be contrasted with the position of judges, who can only be removed by the Governor 'on an address from both Houses of Parliament in the same session, seeking removal on the ground of proved misbehaviour or incapacity': see *Constitution Act 1902* (NSW) s 53(1). While it is true that a decision to remove a non-presidential member might be reviewable, the fact remains that it does not provide the same protection as that conferred on judges.

190. The combination of these factors means that, in my view, the State legislature did not intend the Tribunal to be a 'court of a State' for the purpose of Chapter III of the

> Constitution and that the Tribunal did not have the necessary degree of independence and impartiality to constitute such a court. Thus, irrespective of the approach adopted, the same conclusion is reached.[6]

Similarly, in *Director of Housing v Sudi*, the Victorian Supreme Court of Appeal held that VCAT was not a court because most of its members could not be said to "enjoy judicial independence" as their fixed-term appointments resulted in a perception that VCAT was comprised of members "beholden to the government".[7] VCAT has since been recognised as a body which "resembles a court exercising judicial power" and is vested with state judicial power in *Qantas Airways Ltd v Lustig*.[8] However, in line with the New South Wales decisions on NCAT in *Meringnage v Interstate Enterprises Pty Ltd*, the Victorian Supreme Court of Appeal confirmed that VCAT was not a "court of the state" for the purposes of Chapter III of the *Constitution* and could not determine matters in which the Commonwealth was a party.[9] Conversely, in Queensland, in *Owen v Menzies,* the Queensland Supreme Court of Appeal held that QCAT is a "court of a state" in part because its establishing legislation expressly designates it as a "court of record".[10]

Whether or not the "super tribunals" — NCAT, VCAT, QCAT and others — are officially courts, they undisputedly resemble courts in most respects. As such, the decisions of these super tribunals cannot be considered ADR, not least because, in many cases, parties are required by legislation to attend the tribunal in the first instance to resolve their dispute rather than a court with only appeal rights to the relevant Supreme Court. This chapter concerns these government-run tribunals rather than the privately organised arbitral tribunals discussed in Chapter 4.6.

7.2.2 Tribunal decisions are binding

The decision of a tribunal is binding on all parties. Although most tribunal decisions are appealable in court, the grounds of appeal are often limited to those available in appeals from court decisions as discussed in Chapter 16.6. Courts hearing appeals of tribunal decisions may have broader powers to override tribunal decisions than they do for appeals from court decisions, but such courts will not usually have the ability to re-call witnesses or re-hear evidence.

As with court decisions, tribunal decisions are enforceable through the courts or, in some cases, using enforcement powers of the tribunal itself.[11]

6 Ibid [184]-[190] (Bathurst CJ). See *Civil and Administrative Tribunal Act 2013* (NSW) pt 3A; *Burns v Corbett* (2018) 265 CLR 304; *Gaynor v Attorney-General (NSW)* (2020) 102 NSWLR 123. See Chapter 7.5 for further analysis of the jurisdictional difficulties faced by NCAT in relation to matters involving disputants from different states.

7 *Director of Housing v Sudi* (2011) 33 VR 559, [201] (Weinberg JA).

8 *Qantas Airways Ltd v Lustig* (2015) 228 FCR 148, [65] (Perry J).

9 *Meringnage v Interstate Enterprises Pty Ltd* (2020) 60 VR 361.

10 *Owen v Menzies* [2013] 2 Qd R 327. Bathurst CJ accepts this distinction as a justification for the differing determination that NCAT is not a court of a state in *Attorney-General (NSW) v Gatsby* (2018) 99 NSWLR 1, [191].

11 See Chapter 16.7.

7.2.3 Tribunal structure

The structure of tribunals varies significantly between different states, despite the fact that all states and territories, except Tasmania, now have a central civil and administrative tribunal (the "super tribunal") which hears a large range of disputes. The jurisdiction of each super tribunal is determined by state-based legislation on the basis of perceived need. Accordingly, the nature and business of divisions within each super tribunal varies depending on the needs of the state jurisdiction. For example, the Northern Territory, which is sparsely populated but has significant mining interests, has a strong focus on land, planning and mining disputes. Conversely, New South Wales, which has a high population and a significant volume of commerce, has a greater focus on consumer, residential and professional practice disputes.

All the super tribunals have been introduced relatively recently, with Victoria being the first in 1998. There are advantages and disadvantages to centralising tribunals. While administration costs and the complexity of determining where to litigate is increased by large numbers of tribunals, the ability of such tribunals to develop efficient internal procedures and expertise increases with specialisation. Conversely, it is easier to share resources such as buildings, administrative staff and even tribunal members in a centralised tribunal.

Tribunals are generally constituted by presidents, deputy presidents, senior members and members. The presiding tribunal member is commonly a Supreme Court judge (or Federal Court judge for federal tribunals). Less senior members may be professionals or persons with other specialist expertise who sit on disputes where their expertise is particularly relevant. Unlike members of the judiciary, tribunal members are not necessarily lawyers, although many are. Important cases are more likely to be determined by presidential members, while junior members are more likely to provide non-legal specialist expertise in a three-person tribunal in a dispute relating to that member's specialist knowledge.

7.2.4 Sources of tribunal law

Tribunals are governed by legislation which usually includes an Act dedicated to the operation of the tribunal. There are more than a thousand Australian Acts which influence the operation of tribunals. In addition to specific legislation enabling the existence of each tribunal, jurisdiction for tribunals to hear particular disputes is usually granted by the substantive law governing the dispute. Tribunal procedure is also often influenced by civil procedure legislation and administrative law. For example, the jurisdiction of a state super tribunal to hear discrimination disputes includes provisions of the relevant state-based discrimination Act; for example, the *Discrimination Act 1991* (ACT) for ACAT, or the *Anti-Discrimination Act 1977* (NSW) for NCAT.

7.2.5 Tribunal procedure

Procedure varies considerably between different tribunals, depending on the powers, purposes and resources of the tribunal. In general, tribunals have greater flexibility in their procedure than courts and their procedures tend to be more informal, less adversarial and faster than court procedures. Tribunals do not generally follow the rules of evidence discussed in Chapters 8 and 9 of this book. Tribunals often have no discovery process and may not have affidavits or witness evidence. Settlement negotiations, conciliation and mediation can all be built into tribunal procedures. Aspects of pre-trial procedure and even tribunal hearings may be conducted by telephone conference or entirely on the basis of written submissions.

The Australian Capital Territory case of *Chief Psychiatrist and A (Mental Health)*[12] contains an excellent summary of tribunal procedures. It concerned an order by ACAT, constituted by General President Crebbin and Senior Member Dr Drew, for a six-month Psychiatric Treatment Order (PTO) to apply to A against his will on application by the Chief Psychiatrist. The PTO was made, pursuant to the *Mental Health (Treatment and Care) Act 1994* (ACT), following an inquiry at Canberra Hospital where A was an inpatient. The respondent, A, was concerned that he had not had the opportunity to examine witnesses at the inquiry. General President Crebbin set out in her reasons an excellent summary of general procedure for the Tribunal as well as the rules for private inquiries for inpatients pursuant to the *Mental Health (Treatment and Care) Act 1994* (ACT). The specific procedures for inpatients pursuant to the *Mental Health (Treatment and Care) Act 1994* (ACT) demonstrate the ability of tribunals to operate flexibly so as to accommodate specialist proceedings and to balance competing interests such as procedural fairness, human rights and personal safety:

> **Tribunal procedures generally**
>
> 4. The Tribunal can determine its own procedure. The rules of evidence do not usually apply. Tribunal hearings are not however, a 'free-for-all'. The Tribunal must observe natural justice and procedural fairness. These are interchangeable concepts.
>
> 5. Procedural fairness requires that reasonable notice be given of a hearing and of the matters that are in issue. Participants need to have time to adequately prepare for a hearing. Participants also need to have an adequate opportunity to address the matters in issue.
>
> 6. The procedures adopted in a hearing are largely determined by the nature of the application before the Tribunal. What is reasonable and adequate may vary according to both the authorising law relevant to the application and the issues raised by the particular application. Some cases require a procedural framework that is similar to frameworks used in adversarial proceedings in courts. Other cases will require much less formality and greater flexibility.
>
> 7. The Tribunal may inform itself as it thinks fit. Some cases will have 'parties' who are adversaries presenting their information to the Tribunal. Other cases engage participants in an inquisitorial process in which the Tribunal itself determines and obtains much of the information on which it relies.
>
> 8.Information can be provided in documents or by witnesses giving oral or written evidence. There is no general right for a person to cross-examine witnesses. The Tribunal may draw on its own expertise and experience when evaluating information. Participants should be told when tribunals are relying on the expertise and knowledge of its members.
>
> 9. The Tribunal may, in some circumstances, decide that participants should not be given copies of documents containing information on which it relies; for example, documents that are subject to confidentiality restrictions. If copies of documents that

12 *Chief Psychiatrist and A (Mental Health)* [2011] ACAT 21.

are before Tribunal members are withheld, participants must at least be aware of the general content of those documents and have, save in exceptional circumstances, an opportunity to respond to matters that the Tribunal may take into account.

10. Ultimately, Tribunal decisions must be based on relevant information that tends, logically, to prove what is asserted. The information must have, in other words, probative value.[13]

7.2.6 Council of Australasian Tribunals

In recognition of the growing importance of tribunals in Australia, in 2002, the Council of Australasian Tribunals (COAT) was formed to "establish a national network for members of tribunals to consult and discuss areas of concern or interest and common experiences".[14] COAT maintains a website representing Australian and New Zealand tribunals.[15] Several objectives of COAT relate to tribunal practice and procedure, including developing best practice or model procedural rules, encouraging publication of papers, commentary and articles concerning tribunal practices and procedures, and promoting lectures, seminars, reports and commentaries on tribunal practice and procedure.[16] COAT holds an annual conference for tribunal members, increasing education of tribunal members on issues ranging from the use of interpreters to social media and written and oral communication skills. In 2016, COAT published a *Best Practice Guide to Tribunal Independence in Appointments* to assist governments and tribunals in maximising the independence of tribunal appointments to maintain public trust in the integrity of tribunals.[17]

7.2.7 National laws for state-based tribunals

It is possible for state tribunals to apply national law and for there to be a level of national uniformity in relation to matters resolved by state-based tribunal decisions. For example, the Health Practitioner Regulation National Law in force in each state and territory provides for dispute resolution for professional misconduct by health professionals through tribunals where the matter is of sufficient seriousness for the relevant National Board to refer the matter to a tribunal.[18] Matters which the relevant National Board reasonably considers constitute professional misconduct are referred to the tribunal of the state where the misconduct occurred. For those states with a super tribunal, health disciplinary matters are generally handled by that consolidated tribunal in compliance with the *Health Practitioner Regulation*

13 Ibid [4–13]. Many, if not all, of these tribunal procedures are similarly applicable to other state, territory and federal tribunals.

14 Council of Australasian Tribunals, *An Overview of its Objects and Activities* (24 August 2004) <https://www.aat.gov.au/about-the-aat/engagement/speeches-and-papers/the-honourable-justice-garry-downes-am-former-pres/the-council-of-australasian-tribunals-an-overview->.

15 Council of Australasian Tribunals (Web Page) <https://coat.asn.au/>.

16 *Constitution of the Council of Australasian Tribunals Inc*, [3], <http://coat.asn.au/wp-content/uploads/2018/10/COAT_Constitution_2017-_Final.pdf.

17 Council of Australasian Tribunals, *Tribunal Independence: A Best Practice Guide* (2016).

18 Australian Health Practitioner Regulation Agency & National Boards, 'Tribunal Hearings' (Web Page) <https://www.ahpra.gov.au/Notifications/Further-information/Guides-and-fact-sheets/Tribunal-hearings.aspx>.

National Law while, in Tasmania, such matters are handled by the Health Practitioners Tribunal.[19]

Health Practitioner Regulation National Law regulates 16 health professions, enabling review of decisions from the following national disciplinary boards:[20]

- Aboriginal and Torres Strait Islander Health Practice Board of Australia
- Chinese Medicine Board of Australia
- Chiropractic Board of Australia
- Dental Board of Australia
- Medical Board of Australia
- Medical Radiation Practice Board of Australia
- Nursing and Midwifery Board of Australia
- Occupational Therapy Board of Australia
- Optometry Board of Australia
- Osteopathy Board of Australia
- Paramedicine Board of Australia
- Pharmacy Board of Australia
- Physiotherapy Board of Australia
- Podiatry Board of Australia
- Psychology Board of Australia.

The tribunal, in a health practitioner disciplinary matter, will usually comprise a member "of the same profession as the health practitioner whose behaviour is under review, a non-health practitioner member and a judicial officer." This example demonstrates that there can be high consistency between different state tribunals where the specific law governing the tribunal is uniform. Despite health matters being commonly heard by super tribunals such as ACAT, NCAT and VCAT, in practice, these hearings are specialised for the nature of the disciplinary action and retain the procedural features of the Health Practitioner Tribunals that preceded their consolidation into the state civil and administrative super tribunals.

7.3 Federal tribunals

There are a number of federal tribunals which have jurisdiction to hear a wide range of disputes, mostly involving federal legislation and government determinations. There have been, and continue to be proposals for, structural changes in relation to both courts and tribunals in the federal sphere.

7.3.1 Specialist federal tribunals

There has been significant recent restructuring of federal tribunals. On 1 July 2015, pursuant to the *Tribunals Amalgamation Act 2015* (Cth), the Administrative Appeals Tribunal (AAT)

19 Health Practitioners Tribunal (Tasmania) (Web Page) <https://www.healthpractitionerstribunal.tas.gov.au/>.

20 Australian Health Practitioner Regulation Agency & National Boards, 'Registration Standards' (Web Page) <https://www.ahpra.gov.au/Registration/Registration-Standards.aspx>.

was amalgamated with the Social Security Appeals Tribunal and the Migration Review Tribunal and Refugee Review Tribunal, with all tribunals being subsumed into the AAT.[21]

In addition to the AAT, there are several other federal tribunals including the Australian Competition Tribunal,[22] the Copyright Tribunal of Australia (administered entirely by the Federal Court),[23] the Defence Force Discipline Appeal Tribunal (DFDAT),[24] the Veterans' Review Board (VRB)[25] and, most recently, the National Sports Tribunal (NST). The NST commenced in March 2020, pursuant to the *National Sports Tribunal Act 2019* (Cth) (*NST Act*).[26] The *NST Act* provides for the establishment and structure of the NST, which includes an Anti-Doping Division and a General Division.[27] The General Division encourages the use of facilitated ADR, including mediation and conciliation and case appraisal[28] while providing arbitration as the determinative means of dispute resolution.[29] The *NST Act* also contains an appellate procedure which is a further arbitration process.[30] The NST was established in response to the *Report of the Review of Australia's Sports Integrity Arrangements* (*The Wood Review*).[31] This new tribunal is designed to enable specialist resolution of sport-related disputes at a reduced cost to disputants.

7.3.2 Operation of federal tribunals

There is a significant variation in how federal tribunals are run and the volume of disputes they hear. In part, this relates to the litigation choices available to prospective litigants. Where legislation forces potential litigants through tribunals, those tribunals are likely to be busy. Where litigants may choose between court and tribunal, courts will often be preferred by litigants unless there are incentives to prefer a tribunal, such as speed, low cost or better appeal rights. In addition, some areas of law have a high incidence of disputes, such as family law, tax law and migration law and, accordingly, the tribunals with jurisdiction for those areas are busy. Accordingly, the volume of cases heard by tribunals varies dramatically.

For example, the Copyright Tribunal of Australia is an independent tribunal established through the *Copyright Act 1968* (Cth) but is administered by the Federal Court, funded through the Federal Court, and housed at the Federal Court. It is very rare for the Copyright Tribunal of Australia to sit at all, such that it handed down only four decisions in 2018 and two in 2019.[32] Most copyright disputes are litigated in the Federal Court of Australia or the Federal Circuit Court of Australia. At the other end of the spectrum, the AAT discussed below, hears thousands of cases annually.

21 Administrative Appeals Tribunal (Web Page) <https://www.aat.gov.au/>.
22 Australian Competition Tribunal (Web Page) <https://www.competitiontribunal.gov.au/>.
23 Copyright Tribunal of Australia (Web Page) <https://www.copyrighttribunal.gov.au/>.
24 Defence Force Disciplinary Appeal Tribunal (Web Page) <https://www.defenceappeals.gov.au/>.
25 Veterans' Review Board (Web Page) <https://www.vrb.gov.au/>.
26 National Sports Tribunal (Web Page) <https://www.nationalsportstribunal.gov.au/>.
27 See *National Sports Tribunal Act 2019* (Cth) s 21 for a simplified outline of the NST's operation.
28 Ibid ss 25–6, 28–30.
29 Ibid ss 23–4, 27.
30 Ibid ss 31–45.
31 Department of Health, *Report of the Review of Australia's Sports Integrity Arrangements* (2018).
32 Copyright Tribunal of Australia, 'Decisions' (Web Page) <https://www.copyrighttribunal.gov.au/decisions/judgments>.

7.3.3 Administrative Appeals Tribunal

The AAT is a federal tribunal with jurisdiction over a wide range of disputes (particularly since the *Tribunals Amalgamation Act 2015* (Cth)), involving a large number of Acts and with a presence in every state and territory other than Northern Territory (which is currently serviced by South Australia).[33]

On 23 July 2019, the Commonwealth Government tabled in Parliament the *Report on the Statutory Review of the Tribunals Amalgamation Act 2015* by the Hon Ian Callinan AC QC, former Justice of the High Court of Australia.[34] The Report was significantly critical of the state of the AAT and its procedures, particularly in the Migration and Review Division (MRD), and recommended numerous measures for employment including the appointment of significant further tribunal members to deal with the significant backlog of cases, most of which existed prior to amalgamation. Justice Callinan noted that:

> Jurisdiction to review decisions made by officials of the Commonwealth is now conferred on the AAT by more than 450 enactments. Several of these require close study. As soon as I started my work, I became aware that, far and away, the heaviest burden upon the AAT was the review of decisions made under the *Migration Act 1958* (Cth) ('Migration Act'). It also became apparent that the operation of the *National Disability Insurance Scheme Act 2013* (Cth) ('NDIS Act'), enacted only five years ago, has generated a large and growing number of reviewable decisions. So too, there are many applications for review of decisions made under the *Income Tax Assessment Act 1936* (Cth), the *Tax Administration Act 1953* (Cth), and the *Income Tax Assessment Act 1997* (Cth), as well as the relevant social security and health insurance laws, which are, in each case, highly complex and large pieces of legislation.[35]

The AAT is a very active tribunal which, as of 25 May 2020, employed 19 presidential and deputy presidential judicial members, 75 non-judicial deputy presidential and senior members, and well over 200 ordinary members. More than 100 of the AAT's tribunal members are employed on a full-time basis. The majority of AAT tribunal members sit in New South Wales or Victoria but there are also a significant number in the other states and the ACT.

At of 2020, the AAT had nine divisions as follows:

- Freedom of Information Division
- General Division
- Migration & Refugee Division (including the Immigration Assessment Authority)
- National Disability Insurance Scheme Division
- Security Division
- Small Business Taxation Division
- Social Services & Child Support Division
- Taxation & Commercial Division

---

33 Refer to Administrative Appeals Tribunal (Web Page) <https://www.aat.gov.au> for further information.

34 Ian Callinan, *Report on the Statutory Review of the Tribunals Amalgamation Act 2015: Final Report* (Attorney-General's Department, 2015).

35 Ibid 30.

- Veterans' Appeals Division.[36]

The AAT was established by the *Administrative Appeals Tribunal Act 1975* (Cth) and is governed by this Act and the *Administrative Appeals Tribunal Regulations 1976* (Cth). Its role is to determine appeals from administrative decisions of government departments, agencies, authorities, ministers and the determinations of some other tribunals. The AAT only has jurisdiction where the relevant legislation authorising the administrative decision grants the Tribunal the power to decide the dispute

The AAT is similar to a court, but its processes are more flexible and less formal. The AAT process usually includes status conferences, during which a conference registrar or tribunal member works with the parties to determine what steps are required, what the issues in dispute are, and whether settlement is possible. Where the matter proceeds to hearing, submissions and witness evidence tend to be mostly oral (although written witness statements are more common in some types of disputes, such as taxation disputes).

Parties may be represented by lawyers (and often are in commercial areas such as taxation) but self-representation is more feasible than in court, because the rules of evidence do not usually apply, unless all the parties and the Tribunal agree they should. This also means most hearings are brief, often less than half a day, although they can take days for complex matters. AAT cases rarely involve discovery or affidavit evidence.

AAT cases are appeals from administrative decisions; accordingly, the reasoning for the decision and the documents available to the decision-maker usually form the bulk of the evidence. As such, the AAT pre-trial process is usually significantly shorter and cheaper than for Supreme Court matters. This is as much a result of the nature of the dispute as the processes of the AAT.

However, the AAT does face significant challenges. In his 2019 *Report on the Statutory Review of the Tribunals Amalgamation Act 2015*, Callinan J noted some of the challenges facing the AAT, concluding:

> The absorption of the Migration Review Tribunal ('MRT') and the Refugee Review Tribunal ('RRT'), because of their very different legislative regimes and practices, into an amalgamated tribunal, was never going to be an easy task. The difficulties have been immensely compounded by the intimidating backlog of cases in the Migration and Refugee Division ('MRD') of the AAT.[37]

7.4 Australian Capital Territory Civil and Administrative Tribunal

The Australian Capital Territory was one of the first Australian jurisdictions to integrate its civil and administrative tribunals into a super tribunal: the Australian Capital Territory Civil and Administrative Tribunal (ACAT) was established in February 2009 pursuant to the *ACT*

36 Administrative Appeals Tribunal, 'Who We Are' (Web Page) <https://www.aat.gov.au/about-the-aat/who-we-are>.

37 Ian Callinan, *Report on the Statutory Review of the Tribunals Amalgamation Act 2015: Final Report* (Attorney-General's Department, 2015) 5.

Civil and Administrative Tribunal Act 2008 (ACT).[38] ACAT replaced the previously existing tribunals: Administrative Appeals Tribunal, Small Claims Court, Discrimination Tribunal, Guardianship and Management of Property Tribunal, Mental Health Tribunal, Residential Tenancies Tribunal, Liquor Licensing Board, Health Professions Tribunal Legal Practitioners Disciplinary Tribunal. ACAT is also responsible for disciplinary proceedings relating to many trades including builders, plumbers, motor vehicle dealers and finance brokers and hears civil disputes involving up to $25,000.

Part 8 of the *ACT Civil and Administrative Tribunal Act 2008* (ACT) deals with referrals and appeals from ACAT to refer to the Supreme Court of the Australian Capital Territory. The High Court case of *Williams v Wreck Bay Aboriginal Community Council* concerned an appeal following referral, under s 84 of the *ACT Civil and Administrative Tribunal Act 2008* (ACT), by ACAT to the Supreme Court of the Australian Capital Territory to determine a question of law raising an issue of public importance.[39] The case concerned the Aboriginal Community Council's obligations in relation to a property rented on a 99-year lease capable of being passed on in the event of death where no payments had been made for over 25 years and the property was in disrepair. The High Court held that the *Residential Tenancies Act 1997* (ACT) was not capable of operating concurrently with the *Aboriginal Land Grant (Jervis Bay Territory) Act 1986* (Cth) only to the limited extent that this would prevent the subletting of Aboriginal land. This meant the majority of residential tenancy obligations applied. ACAT has the ability under s 84 to refer legal questions of public importance to the Supreme Court of its own motion, which enables the creation of authoritative binding precedent which tribunal decisions do not have.

7.5 New South Wales Civil and Administrative Tribunal

In 2013, New South Wales passed the *Civil and Administrative Tribunal Act 2013* (NSW) which gave statutory authority for the establishment of the New South Wales Civil and Administrative Tribunal (NCAT) on 1 January 2014. NCAT is an integrated super tribunal with extensive jurisdiction similar to those of other Australian states and territories (other than Tasmania). NCAT enabled New South Wales to consolidate its many tribunals in an effort to simplify the statutory tribunal dispute resolution in that state.

Many of the original tribunals which were combined into NCAT continue to influence the procedures applicable in different parts of NCAT. This is entirely appropriate, as these procedures are tailored to the nature of the dispute under consideration. For example, NCAT has numerous Procedural Directions and Guidelines that apply to all NCAT divisions covering matters such as service, giving notice[40] and expert

38 See Australian Capital Territory Civil and Administrative Tribunal (ACAT) (Web Page) <https://www.acat.act.gov.au/> for further information on ACAT.

39 *Williams v Wreck Bay Aboriginal Community Council* (2019) 266 CLR 499, [14] (Kiefel CJ, Keane, Nettle and Gordon JJ in a joint judgment allowing the appeal, with Bell J and Edelman J each agreeing in separate judgments, and Gageler J dissenting).

40 New South Wales Civil and Administrative Tribunal, *NCAT Procedural Direction 1: Service and Giving Notice*, 8 January 2018.

evidence[41] as well as procedures specific to NCAT divisions, such as the Guideline on Representation in the Guardianship Division[42] and the Guideline on Professional Discipline Matters in the Occupational Division.[43]

NCAT experienced jurisdictional difficulties in relation to disputes between parties from different states which led to the introduction of pt 3A of the *Civil and Administrative Tribunal Act 2013* (NSW) (*NCAT Act*) which enabled matters where NCAT did not have jurisdiction to refer those disputes to a court. These amendments were passed in anticipation of the High Court finding, in *Burns v Corbett*, that provisions of the *NCAT Act* were invalid to the extent that they purported to confer jurisdiction upon NCAT, where the parties to the dispute were "residents of different States" within the meaning of s 75(iv) of the *Constitution*.[44]

In *Gaynor v Attorney General of New South Wales* ('*Gaynor*'),[45] the New South Wales Supreme Court of Appeal effectively endorsed the validity of pt 3A of the *NCAT Act* and its constitutional validity. The underlying dispute in both *Gaynor* and *Burns v Corbett*[46] concerned a large number of discrimination disputes made by Mr Burns, a New South Wales "self-described gay Australian anti-discrimination campaigner," against Mr Gaynor, a Queensland "conservative blogger focussing on issues regarding national security, politics and the defence of the traditional family unit" which had been sent by the Anti-Discrimination Board to NCAT only to be rejected due to the unconstitutionality of NCAT's jurisdiction regarding interstate claims.[47] *Gaynor* confirms, in relation to pt 3A of the *NCAT Act*, that:

> ... the jurisdiction that is conferred on the authorised court by this section of the NCAT Act is not federal jurisdiction but, rather, the authority to decide matters otherwise assigned by that Act or other enabling legislation such as the ADA to NCAT, that is to say, subject matter jurisdiction ...[48]

NCAT has four divisions that handle all the disputes which used to be managed by 22 separate tribunals before the creation of NCAT:[49]

- **The Administrative and Equal Opportunity Division:** reviews New South Wales Government agency administrative decisions, including on use and access to government

41 New South Wales Civil and Administrative Tribunal, *NCAT Procedural Direction 3: Expert Evidence*, 28 February 2018.

42 New South Wales Civil and Administrative Tribunal, *Representation: Guardianship Division Guideline*, August 2017.

43 New South Wales Civil and Administrative Tribunal, *Professional Discipline Matters; Occupational Guideline*, August 2017. Access to all the general and divisional guidelines can be accessed on NCAT's website.

44 *Burns v Corbett* (2018) 265 CLR 304. The partially invalid provisions were *Civil and Administrative Tribunal Act 2013* (NSW) ss 28(2)(a), 28(2)(c), 29(1), 32. There were also minor amendments to the *Civil and Administrative Tribunal Act 2013* (NSW) pt 3A following the High Court's decision in *Gaynor v Attorney-General (NSW)* (2020) 102 NSWLR 123, [9] (Bell P) discussing the *Justice Legislation Amendment Act (No 3) 2018* (NSW) sch 1 cl 1.6.

45 *Gaynor v Attorney-General (NSW)* (2020) 102 NSWLR 123.

46 *Burns v Corbett* (2018) 265 CLR 304.

47 Ibid [1].

48 Ibid [46] (Bell P).

49 New South Wales Civil and Administrative Tribunal, *What is NCAT?*, (20 August 2020), <https://www.ncat.nsw.gov.au/ncat/about-ncat/what-is-ncat.html>; New South Wales Civil and Administrative Tribunal, *NCAT Divisions and Appeal Panel* (20 August 2020), <https://www.ncat.nsw.gov.au/ncat/how-ncat-works/ncat-divisions-and-appeal-panel.html>.

information and personal information held by government, firearms licences, community services sector and vocational training decisions. This division also resolves discrimination matters referred by the Anti-Discrimination Board relating to discrimination, harassment, victimisation and vilification and reviews decisions of the Board.

- **The Consumer and Commercial Division:** covers residential property issues such as tenancy and fencing disputes and disputes about the supply of goods and services including consumer claims up to $40,000 (as at June 2020).
- **The Guardianship Division**: determines the legal appointment of substituted decision-makers for people with decision-making disabilities, including guardianship orders, financial management orders, consent for treatment, and reviews of enduring guardianship and power of attorney appointments.
- **The Occupational Division**: reviews decisions by government agencies about licensing of professional drivers, security guards, builders, real estate agents, motor dealers and repairers, pawnbrokers and second-hand dealers, stock and station agents, business agents, travel agents, valuers and licensed conveyancers. This division also handles complaints concerning professional conduct and discipline of legal practitioners, health practitioners, veterinary practitioners, architects and building professionals.

NCAT also has an Appeal Panel which hears internal appeals from the above divisions of NCAT where a right of appeal exists. In addition to NCAT, New South Wales also has specialised courts within its hierarchy, including the Land and Environment Court which hears environmental, development, building and planning disputes in New South Wales.

7.6 Northern Territory Civil and Administrative Tribunal

The Northern Territory Civil and Administrative Tribunal (NTCAT) is a super tribunal for the Northern Territory which commenced operating on 6 October 2014. As with other civil and administrative super tribunals, NTCAT hears a broad range of matters including civil claims for sums up to $25,000, tenancy disputes professional misconduct claims guardianship orders, discrimination complaints, unit title holders, development disputes as well as reviews of administrative decisions by government bodies.

The medical misconduct appeal of Dr Liyanage to the Northern Territory Supreme Court in *Liyanage v Medical Board of Australia* provides a useful example of the exercise of NTCAT's powers.[50] The Northern Territory Supreme Court declined Dr Liyanage leave to appeal in relation to effectively a three-year medical licence suspension following inappropriate sexual relationships with patients and dishonesty. The Court noted:

> [2] A party may appeal to the Supreme Court against a decision of the Tribunal on a question of law, however pursuant to s 141 of the *Northern Territory Civil and Administrative Tribunal Act* ('the NTCAT Act') leave is required. Further, an application for leave must be filed with 7 days as provided by *the Supreme Court Rules* (NT) ('the Rules'). The application for leave to appeal was not filed within 7 days as required. As

50 *Liyanage v Medical Board of Australia* [2019] NTSC 11.

will be seen in the reasons that follow, notwithstanding non-compliance with the Rules, the merits of the application have been examined. After hearing an appeal, the NTCAT Act provides the Supreme Court must do one of the following:

(a) confirm the decision of the Tribunal;
(b) vary the decision of the Tribunal;
(c) set aside the decision and:
  (i) substitute its own decision; or
  (ii) send the matter back to the Tribunal for reconsideration in accordance with any recommendations the Supreme Court considers appropriate;
(d) dismiss the appeal.[51]

The Court then refused leave to appeal and endorsed the NTCAT's medical licence suspension determination, holding:

> [27] The Tribunal conducted the hearing in this matter in its original jurisdiction, and was bound to exercise its jurisdiction in accordance with the NTCAT Act and the National Law. Neither of these instruments include any restriction on the Tribunal taking into consideration evidence which arises as a result of the investigation and the hearing.
>
> [28] Further, the objectives and guiding principles of the National Medical Registration and Accreditation Scheme are set out in s 3 of the National Law, and under s 4, the Tribunal was bound to consider them … .
>
> [29] In its reasons, the Tribunal highlighted the applicant's multiple attempts to deceive investigators and continued deceitful conduct during the Tribunal hearing as its most significant concern …
>
> [30] I cannot discern error in the approach of the Tribunal in holding that these matters bear poorly on the applicant's trustworthiness, and indicate he did not have insight into the nature of his conduct …[52]

7.7 Queensland Civil and Administrative Tribunal

Queensland has an integrated civil and administrative tribunal called the Queensland Civil and Administrative Tribunal (QCAT), established in December 2009 pursuant to the *Queensland Civil and Administrative Tribunal Act 2009* (Qld).[53] QCAT is the amalgamation of 18 previously existing tribunals but, unlike some other state super tribunals, QCAT has not replaced all of Queensland's tribunals. Queensland retains its Mental Health Review Tribunal, Mental Health Court, Planning and Environment Court, Land Court, Building and Development Tribunals, Industrial Court, Queensland Industrial Relations Commission and the review functions of the Public Service Commission which fall outside the jurisdiction of QCAT.

51 Ibid [2].
52 Ibid [27]–[30].
53 See Queensland Civil and Administrative Tribunal (Web Page) <https://www.qcat.qld.gov.au/>, for further information regarding QCAT.

QCAT has jurisdiction to hear disputes in the following areas:[54]

- Anti-discrimination: including sexual harassment and discrimination, racial and religious vilification, and victimisation
- Building disputes: including domestic and commercial and review of Queensland Building and Construction Commission decisions
- Children and young people: including child protection matters, adoption applications
- Consumer and trader disputes up to $25,000
- Debt disputes up to $25,000
- Decision-making for adults with impaired capacity: administration and guardianship.
- Minor civil disputes up to $25,000, including debt, consumer, residential tenancy, property damage, fences
- Motor vehicle disputes up to $100,000
- Other civil disputes: tree disputes, body corporate and community management scheme disputes, financial losses caused by motor and property agents, integrated resort development matters, legal cost agreement claims, manufactured home park disputes, retirement village disputes and Sanctuary Cove Resort disputes
- Occupational regulation (disciplinary and licencing decisions) for architects, building personnel, health practitioners, introduction agents, legal practitioners, motor dealers, nursing practitioners, plumbers and drainers, prescribed persons who are public servants or police officers, professional engineers, property agents, racing personnel, second-hand dealers and pawnbrokers, security providers, surveyors, tattooists and tattoo business operators, teachers, tour operators, travel agents, valuers and veterinary surgeons
- Residential tenancy disputes
- Review of administrative decisions by government agencies and statutory authorities.

The potential finality of QCAT decisions is explored in *Pivovarova v Michelsen*. In this case, the Queensland Supreme Court Appeal Division held that the requirement, in s 150(3)(a) of the *Queensland Civil and Administrative Tribunal Act 2009* (Qld), that an appeal from a final decision of the appeal tribunal of QCAT be “may be made only on a question of law” did not comprehend granting leave to appeal a mixed question of fact and law.[55] The Court noted that other rights of appeal from QCAT decisions allowed mixed fact and law appeals (s 149(3)(b)) but that s 150(3) was limited purely to errors of law because it concerned matters which had already been considered and refused on appeal by the QCAT appeal tribunal.[56]

QCAT decisions, like court decisions, require adherence to procedural fairness requirements.[57] The QCAT case of *Lyons v Dreamstarters Pty Ltd* discussed the importance of preserving natural justice through procedures which are fair for the individuals involved in the case while still allowing the Tribunal to meet its statutory objectives of procedural efficiency.[58]

54 Queensland Civil and Administrative Tribunal, ‘Matter Types’ (Web Page) <https://www.qcat.qld.gov.au/matter-types>.
55 *Pivovarova v Michelsen* (2019) 2 QR 508, [2].
56 Ibid [4]–[5].
57 See Chapter 2 for detailed discussion of procedural fairness in CDR.
58 *Lyons v Dreamstarters Pty Ltd* [2011] QCATA 142, [2]-[17].

7.8 South Australian Civil and Administrative Tribunal

The South Australian Civil and Administrative Tribunal (SACAT) commenced on 30 March 2015. SACAT replaced the Guardianship Board, Residential Tenancies Tribunal and Housing Appeal Panel. SACAT also has an appellate jurisdiction providing authority to hear appeals from its own decisions including appeals previously made to the District Court in guardianship, residential tenancy and housing, as well as land valuation appeals previously made to the Supreme Court. SACAT has jurisdiction to review over 70 different types of government administrative decisions, including, for example, Department of Child Protection decisions.[59] Under the *Equal Opportunity Act 1984* (SA), SACAT has jurisdiction to review disciplinary actions in relation to professions governed by the following legislation:[60]

- *Architectural Practice Act 2009* (SA)
- *Building Work Contractors Act 1995* (SA)
- *Conveyancers Act 1994* (SA)
- *Health Practitioners Regulation National Law (South Australia) Act 2010* (SA) (nationally uniform legislation governing a wide range of medical and related professions)
- *Land Agents Act 1994* (SA)
- *Land Valuers Act 1994* (SA)
- *Local Government Act 1999* (SA)
- *Motor Vehicles Act 1959* (SA)
- *Plumbers, Gas Fitters and Electricians Act 1995* (SA)
- *Second-Hand Vehicle Dealers Act 1995* (SA)
- *Survey Act 1992* (SA).

In addition to SACAT, South Australia also still maintains other courts and tribunals. For example, the South Australian Employment Tribunal, which also sits as the South Australian Employment Court, does not form part of SACAT and adjudicates a range of employment matters, including industrial and employment disputes, workers compensation, some equal opportunity claims and dust diseases claims.[61] The District Court of South Australia administers the Pastoral Land Appeal Tribunal, the Police Disciplinary Tribunal and the Wardens Court.[62] South Australia also maintains an Environment, Resources and Development (ERD) Court which resolves disputes, and enforces laws relating to the development and management of land, the natural and built environment and natural resources.[63] South Australia also maintains a Youth Court pursuant to the *Youth Court Act 1993* (SA).[64]

59 South Australian Civil and Administrative Tribunal, 'Review of Government Decisions' (Web Page) <http://www.sacat.sa.gov.au/review-of-government-decisions#>.

60 South Australian Civil and Administrative Tribunal, 'Disciplinary: Professional Disciplinary Applications at SACAT' (Web Page) <http://www.sacat.sa.gov.au/get-started/disciplinary>.

61 South Australian Employment Tribunal (Web Page) <https://www.saet.sa.gov.au/>.

62 Courts Administration Authority of South Australia, 'Appeals and Tribunals' (Web Page) <http://www.courts.sa.gov.au/OurCourts/DistrictCourt/Pages/Appeals-and-Tribunals.aspx>.

63 Courts Administration Authority of South Australia, 'Environment, Resources and Development (ERD) Court' (Web Page) <http://www.courts.sa.gov.au/OurCourts/ERDCourt/Pages/default.aspx>.

64 Courts Administration Authority of South Australia, 'Youth Court of South Australia' (Web Page) <http://www.courts.sa.gov.au/OurCourts/YouthCourt/Pages/default.aspx>.

7.9 Tasmanian tribunals

Tasmania is the only remaining state or territory in Australia that does not have a centralised civil and administrative tribunal. In March 2020, the Tasmanian state government committed to introducing its own super tribunal, TasCAT, promising to undertake a significant amount of work on the project in 2020.[65] Tasmania currently has the following tribunals, which are likely to become part of TasCAT:

- Anti-Discrimination Tribunal
- Asbestos Compensation Tribunal
- Forest Practices Tribunal
- Guardianship and Administration Board
- Health Practitioners Tribunal
- Mental Health Tribunal
- Motor Accident Compensation Tribunal
- Resource Management and Planning Appeal Tribunal
- Workers Rehabilitation and Compensation Tribunal.[66]

Tasmania also has what is known as the Mining Tribunal, but this is actually the Mining Division of the Magistrates Court of Tasmania created pursuant to the *Mineral Resources Development Act 1995* (Tas) s 127.

Tasmania is the only jurisdiction in Australia to maintain a Resource Management and Planning Appeal Tribunal (RMPAT). The RMPAT was established pursuant to the *Resource Management and Planning Appeal Tribunal Act 1993* (Tas) and its objectives are referred to in s 5 and set out in sch 1 of that Act, and include promotion of sustainable development of natural and physical resources, sustainable use of air, land and water, public involvement in resource management and shared responsibility between government, the community and industry.[67] The RMPAT is an example of a specialist tribunal designed to meet the specific needs of a particular state because, in Tasmania, there has been long-standing tension between conservationists and industries reliant on use of natural resources such as timber.

7.10 Victorian Civil and Administrative Tribunal

In 1998, Victoria introduced the Victorian Civil and Administrative Tribunal (VCAT) which replaced 15 boards and tribunals previously operating in Victoria. VCAT is governed by the *Victorian Civil and Administrative Tribunal Act 1998* (Vic) and the *Victorian Civil and Administrative Tribunal Rules 2008* (Vic) and has five divisions with each division being

65 Elise Archer, 'Major Steps Towards a Streamlined Tribunal for Tasmania' (Media Release, 18 March 2020) <http://www.premier.tas.gov.au/releases/major_step_towards_a_streamlined,_single_tribunal_for_tasmania>. The promised work included the creation of a physical space for the planned TasCAT.

66 Tasmanian Government, Department of Justice, 'Tribunals' (Web Page) <https://www.justice.tas.gov.au/tribunals>.

67 *Resource Management and Planning Appeal Tribunal Act 1993* (Tas) sch 1.

divided into a number of lists. The titles of the lists, as set out below, indicate the nature of the disputes covered by that list:[68]

(1) **The Administrative Division:** deals with professional conduct inquiries and applications from people seeking review of decisions made by government and other authorities. It has two lists: (1) Legal Practice and (2) Review and Regulation.
(2) **The Civil Division:** hears and determines a range of civil disputes relating to consumer matters, domestic building works, owners corporation matters, retail tenancies, sale and ownership of property, use or flow of water between properties. Civil Division has three Lists: (1) Civil Claims, (2) Building and Property and (3) Owners Corporations.
(3) **The Human Rights Division:** deals with matters relating to guardianship and administration, powers of attorney, medical treatment and advance care directives, equal opportunity, racial and religious vilification, health and privacy information, the *Disability Act 2006* (Vic), decisions made by the Mental Health Tribunal. Human Rights Division has two Lists: (1) Guardianship, including Powers of Attorney, and (2) Human Rights.
(4) **The Planning and Environment Division:** deals with reviews of decisions made by councils and other authorities. The Planning and Environment Division has only one List: Planning and Environment List.
(5) **The Residential Tenancies Division:** deals with matters involving residential tenants and landlords, public tenants, caravan park residency and site owners and tenants. The Residential Tenancies Division has only one List: Residential Tenancies.

VCAT also has an Administrative Executive and Registry which provides registry listings, customer service and other administrative functions.

There are well over 100 Victorian Acts which allow application and referrals to VCAT, including the *Accident Compensation Act 1985* (Vic); the *Children, Youth and Families Act 2005* (Vic); the *Disability Act 2006* (Vic); the *Equal Opportunity Act 1995* (Vic); the *Fair Trading Act 1999* (Vic); the *Health Services Act 1988* (Vic); the *Legal Profession Act 2004* (Vic); the *Medical Treatment Act 1988* (Vic); the *Occupational Health and Safety Act 2004* (Vic); *Residential Tenancies Act 1997* (Vic); *Retail Leases Act 2003* (Vic); the *Sale of Land Act 1962* (Vic); the *Transport Accident Act 1986* (Vic); and the *Victorian State Emergency Services Act 2005* (Vic).

There have been several VCAT decisions appealed all the way to the High Court of Australia, including *Mann v Paterson Constructions Pty Ltd*, which concerned a contract for construction of townhouses that was wrongfully repudiated and the repudiation was accepted.[69] The VCAT decision in *Mann* was overturned, providing an example of the extent of VCAT's decision-making power but also how the common law of contract can limit the extent of that discretionary power. The High Court held that VCAT had erred in upholding a claim for work, labour and materials on a quantum meruit basis which exceeded the value of the contract as the payment should have been limited to the amount due under the contract. The VCAT claim was made pursuant to s 38 of the *Domestic*

68 Victorian Civil and Administrative Tribunal, 'Our Structure' (Web Page) <https://www.vcat.vic.gov.au/about-vcat/our-structure>.
69 *Mann v Paterson Constructions Pty Ltd* (2019) 267 CLR 560.

Building Contracts Act 1995 (Vic) (*DBC Act*). The *DBC Act* provides for disputes to be determined by VCAT (*DBC Act* s 1) and provides significant discretion to VCAT to "may make any order it considers fair to resolve a domestic building dispute" (*DBC Act* s 53), but the High Court held that this did not entitle VCAT to order payment beyond the contracted amount.

7.11 Western Australia: State Administrative Tribunal

Western Australia has an integrated administrative tribunal called the State Administrative Tribunal (SAT) established in 2005 pursuant to the *State Administrative Tribunal Act 2004* (WA).[70] It is the only super tribunal which is not described as a "civil and administrative tribunal", although it actually has extensive jurisdiction for civil as well as administrative matters.[71] SAT is governed by over 150 enabling Acts set out in the *State Administrative Tribunal (Conferral of Jurisdiction) Amendment and Repeal Act 2004* (WA) including numerous professional and industry acts.[72] The objectives of SAT are set out in s 9 of the *State Administrative Tribunal Act 2004* (WA) as follows:

> ***State Administrative Tribunal Act 2004***
>
> **9. Main objectives of Tribunal**
>
> The main objectives of the Tribunal in dealing with matters within its jurisdiction are —
>
> (a) to achieve the resolution of questions, complaints or disputes, and make or review decisions, fairly and according to the substantial merits of the case; and
>
> (b) to act as speedily and with as little formality and technicality as is practicable, and minimise the costs to parties; and
>
> (c) to make appropriate use of the knowledge and experience of Tribunal members[73]

However, SAT is the busiest Western Australian tribunal, determining over 200 cases per annum. SAT hears cases in four main areas:

- **Human Rights:** including guardianship, administration, appeals from the Equal Opportunity Commissioner regarding discrimination, and appeals from the Mental Health Review Board.
- **Development and Resources**: including government decisions on planning, development, resources, land valuation and compensation.
- **Vocational Regulation:** including disciplinary complaints brought by vocational bodies against members of the vocation or occupation, appeals from decisions made by

70 See State Administrative Tribunal (Web Page) <https://www.sat.justice.wa.gov.au/> for detailed information regarding SAT.

71 See Bertus Villiers, 'Accessibility to the Law: The Contribution of Super-Tribunals to Fairness and Simplicity in the Australian Legal Landscape' (2015) 39(2) *University of Western Australia Law Review* 239 for a detailed discussion of the role and jurisdiction of super-tribunals particularly SAT.

72 State Administrative Tribunal, 'Jurisdiction' (Web Page, 13 February 2015), <https://www.sat.justice.wa.gov.au/J/jurisdiction.aspx>.

73 *State Administrative Tribunal Act 2004* (WA) s 9.

regulatory bodies regarding licences to operate in an occupation, and appeals from decisions regarding fidelity and compensation funds and licensing appeals. Vocations covered by SAT include builders, architects, electricians, debt collectors, lawyers, vets, travel agents, real estate agents, pharmacists and childcare providers.

- **Commercial and Civil**: including taxation, Commissioner of State Revenue, property (strata title, commercial tenancy, retirement village) and certain other commercial and personal disputes.

Although the SAT is designed to simplify and reduce procedural barriers to justice, there can remain significant evidentiary obligations on parties to SAT proceedings due to the enabling legislation underlying the dispute as demonstrated by the High Court decision in *Commissioner of State Revenue v Placer Dome Inc*.[74] This decision reinstated the SAT finding in support of an assessment by the Commissioner of State Revenue, despite its concerns as to the Commissioner's valuation methods. The High Court held that the taxpayer's assessment should be reinstated because the taxpayer failed to discharge to the SAT its onus of proving the assessment to be wrong. Justice Gageler (who delivered a single judgment agreeing with the joint judgment of Kiefel CJ, Bell, Nettle and Gordon JJ) stated:

> The State Administrative Tribunal Act 2004 (WA) [Section 29(1)] read with the Taxation Administration Act 2003 (WA) [Section 37(2)], as the Court of Appeal held in an important aspect of its reasoning unchallenged in the appeal, placed on Barrick as taxpayer the onus of establishing that the assessment to which its objection related was 'invalid or incorrect' [Section 37(2) of the *Taxation Administration Act*].[75]

Western Australia also retains the Western Australian Industrial Relations Commission, which is an independent quasi-judicial tribunal established under the *Industrial Relations Act 1979* (WA) to deal with industrial matters in the State of Western Australia by conciliation and arbitration.[76]

7.12 Conclusion

The complexity of CDR and the potential for procedural differences between state jurisdictions is amply demonstrated by considering the operation of Australia's many statutory tribunals. Super civil and administrative tribunals are set up pursuant to state laws and implement a huge range of state-based legislation designed to meet the particular needs of each jurisdiction. Similar to other aspects of CDR, tribunal law is also becoming more uniform throughout Australia and the relative uniformity of civil and administrative super tribunals contributes to this. However, even with each state and territory using a single civil and administrative tribunal, the differences between the tribunals in different states remains significant and mirrors the differing needs and priorities of each state. Statutory tribunals vary substantially, particularly in terms of the jurisdiction each tribunal enjoys and the vast variations within tribunals and between

74 *Commissioner of State Revenue v Placer Dome Inc* (2018) 265 CLR 585.
75 Ibid [217].
76 Western Australian Industrial Relations Commission (Web Page) <https://www.wairc.wa.gov.au/>.

tribunals in terms of jurisdiction driven by variations in the empowering legislation which includes hundreds of acts.

Statutory tribunals are a fascinating hybrid of litigation and ADR which highlight the case management, access to justice, efficiency and open justice issues which form the key themes of this book. Whilst most statutory tribunals more closely resemble courts than ADR, the procedural shortcuts they make to aid access to justice and efficiency are reminiscent of ADR. The proliferation of statutory tribunal matters is not without risk, as many tribunal disputes are statutorily banned from any formal dispute resolution mechanism other than the tribunal. This means, to the extent such tribunals can be accused of reducing procedural protections, the legislation forcing parties into statutory arbitration presents a threat to justice by depriving disputants of their opportunity to have their day in court. Conversely, the relative efficiency and informality of statutory tribunals increases the accessibility of justice to those who could not have afforded court proceedings.

As many of the cases discussed in this chapter demonstrate, the jurisdiction of statutory tribunals has been repeatedly tested in the appellate courts. This testing is likely to continue as each super tribunal has its jurisdiction informed by an array of legislation which varies depending on the nature of the dispute, leaving the potential for many variations in the scope of statutory tribunal jurisdiction. The plethora of enabling Acts underlying statutory tribunal jurisdiction adds considerably to the volume of CDR options lawyers may need to be aware of. In conclusion, statutory tribunals, while often successfully increasing efficiency and reducing procedural hurdles for individual civil disputants, are also, themselves, sources of considerable procedural complexity.

PART II

LITIGATION: THE CRUCIAL LAST RESORT

8 INTERACTIONS BETWEEN PARTIES AND THE COURTS

8.1 Introduction

The remainder of this book is dedicated to the complex, well-defined and extensively legislated processes of litigation. Chapters 9 to 16 detail the key aspects of litigation in the chronological order most civil disputes progress through. This chapter, however, introduces concepts foundational to, or recurrent in, the litigation process concerning how the key stakeholders — parties (or their lawyers) and the courts themselves — interact with each other.

Despite the benefits of alternative dispute resolution (ADR) discussed in earlier chapters, there is no question litigation is an important aspect of civil dispute resolution (CDR)[1]. There are some cases which require judicial input due to their complexity, their important value as future precedents, the intractable nature of the dispute or the uncompromising approach of the disputants.[2] ADR and litigation ideally have a symbiotic relationship. The existence of litigation, its formality and its enforceability act as a strong incentive for parties to settle their disputes outside court through informal means such as those discussed in Chapter 4. Litigation, thereby, enables ADR to be effective. In turn, ADR protects litigation from overuse and prevents courts from becoming clogged with matters which may be easily resolved through other means.

In the course of a litigation, from commencement to conclusion, parties must interact with the court. In most cases, a party's interactions with the court commence when they file their first pleading in the matter (most commonly a statement of claim, writ, summons or defence). Some disputes involve minimal interactions between the court and parties before trial. More commonly, however, there are numerous interactions following the filing of pleadings before a matter is ready for trial. It is the nature of these interlocutory[3] interactions which will be the focus of this chapter. However, it should be noted that some of the most common issues which result in parties interacting with the courts are not discussed in this chapter because they are considered in detail within other chapters, such as interlocutory discovery disputes (Chapter 11.7), subpoena disputes (Chapter 12.4), privilege disputes (Chapter 13) and witness affidavit disputes (Chapter 14).

The first and, arguably, most important issue in considering the relationship between parties and the court is determining which court has jurisdiction to hear a dispute and who are the proper parties to the litigation.[4] . In addition, this chapter will consider interlocutory hearings,[5] the increasing use of technology in litigation procedure, and the complex interrelationships and interplay between litigants, lawyers and courts.

---

1 Hazel Genn, *Judging Civil Justice* (Cambridge University Press, 2010). The interaction between ADR and litigation was discussed in Chapter 5.

2 See Chapter 3.3.3 and Genn (n 1).

3 The term "interlocutory" is based on the Latin *loquela* meaning "discourse" and *inter* meaning "between". Interlocutory communications are the communications parties have with the court between when they commence proceedings and the final hearing of their matter.

4 Further issues are discussed in Chapter 9 in the context of pre-commencement and commencement of proceedings.

5 Interlocutory hearings are hearings between the parties involving the court which do not resolve the dispute which is the subject of the main proceedings between the parties. Interlocutory proceedings can occur at any time during the course of litigation.

8.2 Themes and theories of court and party interactions

As the High Court made clear in *Aon Risk Services Australia Ltd v Australian National University*,[6] courts have limited resources. The key themes of CDR explored in Chapters 2 and 3 all inform the interactions between courts and parties. For example, if courts are too expensive for parties to litigate, this denies access to justice.[7] Similarly, if courts become overcrowded with lengthy backlogs of cases, this also denies access to justice. These factors militate in favour of brief and limited court and party interactions to decrease costs and increase efficiency. Courts, under pressure to resolve matters as quickly as possible, therefore discourage party interactions with the court as occurred in *Expense Reduction Analysis Group Pty Ltd v Armstrong Strategic Management and Marketing*.[8] Discouraging interactions leave courts little time to explain processes to more vulnerable litigants, which can come at a cost to access to justice and procedural fairness.[9] The relationship between due consideration and efficiency is a complex one, which makes the task of courts interacting with parties more challenging. For example, increasing online court processes may increase access for younger generations who have high computer literacy and access to technology, while decreasing access for older generations who tend to have lower digital literacy and reduced access to technology.[10]

Open justice is also a key theme which affects courts' interactions with parties.[11] Parties generally do not wish to disclose their private affairs in public, but open justice requires them to do so. Interactions with courts are influenced by parties' desires to minimise the aspects of their disputes that are open to the public.[12] The extent to which courts impose rules for the means and circumstances through which parties may communicate with judges and their associates invokes the theme of balancing certainty with flexibility, with some courts more willing to handle matters in chambers and by email than others.[13] Finally, the complexity of balancing party autonomy, such as the right to choose which court to commence in and how to plead their case, with court control exercised through individual case management and practice notes is a theme which critically influences interactions between parties and courts.[14]

8.3 Determining jurisdiction

Sometimes the first interaction between a party and the court will be a dispute as to whether that court has jurisdiction. This is generally a dispute about whether there is a better court or an alternative means for resolving the dispute. Sometimes the alternative means of dispute

6 *Aon Risk Services Australia Ltd v Australian National University* (2009) 239 CLR 175.

7 See Chapter 3.2 for detailed analysis of access to justice.

8 *Expense Reduction Analysis Group Pty Ltd v Armstrong Strategic Management and Marketing Pty Ltd* (2013) 250 CLR 303 was discussed in Chapter 2.4.4.

9 See Chapter 2.3.4 and Chapter 3.2 for a more detailed discussion of these issues.

10 Sonya Willis; 'Could Civil Case Management Benefit from a Litigant Vulnerability Assessment Scheme?' (2018) 7(2) *Journal of Civil Litigation and Practice* 94.

11 See Chapter 3.3 for detailed analysis.

12 See Chapter 2.3.3 for detailed analysis.

13 See Chapter 2.3.2 for detailed analysis.

14 See Chapter 2.3.4 for detailed analysis.

resolution may be arbitration, mediation or negotiation as discussed in Chapters 4 and 5. Courts have the power to determine their own jurisdiction, but that determination can be complex and difficult.

The history of judicial obligation to determine jurisdiction was discussed by Leeming JA in *Gaynor v Attorney-General (NSW)*,[15] a case concerning jurisdiction pertaining to claims of discrimination in an online forum by a New South Wales resident against a Queensland resident. His Honour noted:

> A litigant may purport to invoke the jurisdiction of a court, although in fact the court lacks jurisdiction to hear and determine the claim. It is settled law that the court's 'first duty' is to determine whether or not it has jurisdiction. The words 'first duty' are commonly traced to Griffith CJ's judgment in *Federated Engine-Drivers and Firemen's Association of Australasia v Broken Hill Proprietary Co Ltd* [1911] HCA 31; (1911) 12 CLR 398 at 415; [1911] HCA 31: 'the first duty of every judicial officer is to satisfy himself that he has jurisdiction'. The same language was used in the joint judgment in *Re Nash (No 2)* (2017) 263 CLR 443; [2017] HCA 52 at [16], while in *New South Wales v Kable* (2013) 252 CLR 118; [2013] HCA 26 at [31] the joint judgment emphasised that 'all courts, whether superior or inferior, have the authority to decide whether a claim that is made in the court is within its jurisdiction.' In fact, consideration of whether the jurisdictional limitations of a court have been satisfied preceded the creation of the High Court of Australia by centuries. This is one of the earliest examples of legal reasoning.[16]

Determining which court has jurisdiction to hear a matter can also be influenced by substantive legislation relevant to the particular case. For example, the High Court decision in *Minister for Home Affairs v DMA18* concerned the operation of s 494AB of the *Migration Act 1958* (Cth) and whether it allowed proceedings seeking compensation for injury to young children sustained in asylum-seeker detention to be commenced in the Federal Court rather than the High Court.[17] Although the Minister was successful in his appeal against the Full Federal Court's findings in the specific case, the High Court did not accept the Minister's submission that the Federal Court did not have jurisdiction to hear the matters. The High Court unanimously held against limiting the Federal Court's jurisdiction in part for practical reasons:

> So construing s 494AB as a statutory bar avoids the High Court being made a post box for the commencement of proceedings destined to be remitted to another court. It avoids diverting the High Court away from its central work as the apex court of the Australian judicial system. And, further, it avoids administrative inconveniences for the courts, the profession and litigants in circumstances where the Commonwealth could not identify any purpose or utility in requiring the proceedings to be filed in the High Court only for them to be remitted.[18]

15 *Gaynor v Attorney-General (NSW)* (2020) 102 NSWLR 123.

16 Ibid [130]. This case also, arguably, led to the introduction of pt 3A of the *Civil and Administrative Tribunal Act 2013* (NSW) clarifying the limitations of NCAT's jurisdiction in federal proceedings as discussed in *Gaynor v Burns* [2020] NSWCATAP 203, [2].

17 *Minister for Home Affairs v DMA18 as Litigation Guardian for DLZ18* (2020) 385 ALR 16.

18 Ibid [34] (Kiefel CJ, Bell, Gageler, Keane and Gordon JJ).

Minister for Home Affairs v DMA18 is an excellent example of the significant role the case management requirement of efficient procedure can have even in the interpretation of a statute such as the *Migration Act 1958* (Cth). The High Court rejected the interpretation of the legislation propounded by the Minister, as it would have been inefficient for litigants, lawyers and, most importantly, the High Court itself. This is a further demonstration of how the key themes of access to justice and balancing efficiency and due process were highly relevant to the Court's decision.[19]

Sometimes, multiple courts will believe they have jurisdiction and this can result in difficulties with the finality of a court decision because if multiple courts take jurisdiction there is a risk they may come to different conclusions.[20] To ensure both justice and efficiency, which are key objectives of CDR it is important that jurisdictional issues be resolved as promptly as possible in a way which prevents multiple courts taking jurisdiction for the same matter. When such issues arise between courts of different Australian States, these are resolved through cross-vesting legislation. However, in disputes with overseas courts, the issues become more complex.

8.3.1 Statutory and inherent jurisdiction

The jurisdiction of most courts is determined by statute, but courts also have inherent jurisdiction such as to prevent abuse of their own process. For example, the Federal Court of Australia's jurisdiction derives from the *Federal Court of Australia Act 1976* (Cth) and the *Judiciary Act 1903* (Cth), particularly s 39B(1A)(c), which was, itself, able to be enacted due to s 71 of the *Constitution*.[21]

The jurisdiction of state courts is more straightforward. For example, the jurisdiction of the New South Wales Supreme Court is set out in s 23 of the *Supreme Court Act 1970* (NSW):

> **Jurisdiction Generally**
> The Court shall have all jurisdiction which may be necessary for the administration of justice in New South Wales.

Jurisdiction for territories is slightly different again as demonstrated by the Australian Capital Territory *Supreme Court Act 1933* (ACT) s 20:

> Jurisdiction and powers of Supreme Court
>
> (1) The court has the following jurisdiction:
> (a) all original and appellate jurisdiction that is necessary to administer justice in the Territory;
> (b) jurisdiction conferred by a Commonwealth Act or a law of the Territory.
> (2) Unless it is required to do so by or under a Commonwealth Act or a law of the Territory, the court is not bound to exercise its powers if it has concurrent jurisdiction with another court or tribunal.

19 See Chapters 2 and 3 for detailed analysis.
20 See Chapter 16.4.
21 See James Allsop, 'An Introduction to the Jurisdiction of the Federal Court of Australia' [2007] *Federal Judicial Scholarship* 15 which provides an excellent scholarly analysis for those seeking a detailed understanding of the jurisdiction of the Federal Court.

However, discerning the scope of a court's jurisdiction, particularly its inherent jurisdiction, is more difficult. The High Court has affirmed that determining a Court's inherent jurisdiction is difficult. In *Batistatos v Roads and Traffic Authority of New South Wales*, which concerned the ability of a disabled person to pursue proceedings relating to an accident in 1965 where the proceedings had been commenced and then stayed well beyond the usual statutory limitation, the High Court explains the complex distinction between power and jurisdiction:

> 5. The phrase 'inherent jurisdiction' itself is a slippery one. In *Australian Securities and Investments Commission v Edensor Nominees Pty Ltd*, Gleeson CJ, Gaudron and Gummow JJ remarked:
>
> > 'Jurisdiction' and 'power' are not discrete concepts. The term 'inherent jurisdiction' may be used, for example in relation to the granting of stays for abuse of process, to describe what in truth is the power of a court to make orders of a particular description. In *Harris v Caladine*, Toohey J said:
> >
> > > The distinction between jurisdiction and power is often blurred, particularly in the context of 'inherent jurisdiction'. But the distinction may at times be important. Jurisdiction is the authority which a court has to decide the range of matters that can be litigated before it; in the exercise of that jurisdiction a court has powers expressly or impliedly conferred by the legislation governing the court and 'such powers as are incidental and necessary to the exercise of the jurisdiction or the powers so conferred'.[22]

The inherent jurisdiction of Supreme Courts, while not unlimited, is broad as demonstrated in *PT Bayan Resources TBK v BCBC Singapore Pte Ltd*[23] where the High Court summarised the scope and uncertainty of inherent jurisdiction as:

> 38. The term 'inherent jurisdiction' has been described as 'elusive', 'uncertain' and 'slippery'. The difficulty is minimised if the term is confined to its primary signification: to refer to the power inhering in a superior court of record administering law and equity to make orders of a particular description. For present purposes, inherent jurisdiction can be used interchangeably with 'inherent power'
>
> ...
>
> 40. The rule-making power of the Supreme Court conferred by s 167(1)(a) of the *Supreme Court Act* is relevantly confined to making rules 'regulating and prescribing the procedure ... and the practice to be followed in the Supreme Court' in matters in or with respect to which the Supreme Court has jurisdiction. That rule-making power is available to regulate the range of orders capable of being made by the Supreme Court in the exercise of its inherent jurisdiction, but it is not available to expand the range of those orders ...
>
> 50. The power to make a freezing order in relation to an anticipated judgment of a foreign court, which when made would be registrable by order of the Supreme Court under the Foreign Judgments Act, is within the inherent power of the Supreme Court. That is because the making of the order is to protect a process of registration and enforcement in the Supreme Court which is in prospect of being invoked.[24]

22 *Batistatos v Roads and Traffic Authority of New South Wales* (2006) 226 CLR 256, [5].

23 *PT Bayan Resources TBK v BCBC Singapore Pte Ltd & Ors* (2015) 258 CLR 1.

24 Ibid [38], [40], [50]. See also Chapter 9.2.2.2; *PT Bayan Resources TBK v BCBC Singapore Pte Ltd* (2015) 258 CLR 1, [38]-[50] (French CJ, Kiefel, Bell, Gageler and Gordon JJ (with Keane and Nettle JJ agreeing in a separate judgment)).

Thus, the scope of a court's jurisdiction, while predominantly governed by statute, also continues to develop through the common law and may depend on the particular circumstances of the case before the court.

8.3.2 Choosing the appropriate court in international disputes: *forum non conveniens*

Another limitation on jurisdiction of courts can arise where the dispute in question has a stronger connection with a foreign jurisdiction. This can arise in cases with an overseas element or an interstate element. For cases with interstate aspects, there is cross-vesting legislation and the *Service and Execution of Process Act 1992* (Cth).[25] For cases with overseas elements, conflict of law rules on jurisdiction such as the doctrine of *forum non conveniens* come into play.

In order for a court to take jurisdiction over a dispute with an overseas element, the court must answer two questions. First, does the court have jurisdiction? The answer to this question will be "yes", provided one of the following conditions is met: the defendant is present in the relevant Australian state; the defendant submits to jurisdiction; or there is statutory authority for service. For example, in New South Wales, through the *Uniform Civil Procedure Rules 2005* (NSW) r 11 and sch 6.[26]

The second question the court must ask itself is whether it *should* exercise its jurisdiction or decline to exercise leaving jurisdiction to the other relevant jurisdiction(s). This is a discretionary test to which Australian courts will answer "yes", unless the court is a "clearly inappropriate forum" which is the applicable *forum non conveniens* test in Australia.[27] There are several reasons a court may find itself to be a clearly inappropriate forum, including because the parties have contractually chosen another forum (including arbitration),[28] because of the lack of factors (including the substantive law to be applied to the dispute) connecting the court to the dispute, because another court is already hearing (or has determined) the dispute or because another court has ordered the parties not to proceed in Australia (due to the granting of an anti-suit injunction).[29]

8.3.3 Interstate cross-vesting

In many ways, Australia is eight or nine different jurisdictions, but there are a number of matters, in addition to the Constitution and the Commonwealth jurisdiction, which make relations between state and territory jurisdictions closer than foreign nations and render *forum non conveniens* inapplicable for interstate jurisdiction disputes. Jurisdictional disputes

25 The cross-vesting legislation is discussed in Chapter 8.3.3 and interstate service is discussed in Chapter 9.7.5.

26 See also Chapter 9.7.5.

27 *Puttick v Tenon Ltd* (2008) 238 CLR 265; *Regie National des Usines Renault SA v Zhang* (2002) 210 CLR 491; *Voth v Manildra Flour Mills Pty Ltd* (1990) 171 CLR 538.

28 *Rinehart v Hancock Prospecting Pty Ltd* (2019) 366 ALR 635.

29 See *Puttick v Tenon Ltd* (2008) 238 CLR 265; *Regie National des Usines Renault SA v Zhang* (2002) 210 CLR 491 for key High Court decisions discussing the application and circumstances of the clearly inappropriate forum test. See also *UBS AG v Tyne* (2018) 265 CLR 77 regarding stays of proceedings due to matters being already heard in other jurisdictions.

in interstate cases are subject to cross-vesting legislation, which enables courts to transfer matters between States and to resolve jurisdictional disputes more effectively. The effect of the cross-vesting legislation was explained by the High Court in *BHP Billiton Ltd v Schultz*.[30] This case concerned the application of s 5 of the *Jurisdiction of Courts (Cross-vesting) Act 1987* (NSW) to transfer an asbestosis case from the New South Wales Dust Diseases Tribunal to the Supreme Court of South Australia, with the High Court stating:

> [14] In the context of the *Cross-vesting Act*, one is not concerned with the problem of a court, with a prima facie duty to exercise a jurisdiction that has been regularly invoked, asking whether it is justified in refusing to perform that duty. Rather, the court is required by statute to ensure that cases are heard in the forum dictated by the interests of justice. An application for transfer under s 5 of the *Cross-vesting Act* is brought upon the hypothesis that the jurisdiction of the court to which the application is made has been regularly invoked. If it appears to that court that it is in the interests of justice that the proceedings be determined by another designated court, then the first court 'shall transfer' the proceedings to that other court. There is a statutory requirement to exercise the power of transfer whenever it appears that it is in the interests of justice that it should be exercised. It is not necessary that it should appear that the first court is a 'clearly inappropriate' forum. It is both necessary and sufficient that, in the interests of justice, the second court is more appropriate.
>
> ...
>
> [19] In many cases, there will be such a preponderance of connecting factors with one forum that it can readily be identified as the most appropriate, or natural, forum. In other cases, there might be significant connecting factors with each of two different forums. Some of the factors might cancel each other out. If the action is between two individuals, and the plaintiff resides in one law area and the defendant in another, there may be no reason to treat the residence of either party as determinative, although, as already noted, it will ordinarily be the residence of the defendant that is important to establish jurisdiction. Weighing considerations of cost, expense, and convenience, even when they conflict, is a familiar aspect of the kind of case management involved in many cross-vesting applications.[31]

Thus, if a plaintiff commences proceedings in its home jurisdiction where the defendant is interstate, that matter may be transferred to the defendant's home jurisdiction, particularly where there are other factors linking the dispute to the defendant's jurisdiction, such as the events causing the dispute or the law applicable to the dispute. Where it is not appropriate to transfer a case to a different state, but interstate law applies, courts can apply the laws of the other state without requiring expert evidence to prove that law (as is required in international disputes).[32]

30 *BHP Billiton Ltd v Schultz* (2004) 221 CLR 400.

31 Ibid [14], [19] (Gleeson CJ, McHugh and Heydon JJ). Justice Harrison recently relied on *Schultz*, stating "the relevant legal principles are not in doubt" in *Fuji Xerox Australia Pty Ltd v Documents on Call Pty Ltd* [2018] NSWSC 1862, [5]. In *Fuji*, Harrison J refused to transfer proceedings from New South Wales to Victoria given the parties had contractually agreed to the jurisdiction and laws of New South Wales.

32 The complexity of how and when it is required to prove foreign law is discussed by the High Court in *Neilson v Overseas Projects Corporation of Victoria Ltd* (2005) 223 CLR 331.

8.3.4 Exorbitant jurisdiction

Although courts have wide jurisdictional powers, they are not without limitation. Both governments and courts have limitations on the powers they are able to exert. Courts are commonly described as exercising "exorbitant jurisdiction" where they allow service of process on foreign parties.[33] Although service overseas is an allowable exercise of exorbitant jurisdiction,[34] judges are more wary of asserting jurisdiction where that jurisdiction may be considered exorbitant.[35] In *X v Twitter Inc*, Pembroke J granted an injunction against Twitter, an overseas defendant, who chose not to appear at the hearing other than through a single email, finding that the court's jurisdiction was "uncontroversial".[36] However, his Honour carefully considered the discretionary nature of the injunction, including the practical burden imposed on Twitter and the utility of making worldwide orders[37]

Exorbitancy can be legislative as well as judicial. Courts will not enforce foreign legislation that is exorbitant. This was briefly discussed in a hypothetical context by the High Court in the parliamentary citizenship case of *Re Gallagher*,[38] which determined that Katy Gallagher, a Federal Senator representing the Australian Capital Territory, had not been validly elected due to her British citizenship. The Court confirmed that if mischievous foreign legislation attempted to declare all Australian elected politicians as citizens of that foreign power, that legislation would be held invalid: "In cases of such exorbitant foreign laws both public policy and international law require that the foreign law not be recognised."[39]

8.3.5 Jurisdiction to bind other courts

When considering which court has jurisdiction, it should be remembered that there is a significant level of judicial consistency throughout Australia, due to the common appellate jurisdiction of the High Court and the obligations each state has to follow the decision of other states on equivalent issues. This obligation was explained by the High Court in *Farah Constructions Pty Ltd v Say-Dee Pty Ltd*,[40] which concerned a falling out between distant relatives over the co-development of blocks of land in Burwood, Sydney. The High Court held:

> Intermediate appellate courts and trial judges in Australia should not depart from decisions in intermediate appellate courts in another jurisdiction on the interpretation of Commonwealth legislation or uniform national legislation unless they are convinced that the interpretation is plainly wrong. Since there is a common law of Australia rather than of each Australian jurisdiction, the same principle applies in relation to non-statutory law.[41]

---

33 *Agar v Hyde* (2000) 201 CLR 552, [43] with reference to the United Kingdom decision of *Amin Rasheed Corporation v Kuwait Insurance* [1984] AC 50. See Chapter 9.7.5 for overseas service.

34 *Humane Society International Inc v Kyodo Senpaku Kaisha Limited* (2006) 154 FCR 425, [16].

35 *X v Twitter Inc* (2017) 95 NSWLR 301.

36 Ibid [20].

37 Ibid [30]-[43].

38 *Re Gallagher* (2018) 263 CLR 469.

39 Ibid [54] (Gageler J in a separate judgment, agreeing with the judgment of Keifel CJ, Bell, Keane, Nettle and Gordon JJ).

40 *Farah Constructions Pty Ltd v Say-Dee Pty Ltd* (2007) 230 CLR 89.

41 Ibid [115].

The *Farah v Say-Dee* decision means that parties and judges can, and do, rely on the decisions of courts in other Australian jurisdictions to support their arguments, increasing the consistency throughout Australia even before an issue reaches the High Court.[42]

8.4 Determining the proper parties

One important issue which sometimes involves courts is determining the proper parties to litigation. In a small percentage of cases, it is uncertain whether the potential plaintiff has legal standing to bring the litigation and, somewhat more commonly, there are cases where it is unclear who the proper defendants are. In addition, there are a growing number of cases which involve a large number of plaintiffs, each of whom have individually suffered only a small loss but who, as a class, can mount a significant claim. Determining who falls within the class of plaintiffs in a representative action can be a significant issue for the courts to determine.

8.4.1 Does the plaintiff have legal standing?

In most cases, the plaintiff is easily identified and has an obvious entitlement to commence litigation. There are, however, disputes where the party bringing the dispute is not an appropriate plaintiff. For example, the rules regarding plaintiffs' standing can become complex where shareholders and directors wish to bring claims in relation to companies. Companies are recognised legal entities and proper plaintiffs, but they do not exist as flesh and blood. Companies must be properly represented in court cases but this can be problematic for very small, personally-held companies where the directors or owners cannot afford legal representation or refuse to hire lawyers.[43] Similar complications arise with associations.[44] This is an excellent example of the complexity of the theme of balancing efficiency against due process.[45] It is more efficient for all parties and the courts for litigants to be represented and is likely to achieve a fairer result, but requiring a single person company to have legal representation can result in no hearing at all and this is an example of procedural requirements operating as a bar to access to justice.

One rather tragic example of a company director being unable to represent his company is the dispute between Tibra Capital Pty Ltd and its former employer, Mr Tydeman, and his company Tanamerah Estates Pty Ltd in relation to the buy-back of Tibra shares issued to Mr Tydeman during his employment.[46] Rule 7.2 of the *Civil Procedure Rules 2005* (NSW) requires that directors commencing on behalf of their companies must also file an affidavit

42 See, eg, *Newcrest Mining Ltd v Thornton* (2012) 248 CLR 555, [68] (Crennan and Kiefel JJ in dissent but not on this issue). Where intermediate appellate courts fail to follow others, their decisions may be overruled on that basis as in, for example, the unanimous High Court decision in *R v Falzon* (2018) 264 CLR 361, [49].

43 See *Tanamerah Estates Pty Ltd v Tibra Capital Pty Ltd* [2016] NSWCA 42. It is beyond the scope of this book to detail all the requirements of the *Corporations Act 2001* (Cth) and its interaction with the relevant civil procedure rules for each jurisdiction.

44 *Bandiera v Bilambil Community Preschool and Oosh Inc* [2018] NSWSC 1903, [47] (Robb J).

45 See Chapter 2.3.1.

46 This dispute has spawned over 10 decisions in the New South Wales Supreme Court and Court of Appeal.

as to his or her authority. Further, pursuant to r 7.1(2), directors may only commence on behalf of their company in the Supreme Court where the director is also a proper plaintiff. In *Tanamerah Estates Pty Ltd v Tibra Capital Pty Ltd*[47] (upheld in subsequent appeals including *Tanamerah Estates Pty Ltd v Tibra Capital Pty Ltd*),[48] the New South Wales Supreme Court found that Mr Tydeman could not act on behalf of Tanamerah against Tibra as he did not, personally, have a claim against Tibra.[49] Mr Tydeman refused to hire a lawyer because he did not trust lawyers but it was evident to the Court that he did not have the necessary legal skills to properly bring what was a complex claim on behalf of the company despite being its director. A subsequent attempt by Mr Tydeman to restructure his affairs to enable a claim through trust law was also unsuccessful, resulting in summary dismissal in *Tydeman v Tibra Capital Pty Ltd (No 2)*.[50] However, even in this case, the Court's reluctance to deny Mr Tydeman a hearing is apparent from Parker J's hints as to how such an action might be successfully run:

> Of course, this conclusion does not mean that the claims which arise out of the acquisition of Tanamerah's shares in Tibra cannot be litigated. If, as I have found, the claims arising out of the purported buy-back of the shares are not assignable, equity would usually require the former trustee, Tanamerah, to exercise those legal rights as directed by the new trustees, the Tydemans. But the Tydemans' entitlement to direct Tanamerah in this regard is not absolute. For instance, an equitable assignor is usually entitled to insist on an indemnity being given before pursuing any proceeding at the request of the equitable assignee: see J D Heydon, M J Leeming and P G Turner, Meagher, Gummow and Lehane's *Equity: Doctrines and Remedies* (LexisNexis Butterworths Australia, 5th ed, 2015) [6–160], [6–520]. It is not, however, necessary to explore any further for the purposes of this judgment what the Tydemans might need to do in order to require Tanamerah to pursue the claims. It is enough to say that if they are to be litigated they must be litigated in the name of Tanamerah.[51]

Cases where there are difficulties working out the proper plaintiff are at high risk of summary disposition (as occurred in *Tydeman v Tibra Capital Pty Limited (No 2)*) and a consequent denial of access to justice caused by procedural constraints.[52]

8.4.2 Representative actions (class actions): determining the proper plaintiffs

In some cases, with large numbers of potential plaintiffs determining the appropriate plaintiffs to litigation may, in itself, be a substantial task. One of the fastest growing areas of civil litigation is class action litigation (which is also commonly called "representative action litigation" by courts). "Class actions" and "representative actions" are essentially different

47 *Tanamerah Estates Pty Ltd v Tibra Capital Pty Ltd* (2013) 272 FLR 365.
48 *Tanamerah Estates Pty Ltd v Tibra Capital Pty Ltd* [2016] NSWCA 42.
49 *Tanamerah Estates Pty Ltd v Tibra Capital Pty Ltd* (2013) 272 FLR 365, [90]-[119]; *Tanamerah Estates Pty Ltd v Tibra Capital Pty Ltd* [2016] NSWCA 42, [4]-[5], [32]-[40].
50 *Tydeman v Tibra Capital Pty Ltd (No 2)* [2018] NSWSC 884, [46]-[47], [52].
51 Ibid [53].
52 See Chapter 5 for detailed analysis of summary disposition.

titles for actions involving a large number of plaintiffs with legally identical interests in a dispute.[53] The title "representative actions" is apt because, in such actions, a small number of representative plaintiffs are chosen to represent the entire class in the litigation and become the named plaintiffs in the case. Lawyers and the media also commonly refer to such actions as "class actions" because there are many plaintiffs who fall within the same class regarding their action against the defendant(s).

Representative actions tend to be common in certain types of litigation where a number of plaintiffs have similar, or identical, interests, including faulty product litigation (particularly products which cause injury or harm to consumers or fraudulent financial products),[54] employee disputes against employers,[55] and, increasingly, shareholder litigation.[56]

Representative actions have special procedures, many of which relate to the identification of the class of plaintiffs and their representatives. Representative actions were introduced through pt IVA of the *Federal Court of Australia Act 1976* (Cth) in 1992 and similar state-based legislation followed; for example, pt IVA in the *Supreme Court Act 1986* (Vic) and pt 10 in the *Civil Procedure Act 2005* (NSW), together with court-based practice notes further detailing procedures.[57] Australian representative actions are generally "opt out", which means that every potential plaintiff within a class can benefit from the action unless they specifically "opt out" of the class by choosing not to be in part of the litigation. This is different to North America, where potential plaintiffs must "opt in" to be part of a class. How the class is identified is particularly complex in cases involving large numbers of members of the public, which is common with faulty or negligent product litigation.

Representative actions are often subject to funding arrangements which can further increase the complexity of their procedure. The cost of running representative litigation is usually significant and often professional funders become involved in Australian representative actions to enable the action to run without forcing lawyers to collect fees in advance from the, often large, sometimes uncertain, number of plaintiffs in the class. The funders also usually wear the risk of an adverse costs order for a potential loss, so that individual litigants cannot be found personally liable to pay the defendant's costs if they are unsuccessful. The "opt out" nature of Australian class actions makes it more difficult for litigation funders to reach agreement with the potential plaintiffs in a representative action but, despite this, representative actions are relatively common in Australia compared to most jurisdictions. There are also increasing difficulties for courts where multiple litigation funders and lawyers attempt to commence proceedings against the same defendant in relation to

53 See also Chapter 3.2.5 in relation to class actions.

54 See, eg, *Gill v Ethicon Sarl (No 5)* [2019] FCA 1905 which concerned a claim for injury caused by vaginal mesh implants; *Moore v Scenic Tours Pty Ltd* (2020) 377 ALR 209 which concerned claims by over 1,500 passengers on 13 Scenic Tours severely disrupted by predicted weather issues.

55 See, eg, *Mutch v ISG Management Pty Ltd* [2020] FCA 362 which concerned whether Mr Mutch and over 3,000 others were employees of ISGM or were contractors or employees of other entities.

56 See, eg, *Wigmans v AMP Ltd* (2019) 373 ALR 323; *Wigmans v AMP Ltd* (2020) 102 NSWLR 199 which were interlocutory disputes concerning multiple shareholder class actions against AMP in relation to alleged failures to disclose information to the market which were before the High Court at the time of writing.

57 See, eg, Federal Court of Australia, *Class Action Practice Note GPN-CA* (20 December 2019); Supreme Court of New South Wales, *Practice Note No SC GEN 17: Supreme Court Representative Proceedings* (7 March 2017); Supreme Court of Victoria, *Practice Note SC GEN 10: Conduct of Group Proceedings (Class Actions) (Second Revision)* (13 October 2020).

potentially the same dispute, challenging the courts to choose the best plaintiff/lawyer/funder group to run the proceedings.[58]

Class actions are complex and varied and, therefore, create a myriad of issues for courts trying to manage them.[59] As Gummow, Hayne and Crennan JJ stated in the High Court case of *Campbell's Cash & Carry Pty Ltd v Fostif Pty Ltd*:

> 40. In the submissions, the parties tended to speak of 'class actions' as if there were a single, distinct kind of proceedings available by that name. However, the rules governing representative or group proceedings vary greatly from court to court. Two things of present significance follow from this. The first is that close attention must be given to the particular Rules of the Supreme Court upon which this litigation turns. The second is that the outcome of the present proceedings with respect to those Rules is not to be taken necessarily as indicating that there would have been the same outcome in proceedings under the rules of other courts.[60]

In *Campbell's Cash and Carry Pty Ltd v Fostif Pty Ltd*, Gummow, Hayne and Crennan JJ, with whom Gleeson CJ, Callinan and Heydon JJ agreed (with Kirby J dissenting) held that the litigation was not a representative action under the New South Wales rules, such that the litigation funder was able to require prospective plaintiffs to opt into the litigation despite the representative action rules for New South Wales requiring disputes to be "opt out".[61]

Decisions such as *Money Max Int Pty Ltd v QBE Insurance Group Ltd*[62] and *Money Max Int Pty Ltd (Trustee) v QBE Insurance Group Ltd*[63] demonstrate the complexity and resulting cost which can accrue in class actions. Money Max brought a class action in the Federal Court of Australia against QBE on behalf of itself and shareholders who had acquired shares in late 2013. Eventually, 52% of registered class members — 1,292 people — entered into a funding agreement.[64] The Full Federal Court in *Money Max Int Pty Ltd v QBE Insurance Group Ltd* effectively applied a common fund doctrine to determining the class for the dispute which enabled the class to be closed in October 2017. The parties settled and the 2018 decision confirms the settlement deed and the costs payment including a staggering $21,875,678.51 in legal fees to Maurice Blackburn. Justice Murphy stated:

> 7. On 15 November 2016 the Full Court made orders to the effect that, upon any successful settlement or judgment in the proceeding, the applicant and class members must pay a reasonable Court-approved funding commission from any monies received, prior to distribution of those monies (Common Fund Orders): see *Money Max Int Pty*

58 See, eg, *BMW Australia Ltd v Brewster* (2019) 374 ALR 627.

59 It is beyond the scope of this book to consider class actions in detail due to the complexity of issues raised by them.

60 *Campbell's Cash & Carry Pty Ltd v Fostif Pty Ltd* (2006) 229 CLR 386, [40].

61 Ibid [197]. See Peter Cashman, *Class Action Law and Practice* (Federation Press, 2007) for a detailed examination of the law and issues in representative actions, although it should be noted that the *Civil Procedure Act 2010* (Vic) postdates this text. As the author's background is as a plaintiffs' lawyer, readers may also wish to consider the defendants' lawyers' view which can be gleaned from articles such as Stuart Clark and Christina Harris, 'The Push to Reform Class Action Procedure in Australia: Evolution or Revolution?' (2008) 32(3) *Melbourne University Law Review* 775.

62 *Money Max Int Pty Ltd v QBE Insurance Group Ltd* (2016) 245 FCR 191.

63 *Money Max Int Pty Ltd (Trustee) v QBE Insurance Group Ltd* (2018) 358 ALR 382.

64 Ibid [182].

> *Ltd v QBE Insurance Group Ltd* (2016) 245 FCR 191; [2016] FCAFC 148 (*Money Max*). The orders included the rider that the aggregate funding commission payable by class members could not exceed the aggregate amount that would otherwise be payable by them in the event the Common Fund Orders were not made.[65]

Justice Murphy concluded that the litigation funder payment on settlement of $30.75 million was "fair and reasonable" for numerous reasons, including the significant risk and expenditure incurred by the funder, the fact that the payment represented only 23.2% of the payout which was significantly less that the average of approximately 31%, and less than what many sophisticated institutional shareholders had agreed to pay.[66] However, a subsequent High Court decision of *BMW Australia Ltd v Brewster* rejected the authority of the Federal Court to grant a common fund order as a means of managing litigation classes.[67] The *BMW v Brewster* decision reduces the options available to courts for managing the operation and funding of class actions, making this an area where it is likely that statutory law reform will be required to enable courts to equitably manage the enormous funds involved in running many class actions.[68] Class actions are an area of CDR where enabling access to justice for large numbers of plaintiffs, each with small claims, involves complex and novel case management to enable sufficient financial incentives for lawyers and litigation funders to run these actions on behalf of the litigants.[69]

8.4.3 Who are the proper defendants to the proceedings?

As with determining the proper plaintiffs, in many cases, it is obvious who the defendant is. There are, however, cases where it is unclear who the proper defendant is, and many cases where there are a number of possible defendants. Sometimes, plaintiffs claim against all possible defendants, but this can make the proceedings unnecessarily complex and expensive and can lead to adverse costs orders against the plaintiff. Sometimes, the most obvious defendant, in terms of liability, is impecunious, while a less obvious defendant may have sufficient money to pay the plaintiff if the plaintiff succeeds. In such cases, it can be advisable for the plaintiff to sue the less obvious defendant or both potential defendants to ensure they have a judgement which can actually be enforced.[70]

Determining the proper parties to litigation is one of many areas of civil procedure where knowledge of a substantive area of law may be necessary in order to make the appropriate or optimal procedural decision. For example, it may be necessary to research

---

65 Ibid [7].

66 Ibid [187]-[210]. See also Bernard Murphy, 'Civil Justice Reforms in Class Actions and Litigation Funding' [2018] 19 *Federal Judicial Scholarship* 20.

67 *BMW Australia Ltd v Brewster* (2019) 374 ALR 627, [85]-[90] (Kiefel CJ, Bell and Keane JJ), [125] (Nettle J), [106] (Gageler J in dissent).

68 See, eg, Michael Legg, 'Competing Class Actions: A Suggested Solution through Certification' (2018) 7(1) *Journal of Civil Litigation and Practice* 38 for a proposed solution based on US law. See also AE Crowley, 'Limitations on the Scope of a Court's Power to Make any Order it Thinks Appropriate Under s 33ZF or s 183: The High Court's Decision in the Brewster and Lenthall Cases' (2019) 94(8) *Australian Law Journal* 591 for a more detailed analysis.

69 See Chapter 3 for detailed analysis of access to justice issues.

70 See Chapter 16.7 for more detail on enforcement.

and understand employment law, administrative law, insurance law or corporations law in order to determine the most appropriate defendant to litigation. Common circumstances where it can be difficult to determine the most appropriate defendant include:

1. **Cases involving insurers:** Insurers are able to take on the rights of the parties they insure through the principle of subrogation. In cases involving insurers, the named party may be the insured party, but the case may be run by the insurers seeking to recover the money they have already paid to their insured customer.
2. **Cases involving government bodies:** The government is involved in many enterprises and to varying degrees. Some organisations are really part of the government and claims by or against those organisations will be claims by or against the state or Federal Government. In other cases, government linked organisations are independent corporations which can sue and be sued. Even in these cases, a claim may need to be made directly against the government if the offending actions of the government corporation result from some failure by the government in the establishment or constitution of the government corporation.
3. **Employment and subcontractor cases:** Mistakes are invariably made by individuals, but often individuals are also employees or sub-contractors. When individuals make litigation-worthy mistakes in the course of their employment, or as a sub-contractor, the plaintiff is likely to sue the employer or head contractor, as well as the individual wrongdoer using the principle of vicarious liability. An employer is vicariously liable for the actions (and misdeeds) of its employees, provided the employee was acting in the course of his or her employment. Employers and head contractors are more likely to have the necessary funds or insurance to pay a claim than the wrongdoer and therefore make better defendants from the plaintiff's perspective.
4. **Claims against corporations:** In some actions against corporations, particularly where the corporation may be insolvent, it may also be appropriate to sue one or more directors of the company as directors have significant obligations under corporate law in relation to the running of the company. In other cases, a complex corporate structure may make it challenging for a plaintiff to determine which corporate entity has liability for the dispute.

8.5 Communications between parties and the court

Each court simultaneously operates as a single entity, a collection of sub-entities and a large number of individuals. How often and in what manner parties interact with the court often develops over the course of the proceedings. There is a wide range of experiences in interactions with courts affected by the nature of the matter, the practices of the court, and the approach of the parties and their lawyers. All of these aspects of civil litigation are also being affected by new technology.[71]

71 See Chapter 8.6.

8.5.1 The relationship between parties and the court

In the course of a civil litigation, parties deal extensively with each other and with the court. Most of this communication is in writing and formal in nature. For example, proceedings must commence through personal service of the originating process in accordance with legislative requirements even where parties are well known to each other.[72] Formal aspects of litigation will generally be required to be served through ordinary service, which includes the post and agreed electronic means, commonly lawyers' email addresses, which are specified by the parties in their pleadings.[73] Lawyers acting for parties also have obligations to the courts, which affect their interactions with each other.[74] For example, lawyers may have an obligation to return documents disclosed by mistake, as occurred in the High Court case of *Expense Reduction Analysis Group Pty Ltd v Armstrong Strategic Management and Marketing Pty Ltd*.[75]

Correspondence between parties and the court are also usually formal in nature. The more involved a party or lawyer becomes with the court, the more likely they are to be dealing with known individuals rather than a faceless institution. Traditionally, commencement of proceedings and filing the originating process required attendance at the court registry. As e-filing has become prevalent in many courts, most parties are no longer required to attend court to file documents. In 2020, the COVID-19 global pandemic led to a rapid increase in the use of remote electronic procedures for court documentation to enable matters to progress while courts were physically closed.[76] During the early stages of proceedings, parties are more likely to be interacting with registrars and other court officers, rather than with judges.

Conversely, during and immediately prior to the final hearing of a matter, parties may interact closely with an individual judge (and, often, his or her Associate) who has an in-depth understanding of the parties' case.

In some matters, particularly smaller matters in lower courts, there may be minimal interaction with the court prior to hearing. Complex matters in higher courts are likely to involve many directions hearings, interlocutory disputes and significant interaction between the court and the parties prior to trial.

8.5.2 Use of interpreters

Many users of Australian courts do not speak fluent English. For these individuals, an interpreter may be necessary for them to understand and take part in litigation. The Australian Government provides some interpreting services through the Translating and

72 See Chapter 9.7 for further detail on service in commencing proceedings.

73 See, eg, *Federal Court Rules 2011* (Cth) r 10.31 for ordinary service requirements in the Federal Court. Similar rules exist in state courts.

74 See Chapter 6.2 regarding legal ethics and professional responsibility in CDR.

75 *Expense Reduction Analysis Group Pty Ltd v Armstrong Strategic Management and Marketing Pty Ltd* (2013) 250 CLR 303, [64]-[67]. See Chapter 2.4.5 for more detailed analysis of this case and Chapter 13 for analysis of the law of privilege.

76 See, eg, Federal Court of Australia, *Special Measures Information Note SMIN-1: Special Measures in Response to COVID-19* (30 March 2020) which requires, at [3], for all court documents to be filed electronically to the extent possible.

Interpreting Service (TIS) telephone 131 450, particularly for immigration cases, but many civil litigants fund their own interpreters. There are recognised difficulties with obtaining a skilled interpreter for court work and lack of regulation has meant that interpreters are often insufficiently skilled to undertake the challenging job of interpreting complex legal issues.[77]

In 2011, the Australian Institute of Judicial Administration Incorporated published a report by Professor Sandra Hale entitled *Interpreter Policies, Practices and Protocols in Australian Courts and Tribunals: A National Survey*.[78] Professor Hale's report indicated a concerning lack of qualification among those performing interpreter services in courts and tribunals, widespread dissatisfaction among the judiciary and qualified interpreters, and a lack of differentiation in pay and treatment for those who are properly qualified. Professor Hale's report recommended, among other things, the introduction of a specialist legal interpreter accreditation by the National Accreditation Authority for Translators and Interpreters Ltd (NAATI) and formal legal interpreting training for all interpreters appearing in courts and tribunals.

In 2017, the Judicial Council on Cultural Diversity published Recommended National Standards for Working with Interpreters in Courts and Tribunals.[79] These standards describe interpreters as "officers of the Court"[80] and require interpreters to comply with the Court Interpreters' Code of Conduct.[81] The National Standards also describe the duties of interpreters, including confidentiality obligations and how interpreters should interact with the judicial officer such as their obligation to raise potential cross-cultural misunderstandings with the judicial officer.[82] Courts are increasingly aware of the importance of well-qualified interpreters. For example, in March 2020 the New South Wales Supreme Court introduced *Practice Note SC GEN 21*: *Interpreters in Civil Proceedings* for the purpose of implementing the National Standards for Working with Interpreters in Courts and Tribunals.[83]

8.5.3 Open justice and the public nature of court hearings

One issue of concern for civil litigants is the public nature of civil litigation.[84] The dispute between the parties in civil litigation is essentially private in nature and yet the Australian justice system is open, with most hearings (both final and interlocutory) being open to the public and with most judgments published in court reports and now readily available on the internet at sites such as austlii.edu.au. As Australia has a precedent system, whereby prior cases become binding law, it is critical that prior cases be available to the public. At the same

77 Xin Liu and Sandra Hale, 'Achieving Accuracy in a Bilingual Courtroom: The Effectiveness of Specialised Legal Interpreter Training' (2018) 12(3) *Interpreter and Translator Trainer* 299.

78 Sandra Hale, *Interpreter Policies, Practices and Protocols in Australian Courts and Tribunals: A National Survey* (Australian Institute of Judicial Administration, 2011).

79 The Judicial Council on Cultural Diversity is an initiative of the Council of Chief Justices of Australia and New Zealand.

80 Judicial Council on Cultural Diversity, *Recommended National Standards for Working with Interpreters in Courts and Tribunals* (2018) Standard 18.

81 Ibid Standard 19.

82 Ibid Standard 20, Standard 20.6.

83 Supreme Court of New South Wales, *Practice Note SC GEN 21: Interpreters in Civil Proceedings* (13 March 2020).

84 See Chapter 3.3. for detailed analysis of this issue.

time, most civil litigation constitutes a significant, albeit partially voluntary, invasion of the privacy of the parties to the litigation.

8.5.4 Pre-trial interactions with the court

Most courts direct parties in the preparation of their case for trial. In many courts, this direction occurs at preliminary hearings before court. Such hearings are usually purely procedural, directions are often somewhat standard or formulaic, and they are often, and preferably, made by agreement between the parties in advance of the hearing. Sometimes, courts have other names for preliminary hearings in which the court makes directions or orders such as "status conference". The more complex the proceeding, the more directions hearings are likely to be required.

In practice, most court directions prior to trial are consent orders. The parties will discuss and agree, in advance of the directions hearing, on appropriate orders and the court will then make those orders by consent. Sometimes, courts will reject proposed consent orders from parties; for example, where the judge considers the parties are not being efficient and are asking for too much time to undertake preliminary tasks.

8.5.5 The impact of court structure and court lists

Sometimes, as in the Northern Territory Supreme Court and the Federal Court, the judge who finally hears a case will be assigned early in the proceedings through a docket system.[85] In other courts, such as the New South Wales Supreme Court, a single judge will be responsible for all directions hearings in a particular list of the Court and the directions judge is unlikely to be the judge who finally hears the case. Nonetheless, a judge in charge of directions should have some knowledge of the matter through access to the court file. Some courts may have masters or registrars in charge of directions hearings and interlocutory disputes, and only allocate a hearing judge when the dispute is fully prepared for hearing or where a major interlocutory issue arises.

Some courts (or divisions of courts) endeavour to make directions for the entire preparation of a matter up to trial at the first directions hearing. This reduces the number of preliminary hearings required, provided the parties comply with the directions. Unfortunately, the further into the future directions go, the more likely it is that one or other party will default on a direction which will then usually throw out the remainder of the timetable for that matter necessitating further directions. Other courts take the approach that parties should regularly appear (either in person or by telephone) before the court or correspond with the court regarding progress of the matter to ensure it remains on track.

There are advantages and disadvantages to both systems. The docket system has the advantage that the judge assigned to that matter becomes directly involved from the time of commencement. Such judges are more likely to be in a position to actively case manage to ensure that the matter is run efficiently, that the issues in dispute are reduced to the minimum

85 A docket system is one in which cases are assigned to judges on a random, or semi-random, basis at the commencement of proceedings and remain with that judge through to hearing. This is in contrast to cases which sit in a directions list at the court until they are ready for hearing and are then assigned a judge.

number, and that any appropriate alternative dispute resolution mechanisms such as mediation occur as early as possible. Hearing judges with responsibility from commencement are more likely to spot behaviour patterns, such as unnecessary interlocutory disputes and use of inefficient or delaying tactics.

Conversely, matters which are managed in a directions list are all assigned to a judge who is an expert in pre-litigation procedure, albeit less familiar with the facts of each individual case. Matters in a list have regular access to that list judge, usually at least once a week, if they encounter an interlocutory dispute which requires rapid resolution. In addition, matters in a directions list are only assigned to a hearing judge when they are ready for hearing, which increases the ability of the court to fairly share the load between judges and to ensure that matters are heard as rapidly as possible once ready for hearing. Directions lists reduce the amount of time spent in preliminary matters by most judges, freeing them up to hear trials.

8.5.6 The role of practice notes

This book focuses mostly on the legislated rules which govern procedure, but there are also procedural requirements set out in practice notes applicable to each court and often to specific court divisions and even court lists. These practice notes often include specific procedures required for matters of that type which are particularly efficient or appropriate for such matters.

For example, in New South Wales, the procedure for a matter in the Technology and Construction List of the Supreme Court of New South Wales would be governed by:

- *Civil Procedure Act 2005* (NSW)
- *Uniform Civil Procedure Rules 2005* (NSW)
- *Practice Note SC EQ 1: Supreme Court Equity Division Case Management*
- *Practice Note SC EQ 3: Supreme Court Equity Division – Commercial List and Technology and Construction List.*

Additional practice notes may apply to many matters in that List, such as:

- *Practice Note SC EQ 5: Supreme Court Equity Division — Expert Evidence in the Equity Division*
- *Practice Note SC EQ 11: Disclosure in the Equity Division.*

Lawyers must consider the requirements of the practice notes for each case they run and ensure they stay up to date with changes in practice and procedure. In relation to the New South Wales example above, there have been five versions of *Practice Note SC EQ 1* since the introduction of the Civil Procedure legislation in New South Wales in 2005, with the newest *Practice Note SC EQ 1* (at the time of writing) released in September 2018.

Practice notes are an excellent example of the key CDR theme of balancing certainty with flexibility.[86] Practice notes provide a middle path between individual case management and legislated case management requirements. They provide litigants with a level of certainty as to how matters will be run by the court but are significantly more flexible than legislation,

86 See Chapter 2.3.2 for analysis of this theme.

because the Chief Justice of the Court can amend or issue new practice notes whenever necessary. For example, in 2020, many courts issued specific practice notes to explain the adjustments to processes necessitated by the COVID-19 pandemic.[87]

8.5.7 Undertakings to the court

Another important way in which parties interact with the court is through undertakings to the court. Undertakings may be made by lawyers or parties and range from trivial to long-term obligations. If a lawyer makes an undertaking to the court, that is a firm obligation on the lawyer as an officer of the court.[88]

Many undertakings are very simple in nature. For example, if a party failed to appear at a directions hearing, the lawyer for the party present at the hearing may undertake to telephone the absent party to obtain instructions regarding the hearing and the judge may therefore adjourn the hearing while that undertaking was complied with. Parties may undertake to the court to take, or not take, certain steps in proceedings where they might, in the absence of the undertaking, have been entitled to act differently. Where such undertakings are not mutual (ie only one party needs to undertake to do something or abstain from doing something), there is often a reciprocal damages undertaking from the other party (ie the party benefitting from the undertaking agrees to pay any damages resulting from the undertaking).[89]

It is also possible for parties, or lawyers, to request that the court vary undertakings to the court where appropriate, such as due to material new facts which will cause injustice without variation.[90] However, undertakings must be of material value for a court to accept them. So, for example, in the Queensland Supreme Court case of *Rolleston Coal Holdings Pty Ltd v ICRA Rolleston Pty Ltd*, an injunction was refused because the Court found that the applicant had "failed to satisfy the court that its undertaking ha[d] real value" because the underlying value of the applicant's company was in question and it did not have available liquid assets to pay the undertaking amount if called upon to do so.[91]

8.5.8 Changes in legal representation during proceedings

Interactions between parties and the courts most commonly occur through legal representatives (legal practitioners, solicitors, barristers). Civil procedure is most likely to run smoothly where clients are represented throughout proceedings by the same legal

87 See Family Court of Australia and Federal Circuit Court of Australia, *Joint Practice Direction 3: JPD 3 of 2020 — The COVID-19 List* (28 April 2020). See also Chapter 8.6.

88 Lawyers admitted to practice are officers of the court and consequently have obligations to act in the interests of the court. There is *Legal Profession Uniform Law* which has been adopted into law in New South Wales and Victoria pursuant to the *Legal Profession Uniform Law Application Act 2014* (Vic) and *Legal Profession Uniform Law Application Act 2014* (NSW). See Chapter 6.2 for more detail.

89 See Chapter 9.2.2 for a more detailed example of solicitor undertakings in the context of freezing and search orders.

90 However, the court will not always grant variations. See, eg, *Marello & Marello (No 2)* [2011] FamCA 799, where Kent J relied on the High Court decision in *Adam P Brown Male Fashions Pty Ltd v Philip Morris Inc* (1981) 148 CLR 170 to reject a husband's application to have mutual interlocutory undertakings regarding expenditure varied prior to trial because he had not demonstrated a relevant ground rendering enforcement of the undertaking unjust in the circumstances.

91 *Rolleston Coal Holdings Pty Ltd v ICRA Rolleston Pty Ltd* [2020] QSC 331, [56]-[59].

representatives. Unfortunately, this is not always possible. Lawyers may choose to cease to act for their clients and clients can sack their lawyers at any point in litigation. Hence, courts, parties and lawyers require civil procedure mechanisms to allow for changes in legal representation. This topic is complex and there is only scope to briefly consider it here.

There are two common reasons why lawyers choose to cease acting for clients. The first is that they determine, at some point in proceedings, that their client's claim or defence is unmeritorious but they are unable to persuade their client to cease to act. Where lawyers cannot convince their clients to cease unmeritorious litigation, they have a conflict between their duties to the court and their duties to their client. Ceasing to act may be the only way to resolve this conflict.

The second common reason lawyers voluntarily cease acting is lack of payment. Where a client refuses to pay accrued legal fees in breach of their retainer agreement, ceasing to act may be the only option for the lawyer to minimise their personal financial losses from incurring costs and time without payment. In such instances, a lawyer may exercise a solicitor's lien over the client's file, refusing to pass the file to the client or a new legal representative until outstanding fees are paid. A solicitor's lien can cause significant delays in the ongoing litigation, as the party whose file is being held may be unable to comply with court directions in the absence of relevant work in progress. Such delays can cause frustration for courts, as evident in the judgment of Slattery J in the Supreme Court of New South Wales decision of *Gigi Entertainment Pty Ltd v Macree (No 2)*.[92] Despite his evident frustration, Slattery J determined in favour of an order for satisfactory security for the former solicitor, although the principal case was close to hearing, noting:

> [35]. When the Court considers making orders under *Legal Profession Act*, s 728 and the solicitor has terminated the retainer the Court: does not act automatically but in an equitable manner exercising its discretion having regard to 'the nature of the case, the stage which litigation had reached, the conduct of the solicitor and the client respectively, and the balance of hardship which might result from the order the Court is being asked to make': see *Stark v Dennett* [2008] 2 Qd R 72; [2008] QCA 50 at [41] per Keane JA (Muir JA and Mullins J agreeing), citing Templeman LJ in *Gamlen Chemical Co (UK) Ltd v Rochem Ltd* [1980] 1 All ER 1049 at 625.[93]

Clients can also choose to terminate their legal representatives' retainer. Clients may be unable to pay mounting legal fees or be dissatisfied with the level of service they are receiving or consider their lawyer incompetent, greedy or dishonest. Solicitor's liens also commonly apply where the client terminated the retainer.

Where clients have changed legal representatives mid–litigation, it is often necessary for the court to grant a brief adjournment of proceedings to enable the new legal representatives to learn the background of the case and take up where the previous representatives left off. The willingness of courts to allow time for new solicitors to "get up to speed" varies significantly, depending on the circumstances of the change in solicitor, the nature of the proceedings, the closeness to trial and the culture of the court. A borderline

92 *Gigi Entertainment Pty Ltd v Macree (No 2)* [2011] NSWSC 869.
93 Ibid [35].

vexatious litigant who has changed solicitors three times already in the course of a single proceeding, in an expeditious court on an urgent matter, a week before trial is unlikely to be granted an adjournment for a change in solicitor. Conversely, a litigant whose solicitor has become suddenly ill or died, necessitating an urgent change in solicitor with limited potential for smooth handover, considerably prior to a trial in non-urgent proceedings, is likely to receive significant accommodation from the courts in complying with a pre-existing court timetable.

An example of the reluctance of some judiciary to grant adjournments is the family law case of *Wold v Kleppir (No 3)*, where an adjournment sought a week prior to trial was refused by Barry J who stated:

> [8] … So it is important that there is not a culture of the Court's granting an adjournment. It would be years since I last granted an adjournment and that would be in a case of very serious sudden emergency circumstance. I think one last occasion the wife gave premature birth.[94]

8.6 Technology in civil litigation

Technology continues to change many aspects of civil litigation, including how parties interact with the courts. In the past decade, it has become common for parties to file documents electronically, to engage in email correspondence with judges or their Associates, and to undertake significant aspects of their litigation without leaving their offices. Some courts now even require all matters to be filed online, unless special permission is granted by the court, such as the Equity Division of the Supreme Court of New South Wales.[95]

The COVID-19 pandemic required courts to undertake a rapid uptake of technology in 2020, as they were required to close physical courtrooms during lockdowns but citizens' need for court adjudication continued. Many courts used a combination of telephone and video conferencing to continue conducting court hearings remotely and many, non-urgent matters were deferred. Courts issued information statements, practice notes, or similar documents, covering the period of lockdowns and outlining the changes of procedure and how technology would be deployed to enable the courts to continue functioning without physical courtroom spaces. For example, on 23 March 2020, Allsop CJ released *Special Measures in Response to COVID-19* (SMIN-1) for the Federal Court of Australia, requiring all filing to be electronic wherever possible, temporarily allowing the electronic signing of documents such as affidavits and introducing a triage process whereby only urgent matters received an immediate return date. In Victoria, numerous statements were issued in 2020, including the *Joint Statement on Stage 4 Coronavirus Restrictions* issued by the Victorian Court and VCAT in August 2020, which outlined the requirements to maximise online and remote functions wherever possible in the

94 *Wold v Kleppir (No 3)* [2009] FamCA 232, [8].

95 Supreme Court of New South Wales, *Practice Note No SC EQ 1: Case Management* (9 May 2018), discussed in Chapter 8.6.2.

Supreme Court, the County Court, VCAT, the Magistrates Court, the Children's Court and the Coroner's Court.[96]

In 2014, the Productivity Commission's *Access to Justice Report* summarised the impact of technology on civil procedure as follows:

> In the past decade, many Australian courts and governments have implemented significant reforms aimed at better using technology to make legal processes more efficient. Initiatives have been wide-ranging and include:
>
> - allowing court documents to be filed and court fees to be paid electronically
> - providing online access to court documents
> - conducting procedural hearings through tele- and video-conferencing or tailored 'virtual court' applications
> - using case management systems to better support efficient case flow management and performance reporting functions.
>
> However, consultations and submissions to this inquiry suggest that investment in information technology has been uneven across jurisdictions and that the availability, quality and use of technology varies widely. The Commission considers that greater investment in technology is warranted, given the potential benefits. A lack of resources appears to be the main barrier to the uptake of technology.[97]

The adoption of technology in civil litigation interacts closely with key themes of civil procedure, because it has the potential to increase access to justice and to improve efficiency without reducing due process.[98] Used well, technology has the potential to improve CDR but it can also cause additional complexity in civil disputes.

8.6.1 Types of technology in civil litigation

There are three obvious ways in which technology is infiltrating and influencing civil procedure:

1. **The electronic nature of evidence**: The critical evidence in civil litigation is increasingly electronic in nature, including email correspondence, multiple electronic versions of legal documents and draft legal documents, such as contracts, computer metadata proving electronic communications between parties and, most recently, social media such as Facebook and Twitter. Evidence is also more likely to be stored by parties and shared between parties electronically through virtual discovery rooms and other digital media forms.

96 Supreme Court of Victoria, *Joint Statement on Stage 4 Coronavirus Restrictions* (6 August 2020) authored by The Honourable Chief Justice Anne Ferguson, Chief Justice of the Supreme Court, The Honourable Chief Judge Peter Kidd, Chief Judge of the County Court, The Honourable Justice Michelle Quigley, President of VCAT, Her Honour Judge Lisa Hannan, Chief Magistrate, Her Honour Judge Amanda Chambers, President of the Children's Court and His Honour Judge John Cain, State Coroner.

97 Productivity Commission, *Access to Justice Arrangements* (2014) vol 1, 19.

98 See Chapter 3.2 regarding access to justice and Chapter 2.3.1 regarding balancing efficiency and due consideration.

2. **E-Filing/E-Access:** A growing proportion of pre-trial procedure can now be undertaken remotely through electronic filing in many Australian courts, reducing the need for parties to attend court prior to trial and reducing the administrative costs of compliance with court procedures. Online documents are also more easily accessible to parties. Courts increasingly require parties to use online processes.
3. **E-Trials/Online Courts/Video Evidence:** Courts are using technology during trials more and more, with digitised courtrooms where all parties can simultaneously access and view documents and electronic search functions can assist parties and judges to quickly locate relevant documents for immediate consideration. Experts and lay witnesses can give evidence remotely by video link from interstate or overseas, thereby increasing the likelihood of finding suitable hearing dates and reducing the financial cost and inconvenience of giving evidence. COVID-19 dramatically increased the use of all these forms of technology, but also caused many challenges for courts, practitioners, and litigants in managing suboptimal processes.

8.6.2 Ways of incorporating technology into courts

The rise of technology has necessitated special rules for compliance. Electronic filing, use of electronic documents and other electronic processes often constitute radical departures from the pre-existing civil procedure rules. Most of the means by which courts direct and interact with parties discussed earlier in this chapter are being adapted by courts to incorporate use of technology. In particular, courts are using practice notes, court rules, as well as websites and computer systems to assist litigation users to access the courts through technology:

1. **Special Rules:** For example, in New South Wales, the *Uniform Civil Procedure Rules 2005* contain pt 3 (Electronic Case Management), including r 3.4 on filing electronic documents. In addition, elements of pt 4 div 2 (Filing of Documents) provide specifically for procedures introduced to accommodate new technology. The *Uniform Civil Procedure Rules 2005* (NSW) also contains provisions on video evidence at r 31.3.

   Similarly, the *Uniform Civil Procedure Rules 1999* (Qld) contain ch 22, pt 1, div 4 (Electronic Court Documents), including r 975C which defines the circumstances in which a document may be electronically filed and the circumstances in which a document will be taken to have been successfully electronically filed. The *Uniform Civil Procedure Rules 1999* (Qld) also contains r 392 concerning video evidence.
2. **Practice Notes:** Practices concerning technology are increasingly embedded into Practice Notes of courts. For example, Victorian Supreme Court *Practice Note SC Gen 5 Technology in Civil Litigation (First Revision)*[99] aims "to promote the effective use of technology in the conduct of civil litigation to reduce time and costs".[100] This Practice Note also states that "Dealings in hard copy are to be the exception

99 Supreme Court of Victoria, *Practice Note SC GEN5: Technology in Civil Litigation* (30 January 2017).
100 Ibid [1.2].

rather than the rule in all aspects of civil litigation in the Court";[101] that "Email is the preferred mode of communication with the Court";[102] and that "Electronic filing is also mandated for all documents required to be filed in any proceeding in the Commercial Court, Common Law Division and Costs Court by the Rules of the Court."[103]

Similarly, in the New South Wales Supreme Court *Practice Note SC Gen-18, Supreme Court – Production of and access to subpoenaed material and returning exhibits and subpoenaed material in civil proceedings*, paragraphs 10 to 18 are devoted to directing parties as to the production of material electronically and the non-electronic production of electronic documents where required. [104]

The Supreme Court of New South Wales Practice Note SC EQ 14, *Supreme Court Equity Division – Online Court Protocol*,[105] requires all matters in the Equity Division General List case managed by the Registrar to be registered with the Online Court unless the Court orders otherwise[106] and all represented and self-represented litigants to be registered users of the Online Court.[107]

8.6.3 The additional complexity of technology in civil litigation

Although many of the innovations discussed above are assisting users of courts to access justice through technology, the technology revolution has not been without difficulties. Technology, while designed to make life easier, can create additional procedures and new levels of complexity.

The Victorian Supreme Court case of *Wheelahan v City of Casey (No 9)*, which involved a large number of parties, included discussion regarding the difficulties faced by the e-trial subcommittee trying to set up e-trial protocol for the case. E-trials can result in additional court directions totally unheard of in traditional trials, such as the development of e-trial protocols including for the provision of e-discovery and directions to provide e-trial system and services requirements.[108]

Similarly, the Supreme Court of Queensland case of *Central Queensland Mining Supplies Pty Ltd v Columbia Steel Casting Co Ltd* involved a discovery dispute based upon the suitability of different electronic searches for locating discoverable documents. The directions of Applegarth J in this case demonstrate the infiltration of technology into litigation with

---

101 Ibid [4.3].

102 Ibid [6.1].

103 Ibid [7.1].

104 Supreme Court of New South Wales, *Practice Note SC GEN 18: Production of and access to subpoenaed material and returning exhibits and subpoenaed material in civil proceedings* (30 September 2013).

105 Supreme Court of New South Wales, *Practice Note SC EQ 14: Supreme Court Equity Division – Online Court Protocol* (5 September 2018).

106 Ibid [8].

107 Ibid [5].

108 *Wheelahan v City of Casey (No 9)* [2011] VSC 509, [19]-[20].

parties directed to email documents to the judge's Associate rather than filing in court, and the parties being directed to consider using the court's e-trial facilities.[109]

In the Queensland Land Court[110] decision of *New Acland Coal Pty Ltd v Ashman and Chief Executive, Department of Environment and Heritage Protection (No 4)*, Member PA Smith rejected the proposal for Stage 3 of a coal mine following the longest hearing in the Land Court's 120-year history "almost 100 hearing days before this Court, almost 2,000 exhibits containing many tens of thousands of pages of material, and well in excess of 2,000 pages of submissions".[111] This case demonstrates both the progress in e-trials and the continuing challenges they present in terms of managing ever-growing volumes evidence, which is now all too easily delivered in an electronic format, as stated by the Court:

> [97] Another important feature of the hearing is that it was conducted entirely as an e-trial. Although this did not come without some dramas, the huge amount of material was overall well-handled electronically. The simple fact that there are 1,951 exhibits does not of itself properly identify the immense volume of material placed before the Court. While of course some exhibits are only one or two pages in length, others are many hundreds of pages long. I am in little doubt that the total number of pages made up by the exhibits would be many tens of thousands.
>
> ...
>
> [1655] As this is an e-trial, I have no real idea how much extra material is in fact before me in way of physical size.[112]

Courts are also struggling to develop procedures to assist judges in understanding new methods of communication, such as the growing use of emoji by litigants in relevant communications.[113] While the interpretation of emoji is predominantly an evidentiary problem rather than a procedural one, the way emoji are displayed or not displayed in documentation,[114] whether an emoji expert should assist the court and how to display or explain emoji to juries are relatively new issues caused by technology which require procedural decisions from the judiciary.

8.7 Interlocutory proceedings

In civil litigation, a significant proportion of the time preparing the matter for trial can be taken up with interlocutory disputes. Some parties will dispute everything from parties

109 *Central Queensland Mining Supplies Pty Ltd v Columbia Steel Casting Co Ltd* [2011] QSC 183.

110 The Queensland Land Court is a specialised judicial tribunal and court of record established under the *Land Court Act 2000* (Qld).

111 *New Acland Coal Pty Ltd v Ashman and Chief Executive, Department of Environment and Heritage Protection (No 4)* [2017] QLC 24, [19], [36].

112 Ibid [97], [1655].

113 Marilyn McMahon and Elizabeth Kirley, 'The Emoji Factor: Humanizing the Emerging Law of Digital Speech' (2018) 85(2) *Tennessee Law Review* 517.

114 Some cases display emoji and discuss their meaning in the court's decision. See, eg, *School for Excellence Pty Ltd v Trendy Rhino Pty Ltd* [2018] VSC 514. Other cases, such as *Colin Ramon Reguero-Puente v City of Rockingham* (2018) 276 IR 74, state "emoji" in place of the image, thus appearing to exclude the emoji itself from forming part of the evidence.

through pleadings, discovery, experts and anything in between which arises in the course of preparing their matter for trial. Often, these interlocutory disputes will begin with correspondence between the parties but, where the parties are unable to resolve their differences, even the simplest procedural issues may end up before court for determination as an interlocutory proceeding. This section will demonstrate the, sometimes subtle, differences between "interlocutory matters", "substantive matters", "interlocutory decisions" and "final decisions", the appealable nature of such decisions and why it matters, and what is meant when using terms such as "interlocutory" or "final".

8.7.1 Defining interlocutory proceedings

Terminology can become very confusing when discussing interlocutory disputes. Terms such as "interlocutory" and "final" have different meanings in different contexts. An interlocutory proceeding is a court hearing which relates to a preliminary or procedural aspect of litigation. The decision of a court in an interlocutory proceeding does not determine the outcome of the substantive trial. In practice, however, interlocutory proceedings may be critical to the success or failure of a litigation.

It is important to understand the distinction between interlocutory versus final *proceedings* and interlocutory versus final *decisions*. Although an interlocutory proceeding is one which does not finally determine the substantive dispute between the parties, decisions made in relation to interlocutory matters may themselves be final in nature. To further complicate the issue, a decision being "final" does not mean the decision is not appealable (and may therefore be overturned). Hence, a judge may make a final decision in an interlocutory matter which may then be appealed to a higher court that overturns the original judge's decision on that interlocutory matter.

For example, discovery disputes are interlocutory in nature but a court decision (even one made by way of a consensual discovery order) that a party must discover a document is a final decision. Discovery is an interlocutory procedure because it does not determine the substance of the dispute between the parties.[115] However, once a document has been discovered, it cannot be undiscovered (although it may be able to be excluded from evidence at trial). Failure to make discovery in accordance with a court order is potentially contempt of court. If a judge determines that a particular document should be discovered, that "final" determination must be appealed to a higher court if the party wishes to avoid compliance with the discovery order. In the event of such an appeal, the trial judge will grant a stay of his discovery order until the appeal court determines the appeal.

Whether a *decision* is final or interlocutory is important, as issue estoppel only arises in relation to final decisions as confirmed by the High Court in *Kuligowski v Metrobus*.[116] The Court of Appeal of the Supreme Court of Western Australia case of *Atanasio v BP Refinery (Kwinana) Pty Ltd*,[117] before Buss, Newnes and Murphy JJ, summarised the High Court's analysis of the difference between a "final decision" as opposed to an "interlocutory decision" as follows:

115 See Chapter 11 for detailed analysis of discovery.
116 *Kuligowski v Metrobus* (2004) 220 CLR 363. Issue estoppel is discussed in Chapter 16.4.
117 *Atanasio v BP Refinery (Kwinana) Pty Ltd* [2011] WASCA 95.

> [84] The High Court held that the decision of the majority in *Kuligowski* (Supreme Court) should be reversed. Gleeson CJ, McHugh, Gummow, Kirby, Hayne, Callinan and Heydon JJ said that no issue estoppel had arisen because, although the review officer's decision was final (in that it was effective unless and until rescinded, altered or amended), the issue which it determined was not the same as that which would arise for determination in the common law action. Their Honours made these observations in relation to the nature of a 'final' decision:
>
> (a) A 'final' decision is one which is not of an interlocutory character, but is completely effective unless and until rescinded, altered or amended. The fact that an appeal lies from a decision does not make it any less final. It must be 'final and conclusive on the merits'; 'the cause of action must be extinguished by the decision which is said to create the estoppel': *Carl Zeiss Stiftung v Rayner & Keeler Ltd [No 2]* [1967] 1 AC 853, 935 (Lord Guest) [25].
>
> ...
>
> (c) The critical feature of a final decision, namely, complete effectiveness unless and until it can be amended, may be absent from proceedings of the most formal and elaborate character, and may be present in proceedings of the most informal and brisk character [32].[118]

The majority of decisions in relation to interlocutory disputes (whether they are in relation to pleadings, discovery or affidavit evidence) are final decisions in the sense described by the High Court above. They have immediate effect unless amended, varied or overturned on appeal. However, these decisions on interlocutory matters do not finally determine the dispute between the parties.

8.7.2 Types of interlocutory proceeding

Almost any direction or order from the court can also be the subject of an interlocutory dispute and more. The majority of the cases discussed in Chapters 8 to 16 are decisions on interlocutory disputes.

Issues which may become the subject of interlocutory dispute include:

- the terms of pleadings
- the service of originating process
- the need for further and better particulars to pleadings
- the terms of discovery
- the incompleteness of discovery
- the privilege attaching to discovered documents
- the failure to comply with court timetables
- the failure to file affidavit evidence
- the terms or need for preliminary injunctions
- the separation of proceedings

118 Ibid [84].

- the parties to the proceedings
- complaints about the conduct of the court, the parties, and their lawyers (eg judicial bias or unethical conduct cases).

8.7.3 How to commence interlocutory proceedings

Most interlocutory proceedings are commenced by notice of motion in the court, supported by an affidavit.[119] The affidavit is often an affidavit of the legal representative of the party commencing the proceedings, setting out the correspondence between the parties leading up to the dispute.

8.7.4 The cost of interlocutory proceedings

There are often significant costs associated with interlocutory proceedings, both financial and non-financial. Interlocutory disputes generally necessitate a pause in the preparation of a matter for trial while the dispute is resolved. For example, if parties are disputing the scope of discovery, they cannot commence discovery until that dispute is resolved. Interlocutory disputes swallow legal resources in the preparation of materials, including affidavit evidence (often the affidavits are of the legal representatives) and representation in court. The financial, time, and emotional costs associated with litigation[120] are particularly problematic in interlocutory disputes because these disputes, of themselves, do not resolve the main dispute between the parties but can, instead, increase the animosity between the parties and the sense of wasted time and energy in litigation.

Judges, understandably, become openly critical of overly adversarial behaviour in interlocutory matters such as in the Federal Court of Australia case of *Schutz DSL (Australia) Pty Ltd v VIP Plastic Packaging Pty Ltd*.[121] This case, which related to discovery, was the fourteenth interlocutory dispute which McKerracher J had been required to rule on in the same litigation between Schutz DSL and VIP Plastic Packaging. Some of the earlier disputed issues included requests for interlocutory injunctions, terms of correspondence to third parties, amendment to pleadings and numerous disputes regarding discovery.[122]

Some particularly hard-fought litigation will involve numerous interlocutory disputes, some of which might themselves be appealed to higher courts. Appeal courts are even less enthusiastic than trial courts towards parties who appeal decisions on interlocutory disputes. For example, the New South Wales Supreme Court in *Armstrong Strategic Management and Marketing v Expense Reduction Analysis Group Pty Ltd*[123] (heard shortly after the High Court[124] handed down its privilege determination in relation to the same dispute) suggested

119 See, eg, *Uniform Civil Procedure Rules 2005* (NSW) r 18.1 which requires interlocutory motions to be commenced by motion.

120 See Chapter 2.5.

121 *Schutz DSL (Australia) Pty Ltd v VIP Plastic Packaging Pty Ltd (No 14)* [2011] FCA 1159.

122 Ibid [50].

123 *Armstrong Strategic Management and Marketing Pty Ltd v Expense Reduction Analysis Group Pty Ltd* [2013] NSWSC 1702.

124 *Expense Reduction Analysis Group Pty Ltd v Armstrong Strategic Management and Marketing Pty Ltd* (2013) 250 CLR 303.

that: "The procedural history of this matter could be taken to suggest that the parties have paid less attention to the provisions of s 56 of the *Civil Procedure Act 2005* (NSW) than they have to the process of seeking to grind each other into the dust."[125] Appeal courts are very reluctant to interfere with discretionary procedural decisions of lower courts, as explained by the High Court in *Adam P Brown Male Fashions Pty Ltd v Philip Morris Inc*,[126] which continues to be cited frequently.[127] In *Expense Reduction Analysis Group Pty Ltd v Armstrong Strategic Management and Marketing Pty Ltd*, the High Court further emphasised the undesirability of extensive interlocutory disputes, stating:

> It could hardly be suggested that the pursuit of satellite interlocutory proceedings of the kind here in question in any way fulfils the overriding purpose of the CPA. To the contrary, it is the very kind of conduct which should be avoided if those purposes are to be achieved.
>
> It involved a relatively minor issue relating to discovery, the resolution of which appears to have offered little advantage to the Armstrong parties. Its determination went no way towards the resolution of the real issues in dispute between the parties. Instead, it has distracted them from taking steps to a final hearing, encouraged the outlay of considerable expense and squandered the resources of the Court.[128]

The High Court has made it abundantly clear that it does not consider the key themes of justice and procedural efficiency to be assisted by interlocutory disputes on procedural issues. However, the High Court's ruling in *Expense Reduction* belies the complexity of this issue. Lack of court oversight of interlocutory matters could, inadvertently, encourage less ethical parties to litigate in ways which circumvent the justice and efficiency aims of civil procedure.[129]

Interlocutory proceedings provide an important demonstration of the complex interplay between due process and efficiency because, without them, parties may engage in practices which defeat the aims of fair and proper process, leading to injustice. Conversely, interlocutory processes can themselves be abuses of process designed to bankrupt a party to litigation and prevent the efficient resolution of civil disputes.[130] Interlocutory proceedings are also an example of the key theme of balancing autonomy and control. Parties to a civil dispute must often work together to resolve preparation issues and this can often be achieved through informal negotiation between lawyers. Engaging with the court to resolve an interlocutory dispute indicates the parties have been unable to autonomously agree how to proceed with that aspect of their case preparation and are handing control to the courts.

125 *Armstrong Strategic Management and Marketing Pty Ltd v Expense Reduction Analysis Group Pty Ltd* [2013] NSWSC 1702, [1]. There were numerous subsequent interlocutory decisions in this dispute which further demonstrated the animosity of the parties and its negative affect on the running of the dispute such as this costs decision: *Armstrong Strategic Management and Marketing Pty Ltd v Expense Reduction Analysts Group Pty Ltd (No 10)* [2017] NSWSC 16.

126 *Adam P Brown Male Fashions Pty Ltd v Philip Morris Inc* (1981) 148 CLR 170.

127 See, eg, *Gadzikwa v Comcare* [2020] FCA 1560; *Ah-Chee v Stuart* [2019] FCAFC 165.

128 *Expense Reduction Analysis Group Pty Ltd v Armstrong Strategic Management and Marketing Pty Ltd* (2013) 250 CLR 303.

129 See Sonya Willis, 'Courting Incompetence: Should the High Court More Carefully Consider its Influence on Legal Culture?' (2016) 35(2) *Civil Justice Quarterly* 129 for a detailed analysis of this issue.

130 See Chapter 2.3.1 for further analysis.

Cases such as *Expense Reduction Analysis Group Pty Ltd v Armstrong Strategic Management and Marketing Pty Ltd* are an effort by the courts to encourage increased party autonomy by pushing interlocutory disputes back to the parties in order to conserve limited court resources.

8.8 Conclusion

Interactions between parties and the courts are complex and dynamic. Determining which court should hear a matter can require complex considerations by courts and parties. The advent of the internet and the widespread use of electronic documents in everyday life requires constant evolution by courts and civil litigation. A growing percentage of pre-trial procedure takes place electronically, there is greater use of technology in physical courtrooms, and the critical evidence in trials is increasingly constituted by electronic documents and data. Simultaneously, there is an increase in representative (class) actions and matters with numerous defendants and complex party interrelations. All this contributes to the need for constant revision of the ways parties interact with the court. The efficiency of the interactions between the parties and the court can have a massive impact on the financial, time, and emotional cost of litigation with high levels of interlocutory disputes causing frustration among parties and the judiciary. The way parties interact with each other and the courts in the course of civil litigation demonstrate how the key themes of CDR recur throughout disputes and prove the theory that the complexity of procedures can all be explained by reference to these key themes.

9 COMMENCING PROCEEDINGS

9.1 Introduction

Commencing proceedings is one of the most important steps in litigation and, for most cases, it signals the first involvement of the court in the dispute. However, there are important considerations for a plaintiff before commencing proceedings even when the plaintiff is confident litigation is the best way to proceed. This chapter will also consider these precursors to commencing proceedings.[1]

Commencing proceedings is strongly influenced by key themes of civil dispute resolution (CDR), especially procedural fairness and access to justice. Originating process[2] varies between courts and jurisdictions. Most matters are commenced by statement of claim which is both an originating process and a pleading.

This chapter will identify the relevant provisions in each jurisdiction for commencing proceedings and explore how originating process is affected by key themes of CDR including access to justice and the complexity in balancing justice and efficiency.

9.2 Precursors to commencing litigation

Sometimes parties need the assistance of the court before they can commence litigation or even explore alternatives to dispute resolution. This may occur where there are facts critical to a party's case which they are missing. Preliminary discovery is a court procedure which assists parties to identify information necessary to commence dispute resolution. Alternatively, where a party must be prevented from acting in a way which would threaten the administration of justice by jeopardising the other party's case, the court may order an urgent injunction such as a freezing order (Mareva injunction) or a search order (Anton Piller order).

The main purpose of preliminary discovery is to facilitate the court's processes and, in doing so, preliminary discovery supports the key theme of access to justice.

9.2.1 Preliminary discovery

Preliminary discovery is discovery granted prior to any claim being filed in court.[3] There are limited circumstances where a court will grant discovery before proceedings have commenced. These circumstances are essentially those where it is impossible for the plaintiff to commence its claim without further information.

The most common reason for a court to grant preliminary discovery is where the identity or location of the potential defendant is unknown; for example, *Uniform Civil Procedure Rules 2005* (NSW) r 5.2, or *Federal Court Rules 2011* (Cth) ch 2 pt 7 div 7.3 r 7.22.

1 Some of the important precursors to litigation — namely, jurisdiction and parties to disputes — have already been considered in some detail in Chapters 8.3 and 8.4 respectively.

2 Originating process is the title given the document used to commence proceedings. A statement of claim, an application, and a summons are all common examples of originating process. The statement of claim is also a document which pleads a party's case.

3 Discovery is the process whereby one party provides documents to another party. Discovery will be considered in detail in Chapter 11. Discovery is usually ordered once the pleadings have closed (ie once the parties have set out their claims and defences). Claims and defences and other pleadings will be considered in this chapter.

7.22 Order for discovery to ascertain description of respondent

(1) A prospective applicant may apply to the Court for an order under subrule (2) if the prospective applicant satisfies the Court that:
  (a) there may be a right for the prospective applicant to obtain relief against a prospective respondent; and
  (b) the prospective applicant is unable to ascertain the description of the prospective respondent; and
  (c) another person (the **other person**):
    (i) knows or is likely to know the prospective respondent's description; or
    (ii) has, or is likely to have, or has had, or is likely to have had, control of a document that would help ascertain the prospective respondent's description.

(2) If the Court is satisfied of the matters mentioned in subrule (1), the Court may order the other person:
  (a) to attend before the Court to be examined orally only about the prospective respondent's description; and
  (b) to produce to the Court at that examination any document or thing in the person's control relating to the prospective respondent's description; and
  (c) to give discovery to the prospective applicant of all documents that are or have been in the person's control relating to the prospective respondent's description.

Note 1 **Control** and **description** are defined in the Dictionary.

Note 2 For how discovery is to be made, see rule 7.25.

(3) The prospective applicant must provide the person with sufficient conduct money to permit the person to travel to the Court.

Note **Conduct money** is defined in the Dictionary.[4]

For example, in *Dallas Buyers Club LLC v iiNet Ltd*,[5] Perram J granted preliminary discovery requiring internet service providers (ISPs) to divulge the names and addresses of customers (not necessarily the culprits) associated with 4,726 IP addresses likely to have used BitTorrent to view a US movie, *The Dallas Buyers Club,* which had not yet been released in Australia at the time of the alleged downloads. However, the preliminary discovery was stayed and, in *Dallas Buyers Club LLC v iiNet Ltd (No 5)*,[6] Perram J retained the stay on the basis that some purposes of seeking preliminary discovery are not within proper scope of r 7.22 of the *Federal Court Rules 2011* (Cth). This case shows the narrow scope of preliminary discovery and the importance of limiting its use to matters which enable access to justice rather than for supporting the strategic aims of the litigant.

Preliminary discovery can also be granted in some jurisdictions to enable a potential plaintiff to determine whether it has a cause of action; for example, *Uniform Civil Procedure Rules (2005)* (NSW) r 5.3 and *Federal Court Rules (2011)* (Cth) r 7.23.

4 *Federal Court Rules 2011* (Cth) r 7.22.
5 *Dallas Buyers Club LLC v iiNet Ltd* (2015) 245 FCR 129.
6 *Dallas Buyers Club LLC v iiNet Ltd (No 5)* (2015) 115 IPR 544.

7.23 Discovery from prospective respondent

(1) A prospective applicant may apply to the Court for an order under subrule (2) if the prospective applicant:
  (a) reasonably believes that he or she may have the right to obtain relief in the Court from a prospective respondent whose description has been ascertained; and
  (b) after making reasonable inquiries, does not have sufficient information to decide whether to start a proceeding in the Court to obtain that relief; and
  (c) reasonably believes that:
    (i) the prospective respondent has or is likely to have or has had or is likely to have had in the prospective respondent's control documents directly relevant to the question whether the prospective applicant has a right to obtain the relief; and
    (ii) inspection of the documents by the prospective applicant would assist in making the decision.
(2) If the Court is satisfied about matters mentioned in subrule (1), the Court may order the prospective respondent to give discovery to the prospective applicant of the documents of the kind mentioned in subparagraph (1)(c)(i).[7]

AstraZeneca AB v Alphapharm Pty Ltd[8] is an example of a r 7.23 *Federal Court Rules 2011* (Cth) case. In *AstraZeneca,* preliminary discovery was granted to AstraZeneca to discern potential patent infringement by Alphapharm due to the similarities of the Alphapharm product Noxicid to AstraZeneca's Nexium. Both products used esomeprazole magnesium trihydrate, a proton pump inhibitor to reduce stomach acid. Justice Besanko granted the preliminary discovery order stating that "the costs and risks of litigation are relevant to the decision whether to start a proceeding".

Thus, courts recognise that there are circumstances where a potential plaintiff must be assisted by the court to obtain crucial facts concerning the potential defendant and/or the potential claim without which the claim could not proceed. Preliminary discovery does not occur in the vast majority of litigation as, in most instances, claimants have sufficient information to identify their claim and the defendant(s) to that claim.

9.2.2 Urgent preliminary injunctions: search orders and freezing orders

A small percentage of cases involve a potential party to litigation needing a court to take action on its behalf before it has the opportunity to commence litigation. These are circumstances where the potential benefit of an urgent court order outweighs the potential injustice of making an order based on limited and often *ex parte* information.[9] Search orders and freezing orders are not always preliminary to the commencement of litigation, as the

7 *Uniform Civil Procedure Rules 2005* (NSW) r 5.3; *Federal Court Rules 2011* (Cth) r 7.23.
8 *AstraZeneca AB v Alphapharm Pty Ltd* [2014] FCA 9.
9 *Ex parte* means without other parties present. Justice ordinarily requires that each party has a right to be heard (this is the doctrine of *audi alteram partem*). However, there are circumstances where the injustice of not hearing a party is outweighed by the injustice which would occur if an order were not made in the absence of that party.

need for both can arise after litigation commences, but they are considered here because they do commonly occur pre-commencement.

9.2.2.1 Search orders

Search orders, also known as Anton Piller orders, are granted by courts to allow a party to seize evidentiary material (including documents) without notice from another party where it is likely those materials would otherwise be destroyed by that other party to prevent their use in litigation.[10] Search orders are invariably *ex parte* as notifying the other party would destroy the benefit of the order.

The case of *C.T. Sheet Metal Works Pty Ltd v Hutchinson* concerned the undertakings of a solicitor as part of the terms of a Federal Court search order. The grant of a right to search for documents is usually accompanied by strict obligations on those searching another party's documents and premises. The improper disclosure in *C.T. Sheet Metal Works Pty Ltd v Hutchinson* was actually made by an employee of the solicitor on the record, rather than the solicitor who made the undertaking. No order for contempt of court was made against either solicitor, as the solicitor on the record had voluntarily disclosed the breach in circumstances where it might otherwise not have come to light, and both solicitors expressed suitable remorse for the breach. Justice Kenny discussed the circumstances in which search orders are granted and their effect on the breach of undertaking, as follows:

> [31]. It is appropriate to begin any consideration as to whether there has been a breach of Mr Caligaris' undertaking by identifying the context in which the undertaking was given. A search order, or Anton Piller order, of the kind involved here is, as the current Practice Note on the issue of such orders aptly states: 'An extraordinary remedy in that it is intrusive, potentially disruptive, and made without notice and prior to judgment': see Practice Note CM11 at cl 4. Practice Note CM11 goes on to say the terms of such an order: 'contains provisions which are aimed at achieving permissible objects of a search order, while minimising the potential for disruption or damage to the respondent and for abuse of the Court's process'.
>
> [32]. The permissible objects of a search order of this kind were identified by Flick J in *Metso Minerals (Australia) Ltd v Kalra (No 3)* [2008] FCA 1201 ('Metso Minerals'). That case involved a search order under O 25B of the former Federal Court Rules. In the course of his decision, his Honour pointed out that a search order of this kind is directed to searching for, and preserving evidence, that is relevant to proceedings *not* to obtaining evidence to assist a party to conduct its proceedings. It follows, as his Honour correctly (with respect) observed, that such a search order is not to be used as 'an investigatory tool' or a preliminary step that later facilitates an investigation. …
>
> [33]. Moreover, of particular relevance in this matter, his Honour rejected any notion that the materials seized in executing the search order could be used to second guess the opposite party's compliance with its discovery obligations. … .

10 Anton Piller orders were so named after the United Kingdom case of *Anton Piller KG v Manufacturing Processes Ltd* [1976] 1 Ch 55. Most modern Australian legislation uses the term "search orders", such as in the *Uniform Civil Procedure Rules 2005* (NSW), where search orders are provided for by div 3 rr 25.18–25.24, but lawyers and judges will often revert to the term "Anton Piller" as it is more distinctive.

[34]. Next, it is germane to record that the actual wording of the undertaking that Mr Caligaris gave to the Court in this matter came from the Court's Practice Note in relation to such search orders. Paragraph 18 of the current Practice Note CM11 (which is in almost identical terms to the former Practice Note 24) provides as follows:

Appropriate undertakings to the Court will be required of the applicant, the applicant's lawyer and the independent lawyer, as conditions of the making of the search order. The undertakings required of the applicant will normally include the Court's usual undertaking as to damages. The applicant's lawyer's undertaking includes *an undertaking not to disclose to the applicant any information that the lawyer has acquired during or as a result of execution of the search order, without the leave of the Court.* Release from this undertaking in whole or in part may be sought on the return date.

...

[37]. Applying these principles in this matter, it was quite wrong for Mr Brown to disclose anything about the emails to Mr and Mrs Whitehouse. That extends to their existence, the effect of them and, most obviously, their contents. While Mr Brown denies disclosure of the latter, there can be no doubt he disclosed the former, viz the existence and effect of the string of emails. Indeed, one of his stated purposes was to allow the Whitehouses to consider involving the police. This disclosure in these circumstances was the antithesis of the strict confidentiality that applied to a search order of this kind, as dictated by the authorities, the relevant Court Rules and the Court Practice Note. I therefore consider it is clear that Mr Brown breached the undertaking given by Mr Caligaris by disclosing the information that he did about the emails to Mr and Mrs Whitehouse.[11]

Search orders also impose significant obligations on party served with the order. In *AGL Energy Ltd v Hardy*,[12] Mr Hardy was found guilty of contempt after refusing to permit members of the search party, comprising an independent lawyer, a computer expert and AGL's lawyer to enter the premises so that they could carry out the search and other activities referred to in a search order made pursuant to r 7.42 of the *Federal Court Rules 2011* (Cth). Similarly, in *Sun v He*, Mr He was found guilty of contempt of court and abuse of process for breaches of a search order including applying a factory reset to a number of electronic devices the subject of the order likely to contain relevant WeChat messages in a dispute over $80,000,000.[13] Mr He was, subsequently, sentenced to 6 weeks imprisonment for the contempt of court in breaching the search orders and banned from relying on any evidence relating to the WeChat communications in his defence.[14]

9.2.2.2 Freezing orders

Freezing orders, originally called Mareva injunctions and often called Mareva orders, are an order of the court freezing certain assets of a party so as to prevent those assets being

11 *C.T. Sheet Metal Works Pty Ltd v Hutchinson* (2012) 201 FCR 275, [31]-[34], [37].

12 *AGL Energy Ltd v Hardy* [2017] FCA 420.

13 *Sun v He* [2020] NSWSC 802, [35], [261]-[283], [305].

14 *Sun v He (No 2)* [2020] NSWSC 1298. It is interesting to note that Mr He had also breached an earlier freezing order by paying $238,000 in advance school fees: *Sun v He (No 2)* [2020] NSWSC 1298, [57]-[58].

dissipated or hidden offshore which might render final judgment in the substantive case useless.[15] Freezing orders are often but not always *ex parte*. Freezing orders can include orders instructing third parties, such as banks, to freeze the assets of their customers, such as in the High Court case of *Cardile v LED Builders Pty Ltd*.[16] Freezing orders can even be obtained directly by a creditor to a bankrupt estate to protect an asset of that estate from dissipation.[17] It is becoming increasingly common for courts in some jurisdictions, including the United Kingdom, to make worldwide freezing orders which purport to apply to assets across all jurisdictions, including Australia and the United Kingdom.[18]

In the *ex-parte* Federal Court case of *Deputy Commissioner of Taxation v Greenfield Electrical Services Pty Ltd*, Flick J held that a freezing order should be awarded against Greenfield to protect the Australian Taxation Office's interest in assets following a lengthy investigation. The Federal Court discussed the relevant judicial clarification of the federal freezing order provisions in the *Federal Court Rules 2011* and then demonstrates its application of the relevant factors in exercising its discretion:

> [4]. The source of this Court's powers to make the orders sought is to be found in rr 7.32 and 7.35 of the Federal Court Rules 2011 (Cth).
>
> ...
>
> [6]. ... Rule 7.35, it will be noted, expressly provides for:
>
> - the making of an order in respect to a '*prospective cause of action*' and an order against a '*prospective judgment debtor*'; and
> - the making of an order against '*another person*'.
>
> [7]. In considering the ambit of the power conferred by these provisions, and the manner of exercise of the power, it is important to recall that:
>
> - the '*purpose of such an order is to protect the processes of the Court from abuse not to provide security for the applicant for such an order*': *Elderslie Finance Corporation Ltd v Newpage Pty Ltd* [2007] FCA 61 at [14] per Stone J;
> - the making of an order effects a substantial encroachment on a person's basic right and freedom to deal with property: *KGL Health Pty Ltd v Mechtler* [2007] FCA 1410 at [12]; and
> - '*the justice of the case may require that injunctive relief be granted even before the cause of action arises*': *Patterson v BTR Engineering (Aust) Ltd* (1989) 18 NSWLR 319 at 329 per Gleeson CJ.
>
> It is also to be recalled that:
>
> - the requirement imposed by r 7.35(1)(b) that an applicant have a '*good arguable case*' is '*one which is more than barely capable of serious argument and yet not*

15 Mareva orders were named after the English international law case of *Mareva Companis Naviers SA v International Bulkcarriers SA* [1975] 2 Lloyd's Rep 509. Mareva orders are now more commonly called freezing orders; for example, the *Federal Court Rules 2011* (Cth) ch 2 pt 7 div 7.4 rr 7.31–7.38 and the *Uniform Civil Procedure Rules 2005* (NSW) div 2 r 25.11 both provide for "freezing orders". "Freezing order" is more descriptive of the order's function of freezing a party's assets.

16 *Cardile v LED Builders Pty Ltd* (1998) 198 CLR 380.

17 See *Young v Thomson* (2017) 253 FCR 191 where the appropriateness of this was supported by the Full Federal Court.

18 *Coeclerici Asia (Pte) Ltd v Gujarat NRE Coke Ltd* (2014) 312 ALR 389; *Deputy Commissioner of Taxation v Shi* [2021] HCA 22.

necessarily one the judge considers would have better than a fifty per cent chance of success': *Curtis v NID Pty Ltd* [2010] FCA 1072 at [6] per Edmonds J;
- the '*danger*' referred to in r 7.35(4) and (5) '*does not mean that the court need be satisfied that the risk of dissipation is more probable than not; and there does not necessarily need to be evidence of any intention to dissipate*': *Deputy Commissioner of Taxation v Chemical Trustee Ltd (No 4)* [2012] FCA 1064 at [22], [2012] FCA 1064; (2012) 90 ATR 711 at 717 per Perram J. See also: *Deputy Commissioner of Taxation v Hua Wang Bank Berhad* [2010] FCA 1014 at [8] to [10] per Kenny J; and
- the making of an order involves a discretionary exercise of power — even if the requirements imposed by r 7.35 are satisfied, the court nevertheless retains a discretion to refuse relief: *Patterson v BTR Engineering (Aust) Ltd* (1989) 18 NSWLR 319 at 321 to 322 per Gleeson CJ.

...

The exercise of discretion

[10]. Notwithstanding the urgings advanced by Senior Counsel for the Applicant that it would be a most unusual exercise of discretion (having made the above findings) to refuse relief, it was not understood that a submission was advanced that there nevertheless did not reside in the Court a residual discretion to refuse to do so.

[11]. The exercise of the discretion in the present case, it must be recognised, has not proved an easy task.

[12]. Every case must necessarily depend upon its own facts and circumstances and the present case should certainly not provide any encouragement to the Deputy Commissioner of Taxation to seek a freezing order against a taxpayer merely because of a general apprehension that a taxpayer may make the enforcement of any judgment founded upon an assessment more difficult.

[13]. Notwithstanding considerable misgivings, it has been concluded that the discretion should be exercised favourably to the Deputy Commissioner by reason of the fact that:

- the quantum of the amended assessments and the proposed assessments is quite considerable, especially when measured against the known assets of the taxpayers;
- there is a real danger that assets may be dissipated in the absence of an order being made;
- the scope of the assets the subject of the freezing orders is confined to no more than the quantum of the amended assessments and proposed assessments;
- allegations of deliberate evasion and dishonesty have only recently come to the attention of the taxpayers; and
- the audit period being extended to the years 2007–2011 has also only recently come to the attention of the taxpayers.

An earlier reservation founded upon the taxpayers not having taken any steps in the past to dissipate their assets notwithstanding an audit which commenced in September 2014 and an interview in February 2016, is sufficiently answered by the taxpayers only far more recently being informed of the extent of the allegations now levelled against them, and the more extensive periods of time over which their affairs will now be scrutinised. [19]

In the Victorian case of *Rail Plus Pty Ltd v Hee-Meng Ng*, Ginnane J ordered the continuation of a freezing order against a non-party to a dispute where there was a close relationship between that non-party and the defendant (in this case, she was a former spouse) and the defendant was at risk of bankruptcy.[20]

The High Court decision of *PT Bayan Resources TBK v BCBC Singapore Pte Ltd* dismissed an appeal from the Supreme Court of Western Australia concerning the inherent power of the Western Australian court to grant a freezing order to protect the potential future enforcement in Australian of an expected Singapore court decision. In dismissing the appeal, French CJ, Kiefel, Bell, Gageler and Gordon JJ held: "Even where a court makes a freezing order in circumstances in which a substantive proceeding in that court has commenced or is imminent, the process which the order is designed to protect is 'a prospective enforcement process'."[21] This private international law decision confirms the wide power of the Supreme Courts to grant freezing orders and also reminds litigants that the key purpose of the freezing order is to protect the administration of justice by ensuring that future court decisions will be enforceable.

In the Supreme Court of South Australia case of *Seeley International Pty Ltd v Millennium Electronics Pty Ltd (in liq) (No 2)*, the Court granted interim freezing orders against the respondent and, *ex parte,* against third parties even though a liquidator had been appointed to the respondent.[22] The Court justified its decision with reference to *PT Bayan Resources TBK v BCBC Singapore Pte Ltd*, stating:

> [80]. … In the subsequent decision of *PT Bayan Resources TBK v BCBC Singapore Pte Ltd*, the High Court explained:
>
> The actual holding in *Cardile v LED Builders Pty Ltd* illustrates that the prospective enforcement process that a court might protect by making a freezing order can be a process contingent on factors in addition to the outcome of a substantive proceeding in that court. The holding was that a freezing order can be made against a third party against whom no present cause of action exists and against whom no present proceeding has commenced. It is enough that some future legal process (which might be contingent, for example, on the appointment by another court of a liquidator or a trustee in bankruptcy) may be available pursuant to which the third party may be obliged to contribute to the funds of the judgment debtor to help satisfy the judgment against the judgment debtor.
>
> …

19 *Deputy Commissioner of Taxation v Greenfield Electrical Services Pty Ltd* (2016) 103 ATR 327, [4], [6]-[7], [10]-[13]. See also *Groeneveld Australia Pty Ltd v Nolten Vastgoed BV* [2011] VSC 18; *Curtis v NID Pty Ltd* [2010] FCA 1072; *Deputy Commissioner of Taxation v Hua Wang Bank Berhad* (2010) 273 ALR 194 for additional cases which usefully discuss the background and judicial discretion tests for freezing orders.

20 *Rail Plus Pty Ltd v Hee-Meng Ng* [2013] VSC 429.

21 *PT Bayan Resources TBK v BCBC Singapore Pte Ltd* (2015) 258 CLR 1, [46]. It is interesting to note that the Western Australian Supreme Court considered but rejected an application to vary the freezing orders in *BCBC Singapore Pte Ltd v PT Bayan Resources TBK (No 4)* [2018] WASC 338 (S).

22 *Seeley International Pty Ltd v Millennium Electronics Pty Ltd (in liq) (No 2)* [2020] SASC 211. The third parties were not notified of the proceedings because of their urgency. In this case, the third parties were related parties, being directors of the respondent.

[81]. In the same decision, the Court emphasised that, in *Mercedes Benz AG v Leiduck*, Lord Nicholls had thought there was 'nothing exorbitant' in a Hong Kong court making a freezing order in aid of a prospective judgment of a foreign court, being a judgment 'which will be recognised and enforceable in Hong Kong':

The alternative result would be deeply regrettable in its unfortunate impact on efforts being made by courts to prevent the legal process being defeated by the ease and speed with which money and other assets can now be moved from country to country. The law would be left sadly lagging behind the needs of the international community.

[82]. In making the urgent interim *ex parte* orders against the third parties in this case, I was conscious of the requirements for the making of a freezing order generally, as well as the 'guiding' principle described in *Cardile v LED Builders Pty Ltd*. The application of this principle is a matter of law, though discretionary elements are involved. That is to say, Millennium International has a power of disposition over, or is otherwise in possession of, the respondent's assets through the medium of the Asset Purchase Agreement, as is Millennium HK, through the medium of the charges in its favour. I am satisfied that there is a real risk of dissipation, or further dissipation, though I have, of course, not yet heard from the third parties.

[83]. In addition, whether under the powers available to a liquidator, or under the Statute of Elizabeth, these third parties may be obliged, whether at the suit of the liquidator or a creditor, to disgorge or otherwise surrender these entitlements, so as to assist satisfying any judgment liability obtained against the respondent.[23]

Freezing orders restrict the rights of individuals to deal with their assets, necessitating a balance between protecting the litigant's autonomy and the administration of due process. However, there can be other more complex balances involved where freezing orders are accompanied by ancillary disclosure orders. In the worldwide freezing order case of *Deputy Commissioner of Taxation v Shi*, the High Court was required to balance the interests of justice and protection of the Court's decision that money was due to the Australian Tax Office against the potential for disclosure of assets to cause self-incrimination of Mr Shi in Australia and China.[24] The Court held that an affidavit under s 128A *Evidence Act 1995* (Cth) by Mr Shi claiming self-incrimination privilege must be provided to the Deputy Commissioner of Taxation, noting:

> A freezing order, and an asset disclosure order, have the same fundamental purpose: 'to prevent the abuse or frustration of [a court's] process in relation to matters coming within its jurisdiction'. Freezing orders may be made, and may continue to operate, after final judgment to protect the efficacy of the execution. And for freezing orders to be effective there needs to be timely disclosure of assets. The utility in both orders lies in ensuring that the court's processes for enforcement of a judgment are not frustrated by assets being spirited away between the time of commencement of the proceedings and eventual enforcement.[25]

9.2.3 Non-court precursors to commencing litigation

In some litigation, there are processes that must be undertaken by parties or their lawyer before litigation can commence. A party seeking to recover a specific amount of money owed

23 *Seeley International Pty Ltd v Millennium Electronics Pty Ltd (in liq) (No 2)* [2020] SASC 211, [80]–[83].
24 *Deputy Commissioner of Taxation v Shi* [2021] HCA 22.
25 Ibid [22] (Kiefel CJ, Gageler and Gleeson JJ, with Gordon J agreeing and Edelmen J in dissent).

to it under a contract (known as a "liquidated debt") must send correspondence demanding payment of the debt before commencing litigation to recover the debt; for example, ch 7 of the *Uniform Civil Rules 2020* (SA) sets out pre-action steps designed to use ADR as best as possible to reduce the time, cost and need for litigation. The objects of the pre-action steps set out at r 61.1 are an excellent demonstration of the interaction between ADR and litigation:[26]

> **61.1—Objects**
>
> The objects of this Part are to—
>
> (a) encourage parties to resolve a dispute before commencing litigation;
> (b) facilitate litigation, if unavoidable, proceeding expeditiously, efficiently, at a proportionate cost and on narrowed issues;
> (c) involve insurers at an early stage;
> (d) require parties to take steps before instituting proceedings in accordance with the principle that the time and costs incurred should be proportionate to the amount or value in dispute; and
> (e) require substantial compliance without emphasis on technical matters or minor departures from the requirements.[27]

Some jurisdictions have also introduced mandatory ADR obligations on parties as a precursor to commencing litigation.[28] The strongest example is in the *Civil Dispute Resolution Act 2011* (Cth) which requires the filing of a genuine steps statement at the time of commencing proceedings setting out the steps taken to resolve the dispute prior to litigating.[29] This followed similar moves in the United Kingdom but met with significant reservations from the judiciary and small businesses who suggested compulsory preliminary ADR reduces access to courts and can increase costs and delay in commencing proceedings.[30] The resistance to such provisions was demonstrated by the failed introduction of pre-litigation protocols in New South Wales, where pt 2A *Civil Procedure Act 2005* (NSW) containing pre-litigation protocols was introduced in 2010 but never became operational before being repealed in 2013.[31]

A different sort of precursor to litigation applies to married couples wishing to divorce in the form of 12 months prior separation which must be formally declared in order to divorce.[32]

Some statutory regimes also require procedures prior to commencement of litigation. These include claims relating to motor vehicle accidents and workers compensation claims.

The above areas of litigation have their own complex laws and systems which also vary between different state jurisdictions and are beyond the scope of this work.[33]

---

26 See Chapter 5 for detailed discussion of the interaction between ADR and litigation.

27 *Uniform Civil Rules 2020* (SA) r 61.1.

28 See, eg, *Uniform Civil Rules 2020* (SA) which contain pre-action steps in ch 7 (rr 61–62) prior to commencing proceedings by claim. See also Chapter 5.2.4.

29 *Civil Dispute Resolution Act 2011* (Cth) ss 6–7.

30 Rupert Jackson, *Review of Civil Litigation Costs: Final Report* (Stationery Office, 2009).

31 Inserted pursuant to the *Courts and Crimes Legislation Further Amendment Act 2010* (NSW) sch 6.2 [2]. Excluded from operation pursuant to *the Civil Procedure Amendment (Excluded Proceedings) Regulation 2011* (NSW). Repealed under the *Courts and Other Legislation Further Amendment Act 2013* (NSW) sch 1.6 [2]. Victoria similarly repealed its provisions before they became effective. See also Julie Soars, 'Genuine Steps Obligations and Pre-Litigation Requirements' (2011) (Winter) *Journal of the New South Wales Bar Association* 19.

32 *Family Law Act 1975* (Cth) s 90MP.

33 See Chapter 7 for discussion of specific tribunals.

9.3 Lawyer obligations for commencing litigation

What lawyers do, or fail to do, in the period between a client's first visit in relation to a dispute and the time when litigation has commenced, results in a significant portion of the complaints lodged against lawyers. One of the worst and most common mistakes made by lawyers is failing to commence proceedings in a timely fashion. Another common cause for complaint against lawyers regards the failure of lawyers to sufficiently advise clients in relation to legal costs.[34] Both complaints relate to pre-commencement/commencement responsibilities. Lawyers should, therefore, be extra careful to comply with their obligations to clients preceding commencement of litigation.

9.3.1 The importance of statutory limitations and commencing in time

There is a limited time within which most litigation can be commenced. Determining what the statutory time limit is for any potential litigation may be complicated. The time limit may vary depending on the nature of the claim, the location of the claim, what statutes, if any, govern the claim, and the nature and timing of the loss or damage suffered. The most common time limitations are three years and six years, with six years as the common default period. Determining when the three or six year limitation period commenced can be complex in some areas of law, such as personal injury and construction disputes. For example, actions for breach of contract generally have a six-year limitation period, commencing on the date the contract was breached while personal injury claims are commonly restricted to three years from the date the injury was discoverable. This variation is evident in s 5 of the *Limitation of Actions Act 1958* (Vic), which provides a six-year period for simple contractual and tortious claims (s 5(1)) but a shorter three-year limitation period for personal injury claims (s 5(1AA)) and an even shorter one-year period for defamation claims (s 5(1AAA)). A small number of actions, including those concerning land, can have longer time frames; for example, ss 18–25 of the *Limitation Act 2005* (WA) contains 12-year limitations for certain actions involving real property, land and deeds.[35]

Many relevant limitation periods derive from the statutes set out in Table 9.1. The Limitation Acts listed are not exhaustive as there are numerous additional Acts containing statutory limitations.

Some statutory regimes require significant action prior to commencing proceedings, such as attending conciliation, making settlement offers or attending arbitrations which mean that lawyers must be advising their clients to take preliminary steps many months prior to the expiry date for commencing litigation.

34 Office of the Legal Services Commissioner, *Annual Report 2014–2015* (Report, 2015) 18, 22.

35 See *Western Australian Limitation Act 2005* (WA); Peter Handford, 'A New Limitation Act for the 21st Century' (2007) 33(3) *University of Western Australia Law Review* 387 for a comparison to other Australian jurisdictions.

Table 9.1 Limitation Acts

Australian Capital Territory	*Limitation Act 1985*
New South Wales	*Limitation Act 1969*
Northern Territory	*Limitation Act 1981*
Queensland	*Limitation of Actions Act 1984*
South Australia	*Limitation of Actions Act 1936*
Tasmania	*Limitation Act 1974*
Victoria	*Limitation of Actions Act 1958*
Western Australia	*Limitation Act 2005*

A significant proportion of professional negligence claims against lawyers occur because statutory limitation periods were overlooked, and claims were barred or jeopardised by late commencement of a claim.[36]

9.3.2 Costs disclosure

As discussed in Chapter 6, there are increasing obligations on lawyers to make upfront disclosures to clients concerning the process and cost of the legal work requested. This can be particularly challenging in the case of litigation, as it can be very difficult to predict the path of a litigation prior to commencement and even more difficult to estimate the scope of interlocutory steps (eg discovery and preparation of witness evidence) which may vary significantly depending on the approach taken by the other parties to the litigation and aspects of the evidence which are unknown at commencement.

9.3.3 Document obligations

It is important that potential litigants understand that they are likely to have significant obligations regarding the provision of documents relevant to the litigation. The obligation not to destroy documents potentially relevant to litigation commences prior to the litigation. Clients should be warned not to destroy documents and warned that the litigation process may lead to publication of documents and other evidence which would otherwise be private and confidential. *McCabe v British American Tobacco Australia Services Ltd*[37] provides further information in relation to the obligations of parties anticipating litigation not to destroy relevant documents.[38]

9.3.4 Nationalisation of professional obligations

Legislation regulating the legal profession currently varies from state to state, although there has been discussion on nationalising the profession for many years. On 9 September 2011, the Federal Attorney General, Robert McClelland MP, announced draft legislation, the Legal

36 Legal Practitioners Liability Committee, *Know Your Limits Report* (2017) 1, states that 7.6% of the past five years' claims (for its 16,000 insured Australian solicitors and 1,800 Victorian barristers) averaging $2,445,000 per year resulted from missed limitation periods.

37 *McCabe v British American Tobacco Australia Services Ltd* [2000] VSC 73.

38 See Chapters 11, 12 and 13 for more detailed discussion on documentary obligations.

Profession National Law, drafted in cooperation with New South Wales, Victoria, Queensland, and the Northern Territory through the Council of Australian Governments (COAG). By 2013, every state and territory in Australia had introduced legislation harmonising legal professional obligations, with South Australia being the final state to join through the *Legal Practitioners (Miscellaneous) Amendment Act 2013* (SA). Victoria and New South Wales now both have the *Legal Profession Uniform Law Application Act 2014* (NSW). The *Legal Profession Uniform Law Application Act 2014* (NSW), effective from July 2015, provides, in s 4, that the *Legal Profession Uniform Law* set out in sch 1 to the *Legal Profession Uniform Law Application Act 2014* of Victoria applies in New South Wales, and may be referred to as the "*Legal Profession Uniform Law* (NSW)". However, the present extent of harmonisation remains a long way from the Uniform Legal Profession National Law enacted in all Australian States and Territories, which was the intended outcome of the Federal Attorney Generals 2011 draft legislation and which seems unlikely to be achieved in the near future.[39]

9.4 Defining originating process

Originating process is the document filed by the plaintiff which commences the proceedings. Originating process is also commonly the first pleading in litigation.[40] There are a variety of originating processes, including summons, writ, originating motion and statement of claim.

9.4.1 Originating process is sometimes but not always a pleading

The most common form of originating process is a statement of claim. This form of originating process is also a form of pleading because it pleads the plaintiff's case. This

Figure 9.1 Originating process/pleading Venn diagram

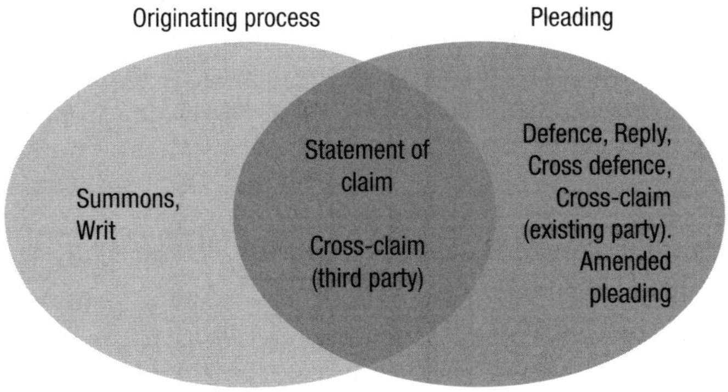

39 Ralph Bonig, 'Another Brick in the Wall: Towards a National Legal Profession' (2013) 35(10) *Bulletin: Law Society of South Australia* 24.

40 Pleadings generally encompass claims, defences, cross-claims, cross-defences and cross-replies. Chapter 10 discusses the structure and rules of pleadings in more detail.

can be contrasted with a summons, which is an originating process, because it commences proceedings but which is not a pleading because it does not plead the plaintiff's case. Whether a document is an originating process is important for the purposes of determining the requirements of service (discussed at Chapter 9.7). A cross-claim against a new party is an originating process because it creates a dispute with a new party and that new party must be properly notified by way of service.

The Venn diagram in Figure 9.1 demonstrates the overlap between pleadings and originating process. Pleadings are discussed in detail in Chapter 10.

9.4.2 Requirements for originating process

Despite the apparent differences between jurisdictions, there is more commonality than difference. Essentially an originating process must identify the parties to the case, what is being claimed, and what basis there is for claiming it. Some types of cases lend themselves to more detail than others and many jurisdictions have different requirements and/or different forms depending on the nature of the claim.

In addition to the formal requirements applying specifically to originating process, there are general requirements applicable to all court documents and requirements specifically applicable to all pleadings. These requirements will be discussed in more detail in Chapter 10 concerning pleadings and particulars, but it is important to note that they apply equally to many originating processes, such as statements of claim, which are also the first pleading in a litigation.[41]

In addition to the differences in form requirements indicated below, there can be circumstances where courts dispense with or limit formal pleading requirements in certain cases to expedite proceedings; for example, in the Commercial List in the Supreme Court of New South Wales, a plaintiff commences with a summons accompanied by a Commercial List Statement rather than a Statement of Claim. The Commercial List Statement is an unverified document designed to be brief, efficient and informal. This is one reason why it is important for lawyers to review the practice notes for courts as well as civil procedure legislation when acting in proceedings in an unfamiliar court or jurisdiction. The role of practice notes will be discussed in more detail in Chapter 10.

9.5 Jurisdiction: choosing the right court to commence proceedings

There are numerous factors to consider when determining the most appropriate court in which to commence proceedings.[42] Essentially, the three aspects of a claim that commonly affect which court is appropriate are the amount in dispute, the location of the dispute (and the location of other relevant factors), and the nature of the dispute. There are

41 When drafting originating process, regard must be had to form requirements applicable to all pleadings, including the need to properly particularise (discussed in Chapter 10) and any form requirements applicable to all documents filed in court. These vary somewhat between jurisdictions.

42 See also Chapter 8.3 on determining jurisdiction.

factors which may complicate all three of these areas and there are many disputes where parties have a choice as to which court they wish to commence proceedings in. There are a number of factors, including statutory limitation periods, enforceability of decisions, appeal options, cost, and convenience which may impact a plaintiff's choice of court.[43] These issues can be particularly complex where the plaintiff's choice is between different jurisdictions.

9.5.1 Monetary guidelines for commencing proceedings

One of the most important factors in determining the appropriate court to commence proceedings is the amount in dispute. Australian states and territories provide guidelines as to which court to commence proceedings in within their jurisdiction, depending on the amount in dispute. These guidelines vary over time, although limits often remain constant for many years. Generally, the maximum amount for claims in lower courts increases as courts are encouraged to push more and more matters to lower courts and to counteract inflation.

Lower courts tend to have simplified procedures and less reliance on process, which makes litigating cheaper and quicker but may compromise the judge's ability to ascertain the relevant facts so as to correctly apply the law. The variation in procedure between different court levels and the consequent different merits of different court levels reflect the key civil procedure theme of balancing efficiency against justice or procedural fairness and the necessity to compromise between these competing objectives of civil procedure.

Sometimes, it is difficult for parties to determine the amount in dispute. Often, the quantum of damage may require expert assessment with parties disagreeing significantly as to the quantum in dispute. In some cases, at the time of commencement, the quantum in dispute may be unknown. In such cases, the plaintiff will commence in the jurisdiction it thinks most likely to be appropriate to the claim.

The monetary guidelines are also not universally applicable. For example, where parties agree to do so, courts will usually allow a claim to commence in a lower court even where the claim exceeds the maximum for that court. This may be attractive to parties where the dispute is legally or factually simple and the lower level of formality often displayed in lower courts is attractive to the parties. Also, court fees and legal costs are usually significantly less in lower courts than in the Supreme Court. The reverse can also happen where matters are significantly more complex than the amount in dispute would indicate and the expertise of a higher court is required.

Either party can apply for a matter commenced in one court to be transferred to a more suitable court and courts can also obtain party consent to transfer matters for the court's convenience either to clear backlogs or because the other court is considered more suitable. There are also certain specific areas of law in some jurisdictions, such as certain dealings with land or money held on trust, where all matters must be commenced in the Supreme

43 In this context, the court is often referred to as the "forum", particularly where the choice is between courts in different jurisdictions. Plaintiffs are sometimes accused by judges of "forum shopping" if the court feels they have selected that court for strategic purposes that may cause injustice to other parties. See *BHP Billiton Ltd v Schultz* (2004) 221 CLR 400, [64].

Court regardless of the amount in dispute or where the monetary limits for lower courts are different than for other types of claim.

To give a general idea of the sort of claims heard by different courts, and the significant variation between different states and territories, the general monetary limits at the close of 2020 for each state and territory are set out below. As discussed in Chapter 7, civil claims, particularly small ones, can also often be heard in the Civil and Administrative Tribunals of many Australian jurisdictions. These amounts will not apply to every type of claim and may change at any time, so readers must check the relevant court websites before commencing any proceedings. For example, the monetary limitations in the Northern Territory increased its local court's monetary jurisdiction in 2015 pursuant to the *Local Court Act 2015* (NT) s 12.

9.5.1.1 Commonwealth: federal jurisdiction

Monetary limits are often not the most relevant factor in Commonwealth courts because the jurisdiction of courts, such as the High Court, are based on the nature of the dispute rather than the amount in dispute. The Federal Circuit Court,[44] until September 2021, sat beneath the Federal Court and Family Court, with jurisdiction for disputes up to $750,000. From 1 September 2021, pursuant to the *Federal Circuit and Family Court of Australia Act 2021* (Cth), the Family Court of Australia amalgamated with the Federal Circuit Court to create the Federal Circuit and Family Court of Australia. The amalgamated Federal Circuit and Family Court of Australia court sits below the Federal Court but has no financial limit for family law disputes. This restructure of Commonwealth courts was partially in recognition of the large number of family law matters under $750,000, which constituted as much as 90% of the Federal Circuit Court's workload prior to amalgamation.[45]

9.5.1.2 Australian Capital Territory

The ACT Magistrates Court hears matters between $25,000 and $250,000 (except for cases concerning land title).[46] Disputes below $25,000 are heard by the ACT Civil and Administrative Tribunal.[47] Disputes in excess of $250,000 and/or concerning title to land are heard in the Supreme Court of the ACT.[48]

9.5.1.3 Northern Territory

In the Northern Territory, the Local Court hears claims up to $250,000 with claims below $25,000 being heard by a separate small claims division of the Local Court. Claims above $250,000 are heard by the Supreme Court of the Northern Territory.

44 Formerly known as the Federal Magistrates Court.

45 There is considerable discussion of the difficulties facing the Family Court and the Federal Circuit Court in relation to family law disputes: see Australian Law Reform Commission, *Family Law for the Future: An Inquiry into the Family Law System* (Report No 135, April 2019). At the time of writing, it is unclear whether the merger of the Family Court with the Federal Circuit Court will resolve any or all of the problems identified by the ALRC, practitioners, and academics in relation to the management of family law matter, particularly those involving allegations of domestic violence.

46 *Magistrates Court Act 1930* (ACT) s 257.

47 Ibid s 266A.

48 Ibid s 264.

9.5.1.4 New South Wales

In New South Wales, the Local Court has jurisdiction for civil claims up to $100,000, including a small claims division hearing matters up to $10,000. The District Court hears motor accident claims of any amount and other claims above $100,000 up to $750,000 (or above if all parties agree or there is no objection by the defendant: *Katter v Melhem*).[49] The Supreme Court hears claims in excess of $750,000.

9.5.1.5 Queensland

The Magistrates Court of Queensland can hear claims less than $150,000. The District Court can hear claims between $150,000 and $750,000, and the Supreme Court hears all claims exceeding $750,000.

9.5.1.6 South Australia

In South Australia, the Magistrates Courts are responsible from claims up to $100,000 (with a small claims division up to $12,000). Claims over $100,000 can be heard by the District Court or the Supreme Court with more complex matters to be commenced in the Supreme Court provided they exceed a minimum of $120,000 (or $50,000 for defamation claims).

9.5.1.7 Tasmania

In Tasmania, the civil division of the Magistrates Court deals with disputes up to $50,000 or more if the parties agree. As there is no District Court in Tasmania, claims above $50,000 are heard in the Supreme Court unless the parties agree to be heard in the Magistrates Court.

9.5.1.8 Victoria

In Victoria, the Magistrates Court has jurisdiction over civil claims up to $100,000. The County Court no longer has an upper monetary limit to its jurisdiction pursuant to the *Courts Legislation (Jurisdiction) Act 2006* (Vic) and its civil jurisdiction covers all claims for personal injury and other personal claims as well as statutorily-conferred jurisdiction in numerous areas. The Supreme Court retains original jurisdiction for civil matters of high complexity or other legal significance.

9.5.1.9 Western Australia

The Western Australia Magistrates Court has jurisdiction for claims up to $75,000, as well as a small claims division for matters up to $10,000. The Western Australia District Court has jurisdiction for claims up to $750,000 and unlimited jurisdiction for personal injury claims. The Supreme Court of Western Australia hears claims in excess of $750,000.

The court hierarchy diagram in Chapter 1 shows the monetary limitations set out above for each court.

9.5.2 The cost of commencing proceedings

All courts charge fees for commencing proceedings and these are usually regulated. The regulations attached to each court governing fees are updated frequently, with some courts, particularly Federal Courts, boasting hefty fees for corporations commencing proceedings.

49 *Katter v Melhem* (2015) 90 NSWLR 164, [95]-[109].

When determining which court to commence in, the amount of fees payable can be a significant factor, which is why most plaintiffs choose to commence proceedings in the lowest court with jurisdiction to hear their claim.

Parties are likely to choose a higher court, despite the higher fees, where they feel the matter is sufficiently complex that it requires a senior judge, where the plaintiff knows that the trial decision is likely to be appealed to a higher court, or where the higher court is considered more efficient (as the Federal Court often is).[50]

The Federal Court charges fees for commencing proceedings, fees for setting down a matter for hearing, and hearing fees. For an example of the costs of commencing proceedings (not including any legal costs), the current fees for commencing proceedings in the Federal Court of Australia are set out in sch 1 of the *Federal Court and Federal Circuit Court Regulation 2012* (Cth).

9.5.3 The substance of the dispute

As noted in Chapter 9.5.1 above, the jurisdictional limits for several jurisdictions vary depending on the nature of the claim; for example, personal injury claims and motor vehicle claims may be treated differently to general claims. Accordingly, the nature of the dispute may determine which court within a state or territory hierarchy is the appropriate court to commence in.

In addition to differences within state hierarchies, it is also important for potential plaintiffs to consider whether the law governing the dispute is Commonwealth law or state-based law. In many cases, it may be a combination of both. Australia is a federal system, in which the Federal Government has limited specified powers and all residual powers fall to the states and territories. Consequently, the Federal Courts have specific areas which fall within their jurisdiction and all other matters fall to state jurisdiction.[51]

Some disputes, such as personal injury, stem from common law and state statutes and generally fall within state or territory legislation. Commercial matters are more complicated, because they often attract both federal jurisdiction through trade-related legislation and state jurisdiction through common law areas such as contract. Hence, parties can often choose between state and federal jurisdictions.

9.5.4 The location of the dispute

Which court to commence in can also be dependent on the location of the dispute. Where both parties are resident in the same state or territory and all the events leading to the dispute are also in that state or territory, then there is no dispute as to the appropriate forum for hearing the dispute. However, with an increasingly global economy and no trade

50 A small number of large commercial cases are likely to be appealed to the highest court possible because the amount of money involved is so significant that no party will accept anything but the most final judgment. Some parties with deep pockets and highly acrimonious disputes may also appeal as far as possible. In such cases, it is sensible to start in the highest court with appropriate original jurisdiction. This is usually a Supreme Court or the Federal Court depending on the nature of the dispute.

51 *Commonwealth Constitution* s 51.

or migration barriers between states, it is very common for parties and events to be spread across multiple jurisdictions.[52]

Where several jurisdictions are available in which to commence proceedings, plaintiffs must weigh up the advantages and disadvantages of each forum. In general terms, it is more convenient for a plaintiff to commence proceedings in its home jurisdiction and plaintiffs are most likely to be familiar with the court and civil procedure rules of their own jurisdiction. In addition, it is often suggested that parties are more likely to receive favourable treatment from the court of their own jurisdiction (despite best judicial efforts to resist bias).[53] On the other hand, it may be easier to enforce a judgment against a defendant if that judgment was made in the jurisdiction where the defendant has assets, which is most often the defendant's place of residence. Enforcement issues can be significant for international disputes, particularly those involving legal systems significantly different to Australia.

Finally, there may be strategic benefits to commencing in one jurisdiction rather than another, such as a variance in statutory limitation periods or the availability of other procedural advantages which favours commencing in one jurisdiction over another.[54]

9.6 Legislative framework for originating process

This book focuses predominantly on Supreme Court proceedings and federal proceedings to source examples of civil procedure in each state, territory and federal jurisdiction. Accordingly, the following examples for each jurisdiction concern the Supreme Court procedure for that jurisdiction. In some jurisdictions, with uniform civil procedure — for example, New South Wales and Victoria — the process will be virtually identical in the lower courts, while other jurisdictions retain separate rules and forms for lower courts.[55] There are significant similarities between the courts within each jurisdiction and between the different jurisdictions.

9.6.1 High Court

The High Court has original jurisdiction, in addition to being the highest appeal court in Australia for all state, territory and Federal Courts. Originating process for matters commenced in the High Court's original jurisdiction is governed by ch 2 of the *High Court Rules 2004*

52 See also Chapter 8.3 which briefly addressed the jurisdictional disputes that can arise as a result of the interstate and international nature of many modern-day disputes.

53 See Chapter 8.3.2.

54 Note that, in Australia, the determination of the applicable limitation period is considered to be a substantive law issue, rather than a procedural one, pursuant to *John Pfeiffer Pty Ltd v Rogerson* (2000) 203 CLR 503. This means an Australian court will determine the law governing the dispute (the choice of law) and then apply the limitation period of that chosen law (which may not be an Australian law) rather than applying the relevant Australian jurisdiction's limitation period. However, not all jurisdictions consider limitation periods to be substantive, so this may remain an issue for consideration depending on the foreign jurisdiction under consideration.

55 It is important to note that, even jurisdictions with uniform civil procedure have some important variations between courts within their hierarchy for reasons such as efficiency. For example, the New South Wales *Uniform Civil Procedure Rules 2005* have significant variations in the rules for service in Local Courts as compared with the Supreme Court.

(Cth). Parts 20 to 29 govern originating process in the High Court, which includes matters commenced by writ of summons, writs of mandamus or prohibition or certiorari and writs of habeas corpus or quo warranto.

For proceedings commenced by writ of summons pursuant to pt 27 of the *High Court Rules 2004* (Cth) (which is the default commencement process), a statement of claim is also required to be filed and served either with the writ of summons or within 21 days of the defendant's appearance pursuant to r 27.03. Pursuant to r 27.01, a summons must be served within 12 months of being issued

Appeals in the High Court are commenced pursuant to ch 4 of the *High Court Rules 2004* (Cth). An appeal commenced in the High Court is also an originating process, as it commences the proceedings in that court, but the rules in relation to appeals differ from those of original trials. Appeals will be considered in more detail in Chapter 16.

9.6.2 Federal Court

Federal Court proceedings are generally commenced by originating application, pursuant to r 8.01 of the *Federal Court Rules 2011* (Cth). The originating application must be in accordance with Form 15.

Pursuant to r 8.02 of the *Federal Court Rules 2011* (Cth), the applicant must, at the time of filing originating process, also file a statement of genuine steps in accordance with Form 16. The statement of genuine steps requires parties to set out the genuine steps they have taken to resolve their dispute prior to commencing the proceedings.[56]

9.6.3 Australian Capital Territory

Pursuant to r 31 of pt 2.2 of the *Court Procedures Rules 2006* (ACT), proceedings may be commenced by an originating claim or an originating application. There is also provision in r 37 for oral originating process, whereby the court gives an oral order, such as for urgent interim injunctive relief,[57] but these are exceptional and are required to be followed by written originating process.

Most proceedings in the ACT are commenced by originating claim pursuant to r 33 of the *Court Procedures Rules 2006* (ACT). The circumstances in which originating application is required are set out in Note 2 to r 34, and include application to identify a defendant, applications to transfer proceedings, and applications to enforce foreign judgments and arbitral awards. Division 2.2.2 sets out the requirements for the originating claim, pursuant to r 50, and the attached more detailed statement of claim, the requirements for which vary as set out in rr 51 to 55.

9.6.4 Northern Territory

In the Northern Territory, proceedings are generally commenced by writ or by originating motion pursuant to ord 4 r 1 of the *Supreme Court Rules 1987* (NT).[58] Most cases are

56 See Chapter 5.2.4.
57 See Chapter 9.1.2.
58 See also *Local Court (Civil Jurisdiction) Rules 1998* (NT) for local court matters.

commenced by writ pursuant to ord 4 r 4. Matters with no defendant are an example commenced by originating motion (ord 4 r 5) and matters where there is no factual dispute and therefore no pleadings or discovery are also commenced by originating motion (ord 4 r 6). Pursuant to ord 5 r 2(1), a writ shall be in Form 5A. Writs are required to contain an endorsement of the claim, generally in the form of a statement of claim pursuant to ord 5 r 4.

9.6.5 New South Wales

In New South Wales, proceedings are generally commenced by statement of claim, pursuant to pt 6 of the *Uniform Civil Procedure Rules 2005* (NSW) which apply to all courts in the New South Wales court hierarchy. Division 2 of pt 6 of the *Uniform Civil Procedure Rules 2005* provides that proceedings should be commenced by statement of claim or summons. In practice, most proceedings are commenced by statement of claim pursuant to r 6.3 which requires a statement of claim be used for numerous types of claims, including liquidated claims, tort claims, fraud claims and possession of land. Rule 6.4 sets out where a summons is required, including proceedings with no defendant, proceedings to transfer proceedings, and preliminary discovery proceedings.

Division 4 of pt 6 of the *Uniform Civil Procedure Rules 2005* (NSW) sets out the requirements for statements of claim and summonses at rr 6.12–6.17. Part 14 of the *Uniform Civil Procedure Rules 2005* (NSW) sets out the form requirements for pleadings and these apply equally to originating process as to defences and other pleadings. The rules of pleading will be discussed in more detail in Chapter 10. New South Wales has a different statement of claim for legally represented litigants (as opposed to self-represented litigants), as lawyers commencing proceedings on behalf of clients must sign a certificate certifying, in accordance with *Legal Profession Uniform Law Application Act 2014* (NSW) s 62 sch 2(2), that the case has reasonable prospects of success.

9.6.6 Queensland

Chapter 2 of the *Uniform Civil Procedure Rules 1999* (Qld) sets out the rules for originating process at all levels of the Queensland court hierarchy. Chapter 2 pt 1 r 8(2) of the *Uniform Civil Procedure Rules 1999* (Qld) sets out the possible originating processes as claims, applications, and notices of appeal. Most cases are commenced by claim, pursuant to r 9, with applications being appropriate pursuant to r 11 for matters where urgent relief is sought or there is no defendant or no factual dispute. Chapter 2 pt 2 of the *Uniform Civil Procedure Rules 1999* (Qld) sets out general rules for originating process (rr 17–20) and pt 3 then sets out rules for claims (rr 21–24).

9.6.7 South Australia

In South Australia, originating process is now governed by ch 6 of the *Uniform Civil Rules 2020* (SA) which applies to Supreme, District and Magistrates Courts and requires proceedings to be commenced by claim (r 51.2) or originating application (r 51.3). As noted in r 51.1:

> Proceedings by way of claim require *pleadings*, discovery and service of *expert reports* and involve several interlocutory steps before proceeding to *trial*. Proceedings by way of

originating application do not usually involve these steps, usually proceed on affidavits when evidence is required and may be finally determined on the *return date*.[59]

It is likely that most cases in South Australia will commence by claim, which covers claims under statute, common law and equity seeking remedies of "damages, compensation, injunction, restitution, specific performance, rescission, rectification or declaration".[60] Actions commenced by originating application are limited to those with specific prescribed forms for application or matters with specific procedures, such as confiscation proceedings, foreign judgment registration proceedings, and contentious probate proceedings.[61]

9.6.8 Tasmania

In Tasmania, originating process is governed by pt 7 of the *Supreme Court Rules 2000* (Tas) concerning proceedings.[62] Most originating process in Tasmania is by way of writ pursuant to r 88. Proceedings not commenced by writ are generally commenced by application pursuant to r 89 and include certain dealings with land and estates. Part 7 div 4 provides general rules for originating process (rr 96–103) and div 5 provides rules for writs (rr 104–107). A writ must be served within six months of filing pursuant to r 107. A writ must generally be endorsed by a statement of claim pursuant to r 108. Accordingly, plaintiffs file the statement of claim as part of the writ and a writ may be set aside by the court if the endorsing statement of claim is inadequate pursuant to r 109.

9.6.9 Victoria

The *Civil Procedure Act 2010* (Vic) affects all civil procedure in Victoria, but each court level has its own rules with the *Supreme Court (General Civil Procedure) Rules 2015* (Vic) providing for originating process in ord 5.[63] Proceedings in Victoria are generally commenced by writ. Proceedings not commenced by writ are commenced by originating motion. A writ is required by ord 5 r 2 to be in Form 5A. Writs are required to contain an endorsement of the claim, commonly an attached statement of claim, pursuant to ord 5 r 4. A writ must be served within a year of being filed pursuant to ord 5 r 12.

9.6.10 Western Australia

In Western Australia, originating process is governed by the *Rules of the Supreme Court 1971* (WA).[64] In Western Australia, originating proceedings may be in the form of a writ, a

59 *Uniform Civil Rules 2020* (SA) commenced on 18 May 2020.

60 *Uniform Civil Rules 2020* (SA) rr 51.2(1)–51.2(2). Claims are explained in ch 7 of the *Uniform Civil Rules 2020* (SA).

61 *Uniform Civil Rules 2020* (SA) ch 8 r 82.1 explains originating applications and include those covered by chs 19–21 of the *Uniform Civil Rules 2020* (SA) which have prescribed forms (r 51.2).

62 See also *Magistrates Court (Civil Division) Rules 1998* (Tas) for smaller disputes.

63 See also *Magistrates' Court General Civil Procedure Rules 2020* (Vic) and *County Court Civil Procedure Rules 2018* (Vic) for less complex or lower value matters.

64 See also *District Court Rules 2005* (WA), *Magistrates Court (Civil Proceedings) Rules 2005* (WA) and *Magistrates Court (Minor Case Procedure) Rules 2005* (WA) for smaller matters. Both sets of *Magistrates Rules* (WA) were significantly updated in June 2020 with new forms designed

summons, or a notice. Order 4 governs the commencement of proceedings and requires that all proceedings be commenced by writ and that proceedings also be commenced by either originating motion or originating summons. Pursuant to ord 5, writs are to be in Form 1 or Form 2. Pursuant to ord 6, a writ must be indorsed by a concise statement of the claim made and the orders sought.

9.7 Service of process

As discussed at the beginning of this chapter, there are many considerations prior to commencing litigation, including the potential for settlement. For this reason, it should be uncommon for a potential defendant to be unaware that litigation is about to be commenced against it. It is, however, important that defendants are notified (by receiving a copy) of the originating process as soon as possible after it has been filed in court. The process of service of documents is based on a key theme of civil procedure — being the entitlement of parties to procedural fairness. Procedural fairness includes the right of parties to be heard. In order to ensure the defendant has sufficient opportunity to be heard, it is first necessary to ensure the defendant has satisfactory notice of the proceedings. For this reason, there are important procedures concerning serving originating process on defendants.

There are a small number of circumstances where plaintiffs may have good reason not to serve immediately on defendants. This includes circumstances where there is ongoing uncertainty at law as to the correct defendant,[65] where there is uncertainty as to the identity of one or more plaintiffs,[66] or where there is uncertainty as to some of the claims made or damages sought but statutory limitations require commencement of the claim. In such cases, plaintiffs may be compelled to file originating process to ensure their right to claim is not lost but wish to defer service of the claim until they can properly clarify the parties, claims and damages. Most civil procedure rules provide a specific period within which a filed originating process must be properly served on all defendants.[67]

9.7.1 The rationale for service of process: notice

It is a critical aspect of our adversarial justice system that both parties have a right to be heard. The administrative law principle of *audi alteram partem* (hear the other side) requires that the defendant receive a reasonable opportunity to be heard before judgment is awarded in favour of a plaintiff.[68] The first step in ensuring a defendant is heard is ensuring that the

to simplify the statement of claim and other pleadings through the *Magistrates Court Rules Amendment Rules 2020* (WA).

65 Where there is uncertainty as to the identity of the defendant, the plaintiff may apply to the court for preliminary discovery, as discussed at Chapter 9.1.1.

66 In representative actions (also called class actions) or ordinary actions involving numerous plaintiffs, it may take years to correctly identify all potential plaintiffs; see Chapter 8.4.2 for further discussion.

67 See, eg, in NSW, where service is required to be made soon as practicable pursuant to *Uniform Civil Procedure Rules 2005* (NSW) r 10.1(1); within six months for all Supreme Court, all Local Court and District Court (outside NSW); and within one month (District Court local service) or *Uniform Civil Procedure Rules 2005* (NSW) r 6.2(4).

68 *Commissioner of Police v Tanos* (1958) 98 CLR 383, 395.

defendant is aware of the proceedings. For this reason, the rules for serving originating process on defendants are stronger than the rules governing service of almost any other court-related document. In most cases, the court will require the plaintiff to personally serve the defendant with originating process as discussed below.

Service of process is not an issue in the majority of proceedings. In most commercial cases where the parties have engaged lawyers and negotiated prior to commencing proceedings, the parties will have already authorised their lawyers to accept service of documents (often including by email and facsimile) and notified each other of this.

It is cases where the defendant is likely to avoid service that proving service of process becomes important. In cases where the plaintiff ends up seeking default judgment or summary judgment against the defendant for failing to defend the proceedings, establishing service of originating process can be critical.[69] Balancing the need for procedures to be efficient while still enabling due process lies at the heart of service requirements.[70]

9.7.2 Personal service

Originating process usually requires personal service.[71] This means that the document must be personally delivered to the defendant (or the principal officer authorised to accept service for corporations) who must acknowledge receipt of the document. In many cases, service will be executed by a process server. Process servers are experts in serving documents. Once they have executed service, they will swear an affidavit as evidence of service.

The relevant court rules for each jurisdiction set out the requirements for service, generally in the provisions immediately following those set out above in this chapter concerning drafting originating process. Lower courts may allow less personal service procedures, such as service by post, particularly for smaller matters to reduce the plaintiff's costs in proceeding to litigation. Once originating process has been personally served, subsequent court documents can be served by ordinary service. The parties specify acceptable means of ordinary service in their pleading documents and these will generally include electronic means, such as email.

For example, the *Federal Court Rules 2011* (Cth) set out the requirements for service in pt 10, with div 10.1 governing personal service, div 10.2 governing service other than by personal service, div 10.3 governing ordinary service, div 10.4 governing service outside Australia, div 10.5 governing service through diplomatic channels and div 10.6 governing service through the *Convention on the Service Abroad of Judicial and Extrajudicial Documents in Civil or Commercial Matters*.

Originating process in the Federal Court is required to be by personal service pursuant to r 8.06. The rules for personal service in the Federal Court are similar to the rules of other Australian jurisdictions. Division 10.1 sets out the requirements for personal service in the

69 See, eg, *Violi v Commonwealth Bank of Australia* [2015] NSWCA 152, [71]. Summary judgment and default judgment were considered in detail in Chapter 5.

70 See Chapter 2.3.1 for detailed analysis of this CDR theme.

71 Subpoenas, which are discussed in Chapter 12, are also generally required to be served personally. This is because subpoenas are usually served on entities or individuals who are not parties to the litigation and, accordingly, may be unaware of the proceedings and their obligations to the court pursuant to the subpoena unless they are properly served with their subpoena.

Federal Court.[72] As with other jurisdictions, the Federal Court Rules deal with service on a wide range of entities, including individuals, corporations, unincorporated associations, organisations, partnerships and people with legal incapacity.

United Group Resources Pty Ltd v Calabro (*United Group Resources*)[73] provides an example of the complexity which may arise in establishing personal service, although it should be noted that the case was decided in accordance with the previous *Federal Court Rules 1979* (Cth), not the current *Federal Court Rules 2011* (Cth).

In the Federal Court case of *United Group Resources*, McKerracher J explains the basis for the rules concerning service and the circumstances in which they apply. The case concerned an application to prevent industrial action by building and construction employees and involved in excess of 1,500 respondents, being the employees of a number of building and construction companies who were the applicants in the case.[74] This case concerned the requirement for personal service and the ability to grant substituted service (discussed below) in circumstances where the defendant (or in this case respondent) could not be unaware of the proceedings. The respondents sought a declaration under ord 9 r 7(1)(c) of the *Federal Court Rules 1979* (Cth) that originating process had not been properly served on several hundred of the respondents.

United Group Resources concerned service on over 1500 respondents who were workers in an industrial dispute with their employers, where significant attempts at personal service had been made and there was wide publicity of the dispute. In the following extract from *United Group Resources*, McKerracher J explains the objectives of personal service with reference to leading cases on service of process, including *Laurie v Carroll*[75] and *Ainsworth v Redd*,[76] before concluding that the respondents' application should fail because they were all properly aware of the proceedings commenced against them despite the defects in personal service.[77]

> [26]. The position as to whether the respondents actually received the originating process is not clear but it must be said that at the commencement of this proceeding a great deal of publicity occurred as disclosed on affidavit evidence. That publicity taken together with the personal letters would explain why there is no evidence that any respondent, especially any conditional respondent, did not become aware that he or she was a party to the proceeding in the manner described in the letter forwarded by the applicants to all respondents at or about the date of the various letters.
>
> [27]. Without the letter, it must be said that simply knowing of the proceeding does not mean that one knows that one is a party to the proceeding, let alone the precise cause of action being pursued. But the letter does at least deal with the important issue of knowledge of those matters.
>
> [28]. Importantly given that the conditional respondents each instructed the solicitors concerned to enter conditional appearances, it must be inferred that the originating process came to their notice.

72 *Federal Court Rules 2011* (Cth).

73 *United Group Resources Pty Ltd v Calabro (No 4)* [2010] FCA 791.

74 Federal Court applications involve "applicants" rather than "plaintiffs" and "respondents" rather than "defendants" but the roles are broadly equivalent.

75 *Laurie v Carroll* (1958) 98 CLR 310.

76 *Ainsworth v Redd* (1990) 19 NSWLR 78.

77 *United Group Resources Pty Ltd v Calabro (No 4)* [2010] FCA 791.

[29]. In *Howship Holdings Pty Ltd v Leslie [No 2]* [1996] NSWSC 314; (1996) 41 NSWLR 542 (at 544) Young J said observed:

> ... personal service merely means that the document in question must come to the notice of the person for whom it is intended. The means by which that person obtains the document are usually immaterial. This is clear in cases that have been considered good law over the centuries, including *Hope v Hope* [1854] EngR 468; (1854) 4 De GM & G 328 at 341–345; [1854] EngR 468; 43 ER 534 at 539–540; *R v Heron; Ex parte Mulder* (1884) 10 VLR 314 at 315; *Pino v Prosser* [1967] VR 835 at 838.
>
> If this were not so, one would get the absurd situation referred to by McInerney J in *Pino v Prosser* (at 837), that the conclusion would be one which is:
>
> > ... remarkable to the point of seeming absurdity, in that the defendant who, on his own affidavit admits that he received the writ ... should be held not to have been served.

[30]. Recently in *Metacorp Pty Ltd v Andeco Construction Group Pty Ltd* [2010] VSC 199 Vickery J said (footnotes omitted):

> 84 As was pointed out by the Lord Chancellor in *Hope v Hope*:
>
> > The object of all service is of course only to give notice to the party to whom it is made, so that he may be made aware of and may be able to resist that which is sought against him; and when that has been substantially done, so that the court may feel perfectly confident that service has reached him, everything has been done as required.
>
> ...

[36]. In my view the declarations sought should not be made as it is clear that all of the conditional respondents have the necessary notice of the originating process. Although they have not all been personally served in the conventional sense under the rules, the cases show that the purpose of the rules as to service has been achieved.[78]

9.7.3 Substituted service

Where all efforts to serve originating process have failed, a plaintiff may apply to the court to grant substituted service.[79] Substituted service is a process whereby the court effectively deems the originating process to have been properly served. In order for the court to award substituted service, the plaintiff must take steps, approved by the court, to ensure that the defendant is aware of the proceedings. Commonly, the agreed steps for substituted service will have already been completed by the plaintiff at the time of the application for substituted service. Courts are reluctant to grant substituted service in circumstances where it is uncertain whether the defendant is actually aware of the proceedings. Conversely, if it appears, from evidence provided by the plaintiff, that the defendant is well aware of the proceedings but is deliberately avoiding service of process, then a court is likely to make an order for substituted service. Forms of substituted service can include service by electronic

78 Ibid [26]-[36].

79 An application for substituted service is an interlocutory application. It is not a final hearing. Interlocutory applications are discussed in more detail in Chapter 8.7.

means, including email and service by social media, as well as more traditional means, such as postage or leaving at an address.[80]

The New South Wales Supreme Court case of *Syndicate Mortgage Solutions Pty Ltd v El-Sayed* indicated the two key requirements for granting substituted service.[81] Justice Brereton does not order substituted service because:

- 'I am not satisfied that the evidence sufficiently establishes the impracticability of service in accordance with the rules.'[82]
- 'Nor am I satisfied that the evidence establishes that the method of substituted service proposed is reasonably likely to bring the proceedings to the notice of Mr Mouhajar.'[83]

In *Violi v Commonwealth Bank of Australia*, the original defendant successfully appealed a decision refusing to set aside default judgment in part due to the substituted service orders which enabled the default judgment.[84] In determining to allow the appeal, Sackville AJA indicated the importance of carefully and clearly drafted substituted service orders:

> The proceedings demonstrate two matters in particular. The first is that care must be taken to frame orders for substituted service clearly and precisely. I agree with Emmett JA's observation (at [63]) that the form of the Substituted Service Order in the present case is to be deplored. The language used in the Order is imprecise and a recipe for uncertainty and disputation.[85]

Courts are more reluctant to grant substituted service where the service is outside Australia because the power to serve goes to the heart of a court's jurisdiction, which must be limited by respect for foreign courts as explained by Edelman J when refusing to grant substituted service in lieu of personal service for a Thai resident in *Park v Tschannen*:

> It would not be consistent with [international] comity for an agreed regime to provide for a form of service outside the jurisdiction if the laws of that jurisdiction permitted a party immediately to substitute an alternative form of service. As Dixon CJ, Williams and Webb JJ remarked, if the position were otherwise, 'the strict conditions regulating and limiting service out of the jurisdiction upon defendants abroad would be ineffective; for they could be avoided by obtaining an order for substituted service within the jurisdiction': *Laurie v Carroll* [1958] HCA 4; (1958) 98 CLR 310, 325. Another reason is the importance of personal service and the need for some reason to exist before orders are made for departure from it. As the High Court observed at 323 in Laurie, service was historically closely associated with jurisdiction and it had been assumed that the

80 *Australian Information Commission v Facebook Inc* (2020) 144 ACSR 88 is an example of service by email; *Polis v Zombor* (2019) 134 ACSR 486 is an example of service by Facebook; *Zervas v Burkitt* [2019] NSWCA 112, [29] is an example of substituted service through leaving at an address and posting.

81 *Syndicate Mortgage Solutions Pty Ltd v El-Sayed* [2009] NSWSC 207, [1]-[9].

82 Ibid [6].

83 Ibid [7].

84 *Violi v Commonwealth Bank of Australia* [2015] NSWCA 152. The decision was 2:1 by Bergin CJ and Sackville AJA with Emmett JA dissenting but even Emmett was highly critical of the substituted service order.

85 *Violi v Commonwealth Bank of Australia* [2015] NSWCA 152, [125].

> foundation of jurisdiction was physical power. That historical foundation is one of the reasons for the importance of personal service. The other is its foundations in natural justice.[86]

However, in the Federal Court decision of *Australian Information Commission v Facebook Inc*, substituted service on overseas defendants was granted in the form of email to Head of Data Protection and Privacy and Associate General Counsel at Facebook and identified individuals at KWM, the lawyers for the respondent, because personal service was deemed too difficult as a result of the COVID-19 pandemic.[87] The Court analysed earlier cases to confirm that the substituted service requirement, in r 10.24 of the *Federal Court Rules 2011* (Cth) that service in the required way is "not practicable" meant: "not sensible or realistic to effect personal service even though it may be possible or feasible"[88] and that the similar r 10.23 "practicable" requirement "does not require the applicant to prove the impossibility of service of documents upon a party in accordance with the rules".[89]

Substituted service is an excellent example of both the challenges courts face in balancing efficiency with due consideration, balancing certainty with flexibility and the complexity of access to justice.[90] Substituted service enables plaintiffs' access to justice through alternate means of serving process, particularly on defendants deliberately avoiding service. Simultaneously, it is critical defendants do not have judgment awarded against them in proceedings they were not even aware of due to an inappropriate and ineffective substituted service order. Courts must have flexible means to enable efficient service while still maintaining due process. The practical complexity of this task becomes apparent in cases such as *Violi v Commonwealth Bank of Australia*,[91] *Park v Tschannen*[92] and *Australian Information Commission v Facebook Inc*.[93]

9.7.4 Personal service on corporations and special entities and in lower courts

There are, however, significant exceptions to the requirements for personal service. For example, service on Australian corporations may be achieved by posting documents to the registered office of a corporation pursuant to s 109X of the *Corporations Act 2001* (Cth) and s 9 of the *Service and Execution of Process Act 1992* (Cth).

Special rules for service can also apply where serving on a child, spouse, mentally ill person, the Crown, prisoners and unincorporated associations or businesses. For example, in New South Wales, the *Uniform Civil Procedure Rules 2005* (NSW) r 10.9 provides for service by post or delivery on a defendant operating under an unregistered business name.

86 *Park v Tschannen* (2016) 341 ALR 452, [16]. See also Chapter 8.3 and Chapter 9.7.5.

87 *Australian Information Commission v Facebook Inc* (2020) 144 ACSR 88, [73]-[74]. This decision was under appeal to the Full Federal Court at the time of writing.

88 Ibid [67] quoting from *Commissioner of Taxation v Caratti (No 2)* [2018] FCA 1500, [10].

89 *Australian Information Commission v Facebook Inc* (2020) 144 ACSR 88, [68] quoting from *Kosmos Capital Pty Ltd v Turiya Ventures LLC* [2019] FCA 528, [50].

90 See Chapter 2.3.1 regarding the balance between efficiency and due consideration. See Chapter 3.2 concerning access to justice.

91 *Violi v Commonwealth Bank of Australia* [2015] NSWCA 152.

92 *Park v Tschannen* (2016) 341 ALR 452.

93 *Australian Information Commission v Facebook Inc* (2020) 144 ACSR 88.

Due to the unreasonable expense service would entail for smaller matters, there is also no requirement of personal service in some local courts.[94]

9.7.5 Service outside the jurisdiction

Service of process can be particularly difficult when the defendant resides in a different jurisdiction to the one in which the proceedings have been commenced. Service within Australia is governed by pt 2 div 1 of the *Service and Execution of Process Act 1992* (Cth). The *Service and Execution of Process Act 1992* (Cth) also deals with the service of subpoenas within Australia but interstate in pt 3 (subpoenas are considered in Chapter 12).

Service interstate is essentially the same as service within the state and does not require leave to serve, pursuant to s 15 of the *Service and Execution of Process Act 1992* (Cth).

Service outside Australia is governed by the civil procedure rules for each jurisdiction. Most Australian jurisdictions allow service outside Australia without leave of court. Whether or not leave of court is required to serve, there must be proper service and there must be a proper nexus between Australia and the cause of action in the claim service to succeed.

The New South Wales Supreme Court case of *Showtime Touring Group v Mosely Touring Inc*[95] concerned objections by an American individual and an American corporation to overseas service of process in proceedings commenced in New South Wales by a Queensland company for breach of contract. Justice Hislop found that personal service had not been effected on the American individual defendant, but granted substituted service on the basis that this defendant was clearly aware of the proceedings being in control of the related corporation (which had been properly served) and having retained counsel to dispute jurisdiction. However, Hislop J then set aside service on both American parties, in reliance on the High Court authority of *Agar v Hyde*[96] and *Voth v Manildra Flour Mills Pty Ltd*,[97] on the basis that the nexus of the dispute to the New South Wales jurisdiction was not made out by the plaintiff.[98]

In *Flo Rida v Mothership Music Pty Ltd*,[99] the New South Wales Court of Appeal also confirmed that only the New South Wales Supreme Court has authority, under the *Civil Procedure Act 2005* (NSW), to allow service of process out of Australia, holding that the New South Wales District Court does not have the power to order service offshore.[100]

Service overseas has a significantly higher risk of failing to achieve the core objective of service, which is to provide the defendant the opportunity to be heard by ensuring it has satisfactory notice of the proceedings. The entitlement of the defendant to procedural fairness is the sole theoretical justification for service. This makes it critical to ensure that

94 See, eg, in New South Wales where the *Uniform Civil Procedure Rules 2005* (NSW) r 10.20(2)(b) enables local court service at a business or residential address including service by the Local Court using the post.

95 *Showtime Touring Group v Mosely Touring Inc* [2010] NSWSC 974.

96 *Agar v Hyde* (2000) 201 CLR 552.

97 *Voth v Manildra Flour Mills Pty Ltd* (1990) 171 CLR 538.

98 *Showtime Touring Group v Mosely Touring Inc* [2010] NSWSC 974 at [19–27], [47].

99 [2013] NSWCA 268.

100 *Flo Rida v Mothership Music Pty Ltd* [2013] NSWCA 268 (Macfarlan JA with Ward and Gleeson JJA agreeing) overruled substituted service by the New South Wales District Court in relation to a US rap artist, Flo Rida, in a suit by the festival organisers, Mothership, after he failed to appear in the "Fat as Butter" music festival in 2011.

service does, as far as possible, equate with genuine notice wherever possible. As discussed in Chapter 9.7.3, this increases judicial reluctance to granting substituted service outside the jurisdiction, although it remains possible, as demonstrated in *Australian Information Commission v Facebook Inc*.[101]

It is important to be aware that legislative provisions governing the circumstances in which overseas service is allowed are informed by the complex jurisdictional aspects of conflicts of law. This explains the complexity of, for example, sch 6 of the *Uniform Civil Procedure Rules 2005* (NSW) and its equivalent provisions in other Australian jurisdictions.[102]

9.8 Conclusion

Commencing proceedings is often the most difficult step in litigation and requires the plaintiff to carefully consider the nature, amount and location of the claim, and other factors such as enforceability, efficiency and cost in order to determine the best court to commence proceedings in. The plaintiff has the most control over the proceedings at the point of commencement and plaintiffs who wish to succeed should ensure this advantage is not wasted.

The key themes of CDR inform and influence the commencement of litigation in significant ways. Most notably these are:

1. Access to justice which drives governments to devise more simple and cost effective court procedures for commencement.[103]
2. The balance between efficiency and due consideration which underpins the need for efficient service of process to ensure defendants are aware of the claims against them without unduly burdening the plaintiff with service obligations.[102]
3. The importance of access to justice and the difficult balance between efficiency and due process and between flexibility and certainty is also evident in statutory limitations on timing of commencement, the jurisdictional hierarchy of the courts, and the form and requirements of originating process which focus on brevity.[103] Courts must enable parties to proceed as efficiently as possible and with maximum certainty while still managing the complexity and variability of disputes.
4. The desire for open justice and transparency, which is evidenced through the disclosure requirements of originating process.[104]

Whilst the details and titles of originating process vary significantly between jurisdictions, these key requirements for commencing proceedings persist across all Australian jurisdictions.

101 *Australian Information Commission v Facebook Inc* (2020) 144 ACSR 88.
102 See also Chapter 8.3.
103 See Chapter 3.2.
104 See Chapter 2.3.
105 See Chapter 2.3.
106 See Chapter 3.3.

10 PARTIES AND PLEADING

10.1 Introduction

This chapter considers the issues arising in relation to the pleading phase of litigation, which is the first phase of court proceedings. After proceedings have been commenced by the originating process (which is often itself a pleading), the defendant (or defendants) must decide whether, and how, to defend the proceedings. The pleading process continues many of the key themes of civil dispute resolution (CDR) discussed in Chapters 8 and 9. The procedures for pleading a case emanate from the same aims as the originating process of making justice accessible, maximising efficiency, giving all parties the right to be heard and ensuring open justice.[1] Matters can involve large numbers of pleadings, with the most common types of pleadings required being defences, cross-claims, cross-defences and replies. Once all the pleadings have been filed and served, including any amendments to pleadings required and allowed by the court, the pleadings are said to have closed. The parties can then complete evidence gathering and preparation for trial.

1 See Chapter 2.3 and Chapter 3.

The nature and number of pleadings required for litigation vary depending on the complexity of the matter and the number of parties involved. In mega-litigation, such as *Bell Group Ltd (in liq) v Westpac Banking Corporation (No 9)*,[2] there may be numerous (sometimes hundreds) of pleadings, including:

- separate defences for each defendant
- cross-claims
- cross-defences
- replies to defences
- cross-defences (to further clarify issues in dispute).

Conversely, in many proceedings there will be only two pleadings: the statement of claim (the originating process) filed by the plaintiff; and the defence, filed by the defendant in response to that originating process.

This chapter will consider the role of pleadings in the context of the conflicting aims of open justice, access to justice, the right to be heard and efficiency.

10.2 Rules and requirements for pleading

There are numerous rules and requirements that apply to any party wishing to file pleadings in a court. Many of these rules govern all documents filed in courts. These range from highly technical requirements as to the size, format, and layout of court documents, to important substantive obligations to tell the truth in court documents (particularly sworn documents such as affidavits). Increasingly, pleading requirements include electronic obligations for litigants as courts move such processes online.[3] Breaches of these obligations may constitute contempt of court and thereby possibly attract criminal sanctions.

The rules and requirements of pleadings, like all aspects of CDR can be explained by the key themes outlined in Chapters 2 and 3. The process of pleading frequently attracts criticism on the basis that it is too complex and to formulaic to enable access to justice.[4] However, where the formal structure of pleadings is removed, the increased flexibility and efficiency this gives to litigants also reduces the certainty of process and the protection of due process.[5] So the need to balance these conflicting imperatives provides incentives to retain significant formality of process, particularly in matters which are inherently complex and high value. Pleading processes aim to maximise efficiency while protecting due process. The requirements of pleadings also engage with the key theme of balancing autonomy with control.[6] Litigation is the most formal CDR process, so it is to be expected that party autonomy will be reduced, as compared to ADR, in favour of court control. The formal requirements of pleadings assist courts in controlling the litigation process while still allowing party autonomy to the extent of deciding how to respond to substantive

2 *Bell Group Ltd (in liq) v Westpac Banking Corporation (No 9)* (2008) 39 WAR 1.

3 See, eg, the Equity Division of the Supreme Court of New South Wales which, from 3 September 2018, required all proceedings to commence through online filing pursuant to Supreme Court of New South Wales, *Practice Note SC EQ 14: Online Court Protocol* (9 May 2018).

4 Camille Cameron and Elizabeth Thornburg, 'Defining Civil Disputes: Lessons from Two Jurisdictions' (2011) 35(1) *Melbourne University Law Review* 208.

5 See Chapter 2.3.1 and Chapter 2.3.2 for detailed analysis of these themes.

6 See Chapter 2.3.4 for detailed analysis of this issue.

issues. However, it is a complex balancing act which risks denying access to justice, particularly where litigants are self-represented and struggle to comply with the pleading requirements.[7]

10.2.1 Detailed obligations: brevity, completeness, clarity and more

In addition to general rules regarding documents filed in court, there are specific rules regarding the preparation and filing of pleadings. These pleading rules tend to be detailed in an effort to ensure that the parties and the court are properly aware of the case and the issues in dispute. The pleading requirements set out in div 2.6.2 of the *Court Procedures Rules 2006* (ACT) (rr 405–9) provide an excellent example of the rules imposed on litigants regarding pleadings.[8] The requirements set out in these rules include the following critical principles:

- pleadings should be as brief as possible (this ensures maximum efficiency)[9]
- pleadings must state material facts but not provide evidence of those facts and there are exceptions where the law presumes facts (this ensures evidentiary processes are respected so that every party has a fair opportunity to put their case in open court)[10]
- pleadings must set out the relief (remedies) sought from the court (this ensures that the parties and the court are on notice as to what is sought protecting the right to be heard and access to justice)[11]
- pleadings must meet a number of formatting requirements to ensure they are easily navigable; e.g. be in writing, set out clearly with each new issue in a new paragraph numbered sequentially (this protects access to justice and efficiency)[12]
- pleadings must state everything which, if not stated, would cause surprise to the other parties (to ensure both efficiency and justice)[13]
- pleadings (including defences) must explicitly plead certain matters, such as fraud, illegality, duress, estoppel, breach of contract, trust or statutory duty, malice, ill will, negligence and misrepresentation (this prevents surprise, particularly where it might otherwise be obscured by a denial in a defence pleading and ensures that parties properly understand what evidence will be required to prove their case).[14]

10.2.2 All parties must plead positively

All parties must ensure that they comply with their obligation to clearly and positively plead all matters which are essential to their case, including issues such as fraud. The failure to positively

7 See Chapter 3.2 for more detailed analysis of barriers in access to justice.
8 *Court Procedures Rules 2006* (ACT) rr 405–9.
9 Ibid r 406(1)(a).
10 Ibid rr 406(1)(b), 409 (for exceptions).
11 Ibid rr 406(1)(d), 405(3), 407A(3), 407B(2)(c). It should be noted that the court may grant relief not pleaded per r 419.
12 Ibid rr 405, 406.
13 Ibid r 406(1)(c).
14 Ibid r 407 (which includes numerous additional matters not listed here).

plead is most commonly an issue for defendants, which sometimes simply deny matters instead of positively pleading matters, such as fraud, to explain their denials.[15] However, the importance of positive pleading obligations applies to all parties, including plaintiffs, as demonstrated by the High Court decision of *Forrest v Australian Securities and Investments Commission*.[16]

In *Forrest v Australian Securities and Investments Commission* (*Forrest*), the High Court held that Fortescue Metals Group Ltd and its owner, Mr Forrest, had not contravened s 1041H of the *Corporations Act 2001* (Cth) because the Court held that statements made to the market were not misleading or deceptive. The Australian Security and Investment Commission (ASIC) failed in its regulatory action against Forrest and Fortescue, in part due to its failures to plead its case to the High Court's satisfaction. Chief Justice French and Gummow, Hayne and Kiefel JJ held:

> [25]. This is no pleader's quibble. It is a point that reflects fundamental requirements for the fair trial of allegations of contravention of law. It is for the party making those allegations (in this case ASIC) to identify the case which it seeks to make and to do that clearly and distinctly. The statement of claim in these matters did not do that.
>
> [26]. Contrary to ASIC's submissions in this Court, a case of fraud cannot properly be seen as a 'fallback' claim to be made against the possibility that the party accused of engaging in misleading or deceptive conduct by publishing notices in relation to a financial product may seek to characterise them as statements of opinion, not fact. It is fundamental, and long established, that if a case of fraud is to be mounted, it should be pleaded specifically and with particularity. A pleading of fraud will necessarily focus attention upon what it was that the person making the statement intended to convey by its making. And the pleading must make plain that it is alleged that the person who made the statement knew it to be false or was careless as to its truth or falsity. If an alternative case of misleading or deceptive conduct is to be advanced, it is necessary to identify that claim as separate from the allegation of fraud. And for the purposes of the misleading or deceptive claim the pleader must identify what it is alleged that the impugned statements conveyed to their intended audience. Of course there may be circumstances in which it is appropriate to plead alternative cases of misleading or deceptive conduct or alternative cases of fraud and misleading or deceptive conduct. But it is greatly to be doubted that it will ever be appropriate to pile, one on top of the other, as many alternative allegations as were made in this case. Doing so risks contravention of what, in *Gould and Birbeck and Bacon v Mount Oxide Mines Ltd (in Liquidation)*, Isaacs and Rich JJ said was 'the fundamental principle that no man ought to be put to loss without having a proper opportunity of meeting the case against him' which requires that 'pleadings should state with sufficient clearness the case of the party whose averments they are'.
>
> [27]. The task of the pleader is to allege the facts said to constitute a cause of action or causes of action supporting claims for relief. Sometimes that task may require facts or characterisations of facts to be pleaded in the alternative.[17]

The High Court's analysis of pleading requirements in *Forrest* demonstrates both the inherent importance of pleadings and the fact that, at the heart of the need to plead positively, lies the need to avoid surprise and to enable the opponent to properly understand the case it

15 See Chapter 10.3.
16 *Forrest v Australian Securities and Investments Commission* (2012) 247 CLR 486.
17 Ibid [25]–[27].

must prove or defend. This is an important example of how complex procedural pleading requirements are essential to ensuring due process. Whilst it might seem efficient to reduce the complexity of pleading obligations, cases such as *Forrest* demonstrate that correctly pleading can be essential to justice by enabling both due process and efficiency through preventing surprise and consequential failure to prepare necessary evidence.[18]

Figure 10.1 The steps in defending proceedings

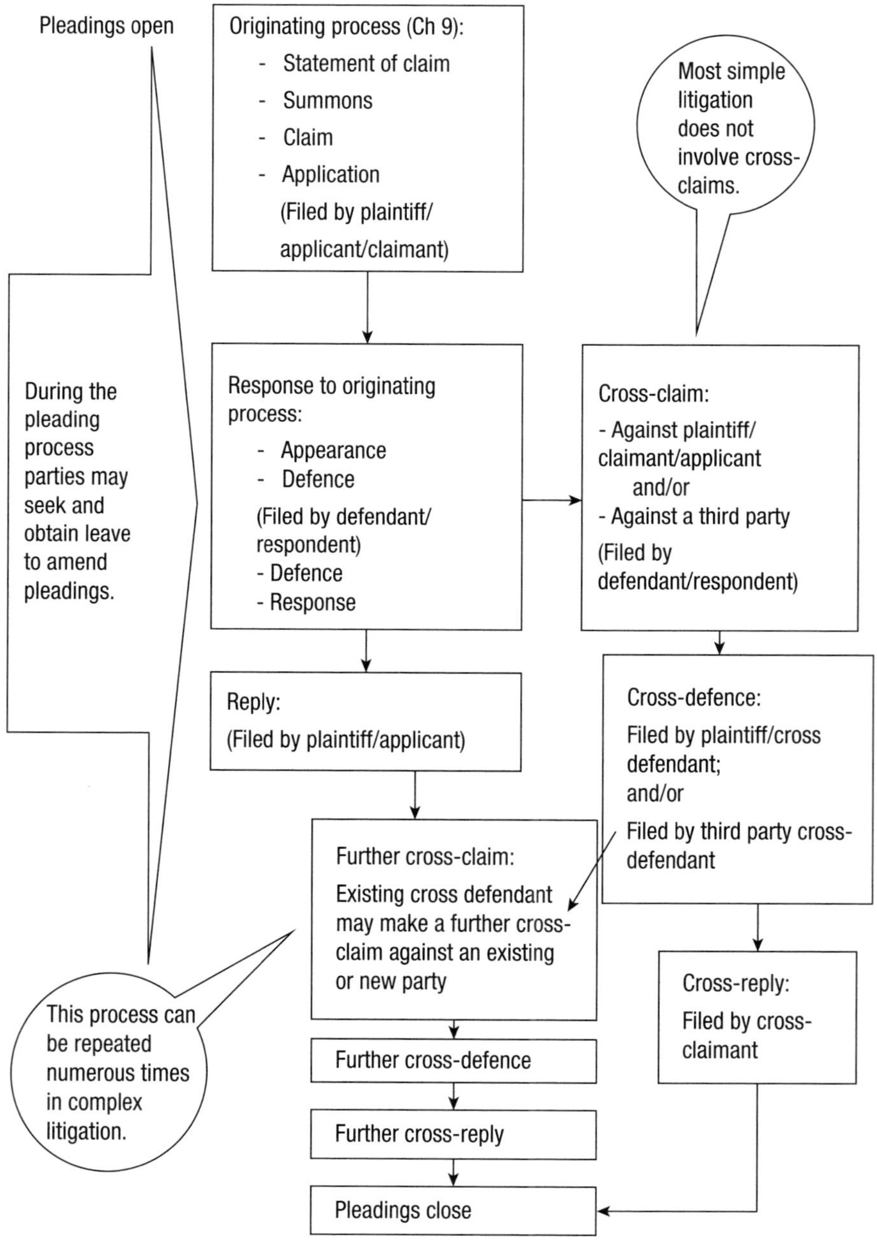

18 See Chapter 2.3.1 for detailed analysis of the balance between efficiency and due process.

10.3 Defending proceedings

In most litigation, the two main pleadings are the plaintiff's claim[19] and the defendant's defence to that claim.

After the defendant has been served with the originating process, it must decide whether it wishes to defend the proceedings and, if so, on what basis. Regardless of how it intends to proceed, the originating process requires the defendant to respond to the process served. This is usually achieved, in the first instance, by filing a notice of appearance.

10.3.1 Appearing in proceedings

Appearance in proceedings is a form of notice to both the plaintiff and the court. Notice is another key requirement for ensuring due process through preventing surprise.[20] There are essentially three types of appearance. The first is an appearance from a defendant intending to defend the proceedings. This is sometimes called an "unconditional appearance", and it is by far the most common type of appearance. The other types of appearances are conditional appearances and an appearance submitting to the court's jurisdiction. Both are discussed below. If a defendant disputes the jurisdiction of the court, it may file a conditional notice of appearance noting that it has been served with the original process but disputing the jurisdiction of the court to hear the dispute.

Disputes concerning court jurisdiction are common in international matters. They sometimes arise in interstate matters. If a defendant files an unconditional appearance, that appearance may be taken as submitting to the jurisdiction — hence, preventing its right to contest jurisdiction where it might be arguable that the court is not the appropriate forum.[21] In the extraordinary case of *Mentyn v Falcone*,[22] the Full Court of the Tasmanian Supreme Court confirmed on appeal that filing a conditional appearance does not affect the jurisdiction of the court where there is no basis for arguing that the court is an inappropriate forum. In that case, Mr Mentyn, who was involved in numerous cases as an unrepresented litigant, was under the misapprehension that he could prevent the court's jurisdiction by filing a conditional appearance. Mr Mentyn was later declared a vexatious litigant.[23] Justice Underwood (with whom Slicer and Evans JJ agreed) explained the role of conditional appearances and the operation of *Supreme Court Rules 2000* (Tas) r 168 governing applications to set aside originating process:

> [9]. … The appellant's understanding of the nature of a conditional appearance is misconceived. The filing of a conditional appearance does not affect the jurisdiction of the Court. It merely gives notice that a respondent or a defendant reserves the right for up to 14 days to argue that the Court does not have jurisdiction to make the orders sought. If the respondent or defendant wishes to pursue that argument, he or she must file an application (as did the appellant) seeking an order that the originating process or its service be set aside. Jurisdiction is not affected by the simple expedient of filing and serving a conditional appearance, nor is it affected by filing and serving a r168 application. It can only be affected by an order of the Court made upon the determination of a r168 application.[24]

19 This is the most common form of originating process and is discussed in Chapter 9.
20 See also Chapter 9.6.1 for discussion of this in the context of service of originating process.
21 See Chapter 8.3 for discussion of jurisdiction.
22 *Mentyn v Falcone* (2004) 12 Tas R 461.
23 See Chapter 5.5.4 for discussion of vexatious litigants.
24 *Mentyn v Falcone* (2004) 12 Tas R 461, [9].

The third type of appearance is a submission whereby the defendant agrees to accept whatever order the court makes without actively defending proceedings. Appearances submitting to the court's orders are rare because most disputes where the defendant does not intend to defend itself settle before commencement. One case of an appearance submitting to court orders was the case of *Evergreen Tours Pty Ltd v McLaren*.[25] The judgment of Tamberlin AJ demonstrates how even simple procedures, such as appearing before the court, may prove confusing and problematic for defendants faced with unwanted litigation. In *Evergreen Tours Pty Ltd v McLaren*, Tamberlin AJ allowed the defendant to withdraw his appearance submitting to the court's orders so that the defendant could contest the claim. The following extracts from *Evergreen* discuss the court rules governing appearances (in this case, the *Uniform Civil Procedure Rules 2005* (NSW)), the principles of appearances, the balance between the right to be heard and, the need to comply with procedures:

> [15]. In substance, the defendants say that at the time the submitting appearance was filed Mr McLaren, who controls Burlington, was of the opinion that he did not have and could not access funds to defend the Summons and he had not received legal advice as to the merits of the claims in the Summons. Consequently, Mr McLaren decided not to defend the Summons because of lack of funds. …
>
> [16]. Mr McLaren was cross-examined and stated that he was unfamiliar with legal process and was confused as to the nature of his legal rights and liabilities. In cross-examination, it appeared that he had previously been bankrupt. I do not accept that he was unfamiliar with legal process. However I do accept that Mr McLaren was unsure of his legal position at the time when the submitting appearance was filed. I also accept his explanation as to his then shortage of funds.[26]
>
> **Legal principles**
>
> [17]. As a general principle the interests of justice require that a defendant with an arguable case should not be shut out from presenting a case unless there are substantial countervailing considerations.
>
> …
>
> [19]. Although there is no general rule for the way in which the discretion to grant leave to withdraw and defend should be exercised some useful guidelines are indicated in the authorities. In *Somportex Ltd v Philadelphia Chewing Gum Corp* [1968] 3 All ER 26 at 28 and 29 the Court of Appeal observed that generally leave may be granted when an appearance has been entered by accident or mistake but may not be granted in circumstances where a deliberate informed choice has been made after taking legal advice. That was a case involving submission to jurisdiction. This reasoning was applied by McDougall J in *Garsec v His Majesty the Sultan of Brunei* [2007] NSWSC 882 at [48]–[53]. The grounds for the exercise of the discretion to grant leave are not spelt out and it is a broad discretion but the discretion must be exercised judicially: see *Firth v John Mowlem and Co Ltd* [1978] 3 All ER 331. Another relevant and important consideration is whether the defendant has an arguable defence within the principles referred to in *General Steel Industries Inc v Commissioner for Railways* [1964] HCA 69; (1964) 112 CLR 125 at 129; *Hilton v Gidley* at [19]–[31] per Hislop J.

25 *Evergreen Tours Pty Ltd v McLaren* [2010] NSWSC 1362.
26 Ibid [15]–[17], [19].

However, courts are less likely to exercise their discretion to allow a party to withdraw a submitting appearance where the party has been represented at all times and there is no other vitiating factor, such as an amendment to the plaintiff's claim.[27]

Defendants will sometimes file a submitting appearance where another defendant is actively defending the proceedings or where the issue in dispute does not directly affect them. This may occur where the defendant is a subsidiary of another defendant, or a government authority, or tribunal involved in a previous stage of proceedings subject to appeal.[28] The main advantage of a submitting claim is to save legal costs and increase efficiency of proceedings by not actively defending the matter. Courts are also less likely to award adverse costs against a submitting party where that party loses and submitting appearances are often described as being "save as to costs".[29] However, the plaintiff must still prove its case even where all defendants have filed submitting appearances, so this remains a costlier process than settlement out of court through ADR.[30] *Lou v IAG Ltd*[31] was an example of a successful costs appeal from a decision to award costs against a submitting defendant where the NRMA had appealed a claims assessors decision in a motor vehicle injury case.[32] The New South Wales Supreme Court of Appeal held that, although there was no rule against a submitting defendant being required to pay costs, the submitting first defendant should not have been ordered to pay costs. The Court in *Lou v IAG Ltd* held the mistake of the claims assessor was no fault of the defendant, the proceedings were review proceedings which could not be resolved by consent, and there was no evidence the NRMA would have saved any costs if the defendant had signed a consent order rather than filing a submitting appearance.[33]

10.3.2 Filing a defence: traversing the originating process

In addition to the formal requirements of pleadings discussed above, there are particular requirements peculiar to defences. A defence must traverse all the claims made in the originating process.[34] Failure to traverse an aspect of a claim will constitute admission of that aspect of the claim.[35]

---

27 *Re Italian Forum Ltd (subject to a deed of company arrangement) (No 2)* [2015] NSWSC 1382, [25].

28 See, eg, *Council of the Law Society of the ACT v The Legal Practitioner D3* (2018) 331 FCR 132. The Australian Capital Territory Civil and Administrative Tribunal (ACAT) filed a submitting appearance as the second defendant in a dispute between the ACT Law Society and an ACT solicitor.

29 See, eg, *Dyczynski v Gibson* (2020) 381 ALR 1, [406] where the Court recommended the defendant should have filed a "submitting appearance save as to costs". See Chapter 6.5.1 for a discussion of adverse costs orders.

30 It should be noted that there is no rule that a submitting party will not be ordered to pay costs: see *Seller v Jones* [2014] NSWCA 19, [55], [59] (McColl JA with Basten and Ward JJA agreeing).

31 *Lou v IAG Ltd* (2019) 101 NSWLR 606.

32 Ibid (Payne JA with Gleeson JA agreeing and Brereton JA in dissent).

33 Ibid [44] (Payne JA with Gleeson JA agreeing).

34 *Hancock Prospecting Pty Ltd v Wright Prospecting Pty Ltd* [2019] WASCA 141.

35 See, eg, in New South Wales this is pursuant to *Uniform Civil Procedure Rules 2005* (NSW) r 14.26(1) as applied by the New South Wales Supreme Court in *Cohen v Cohen* [2016] NSWSC 336, [54].

Traversing a claim or allegation means responding by either not admitting or denying that allegation.[36] To properly traverse originating process, the defendant must separately deny or not admit each claim within that originating process.[37]

There are, essentially, three possible responses available for a defendant regarding each allegation, as follows:

1. admit
2. do not admit
3. deny.

Most defences will contain a combination of admissions, denials and non-admissions. Each of the three possible responses imposes a different obligation on the plaintiff in regard to proving its claim.

10.3.2.1 Admissions

Where a matter is admitted, the claimant is not required to prove that aspect of the claim as it is agreed between the parties. In most matters, there will be at least a few preliminary claims (such as the names of the parties and perhaps aspects of their relationship with each other) that are not in dispute. However, for judgment to be awarded against a party on the basis of an admission, the admission must be "clear and unambiguous" and the court's power to make such an order is discretionary.[38]

10.3.2.2 Non-admissions

Where a claim is not admitted, the plaintiff must prove that aspect of its claim. The matters that a defendant does not admit should be limited to matters about which the defendant has no knowledge. For example, a plaintiff may make claims concerning the plaintiff's state of mind or knowledge at a particular time. The defendant may not be in a position to deny those allegations, as it was unaware of the plaintiff's relevant state of mind. Equally, however, the defendant does not admit that the plaintiff is correct. This is the type of allegation where it is appropriate for the defendant to not admit the plaintiff's claim.

Defendants may be faced with adverse costs orders where they are found to have unnecessarily put the plaintiff to proof on matters by not admitting matters they should have admitted.

10.3.2.3 Denials

The most important part of a defence is the denials. These are the matters that are in dispute between the parties. They often form the bulk of the defence. In some instances, a simple denial is sufficient and no further particulars are required. In other cases, denials should be particularised.[39]

36 Only non-admissions and denials are technically traversals, as an admission does not, technically, cross the plaintiff's pleading. See, eg, *Alcoa of Australia Ltd v Apache Energy Ltd (No 3)* [2013] WASC 334, [13] applying ord 20 r 14(2) of the *Rules of the Supreme Court 1971* (WA).

37 Although it can be possible for there to be both admissions and traversals by necessary implication, as discussed by the New South Wales Supreme Court in *Tanwar Enterprises Pty Ltd v Bradshaw* [2013] NSWSC 1276, [56]–[57].

38 *Moon v Mun* [2013] NSWCA 217, [40] (Barrett JA with Basten and Ward JJA agreeing).

39 Particulars are discussed in more detail in Chapter 8.9.

10.3.2.4 Positive pleadings in defences

In addition to admissions, denials and non-admissions, there is a fourth category of pleading that arises in some defences. These are matters that do not directly traverse the plaintiff's claim but plead a matter relevant to the traversal of that claim. There are a number of circumstances in which matters must be positively pleaded where a defendant is intending to rely on them at trial.[40] For example, if the defendant relies on an allegation of fraud on the part of the plaintiff to defend against the plaintiff's claim, such fraud must be positively pleaded by the defendant. Rule 407 of the *Court Procedures Rules 2006* (ACT) (extracted in Chapter 9.1) lists the matters requiring positive pleading, including fraud (r 407(h)).

Australian Competition and Consumer Commission v Australialink Pty Ltd (No 3)[41] considered the Federal Court Rules for filing defences, as set out in ord 11 of the *Federal Court Rules 1979* (Cth). In particular, it considered the obligation to traverse all aspects of the claim, as well as the risk of unintended admissions resulting from careless drafting of denials. Readers should note that the *Federal Court Rules 1979* (Cth) discussed in this case was replaced by the *Federal Court Rules 2011* (Cth), which set out the requirements for traversing pleadings in pt 16 div 16.1 r 16.07. The 2011 requirements are relevantly similar to the old rules. Rule 16.07(2) provides "Allegations that are not specifically denied are taken to be admitted".

In *Australian Competition and Consumer Commission v Australialink Pty Ltd (No 3)*, Spender J allowed the defendant to file a fresh defence properly compliant with the obligations to traverse the claim. Justice Spender also referred to *Banque Commerciale SA (En Liquidation) v Akhil Holdings Ltd*,[42] which discussed the function of pleadings. This case provides a good example of where particulars of a denial are required. The following extract demonstrates the complexity of traversing a claim and the key role of natural justice (another term for procedural fairness) in pleadings:

> [14]. Paragraph 20 is really a broad-brush general denial. Proper pleading of the Defence would require a statement as to whether knowledge of each of the matters alleged in par 26 of the Statement of Claim is contested … .
>
> …
>
> [17]. The function of pleadings is to state with sufficient clarity the case that must be met and to define the issues for decision: *Banque Commerciale SA En Liquidation v Akhil Holdings Ltd* [1990] HCA 11; (1990) 169 CLR 279 per Mason CJ and Gaudron J at 286.
>
> [18]. Burchett J said in *Multigroup Distribution Services Pty Ltd v TNT Australia Pty Ltd* [1996] ATPR 41–522, at 42,679:
>
>> The primary function [of a statement of claim] is to tell the defending party what the claim is that he has to meet. That is a matter of elementary and natural justice; the claim cannot be answered until it is known. When a sufficient defence has been filed to a sufficient statement of claim, a further function will generally have been performed—that of defining the question or questions for decision. This definition is required, of course, from an early stage, or else discovery and other interlocutory procedures are likely to prove misdirected, wasteful and unproductive.
>
> …

40 See Chapter 10.1.2.
41 *Australian Competition and Consumer Commission v Australialink Pty Ltd (No 3)* [2009] FCA 332.
42 *Banque Commerciale SA (en liquidation) v Akhil Holdings Ltd* (1990) 169 CLR 279.

> [28]. I will direct that the respondents have leave to file and serve a Defence on or before 4 pm on 29 May 2009, and that such Defence:
> (i) Specifically plead to each allegation in each paragraph and sub-paragraph of the Statement of Claim, and specifically identify the matter in issue, if any, in each paragraph and sub-paragraph of the Statement of Claim;
> (ii) Specifically traverse any matter that is not admitted.
> (iii) Be accompanied by a certificate in accordance with Form 15B signed by a legal practitioner, and otherwise comply with O 11 r 1B.[43]

Most cases which discuss the requirements of pleadings do so in the context of pleadings which require amendment.[44] Assisting parties to plead properly is an example of where judicial case management can support justice and efficiency simultaneously, even where there is a time cost to allowing pleading amendment because pleading properly should enable the remainder of the case to run more fairly and efficiently.[45] As the New South Wales Supreme Court noted in *Hordern v New South Wales*: "pleadings serve to define the issues for decision and ensure the basic requirement of procedural fairness that a party should have the opportunity of meeting the case against him or her: *Banque Commerciale SA En Liquidation v Akhil Holdings Ltd* [1990] HCA 11; (1990) 169 CLR 279 at 286–287 and 302–3."[46]

10.4 Further and better particulars

Notice is a key aspect of the efficiency and due process themes present in CDR. Further and better particulars are a key example of notice. The ability of the court and the parties to litigate to a just resolution is increased where relevant facts are known. The earlier details are provided, the more efficient the process is likely to be.

10.4.1 Particulars within pleadings

Pleadings invariably require particularisation. Where possible, this should form part of the pleading. Often, however, pleadings do not provide sufficient particulars and requests are made by parties in correspondence for further and better particulars.

In *Hercules v Magistrates' Court of Victoria*, the unrepresented Mr Hercules took umbrage with the Magistrates Court's failure to strike out a defence due to lack of particulars. President Maxwell and Redlich JA delivered a joint judgment rejecting Mr Hercules appeal. They summarised the purpose and requirements for pleadings and particulars as follows:

> [11]. Where explanatory reasons are required to be given, and can meaningfully be given, the intention of the rule is presumably that they should be provided in the form of particulars. By this means the plaintiff, whose allegation has been denied, is informed more fully than a bare denial might do of the case which the defendant

43 *Australian Competition and Consumer Commission v Australialink Pty Ltd(No 3)* [2009] FCA 552, [14], [17], [18], [28].

44 See Chapter 10.8 for more detail regarding amending pleadings.

45 See Chapter 2.3 and Chapter 2.4 for further detail on the key themes of balancing efficiency and due process and autonomy with control as well as case management.

46 *Hordern v New South Wales* [2018] NSWSC 1515, [12].

> will make. That is of course the function of pleadings and, specifically, the function of particulars. ... Accepting that the defendant was obliged by the rule to give the reasons for each denial of a statement of fact, Mr Hercules had a legitimate objection to make. There is no qualification in the rule and it is expressed in mandatory terms. But, as with the rule in this Court requiring particulars to be given, the particulars to be given will only be such as the defendant is reasonably capable of giving, having regard to the allegation pleaded and denied.
>
> ...
>
> [13].... A pleading issue is a quintessential matter of practice and procedure and is properly to be regarded as under the control of the court in which the proceeding is being conducted. The circumstances in which an appeal court would be likely to intervene in a decision about particulars of a pleading must be quite exceptional.[47]

The Victorian Court of Appeal in *Hercules v Magistrates' Court of Victoria*, in upholding the magistrate's decision, confirmed that the appropriate remedy for insufficient particularisation would be rectification, rather than striking out of the defence.[48]

Similarly, the Queensland Supreme Court ordered rectification of pleadings and particulars and rejected both parties' requests for permanent pleadings strike outs in the Queensland construction case of *Alexanderson Earthmover Pty Ltd v Civil Mining & Construction*, which involved "skirmishes aplenty".[49] The case concerned the actions of subcontractors in building holding dams at a coal export terminal. The Court cited *Equititrust Ltd v Tucker (No 2)*[50] with approval that:

> [14] ... Particulars are not meant to be used to fill material gaps in a pleading. They serve a different purpose, which is 'to fill in the picture of the plaintiff's cause of action with information sufficiently detailed to put the defendant on his guard as to the case he has to meet'; although in practice the distinction may be difficult to discern.[51]

In *Alexanderson Earthmover Pty Ltd v Civil Mining & Construction*, the Court made detailed and explicit orders for amending particulars which provide excellent examples of the type of details which constitute particulars as opposed to pleadings, including:

> ...
>
> - in every paragraph in which the defendant has asserted that it did provide the plaintiff with 'sufficient access' — particulars of when and where it gave the plaintiff 'sufficient access' and how and when the fact of access was communicated to the plaintiff; and
> - in every paragraph in which the defendant has referred to "the plaintiff's own delays' or 'delays for which the plaintiff was responsible' or similar — particulars of the nature of the plaintiff's delays.[52]

47 *Hercules v Magistrates' Court of Victoria* [2008] VSCA 1, [11], [13].
48 Ibid [12].
49 *Alexanderson Earthmover Pty Ltd v Civil Mining & Construction* [2019] QSC 259, [14].
50 *Equititrust Ltd v Tucker (No 2)* [2019] QSC 248.
51 *Alexanderson Earthmover Pty Ltd v Civil Mining & Construction* [2019] QSC 259, [49] citing *Equititrust Ltd v Tucker (No 2)* [2019] QSC 248, [14] with approval.
52 *Alexanderson Earthmover Pty Ltd v Civil Mining & Construction* [2019] QSC 259, [762].

It is unusual for a court to take the level of control taken by the court in *Alexanderson Earthmover Pty Ltd v Civil Mining & Construction*. However, this reduction in the parties' autonomy with their pleadings was necessary and justified due to the parties' inability to cooperate.[53]

10.4.2 Particulars additional to pleadings

Particularising pleadings is an important aspect of the pleadings themselves. It is also common, however, for further and better particulars to be sought by an opposing party after a pleading has been filed. Courts will sometimes include orders for the service of further and better particulars as part of court timetables for case preparation or in response to a court motion.[54]

In some types of matters, such as complex commercial matters, it is common for the defendant to seek further and better particulars of a claim prior to filing its defence. Rather than requiring amendment to the claim, the defendant simply serves a letter on the plaintiff setting out the further and better particulars required. This letter is usually faxed, emailed or posted in accordance with the accepted methods for ordinary service agreed to by the plaintiff in its claim or in subsequent correspondence with the defendant. The defendant responds by letter sent in the same agreed way setting out the particulars.

Sometimes, there may be the need for several further requests and responses if there are matters which remain unclear to the defendant. Neither the request nor the response is filed in the court. The court has no involvement unless the parties make an interlocutory application in relation to particulars because a dispute has arisen.

Once the defendant files its defence, the plaintiff may need to seek further and better particulars of the defence. This process operates the same way as the request for particulars of a claim; that is, by correspondence served on the opposite party in an agreed format but without being filed in court.

10.5 Other pleadings: cross-claims, cross-defences and replies

Originating process and defence are the only pleadings in many cases. There are, however, a significant number of cases which involve cross-claims, cross-defences and replies.

53 See Chapter 2.3.4 for further discussion of the theme of balancing autonomy and control.

54 See, eg, *De Saram v Brown* [2015] VSCA 142, [24] where the "further and better particulars" order was originally part of a consent order agreed by the parties but then required an express order following a court motion: [31]. A motion for further and better particulars can also be brought by the party wishing to provide the particulars to ensure the adequacy of its pleading. See, eg, *Upaid Systems Ltd v Telstra Corporation Ltd* (2016) 122 IPR 190 where the Full Federal Court gave the applicant leave to file further and better particulars of a patent infringement.

10.5.1 Cross-claims

A cross-claim is a claim made by the defendant either against the plaintiff or against a third party. Where the cross-claim is against a third party, it must relate to the original claim made against the defendant. A common example of a cross-claim against a third party is a construction dispute where party A sues party B for a fault in construction. Party B had subcontracted some of the work to party C. Party B then files a cross-claim against party C in the proceedings commenced by party A. For example, s 22 of the *Civil Procedure Act 2005* (NSW) provides the cross-claiming defendant with all the entitlements a plaintiff would receive in relation to an original claim.[55]

A common example of a cross-claim against a plaintiff is a contractual dispute where the plaintiff claims the defendant has breached the contract. The defendant, as well as denying some or all of its alleged breaches, also wishes to claim that the plaintiff breached the contract, or other contracts, between the parties. The breaches alleged by the defendant are properly the subject of a cross-claim, while the denials as to its own breaches form part of its defence.

Cross-claims should be distinguished from claims for offset. In some cases, a defendant may claim that the money it potentially owes the plaintiff is offset by money the plaintiff owes the defendant. This, more simple, trade-off in amounts owing may be able to form part of a defence (rather than requiring a separate cross-claim); for example, as set out in s 21 of the *Civil Procedure Act 2005* (NSW).[56]

10.5.2 Cross-defences

A cross-defence is a defence to a cross-claim. Where the cross-claim is against the plaintiff, the plaintiff then becomes the plaintiff/cross-defendant. In other cases, the cross-defendant is a new party to the litigation whose only role is as cross-defendant (unless it also then wishes to cross-claim against another party). In large commercial litigation, it is not uncommon for parties to have titles such as "twelfth defendant/cross claimant to the fourth cross-claim/ cross-defendant to the sixth cross-claim".

10.5.3 Replies

It is not uncommon for parties to file replies to defences and cross-defences. Replies are usually very brief and must be careful not to reiterate the claim or cross-claim. The purpose of a reply is to respond to an allegation or statement raised in the defence or cross-defence that was not addressed by the claim or cross-claim. For example, in defence to a claim for breach of contract, a defendant may plead fraud or illegality by the plaintiff.[57] Assuming the plaintiff denied any such fraud or illegality, it would be necessary for the plaintiff to file a reply denying the fraud or illegality. The reply should not traverse other denials or non-admissions in the defence, provided those matters are already the subject of the original claim that continues to stand as part of the pleadings.

55 *Civil Procedure Act 2005* (NSW s 22

56 *Civil Procedure Act 2005* (NSW s 2

57 See Chapter 10.1.2.

10.6 Joinder

An important issue which arises in all litigation is who will be involved in the litigation and what will be in dispute between those parties. The ability of parties, actions and causes to be joined is critical to the balance between efficiency and access to justice. It is efficient for identical matters to be heard together and for related issues between identical parties to be resolved in a single hearing.[58] Thus, joining parties and joining actions can be efficient and improve access to justice.

10.6.1 Joinder of parties and causes of action

Courts must balance the rights of parties to manage litigation and to choose what issues to litigate[59] with the need for case management and efficiency. A party should be joined where it has an interest in proceedings, and a cause of action should be joined where it is in the interests of the courts or parties to resolve the matters together, particularly where this is necessary to avoid operation of the finality doctrines.[60] Joining parties and joining causes of action are both procedural actions which should minimise the number of matters appearing before the court.

John Alexander's Clubs Pty Ltd v White City Tennis Club Ltd[61] was a dispute about the sale of the White City tennis courts which demonstrates the requirements and purpose of joinder. The issue of joinder in *John Alexander's Clubs v White City Tennis Club Ltd* arose due to the role of Walker, which provided funds to the purchaser but which had not been a party to proceedings. In the High Court, French CJ, Gummow, Hayne, Heydon and Kiefel JJ held that Walker should have been joined as a party because its interests were directly affected by the proceedings:

> The Court of Appeal majority's belief that adequate protection of Walker Corporation's position would be achieved by pursuing its claim to an equitable interest in 'separate proceedings' took no account of s 63 of the *Supreme Court Act 1970* (NSW). Section 63 provides:
>
>> The [Supreme Court] shall grant, either absolutely or on terms, all such remedies as any party may appear to be entitled to in respect of any legal or equitable claim brought forward in the proceedings so that, as far as possible, all matters in controversy between the parties may be completely and finally determined, and all multiplicity of legal proceedings concerning any of those matters avoided.
>
> The question is not whether any problem arising in the original proceedings could be resolved in separate proceedings, but, as explained above, whether that problem should have been resolved in the original proceedings without the need for separate proceedings.[62]

---

58 The parties to disputes were considered in some detail in Chapter 8.4, including consideration of representative actions (class actions) where numerous plaintiffs have a substantially identical dispute against the same defendant.

59 See Chapter 9 regarding commencing proceedings.

60 See Chapter 10.8 and Chapter 16.4.

61 *John Alexander's Clubs Pty Ltd v White City Tennis Club Ltd* (2010) 241 CLR 1.

62 Ibid [135].

However, joinder is not always a straightforward issue. In the rather unusual New South Wales case of *National Australia Bank Ltd v Charlton (No 3)*,[63] Mr O'Brien unsuccessfully attempted to be joined as a defendant to proceedings by the National Australia Bank against his daughter, Ms Charlton, in relation to a farm debt for which he claimed to be sole trustee of a trust owning the property. This case provides an excellent example of a joinder provision and accepts but distinguishes *John Alexander's Clubs Pty Ltd v White City Tennis Club Ltd*.[64] In determining that Mr O'Brien could not be joined as a defendant, Walton J gave careful consideration to the circumstances in which a person whose rights were affected by a judicial decision should be joined as a party to that decision, stating:

> [15]. If the Court were to consider the exercise of a discretion to join Mr O'Brien as a party, there are substantial reasons to refuse an exercise of discretion in his favour. The reasons for that conclusion may be briefly stated as follows:
>
> > The application was made far too late — not only was the application made on the eve of the hearing of the respective applications for debt and possession and judicial review, but Mr O'Brien had been on notice of NAB's claim for debt and possession since at least 3 August 2015 (when he issued his cross-claim against NAB). No application was made to be joined as a defendant to NAB's claim from the date of that cross-claim, notwithstanding the subsequent commencement of judicial review proceedings.
>
> As I will discuss below, the effect of an order on Mr O'Brien as a non-party in the present context may be characterised as only indirect or consequential. This is a significant consideration in the determination of whether or not Mr O'Brien ought to be joined: *News Ltd v Australian Rugby Football League Ltd* (1996) 64 FCR 410 at 525 (per Lockhart, von Doussa and Sackville JJ).[65]

A comparison of *John Alexander's Clubs Pty Ltd v White City Tennis Club Ltd*[66] with *National Australia Bank Ltd v Charlton (No 3)*[67] demonstrates two of the key CDR themes: the balance between efficiency and due process, and the balance between autonomy and control.[68] Adding parties to disputes which were not chosen by the plaintiff to be parties is a decision which goes against the autonomy of the parties and is likely to increase the costs of the dispute. On the other hand, denying a non-party the right to participate in proceedings which affect it can constitute a denial of due process and operate as a bar to accessing justice. Preventing joinder of a non-party also negatively impacts the autonomy of that non-party. In controlling the joinder of parties, the courts must carefully balance these competing aspects resulting in the complexity of the test in *National Australia Bank Ltd v Charlton (No 3)*.[69]

10.6.2 Joinder of issues

Joinder of parties or causes of action should not be confused with joinder of issue. Joinder of issue is relevant for pleadings but is different to joinder of parties or causes of action. Joinder

63 *National Australia Bank Ltd v Charlton (No 3)* [2018] NSWSC 970.
64 *John Alexander's Clubs Pty Ltd v White City Tennis Club Ltd* (2010) 241 CLR 1.
65 *National Australia Bank Ltd v Charlton (No 3)* [2018] NSWSC 970, [15].
66 *John Alexander's Clubs Pty Ltd v White City Tennis Club Ltd* (2010) 241 CLR 1.
67 *National Australia Bank Ltd v Charlton (No 3)* [2018] NSWSC 970.
68 See Chapter 2.3.1 and Chapter 2.3.4.
69 *National Australia Bank Ltd v Charlton (No 3)* [2018] NSWSC 970.

of issue is the term used (somewhat counterintuitively) to describe the situation where an allegation made by one party is disputed by another party. Therefore, if a defendant "joins issue" with something the plaintiff alleges, the defendant has "taken issue" with that allegation, identifying that this issue is in dispute between the parties.

The defendant is not assumed to have joined issue with the statement of claim until it files a defence in which it denies or does not admit liability.[70]

Once the defendant has denied some or all of the claim, the parties are then assumed to take adversarial positions. If the plaintiff does not reply to the defence, it is assumed the plaintiff disagrees with everything in the defence. This holds true for any subsequent pleadings. Therefore, parties are assumed to be in complete opposition where they do not specifically plead, with the notable exception of the original defence where the defendant is assumed to agree entirely with the plaintiff's allegations except where it has specifically indicated lack of agreement (or disagreement).[71]

10.7 Amending pleadings

It is commonplace for pleadings to be amended and the originating process is the most frequently amended pleading.[72] This is not a reflection of incompetence on the part of parties or their legal counsel — although there are instances where incompetence can occasion a need to amend originating process or other pleadings.[73] In most cases, amendment is required because more is known about the litigation and the real issues in dispute. It is increasingly common for civil procedure rules to require parties to narrow the issues in dispute. Sometimes, having received the defence and, possibly, the discovered documents or other evidence, it becomes clear to a plaintiff that its statement of claim does not truly reflect the issues in dispute.

Courts and parties are should always take steps to narrow the issues wherever practicable. This ensures that the court hears only the real issues in dispute. Accordingly, many amendments to pleadings are consensual and court approval is common. Occasions do arise, however, where further amendment would be so prejudicial to the other parties or would constitute an unreasonable imposition on the resources of the court that amendment is not allowed. This is despite the potential injustice caused to the party seeking to amend by denying that amendment. Leave to amend pleadings is most likely to be refused where there is delay in seeking the amendment, particularly where such delay was a deliberate tactic.[74]

If pleadings are particularly problematic, a court may strike the pleading out altogether. Even in such cases, it is likely the offending party will be given the opportunity to replead

70 See Chapter 10.3.

71 See, eg, *Uniform Civil Procedure Rules 2005* (NSW) r 14.27.

72 The majority of cases discussed in this chapter are themselves amendment of pleading cases, as disputes about pleadings and their amendment represent the interlocutory disputes that require courts develop principles of pleading.

73 See, eg, *Hordern v New South Wales* [2018] NSWSC 1515, [14]–[34] where the Court provides justification for striking out many paragraphs, allowing for some to be repleaded but others not because they have "no reasonable prospects of success" [27] or are "stream of consciousness" [16].

74 See Chapter 2.4.4, with reference to *Aon Risk Services Australia Ltd v Australian National University* (2009) 239 CLR 175.

their case so as to prevent a denial of access to justice.[75] This occurred in the Victorian Supreme Court case of *McIntyre v Hipkin* where the Court found that the objectionable aspects of a statement of claim were so numerous and the drafting was so poor that it struck out the entire pleading but stopped short of staying the proceedings for abuse of process, thus allowing the plaintiffs to replead their case.[76]

10.8 Pleading completeness: avoiding the finality doctrines

It is important that parties ensure their pleadings are as complete as possible. There are several doctrines that protect the finality of court proceedings by restricting the ability of a party to bring new actions or claims in relation to matters already litigated. These doctrines of finality include:

- *res judicata*
- issue estoppel
- Anshun estoppel.[77]

Res judicata means "a thing judged" and describes the principle that parties may not re-litigate matters already determined by the court.[78] Issue estoppel prevents a new claim that would require the new court to reconsider an issue already determined by virtue of prior proceedings.[79] Anshun estoppel extends issue estoppel to prevent a new claim in relation to an issue which is so closely related to the issues in dispute that it should have been raised during the original litigation.[80]

The effect of these doctrines is that if a party fails to recognise a possible cause of action or aspect to its claim in its pleadings and runs its case without that aspect, it may be barred from bringing subsequent proceedings to litigate the overlooked aspect of its claim. In addition, the recent general efficiency objectives of most Australian jurisdictions must consider whether separate cases that could have been run together potentially breaches those objectives and should, therefore, be struck out.[81]

The law in relation to this area is complex because it is not necessary for a party to bring every possible claim it may have against a potential defendant simultaneously. Courts must, therefore, distinguish between claims that are separate and entitled to be the subject of separate proceedings and claims that are so inextricably linked that they must be run in a single proceeding. The interaction of the doctrines is demonstrated by Sackar J in *Telesto Investments Ltd v UBS AG*.[82]

75 See Chapter 3.2 for detailed consideration of access to justice issues.

76 *McIntyre v Hipkin* [2020] VSC 30, [55], [77]. See Chapter 5.4.2 for detail on abuse of process.

77 See Chapter 16.4 for a discussion of the finality doctrines.

78 *UBS AG v Tyne* (2018) 265 CLR 77.

79 Ibid; *Telesto Investments Ltd v UBS AG* (2013) 94 ACSR 29.

80 *Port of Melbourne Authority v Anshun Pty Ltd* (1981) 147 CLR 589; *UBS AG v Tyne* (2018) 265 CLR 77.

81 See Chapter 2 for detailed discussion of efficiency objectives and case management provisions in civil procedure legislation.

82 See Chapter 16.4. See also *UBS AG v Tyne* (2018) 265 CLR 77. See *Habib v Radio 2UE Sydney Pty Ltd* [2009] NSWCA 231 (McColl JA with Giles and Campbell agreeing) for an excellent analysis of the finality doctrines and efficiency consideration.

10.9 Conclusion

The pleading process gives all parties an opportunity to define the dispute clearly for each other and the court. Where optimally undertaken, the pleading process should simultaneously enable efficient dispute resolution and due process.

The nature and form of pleadings are entirely driven by the key civil procedure themes. Pleadings can appear overly formal and complex but, hopefully, this chapter has demonstrated why there is a need for the formality and complexity inherent in the pleading exercise. Underlying the complexity of pleadings is the complexity of substantive law and dispute resolution procedures. Within this complexity, key civil procedure themes which inform the pleading process include:

1. The balance between efficiency and due process informed by:
   - the right to be heard (procedural fairness) which underpins the entitlement of parties to plead
   - the need for efficiency which is evident in the timeframes for pleadings, the succinctness requirements of pleadings and the abilities, but also the limitations on joining parties and actions and on amending pleadings
2. The balance between party autonomy and judicial control demonstrated through:
   - the formal requirements for pleadings which limit party control (by requiring no surprise and positive pleading) contrasting with the significant scope for parties to choose what to plead (predominantly the plaintiff's decision) and which matters will be put to proof (predominantly the defendant's decision)
3. The need to maximise access to justice which is evidenced through:
   - requirements that pleadings must fully disclose issues in dispute enabling fair judicial decision making in full knowledge of the real issues in dispute
   - judicial willingness to allow pleading amendment so as to minimise the barrier to accessing justice caused by the complexity of the pleading process.

The details and titles of originating process and pleadings vary between jurisdictions but these key requirements and their purposes persist across all Australian jurisdictions.

11 PARTY DOCUMENTS: THE VOYAGE OF DISCOVERY

11.1 Introduction

Discovery is the term used to describe the process whereby parties to litigation provide each other with documentary evidence which might be relevant to a case before the courts. Discovery of documents between parties, also called "disclosure" in some jurisdictions, is a critical part of civil litigation and a significant differentiator from ADR processes where parties rarely have access to each other's documents.[1] Where general discovery is ordered by a court, parties must provide each other with access to all relevant documents, generally including all documents on which they wish to rely in court prior to the hearing.

1 See Part 1 of the book for detailed analysis of the interaction between ADR and litigation.

Discovery was aptly described in the unanimous High Court decision of *Expense Reduction Analysts Group Pty Ltd v Armstrong Strategic Management and Marketing Pty Ltd*:

> [44]. ... discovery is a practice peculiar to common law systems, whereby parties to litigation can be compelled to produce to one another, for inspection and copying, all the documents in their possession or control which contain information that may assist another party to advance its own case or to damage the case of the disclosing party. ... '[t]he use of discovery involves an inroad, in the interests of achieving justice, upon the right of the individual to keep his own documents to himself'.
>
> [45]. Although discovery is an inherently intrusive process, it is not intended that it be allowed to affect a person's entitlement to maintain the confidentiality of documents where the law allows ... .[2]

The preceding statement of the High Court demonstrates the heart of discovery as a process requiring parties to reveal information to each other to which they would, otherwise, not have access. This raises issues of balancing privacy against openness and efficiency with fairness.[3] The obligations placed on parties through discovery also present some of the most significant ethical challenges for civil dispute resolution (CDR) lawyers because they commonly require the production of materials which are damaging to a client's case.[4] This creates a conflict between a lawyer's obligation to act in their client's best interests and their higher duty as officers of the court to ensure that the litigation process is fair by providing all parties with access to relevant information.[5]

The majority of critical evidence in most cases is documentary evidence. As our society embraces social media, email, text messaging and other written and recorded forms of communication, the percentage of evidence in litigation constituted by contemporaneous documentary material correspondingly increases. Reviewing documents and determining which ones are discoverable is, therefore, often a long and tedious process which causes many junior lawyers to abandon thoughts of a career in litigation. Discovery is, increasingly, sent overseas by large firms to take advantage of cheaper labour rates in developing countries. This is problematic because, as this chapter and Chapter 13 will demonstrate, discovery is difficult and requires a sophisticated and nuanced understanding of law and the potential evidence. The process benefits considerably from being undertaken by personnel with Australian legal qualifications and strong English language skills.

Television shows and movies about the law commonly focus on litigation but rarely focus on discovery. This is because discovery, while critical, is possibly the least glamourous aspect of litigation. Preparing a client's documents for discovery is, generally, the most difficult and time-consuming aspect of the discovery process. Reviewing documents discovered by opposing parties is far more interesting and usually less time-consuming

2 *Expense Reduction Analysis Group Pty Ltd v Armstrong Strategic Management and Marketing Pty Ltd* (2013) 250 CLR 303 (French CJ, Kiefel, Bell, Gageler and Keane JJ). This case was introduced in Chapter 2 as it is a key High Court case management decision.

3 See the analysis at Chapter 11.2 on themes, and Chapter 2.3 and Chapter 3.3 in particular.

4 See *Brookfield v Yevad Products Pty Ltd* [2004] FCA 1164, [368] cited with approval in *Clifton (Liquidator) v Kerry J Investment Pty Ltd* (2020) 379 ALR 593, [137].

5 See Chapter 6.2 for further analysis of professional responsibility for lawyers.

provided the opposing parties have been diligent in the removal of unnecessary duplication and irrelevant material.

This chapter should be read in conjunction with Chapters 12 and 13. Chapter 12 deals with procedures for obtaining documents and written evidence other than interparty discovery. Chapter 13 discusses the rules of privilege which are critical to inter party discovery and most other documentary production. The 2013 decision of the High Court in *Expense Reduction Analysis Group Pty Ltd v Armstrong Strategic Management and Marketing Pty Ltd*[6] is also important to this chapter and Chapter 13 as the underlying dispute related to a failure to a discovery dispute concerning claiming privilege. It is relatively rare for cases concerning discovery to ascend to the High Court.[7]

11.2 Themes and theories of discovery

Discovery engages with numerous key themes of civil procedure, but most strongly with the balance between efficiency and due consideration and the balance between privacy and openness.[8] The discovery of relevant documents is partially motivated by the same key theme of notice, ensuring due process, which motivated the service of process requirements.[9] Parties must not be surprised during proceedings by previously unseen material produced in court by another party. However, preventing surprise is probably not the most important purpose of discovery. Discovery requires parties to provide each other with documents which are relevant to the dispute but which are unhelpful to their own case. In order for judges to rule fairly, it is important that they have all relevant evidence before them, even in cases where the most important documents were originally only in the possession of a party for whom they are unfavourable.

The case management provisions common in civil procedure rules aim to reduce litigation to the real issues in dispute thereby increasing efficiency.[10] Ascertaining the real issues in dispute should be assisted by the discovery of relevant documents between parties. However, despite the evident value of important documents being provided to opposing parties early, there are efforts in many jurisdictions to reduce the scope and frequency of discovery. For example, the *Federal Court Rules 2011* (Cth) prevent discovery except where there is a court order based on an application which can only be made where discovery will facilitate quick and inexpensive litigation. The rationale behind reduced use of discovery is the need to balance efforts to ensure due process with the need to maximise efficiency to reduce the barriers to accessing justice.[11] The time and money cost of discovery is enormous and can be prohibitive of access to justice.

6 *Expense Reduction Analysis Group Pty Ltd v Armstrong Strategic Management and Marketing Pty Ltd* (2013) 250 CLR 303.

7 See *Glencore International AG v Commissioner of Taxation* (2019) 265 CLR 646 where there was a brief mention of discovery (but that case did not concern discovery).

8 See Chapter 2.3.1 and Chapter 2.3.3.

9 See Chapter 9.7.

10 See Chapter 2 for more detail of case management and the balance between due process and efficiency.

11 See *Construction, Forestry, Maritime, Mining and Energy Union v Os Mcap Pty Ltd* [2020] FCA 1435, [18]. See Chapter 2.3.1 and Chapter 3.2 regarding the key themes.

The scale of discovery should not be underestimated. For example, in the Federal Court litigation, *Seven Network News Ltd v News Ltd* ('*C7*'), Sackville J noted in his case summary:

> The outcome of the processes of discovery and production of documents in this case was an electronic database containing 85,653 documents, comprising 589,392 pages. Ultimately, 12,849 'documents', comprising 115,586 pages, were admitted into evidence. The Exhibit List would have been very much longer had I not rejected the tender of substantial categories of documents that the parties, particularly Seven, wished to have in evidence.[12]

In most cases, only a small portion of documents reviewed by lawyers in preparing discovery are actually discovered. It is likely that, in the *C7* case, the lawyers reviewed hundreds of thousands of documents to result in them discovering 85,653.

The scale of discovery costs in complex disputes is evident from the costs hearing in the class action dispute of *Money Max Int Pty Ltd (Trustee) v QBE Insurance Group Ltd*, which involved an independent costs assessor assessing discovery costs at $6.7 million which the court-appointed costs referee reduced by only $52,000.[13]

Discovery is the subject of much criticism and is, arguably, one of the key causes of the constant calls for civil procedure reform. The criticism extends to the judiciary and law reform reports. For example, the Australian Law Reform Commission's 2011 *Managing Discovery — Discovery of Documents in Federal Courts* made 27 recommendations for reform, noting that "[a] process that may have been fair and aided the administration of justice can become unfair and obstructive of the administration of justice in the contemporary information context — unless tightly controlled".[14]

In *Armstrong Strategic Management and Marketing Pty Ltd v Expense Reduction Analysis Group*,[15] decided a week after the High Court privilege decision,[16] McDougall J ordered the defendants to comply with discovery order despite the *Practice Note SC EQ 11*[17] (discussed below) because their "wholesale non-compliance" with the previous court order led to failure to review a further 100,000 potentially discoverable documents. The extent to which inefficiencies in discovery can become a bar to justice is evident from McDougall J's observation that:

> The procedural history of this matter could be taken to suggest that the parties have paid less attention to the provisions of s 56 of the *Civil Procedure Act 2005* (NSW) than they have to the process of seeking to grind each other into the dust.[18]

12 *Seven Network News Ltd v News Ltd* [2007] FCA 1062, [4].

13 *Money Max Int Pty Ltd (Trustee) v QBE Insurance Group Ltd* (2018) 358 ALR 382, [166]–[167]. Although, it should be noted, this was only a small portion of the total approved for legal costs of $21,875,678.51 and the $30.75 million paid to the litigation funders. This case was also discussed in Chapter 8.4.2.

14 Australian Law Reform Commission, *Managing Discovery: Discovery of Documents in Federal Courts* (Report No 115, May 2011) 60.

15 *Armstrong Strategic Management and Marketing Pty Ltd v Expense Reduction Analysis Group* [2013] NSWSC 1702.

16 *Expense Reduction Analysis Group Pty Ltd v Armstrong Strategic Management and Marketing Pty Ltd* (2013) 250 CLR 303.

17 Supreme Court of New South Wales, *Practice Note No SC EQ 11: Disclosure in the Equity Division* (22 March 2012).

18 *Armstrong Strategic Management and Marketing Pty Ltd v Expense Reduction Analysis Group* [2013] NSWSC 1702, [1].

However, there are indications that court management of discovery is improving. The *Access to Justice: Productivity Commission Report* in December 2014 noted that rules around discovery stood out as an area that had reformed to reduce costs, although to varying degrees across jurisdictions:[19]

Discovery is undeniably important for due process and access to justice, but it is also one of the most common causes of expense and inefficiency in the court which can act as a barrier to justice, making discovery a significant example of the key theme of balancing efficiency with due process.

The key theme of balancing privacy with openness is also a critical motivator in managing discovery.[20] Discovery is an invasion of privacy, particularly where discovered documents may be put before open court. However, failing to disclose relevant documents clearly limits the potential of the court to do justice, as well as defeating the concept of open justice.[21] Simultaneously, parties may become reluctant to litigate where the breach of confidentiality caused by discovery obligations is too high.[22] Thus the personal, commercial or reputational need to maintain confidentiality can become a barrier to accessing justice where litigation presents too high a confidentiality risk.[23] Australian courts have approved the English view of discovery as a "serious invasion of the privacy and confidentiality of a litigant's affairs" existing in civil procedure because "the public interest in securing that justice is done between the parties is considered to outweigh the private and public interest in the maintenance of confidentiality".[24] The courts must balance these competing objectives of protecting confidentiality while promoting openness and justice when managing party discovery obligations.

11.3 Legislative framework for interparty discovery and disclosure

Although the key concepts in discovery are consistent throughout Australia, there are some surprisingly significant variations in terminology and rules as demonstrated by the brief summaries below of the relevant court rules for interparty provision of documents.

There are several terms commonly used by different jurisdictions to describe the provision by parties of documents to each other in the course of pre-trial proceedings. The

19 Productivity Commission, *Access to Justice Arrangements* (2014) 15.

20 See Chapter 13. This theme is particularly evident in the application of privilege to discovered documents.

21 See Chapter 2.3.3 and Chapter 3.3.

22 See *Cargill Australia Ltd v Viterra Malt Pty Ltd* [2018] VSCA 260 where the high cost of discovery in the context of parties in commercial competition with each other is evident.

23 See Chapter 3.3.

24 *Russel v Macquarie Bank Ltd* [2020] FCA 1332, [64] citing the UK case of *Home Office v Harman* [1983] 1 AC 280, 308 with approval. See also *Mobil Oil Australia Ltd v Guina Developments Pty Ltd* [1996] 2 VR 34, 37.

most common term used is "discovery", with "disclosure" and "production" also common. The Federal Court, New South Wales, the Northern Territory, Victoria, Tasmania, Western Australia and South Australia generally use the term "discovery" to describe the provision by parties of documents to each other in the course of pre-trial proceedings. Queensland uses the term "disclosure" to describe essentially the same process. The ACT Rules refer to "disclosure" but also talk in terms of "discoverable documents". Court rules often refer to the "production" of documents in relation to both discovery and other court processes, including subpoenas.[25]

One important area of variation between jurisdictions is the relevance test which lies at the heart of determining which documents are discoverable. Queensland and South Australia are examples of disclosure/discovery rules, using the direct relevance test (ie discovery limited to documents directly relevant to pleaded issues). Conversely, the Tasmanian provisions demonstrate a broader relevance test which can require discovery of indirectly relevant documents. Determining relevance is discussed later in this chapter. Another key difference between jurisdictions is the level of autonomy parties have over discovery which engages with the key theme of balancing autonomy with control.[26] Some courts require a court order for parties to undertake any discovery, and such orders may be limited, while other jurisdiction give parties more control over the discovery process. Increased court control over discovery is usually aimed at increasing efficiency, further demonstrating the link between reductions in party autonomy and efforts to increase efficiency.

It should be noted that parties may always agree informally to provide each other with documents, and such informal discovery is often encouraged by courts. Informal discovery is actually a form of negotiation and can be considered a non-court ordered ADR process occurring within litigation.[27] However, informal discovery can increase the risk that important documents are not discovered because the obligation to provide documents is less clear and less likely to be reviewed by lawyers than formal discovery.[28] The rules governing discovery can be contrasted with the rules governing the admissibility of evidence, which are significantly more uniform due to the existence of the Uniform Evidence Law, applicable in New South Wales, Victoria, Tasmania, the Australian Capital Territory and the Commonwealth, also potentially impacts and govern the admissibility of documents in proceedings[29] and privilege.[30]

11.3.1 Federal Court

Discovery and inspection of documents by parties to proceedings in the Federal Court is governed by ch 2 pt 20 of the *Federal Court Rules 2011* (Cth). Rule 20.12 requires that a party must not give discovery without a court order. Accordingly, the Federal Court can be

25 See Chapter 12 for a discussion of subpoenas.
26 See Chapter 2.3.4.
27 See Chapters 4 and 5 for further discussion of ADR and its interaction with litigation.
28 See, eg, *Hookway v Hookway* [2017] TASFC 4, [90].
29 See Chapters 14 and 15.
30 See Chapter 13.

considered a jurisdiction with lower autonomy and higher court control over the discovery process.[31] Rule 20.11 requires that a party may only apply for a discovery order where the order sought will "facilitate the just resolution of the proceeding as quickly, inexpensively and efficiently as possible". Part 20 div 20.2 requires the discovery application to specify whether standard discovery (r 20.14) or non-standard or extensive discovery (r 20.15) is required and provide reasons in an affidavit where extensive discovery is sought. Discovery by categories is now limited to extensive discovery cases. The relevance test for Federal Court discovery is for documents "directly relevant to the issues raised by the pleadings or in the affidavits" which can be located by reasonable search.[32] Further definition of r 20.14(1)(a) is provided in r 20.14(2) as documents which the discovering party intends to rely on and documents which "support" or "adversely" affect a party's case. Documents which support the discovering party's case are only discoverable where it is intended for that party to rely on them, reducing the discovery of repetitive and unnecessary documents.

The non-standard or extensive discovery envisaged by r 20.15 is even more difficult to obtain court permission for, as demonstrated in *Australian Competition and Consumer Commission v Colgate-Palmolive Pty Ltd*.[33] Justice Wigney, in *Australian Competition and Consumer Commission v Colgate-Palmolive* refused to require Colgate to discover information regarding the New Zealand laundry detergent market which the ACCC said it needed to brief its expert witness so that witness could compare jurisdictions to prove breaches of the *Competition and Consumer Act 2010* (Cth). The Federal Court was not satisfied the special discovery sought would "facilitate the just resolution of the proceedings as quickly, inexpensively and efficiently as possible" because the ACCC's evidence did not support the necessity of the special discovery order sought and it was likely to increase the cost and complexity of the trial.[34]

11.3.2 Australian Capital Territory

Chapter 2 pt 8 of the *Court Procedures Rules 2006* (ACT) sets out the rules for disclosure of documents. Part 2.8 divs 1–5 rr 600–641 essentially provide for the disclosure of discoverable documents between parties. The *Court Procedures Rules 2006* (ACT) have a broad test for relevance requiring disclosure of any document which "relates, directly or indirectly, to a matter in issue in the proceeding" or "is mentioned, expressly or by necessary implication, in a pleading or notice filed in the proceeding."[35] Discovery may be instigated by parties or the court in the Australian Capital Territory, making it a jurisdiction with relatively high party autonomy regarding discovery.[36]

31 See Chapter 2.3.4.
32 *Federal Court Rules 2011* (Cth) r 20.14(1)(a).
33 *Australian Competition and Consumer Commission v Colgate-Palmolive Pty Ltd* [2015] FCA 1520.
34 Ibid [3], [13].
35 *Court Procedures Rules 2006* (ACT) r 605(1). Although there are exceptions set out in r 605(2), but these are mostly standard exclusions such as for documents already filed in court and correspondence between the parties.
36 Ibid r 606 (court-ordered), r 607 (by party notice). The court also has the power to limit a party's discovery duty (r 606(1)(a)).

11.3.3 Northern Territory

In the Northern Territory, rules for discovery and inspection of documents by parties are governed by ord 29 of the *Supreme Court Rules 1987* (NT).[37] Order 29 applies to proceedings commenced by writ[38] and provides for discovery to occur after pleadings close, unless the parties agree otherwise.[39] The relevance test in the Northern Territory provides for documents relating to questions raised by the pleadings but expressly excludes documents which are relevant only because they may lead to a chain of enquiry.[40] The Northern Territory rules indicates a balance towards due process and the opportunity to be heard rather than on reducing discovery to maximise efficiency. This is consistent with there being relatively fewer large-scale document-heavy commercial cases in the Northern Territory than in jurisdictions such as New South Wales and Victoria.

11.3.4 New South Wales

In New South Wales, discovery between parties is addressed in pt 21 div 1 of the *Uniform Civil Procedure Rules 2005* (NSW) rr 21.1–21.8. New South Wales also allows for notices to produce, governed by pt 21 div 2 rr 21.9–21.13 for pre-trial production and pt 34 for production at trial. Notices to produce enable interparty production of specific documents but require a party seeking production under such a notice to pay the reasonable costs of the party producing.

However, due to the prohibitive cost of discovery which thereby reduces access to justice, New South Wales is an excellent example of legislative and court-based solutions aimed at reducing the discovery burden wherever possible. For example, the *Uniform Civil Procedure Rules 2005* (NSW) r 21.8 provides that there is no order for discovery in personal injury claims unless "special reasons" exist. Effective 26 March 2012, Bathurst CJ introduced *Practice Note SC EQ 11* in the Equity Division of the Supreme Court of New South Wales, which provides for no discovery orders in the New South Wales Supreme Court Equity Division unless necessary to resolve the "real issues in dispute".[41] In addition, discovery is not to occur prior to parties serving evidence "unless there are exceptional circumstances necessitating disclosure".[42]

Practice Note SC EQ 11 has significantly reduced the volume of discovery in the Equity Division, including the Corporate and Commercial List which had, perhaps, been guilty of the most voluminous discoveries.[43] However, it has also spawned a substantial series of

37 The Northern Territory Supreme Court Rules on discovery are parallel to the *Supreme Court (General Civil Procedure) Rules 2015* (Vic) (which are based on the 2005 rules of the same name) but the Northern Territory rules do not contain the significant amendments made to the Victorian Rules in 2010.

38 *Supreme Court Rules 1987* (NT) r 29.01. Northern Territory proceedings are commenced by either writ or originating motion (see ord 4 for more details).

39 *Supreme Court Rules 1987* (NT) r 29.02.

40 *Supreme Court Rules 1987* (NT) r 29.02(3). The "chain of enquiry" test is the common law test. See Chapter 11.5.2 for more detail.

41 New South Wales Supreme Court, *Practice Note No SC EQ 11: Disclosure in the Equity Division* (22 March 2012) [5].

42 Ibid [4].

43 In May 2015, the limitations on discovery were extended to the Real Property List by New South Wales Supreme Court by *Practice Note No SC EQ 12: Real Property List* (20 May 2015).

decisions predominantly interpreting the meaning of "necessary" in the context of discovery. One of the leading decisions in relation to *Practice Note SC EQ 11* is *Leda Manorstead Pty Ltd v Chief Commissioner of State Revenue*, where Gzell J refused to grant the Commissioner of Taxation discovery before witness evidence in a taxation dispute, stating:

> [T]o be exceptional the circumstance need not be unique or unprecedented or very rare. What is needed is an appraisal of all the circumstances and the context in which the expression must be satisfied. Are there circumstances necessitating disclosure before evidence in the sense that the party's case cannot be put without the disclosure? Are those circumstances exceptional?[44]

In a subsequent decision in the same dispute (after witness evidence was served), Gzell J did allow discovery "limited to the cattle grazing use of the land", holding that the Commissioner had demonstrated exceptional circumstances because the relevant documents were wholly within Leda's control and the Commission could not compulsorily obtain access to them.[45]

The Court Practice Notes in the New South Wales Supreme Court, and the decisions in relation to them, focus closely on the s 56 *Civil Procedure Act 2005* (NSW) requirements of "just, quick and cheap" procedure as demonstrated in the 2015 decision of *Thiess v Parsons Brinckerhoff Australia*. This case concerned a dispute in relation to the construction and partial collapse of the Lane Cove tunnel. The New South Wales Supreme Court denied the application for discovery, holding the discovery sought was not consistent with "the just determination of the proceedings, the efficient disposal of the Court's business, the efficient use of Court and other resources, and the timely and cost effective disposal of the real issues in the proceedings".[46]

The emphasis on "just, quick and cheap" was even more pronounced in *Re Felan's Fisheries Pty Ltd*, where Black J refused discovery because the applicant had failed to comply with the requirements of *Practice Note SC EQ 11*,[47] noting: "The decisions which have considered Practice Note Supreme Court Equity 11 emphasise its importance in giving effect to the policies contemplated by s 56 of the *Civil Procedure Act 2005* (NSW) and, in particular, the Court's obligation to promote the just, quick and cheap resolution of the real issues in dispute in the proceedings."[48] The close connection between the *Civil Procedure Act 2005* (NSW) ss 56–8 overriding case management requirements and the decisions on *Practice Note SC EQ 11* demonstrate the key balance between due process and efficiency and autonomy and control which pervade the discovery process.[49] However, there are also numerous cases where discovery has been granted as necessary under

---

44 *Leda Manorstead Pty Ltd v Chief Commissioner of State Revenue* (2012) 89 ATR 102, [17]. This excerpt was subsequently cited with approval in *Schofields Property Development Pty Ltd v Lindsay-Owen* [2014] NSWSC 220, [30] in which Stephenson J refused to order disclosure prior to finalisation of expert witness report on basis grounds not exceptional as expert had access to relevant materials.

45 *Leda Manorstead Pty Ltd v Chief Commissioner of State Revenue (No 2)* [2013] NSWSC 89, [26].

46 *Thiess v Parsons Brinckerhoff Australia* [2015] NSWSC 326, [38].

47 Supreme Court of New South Wales, *Practice Note No SC EQ 11: Disclosure in the Equity Division* (22 March 2012).

48 *Re Felan's Fisheries Pty Ltd* [2017] NSWSC 1273, [4].

49 See Chapter 2.3 and Chapter 2.4. See also *Re Pure Nature Sydney Pty Ltd* [2018] NSWSC 482, [26] for another example of judicial reliance overriding case management requirements of justice and efficiency in making *Practice Note SC EQ 11* determinations.

Practice Note SC EQ 11.[50] In *Lam v Rolls Royce plc (No 3)*, the class action representative plaintiff's request for discovery was rejected but Beech-Jones J raised the possibility that class actions may require a more flexible approach than was available pursuant to *Practice Note SC EQ 11*.[51] This case demonstrates how the key theme of balancing certainty with flexibility also arises in the discovery context.[52] Limiting discovery increases certainty, but reduces the court's flexibility to allow discovery. *Practice Note SC EQ 11* constitutes a relatively sophisticated balancing of these competing objectives by allowing limited discovery upon proof of necessity. However, the need for an interlocutory court hearing to determine whether to allow discovery itself creates additional costs which sacrifice efficiency and may create barriers to justice. The interplay between the key themes is, thus, particularly complex in the discovery context.[53] The introduction of *Practice Note SC EQ11* has also led to increasing use and misuse of notices of production and subpoenas by parties desperate to obtain documentary evidence in the absence of an order for discovery. In *VPlus Holdings Pty Ltd v Bank of Western Australia Ltd*, the Supreme Court made it clear that it will not allow parties serve notices to produce which are really requests for discovery before evidence has been served in order to circumvent the effect of *Practice Note SC EQ 11*.[54]

11.3.5 Queensland

Chapter 7 pt 1 of the *Uniform Civil Procedure Rules 1999* (Qld) sets out the rules for disclosure of documents by parties. The following extract sets out the most critical Queensland provisions.[55] Queensland requires the discovery of documents "directly relevant to an allegation in issue in the pleadings" (or proceeding) which is the more limited discovery test than its common law predecessor.[56] The presumption that discovery will occur in Queensland cases increases certainty for the parties and ensures due process, but may come at a significant efficiency cost in some matters which may constitute a barrier to justice. However, there is scope for Queensland courts to order deferral of disclosure or order that certain documents not be disclosed.[57] Queensland courts can be involved in disclosure protocols, but this can, itself, lead to interlocutory disputes which threaten efficiency as occurred in the coal seam gas contracting decision in *Santos Ltd v Fluor Australia Pty Ltd*.[58]

11.3.6 South Australia

In South Australia, discovery of documents between parties is governed by ch 7 pt 13 of the *Uniform Civil Rules 2020* (SA) (r 73).

50 See, eg, *Skyscanner Ltd v Hotels Combined Pty Ltd* [2016] NSWSC 183; *Re Metal Storm Ltd* [2016] NSWSC 306; *Micro Machinery Manufacturing Pty Ltd and Micron Group Pty Ltd* [2017] NSWSC 289.
51 *Lam v Rolls Royce plc (No 3)* [2015] NSWSC 83, [10].
52 See Chapter 2.3.2.
53 See Chapter 2.3 and Chapter 3.2.
54 *VPlus Holdings Pty Ltd v Bank of Western Australia Ltd* (2012) 91 ACSR 545, [89]–[90].
55 *Uniform Civil Procedure Rules 1999* (Qld) ch 7 pt 1.
56 Ibid r 211.
57 Ibid r 223.
58 *Santos Ltd v Fluor Australia Pty Ltd* [2020] QCA 254, [29].

The current South Australian test for discovery is set out in r 73.7(5) and requires disclosure only of documents directly relevant to an issue raised by the pleadings. The *Uniform Civil Rules 2020* (SA) provide for general discovery (r 73.7), discovery by category (r 73.8) and specific discovery (r 73.9). The *Uniform Civil Rules 2020* (SA) also provide separate protocols for physical discovery, protocols where electronic discovery is not needed or justified (r 73.4), protocols for simple electronic discovery (r 73.5 and sch 4 pt 2)) and protocols for complex electronic discovery (r 73.6 and sch 4 pt 3). The court may modify the operation of the rules pursuant to r 73.14 and can make orders to ensure compliance with discovery obligation, such as requiring a person to verify their discovery list on oath or even appear before court for examination (r 73.15).

11.3.7 Tasmania

In Tasmania, discovery between parties is governed by pt 13 divs 1, 1A and 2 (rr 381–403) of the *Supreme Court Rules 2000* (Tas). In Tasmania, discovery occurs mutually after pleadings subject to agreement of the parties or court orders.[59] The Tasmanian test requires parties to discover documents located after a "reasonable search" that they intend to rely on or which support the other side's case or are adverse to any party's case "that are directly relevant to the issues raised by the pleadings".[60] This is a direct relevance test which is considerably narrower than the original common law test and the original *Supreme Court Rules 2000* (Tas) r 382.[61]

11.3.8 Victoria

The *Supreme Court (General Civil Procedure) Rules 2015* (Vic) provide for discovery and inspection of documents in ord 29 (rr 29.01–29.17). Victoria provides for general discovery, category discovery, particular discovery and expanded discovery and courts can make discovery orders during the discovery process based on circumstances. The Victorian *Supreme Court (General Civil Procedure) Rules 2005* (Vic) discovery rules were amended substantially in 2010 and the *Supreme Court (General Civil Procedure) Rules 2015* (Vic) discovery rules closely mirror their predecessor provisions. Rule 29.01.1 sets out the scope of discovery where there is no express court order, while r 29.05 provides for court orders limiting discovery including to discovery by categories.[62]

In addition to the discovery obligations set out in ord 29 of the *Supreme Court (General Civil Procedure) Rules 2015* (Vic), Victoria also sets out an overarching disclosure obligation in s 26 of the *Civil Procedure Act 2010* (Vic) as part of the Act's overarching obligations. The s 26 obligations require the disclosure of documents which ought reasonably be considered "critical" to the resolution of the dispute[63] and do not limit or affect a party's discovery obligations.[64]

59 *Supreme Court Rules 2000* (Tas) r 382.
60 Ibid r 382(1).
61 See *Fingal Pastoral Pty Ltd v Page Seager Lawyers* [2017] TASSC 24, [28]–[36].
62 *Supreme Court (General Civil Procedure) Rules* 2015 (Vic) r 29.05.1 allows for general discovery, r 29.05.2 allows for expanded discovery.
63 *Civil Procedure Act 2010* (Vic) s 26(1)(b).
64 Ibid s 26(4)(b).

11.3.9 Western Australia

In Western Australia, Supreme Court discovery is governed by ord 26 of the *Rules of the Supreme Court 1971* (WA), with ord 26A concerning discovery by potential parties and non-parties.[65] Pursuant to ord 26 r 1, any party may give notice in writing to another party to give discovery of all documents relating to any matter in question in the proceeding without court order. This gives parties an unusually high level of autonomy over the discovery process compared to most jurisdictions in Australia. Order 26 r 16A requires practitioners of parties providing discovery to file a signed certificate with the court stating that the duty of discovery has been fully explained to the party.

11.4 Timeline for producing interparty documents

There are several steps (as shown in Figure 11.1) which a legal practitioner must take before being in a position to determine whether a document is relevant as follows:

1. **Establish the issues in dispute**: In order to locate relevant documents and/or draft categories of discovery, lawyers must understand what the issues in dispute are. In complex matters with many pleadings, determining what issues are actually in dispute may be a significant task.
2. **Draft categories of discovery**: Where discovery is to be by category, rather than general, lawyers must draft the categories of documents they require. Categories must be drafted very carefully and drafting is a difficult task. On the one hand, the court requires the discovery categories to be as narrow as possible to limit the scope of discovery and thereby reduce the timeframe and cost of discovery. This is also in the parties' interest. On the other hand, if categories are too narrow, there is a risk that lawyers will use the narrowness of the category as a basis to exclude documents from their client's discovery which are potentially relevant but fall outside the scope of the category (particularly if such documents may have potential to be unfavourable to their client's case or otherwise confidential or embarrassing to their client).
3. **Brief client on discovery obligations**: It is common, particularly in complex litigation, multi-party litigation, and litigation involving companies for lawyers to have a far better understanding of the issues than their clients by the time pleadings close. Unfortunately, the relevant discoverable documents belong to the client and are in the possession of the client rather than the lawyer. Lawyers must, therefore, to a certain extent, rely on their clients to provide them with the necessary documents to enable preparation of the client's discovery. The extent to which this can prove problematic is demonstrated in the New South Wales Supreme Court case of *Ange v Fairfax Media Publications Pty Ltd*,[66] where the client refused to provide any documents to his lawyer.

65 See Chapter 12.2.10.
66 *Ange v Fairfax Media Publications Pty Ltd* [2010] NSWSC 1200.

Figure 11.1 Discovery flowchart

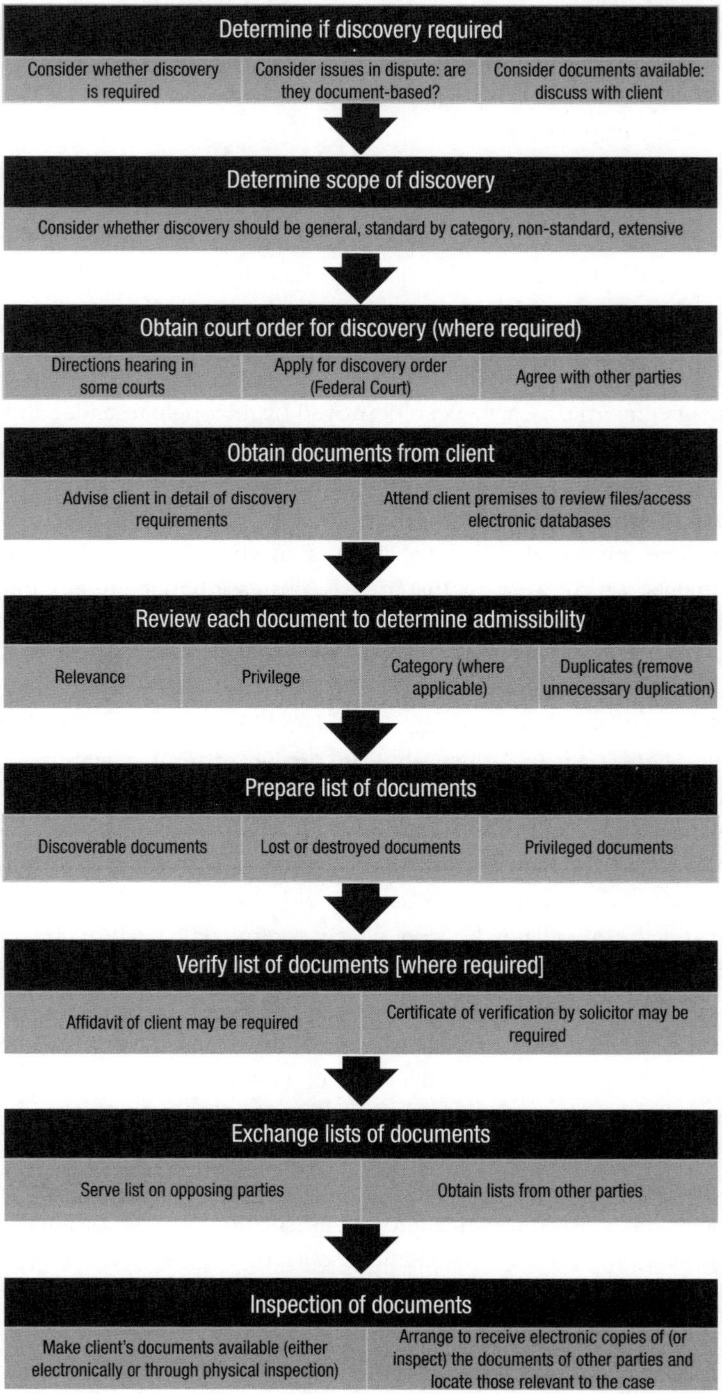

4. **Locate client documents:** Once the client understands its discovery obligations, it must then locate all the documents it thinks might possibly be relevant for its lawyers to review. Sometimes, this task is also performed by the lawyers but, even where the lawyers are locating the documents, the client must provide the necessary access and tell the lawyers what to look at (particularly now that most documents are stored electronically).
5. **Search electronic sources:** The task of locating all the relevant documents has potentially become more complex as a result of the increased use of electronic media. Documents are now routinely emailed which makes it much easier to provide a document to many different individuals at once. This means that, for a complex commercial litigation, there may be hundreds of individuals who may potentially have received and retained a relevant document received by email. It is also possible that a relevant document (such as an email discussing possible terms of an agreement) may have been destroyed by the original sender and recipient but may still exist on a backup tape owned by the party or in an email inbox of another employee who received a copy and did not happen to delete it. That remaining copy is discoverable.
6. **Determine missing documents:** There is an obligation on parties to list relevant documents which were in that party's possession but are no longer. See, for example, *Uniform Civil Procedure Rules 2005* (NSW) r 21.3(2)(a)(ii), which requires the listing of all discoverable documents no longer in the party's possession which were in the party's possession up to six months prior to the commencement of proceedings. Describing missing documents can require lengthy discussions with clients. Parties can find themselves in significant trouble with the courts where documents have been destroyed at a time where litigation was anticipated. The obligation not to destroy documents when litigation is anticipated is discussed by the Victorian Supreme Court in relation to the destruction of documents relating to the dangers of smoking in *McCabe v British American Tobacco Australia Services Ltd*[67] and the appellate decision which overruled it (*British American Tobacco Australia Services Ltd v Cowell*).[68]
7. **Review documents for relevance:** Once all the potentially relevant documents have been located, the lawyers must review those documents to determine those of relevance. They must also consider issues of duplication, whether documents fit within categories, and whether a claim for privilege should be made. These issues will be considered elsewhere in this chapter and, in the case of privilege, in Chapter 13.
8. **Review documents for privilege:** Where parties which to claim privilege over a document, it is critical that the document be listed accordingly and that the description of the document is limited so as to prevent waiver of privilege through inadvertent disclosure. Privilege is the subject of Chapter 13.

---

67 *McCabe v British American Tobacco Australia Services Ltd* [2002] VSC 73.

68 *British American Tobacco Australia Services Ltd v Cowell* (2002) 7 VR 524. The destruction of documents by British American Tobacco led to further proceedings including *British American Tobacco Australia Services Ltd v Sharon Y Eubanks for the United States of America* (2004) 60 NSWLR 483; *British American Tobacco Australia Ltd v Gordon (No 3)* [2009] VSC 619.

9. **Review documents for duplication:** It is not necessary to discover duplicates in most cases. There is an important exception to this rule. Where the duplicates have markings which are different and significant or where the very fact of a particular individual having possession of a copy is significant, it may be necessary to discover multiple versions of the same document. For example, there may be two copies of a draft document which are essentially identical except that each contains underlining of different words and which words were underlined is significant in demonstrating understanding of the document. For example, in *Clone Pty Ltd v Players Pty Ltd (in liq)*, the South Australian Full Court of the Supreme Court upheld the setting aside of a judgment due to the failure to discover third and fourth copies of a disputed agreement which constituted malpractice.[69] In commercial cases involving disputes as to terms of a contract, it is not uncommon for hundreds of different versions, and differently annotated versions, of the same contract to be discovered. A significant task commonly performed by discovery software is the removal of unnecessary duplicated documents.
10. **Prepare document list:** Once all the discoverable documents have been located and irrelevant duplicates removed, a list of all the documents must be prepared. Lists of documents for discovery or disclosure may be very large. In the *C7* case extracted above, over 85,000 documents were discovered by the parties.[70]
11. **Verify list:** In most cases, once the list is prepared and finalised, it is necessary for the client to swear an affidavit verifying the discovery. This affidavit essentially attests that the party understands its discovery obligations, that the list is complete, that all discoverable missing documents have been listed and that privilege is properly claimed. Lawyers also need to certify discovery in some courts.
12. **Serve list:** Once the list is completed and verified, it must be served on the other parties to the litigation. Sometimes, parties will serve informal discovery lists so that inspection can commence if there is a delay in obtaining verification. Commonly, parties provide discovery lists simultaneously but, in some cases, it may be appropriate for the plaintiff to provide discovery first.
13. **Arrange for inspection of documents:** Once the lists have been exchanged, parties must arrange for each other to have access to their discovered documents. Generally, documents are held by the lawyers and inspection is also carried out by the lawyers. It is important for lawyers to ensure that the documents are ready in accordance with the list of discovered documents and that all privileged documents are held separately and away from the remainder of the discovery, such that they are not seen by the other parties. In modern cases, it is increasingly common for documents to be maintained on electronic databases rather than in physical rooms. Where documents are maintained electronically, inspection can sometimes be organised remotely in an electronic discovery room.
14. **Inspect other parties' documents:** An important aspect of litigation is reviewing the discovery of other parties. The critical documents upon which a party will

69 *Clone Pty Ltd v Players Pty Ltd (in liq)* (2016) 127 SASR 1.

70 *Seven Network News Ltd v News Ltd* [2007] FCA 1062, [4].

seek to rely in court must form part of its discovery. In addition, unfavourable documents are also often discoverable and so weaknesses in a party's case are often found in their discovery. Inspecting documents is time-consuming and may be dull. Consequently, inspection is often delegated to junior lawyers or paralegals. This is a risky strategy unless the juniors are very well briefed and genuinely understand the issues in dispute and how documentary evidence may impact those issues.

15. **Arrange for provision of copies of requested documents:** Once documents have been inspected, parties are entitled to request copies of those of interest to them. Where documents are in hard copy only, photocopying is expensive and can take time. The copying expenses are on-charged to the party requesting the copies, usually at a pre-agreed rate. Where discovery is electronic, as is increasingly the case, copies may be automatically available at the time of inspection.

11.5 Determining which documents are discoverable

The legislative provisions discussed above set out the guidelines for what is discoverable in each jurisdiction, including what constitutes a "document", whether the document is considered to be in the party's possession, custody or control, and what relevance to proceedings is required. Essentially, parliaments and courts take a broad view of what constitutes a document for the purposes of discovery, a broad view of what is within a party's control, and a somewhat variable view about which documents are relevant.

It is obvious that the court is unlikely to meet the interests of justice if parties are required to discover irrelevant documents. Whether discovery is to be general (all relevant documents) or by category (all documents relating to X and all documents relating to Y etc), documents are only discoverable if they are of some relevance to the proceedings. However, what may or may not be relevant to proceedings is often a difficult and complex matter.

The question of which documents are discoverable can also depend on the wording of the applicable rules (which varies from jurisdiction to jurisdiction). In jurisdictions which apply the Uniform Evidence Law, s 55(1) of the *Evidence Act* defines relevant evidence as "evidence that, if it were accepted, could rationally affect (directly or indirectly) the assessment of the probability of the existence of a fact in issue in the proceeding".[71]

Where discovery is by category, which documents are relevant may also be influenced by the wording of the discovery categories.

11.5.1 Relevance in discovery by category

Where discovery is by category, interlocutory disputes often arise before discovery even commences with disputes as to the appropriateness of the categories. Parties must craft

71 The application of the Uniform Evidence Law is discussed further in Chapter 13.4 and Chapter 14.

categories broad enough to encompass all the relevant documents they believe might be held by another party but not be guilty of a "fishing expedition".[72]

The New South Wales Supreme Court case of *Ashton v Pratt*[73] was an *ex tempore* judgment of Brereton J which concerned several discovery issues resulting from an apparent mismatch between the categories for discovery and the issues in dispute and led to a request to amend pleadings. *Ashton v Pratt* also emphasised that discovery categories should be drafted by reference to the issues raised by the pleadings, rather than as if they were subpoena categories.[74]

Clifton (Liquidator) v Kerry J Investment Pty Ltd demonstrates the potential complexity of complying with discovery categories with multiple parties, including liquidators in the modern environment when documents are stored on the cloud.[75] In remitting the matter back to a single Federal Court judge, the Full Court also grappled with the more complex matter of attempting to rectify on appeal where inadequate discovery was not acknowledged in the initial hearings and innocent parties were inconvenienced by the rehearing, but this was necessary due to the discovery failure.[76]

11.5.2 The related documents relevance test: *Peruvian Guano*

Determining whether documents are properly discoverable depends on the test applied for relevance. As discovery has become more onerous, jurisdictions have introduced legislation which limits discovery to more directly relevant documents. For example, in the Tasmanian case of *Campbell v Biernacki*,[77] Blow J applied the old English case of *Compagnie Financière du Pacifique v Peruvian Guano Co*[78] (often referred to as the "*Peruvian Guano* test") to allow discovery of secondary school reports requested by the defendant's psychologist as relevant to whether the plaintiff's alleged mental condition preventing his employment was caused entirely by his accident.[79] The Tasmanian discovery rules at the time required "documents relating to any matter in question" to be discovered but have since been amended to restrict discovery to directly relevant documents as emphasised by the Supreme Court of Tasmania in *Fingal Pastoral Pty Ltd v Page Seager Lawyers*.[80]

It is perhaps unsurprising that indirectly relevant documents were considered to be discoverable, given the test for admissibility of documents in the *Evidence Act 2001* (Tas)

72 Parties requesting documents in categories considered too broad by the courts are often said to be on a "fishing expedition". This is a phrase long associated with the drafting of subpoenas and will be discussed further in Chapter 12.

73 *Ashton v Pratt* [2010] NSWSC 1376.

74 Ibid [6]–[9]. The ongoing litigiousness of these parties was evidenced by the numerous hearings ending with a costs hearing in *Ashton v Pratt No 2* [2015] NSWCA 134. See Chapter 12.4 for a discussion of subpoenas.

75 *Clifton (Liquidator) v Kerry J Investment Pty Ltd* (2020) 379 ALR 593, [168]–[189].

76 Ibid [197]–[209].

77 *Campbell v Biernacki* (2009) 19 Tas R 345.

78 *Compagnie Financière du Pacifique v Peruvian Guano Co* (1882) 11 QBD 55.

79 *Campbell v Biernacki* (2009) 19 Tas R 345.

80 *Fingal Pastoral Pty Ltd v Page Seager Lawyers* [2017] TASSC 24, [29]. The *Supreme Court Rules 2000* (Tas) r 382 was substantially amended effective 1 December 2012 replacing the broad relevance test with a direct relevance test.

(a Uniform Evidence Law Act) at s 55(1) states that "evidence that is relevant in a proceeding is evidence that, if it were accepted, could rationally affect, *directly or indirectly*, the assessment of the probability of the existence of a fact in issue in the proceeding" (emphasis added). However, even Uniform Evidence Law jurisdictions have been forced to limit their discovery because of the need to balance due process with efficiency and to prevent discovery becoming too significant burden on litigants.[81]

11.5.3 The direct relevance test

Increasingly, jurisdictions have disclosure provisions in their rules which focus on direct relevance. Some jurisdictions have had direct relevance rules for decades, such as South Australia where the direct relevance rule (r 73.7(5)) of the new *Uniform Civil Rules 2020* (SA) is consistent with its predecessors.[82] Similarly, Queensland's *Uniform Civil Procedure Rules 1999* (Qld) r 211 also requires directly relevant evidence.[83]

However, introducing direct relevance rules creates its own difficulties. Chief Justice Doyle, in the South Australian case of *Rehn v Australian Football League*,[84] discussed the complexity of the distinction between direct and indirect relevance, including reference to the High Court authority of *Mulley v Manifold*.[85] *Rehn v AFL* explained the purpose of direct relevance rules as being to reduce the cost of discovery which was "disproportionate" to its contribution to the "just and efficient disposal" of proceedings, but noted the difficulty in defining the adverb "directly".[86] The debate as to the meaning of "directly relevant" is unlikely to ever be settled, with Flick J noting in *Australian Licenced Aircraft Engineers Association v Qantas Airways Ltd* that "it is probably not possible to define exhaustively that which is 'directly relevant', and would in any event be imprudent to attempt to do so given that it is a phrase which is to be applied by reference to the facts and circumstances of each individual case".[87]

In *Clifton (Liquidator) v Kerry J Investment Pty Ltd*, the Full Federal Court confirmed that discovery by categories (described as "non-standard" discovery in *Federal Court Rules 2011* (Cth) r 20.15) was still required to be limited to directly relevant documents. This is because the aim of such discovery was to further narrow the discoverable documents, so it would make no sense to broaden what was discoverable beyond the "directly relevant" requirement for standard discovery (*Federal Court Rules 2011* (Cth) r 20.14).[88] This serves as a reminder

81 See Chapter 2.3.1 and Chapter 11.2.

82 The predecessor to r 73.7(5) of the *Uniform Civil Rules 2020* (SA) was the *Supreme Court Civil Rules 2006* (SA) r 136. However, the direct relevance rule in South Australia pre-dated 2006, having been introduced through r 58A.03 of the *Supreme Court Rules* 1987 (SA).

83 Queensland has also grappled with the direct relevance test: see, eg, *Peninsula Shipping Lines Pty Ltd v Adsteam Agency Pty Ltd* [2008] QSC 317, [41]–[43]. See also Chapter 11.3.5 and Chapter 11.3.6.

84 *Rehn v Australian Football League* [2003] SASC 159.

85 *Murray v Manifold* (1959) 103 CLR 341 cited in *Rehn v Australian Football League* [2003] SASC 159, [23]. The explanation of "directly relevant" provided in *Rehn* is still commonly cited in South Australian cases. See, eg, *Amaca Pty Ltd v Werfel* (2019) 132 SASR 585, [14].

86 *Rehn v Australian Football League* [2003] SASC 159, [22], [24]–[25].

87 *Australian Licenced Aircraft Engineers Association v Qantas Airways Ltd* (2018) 280 IR 47, [152]. It should be noted that this case was not concerned with litigation discovery but with s 482 of the *Fair Work Act 2009* (Cth) which also required production of documents "directly relevant".

88 *Clifton (Liquidator) v Kerry J Investment Pty Ltd* (2020) 379 ALR 593, [173].

that most legislative modifications to discovery (including discovery by categories and the "directly relevant" test) are aimed at increasing the efficiency of the discovery process while sacrificing as little as possible the due process aim of discovery which is ensuring the parties have maximum access to each other's documents.[89]

11.5.4 Documents within a party's possession, custody or power

Having determined what documents are relevant, it is necessary to consider what documents are within a party's power to discover. It is futile for parties to be ordered to produce documents they do not possess and are unable to obtain. Courts also take a broad view of what documents a party is able to produce and this may include documents held offshore or by companies or individuals related to a party, where the party to the action has control over those related entities. In *UDP Holdings Pty Ltd v Esposito Holdings Pty Ltd (No 3)*, the Victorian Supreme Court confirmed that documents to be discovered by the second defendant, AE Brighton, went beyond just physical possession. The Court held that the test in the rules for "possession, custody or power" included documents held under lien by AE Brighton's former lawyer (K&L Gates) and accountant (PWC) where there was no evidence that those third parties were insisting on their liens nor that AE Brighton was unable to discharge those liens.[90] Just as parties may not destroy documents in anticipation of litigation, so the courts frown on parties attempting to send documents offshore or avoid discovery of documents within their power.[91] On the other hand, courts only require parties to make enquiries to obtain documents which have never been in their possession, custody or power in limited circumstances, as explained by Le Miere J in the Western Australian Supreme Court case of *Absolute Analogue Inc v Sundance Resources Ltd*.[92]

The potential complexity of the terms "power" and "control" in a discovery context is demonstrated by the South Australian Full Court of the Supreme Court decision in *Clone Pty Ltd v Players Pty Ltd (in liq)* ('*Clone*').[93] *Clone* concerned a lease agreement where it was disputed whether a term crossed out in pen had been agreed and where the original document was lost making copies important in terms of the disputed alteration. The Full Court in *Clone* reached differing split decisions on their conclusion as to whether a crucial third copy of the document, held by the Liquor and Gaming Commissioner but inspected by Clone's lawyers and the subject of a Notice to Produce by Clone was in the power and custody of Clone (the appellant). The majority (Blue and Stanley JJ) concluded the third copy of the document was in the custody of Clone and therefore properly discoverable such that the trial judge was correct in finding Clone culpable for non-discovery.[94] However, Stanley J agreed with Debelle J (with Blue J in dissent) to create

89 See Chapter 2.3.1 and Chapter 11.2.

90 *UDP Holdings Pty Ltd v Esposito Holdings Pty Ltd (No 3)* [2020] VSC 260, [55]–[59].

91 *McCabe v British American Tobacco Australia Services Ltd* [2002] VSC 73; *British American Tobacco Australia Services Ltd v Cowell* (2002) 7 VR 524.

92 *Absolute Analogue Inc v Sundance Resources Ltd* [2008] WASC 259, [30]–[35].

93 *Clone Pty Ltd v Players Pty Ltd (in liq)* (2016) 127 SASR 1.

94 Ibid. Findings on custody: Blue J [148], Stanley J [469], Debelle J (in dissent), [598]; culpability for discovery: Blue J [197], Stanley J [423], Debelle J (in dissent) [607].

a different majority on the issue of power, finding that the third copy document was not in the power of Clone.[95]

11.6 Discovering privileged documents

Privilege over documents is an area of significant complexity which impacts both interparty disclosure of documents and the production of documents by non-parties through non-party discovery, subpoenas and other means. Privilege is the subject of Chapter 13. It is important to note in this chapter, however, the role privilege plays in interparty lists of documents. Parties must discover their privileged documents, but they need not disclose them to the other party. This means that the list of documents provided to the other side must include a list of the documents which will not be produced because privilege is claimed over those documents. Without this list, it would be impossible for courts to verify claims for privilege and the scope for incompetence or deliberate abuse of obligations to produce documents would be arguably too great.[96]

11.7 Interlocutory disputes in the discovery and disclosure process

A common cause of interlocutory (pre-trial) disputes is the discovery and disclosure of documents between parties. Parties in dispute are often adversarial and have commonly lost faith in each other; hence, necessitating their reliance on the court to resolve their dispute. In these circumstances, it is unsurprising that parties often do not trust each other to honestly comply with their discovery obligations. Interlocutory discovery disputes include disputed claims for privilege, disputes as to appropriate categories of documents (where discovery is by category), disputes that discovery provided is inadequate, and disputes that discovery orders have not been complied with in a timely manner resulting in prejudice to one or more parties.

Sunland Waterfront (BVI) Ltd v Prudentia Investments Pty Ltd (No 8)[97] was a Federal Court case before Logan J, in which the fourth respondent was ordered to provide a further affidavit regarding documents within certain categories, including listing all documents within its power, separately listing all documents which had been but were no longer in its power and when they ceased to be and, in relation to documents not located, what searches had been made for those documents. It should be noted that the *Federal Court Rules 2011* (Cth), which did not apply in *Sunland,* only provide for discovery by categories pursuant to r 20.15 "Non-standard and extensive discovery". This mode of discovery can now only be applied for in the Federal Court, where the application sets out the proposed categories (r 20.15(2)(b)) and is accompanied by an affidavit stating why the order should be made

95 Ibid. Findings on power: Stanley J [421], Debelle J [588], Blue J (in dissent) [185].

96 The difficult task of describing privileged documents sufficiently to meet disclosure obligations but not so much as to waive privilege will be discussed further in Chapter 13. Privileged documents are *discoverable* and must appear on the document list provided to other parties. It is a common error to describe privileged documents as not discoverable. Privileged documents are not available for *inspection* but they are discoverable.

97 *Sunland Waterfront (BVI) Ltd v Prudentia Investments Pty Ltd (No 8)* [2011] FCA 221.

(r 20.15(3)). The opening comments of Logan J in *Sunland* exemplify the frustration of the judiciary in resolving disputes as to discovery:

> This is the third occasion in which it has proved necessary in this matter to resolve a dispute between the parties in relation to discovery. That was after an initial expectation in the course of pre-trial management that all disputes on this subject would be brought forward and resolved but once by an interlocutory judgment, and thence, with the benefit of the reasons for judgment for that resolution, by such mutual co-operation between solicitors in the interests of justice, as the Court is entitled to expect of officers of the Court. So much for expectations.[98]

Interlocutory disputes in relation to litigation often involve the verification of discovery. Where parties do not have great faith in each other's honesty, disputes as to the veracity of discovery are perhaps unsurprising. Courts have historically been reluctant to question the truth of a document sworn on oath, but courts will sometimes question an affidavit verifying discovery where there are obvious defects in the discovery.

In the Supreme Court of New South Wales case of *Ange v Fairfax Media Publications Pty Ltd*,[99] Garling J allowed the cross-examination of a plaintiff on his affidavit verifying discovery. In New South Wales, parties and their lawyers are required to certify the veracity of discovery by affidavit. Lawyers are required to certify that they have properly explained the obligations of discovery to their clients, and clients must swear an affidavit as to the correctness and completeness of their discovery. In most cases, this affidavit may seem little more than a formality, but the court's power to test the veracity of discovery should not be overlooked and it is crucial that litigants take their obligations to verify discovery seriously.

In *Ange v Fairfax Media Publications Pty Ltd*, Garling J was persuaded that Mr Ange's lawyer had properly explained to Mr Ange his discovery obligations but that, despite this, the discovery verified as complete and correct by Mr Ange seemed very likely, on the evidence known, to be inadequate. Mr Ange's discovery, which was provided following six court orders requesting its provision, listed only a number of newspaper articles, despite there being evident relevance in business documents which Garling J found Mr Ange would have been required to retain pursuant to taxation and corporations law.[100]

The role of discovery in a litigation can also be relevant to the determination of interlocutory applications for unrelated procedures, such as summary disposition.[101] For example, in the High Court decision of *Trkulja v Google LLC*, the High Court overruled the Victorian Court of Appeal and upheld the primary judge's refusal to set aside Trkulja's defamation case against Google as having no real prospects of success.[102] One of the key reasons why the High Court overruled the summary disposition of the Court of Appeal was because it found that " ... contrary to the Court of Appeal's approach, there can be no certainty as to the nature and extent of Google's involvement in the compilation and publication of its search engine results until after discovery".[103] The High Court held that the untested assertions of Google

98 Ibid [2].
99 *Ange v Fairfax Media Publications Pty Ltd* [2010] NSWSC 1200.
100 Ibid.
101 See Chapter 5 for detailed analysis of summary disposition.
102 *Trkulja v Google LLC* (2018) 263 CLR 149.
103 Ibid [39].

deponents could not be relied on as a basis for summary disposition and that discovery was a necessary precursor to summary disposition given the nature of the claim.

An additional incentive for parties to comply carefully with their discovery obligations is that courts may grant summary disposition against them or make other unfavourable orders due to failures to comply with discovery obligations. In *National Builders Group IP Holdings v ACN 092 675 165 Pty Ltd (in liq)*,[104] the Victorian Court of Appeal allowed the appeal against a defence strike out solely because the original decision might lead to inconsistent decisions where one defendant's proceedings were struck out and another's not. However, the Court otherwise strongly supported the decision to strike out for persistent failure to meet discovery obligations, noting that:

> ... the effect of the order would be to deny Holdings a hearing, but the statutory language leaves no room for doubt that this is what the provision was intended to authorise the Court to do. Nor was the sanction disproportionate, given the persistent and unexplained non-compliance of Holdings with the orders for discovery.[105]

Similarly, courts may be reluctant to allow new evidence to be brought where that evidence should have been discovered earlier and may order a retrial where a successful party failed to comply with its discovery obligations.[106]

11.8 Conclusion

Discovery, or disclosure, of documents between parties to litigation is often one of the most time-consuming, costly and complicated aspects of litigation. Discovery causes many interlocutory disputes and often generates much interparty correspondence due to the complexity of determining what is relevant and appropriate for discovery. The conversion in recent decades to electronic discovery has reduced the vast amounts of paper previously dedicated to the discovery process, but volumes of documents have increased exponentially as a result of the increased use of electronic media. The increased volume of relevant documents per dispute more than makes up for the reduced processing time per document which technology has made possible. These factors combine to make discovery one of the greatest challenges for courts seeking to balance the competing objectives underlying CDR.

Discovery requires courts and parties to engage with all the key balancing themes of CDR.[107] Discovery is one of the strongest examples of the potential for efficiency aims to conflict with the need for due consideration. Documentation essential to one party's case may be entirely in the possession of the other party, meaning that the process of discovery can be essential to enabling the court to do justice. The availability of discovery can be considered one of the key procedural protections missing from ADR. Simultaneously, however, discovery is often the costliest aspect of litigation with the highest potential for

104 *National Builders Group IP Holdings v ACN 092 675 165 Pty Ltd (in liq)* [2015] VSCA 260.

105 Ibid [5].

106 See *Adaz v Castleway (No 2)* [2020] VSCA 293; *Commonwealth Bank of Australia v Quade* (1991) 178 CLR 134; *Clifton (Liquidator) v Kerry J Investment Pty Ltd* (2020) 379 ALR 593.

107 See Chapter 2.3.

abuse of process. Unfortunately, the resources which would be required to locate and analyse all the relevant documentation for discovery is frequently disproportionate to the amount at stake in the dispute. As this chapter has demonstrated, most legislative changes to discovery are aimed at limiting discovery and reducing its scope in order to reduce costs which create barriers to accessing justice.

Discovery also engages with the other three key CDR themes: balancing certainty with flexibility, balancing privacy with openness, and balancing autonomy with control. Legislative provisions defining discovery and court-based case management rules, such as the New South Wales Supreme Court's *Practice Note SC EQ 11*, have built in court discretion which provides a necessary level of flexibility to enable limited discovery where required, but comes at a cost to certainty for parties. Discovery inherently entails an invasion of each party's confidential documents, but this is essential to enable the court to openly hear each case. Again, this provides a contrast to ADR where confidentiality is crucial and there is no open justice. The variation between jurisdictions as to whether discovery is an entitlement or requires court order, and whether it is formal or informal and by party agreed categories or general, provide examples of how CDR requires a balance between party autonomy and court control. The process of discovery itself frequently involves considerable ADR in the form of negotiated agreements as to discovery categories, informal discovery, inspection regimes and electronic protocols. However, discovery is also, arguably, the best example of the differences between ADR and litigation because it so strongly exemplifies both the advantages and disadvantages of litigation.

12 OBTAINING RELEVANT INFORMATION: ALTERNATIVES TO INTERPARTY DISCOVERY

12.1 Introduction

This chapter focuses on obtaining information and documents other than through interparty discovery. As for interparty discovery,[1] this chapter concerns the pre-trial collection of information and potential evidence which is critical to all four of the key balancing themes in civil procedure, particularly balancing efficiency with due process and balancing privacy and openness.[2] The ability of parties to access relevant information to prove their case is

1 See Chapter 11.
2 See Chapter 2.3.

essential for due process, but can be costly and inefficient if not managed well and can impose unfair burdens on unrelated parties whose only involvement is their possession of relevant information. The processes discussed in this chapter (other than FOI applications) are all interlocutory procedures which are commonly commenced through motions in court or as part of agreed court timetables.[3]

Although interparty discovery remains the most common way parties acquire documentary evidence relevant to a dispute, this chapter considers the numerous other ways parties obtain and create documentary evidence. As courts become more reluctant to grant discovery,[4] the means of obtaining documents discussed in this chapter become increasingly important. Subpoenas, notices to admit and produce, interrogatories and Freedom of Information (FOI) applications are all important ways to obtain evidence pre-trial.

If there are factual matters which should be within another party's knowledge, but not necessarily the subject of a document or not readily extractable from documents, interrogatories or notices to admit can prove useful. It is common in litigation for non-parties to have documents which are relevant to the dispute. Doctors, accountants, banks and government bodies are all non-parties who commonly hold information relevant to civil litigation. There are several ways in which such information may be obtained. Where the entity holding information is the government or a government-controlled body, documents may also be obtained through non-court processes such as a Freedom of Information (FOI) application.

This chapter provides another excellent demonstration of how the key balancing themes of civil dispute resolution (CDR) drive the litigation procedures available to parties and the management of those procedures by the courts. The most significant balancing act for the courts is balancing the need for due process against the need for efficiency.[5] The more information available to the parties to prove their cases, the more likely the court can come to a just decision. However, the accrual of this information comes at a significant cost, including to third parties required to engage in the process through court orders such as subpoenas. The courts must balance their desire for the full picture against the need to manage the limited resources of the courts, the parties (who may find high cost a barrier to accessing justice), and non-parties dragged into the process.[6] This balance is usually achieved by the courts imposing significant control over the employment by parties of the tools discussed in this chapter for obtaining information. For example, courts commonly limit the use and content of subpoenas, interrogatories, and notices to admit and produce. In controlling the use of such processes, the courts are balancing the desirability of autonomy of the parties against the need for courts to control processes, which is another key theme of CDR.[7]

Obtaining documents for litigation, particularly from non-parties, also engages with the key theme of balancing privacy and openness.[8] While judicial decision-making benefits from maximum information, most cases involve a significant amount of private information and it can often be the privacy of third parties which is interfered with by the document-

3 See Chapter 8.7 for a discussion of interlocutory applications.
4 See Chapter 11.3.4.
5 See Chapter 2.3.1 for analysis of the efficiency versus due process theme.
6 See Chapter 3.2 regarding access to justice.
7 See Chapter 2.3.4.
8 See Chapter 2.3.3.

gathering processes. For example, non-parties who are subjected to a subpoena may be required to disclose confidential information to the court and the parties to the dispute. The wide variation in civil disputes and the documentation relevant to them is one reason why it is common for courts to actively manage the process of obtaining information. This engages with the remaining key theme of balancing certainty with flexibility.[9] Obtaining documentation from non-parties is one area of CDR where a high level of flexibility is required. In many matters, interrogatories and notices to admit are entirely inappropriate, and other processes discussed in this chapter should occur in a limited fashion. However, there are some matters where procedures, such as a notice to admit facts or a well-drafted interrogatory, may save the court and parties significant time and expense in resolving the dispute. This makes it an important area for legislation and practice notes to sacrifice certainty in favour of flexibility.

12.2 Legislative framework for obtaining pre-trial materials

As with interparty discovery,[10] there are variations between different jurisdictions in relation to other means of obtaining documents and facts pre-trial. Courts allow most or all of non-party discovery, notices to produce, notices to admit, interrogatories and subpoenas, and each of these are governed by the relevant civil procedure rules. The only form of information gathering discussed in this chapter which occurs outside the litigation process is FOI applications that are also governed by separate FOI legislation for each state and territory.[11]

A brief reference to relevant provisions in each jurisdiction is set out below.[12] Many courts will also have relevant practice notes which apply for the processes discussed in this chapter.[13] Due to limitations in scope, this chapter will primarily focus on the procedures for obtaining documents from non-parties in Supreme Court proceedings and Federal proceedings.[14]

12.2.1 High Court

The High Court has rules for the issue of subpoenas pursuant to pt 24 in ch 2 of the *High Court Rules 2004* (Cth) concerning the original jurisdiction of the Court.

12.2.2 Federal Court

Discovery of documents by non-parties in the Federal Court is governed by r 20.23 of the *Federal Court Rules 2011* (Cth). Issue of subpoenas is governed by pt 24 and interrogatories are addressed by pt 21 of the *Federal Court Rules 2011* (Cth).

9 See Chapter 2.3.2.
10 See Chapter 11.
11 In New South Wales, the FOI process is commonly referred to as GIPAA after the *Government Information (Public Access) Act 2009* (NSW).
12 See Chapter 11 for excluding interparty discovery.
13 See Chapter 8.5.6 for explanation of the role of practice notes in civil procedure.
14 For those jurisdictions with Uniform Civil Procedure rules (Queensland, New South Wales, Victoria and South Australia), the rules for these procedures apply equally to lower-level courts.

12.2.3 Australian Capital Territory

In the Australian Capital Territory, rules for non-party production of documents are governed by ch 2 pt 8 div 7 of the *Court Procedures Rules 2006* (ACT) (rr 660–7); interrogatories by ch 2 pt 8 div 4; and subpoenas are governed by ch 6 pt 9 (rr 6600–6615).

12.2.4 Northern Territory

In the Northern Territory, rules for discovery and inspection of documents by non-parties are governed by ord 32 of the *Supreme Court Rules 1987* (NT); interrogatories by ord 30; and subpoenas are governed by ord 42.[15]

12.2.5 New South Wales

In New South Wales, discovery between non-parties is governed by pt 5 rr 5.4–5.5 of the *Uniform Civil Procedure Rules 2005* (NSW); interrogatories by pt 22 rr 22.1–22.6; and subpoenas by pt 33 rr 33.1–33.13.

12.2.6 Queensland

In Queensland, the rules for disclosure of documents by non-parties are governed by ch 7 pt 2 of the *Uniform Civil Procedure Rules 1999* (Qld); interrogatories by ch 7 pt 1; admissions by ch 6 pt 5 div 3 (with r 189 specifically providing for notices to admit facts or documents); and subpoenas by ch 11 pt 4.

12.2.7 South Australia

In South Australia, disclosure of documents between non-parties is governed by ch 10 pt 6 of the *Uniform Civil Rules 2020* (SA) (r 116); subpoenas by ch 13 pt 6 (r 156); and notices to admit facts or documents and interrogatories are governed by ch 10 pt 7 (r 117).

12.2.8 Tasmania

In Tasmania, discovery between non-parties is provided for in pt 13 div 2A (r 403FA) of the *Supreme Court Rules 2000* (Tas); interrogatories in pt 13 div 3 (rr 404–413); and subpoenas in pt 19 div 3 (rr 494–500F).

12.2.9 Victoria

In Victoria, interrogatories are governed by ord 30 of the *Supreme Court (General Civil Procedure) Rules 2015* (Vic); discovery by oral examination in ord 31; preliminary discovery and discovery from non-parties in ord 32; and subpoenas in ord 42.

15 *Supreme Court Rules 1987* (NT) are essentially uniform with the *Supreme Court (General Civil Procedure) Rules 2015* (Vic).

12.2.10 Western Australia

In Western Australia, discovery by non-parties is governed by the *Rules of the Supreme Court 1971* (WA): non-party discovery is governed by ord 26A; and issue of subpoenas is governed by ord 36B. Order 36B was amended significantly in May 2017 in relation to service, attendance, production, inspection and setting aside of subpoenas, together with treatment of subpoenaed documents and contempt for non-compliance with subpoena orders.[16] Interrogatories are governed by ord 27 and notices to admit by ord 30.[17]

12.3 Discovery from non-parties

Where a non-party has relevant information, it is more common for that entity to be subpoenaed and for discovery to be reserved for the parties. As the cases below demonstrate, non-party discovery is difficult to obtain. However, there are circumstances — such as where there are parallel, or related, proceedings involving different parties, and where non-parties have sufficient relevant documents and knowledge of the issues — where the courts can order non-party discovery. For example, in the South Australian Supreme Court case of *Commissioner of Police v Channel Seven Adelaide Pty Ltd*,[18] Channel Seven requested non-party discovery by the Commissioner of Police to assist Channel Seven in making the defence of justification against a claim for defamation by Mr Sands. The plaintiff was seeking to strike out the justification defence of Channel Seven. The defamation action concerned an advertisement by Channel Seven in which Mr Sands was associated with Ms Patricia Draper, a federal politician with whom he had made a taxpayer funded overseas trip, and Ms Corrina Marr who was murdered on 4 July 1997, in relation to which murder Mr Sands had been interviewed by police.[19]

In the South Australian case of *Commissioner of Police v Channel Seven Adelaide Pty Ltd*,[20] White J held that Channel Seven was entitled to discovery from the Commissioner of Police, but imposed limitations on the scope of the discovery to reduce the burden on the police. Justice White also addressed the argument that the application was a "fishing expedition". This is a complaint regularly made in relation to subpoenas and also interparty discovery where parties consider the scope of the request to be unfairly broad. In this case, White J found the proposed discovery was not a fishing expedition because Channel Seven had good reason, based on a police affidavit, to believe the police had relevant evidence and that, despite the resource cost to the police, limited non-party discovery should be granted.[21]

There are also limitations on non-party discovery where interparty discovery options have not been exhausted. In the South Australian Supreme Court case of *Viscariello v Macks*

16 Order 36A rr 4, 5, 5A, 6, 7, 8, 8A, 8B, 9, 10, 12, 13.

17 Interrogatories can only be administered with leave of the court unless they are personal injury interrogatories falling within the limited categories set out in r 47 of the *District Court Rules 2005* (WA).

18 *Commissioner of Police v Channel Seven Adelaide Pty Ltd* [2008] SASC 164.

19 See *Sands v Channel Seven Adelaide Pty Ltd* (2009) 104 SASR 452 (Bleby J) for the substantive decision in relation to the litigation, whereby the plaintiff's defamation case against both Channel Seven and the ABC failed.

20 *Commissioner of Police v Channel Seven Adelaide Pty Ltd* [2008] SASC 164.

21 Ibid [14]–[38].

(No 6),[22] Master Lunn held that there was no general right of a party to obtain discovery from non-parties where it was uncertain the other party had made proper discovery. *Viscariello v Macks (No 6)*, which also referred to *Commissioner of Police v Channel Seven Adelaide Pty Ltd*[23] above with approval, involved the plaintiff's request for non-party discovery against six different entities. This request was rejected against all six entities because the plaintiff had not exhausted his avenues of discovery against the other party.

> [28]. The plaintiff's counsel contended that the plaintiff ought to be entitled as a matter of fairness to get the most complete picture by way of discovery as he was able to get from all of the documents in the interests of justice, and, if he could not get it from the defendant, the Court should require non-parties to give it to him. No authority was cited for this proposition. In my view, it is contrary to the authorities and the rules.
>
> ...
>
> [34]. ... I do not consider that the plaintiff has brought himself within an exception to the principle that he must first exhaust his rights of discovery against the defendant before being able to resort to non-party discovery.[24]

In the Western Australian Supreme Court case of *Lafferty v Waterton (No 2)*, the plaintiff filed nine applications for discovery against non-parties in a dispute between family members in relation to their inheritance from their deceased parents while the second defendant sought discovery from the plaintiff's husband, another non-party.[25] The Court rejected most of the applications, including several applications against law firms where it considered the documents properly belonged to the clients of the law firms who were entitled to claim privilege.[26] However, the Court did grant the plaintiff non-party discovery of financial documents from a school in relation to fees paid as a gift and also granted limited discovery for the second defendant against the plaintiff's husband.[27] In *Lafferty v Waterton (No 2)*, the Court noted the similarity between non-party discovery and subpoenas noting that both constitute "an intrusion into a person's right to keep his documents to himself".[28]

In the Federal Court case of *Mayfield Development Corporation Pty Ltd v NSW Ports Operations Hold Co Pty Ltd*, Yates J upheld the primary judge's decision not to allow non-party discovery in circumstances where no defence had yet been filed and the proceedings had been stayed, pending related proceedings by the ACCC.[29] The judge approved the consideration by the primary judge of r 20.11 of the *Federal Court Rules 2011* (Cth) and the case management provision of s 37M of the *Federal Court of Australia Act 1976* (Cth) which required a broad perspective and limited discovery, including non-party discovery to cases where it would "facilitate the just resolution of the proceeding as quickly, inexpensively and efficiently as possible".[30] The judge also noted the further limitation

22 *Viscariello v Macks (No 6)* [2010] SASC 303.
23 *Commissioner of Police v Channel Seven Adelaide Pty Ltd* [2008] SASC 164.
24 *Viscariello v Macks (No 6)* [2010] SASC 303, [28], [34].
25 *Lafferty v Waterton (No 2)* [2017] WASC 84.
26 Ibid [46]–[48], [53]–[55]. See Chapter 13 for detailed analysis of privilege.
27 *Lafferty v Waterton (No 2)* [2017] WASC 84, [31]–[34], [69]–[70] respectively.
28 Ibid [46].
29 *Mayfield Development Corporation Pty Ltd v NSW Ports Operations Hold Co Pty Ltd* [2020] FCA 1334.
30 Ibid [25].

for federal non-party discovery under r 20.23 of the *Federal Court Rules 2011* (Cth) to documents of "direct relevance" and the impossibility of determining such relevance given the state of the proceedings with no defence having yet been filed.[31]

The cases demonstrate that non-party discovery is not easily obtained and that courts will apply case management principles, including the balance between due process and efficiency, in exercising their discretion whether to grant non-party discovery.[32]

12.4 Subpoenas to produce documents

Many of the same issues arising in discovery cases for parties[33] and non-parties also arise in relation to the terms of, and compliance requirements for, subpoenas to produce documents. Subpoenas must generally be served personally and so give rise to similar issues regarding service as occur for originating process.[34] Disputes also commonly arise as to the scope of subpoenas and claims for privilege may be made in relation to subpoenaed documents by either the subpoenaed party or by one of the parties to the litigation. Subpoenaed documents are produced to court and are then made available to parties for inspection.

12.4.1 What is a subpoena?

A subpoena is essentially an order of the court for the person or entity subpoenaed to appear before the court on a specified date or to produce documents to the court by a specified date. Failure to comply with a subpoena can constitute contempt of court which can attract criminal sanctions.[35] In reality, delay in compliance with subpoenas, particularly subpoenas to produce documents, in civil law matters does not commonly attract criminal sanctions and is more likely to be resolved through informal negotiation and costs orders.[36]

The rules concerning subpoenas are located among the trial provisions of court rules rather than among the pre-trial procedures. Appearing as a subpoenaed witness in court is usually part of trial procedure and producing documents to court can also occur during trials.[37]

Although subpoenas are orders of the court, they are generally drafted by a party to the proceedings, filed in court, and then served by the party seeking the subpoenaed documents on the subject of the subpoena. It is common for subpoenas to be issued shortly after the completion of discovery and court timetables for cases will often include a timeframe for the issue of subpoenas to produce.

31 Ibid [36].

32 See Chapter 2.3 for the key themes of CDR.

33 See Chapter 11.

34 See Chapter 9 for a discussion of originating process..

35 *Schneider v Caesarstone Australia Pty Ltd* [2012] VSC 126 discusses these sanctions in the context of court reluctance to subpoena overseas parties where it would be impossible to enforce sanctions for non-compliance.

36 See, eg, *Allstar Capital Pty Ltd v FIP Holdings Victoria Pty Ltd* [2019] NSWSC 693. See also *Pentridge Village Pty Ltd (in liq) v Construction, Forestry, Maritime, Mining and Energy Union* [2020] VSC 47 where the delays were by the issuing parties as well as the subpoenaed parties.

37 See Chapter 15.3.2 for a discussion of subpoenas to give evidence (rather than to produce documents).

12.4.2 Return of subpoena

Subpoenaed documents are often produced pursuant to subpoenas long before trial and most courts hold return of subpoena hearings for this purpose. At such hearings, entities and individuals who have been subpoenaed appear to produce documents. Parties to proceedings also appear at the return of subpoena hearing to determine what documents have been produced to court pursuant to subpoenas and, in some circumstances, one party will be granted first access to the subpoenaed documents to review for possible privilege claims before the other parties are allowed to inspect the subpoenaed documents.[38] Most courts will have all subpoena matters heard together in the same courtroom and may have one day each week where subpoenas are returned. Courts will often set out procedures for subpoenas in practice notes and these may not require any court appearance where the subpoena is for production of documents. For example, in the Western Australia Supreme Court, inspection for non-contentious subpoenas returned before trial is in accordance with the Supreme Court of Western Australia *Consolidated Practice Directions*.[39]

12.4.3 Scope of subpoenas to produce documents

Disputes arise as to the scope of subpoenas to produce documents, similar to the disputes discussed in relation to the scope of discovery in Chapter 11. Subpoenas should not be used as de facto discovery and courts are often highly critical of parties who try to use subpoenas as if they were discovery.[40] As they are imposing obligations on non-parties, courts are even more concerned not to impose unreasonable obligations on non-parties to produce documents to court. The Federal Court case of *Dorajay Pty Ltd v Aristocrat Leisure Ltd*[41] concerned the extent of the obligation of an entity to produce documents not in its possession and relied on the High Court decision in *Rochfort v Trade Practices Commission*.[42] In *Dorajay Pty Ltd v Aristocrat Leisure Ltd*, Stone J held that the Australian arm of PricewaterhouseCoopers (an international accounting firm) was not required to produce documents which might be held by its non-Australian affiliated partnerships because the documents were not in the "possession, power or control of PwC" (PricewaterhouseCoopers) because the affiliation was "equally consistent with the relationship being one of independent contracting parties".[43]

In the Federal Court case of *Campaign Master (UK) Ltd v Forty Two International Pty Ltd (No 4)* ('*Campaign Master*'),[44] Yates J rejected an application by two non-parties, Messrs Barnes and Hawksley, for strike out of a subpoena on the basis that it potentially disclosed information against them. Justice Yates found that a non-party could potentially have standing to seek to have a subpoena struck out and that, in addition, the court could, of its own volition, strike out a subpoena as abuse of process. However, in *Campaign Master*, the claims of the non-parties were not made out and the documents produced on subpoena

38 See Chapter 13 for detailed explanation of privilege.
39 Supreme Court of Western Australia, *Consolidated Practice Directions* (2020), 4.3.7 [15]–[27].
40 See Chapters 11.3.4 and 11.5.1.
41 *Dorajay Pty Ltd v Aristocrat Leisure Ltd* (2006) 230 ALR 549.
42 *Rochfort v Trade Practices Commission* (1982) 153 CLR 134.
43 *Dorajay Pty Ltd v Aristocrat Leisure Ltd* (2006) 230 ALR 549, [18], [16] respectively.
44 *Campaign Master (UK) Ltd v Forty Two International Pty Ltd (No 4)* (2010) 269 ALR 76. This case was decided under the old Federal Court Rules.

by National Australia Bank were therefore not an abuse of process. The *Campaign Master* provides a detailed analysis of many cases concerning validity of subpoenas.[45]

There are a number of key factors which a court needs to consider when a non-party challenges the scope of a subpoena, as occurred in the Federal Court case of *Kitchen v Director of Professional Services Review under s 83 of the Health Insurance Act 1973 (Cth) (No 3)* ('*Kitchen*').[46] *Kitchen* involved a professional review of Dr Kitchen in relation to using Medicare rebate codes while providing ophthalmology services. The subpoena was issued by Dr Kitchen on the Chief Executive, Medicare, who was responsible for the original review of Dr Kitchen's services but was not a party to the proceedings. The case included a dispute as to the selection of the items reviewed and the subpoena, therefore, sought documentary evidence of the computer program used to generate the review items. Dr Kitchen's limited knowledge of the Department of Human Services or Medicare's computer systems, the complex structure of the relevant government department and its chains of responsibility, and the COVID-19 crisis all contributed to the complexity of this case. Justice Collier held that the scope of the subpoena was appropriate, provided sufficient time was allowed for compliance given the stress COVID-19 had imposed on the Chief Executive, Medicare.[47] In upholding the scope of the subpoena, the Federal Court considered the following four issues:

1. Had the issuer of the subpoena (Dr Kitchen) identified "with reasonable particularity" the documents he sought under the subpoena? The Court concluded he had.[48]
2. Were the documents sought in correspondence outside the subpoena outside the "scope" of the subpoena categories? The Court concluded that Dr Kitchen was entitled to seek the documents listed in correspondence and that these were within the scope of the subpoena.[49]
3. Were the documents "relevant" to the substantive proceedings and did they have a "legitimate forensic purpose"? The judge concluded: "I am satisfied that documents in categories 2, 4 and 5 of the subpoena are not sought in the course of a 'fishing exercise,' but are adjectivally relevant to the substantive proceeding and have a legitimate forensic purpose in relation to issues in the proceedings."[50]
4. Was it oppressive to require the Chief Executive, Medicare to produce under the subpoena due to "impermissible breadth or lack of clarity of description"? The Court concluded the scope of the subpoena was not oppressive provided sufficient time was allowed due to the exigencies of COVID-19.[51]

The potential complexity of determining the proper scope of a subpoena is demonstrated by the split decision of the New South Wales Supreme Court of Appeal in *Lowery v Insurance Australia Ltd*.[52] Basten and Emmett JJ (with Adamson J dissenting) overruled the primary judge and agreed to set aside subpoenas by the insurer in relation to a motor vehicle insurance claims as fishing, expeditions including a subpoena to the New South Wales Police in relation

45 Ibid [31], [32], [38], [40], [43], [44], [45], [63].
46 *Kitchen v Director of Professional Services Review under s 83 of the Health Insurance Act 1973 (Cth) (No 3)* [2020] FCA 634.
47 Ibid [85]–[86].
48 Ibid [29]–[46].
49 Ibid [47]–[64].
50 Ibid [65]–[76] (quotation at [72]).
51 Ibid [77]–[90].
52 *Lowery v Insurance Australia Ltd* (2015) 90 NSWLR 320.

to the entire criminal record of the plaintiffs and their son. However, the Court also accepted that new subpoenas could be drafted by the insurer with a more appropriate scope.[53]

12.4.4 Setting aside subpoenas

It is not uncommon for subpoenas to be set aside, often as an abuse of process, and many of the cases discussed above concern applications to set aside subpoenas. Commonly applications to set aside subpoenas are made either by the opposing party to the litigation or by the recipient of the subpoena (which is most commonly not a party to the litigation). Judicial decisions on applications to set aside subpoenas also provide the most thorough discussions of the purpose of subpoenas and how they fit with the theory of CDR. Subpoenas can be an important source of crucial information. However, subpoenas are also a significant imposition on the recipient of the subpoena and, depending on the level of review for privilege required,[54] also on parties to the dispute. As such, they engage the key CDR theme of balancing efficiency against enabling due process.[55]

In *Secretary of the Department of Planning, Industry and Environment v Blacktown City Council*,[56] the New South Wales Court of Appeal upheld the Land and Environment Court's decision not to set aside a subpoena seeking information from the Department in relation to a compulsory acquisition of land dispute. The case contains a detailed analysis from Bell P on the law of civil subpoenas, concluding that there should not be a definitive test for setting aside subpoenas as follows:

> [32] As explained below, where it can be shown that the documents sought on subpoena are likely materially to assist the party that issued the subpoena, it will generally not be possible for the subpoenaed or some other interested party to contend that the subpoena should be set aside on the grounds of abuse of process or that the issuing party lacked a legitimate forensic purpose. The converse does not, however, follow….
>
> [56] In *Lane v The Registrar of The Supreme Court of New South Wales (Equity Division)* (1981) 148 CLR 245 at 259 … the High Court observed that a 'subpoena to produce documents is an important means of establishing the facts in issue in litigation and thereby enabling justice to be done.' Again one can see the correlation drawn between the use of subpoenas to facilitate justice by requiring production of documents apparently relevant to or capable of casting light on the matters in issue in the litigation….
>
> [57] This is no doubt one of the reasons why medical and telephone records, for example, are frequently the subject of subpoenas, even though it will not be known or knowable ex ante whether or not the subpoenaed material will, or is likely to, assist the party issuing the subpoena. To insist on such an added requirement would, as Brereton J observed in *A v Z*, 'require an issuing party to be able to predict the contents of documents potentially relevant, and would unduly constrain the ability of litigants to investigate the facts': at [18]. So long as the subpoena can plausibly be seen to relate to an issue or issues in the proceedings or to "cast light" on such an issue (see *R v McPhail* (1988) 36 A Crim R 390 at 404-405), and the subpoena is not in other respects either too vague or oppressive, it should not be set aside, nor should the inspection of documents produced be refused.

53 Ibid [26] (Basten JA), [54] (Emmett JA).
54 See Chapter 13.
55 See Chapter 2.3.1.
56 *Secretary of the Department of Planning, Industry and Environment v Blacktown City Council* [2021] NSWCA 145.

> [58] … Examining the question more than 40 years later, one important contemporary contextual matter that informs the Court's consideration of the proper use of subpoenas in civil litigation is s 56 of the *Civil Procedure Act* and its identification of the overriding purpose of that Act and of the *Uniform Civil Procedure Rules* in their application to civil proceedings, namely to 'facilitate the just, quick and cheap resolution of the real issues in the proceedings'. An appropriately targeted subpoena may advance the overriding purpose in a particular case, even though it may not be able to be shown that the documents subpoenaed either will or will be likely to assist the case of the party that has issued the subpoena.
>
> [59] … The importance of the procedural context in which a subpoena is issued has been identified by Benjamin Coles in "The Confetti of the Justice System – Subpoenas, Justice and Third Parties" (2016) 42(3) *Australian Bar Review* 385 at 396-398, 407-408.
>
> [60] There is a danger in using the language of 'tests' for the setting aside of subpoenas and such terminology should, in my opinion, be eschewed. It is sufficient to observe that subpoenas will and should be set aside when they can be seen to involve or amount to an abuse of process as part of the Court's general power to regulate and protect its own processes. Such a power is not to be restricted to defined and closed categories: see *CSR Limited v Cigna Insurance Australia Limited* (1997) 189 CLR 345 at 392 … The variety of grounds on which a subpoena may be set aside is illustrated by the list of examples supplied by Powell J in *Botany Bay* [*Botany Bay Instrumentation and Control Pty Limited v Stewart* [1984] 3 NSWLR 98] at 100.[57]

Inappropriate scope causing the subpoena to become a fishing expedition and lack of relevance remain the most common reasons for subpoenas to be set aside or required to be altered.

12.4.5 Costs of compliance with subpoenas

Generally, the party issuing the subpoena will also be required to pay the reasonable costs of the subpoenaed entity in complying with the subpoena. The costs of complying with a subpoena may be significant; for example, when lawyers are subpoenaed for files relating to a previous litigation, thousands of documents may need to be individually reviewed to determine relevance and possible claims for privilege.[58]

The obligation to pay subpoena costs was discussed by the Supreme Court of New South Wales in the case of *Frontier Assets Pty Ltd v Fishburn*,[59] in which costs of $84,179.87 were sought by a non-party whose former solicitors had been subpoenaed. In *Frontier Assets Pty Ltd v Fishburn*, Harrison J found that the non-party solicitor was entitled to costs sought under the New South Wales *Uniform Civil Procedure Rules 2005* (NSW), acknowledging that the client would, otherwise, ultimately bear the expense of its solicitor (or former solicitor) being subpoenaed.[60]

Where a subpoena is inappropriate, the party subpoenaed may seek costs for compliance or costs for applying to set aside the subpoena on an indemnity basis as occurred in the Victorian

57 Ibid [32], [56–60], with McCallum JA at [98] expressly endorsing Bell P's concerns as to the dangers of purporting to formulate a definitive test for setting aside subpoenas].
58 See Chapter 13 for analysis of client ownership of client legal privilege.
59 *Frontier Assets Pty Ltd v Fishburn* [2011] NSWSC 187.
60 Ibid [17]–18].

Supreme Court case of *Naumovski v Ugrinovski*.[61] *Naumovski v Ugrinovski* is an excellent example of how the overarching case management obligations, aimed at ensuring efficient and fair procedure, can interact with other processes. In *Naumovski v Ugrinovski*, the plaintiff did not resist the application to set aside the problematic subpoenas, but the application followed significant failures to respond properly to correspondence from the subpoenaed parties' lawyers seeking clarification and amendment of the subpoenas. The Victorian Supreme Court held that that the plaintiff's subpoenas were unsustainable and in breach of the plaintiff's obligation, in s 19 of the *Civil Procedure Act 2010* (Vic), to only take steps necessary to resolve the dispute.[62] The Court also found that the plaintiff's failure to properly respond to reasonable correspondence from the solicitors of a non-party subpoenaed by the plaintiff in relation to the scope and legitimate forensic purpose of the subpoena amounted to a breach of its obligation, in s 20 of the *Civil Procedure Act 2010* (Vic), to cooperate in the conduct of civil proceedings.[63] The Victorian Supreme Court then awarded indemnity costs payable immediately by the plaintiff pursuant to s 29 of the *Civil Procedure Act 2010* (Vic) on the basis that "the demands of justice require a departure from the general rule".[64]

The breadth of the power to award costs for subpoenas was explored by the New South Wales Supreme Court in *R v Obeid*.[65] *R v Obeid* concerned a subpoena issued to KEPCO Bylong Australia Pty Limited (Kepco), a subsidiary of Korean Electric Power Corporation, by lawyers for Moses Obeid (son of disgraced former New South Wales Labor politician Eddie Obeid) in relation his indictment for conspiracy with his father and former minister Ian Macdonald. Justice Beech-Jones held that much of r 33 of the *Uniform Civil Procedure Rules 2005* (NSW) applied in relation to the subpoena dispute, despite that dispute relating to a criminal prosecution. The Court ordered Obeid to pay $26,980 for Kepco's costs of complying with the subpoena, being the costs of Kepco's solicitors, Minter Ellison, and the costs of a junior barrister and consultant, but not Kepco's internal costs.[66] However, Kepco were unsuccessful in recovering costs for successfully setting aside an earlier subpoena with Beech-Jones J finding:

> In proceedings on indictment in this Court, the Court does not have power to award costs against an accused person in favour of the recipient of a subpoena who successfully applies to set it aside.[67]

In *R v Obeid*,[68] the Court discussed the difference between civil and criminal proceedings and between the costs of setting aside a subpoena and costs of compliance, holding that the *Uniform Civil Procedure Rules 2005* (NSW) were applicable in relation to compliance costs even for a subpoena issued by the accused in a criminal prosecution, but that the *Uniform Civil Procedure Rules 2005* (NSW) application did not extend to recovery for the motion to set the subpoena aside.

61 *Naumovski v Ugrinovski* [2015] VSC 49.
62 Ibid [46]–[48].
63 Ibid [49]–[54]. The Court also indicated a breach of ss 23 and 24 of the *Civil Procedure Act 2010* (Vic) by the plaintiff in failing to narrow the issues and failing to ensure costs were reasonable and proportionate, respectively: [55]–[58].
64 *Naumovski v Ugrinovski* [2015] VSC 49, [74]–[75].
65 *R v Obeid* [2018] NSWSC 1024.
66 The Court reduced the payment to account for what it considered to be unreasonably high charge-out rates of Minter Ellison and the junior counsel.
67 *R v Obeid* [2018] NSWSC 1024, [54].
68 Ibid.

12.5 Freedom of Information

Documents can be sought from government bodies pursuant to Freedom of Information (FOI) legislation, which is state-based and Federal.[69] In New South Wales, FOI has been renamed GIPA due to its being governed by the *Government Information (Public Access) Act 2009* (NSW). FOI requests are a common way for potential plaintiffs in actions against government bodies to obtain documentary evidence prior to commencing litigation. It can also be an effective way to obtain documents from non-party government bodies without having to obtain court orders for subpoenas or non-party discovery. FOI applications can also be made by parties not involved in litigation seeking information from government bodies. Therefore, unlike the other documentary tools discussed in this chapter, FOI is a tool which can also be used to obtain information in alternative dispute resolution (ADR) including negotiation, mediation and arbitration.[70] There are documents which are exempt from production pursuant to FOI legislation, including documents which would attract legal privilege were they the subject of litigation.[71]

FOI applications are separate from the courts and an FOI request does not form part of litigation. As administrative decisions, they are appealable and the correctness of a decision regarding an FOI application may itself become the subject of litigation, as in the High Court case of *Osland v Secretary to the Department of Justice*. This case considered the purpose of the Victorian FOI legislation and its exemptions, including the protection of client legal privilege and documents which should not be released in order to protect the public interest.[72]

However, there are significant limitations on the documents which are able to be made available pursuant to an FOI request. Some of the limitations of the *Freedom of Information Act 1982* (Cth) were tested by the High Court in *Kline v Official Secretary to the Governor-General*.[73] Kline was seeking information, including working manuals, policy guidelines and criteria, from the Secretary of the Governor General in relation to two unsuccessful nominations she had made for someone to be awarded an Order of Australia. The High Court unanimously (in two separate judgments) dismissed Kline's appeal. All the courts who heard the matter, including the High Court, held that the information Kline was seeking was not within the relevant provision, s 6A of the *Freedom of Information Act 1982* (Cth), because it was not administrative in nature.

12.6 Interrogatories and notices to admit and produce

As discussed in Chapter 2, all courts and legislators aim to reduce the time, cost and complexity of litigation. One way to reduce the scope of litigation is for the parties to

69 *Freedom of Information Act 1982* (Cth).
70 See Chapters 4 and 5.
71 See Chapter 13 for the impact of privilege on disclosure of documents and the public interest in disclosure.
72 *Osland v Secretary, Department of Justice* (2008) 234 CLR 275, [7]–[10]. See Chapter 13 for analysis of legal professional privilege and public interest immunity.
73 *Kline v Official Secretary to the Governor-General* (2013) 249 CLR 645.

agree on as many facts and matters as possible. Notices to admit, notices to produce and interrogatories can all be effective means for parties to agree on facts in a formal way which avoids the requirement to prove those facts in court. Notices to produce and to admit and interrogatories must be used sparingly as they are processes which can be easily overused, or inappropriately used, by practitioners.[74] However, a failure to ask appropriate interrogatories or service notices to admit, can be equally problematic; for example, where a party is claiming insufficient evidence of reasoning, but that party has not sought such evidence through available civil procedures.[75]

12.6.1 Notices to produce

The rules governing notices to produce vary between jurisdictions, but generally cover the specific process of producing documents — either to another party or to court — which are significant to the proceedings[76] Notices to produce are similar to subpoenas in many ways, including that the documents sought must have a legitimate forensic purpose and that the process should not be used as a fishing expedition nor as substitute for discovery (particularly where discovery is not allowed).[77] Notices to produce, similar to subpoenas, may be set aside by the court where they breach these requirements.[78] However, notices to produce are requests to other parties to a dispute and are not orders of a court; whereas subpoenas are commonly issued to non-parties to a dispute and are orders of the court.[79]

12.6.2 Notices to admit

If there are documents or facts which are critical to one or more party's case, it may be important to agree that the documents are authentic or the facts correct. A party seeking to rely on documents can serve a notice to admit authenticity of documents. All the documents referred to in the notice are then admitted to be authentic unless the notified party objects promptly in response to the notice. If a party objects to authenticity, the other party must prove the authenticity of the document. Putting another party to proof may attract negative costs consequences where there was no basis for questioning authenticity.

Similarly, if there are facts which one party wishes to rely on but which might be time-consuming or expensive to prove, that party may serve a notice to admit facts which will then

---

74 *Australian Competition and Consumer Commission v Australia and New Zealand Banking Group Ltd* [2010] FCA 230 discussed at Chapter 12.6.2.

75 *Minister for Home Affairs of the Commonwealth v Zentai* (2012) 246 CLR 213, [94].

76 See, eg, *Federal Court Rules 2011* (Cth) r 20.31 (for production to another party) and r 30.28 (for production to court); *Uniform Civil Procedure Rules 2005* (NSW) r 21.10 (for production to another party) and r 34 (for production to court); *Supreme Court (General Civil Procedure) Rules 2015* (Vic) r 35.08.

77 *Gloucester Shire Council v Fitch Ratings Inc* [2016] FCA 587, [21–24]; *Kazal v Independent Commission Against Corruption* [2018] NSWSC 1370, [25]; *ICAP Australia Pty Ltd v Howell* [2019] NSWSC 1024, [31]; *Klein v National Australia Bank Ltd* [2016] VSCA 144, [50]; *Arnot and Arnot v Commissioner of Fire and Rescue NSW* [2021] NSWIRComm 1030, [15–16].

78 *Tucker v Victoria (Notice to Produce)* [2019] VSC 689, [7], [22], [35], [48].

79 *Clone Pty Ltd v Players Pty Ltd (in liq)* (2016) 127 SASR 1, [626]; *Australian Securities and Investments Commission v Macks* [2018] SASC 132, [90] (approving *Suzlon Energy Ltd v Bangad* (2011) 198 FCR 1, [13]–[14]).

be assumed to be admitted unless the party served with the notice objects. Again, there can be adverse costs consequences for a party who disputes the truth of a fact inappropriately.

Notices to admit can also be particularly useful in circumstances where a person's decision-making processes are an issue in the case. For example, in the Full Federal Court case of *Folau v Minister for Immigration and Border Protection*, a notice to admit was used to establish that the Minister for Immigration and Border Protection had signed every visa refusal and cancellation prepared in draft by the Department of Immigration and Border Protection without alteration.[80] Although the Full Federal Court dismissed the appeal, finding that the admissions made were insufficient to demonstrate that the Minister had made the visa refusal and cancellation decisions unthinkingly, the Court clearly acknowledged the significant evidentiary value of the Notice to Admit stating:

> Whether the Minister gave proper, genuine and realistic consideration to the merits of Mr Folau's case is one of fact. It was not straightforward for Mr Folau (or indeed any person adversely affected by a visa cancellation decision) to establish that the Minister did not give proper consideration to the merits of the case but that may not be the position in every case. Depending on the case, further evidence adduced through, for example, a more detailed notice to admit or targeted interrogatories may assist an affected person in bridging the evidentiary gap.[81]

In *EMS18 v Minister for Immigration, Citizenship, Migrant Services and Multicultural Affairs*, the Full Federal Court arguably encourages lawyers for immigrants to make better use of notices to admit and other processes to assist the courts in understanding the immigration decision-making processes of the Department.[82]

12.6.3 Interrogatories

In some cases, there are key facts which are unknown to a party but which that party believes are within another party's knowledge. If such facts can be established prior to the trial, it may reduce the cost and complexity of the case. In such cases, it may be appropriate to issue interrogatories, but interrogatories are only issued after pleadings have closed.

In many cases, interrogatories are unnecessary because the pleadings and further and better particulars establish the relevant facts in dispute. There can be adverse costs consequences for issuing inappropriate interrogatories and interrogatories must not be used for improper tactical purposes. Interrogatories are most commonly requested in personal injury cases, even though there must be special reasons for interrogatories in such cases and they are difficult to get right. In *Booth v Navarro*,[83] the Supreme Court of the Australian Capital Territory grappled with the appropriateness and restrictions of interrogatories in a personal injury case involving a fall at a friend's house which resulted in brain damage. Both parties disputed some interrogatories and some were set aside and others given leave to be

80 *Folau v Minister for Immigration and Border Protection* (2017) 256 FCR 455, [64].

81 Ibid [91]. At [71]–[73] the Full Federal Court also sets out the notice to admit and discusses the operation of the relevant *Federal Court Rules 2011* (Cth) rr 22.01, 22.02, 22.04.

82 *EMS18 v Minister for Immigration, Citizenship, Migrant Services and Multicultural Affairs* [2020] FCAFC 174, [58].

83 *Booth v Navarro* [2017] ACTSC 353.

redrafted. Associate Justice McWilliam considered rr 631 and 632 of the *Court Procedures Rules 2006* (ACT) and the requirements and purpose of interrogatories, noting:

> [12]. … It need hardly be said that interrogatories and answers should be expressed in language of the most rigorous precision. The requirement is not mere pedantry. The nature and purpose of interrogatories and answers (being the seeking and the supply, respectively, of evidence in writing on oath) call for the strictest adherence to the letter of the words used. There is no place in interrogatories and answers for 'reading between the lines', adopting a liberal construction, or seeking the author's intention rather than the meaning the words bear on their face …
>
> …
>
> [16]. The object of interrogatories is to enable a party to obtain discovery of material facts in order to support or establish proof of that party's case, or to find out the case to be met, or to destroy or damage the opposing case …
>
> …
>
> [19]. The purpose of interrogatories is not to elicit evidence, nor to serve as a means of cross-examination …[84]

Issues can arise where interrogatories are asked of a corporation, because corporations are legal fictions so it must be an individual who answers the actual questions. In *Commonwealth v Helicopter Resources Pty Ltd*, the High Court determined it was not improper for an officer to be subpoenaed to give evidence in a coronial inquest.[85] The Court confirmed that the evidence of a proper officer of a company given in interrogatories remained the evidence of that individual even if the representations are able to be attributed to the employer and binding upon the company.[86]

The majority of proceedings do not involve interrogatories and their utility has been questioned by senior members of the judiciary. The Federal Court case of *Australian Competition and Consumer Commission v Australia and New Zealand Banking Group Ltd*[87] reviewed the law of interrogatories. This case was decided under the old Federal Court Rules, not the *Federal Court Rules 2011* (Cth). The 2011 r 21.01 is similar to the old rule, and requires a party to apply to the court for interrogatories supported by an affidavit. In *Australian Competition and Consumer Commission v Australia and New Zealand Banking Group Ltd*, Greenwood J made an order for interrogatories, some of which were required to be reformulated, despite his overall dissatisfaction with interrogatories. Justice Greenwood made the following statements in relation to the law of interrogatories, including reference to a speech by French CJ of the High Court:

> [9]. On 7 March 2009, his Honour, as Chief Justice of Australia, delivered an address to the annual conference of the Bar Association of Queensland on the topic *The Future of Litigation: Dispute Resolution in Jurassic Park?* In that address, on the topic of interrogatories, the Chief Justice at p 7, point 2, said this:
>
>> *Interrogatories.* The Federal Court Rules required leave to interrogate. Experience with interrogatories over a period of time persuaded me of their

84 Ibid [12], [16], [19].
85 *Commonwealth v Helicopter Resources Pty Ltd* (2020) 377 ALR 191.
86 Ibid [57].
87 *Australian Competition and Consumer Commission v Australia and New Zealand Banking Group Ltd* [2010] FCA 230.

> extremely limited utility, if not total uselessness. Parties had to be reminded that interrogatories were not a form of pre-trial cross-examination. Applicants for leave were urged to agree all facts of which they sought admissions and to do so without resort to interrogatories unless there was a fact on which agreement could not be reached and the Court could be persuaded that it was appropriate to grant leave. Today interrogatories are something of a rarity.
>
> ...
>
> **Preferred practice**
>
> [14]. As a matter of general practice, I am satisfied that no good purpose is served either in a case management sense or as a vehicle for serving the public interest by granting general leave to administer interrogatories. ...
>
> [15]. For all the reasons mentioned by the Chief Justice of Australia in his 2009 address, the practice of first drafting the interrogatories and circulating the proposed interrogatories to the relevant parties and the Court, is to be preferred.
>
> ...
>
> [94]. In principle, an interrogatory ought only to be allowed if the end sought to be achieved by administering the question is reasonably proportionate to the effort required in answering the question.[88]

The above recommendation that interrogatories be reviewed and approved by courts demonstrate that this is an area where courts commonly exert significant control, thereby reducing party autonomy in order to prevent abuse of the processes.[89]

In *Palmer v Magistrates Court of Queensland*,[90] the Court of Appeal of the Supreme Court of Queensland rejected an appeal by Clive Palmer and a related entity following a strike out of Palmer's proceedings against the Magistrates Court, the Commonwealth Department of Public Prosecutions and Australian Securities Investments Commission. In relation to Palmer's allegations that the strike out denied him the opportunity to issue interrogatories which might strengthen his case, the Court noted:

> The fact that the appellants will have no opportunity to seek leave to administer interrogatories — an order which is rarely made in any case — could not justify permitting the appellants' speculative claims to proceed.[91]

12.7 Conclusion

There are numerous ways in which parties to litigation can obtain documents and information pertinent to pursuing the dispute to trial or resolving it prior to trial. Although interparty discovery[92] is important, the means of obtaining documents discussed in this chapter, including information from non-parties, can be just as critical. For this reason, use of non-

88 Ibid [9], [14]–[15], [94].

89 See Chapter 2.3.4.

90 *Palmer v Magistrates Court of Queensland* (2020) 3 QR 546.

91 Ibid [85] (Fraser JA with Morrison JA and Boddice J agreeing). See Chapter 5.5 for further analysis of summary disposition for problem plaintiffs.

92 See Chapter 11.

party discovery, subpoenas, interrogatories, notices to admit and FOI applications are all common in civil litigation. Restrictions and rules apply to each of the methods discussed in this chapter of extracting, locating and clarifying relevant information, and those rules vary somewhat between jurisdictions and between courts within jurisdictions. It is important, therefore, when gathering information for a trial, to consider carefully, with close reference to the relevant rules and practice notes, which means of information gathering is most likely to efficiently and cost effectively extract the required evidence.

Any or all of the above means of obtaining information and documents in preparation for trial may be used in the course of the same litigation. However, courts will carefully consider balancing the key case management obligations of efficiency and due process when determining which processes are appropriate and adverse costs may be awarded particularly where courts determine that a chosen process amounts to an abuse of process. As with all CDR processes, the key themes of CDR guide the appropriateness of the civil procedures discussed in this chapter and create complex balancing issues for the courts, including the appropriate level of court control over such processes, balancing the benefits of information against the intrusion on privacy of requiring such information (particularly from non-parties) and the risk to efficiency from adding potentially time-consuming processes.[93] Therefore, parties (and their lawyers) contemplating the use of the processes discussed in this chapter must carefully consider the scope and purpose of the information they seek, the appropriateness of the processes chosen, and the reasonableness of the costs likely to be incurred in the processes.

93 See Chapter 2.3 regarding the key themes.

13 PROTECTION OF DOCUMENTS: PRIVILEGE AND CONFIDENTIALITY

13.1 Introduction

This chapter considers the protection afforded to documents as part of the litigation process. The documents in question include both the pre-trial documents discussed in both Chapter 11 and Chapter 12 and documents that are produced at trial. It is more difficult to protect the confidentiality of documents produced at trial because most trials are held in open court. Civil dispute resolution (CDR) inevitably involves the provision of information between parties and this can come at a significant cost to party confidentiality. Litigation involves an even greater sacrifice of confidentiality as the key requirement for open justice means that confidential material discussed in open court can become public knowledge through judgments, court transcripts or media reporting of open court hearings.[1] However, even litigation attempts to minimise the invasion of party privacy, and privilege is one of the key protections the law provides to ensure that the need to put material before the court does not create perverse incentives for parties.

Most of this chapter is dedicated to the complicated area of privilege, with a brief discussion about non-privileged confidential documents and the confidentiality applicable to all documents produced pursuant to litigation. Privilege can protect documents from disclosure to other parties and the court during both pre-trial and trial processes. This chapter will focus on pre-trial processes, because pre-trial claims for privilege are often the subject of dispute and many litigators spend a disproportionate percentage of their time considering the application of privilege to documents pre-trial. It is not uncommon for privilege disputes to be appealed as far as the High Court, although the High Court itself has strongly discouraged lengthy appeals on interlocutory matters such as privilege.[2] Privilege also applies to trial itself and the privileges discussed in this chapter also apply to written witness evidence prepared for trial[3] and the trial itself.[4] Accordingly, there will be further references to privilege in the following chapters.

In order to explain the operation of privilege, it is necessary to delve into the law of evidence and the Uniform Evidence Law (UEL).[5] Those states which have not introduced the *UEL* (Queensland, South Australia and Western Australia) are governed by the common law in relation to claims for privilege. These non-UEL states also have their own *Evidence Acts* which will be relevant in subsequent chapters but do not govern the operation of privilege.

1 See Chapter 3.3 for analysis of open justice.
2 See *Expense Reduction Analysis Group Pty Ltd v Armstrong Strategic Management and Marketing Pty Ltd* (2013) 250 CLR 303. This case is discussed in detail below under inadvertent waiver of privilege in Chapter 13.8.3.
3 See Chapter 14.
4 See Chapter 15.
5 See Chapters 14 and 15.

13.2 The rationale for privilege

"Privilege" is a term used to describe the right not to disclose information of a privileged nature. Privilege has been held by the High Court to be a substantive legal right and not merely a rule of evidence in *Attorney-General (NT) v Maurice*.[6] Accordingly, privilege applies regardless of the existence of legal proceedings and applies to any phase of proceedings.[7] As an example, the application of privilege to a Freedom of Information (FOI) application is discussed later in this chapter.

Privilege engages significantly with the key themes and theories of civil procedure, particularly the theme of balancing privacy and openness, and the role of open justice.

13.2.1 Why are some documents privileged?

Privilege attaches to information rather than documents themselves. If a document discloses privileged information, then the document is said to attract privilege and need not be produced to other parties in order to protect that privilege.

Privilege essentially exists for policy reasons. If you consider a particular civil litigation in isolation, the court would be assisted by every relevant document in existence being produced. Therefore, it would seem that requiring full disclosure of all relevant documents would assist the requirements of justice and notice by providing maximum information to assist the decision-making process. However, adopting such a policy would rapidly result in a culture of non-disclosure, particularly among those who least understood the legal process. For example, clients might deliberately withhold important information from their lawyers for fear it may have unknown negative ramifications and be held against them in court. Other types of confidential information would be similarly adversely affected. Journalists would find it difficult to obtain information confidentially, people would be scared to confess sins to their religious leaders, or to tell their doctors or counsellors the events causing them injury or trauma.[8] Lawyers, and other professionals, would be reluctant write down anything clients told them due to its adverse evidentiary potential. Similarly, parties would be unwilling to offer settlement for fear their offers would adversely influence judicial decision-making explaining the rationale for negotiations privilege. Removing privilege would simply result in less informed lawyers and more distressed clients which would not assist the courts. It is important that some information attracts privilege to ensure that parties, lawyers and other professionals can maintain confidentiality, thereby encouraging full disclosure; maximum use of ADR to settle disputes wherever possible; and protection of the public interest.

6 *Attorney-General (NT) v Maurice* (1986) 161 CLR 475, 490 (Deane J).

7 Although, in this regard, it should be noted that there is some difference as to whether the pre-trial privilege is covered by a statutory regime or the common law depending on whether the relevant jurisdiction has enacted the UEL with s 131A, which extends the application of statutory privilege to pre-trial processes.

8 Professionals may be protected from having to disclose this sort of information by various privileges, such as journalist privilege, religious confession privilege, professional confidential relationship privilege, marital privilege, sexual assault counselling privilege, medical privilege, and communication to a counsellor privilege.

In practice, claims for privilege most commonly arise in relation to the forms of document production[9] and in relation to witness evidence.[10] There are the key circumstances where it would be advantageous to the parties and courts to have information, but the possible value of the information would be outweighed by the possible future negative consequences. In determining the extent of privilege, courts must balance the policy objectives of privilege against the value to the courts and parties of obtaining information in order to deliver justice, which is one of the most challenging of the key balancing acts in CDR.[11] This balancing act was recently summarised, in the context of legal professional privilege, by the High Court in *Glencore International AG v Commissioner of Taxation*, as follows:

> It was recognised in *Grant v Downs* that there was another, more general, public interest which legal professional privilege did not promote. That public interest lies in the fair conduct of litigation, which requires that all relevant documentary evidence be available. But the public interest which supports the privilege is paramount to the more general public interest. In the provision of the privilege the law has struck the balance between two competing public interests. Consequently, once the privilege is found to exist, no more is required for effect to be given to it.[12]

13.2.2 Types of privilege

The application of the UEL is discussed in detail in the following section as this legislation applies to most Australian jurisdictions. However, the UEL is based on the common law. Accordingly, the extracts from its provisions below provide a useful outline of the relevant different types of privilege, even for jurisdictions retaining the common law.

The three types of privilege which tend to arise in pre-trial production of documents are: client legal privilege (or its common law equivalent, legal professional privilege), negotiations privilege, and public interest immunity (also described as Crown privilege). There are also privileges against self-incrimination, religious confession privilege, professional confidential relationship privilege, marital privilege, sexual assault counselling privilege, medical privilege, communication to a counsellor privilege and penalty privilege — most of which tend only to arise more commonly in criminal law cases rather than civil litigation, and some of which only apply in a small number of Australian states.[13] This chapter will address the three most common types of privilege for civil litigation: legal privilege, negotiations privilege, and public interest immunity which apply in all states and territories in one format or another.

9 See Chapters 11 and 12.

10 See Chapter 14.

11 See Chapter 2.3.3.

12 *Glencore International AG v Commissioner of Taxation* (2019) 265 CLR 646 is a unanimous seven-judge High Court decision discussed further in Chapter 13.2.3.

13 Most of these privileges are statute-based, such as the statutory discretion to exclude prejudicial evidence which is covered by ss 135–6 of the UEL. However, privilege also continues to be developed through common law, such as penalty privilege in *Fair Work Ombudsman v Hu* [2017] FCA 1081.

13.2.3 Scope of privilege

Privilege has a limited scope due to its policy-based rationale. The scope of privilege was tested in the High Court in *Glencore International AG v Commissioner of Taxation*.[14] Glencore had employed Bermudan law firm Appleby on tax-related legal matters.[15] Appleby had privileged advice documents, known as the Paradise Papers, stolen and leaked to global media including documents of Glencore which were disseminated widely including to the Australian Taxation Office (ATO).[16] Glencore commenced in the High Court in its original jurisdiction seeking an injunction restraining ATO use of the stolen documents.[17] The High Court held that legal professional privilege does not found a cause of action.[18] The privilege is only an immunity from the exercise of powers that would otherwise compel disclosure. It does not give rise to an actionable legal right or need for further relief beyond ensuring that privileged documents need not be produced. Although there was no question the stolen documents were privileged and, therefore, exempt from production by court process or statutory compulsion, there was no juridical basis upon which Court could restrain use of the documents.[19]

The documents were in the public domain (due to the theft) and ATO did not behave wrongly in any way in obtaining them.[20] In rejecting Glencore's request for injunction, the High Court noted that granting the injunction would require the ATO to assess the Australian Glencore entities for income tax "on a basis which may be known to bear no real relationship to the true facts".[21]

13.3 Jurisdictional framework

The law applying to privilege is complex. As mentioned above, some states and territories have enacted the Uniform Evidence Law (UEL) and others have not. All Australian jurisdictions have an *Evidence Act* containing provisions which potentially affect the law of privilege in that state. The states which have adopted the UEL have their law of privilege significantly governed by that legislation. The states which have not enacted the UEL have privilege predominantly governed by common law. There are also references to privilege in the relevant court rules for most jurisdictions. The interaction of the common law and evidence legislation between different states and territories will be considered in more detail in the next section of this chapter.

13.3.1 Federal jurisdiction

In 1995, the Commonwealth Government introduced the *Evidence Act 1995* (Cth) applicable in all federal courts (including the High Court) and the Australian Capital Territory. The *Evidence Act 1995* (Cth) codified much of the law of privilege. It has been amended several times, including

14 *Glencore International AG v Commissioner of Taxation* (2019) 265 CLR 646.
15 Bermuda is well known as a tax haven.
16 *Glencore International AG v Commissioner of Taxation* (2019) 265 CLR 646, [2].
17 See Chapter 8.7 and Chapter 9.2 for information on interlocutory applications and preliminary injunctions.
18 *Glencore International AG v Commissioner of Taxation* (2019) 265 CLR 646, [12].
19 Ibid [34], [37].
20 Ibid [7].
21 Ibid [33].

by the *Evidence Amendment Act 2008* (Cth) which amended s 117 and s 118 (concerning client legal privilege), replaced s 122 (concerning privilege waiver) with a new version, replaced s 128 with a new version, and introduced s 128A (the last two both concerning self-incrimination privilege).[22] There are also rules relating to privilege in the relevant court rules, such as r 20.19 of the *Federal Court Rules 2011* (Cth) which prevents a claim for privilege solely on the basis that a document is only relevant and beneficial to the party required to discover it.

13.3.2 Australian Capital Territory

Privilege in the Australian Capital Territory is governed by the *Evidence Act 2011* (ACT), which is part of the UEL. The 2011 Act is, therefore, uniform with the Commonwealth, New South Wales, Victorian and Tasmanian legislation but, as with the other states, contains variations from the Commonwealth *Evidence Act 1995*. The ACT *Evidence Act 2011* includes s 131A (discussed below in relation to New South Wales) that extends privilege to pre-trial procedures and represents its most significant variance from the *Evidence Act 1995* (Cth) in relation to privilege.

13.3.3 New South Wales

Privilege in New South Wales is essentially governed by the *Evidence Act 1995* (NSW) which is part of the UEL. In 2009, New South Wales introduced s 131A of the *Evidence Act 1995*, which applied the *Evidence Act 1995* to pre-trial procedures as well as trial procedures for privileges covered by div 1 (Client Legal Privilege), div 1A (Professional Confidential Relationship Privilege) and div 3 (Public Interest Immunity).

Section 131A has since been adopted in other states and territories with UEL (but not the federal legislation, where s 131A is limited to s 126K matters involving journalist privilege relating to informants). There is also reference to privilege in the *Uniform Civil Procedure Rules 2005* (NSW), in which the Dictionary of the *Uniform Civil and Procedure Rules 2005* (NSW) defines a "privileged document" as "a document that contains privileged information" and a "privileged information" largely in terms of pt 3.10 of the *Evidence Act 1995* (NSW).[23] The operation of s 131A has been confirmed to apply to all pre-trial cases, including subpoenas, pre-trial discovery, non-party discovery, interrogatories and notices to produce.[24]

The complexity of claiming pre-trial privilege is demonstrated in *Griffiths v German*, which concerned the operation of r 1.9 of the *Uniform Civil Procedure Rules 2005* (NSW) and s 131A of the *Evidence Act* in the context of whether a solicitor producing documents under subpoena could claim privilege and not produce documents to the court at all.[25] In *Griffiths v German*, the Supreme Court of New South Wales held in obiter dicta: "Where UCPR r 1.9 applies, a party who receives a subpoena and claims privilege over documents covered by the subpoena is entitled to refuse to produce the documents at all, and the Court

22 The complexity of of s 128A is evident from the High Court's decision in *Deputy Commissioner of Taxation v Shi* [2021] HCA 22 where Mr Shi was ordered to provide a s 128A privilege affidavit to the Deputy Commissioner of Taxation in the context of a worldwide freezing order and accompanying disclosure orders aimed at enforcing payment of $42,297,437.65 in unpaid taxes.

23 Part 3.10 of the UEL is discussed in Chapter 13.4.1, Chapter 13.5.2, Chapter 13.6.1 and Chapter 13.7.1.

24 *Singtel Optus Pty Ltd v Weston* (2011) 81 NSWLR 526.

25 *Griffiths v German* [2017] NSWSC 1392.

is not entitled to require production unless and until it has ruled on any claim for privilege".[26] However, in that case, because the producer under the subpoena was the solicitor and the privilege belonged to the client, r 1.9 was held not to apply.

13.3.4 Northern Territory

Effective from 1 January 2013, the Northern Territory adopted the UEL by way of the *Evidence (National Uniform Legislation) Act 2011* (NT). The current version of this Act commenced on 21 April 2018. The *Evidence (National Uniform Legislation) Act 2011* (NT) most closely mirrors the Commonwealth, New South Wales and Victorian UEL.[27] The Act contains s 131A, similar to that of New South Wales, Victoria, Tasmania and the ACT, which applies statute-based privilege to pre-trial procedures.

13.3.5 Queensland

Queensland has not adopted the UEL. It retains the *Evidence Act 1977* (Qld) and the common law for governing privilege.

13.3.6 South Australia

South Australia has not adopted the UEL and retains the *Evidence Act 1929* (SA) which does not codify privilege although it does contain a small number of statutory privileges. Privilege is essentially governed by the common law.

13.3.7 Tasmania

In 2001, Tasmania introduced the *Evidence Act 2001* (Tas) which is essentially uniform with the federal, New South Wales and, since 2008, Victorian *Evidence Acts*. Tasmania's s 131A is similar to that of New South Wales, Victorian, Australian Capital Territory and Northern Territory and, accordingly, the *Evidence Act 2001* (Tas) governs the operation of most privileges pre-trial as well as during trial consistent with the UEL.

13.3.8 Victoria

In 2008, Victoria joined New South Wales, Tasmania, the Australian Capital Territory and the federal jurisdictions in introducing UEL in the form of the *Evidence Act 2008* (Vic). Victoria's s 131A is similar to that of New South Wales, the Australian Capital Territory, the Northern Territory and Tasmania, such that most privileges are governed by the *Evidence Act 2008* (Vic) pre-trial as well as during trial.

13.3.9 Western Australia

Western Australia has not adopted the UEL and maintains the *Evidence Act 1906* (WA). Privilege is, therefore, mostly governed by the common law.

26 Ibid [16].
27 *Evidence (National Uniform Legislation) Act 2011* (NT) s 2A.

13.4 Legal framework

Although the legal framework for privilege is complex, each of the privileges common to civil litigation is substantially similar across the common law and legislative provisions. This means the basic legal concepts of privilege are essentially uniform, despite the complexity regarding which provisions apply in which jurisdictions.

As set out above, the federal, Australian Capital Territory, New South Wales, Tasmanian, Victorian and Northern Territory courts are all governed by the UEL. Queensland, South Australia and Western Australia have not enacted the UEL. To further complicate matters, those states and territories which have enacted the UEL have all amended their legislation such that it is no longer entirely uniform as regards privilege.

Where the UEL applies, ch 3 pt 3.10 governs privilege, at least as regards trial procedures (but not always pre-trial procedures). To a large extent, jurisdictions not governed by the UEL follow the common law regarding privilege.

Although the operation of the UEL is complicated, the Acts essentially codify the common law and, accordingly, the codified law of privilege (where applicable) is not radically different to the common law.

13.4.1 Uniform Evidence Law

Lawyers, governments and law reform bodies have made considerable efforts over the past decade to introduce uniform laws of evidence across Australia, with only partial success.[28] In 1995, the Commonwealth and New South Wales both introduced a new *Evidence Act 1995* (Cth) and *Evidence Act 1995* (NSW) which were essentially uniform. The *Commonwealth Act* applied in the Australian Capital Territory as well as in federal proceedings. Tasmania and Victoria followed with essentially uniform legislation, the *Evidence Act 2001* (Tas) and the *Evidence Act 2008* (Vic), with most provisions commencing effect on 1 January 2010. The Australian Capital Territory then introduced its own *Evidence Act* in 2011, followed by the Northern Territory's *Evidence (National Uniform Legislation) Act* effective from 1 January 2013.

Queensland, South Australia, and Western Australia have not introduced the Uniform Evidence Law (UEL) and remain governed by common law in relation to privilege.[29]

13.4.2 Common law or Uniform Evidence Law: which applies?

Originally, the provisions in the UEL governing privilege (ch 3 pt 3.10 of the UEL) applied only to pre-trial proceedings. Now all jurisdictions have also enacted s 131A, which extends

28 There are different levels of uniformity within civil procedure law: the *Uniform Civil Procedure Rules*, which exist in some Australian states (eg NSW) are only uniform throughout that state; whereas the UEL is uniform across all the states which have adopted it and the Commonwealth. The rules of evidence, including privilege, are also already essentially uniform throughout different courts in each state and territory as they are situated in the relevant evidence legislation or common law, rather than court-based rules which might vary within a state's court hierarchy.

29 The legislative regime for evidence law discussed in this chapter is also relevant to Chapters 14 and 15 concerning witness evidence and trial procedures.

the operation of the UEL to certain pre-trial procedures. Unfortunately, the content of s 131A is not uniform between states, resulting in significant variation as to which pre-trial procedures each *Evidence Act* applies.

In the federal jurisdiction, the common law continues to govern privilege for most pre-trial matters. In the federal *Evidence Act 1995* (Cth), the application of s 131A is limited (essentially, it applies in relation to s 126K concerning journalist privilege relating to the identity of an informant). In New South Wales, Tasmania, Victoria, the Australian Capital Territory and the Northern Territory, s 131A of the *Evidence Act* governs privilege for most pre-trial procedures.

The application of the common law and/or the UEL to the three key privileges discussed in this chapter for each Australian jurisdiction is listed in Table 13.1.

Table 13.1 Privilege source of law chart (operation of *Evidence Act* including s 131A)

State or Territory	Applicable law	
	Pre-trial	Trial
Commonwealth (Federal)	Common Law	*Evidence Act*
Australian Capital Territory	*Evidence Act*	*Evidence Act*
Northern Territory	*Evidence Act*	*Evidence Act*
New South Wales	*Evidence Act*	*Evidence Act*
Queensland	Common Law	Common Law
South Australia	Common Law	Common Law
Tasmania	Evidence Act	Evidence Act
Victoria	Evidence Act	Evidence Act
Western Australia	Common Law	Common Law

Table 13.1 applies to legal privilege (legal professional privilege in common law and client legal privilege in the UEL Div 1); negotiations (settlement) privilege (UEL Div 3); and public interest immunity (UEL Div 3).

Table 13.1 considers only the three types of privilege most common to civil litigation. As such, it belies the complex non-conformity of the law of privilege for several reasons.

First, there are some provisions in the *Evidence Acts* of non-UEL states which affect privilege; for example, s 32A of the *Evidence Act 1906* (WA) derogates from common law privilege in relation to expert evidence. This means it cannot be said that only common law applies in relation to privilege in states which have not enacted the UEL.

Second, amongst the other privileges, the application of the uniform evidence legislation is more complex. For example, div 1A of the *Evidence Act* (concerning professional confidential relationship privilege in s 126A-F) applies to pre-trial processes in the Australian Capital Territory and Federal Courts, in New South Wales and in Tasmania pursuant to s 131A, but not in Victoria or the Northern Territory where div 1A does not exist. Tasmania also has added protections for medical communications (s 127A *Evidence Act 2001* (Tas)) and communications to counsellors (s 127B *Evidence Act 2001* (Tas)), both of which apply to trial and pre-trial procedures.

Third, there are special statutory privileges which apply in some of the UEL states, but not all, and also apply in some of the non-UEL states. For example, counsellor communications in cases involving sexual assault may be privileged in New South Wales through pt 3.10 div 1B ss 126G-I of the *Evidence Act 1995* (NSW); in Tasmania through ss 127A or 127B (in div 2 pt 3.10 of the *Evidence Act 2001* (Tas); and in the non-UEL state of South Australia (*Evidence Act 1929* (SA) s 67F). The application of most of these provisions rarely arises in civil law cases.

The original legislation applied only to trial procedures. Hence, in the case of *Esso Australia Resources v Commissioner of Taxation*,[30] extracted below, the High Court ruled on the operation of legal professional privilege rather than client legal privilege even though the case was a Federal Court case to which the uniform *Evidence Act 1995* (Cth) applied. This was because the dispute arose in relation to discovery of document which was a pre-trial procedure to which the *Evidence Act 1995* (Cth) did not apply. The insertion of s 131A of the *Evidence Act* in New South Wales, Victoria, Tasmania, Australian Capital Territory and Northern Territory was to overcome this difficulty.

13.5 Legal privilege

Arguably, the most important privilege in civil litigation is the privilege which protects many of the documents created by lawyers for their clients. Parties are not required to disclose legal advice or advice given in anticipation of litigation and need not produce documents which would disclose communications made for that dominant purpose. This privilege exists to ensure that parties feel free to disclose all relevant facts to their lawyers, which assists in the administration of justice.

At common law, this is called legal professional privilege (LPP). In the UEL, it is called client legal privilege (CLP). The differences between CLP and LPP have been the subject of High Court litigation.

There are two types of CLP/LPP:

1. **Legal advice:** documents created for the dominant purpose of providing legal advice
2. **Litigation privilege:** documents created for the dominant purpose of advising relation to litigation or anticipated litigation.

13.5.1 The basis for legal privilege

A useful summary of the policy basis for legal professional privilege is extracted in *Osland v Secretary, Department of Justice*.[31] The majority of the High Court approved the earlier High Court judgments of *Grant v Downs*[32] and *Baker v Campbell*[33] as follows:

> First it is necessary to restate the purpose of the confidentiality which the privilege preserves. In *Grant v Downs*, Stephen, Mason and Murphy JJ said:

30 *Esso Australia Resources Ltd v Commissioner of Taxation* (1999) 201 CLR 49.

31 *Osland v Secretary, Department of Justice* (2008) 234 CLR 275, discussed and extracted further in the privilege waiver section of this chapter.

32 *Grant v Downs* (1976) 135 CLR 674.

33 *Baker v Campbell* (1983) 153 CLR 52.

> The rationale of this head of privilege, according to traditional doctrine, is that it promotes the public interest because it assists and enhances the administration of justice by facilitating the representation of clients by legal advisers, the law being a complex and complicated discipline. This it does by keeping secret their communications, thereby inducing the client to retain the solicitor and seek his advice, and encouraging the client to make a full and frank disclosure of the relevant circumstances to the solicitor.[34]

This incentive for the client to fully and frankly disclose to its lawyer which requires protection of documents from disclosure in court must then be balanced against the need to conduct litigation fairly with the maximum possible information, as noted by the High Court in *Glencore v Commissioner of Taxation*.[35] The development of the law of privilege must be done carefully to best balance these competing interests of privacy and openness.[36]

13.5.2 The statutory law

Sections 118 and 119 of the UEL (contained pt 3.10, div 1) set out the basic privileges contained within CLP. These provisions essentially mirror the common law (LPP). Section 118 sets out legal advice privilege, while s 119 covers litigation privilege.[37] Both s 118 and s 119 contain a "dominant purpose" test and both limit the privilege provided to "confidential communications". It is common for documents to fall within s 118 and s 119 simultaneously, such as legal advice on litigation prospects, and for parties to claim that both s 118 and s 119 apply to the same document.[38] There are also many documents which fall solely within s 118, such as legal advice provided to a client in relation to a transaction such as the acquisition or sale of land or a business.[39] It is also possible for documents to fall solely within s 119, such as a communication between an expert witness and a lawyer in relation to the preparation of expert witness evidence.[40]

13.5.3 The dominant purpose test for legal privilege

Both CLP and LPP require that the privileged purpose must be the dominant purpose of a document for privilege to apply. In relation to common law LPP, the "dominant purpose" test was introduced by the High Court in the case of *Esso Australia Resources Ltd v Commissioner of Taxation* ('*Esso*'),[41] which reversed the common law "sole purpose" test which applied between 1976 and 1999 following the earlier High Court decision of *Grant v Downs*.[42] *Esso* also discussed why LPP/CLP existed and the policy reasons behind it.

34 *Osland v Secretary, Department of Justice* (2008) 234 CLR 275 [35], approved [50].
35 *Glencore International AG v Commissioner of Taxation* (2019) 265 CLR 646, [29].
36 See Chapter 2.3.3.
37 UEL; applicable in Commonwealth, ACT, Tasmania, New South Wales, Victoria, Northern Territory.
38 *Re Whitebox Trading Pty Ltd* [2017] FCA 324 provides a useful analysis of ss 118 and 119 in the context of specific documents which the Federal Court held were not privileged under either provision.
39 *Molenaar v Andonovski* [2020] NSWSC 1258 (although s 119 was also raised in relation to some documents in dispute in this case).
40 *Desane Properties Pty Ltd v New South Wales* [2018] NSWSC 173, [212].
41 *Esso Australia Resources Ltd v Commissioner of Taxation* (1999) 201 CLR 49. Cases decided before 1999 refer to the "incorrect purpose test".
42 *Grant v Downs* (1976) 135 CLR 674.

In *Esso*, the majority decision of Gleeson CJ, Gaudron and Gummow JJ chose the dominant purpose test after discussing the difficult balancing act between the competing public interests of privacy and openness:

> [2]. The test in the *Evidence Act 1995* is whether the communication was made, or the document was prepared, for the dominant purpose of the lawyer providing legal advice or legal services. The dominant purpose test accords with the common law test now adopted in England, New Zealand, Ireland, and most Canadian Provinces.
>
> ...
>
> [35]. Legal professional privilege (or client legal privilege) protects the confidentiality of certain communications made in connection with giving or obtaining legal advice or the provision of legal services, including representation in proceedings in a court. In the ordinary course of events, citizens engage in many confidential communications, including communications with professional advisers, which are not protected from compulsory disclosure. The rationale of the privilege has been explained in a number of cases, including *Baker v Campbell*, and *Grant v Downs* itself. The privilege exists to serve the public interest in the administration of justice by encouraging full and frank disclosure by clients to their lawyers. In *Waterford v The Commonwealth*, Mason and Wilson JJ explained that legal professional privilege is itself the product of a balancing exercise between competing public interests and that, given the application of the privilege, no further balancing exercise is required. As Deane J expressed it in *Baker v Campbell*, a person should be entitled to seek and obtain legal advice in the conduct of his or her affairs, and legal assistance in and for the purposes of the conduct of actual or anticipated litigation, without the apprehension of being prejudiced by subsequent disclosure of the communication. The obvious tension between this policy and the desirability, in the interests of justice, of obtaining the fullest possible access to the facts relevant to the issues in a case lies at the heart of the problem of the scope of the privilege. Where the privilege applies, it inhibits or prevents access to potentially relevant information. The party denied access might be an opposing litigant, a prosecutor, an accused in a criminal trial, or an investigating authority. For the law, in the interests of the administration of justice, to deny access to relevant information, involves a balancing of competing considerations. This Court is now asked to reconsider the balance that was struck in *Grant v Downs*.
>
> ...
>
> [61] ... The dominant purpose test should be preferred. It strikes a just balance, it suffices to rule out claims of the kind considered in Grant v Downs and Waugh, and it brings the common law of Australia into conformity with other common law jurisdictions.[43]

Esso led to a series of cases considering the meaning of "dominant" and the evidentiary burden for proving that dominant purpose. *Ensham Resources Pty Ltd v AIOI Insurance Co Ltd* concerned loss adjuster reports prepared by insurers.[44] The Court considered whether lawyers requiring a new retainer through the lawyers increase the likelihood of the report being in anticipation of litigation had the desired effect and rendered the report privileged. In *Ensham Resources Pty Ltd v AIOI Insurance Co Ltd*, the full Federal Court upheld the

43 *Esso Australia Resources Ltd v Commissioner of Taxation* (1999) 201 CLR 49, [2], [35], [61].

44 *Ensham Resources Pty Ltd v AIOI Insurance Co Ltd* (2012) 209 FCR 1.

primary judge's decision that it did.[45] Lander and Jagot JJ held that "purpose may not be divined solely by reference to the person who sought the creation of the document".[46]

In *Victoria v Tabcorp Holdings Ltd*, the Victorian Supreme Court of Appeal denied leave to appeal a finding that the State of Victoria had not given sufficient evidence to establish the dominant privileged purpose of 105 documents.[47] Hansen JA (with Ashley JA agreeing) summarises the tests from earlier cases on dominant purpose before upholding the primary judge's finding "that the State had failed to establish that the dominant purpose of the documents was the provision of legal advice":[48]

> [20]. His Honour noted that it was necessary that the State identify and prove that the 'dominant purpose' which led to the making of a confidential communication was the provision of legal advice by the lawyer to a client, 'dominant purpose' referring to the 'ruling, prevailing, or most influential purpose'. If there was more than one purpose, and they were of equal weight, no privilege inhered in the communication. The dominant purpose was to be determined objectively, having regard to the evidence, the whole of the documents and the parties submissions. Further, the support for the claim should be 'focussed and specific', verbal formulae and conclusory assertions of purpose not being sufficient. And, in *Bailey v Director-General, Department of Land and Water Conservation*, the New South Wales Court of Appeal held that particularly where the State, or agencies of the State are involved, 'every effort should be made to ensure that evidence in support of a claim of privilege is in all respects adequate and compelling'.[49]

13.5.4 Legal privilege for documents involving third parties

Further complexity often arises in relation to claiming legal privilege (both CLP and LPP) when communications involve people other than lawyers and their clients. The courts and legislators have struggled with documents between lawyers and expert witnesses, documents involving accountants (especially those providing advice regarding taxation law), documents created by (or prepared for) in-house counsel (lawyers employed by companies), and the circulation of legal advice within an organisation and by an organisation to third parties such as accountants or financiers.

There is now significant authority that a range of third-party documents can attract privilege where their purpose complies with the requirements of legal privilege (whether client legal privilege or legal professional privilege). However, third parties are not equivalent to lawyers or clients when it comes to attracting privilege.

In *New South Wales v Betfair Pty Ltd*,[50] the New South Wales Court of Appeal (Kenny, Stone and Middleton JJ) held that email communications between Racing NSW and Harness Racing NSW and the NSW Office of Liquor, Gaming and Racing (OLGR), as part of a working

45 Lander and Jagot JJ refused leave to appeal and Buchanan J granted leave but agreed with the primary judge that the report was in anticipation of litigation. Law firm King & Wood Mallesons were genuinely concerned about potential litigation, and this was basis for seeking to categorise the report as anticipated litigation privilege.

46 *Ensham Resources Pty Ltd v AIOI Insurance Co Ltd* (2012) 209 FCR 1, [77].

47 *Victoria v Tabcorp Holdings Ltd* [2013] VSCA 180.

48 Ibid [44].

49 Ibid [20].

50 *New South Wales v Betfair Pty Ltd* (2009) 180 FCR 543.

group to develop legislative drafting instructions for Parliamentary Counsel, were the subject of legal professional privilege. The State of New South Wales intervened in the proceeding, claiming legal professional privilege over documents that Racing NSW and Harness Racing NSW had discovered. Their Honours relied on and clarified the operation of *Pratt Holdings Pty Ltd v Commissioner of Taxation*, finding:

> 40 The distinction that Betfair urged us to make is an entirely artificial one. In our view, the case for privilege attaching to the communications at issue is at least as strong as, perhaps stronger than, in Pratt Holdings. … In the present case, emailed communications created a virtual meeting room in which OLGR and the Working Group were present. For the purposes of legal professional privilege, there can be no sensible distinction between emailed communications emanating from OLGR and sent to the members of the Working Group and emailed communications from Working Group members to OLGR. The rationale for legal professional privilege as outlined in Pratt Holdings would not support such an artificial distinction. Provided a communication is made with the dominant purpose of the client seeking or obtaining legal advice, we see no reason why privilege should not protect communications between the client and third parties whose knowledge is desirable or necessary for the client to obtain the legal advice the client desires, as in this case. Accordingly, we rejected Betfair's submissions as to the inapplicability of Pratt Holdings.[51]

In the Federal Court case of *Granitgard Pty Ltd v Termicide Pest Control Pty Ltd (No 2)*,[52] Logan J considered a claim for privilege by one party over documents produced under subpoena by expert witnesses to the case. Justice Logan, with reference to the Queensland decision of Pincus J in *Interchase Corporation Ltd (in liq) v Grosvenor Hill (Qld) Pty Ltd (No 1)*,[53] concluded that there was no blanket privilege for subpoenaed expert witness documents, that documents created by experts to assist in making opinions are generally not privileged, and that the party seeking privilege had to make out its legal privilege claim in relation each document.[54]

13.6 Without prejudice privilege: privilege for settlement negotiations

Parties are not required to disclose to the court, without prior agreement, information disclosing settlement negotiations. This ensures offers and admissions made in pre-trial negotiations do not influence the court's view of any party's prospects, because this possibility would negatively affect the likelihood of open negotiation and reduce prospects of settlement. Negotiation privilege is an area of litigation which interacts closely with ADR.[55] The main purpose of settlement negotiation is to resolve disputes without the need for a full trial. However, the law of privilege in relation to negotiations is designed to ensure

51 *Pratt Holdings Pty Ltd v Commissioner of Taxation* (2004) 136 FCR 357, [40] (see also [267].
52 *Granitgard Pty Ltd v Termicide Pest Control Pty Ltd (No 2)* [2008] FCA 1451.
53 *Interchase Corporation Ltd (in liq) v Grosvenor Hill (Qld) Pty Ltd (No 1)* (1999) 1 Qd R 141.
54 *Granitgard Pty Ltd v Termicide Pest Control Pty Ltd (No 2)* [2008] FCA 1451, [15], [16]. [21], [27], [28].
55 See Chapter 5.

that parties are not discouraged from negotiating by their fears of a court being adversely affected by the negotiation if it is not successful.

The privilege is variously described as "negotiations privilege", "settlement privilege", "settlement negotiations privilege" and "without prejudice privilege". The privilege does not apply to negotiations in relation to the formation of a contract but only to negotiations in relation to settlement of a dispute. Once the substantive issues are determined, parties may disclose the terms of settlement negotiations to assist the court in making a fair order as to costs. Settlement negotiations and offers to settle are usually stated to be "without prejudice except as to costs". This phrase denotes an intention that the materials be unable to influence a court except on the matter of costs.[56]

13.6.1 Uniform Evidence Law: settlement negotiations

The essence of negotiations privilege is set out in s 131(1) (pt 3.10 div 3) of the UEL.[57] There is then a lengthy list of exceptions in s 131(2) of the UEL including, most significantly, disclosure with consent (ss 131(2)(a)-(d)), existing evidence would be misleading without the settlement negotiation evidence (s 131(2)(g)), the evidence is relevant to determining liability for costs (s 131(2)(h)), and the communication was made in furtherance of fraud or abuse of power (ss 131(2)(j) and (k) respectively). The most commonly applied exception to settlement negotiation privilege is s 131(2)(h) which applies whenever a party asks the court to take into consideration a rejected settlement offer when determining costs after a court hearing.[58]

There are further provisions (ss 131(3)–(6)) which explain certain of the exclusions in more detail.

13.6.2 The principles of negotiations privilege

Negotiations privilege presents similar challenges to the courts in the key theme of balancing privacy and openness as legal professional privilege (or client legal privilege).[59] One area where courts struggle involves cases where there are multiple disputes and where parties seek to use documentation from negotiations held in one dispute to assist with proving their case in a related dispute. In such cases, the public interest of protecting the privilege in the negotiations in order to encourage the parties to settle is, arguably, reduced as the material is being used for a different dispute. However, it could also be argued that the potential for confidential negotiations material to be disclosed in relation to any related dispute provides a similar disincentive to negotiate freely that is worthy of protection through privilege.

In the Full Court of the Supreme Court of South Australia case of *Yokogawa Australia Pty Ltd v Alstom Power Ltd*,[60] Duggan J (with Sulan and Kourakis JJ agreeing) determined that the primary judge had been correct in upholding Alstom's claim for without prejudice privilege in relation to documents prepared in the course of related negotiations, and that without

56 See Chapter 6.8 for a discussion on the impact of negotiations on costs.
57 UEL; applicable in Commonwealth, Australian Capital Territory, Tasmania, New South Wales, Victoria and Northern Territory.
58 See Chapter 6.8 for analysis of the effect of settlement offers on costs.
59 See Chapter 2.3.3 for analysis of this key theme.
60 *Yokogawa Australia Pty Ltd v Alstrom Power Ltd* (2009) 262 ALR 738.

prejudice privilege applies irrespective of whether settlement was reached and had not been waived in this case. In their judgment, the Full Court relied on the decision of Gleeson CJ (then Chief Justice of the Supreme Court of New South Wales) in the case of *Hong Kong Bank of Australia Ltd v Murphy*[61] and on the decision of the Queensland Court of Appeal in *Village/Nine Network Restaurants & Bars Pty Ltd v Mercantile Mutual Custodians Pty Ltd.*[62] This was based solely on the common law, as South Australia has not enacted the UEL.

> [70]. The rationale of 'without prejudice' privilege was stated by Oliver LJ in *Cutts v Head* in a passage cited by Gleeson CJ in *Hong Kong Bank of Australia Ltd v Murphy*:
>
>> That the rule rests, at least in part, upon public policy is clear from many authorities, and the convenient starting point of the inquiry is the nature of the underlying policy. It is that parties should be encouraged so far as possible to settle their disputes without resort to litigation and should not be discouraged by the knowledge that anything that is said in the course of such negotiations (and that includes, of course, as much the failure to reply to an offer as an actual reply) may be used to their prejudice in the course of the proceedings. They should … be encouraged fully and frankly to put their cards on the table … The public policy justification, in truth, essentially rests on the desirability of preventing statements or offers made in the course of negotiations for settlement being brought before the court of trial as admissions on the question of liability.
>
> …
>
> [83]. It is unnecessary to decide in the present case whether the privilege is wide enough to prevent disclosure to all third parties except in cases of fraud or other recognised exceptions. However, it is my view that the privilege should apply in a case such as the present where the litigation has a connection with the same subject matter as the negotiations.
>
> [84]. In such a case the result should not turn on the question whether all concerned are joined in the same action. The rationale for without prejudice privilege which is relied upon in authorities such as *Rush & Tompkins*, is equally applicable in cases where the negotiations and the litigation arise out of the same subject matter and the negotiations and settlement (if achieved) are of potential relevance to subsequent litigation between one of the parties to the negotiation and a party involved in the litigation.[63]

In contrast to the *Yokogawa Australia Pty Ltd v Alstrom Power Ltd* decision above, in the Federal Court case of *Verge v Devere Holdings Pty Ltd,*[64] McKerracher J found without prejudice privilege did not apply to negotiation communications from a previous dispute. In *Verge v Devere Holdings Pty Ltd,* McKerracher J considered whether privilege applied to settlement negotiations in different but related proceedings. Justice McKerracher found that

61 *Hong Kong Bank of Australia Ltd v Murphy* (1992) 28 NSWLR 512.

62 *Village/Nine Network Restaurants & Bars Pty Ltd v Mercantile Mutual Custodians Pty Ltd* [2001] 1 Qd R 276.

63 *Yokogawa Australia Pty Ltd v Alstom Power Ltd* (2009) 262 ALR 738, [70], [78], [83], [84]. This case has also been cited in numerous UEL jurisdiction cases. See, eg, *Verde Terra Pty Ltd v Central Coast Council (No 8)* NSWLECV 148, [80]; *Australian Competition and Consumer Commission v NSW Ports Operations Hold Co Pty Ltd* [2020] FCA 1232, [54].

64 *Verge v Devere Holdings Pty Ltd* (2009) 258 ALR 464.

the subject matter and the parties to the current litigation were different to the documents over which privilege was sought. Furthermore, the party seeking to assert privilege had relied on the settlement negotiations in another matter in its defence, which made the negotiations an issue in the proceedings inconsistent with the maintenance of privilege. *Verge v Devere Holdings Pty Ltd* concerned the pre-trial process of discovery in the Federal Court and, accordingly, the common law applied. The judge noted that s 131 of the *Evidence Act 1995* (Cth) would have application should any of the discovered documents be sought to be tendered in evidence at trial.[65]

Similarly, in the New South Wales Supreme Court Case of *Dowling v Ultraceuticals Pty Ltd*, the plaintiff, Dowling, was unsuccessful in claiming negotiations privilege in relation to documents the defendant, Ultraceuticals, had subpoenaed from a non-party, Star, in relation to a previous dispute between Star and Dowling.[66] In *Dowling v Ultraceuticals Pty Ltd,* the parties agreed that s 131 of the *Evidence Act 1995* (NSW) did not apply, despite New South Wales being a UEL jurisdiction, because the person raising the privilege, Dowling, was not the recipient of the subpoena leading to production of the communications in relation to which privilege was being claimed.[67] In *Dowling v Ultraceuticals Pty Ltd,* Hammerschlag J confirmed that the onus of proving privilege was on the party claiming it and reviewed the documents himself to assist in his decision making.[68] The Court found that "privilege extends to cover disclosure to third parties in a subsequent dispute provided there is sufficient connection between the subject matter of the original dispute and the later one" but that the necessary connection had not been consistently articulated in the case law.[69] In this case, the claim for privilege failed as the only real connection between the disputes was that "things done and said to settle the first dispute falsifies things later done and said in a different context by the party resisting disclosure".[70]

13.6.3 Exceptions to the exclusion for negotiation privilege

Understandably, there are circumstances where it is not appropriate to afford people protection for their negotiations. The most obvious circumstance where privilege should not apply being where the parties all consent to the negotiations being disclosed to the court (*Evidence Act 1995* (Cth) s 131(2)(a)). The other very common exception to the exclusion is where there is a dispute as to costs. Almost all negotiation correspondence is described as being "without prejudice except as to costs". This is precisely so that costs information can be disclosed to the court for the purposes of determining whether the offers made by parties should influence the courts' decision.[71]

The other exclusions to the costs exception arise less commonly but are important and demonstrate the balancing act involved between disclosure and confidentiality inherent in most privilege questions. In the Family Court case of *Kelly v Lomax*, the wife sought to admit evidence of secretly recorded conversation with the husband about the ownership

65 Ibid [44]–[51] (McKerracher J).
66 *Dowling v Ultraceuticals Pty Ltd* (2016) 93 NSWLR 155. See Chapter 12.4 for analysis of subpoenas.
67 *Dowling v Ultraceuticals Pty Ltd* (2016) 93 NSWLR 155, [4]. [4].
68 Ibid [20], [21].
69 Ibid [28], [34].
70 Ibid [44], [45].
71 See Chapter 6.8.

or control of corporations and professional indemnity insurance.[72] The husband argued the disclosure breached the *Evidence Act 1995* (Cth) s 131 negotiations privilege. Justice Tree held the communications were in the course of settlement under s 131, but that the s 131(2)(j) exception applied because purpose of proposed settlement was fraudulent and the communications were, therefore, not privileged. *Kelly v Lomax* required the Court to consider s 131(2)(g) (misleading evidence), s 131(2)(i) (rights directly affected by communication) and s 131(2)(j) (communication in furtherance of fraud). Justice Tree held that ss 131(2)(g) and (i) failed, but s 131(2)(j) succeeded because the settlement negotiations, which were secretly taped by the wife and sought to be put into evidence, included discussions of company structure which attempted to defraud the wife's creditors (the litigation funder and counsel) of their legal fees and were thus not protected by settlement privilege:

> Here, the expressly stated purpose for the proposed structure of the settlement was to prejudice the interests of the applicant's creditors by making the prospects of them being able to recover their debts more difficult, if not impossible. There seems no logical distinction between the prejudice to the bank in *Barclays Bank v Eustice* and the prejudice proposed to creditors here. I therefore conclude that the proposed settlement, or more precisely the proposed consent orders of a 90/10 division in favour of the respondent, would have comprised fraud as that term is used in section 131(2)(j).[73]

13.7 Public interest immunity

Information should not be disclosed where the public interest in preserving the confidentiality or secrecy of that information outweighs the litigation benefit of its disclosure. Public interest immunity is not technically privilege but constitutes a similar reason for resisting disclosure and appears within the privilege division (ch 3 pt 3.10 of the *Evidence Act*). Public interest immunity was historically often referred to as "Crown privilege" but now extends beyond purely government matters both at common law and pursuant to the UEL. The recent High Court decision of *Graham v Minister for Immigration and Border Protection* contains a detailed discussion of the history and theory of public interest immunity, particularly the decision of Edelman J.[74]

13.7.1 The Uniform Evidence Law: public interest immunity

A non-exhaustive list of matters where public interest in retaining confidentiality may outweigh disclosure is set out in s 130(4) (pt 3.10 div 3) of the UEL.[75] Of the s 130(4)

72 *Kelly v Lomax* [2013] FamCA 556 was a very hard-fought divorce case with a large number of decisions on a wide range of issues involving property and child custody.

73 Ibid [44].

74 *Graham v Minister for Immigration and Border Protection* (2017) 263 CLR 1 was a *Migration Act 1958* (Cth) case, not a public interest immunity case but, because it tried to draw an analogy to public interest immunity, Edelman J discusses the pre-federation history of public interest immunity and considers to what extent the Court can and should accept the word of the "Executive" as to the public interest in documents the Executive are not wishing to disclose.

75 UEL; applicable in Commonwealth, Australian Capital Territory, Tasmania, New South Wales, Victoria and Northern Territory.

list, many directly involve the functions of government including s 130(4)(a): "prejudice the security, defence or international relations of Australia" which is probably the most commonly applied provision.

13.7.2 The principles of public interest immunity

Public interest immunity involves balancing the public interest in full disclosure against the public interest of preserving secrecy or confidentiality of certain matters such as national security.[76] The principle of public interest immunity was recently described in *Graham v Minister for Immigration and Border Protection* by the High Court in explaining why it was an incomplete analogy to the operation of s503A(2)(c) of the *Migration Act 1958* (Cth):

> The fact that a successful claim for public interest immunity 'handicaps one of the parties to litigation' is, of course, 'not a reason for saying that the Court cannot or will not exercise its ordinary jurisdiction', as has been explained earlier in these reasons. A case in which a claim for public interest immunity is made and is successful, however, is a case in which 'the veil of secrecy is not absolutely impenetrable, for the public interest in litigation to enforce the limitation of function ... is never entirely excluded from consideration'. The court in such a case has not been deprived of access to the material in limine. The court has rather been able to weigh, and has weighed, the public interest in non-disclosure of the particular information against the interests of justice in the particular circumstances of the case before it and has made an assessment that the former outweighs the latter.[77]

The New South Wales Supreme Court case *Re OPEL Networks Pty Ltd (in liq)* concerned a claim for public interest immunity by the Department of Broadband Communications and the Digital Economy (essentially, the Commonwealth) over six Cabinet-related documents sought by the liquidators of OPEL in relation to the Broadband Connect Infrastructure Program.[78] OPEL was a corporation formed by Optus and Elders which was forced into liquidation when its funding arrangement with the Commonwealth was terminated soon after the 2007 change in Federal Government. The liquidators of OPEL sought to determine whether the termination was proper.

In *Re OPEL Networks Pty Ltd (in liq)*, Austin J determined that three of the documents were entitled to immunity without the need for inspection and that it was necessary for him to inspect the other three as their entitlement to immunity would depend on their actual content. As a New South Wales case, s 130 of the *Evidence Act 1995* (NSW) applied, but the Court also utilised pt 1 r 1.9(3) of the *Uniform Civil Procedure Rules 2005* (NSW).[79] In making his decision, Austin J relied on the common law principles of public interest immunity, including those set down by the High Court in *Sankey v Whitlam*,[80] in *Commonwealth v Northern Land Council*[81] and in *Lanyon v Commonwealth*.[82] Justice Austin relevantly stated as follows:

76 This is another key example of the key CDR theme of balancing privacy and openness introduced in Chapter 2.3.3.
77 *Graham v Minister for Immigration and Border Protection* (2017) 263 CLR 1, [61] (Kiefel, Bell, Gagler, Keane, Nettle and Gordon JJ; Edelman J delivered a separate judgment).
78 *Re OPEL Networks Pty Ltd (in liq)* (2010) 77 NSWLR 128.
79 Ibid [16]–[18], [74].
80 *Sankey v Whitlam* (1978) 142 CLR 1.
81 *Commonwealth v Northern Land Council* (1993) 176 CLR 604.
82 *Lanyon v Commonwealth* (1974) 129 CLR 650.

Public interest immunity

[73]. A claim for public interest immunity in relation to documents that are subject to a compulsory discovery process under court rules seeks to preserve the confidentiality of documents if disclosure would have the potential to harm the public interest. The *Evidence Act 1995* (NSW), s 130, recognises that the public interest in admitting into evidence a document relating to matters of state may be outweighed by the public interest in preserving secrecy or confidentiality in relation to the document, and if that is so, the Court is empowered to direct that the document not be adduced as evidence. The statutory 'balancing exercise' reflects the general law with respect to public interest privilege, as explained in such cases as *Sankey v Whitlam* [1978] HCA 43; (1978) 142 CLR 1; see also *Penrith Rugby League Club Ltd v Brown* [2004] NSWSC 1182 at [27]–[28]. The Court has to balance competing public interests: on the one hand, the public interest in the administration of justice, which could be frustrated or impaired if access to relevant documents were denied; and on the other hand, the public interest that harm should not be done to the nation or government by disclosure of confidential matters: *Sankey v Whitlam*, at 38–39 per Gibbs ACJ, 60–61 per Stephen J, 95–96 per Mason J.

...

[75]. Several matters of principle are relevant to the assessment of the Commonwealth's claim to public interest immunity:

(a) a claim for public interest immunity has no automatic operation; it always remains the function of the Court to determine upon that claim (*Sankey v Whitlam*, at 58 per Stephen J);
(b) those who urge privilege for classes of documents, regardless of particular contents, carry a heavy burden of proof (*Sankey v Whitlam*, at 62 per Stephen J);
(c) the character of the proceedings and the issues raised are relevant: where the proceedings are centrally concerned with the government's conduct or a decision it has made, claims for public interest immunity over documents relating to that conduct or decision are less likely to succeed (*Sankey v Whitlam*, at 56 per Stephen J);
(d) the Court may examine the documents for the purpose of determining claims for public interest immunity (*Sankey v Whitlam*, at 47–8 per Gibbs ACJ), a step that may be appropriate where it is 'on the cards' that the documents contain relevant information (*Attorney-General (NSW) v Chidgey* [2008] NSWCCA 65; (2008) 182 A Crim R 536 at [58]–[80]; *Watson v AWB Ltd (No 2)* [2009] FCA 1047 at [58]).

[76]. In the present case the Court is required to consider the public interest in preserving the confidentiality of the Commonwealth Government's Cabinet process. ...

[77]. The confidentiality of Cabinet deliberations is important in order to preserve the principle of collective responsibility, which requires that Cabinet decisions, once made, must be supported by all ministers, irrespective of personal views (see *Commonwealth of Australia v Northern Land Council* [1993] HCA 24; (1993) 176 CLR 604, at 615). Collective Cabinet responsibility is intended to bring about effective and efficient government by facilitating finality in decision-making; whatever the range of private views put by Ministers in the Cabinet, once decisions are arrived at and announced they are expected to be supported by all Ministers.[83]

83 *Re OPEL Networks Pty Ltd (in liq)* (2010) 77 NSWLR 128, [73], [75]–[77].

Public interest immunity faces, perhaps, its most troubling balancing act when weighing the administration of justice interest against the interest in national security interests in immigration cases. While it is highly desirable for powerful national security bodies such as Australian Security and Intelligence Organisation (ASIO) to be subject to judicial oversight, challenging security decisions requires a risk to national security which courts can almost never afford to take. No judge wishes to be responsible for breaching national security. This was demonstrated by the decision of Tracey J in *Plaintiff M46 of 2013 v Minister for Immigration and Border Protection* where the appellant was refused a visa due to security information which was unknown to both the appellant and the Court. Tracey J held:

> 89. The first is that the courts will give 'very considerable weight' to the agency's view of what national security requires in any particular instance: see Alister at 435 (per Wilson and Dawson JJ). This dictum was applied by the Full Court in Leghaei when dealing with an adverse security assessment, made under the ASIO Act: see at 147. That is not to say that the Court must, in all cases, accept the security organisation's assessment. Such deference is, however, an acknowledgement of the practical difficulty faced by a court in evaluating evidence adduced in support of public interest immunity claims on the grounds of harm to national security.[84]

Similarly, in *BSX15 v Minister for Immigration and Border Protection*, Markovic J rejected claims of procedural unfairness by the Minister and also allowed the exclusion of security assessments on the grounds of public interest immunity, finding:

> The authorities establish that where a claim for public interest immunity privilege is properly made there will be evidence that is not available to an applicant to assist in establishing his or her case. That may make it very difficult for an applicant to discharge his or her onus of proof but that is the effect of such a claim properly made. The effect of the claim is not, as the applicant submitted, limited to a properly made claim not to produce documents before trial. In my opinion, the Director-General's claim, which the applicant conceded, with the exception of one document, was properly made, precludes that material from disclosure by the Director-General in the proceeding.[85]

13.8 Waiver of privilege

Privilege is a right not to disclose information rather than a requirement not to disclose. The owner of privileged information (often a party to the litigation) can choose to waive their privilege at any time. Once privilege has been waived, the information disclosed is no longer privileged. Disclosure of a document which refers to the existence of privileged information (such as a reference to legal advice) may waive the privilege on the document(s) referred to (such as the letter of legal advice itself). Waiver of privilege is governed by s 122 of the UEL.

Discovery or production of privileged documents must be made carefully so as not to inadvertently waive privilege. The existence of privileged documents must be disclosed pursuant to any court order to discover or produce documents but must be done in a way that does not disclose the privileged information.

84 *Plaintiff M46/2013 v Minister for Immigration and Border Protection* (2014) 139 ALR 277, [89].
85 *BSX15 v Minister for Immigration and Border Protection* [2016] FCA 1432, [34].

Although it is possible to waive privilege by negligence, courts will try to preserve privilege where possible. Inadvertent waiver will often be rectified by the courts and privilege preserved, and even deliberate disclosure of some aspect of a privileged communication will not necessarily result in a waiver of the entire communication.

Privilege waiver is one way in which courts shift the balance between privacy and openness.[86] Where parties have acted in a way which reduces their entitlement to maintain their privacy, the balance between the public interest in preserving confidentiality and the public interest in disclosure may shift sufficiently that a court finds the privilege has been waived and the court is entitled to disclosure of the confidential communication.

13.8.1 Waiver by intentional disclosure and common interest privilege

An intentional reference to legal advice does not necessarily waive privilege in the entire contents of that advice. The High Court decision of *Osland v Secretary, Department of Justice* ('*Osland*') sets out the High Court position on the issue of waiver of privilege.[87] *Osland* concerned the application of the common law, and the High Court noted the possibility for variation in the application of s 122 of the *Evidence Act 1995* (Cth).[88] The *Osland* decisions concerned petitions for the release of Mrs Osland from a jail sentence for the murder of her husband.[89] The murder followed 13 years of torture and abuse by the husband against Mrs Osland and her children. Despite the criminal nature of the *Osland* case, the High Court decisions discussed here and below concern issues of privilege entirely relevant to civil procedure. The 2008 *Osland* case concerned the waiver of privilege over legal advice obtained by the Department of Justice through a press release referring to the advice and stating: "The joint advice recommends on every ground that the petition should be denied."[90]

The majority decision of Gleeson CJ, Gummow, Heydon and Kiefel JJ in *Osland* in 2008 supported the decision of Maxwell P in the Court of appeal below and approved Maxwell P's reasoning that privilege in the advice had not been waived.[91] The *Osland* decision relied on earlier High Court cases including the important decision in *Mann v Carnell*.[92]

> [32]. [President Maxwell in the Court of Appeal] began by referring to the statement in *Mann v Carnell*:
>
> > Legal professional privilege exists to protect the confidentiality of communications between lawyer and client. It is the client who is entitled to the benefit of such confidentiality, and who may relinquish that entitlement. It is inconsistency between the conduct of the client and maintenance of the confidentiality which effects [an implied or imputed] waiver of the privilege.
> >
> > ...

86 See Chapter 2.3.3.
87 *Osland v Secretary, Department of Justice* (2008) 234 CLR 275.
88 Ibid [49].
89 The final decision of the High Court concerning Mrs Osland's case, *Osland v Secretary, Department of Justice (No 2)* (2010) 241 CLR 320, is discussed below and concerned public interest override in freedom of information applications.
90 *Osland v Secretary, Department of Justice* (2008) 234 CLR 275, [15].
91 Ibid [50].
92 *Mann v Carnell* (1999) 201 CLR 1.

> [45] Waiver of the kind presently in question is sometimes described as implied waiver, and sometimes as waiver 'imputed by operation of law'. It reflects a judgment that the conduct of the party entitled to the privilege is inconsistent with the maintenance of the confidentiality which the privilege is intended to protect. Such a judgment is to be made in the context and circumstances of the case, and in the light of any considerations of fairness arising from that context or those circumstances. …
>
> [49]. Whether, in a given context, a limited disclosure of the existence, and the effect, of legal advice is inconsistent with maintaining confidentiality in the terms of advice will depend upon the circumstances of the case. As Tamberlin J said in *Nine Films and Television Pty Ltd v Ninox Television Ltd*, questions of waiver are matters of fact and degree. It should be added that we are here concerned with the common law principle of waiver, not with the application of s 122 of the *Evidence Act 1995* (Cth) which, as was said in *Mann v Carnell*, has the effect that privilege may be lost in circumstances which are not identical to the circumstances in which privilege may be lost at common law.[93]

More recently privilege waiver in the context of a deliberate disclosure arose in the Federal Court Case of *Cantor v Audi Australia Pty Ltd*[94] which was a class action claiming misleading conduct by Volkswagen in relation to its diesel cars. The Federal Court held that privilege was not waived by Volkswagen providing certain information to KBA (a German authority) in response to a request which was not compulsory at law, but which commercially and practically had to be complied with.

It is also possible for different parties to have a common interest in otherwise privileged communications, such that disclosure between those parties does not waive privilege but those parties cannot maintain privilege against each other in relation to such communications. For UEL jurisdictions, ss 122(5)(b) and 122(5)(c) of the *Evidence Act* enables privilege to continue where a party discloses to another person where the same lawyer is providing advice to both people, or where both parties have a common interest in proceedings or anticipated proceedings. Common interest privilege is not a privilege in its own right but, rather, an exception to waiver of privilege to enable the party to maintain privilege over the communication against the world at large and the other parties to a dispute despite having intentionally disclosed the privileged communication to the third party with whom the common interest is said to apply.[95]

Common interest privilege is a difficult area, with the Supreme Court of Victoria describing the authorities on what constitutes a sufficient common interest as "not easily reconcilable."[96] The use of common interest privilege is becoming more complex with increases in class actions and even competing class actions where there are sometimes changing groups of plaintiffs and plaintiff witnesses with potential common interests in disputes.[97] Sometimes, it may be necessary for the judge to inspect the documents over which common interest privilege is argued in order to determine whether the client legal privilege has been waived or whether the common interest is sufficient to allow limited disclosure without waiver.[98]

93 *Osland v Secretary, Department of Justice* (2008) 234 CLR 275, [32], [45], [49].

94 *Cantor v Audi Australia Pty Ltd* [2016] FCA 1391.

95 *Timbercorp Finance Pty Ltd v Tomes* [2019] VSC 445, [21], [47]–[55].

96 Ibid [50]. Associate Justice Lansdowne discusses the variance in the cases, particularly in relation to communications with litigation funders in class action cases at [51]–[54].

97 Ibid [49].

98 *Molenaar v Andonovski* [2020] NSWSC 1258, [73].

13.8.2 Implied waiver of privilege

In *Mann v Carnell,* referred to above, the High Court noted that the same rationale applied to deliberate and implied waiver of privilege, noting:

> Waiver may be express or implied ... What brings about the waiver is the inconsistency, which the courts, where necessary informed by considerations of fairness, perceive, between the conduct of the client and maintenance of the confidentiality; not some overriding principle of fairness operating at large.[99]

Implied waiver of privilege was also more recently discussed by the Full Federal Court in *Macquarie Bank Ltd v Arup Pty Ltd.*[100] This case was a dispute about the common law legal professional privilege attaching to documents required for discovery in the Federal Court in relation to a dispute between BrisConnections (of which Macquarie were a consortium member) and Arup which provided traffic forecasts in relation to the Brisbane Airport Link toll road. The Full Federal Court of Middleton, Robertson and Gleeson JJ denied Macquarie leave to appeal because they held the primary judge had been correct in finding no waiver of privilege had occurred. The Full Federal Court held:

> This proceeding merely involves the pleading by Arup of reliance and the discovery of privileged documents. Whilst such documents are relevant to the proceeding (and hence discoverable), this is not sufficient to constitute waiver. If it were, then as the primary judge observed, this would 'come perilously close to, if not amount to, a proposition that a mere pleading of reliance would itself be sufficient to constitute a waiver of privilege'.[101]

13.8.3 Inadvertent waiver of privilege

In addition to cases such as *Osland*[102] and *Macquarie Bank Ltd v Arup Pty Ltd*, concerning the impact of a partial deliberate waiver or implied waiver, there are also cases concerning inadvertent waiver of privilege. These cases generally involve lawyer error and courts are reluctant to allow such errors to result in detriment to the litigant.

This reluctance was strengthened by the High Court in *Expense Reduction Analysis Group Pty Ltd v Armstrong Strategic Management and Marketing Pty Ltd* (*Expense Reduction Analysis Group*).[103] *Expense Reduction Analysis Group* has been discussed in previous chapters because it provides High Court precedent in relation to case management, court procedural powers and professional obligations of solicitors.[104] However, it was, substantively, a case concerning the unintentional waiver of client legal privilege.

The Armstrong parties (plaintiffs/High Court respondents: 3 parties) commenced proceedings against the Expense Reduction Analysis Group (ERA) parties (defendants/High Court appellants: 10 parties) for alleged contractual breaches pertaining to an insurance

99 *Mann v Carnell* (1999) 201 CLR 1, [49].
100 *Macquarie Bank Ltd v Arup Pty Ltd* [2016] FCAFC 117.
101 Ibid [41].
102 *Osland v Secretary, Department of Justice (No 2)* (2010) 241 CLR 320.
103 *Expense Reduction Analysis Group Pty Ltd v Armstrong Strategic Management and Marketing Pty Ltd* (2013) 250 CLR 303.
104 Ibid. This case had been cited by courts in over 300 reported decisions by 2020, but most cases cite the decision's findings on case management and professional obligations rather than waiver of privilege.

expense reduction business. The Armstrong Parties, represented by Marque Lawyers, commenced in the District Court of New South Wales and were transferred to the Supreme Court of New South Wales, which ordered general discovery by the parties. The High Court proceedings concerned the inadvertent disclosure by Norton Rose, solicitors for the defendant ERA Parties, of 13 documents which were properly the subject of client legal privilege. Norton Rose (on behalf of ERA) requested the return of the inadvertently disclosed documents and Marque Lawyers (on behalf of Armstrong) refused on the basis that the privilege had been waived by the disclosure.

Each of the three courts which heard the privilege dispute decided differently, indicating the complexity of the issue. At the original trial, Bergin J (in the Supreme Court of New South Wales), held that 9 of the 13 documents had been inadvertently disclosed and should be returned by Marque Lawyers (for Armstrong) to Norton Rose (for ERA).[105] Justice Bergin accepted that there was sufficient evidence that the disclosure was due to error manipulating the computer system because there were copies of the 9 documents listed in the privileged documents discovered. Justice Bergin held privilege had been waived on the remaining 4 documents because the document reviewers (Norton Rose employees) were unable to evidence an intention to claim privilege on those documents. The New South Wales Court of Appeal overruled Bergin J regarding the 9 documents and allowed Armstrong's appeal against ERA (ie the Court of Appeal allowed Armstrong access to all 13 privileged documents).[106] The High Court overruled the New South Wales Court of Appeal and held that all 13 documents were privileged and must be returned by Marque Lawyers/Armstrong to Norton Rose/ERA as the disclosure was inadvertent and did not waive the client's privilege.

There were 60,000 documents involved in ERA's discovery process and an electronic database was used which had a privilege field. Unless the privilege field was tagged "yes" or "part", the document was not treated as privileged. Numerous documents were not marked as privileged which should have been marked privileged, including the final 13 documents the subject of the High Court litigation.[107] There were numerous errors in the discovery which the Court accepted as inadvertent because there was no evidence of any intention to waive privilege (other than the failure to tag the document as privileged in the database and its subsequent inclusion on the non-privileged list of discovered documents). The High Court indicated that the parties should have consensually rectified the error without cause for court intervention and then awarded costs against Armstrong in respect of the proceedings for incorrectly asserting privilege waiver.

In their joint judgment, French CJ, Kiefel, Bell, Gageler and Keane JJ held in relation in relation to discovery, privilege and privilege waiver:

> [44]. As Lord Diplock observed in *Harman v Secretary of State for the Home Department* [[1983] 1 AC 280 at 300], … '[t]he use of discovery involves an inroad, in the interests of achieving justice, upon the right of the individual to keep his own documents to himself'.
>
> [45]. Although discovery is an inherently intrusive process, it is not intended that it be allowed to affect a person's entitlement to maintain the confidentiality of documents

105 *Armstrong Strategic Management and Marketing Pty Ltd v Expense Reduction Analysts Group Pty Ltd* (2012) 295 ALR 348.

106 Ibid.

107 *Expense Reduction Analysis Group Pty Ltd v Armstrong Strategic Management and Marketing Pty Ltd* (2013) 250 CLR 303.

> where the law allows. It follows that where a privileged document is inadvertently disclosed, the court should ordinarily permit the correction of that mistake and order the return of the document, if the party receiving the documents refuses to do so.[108]

The High Court's decision in *Expense Reduction Analysis Group* is, however, dangerous to civil procedure in one important respect. It effectively condones the sloppy work performed in reviewing privilege by ERA including the use of inexperienced and poorly qualified employees with ostensibly insufficient review by more senior lawyers resulting in the inadvertent disclosure of privileged documents. In *Expense Reduction Analysis Group*, the onus, and cost, of rectification of the errors in discovery ultimately fell on the party observing the error rather than the party committing it. Such acceptance of poor standards of legal work may lead to unforeseen inefficiencies in future litigation and should, perhaps, be a cause for concern to potential future litigants forced to rely on the services of such law firms.[109] *Expense Reduction Analysis Group* is also an excellent example of the courts balancing efficiency with due process and balancing autonomy with control.[110] The High Court's discouragement in *Expense Reduction Analysis Group* of parties bringing interlocutory privilege disputes aims to increase efficiency and party autonomy but potentially does so at a cost to due process and court control.

Expense Reduction Analysis Group treated a more significant erroneous disclosure as inadvertent than earlier cases such as the Federal Court case of *CMA Corporation Ltd v Rowe*.[111] In *CMA Corporation Ltd v Rowe,* Buchanan J held that privilege in part of an email exhibited in an affidavit had not been waived because the exhibit of that part of the communication was inadvertent and had been rectified promptly. The affidavit and exhibits had been "e-lodged" at 3:57pm following an urgent order earlier that day for the party to demonstrate by 4:00pm by affidavit the steps it had taken to comply with an order imposing interlocutory restraints. The solicitor attempted to retract the erroneous e-lodgement and re-serve the affidavit and exhibits without the inadvertent privilege waiver by 4:57pm (an hour later). She also corresponded with the other party and the court before 6:00pm, confirming there was no intention to waive privilege.

13.8.4 Issue waiver

A fourth type of waiver occurs where parties to litigation raise a matter in the course of the litigation which, by its very nature, waives privilege in documents which might otherwise attract such privilege. The Federal Court case of *Hine v New South Wales Land and Housing Corporation* concerned a notice given pursuant to clause 16 of a contract regarding prohibition on the use of a subcontractor. Clause 16 relevantly provided that prohibition was allowed where "the first respondent's representative reasonably regarded that person or subcontractor as incompetent, negligent or otherwise unsuitable".[112] The applicants argued that the opinion of the respondent's representative used to invoke clause

108 Ibid [44]–[45].

109 Sonya Willis, 'Courting Incompetence: Should the High Court More carefully Consider its Influence on Legal Culture?' (2016) 35(2) *Civil Justice Quarterly* 129.

110 See Chapters 2.3.1 and 2.3.4 respectively.

111 *CMA Corporation Ltd v Rowe* (2010) 277 ALR 163.

112 *Hine v New South Wales Land and Housing Corporation* [2009] FCA 502, [4].

16 of the contract was not reasonable. Justice Jagot held that privilege had been waived over certain documents relating to exercise of the opinion to prohibit the subcontractor due to issue waiver:

> [12]. Second, the applicants say that the doctrine of issue waiver applies. The touchstone for issue waiver is whether there is inconsistency between the maintenance of the privilege and the conduct of the respondents.
>
> ...
>
> [16]. Having looked at the documents and heard the submissions, I accept that this is a case where there is not a mere denial of an obligation as in *DSE (Holdings) Pty Ltd v Intertan Inc* (2003) 127 FCR 499; [2003] FCA 384. It is a case where the circumstances necessarily lay open to scrutiny certain confidential communications. I am satisfied, at least in respect of some of the documents I have seen, that there is an inconsistency between the maintenance of the privilege and the conduct of the respondents, being their conduct in issuing the notice under clause 16 itself, and expressly relying upon and pleading the entirety of the clause in their defence, and otherwise denying the applicants' assertion of the unreasonableness of the opinion. In other words, the respondents' conduct has itself put in issue certain matters which might otherwise attract legal professional privilege.[113]

13.9 Public interest override

As set out at the beginning of this chapter, privilege exists for reasons of public policy. If the public benefit in disclosing a document outweighs the public interest in preserving privilege, a court may override that privilege pursuant to the doctrine of public interest override. Override is similar to waiver in the sense that it prevents the operation of privilege but, unlike waiver, is not caused by the actions of the privileged party but by the underlying public interest as determined by the court. Public interest override is unlikely to arise in most civil litigation involving purely private parties but arises in relation to government-held privilege. The High Court case of *Osland v Secretary, Department of Justice (No 2)* ('*Osland (2010)*')[114] found that the entitlement to privilege may be overruled by the public interest benefit of disclosure.

As previously noted, privilege is not limited to legal proceedings and so can apply to non-court proceedings such as FOI Applications. *Osland (2010)* concerned the FOI application by Mrs Osland (who was serving a jail sentence for the murder of her husband) for documents advising the Governor of Victoria (via the Attorney-General) not to exercise the Royal prerogative of mercy and therefore not to pardon Mrs Osland. The High Court, comprising six judges in three separate judgments, French CJ, Gummow, Hayne, Heydon, Kiefel and Bell JJ unanimously allowed Mrs Osland's appeal for access to documents relating to the decision on the basis that it was in the public interest for the documents to be released. The decision of French CJ, Gummow and Bell JJ concluded that public interest in disclosure outweighed the public interest in protection of privilege as follows:

113 Ibid [12], [16].
114 *Osland v Secretary, Department of Justice (No 2)* (2010) 241 CLR 320.

> [46]. This Court, in the course of the present appeal, has looked at the disputed documents and received detailed written submissions respecting the terms in which they were expressed. A consideration of the content of the disputed documents in light of the terms of the press release indicates that important elements of the differences between the advices were not based upon different views of the applicable law. The substance of the most important differences turned upon normative judgments on matters which the authors of the advices thought relevant to the exercise of the prerogative of mercy.
>
> ...
>
> [48]. The nature of the differences between the advices, throwing up opinions about the fairness and authority of the criminal justice system, the circumstances of Mrs Osland's situation, and asserted inadequacies in the law in relation to chronic domestic violence, was such as to be capable of supporting the formation of an opinion that the public interest required the disclosure of the documents. It was, at the very least, arguable, in the circumstances of the case, that the high-threshold public interest standard was met and that the public interest required disclosure of the contending, essentially normative propositions which the Attorney-General had before him when he recommended that Mrs Osland's petition be denied. The differences between the authors of the advices were on questions readily comprehensible by members of the public. They did not turn upon arcane disagreements, likely to be misunderstood, about the interpretation of the relevant law. Against the weight of such considerations, in applying s 50(4) of the *FOI Act* the interests protected by legal professional privilege, and recognised by s 32(1) of that Act, in the particular case were arguably of diminished importance. When the Attorney-General received the advices which he did from various members of the legal profession, he did so on behalf of the public and not as a private citizen. Such continuing public interest as there was in the privilege attaching to the documents in the circumstances of this case was capable of being put to one side against the public interest in disclosure.[115]

13.10 Statutory discretion to exclude evidence

The UEL also contains pt 3.11 ss 135 and 136, which infer a general discretion on the court to exclude evidence (s 135) or limit its use (s 136) where there is a danger the evidence may be unfairly prejudicial to a party or be misleading or confusing. The court may also exclude evidence where that evidence may result in undue waste of time (s 135(c)). For evidence to be excluded (s 135), the danger of prejudice or confusion must "substantially outweigh" the probative value of the evidence. For use to be limited (s 136), there need only be a danger that the limited use would cause prejudice or confusion.

An example of use of s 136 is the defamation case of *Winnel v Byron*[116] in the Supreme Court of the Australian Capital Territory, where Master Harpur admitted a copy of an advertisement into evidence but limited its use such that it was not taken as evidence of the truth of its contents. Similarly, in the New South Wales Supreme Court case of *Australian Securities and Investments Commission v Sydney Investment House Equities Pty Ltd*, Barrett J stated:

115 Ibid [46], [48].
116 *Winnel v Byron* [2009] ACTSC 146.

> [21]. … while evidence that is admitted will be admitted for all purposes, any demonstrated danger of unfair prejudice arising from its use against a particular defendant will be capable of resolution pursuant to s.136 of the *Evidence Act 1995*: see *Australian Securities and Investments Commission v Vines* [2003] NSWSC 995; (2003) 48 ACSR 282 at [24]. That, as the plaintiff submits, is something best dealt with by the trial judge in the course of the trial, should the need arise.[117]

However, the application of ss 135 and 136 is limited as explained by Gzell J in *Australian Securities and Investments Commission v Macdonald* where he declined to apply ss 135 or 136, stating:

> [8]. … s 56 of the *Evidence Act* is subject to other provisions of the Act including the discretions to exclude evidence in Pt 3.11 and, in particular, s 135 and 136.
>
> [9]. But the circumstances in which the discretions may be exercised are circumscribed. The occasion for the exercise or non-exercise of the discretions only arises if the probative value of the evidence is substantially outweighed by the danger that the evidence might be unfairly prejudicial or misleading or confusing or, in one case, might cause or result in undue waste of time.
>
> [10]. One would have thought that care should be taken not to exercise the discretions liberally for that would undermine the general proposition that all evidence relevant to an issue in a proceeding is admissible for all purposes.[118]

Interestingly, Gzell J applied both s 135 and s 136 as an additional basis to *Browne v Dunn*[119] to prevent the late tender of analysts' reports in a subsequent interlocutory dispute in the same litigation *Australian Securities and Investments Commission v Macdonald (No 10)*.[120]

Sections 135 and 136 more commonly apply in criminal proceedings than civil and the remainder of pt 3.11 applies solely to criminal proceedings.

13.11 Confidentiality in the absence of privilege

Confidentiality is not the same as privilege and does not attract the same rights. However, confidentiality can be critical, particularly in commercial cases. Commercial litigation may involve contracts, trading terms and other strategic business documents, the secrecy of which would usually be guarded with utmost care. The courts are sympathetic to the invasion of privacy caused by civil litigation and will sometimes allow the partial masking of documents to protect confidential information where the confidential information is not of itself relevant to the litigation. This protection is even more likely to be allowed where the confidential material in question belongs to a third party (eg the documents produced under subpoena).

117 *Australian Securities and Investments Commission v Sydney Investment House Equities Pty Ltd* [2007] NSWSC 34, [21].

118 *Australian Securities and Investments Commission v Macdonald* (2008) 68 ACSR 126, [8]–[10].

119 *Browne v Dunn* [1893] 6 R 67.

120 *Australian Securities and Investments Commission v Macdonald (No 10)* [2009] NSWSC 53.

The New South Wales Supreme Court case of *NAK Australia Pty Ltd v Starkey Consulting Pty Ltd*[121] was an *ex tempore* judgment[122] in which the defendants were exempted from discovering certain confidential documents, were allowed to mask other discoverable documents, and were allowed to withhold discovery of documents relevant only to quantum (ie the amount in dispute) until a determination as to liability had been made. Justice Brereton set out the relevant case law on the issue of confidentiality of documents in the extract below:

> [4]. Before turning to the particular matters in dispute, it is convenient to summarise a number of the principles that I will apply. First, as Lord Wilberforce pointed out in *Science Research Council v Nasse* [1980] AC 1028, 1065, in a passage cited by Spender J in *Mackay Sugar Co-operative Associated Ltd v CSR Ltd* (1996) 63 FCR 408, 412, and again by Branson J in *Gray v Associated Book Publishers (Australia) Pty Ltd* (in *liq*) [2002] FCA 1045, there is no principle in our law by which documents are protected from discovery by reason of confidentiality alone. Nonetheless, it is recognised that discovery constitutes a serious invasion of the privacy and confidentiality of a litigant's affairs and, while the process forms part of civil procedure because of the public interest in ensuring that justice is done between the parties, it ought not be allowed to place upon the litigant any harsher or more oppressive burden than is required to permit justice to be done [*Harman v Secretary of State Home Department* [1983] 1 AC 280, 308 (Lord Keith of Kinkel); see also *Gray v Associated Book Publishers*].
>
> [5]. Secondly, in the context of invasion of confidentiality by discovery, it is important to bear in mind that a party obtaining documents by compulsory process remains under an implied obligation imposed by law to use the information derived from that process solely for the purpose of the litigation in which the documents are produced, as recently recognised by the High Court in *Hearne v Street* [2008] HCA 36.
>
> [6]. Thirdly, nonetheless, a practice has become established whereby inspection is provided of discovered documents with parts of those documents masked [*Grofam Pty Ltd v Australian & New Zealand Banking Group Ltd* (1993) 43 FCR 408; *Optus Communications Pty Ltd v Telstra Corporation Ltd* [1995] FCA 254; *GEC Marconi Systems Pty Ltd v BHP Information Technology Pty Ltd* [2000] FCA 593; *Fort Dodge Australia Pty Ltd v Nature Vet Pty Ltd* [2002] FCA 501; *GE Capital Corporate Finance Group Ltd v Bankers' Trust Co* [1995] 1 WLR 172; *Telstra Corporation v Australis Media Holdings* (NSWSC, McLelland CJ in Eq, 10 February 1997 unreported); *Gray v Associated Book Publishers*]. In *Telstra v Australis Media Holdings* and in *Gray v Associated Book Publishers*, McLelland CJ in Eq and Branson J respectively recognised that where masking was undertaken pursuant to a valid claim for privilege in respect of the relevant portion of the document, it is based on a positive right to withhold from inspection a part of the document; but that there is no such positive right in respect of documents sought to be withheld on grounds of confidentiality or irrelevance, as distinct from those of privilege. … .
>
> … .

121 *NAK Australia Pty Ltd v Starkey Consulting Pty Ltd* [2008] NSWSC 1136 which has subsequently been approved in a number of decisions as noted by Edelman J (then of the WA Supreme Court) in *Co-operative Bulk Handling Ltd v Brookfield Rail Pty Ltd (No 2)* [2014] WASC 38, [8].

122 An *ex tempore* judgment is one given at the time of the hearing and such judgments are usually brief, delivered orally and contain little reference to authority. In *NAK Australia Pty Ltd v Starkey Consulting Pty Ltd* [2008] NSWSC 1136, the judgment was actually given on the Monday, three days after the hearing on the previous Friday which may explain how Brereton J was able to deliver such a well-researched *ex tempore* judgment.

> [8]. Fourthly, as I sought to explain in *Portal Software International Pty Ltd v Bodsworth* [2005] NSWSC 1115, it has long been the practice that restrictions be imposed on the access of a party to documents produced on discovery, or on subpoena, particularly in cases concerning patents and trade secrets. … . Protective limitations are sometimes introduced at the time of the production or inspection — such as orders for inspection by an independent solicitor or expert, or limiting access (for example) to the plaintiff's expert but not the plaintiff, or inspection by the plaintiff's solicitor but not by the plaintiff.
>
> …
>
> [10]. Ultimately, the fact that giving discovery would involve the loss of a party's own trade secrets or confidences is of itself no objection to discovery, but courts more closely scrutinise the discovery sought to ensure that it truly is material and not oppressive in such a case [*Great Western Colliery Co v Tucker* (1874) LR 9 Ch App 376; *Moore v Craven* (1870) LR 7 Ch App 94; *Carver v Pinto Leite* (1871) LR 7 Ch App 90; *Aktiebolaget Hassle v Pacific Pharmaceuticals Ltd* [1991] 3 NZLR 186; Matthews & Malek, *Discovery*, (1992) Sweet & Maxwell, [6.23]].[123]

Thus, the use of redacting documents to protect confidentiality represents another way in which the courts balance the need to protect privacy against the need for open disclosure separate from invoking privilege.[124]

13.12 Restricted use of documents produced in litigation

Even where documents have not been excluded or masked due to privilege or confidentiality, they remain confidential to the litigation. When non-privileged documents have been produced to court through litigation, restrictions continue to apply to their use during and after the litigation. Parties granted access to documents in proceedings make an implied undertaking only to use those documents for the purposes of that litigation. Breaching this undertaking may constitute contempt of court, attracting criminal sanctions. Once a document is read in open court during a hearing; however, the confidentiality in that document is usually lost.

In the Victorian Supreme Court case of *Ambridge Investments Pty Ltd (in liq) (rec apptd) v Baker (No 3)*,[125] Vickery J relied on the High Court decision of *Hearne v Street*[126] in refusing to lift the implied undertaking not to use documents produced in litigation for any other purpose. Justice Vickery discussed the balancing of private rights, public interest and the administration of justice requiring special circumstances to lift the implied undertaking of confidentiality:

> [20]. Where a person is compelled, by reason of a rule of court, a specific order of the court, or other coercive process, to disclose documents or information in the course of a proceeding in court, the person obtaining the disclosure cannot, without the leave of the court, use it for any purpose other than that for which it was given, unless it is received into evidence. As to the continued applicability of the rule in circumstances

123 Ibid [4]–[6], [8]–[10] (footnotes included).
124 See Chapter 2.3.3.
125 *Ambridge Investments Pty Ltd (in liq) (rec apptd) v Baker (No 3)* [2010] VSC 545.
126 *Hearne v Street* (2008) 235 CLR 125.

where a document is used in open court but where the document is not admitted into evidence, reference is made to the detailed analysis of Hargrave J in *Citicorp Life Insurance Ltd v Lubransky; Bagiotas v Citicorp Life Insurance Ltd.*

[21]. The rule has a wide scope in its application to a range of documents. As noted by the High Court in *Hearne v Street*, included within the reach of the principle, for example are: documents inspected after discovery, answers to interrogatories, documents produced on subpoena, documents produced for the purposes of taxation of costs, documents produced pursuant to a direction from an arbitrator, documents seized pursuant to an Anton Piller order, witness statements served pursuant to a judicial direction and affidavits.

[22]. The importance attributed to the obligation is reflected in the approach of the courts to its breach. A contravention is treated as contempt.

[23]. Further, the reach of the principle is extended to third parties who use the documents with knowledge of the circumstances of their production before a court. …

[25]. The fundamental principle is that the Court ought not to exercise its discretion to release or modify the implied undertaking unless there are 'special circumstances' present which justify taking this course. So much was common ground.

…

[28]. The rule has the purpose of protecting both private and public interests. The two are interrelated.

[29]. Protection of a private right to keep one's documents to oneself, yielding only so far as is necessary to the interests of justice for the purposes of a proceeding in which the documents are compelled to be produced, is clearly championed by the rule. The rationale is to ensure that the privacy of the person from whom otherwise private or confidential information is coercively obtained is invaded no more than is necessary for the purposes of the administration of justice.

[30]. Of no less import is the public interest in maintaining privacy and confidence in relation to documents produced to a court under compulsion. This arises directly from protection of the private interest. Protection of the confidentiality of a person's private documents encourages the full and proper disclosure of documents that the administration of justice requires. As such, it is an important element in maintaining public confidence in the conduct of legal proceedings in court and by this means securing constructive participation in its processes.

…

[32]. In my opinion, it is not possible nor desirable to confine the notion of 'special circumstances' to an exhaustive list of factors. …

[33]. … 'special circumstances' may arise where there are special features (or a special feature) of the case which afford good reason for modifying or releasing the undertaking, being circumstances which are of sufficient gravity to override the private and public interest in protection of the confidentiality of a person's private documents which are required by law to be produced to a court.[127]

Therefore, the restrictions in use of discovery documents constitutes yet another balancing act between privacy and openness which is the key theme of CDR that pervades this chapter.[128]

127 *Ambridge Investments Pty Ltd (in liq) (rec apptd) v Baker (No 3)* [2010] VSC 545, [20]–[23], [25], [28]–[30], [32]–[33].

128 See Chapter 2.3.3.

13.13 Conclusion

The law of privilege demonstrates some of the conflicts which lie at the heart of civil disputes and how such conflicts are resolved to protect legal process and the rule of law. As with all CDR, privilege involves complex judicial balancing and engages particularly with the key theme of balancing openness with confidentiality.[129] The courts' efforts to efficiently resolve interlocutory privilege disputes also engage with the key themes of balancing efficiency with due process and balancing autonomy with control. While judges are charged with finding the truth and delivering justice, they must do so in a way which preserves the procedures which protect access to justice and the efficient resolution of disputes. It is important that parties can discuss their issues freely and efficiently with their lawyer and thus client legal privilege is essential. It is important that parties can attempt settlement openly and in good faith and thus negotiation privilege must be preserved. Similarly, important government duties including the protection of national security should not be threatened by the operation of the courts nor should the courts be at risk of disclosing state secrets and, thus, public interest immunity is also crucial to civil procedure. The complexity of these competing objectives and the potential for current decisions to influence future behaviour make privilege one of the most difficult areas of CDR.

129 *Glencore International AG v Commissioner of Taxation* (2019) 265 CLR 646, [29].

14 WITNESS EVIDENCE PRE-TRIAL

14.1 Introduction

This chapter concerns the role of witnesses in litigation pre-trial and will focus on the preparation of affidavits and witness statements for use in trials but will also consider affidavits used in interlocutory disputes.[1] Obtaining evidence from witnesses, both lay and expert, is one of the key procedures available in litigation which is absent from other forms of civil dispute resolution (CDR). Witness evidence is also one of the most time-consuming and expensive aspects of case preparation, particularly expert evidence as experts can be extremely costly.[2] Expert witnessing has been the subject of considerable contention, reform and debate, both within the legal fraternity and in the broader community. The preparation of expert evidence demonstrates many of the key conflicts explored in Chapter 2.3, particularly the balancing of efficiency with due consideration. The preparation of witness evidence also engages with the key CDR issues of access to justice and open justice. The time and expense associated with locating witnesses and preparing affidavits highlights the potential for the wealthy to be unfairly advantaged when preparing for litigation.[3] Similarly, the disincentives to litigate associated with open justice[4] are particularly prominent in the preparation of witness evidence which commonly raises issues of breach of privacy and confidentiality.

This chapter will explain the structure of evidence law in Australia, which is partially uniform, and introduce briefly the rules of evidence most relevant to drafting affidavits in preparation for civil trials. Evidence is a substantial area of law in its own right and cannot be considered exhaustively in a chapter. However, consideration of evidentiary rules in affidavit preparation is essential because failure to comply with evidentiary rules may render witness evidence inadmissible at trial.[5]

14.2 Preparing affidavits

An affidavit is a sworn statement.[6] Many affidavits are statements made by witnesses, but it is also common for lawyers to swear affidavits, particularly in interlocutory proceedings.[7] In civil litigation, where parties are represented by lawyers, it is usual for lawyers to assist in the preparation of affidavits. This is largely due to the evidentiary rules which apply for affidavits to be admissible in court, as discussed later in this chapter.

1 An "affidavit" is a sworn statement. Affidavits are either sworn on oath or affirmed. The deponent, being the person who makes the affidavit, must swear or attest that the statement is correct. An "interlocutory dispute" is a disagreement between the parties as to an aspect of the trial preparation. Interlocutory disputes are common in civil litigation, particularly in complex commercial disputes. Interlocutory disputes may arise in relation to pleadings, particulars, discovery, subpoenas and privilege. Interlocutory disputes were considered in more detail in Chapter 8.7.

2 See Chapter 14.5.

3 See Chapter 3.2.

4 See Chapter 3.3.

5 See Chapter 15 for further consideration of evidentiary issues arising during trial.

6 Affidavits may be sworn under oath or affirmed (as discussed in Chapter 14.2.1) but both forms are commonly referred to as "sworn" and references to "sworn" in this chapter, other than in Chapter 14.2.1, should be taken to refer to sworn or affirmed.

7 The person — for example, a witness — making the affidavit is known as the "deponent".

14.2.1 What are the form requirements for an affidavit?

The form of an affidavit may vary somewhat from court to court, but affidavits are formal court documents. Affidavits are either sworn, where the deponent is religious and takes an oath, or affirmed, where the deponent is not religious. The deponent, being the person who makes the affidavit, must swear or affirm that the affidavit is true and correct to the best of the deponent's information, knowledge and belief. The attestation is made in front of a witness, commonly the party's solicitor, who then signs the attestation clause of the affidavit.

The Uniform Evidence Law (UEL) sets out the requirements for oath and affirmation which apply to affidavit evidence as well as oral evidence given in court:

21 Sworn evidence of witnesses to be on oath or affirmation

(1) A witness in a proceeding must take an oath or make an affirmation before giving evidence.

(2) Subsection (1) does not apply to a person who gives unsworn evidence under section 13 (Competence—lack of capacity).

(3) A person who is called only to produce a document or thing to the court need not take an oath or make an affirmation before doing so.

(4) The witness must take the oath, or make the affirmation, in accordance with the appropriate form in schedule 1 or in a similar form.

(5) An affirmation has the same effect for all purposes as an oath.[8]

If an affidavit contains a deliberate lie, its tender in court may constitute contempt of court by the deponent or perjury and may attract criminal sanctions, including, potentially, a jail sentence.[9] This does not mean that a witness whose evidence is not accepted by court is likely to be tried for contempt of court. Most cases include conflicting witness evidence, even where all witnesses are completely honest simply because human recall is imperfect and recollection is coloured by the rational and emotional interpretation subconsciously made by all witnesses in relation to what they experienced.

In addition to the attestation clause, or oath, there are various other form requirements for affidavits which vary from court to court. Most form requirements for affidavits are largely common sense, such as ensuring that all pages are numbered and that annexures or exhibits are correctly identified and annexed/exhibited. In some jurisdictions, each page of every affidavit must be signed by the deponent and the witnessing legal practitioner. The most significant requirement is that affidavit evidence be in admissible form; that is, the affidavit must comply with the rules of evidence discussed in Chapter 14.6.

As discussed by the Western Australian Supreme Court of Appeal in *Walsh v Adrian Sloan as Executor of the Estate Keddie*, parties are entitled to object to affidavits which are not in admissible form, but such objections must be reasonable, should be made at the time when the evidence is tendered or, for affidavits, read and made explicitly to the court rather

8 *Evidence Act 2011* (ACT). The UEL applies almost uniformly in New South Wales, Victoria, Tasmania, Australian Capital Territory, and Federally.

9 See, eg, *Oaths Act 1900* (NSW) s 29; *Collier v Country Women's Association of New South Wales* [2018] NSWCA 36, [84]; *Oueik v Girgis* [2018] NSWDC 164 where Girgis' swearing of a false affidavit was referred to the Department of Public Prosecutions.

than being merely foreshadowed in a written schedule.[10] Objections to affidavits due to inadmissibility can be costly and time-consuming for all parties and can reduce the evidence before the court in support of a party's case where they are upheld, resulting in some or all of an affidavit being struck out of the material before the court for consideration.

Where an affidavit refers to annexures or exhibits, it should not explain the contents of the annexures or exhibits, as such documents speak for themselves. An example of the sort of reference commonly made to annexures and exhibits is set out below in relation to interlocutory affidavits which often contain many such references. Where an annexure or exhibit requires explanation, that should be included in the body of the affidavit.

It is advisable to write affidavits in first person, and some jurisdictions, such as the Federal Court, require affidavits to be written in first person.[11] Where an affidavit attests to a conversation, that conversation should be in direct speech wherever possible. This improves the clarity of the affidavit and also forces the deponent to think carefully about their recollection of the conversation. However, judges do not expect that witnesses will actually be word for word correct in their recollection of conversations and, for this reason, the phrase "words to the effect of" is commonly used before a direct statement of what was said to confirm the likely imperfection of the deponent's memory.[12] In *Qube Ports Pty Ltd v Maritime Union of Australia*,[13] the Full Federal Court of Australia noted that direct speech, although not compulsory, was still desirable even where the evidence related to events long past where exact recollection could not be expected:

> [115]. It is true that much of the content of the affidavits containing the evidence in chief was conclusionary in form and made liberal use of indirect speech.
>
> [116]. Given that the witnesses were giving evidence of conversations which had occurred approximately 16 years earlier, it was probably unrealistic to expect that any would have been able to give an account of them using direct speech. However, that circumstance did not mean that no evidence could be given of the conversations. In *Hamilton-Smith v George* [2006] FCA 1551; (2006) 247 FCR 238, Besanko J said at [83]:
>
>> In my opinion, there is a rule of practice at common law that requires a witness to recount the actual words used in a conversation if he or she is able to do that: ... If the witness is unable to recall the actual words used, he or she can give evidence of the substance or effect of what was said. ... [Citations omitted]
>
> [117]. In *LMI Australasia Pty Ltd v Baulderstone Hornibrook Pty Ltd* [2001] NSWSC 688; (2001) 53 NSWLR 31, Barrett J said at [8]:
>
>> There is no rule of law, whether under the *Evidence Act* or otherwise, which makes inadmissible evidence of a conversation given in indirect speech, but there are obviously very good reasons why courts have, over the years, been astute to regard the direct speech form as the best form.[14]

10 *Walsh v Sloan as Executor of the Estate of Keddie* [2019] WASCA 107, [74]–[76]. See also *Fodare Pty Ltd v Shearn* (2010) 240 FLR 187 for limitations on what is a reasonable objection.

11 *Federal Court Rules 2011* (Cth) rule 29.02(1). It is also, for example, a requirement in Queensland pursuant to the *Uniform Civil Procedure Rules 1999* (Qld) r 431(3).

12 See, eg, *Parker v Australian Building and Construction Commissioner* (2019) 270 FCR 39, [28], [46], [52], [56], [58], [59], [62], [67], [71], [75], [76], [77], [79], [81], [82], [84]. See also *Zreika v Royal* (2019) 271 FCR 65, [246].

13 *Qube Ports Pty Ltd v Maritime Union of Australia* [2018] FCAFC 72.

14 Ibid [115]–[117].

14.2.2 What is the difference between an affidavit and a witness statement?

Some courts and tribunals allow parties to file witness statements rather than affidavits. Witness statements are generally somewhat less formal than affidavits in form although their substantive purpose is identical. Witness statements need only be signed rather than sworn and may not include the formal court document information contained in affidavits. Affidavits are court documents that include all the formal information as to parties and courts which are contained in pleadings. Affidavits are read into evidence, while witness statements must be tendered. However, once a witness has been called and asked to verify his or statement, a witness statement becomes evidence in much the same way as an affidavit.[15] Some courts or tribunals may also require, or accept, a statutory declaration rather than an affidavit in support of a claim or defence.

This chapter will focus on affidavits, but readers should note that other forms of written witness evidence, such as those mentioned above, will engage many of the same rules and requirements as for affidavits.

14.2.3 Exhibits and annexures

Documentary evidence is often a critical part of civil litigation. Many interactions in modern society involve written contracts, receipts, tickets, letters, notices, emails, text messages, tweets, and other documents, including all forms of social media which may be relevant evidence for a dispute. There are two common ways to bring the court's attention to a document through an affidavit. One is to annex the document and the other is to exhibit it. Where a document is annexed to an affidavit, the document forms part of the affidavit and is filed and served with the affidavit. Where a document is exhibited to the affidavit, the document is referred to in the affidavit rather than being attached to it. Parties filing and serving affidavits must still serve a copy of the exhibit bundle when serving the affidavit on another party but will not file the exhibits with the court. Some documents may not be purely in electronic formats that are only capable of reproduction electronically. Not all courts require affidavits to be filed in court and, in such jurisdictions, there are less likely to be length limitations on affidavits. Even where affidavits are not filed in court prior to trial, it is useful for parties to have their affidavits in the most efficient and easy to review format so they are of maximum use at trial.

Whether it is better to annex or exhibit depends to some extent on the rules of the court. Courts, through practice notes, or judges, on a case-by-case basis, may impose a maximum length for affidavits. Annexures to an affidavit are included in its page count, while exhibited documents are not. This means lengthy affidavits, and/or those referring to numerous documents, or material incapable of pagination (such as YouTube videos) may require exhibits rather than annexures. There can also be significant benefits to exhibiting documents in cases where there are a large number of witnesses attesting to many of the same documents. In such cases, a single exhibit bundle containing all relevant documents can significantly reduce the total bulk of documents as compared to each witness separately annexing the same documents to their affidavit.

15 See Alan Sullivan, *Written Evidence: Witness Statements and Affidavits as an Alternative to Oral Evidence* (New South Wales Bar Association, 2015).

14.2.4 The role of lawyers in preparing affidavits

An affidavit belongs to the deponent and it is the deponent who must swear that its contents are true and correct. However, due to the complex form and evidentiary requirements of affidavits, most non-lawyers are not able to prepare their own affidavits. Instead, most affidavits are drafted by lawyers. An important aspect of a civil dispute lawyer's job is the ability to effectively interview witnesses giving consideration, during the interview process, to the form and evidentiary requirements of affidavits. For example, without prompting during interview, witnesses may not proffer the actual words they believe were used in a conversation as required for a properly prepared affidavit.

Witnesses do not always know or understand the matters in dispute and may not properly understand the significance of their role in the dispute. It is the lawyer's job to ask a witness the questions necessary to extract this information. Often, what a witness relevantly knows or did will not be understood by the lawyer until he or she actually interviews the witness so, while some questions may be drafted in advance of an interview, lawyers must be flexible in interviewing their witnesses.

If a lawyer fails to uncover an important and relevant adverse fact and this fact is then uncovered by the other side's lawyers in cross-examination, such a failure may be fatal to their client's case or, at least, may impact the strength of the case, adversely impact the utility of prior settlement negotiations, or prove deleterious to the credibility of the witness. It is therefore critical that witness interviews are probing and well thought out.

Once a lawyer has obtained all the relevant information from the witness, it is the lawyer's task to establish the most efficient way to set out the affidavit, ensuring compliance with the form requirements referred to above and the evidentiary requirements discussed below. In many instances, a simple chronological approach may suffice. In other instances, it may be more useful to the court to set out the affidavit dealing with each disputed issue sequentially or, where there is a central exhibit bundle, by reference to the order of the relevant documents in the bundle.

Once the affidavit is drafted, it must be reviewed by the witness and the lawyer must ensure that the witness understands and agrees with everything in the affidavit before swearing to its correctness. Complex or lengthy affidavits may require many iterations to ensure the affidavit is entirely correct and accurately represents the witness's evidence.

14.2.5 Affidavits in interlocutory proceedings

As discussed in prior chapters, it is common for civil litigants to have disputes in relation to interlocutory matters, such as discovery, subpoenas, privilege, pleadings and particulars. In most such disputes, there has been correspondence between the parties in relation to the matters in dispute which has not been seen by the court. When parties bring interlocutory disputes to court for resolution, their claims are usually set out in a notice of motion supported by one or more affidavits. These affidavits are often deposed to by the party's lawyers and will usually annex or exhibit the relevant written correspondence between the parties and attest to any telephone discussions or meetings. In this way, the court is able to review the actions of the parties and determine the dispute.

The affidavits of lawyers in interlocutory disputes are often brief, with lengthy annexures or exhibits. For each piece of correspondence annexed or exhibited, the deposing lawyer will often make only the briefest statement. An extract from the supporting affidavit of a lawyer acting for his or her client in an interlocutory dispute might read something like this:

> 3. On 10 April 2020, I caused to be emailed to the defendant's solicitor, X Firm, a letter dated 10 April 2020, a copy of which is annexed to this affidavit and marked 'A.'
> 4. On 18 April 2020, I received by email from the defendant's solicitor, X Firm, a letter dated 18 April 2020, a copy of which is annexed to this affidavit and marked 'B.'
> 5. On 19 April 2020, I telephoned the Ms B, at X Firm.
>
> I said words to the effect of:
>
> 'Thank you for your letter dated 18 April but I still don't understand why your client is unable to provide the particulars of the defence requested at numbers 4, 5 and 6 of our letter dated 15 April and you haven't explained that in your response.'
>
> Ms B replied words to the effect of:
>
> 'I will have to get instructions from my client in relation to 4, 5 and 6.'
>
> I replied words to the effect of:
>
> 'How long will that take because your particulars were due a week ago and we are supposed to file our reply by 28 April.'
>
> Ms B replied words to the effect of:
>
> 'I should be able to get back to you in the next 2 days.'
>
> 6. On 25 April 2020 I sent correspondence by email to Ms B, a copy of which is annexed to this affidavit and marked 'C.'[16]

14.3 Legislative framework

The rules as to admissibility of evidence are critical to the drafting of affidavits and witness statements in preparation for trial. The rules of evidence are governed by the *Evidence Act* enacted in each state or territory or the Commonwealth *Evidence Act* for matters within federal jurisdiction. For states which have not enacted laws based on the Uniform Evidence Law (UEL), many of the rules of evidence remain governed by the common law.

As discussed in Chapter 13, some states and territories have enacted legislation mirroring, the UEL template and others have not.[17] All states, including non-UEL states, have an *Evidence Act* which imposes obligations on parties regarding the production of evidence at trial. In states where the UEL applies, these rules are relatively uniform and are set out, mostly in in chs 2–4, of each *Evidence Act* with rules concerning admissibility set out in ch 3. Where the UEL does not apply, the common law governs many key principles of admissibility. The common law is relatively uniform across the states where it still applies and contains many of the same key concepts as the UEL, which owes its core foundation to the common law. However, the UEL was designed to reform the common law and, accordingly, there can be significant differences between jurisdictions which have

16 This is a hypothetical sample affidavit extract.

17 The UEL states and territories are New South Wales, Victoria, Tasmania, the Australian Capital Territory and the Northern Territory together with the federal jurisdiction. The non-UEL states are Queensland, South Australia and Western Australia.

legislated based on the UEL and those which have not.[18] Jurisdictions which have not enacted legislation based on the UEL may also make their own legislative amendments to the common law which mirror ch 3 of the UEL's variation from the common law (eg the expert witness exception to the opinion rule).

Affidavits must also comply with the formal rules for court documents set out in the civil procedure legislation for each jurisdiction; for example, the Uniform Civil Procedure Rules or Supreme Court Rules (depending on the state or territory in question), which have been discussed in prior chapters.

14.3.1 Federal jurisdiction

Admissibility of evidence in the Federal Courts (including the High Court) is governed by ch 3 of the *Evidence Act 1995* (Cth) which mirrors the UEL. However, the *Evidence Act 1995* (Cth), like most state legislation based on the UEL, has been amended several times and is, therefore, not identical to the *Evidence Acts* of other states. In addition to the *Evidence Act*, the *Federal Court Rules 2011* (Cth) pt 23 (rr 23.01–23.15) set out guidelines for appointing court experts and party experts, for calling expert evidence, and for the provision of expert reports in the Federal Court.[19]

14.3.2 Australian Capital Territory

The *Evidence Act 2011* (ACT) is based on the UEL and is mostly uniform with the *Evidence Act 1995* (Cth), which previously applied in the Australian Capital Territory. However, the *Evidence Act 2011* (ACT) differs from the *Evidence Act 1995* (Cth) in places where required to comply with the *Human Rights Act 2004* (ACT), including overarching provisions on the right to a fair trial. The Australian Capital Territory also sets out procedures for expert evidence in pt 2.12 of the *Court Procedures Rules 2006* (ACT).[20]

14.3.3 Northern Territory

The *Evidence (National Uniform Legislation) Act 2011* (NT) applies in the Northern Territory in conjunction with the *Evidence Act 1939* (NT). Section 6 of the *Evidence Act 1939* (NT) states that it applies in addition to but does not affect the operation of the *Evidence (National Uniform Legislation) Act 2011. The Evidence (National Uniform Legislation) Act 2011* mirrors the UEL, including the rules as to admissibility of evidence in ch 3. The *Supreme Court Rules 1987* (NT) ord 44 provide procedures for expert evidence.[21]

14.3.4 New South Wales

The *Evidence Act 1995* (NSW) mirrors the UEL, with admissibility of evidence in New South Wales governed by ch 3. New South Wales was an early adopter of the UEL and,

18 See, eg, *CSR Ltd v Amaca Pty Ltd* (2016) 62 VR 359, [74]. The Victorian Court of Appeal noted, in relation to the *Evidence Act 2008* (Vic) which is based on the UEL, that: "It is acknowledged that the Act did not simply adopt or incorporate common law principles and doctrines. In a number of significant respects, the Act abrogated, altered, adjusted or supplemented existing common law approaches to the law of evidence."

19 There are similar rules for the Federal Circuit Court at *Federal Circuit Court Rules 2001* (Cth) pt 15 div 2 (rr 15.06A–15.12).

20 *Court Procedures Rules 2006* (ACT) rr 1200–1246.

21 *Supreme Court Rules 1987* (NT) rr 44.01–44.05 for Supreme Court cases.

like the Commonwealth, now has over 20 years of case law interpreting its provisions. In addition, the *Uniform Civil Procedure Rules 2005* (NSW) pt 31 sets out procedural rules for the manner of giving evidence, including detailed rules in relation to the calling of expert witnesses,[22] expert witness reports,[23] parties' single experts,[24] and court-appointed experts.[25]

14.3.5 Queensland

Queensland has not adopted the UEL. It retains the *Evidence Act 1977* (Qld) with the rules as to admissibility of evidence predominantly governed by the common law. The *Evidence Act 1977* (Qld) contains s 92 which specifically enables use of affidavit evidence to establish facts in issue. The *Uniform Civil Procedure Rules 1999* (Qld) contains ch 11 on evidence, including ch 11 pt 5 setting out procedures for expert evidence.[26]

14.3.6 South Australia

South Australia has not adopted the UEL and maintains the *Evidence Act 1929* (SA), with the rules as to admissibility of evidence predominantly governed by the common law. The *Evidence Act 1929* (SA) contains s 34C specifically enabling the admissibility of affidavit evidence where it constitutes documentary evidence as to facts in issue. Procedures concerning expert reports in South Australia are governed by the *Uniform Civil Rules 2020* (SA) ch 7 pt 14 r 74.

14.3.7 Tasmania

Tasmania introduced the *Evidence Act 2001* (Tas) mirroring the UEL and, therefore, largely consistent with the federal, New South Wales, Australian Capital Territory, Northern Territory and Victorian *Evidence Acts* setting out the rules for admissibility of evidence in ch 3. The *Supreme Court Rules 2000* (Tas) pt 19 also contain procedural provisions on evidence, including div 5 on expert opinion evidence.[27]

14.3.8 Victoria

Victoria introduced the *Evidence Act 2008* (Vic), effective in 2010, mirroring the UEL and, therefore, mostly identical to the other states and territories following the UEL. In addition to introducing the *Evidence Act 2008* (Vic), Victoria introduced the *Charter of Human Rights and Responsibilities Act 2006* (Vic) which potentially impacts the interpretation of the *Evidence Act 2008* (Vic) through its requirement (in pt 3 div 3 ss 32–3) that Victorian statutes be interpreted compatibly with human rights or may be referred to the Supreme Court to make a declaration when that is not possible. Chapter 3 of the *Evidence Act 2008* (Vic) governs admissibility of evidence. Chapter 4 pt 6 of the *Civil Procedure Act 2010* (Vic) contains procedures governing expert witnesses and expert evidence.[28]

22 *Uniform Civil Procedure Rules 2005* (NSW) pt 31 div 2.
23 Ibid rr 31.27–31.36.
24 Ibid rr 31.37–31.45 where parties jointly appoint a single expert to provide expert evidence.
25 Ibid rr 31.46–31.54.
26 *Uniform Civil Procedure Rules 1999* (Qld) rr 423–429S.
27 *Supreme Court Rules 2000* (Tas) rr 514–517 govern expert evidence, including service of statements at r 515 for Supreme Court cases.
28 *Civil Procedure Act 2010* (Vic) ss 65F–65Q.

14.3.9 Western Australia

Western Australia, like Queensland and South Australia, has not adopted the UEL and maintains the *Evidence Act 1906* (WA) with the common law predominantly governing admissibility of evidence. Sections 79B-F of the *Evidence Act 1906* (WA) contain provisions governing expert evidence and the admissibility of business records and other documentary evidence. The *Rules of the Supreme Court 1971* (WA) ord 36A r 1 governs expert evidence through a single provision prohibiting adducing of expert evidence except where ordered by the case manager and in compliance with the directions given by the case manager in relation to the evidence.[29]

14.4 Lay witnesses

Most civil litigation involves at least one lay witness, and a complex litigation may boast dozens of lay witnesses. The admissibly of lay witness evidence in litigation is generally more straightforward than the admission of expert witnesses, because lay witness evidence rarely engages with the exception to the opinion evidence rule.[30] The role of most lay witnesses is to recount their knowledge of relevant past events. Statements for these lay witnesses of fact must consider evidentiary rules such as hearsay but need not consider the opinion evidence exception except to the extent the lay witness is providing opinion on the facts. In such cases, the admissibility rules applicable to their lay evidence is more complicated.[31]

14.4.1 What is a lay witness?

A lay witness essentially provides evidence of relevant facts in the dispute. Increasingly, such evidence is provided in a written statement, such as an affidavit, and much of the evidence may be in the form of documentary annexures or exhibits to that statement rather than oral statements made in court. In much civil litigation, witnesses are not examined in chief but rather provide all their evidence-in-chief by affidavits or witness statements and will only appear at a trial if they are required for cross-examination. This chapter will focus on the preparation of such written statements.[32]

Some common examples of lay witnesses include:

- parties to contracts in contractual disputes
- drivers, passengers and bystanders in motor vehicle accident cases
- property owners, developers and builders in property disputes
- husbands, wives, neighbours, family members in family law disputes
- employees and officers of financial institutions, insurers and corporations in a range of disputes including consumer disputes
- employees and officers of government bodies, government corporations, government authorities and councils in a wide range of disputes.

---

29 This provision applies only in the Western Australian Supreme Court.
30 See Chapter 14.6.4.
31 See Chapter 14.6.4 regarding opinion evidence.
32 See Chapter 15 for the role of witnesses at trial.

14.4.2 Selecting the appropriate lay witnesses

There are several considerations, practical and legal, when deciding the appropriate witnesses for a case, many of which relate to the key aspects of CDR discussed in Chapters 2 and 3. By this stage of the proceedings, parties are in possession of the pleadings and, sometimes, discovered documents and so should be well placed to identify the outstanding issues in dispute and the evidence required to prove their case.

There are, however, good reasons why parties do not necessarily prepare affidavits for every possible witness to a case. Preparing affidavits is a time-consuming and, therefore, costly process. Any witness who gives evidence which is then relied on by a party (whether in person or by affidavit) is likely to be required for cross-examination by the other party or parties. Attending court as a witness for cross-examination is not only time-consuming and expensive, but also extremely stressful and, for most witnesses, very unpleasant. In addition, an unreliable witness may do more damage to a client's case than good. A witness who the court finds to be dishonest or unreliable may cause evidence to be questioned which might otherwise have been readily accepted. Finally, the time and cost to the court and the parties in general also needs to be minimised to comply with the obligations on parties to undertake litigation as efficiently as possible.[33] A failure to comply with efficiency requirements may result in adverse costs orders.[34]

On the other hand, it can be potentially fatal to a client's prospects of success to call insufficient witnesses for two reasons. First, evidence is usually a prerequisite to proving a party's case. The fewer witnesses are called, the greater the likelihood that insufficient evidence is led to persuade the court of the merits of the case. The second risk from calling insufficient witnesses is that an adverse inference may be drawn by the court regarding missing witness evidence.. This is known as the *Jones v Dunkel* inference, after the High Court case *Jones v Dunkel*,[35] and provides the court with a discretion (rather than an obligation) to make an adverse finding where no explanation has been provided for an expected witness's absence. The adverse inference is that the missing witness would not have assisted the party who might have been expected to call them. The *Jones v Dunkel* inference can become complicated in relation to witnesses who do not obviously belong to any party or where it is desirable to draw an adverse inference against more than one party and the parties do not share the same relationship with the uncalled witness.[36]

14.5 Expert witnesses

Expert witnessing is one of the most contentious areas of civil procedure. The use of experts is prevalent in many types of civil litigation and yet their role is increasingly questioned. The key concerns relate to costs, which can be prohibitive, and issues surrounding the independence of evidence given by an expert who is recruited and paid by one party.[37] However, the complexity of modern life means that there are an increasing

33 See Chapter 2.4.
34 See Chapter 6.5.1.
35 *Jones v Dunkel* (1959) 101 CLR 298.
36 See Chapter 15.6.4 for more detail.
37 See Chapter 6 for detailed analysis of costs issues.

number of matters upon which a judge cannot be expected to have sufficient expertise to properly assess the factual evidence and determine which party should succeed without the assistance of expert evidence. Expert evidence is, therefore, an important example of the key CDR theme of balancing efficiency and due process because expert evidence can be simultaneously a necessity for a fair hearing and an expense so significant it renders litigation inaccessible.[38]

14.5.1 What are expert witnesses?

Expert witnesses are witnesses with relevant specialist expertise, gained through "training, study or experience", who provide an expert opinion to the court rather than evidence of facts.[39] Expert evidence is a key exception to the general evidentiary rule that opinion evidence is inadmissible.[40] An expert is often retained by a single party with multiple experts providing differing opinions for different parties on the same matter. An expert may, however, be retained by a court or agreed on by all parties as a single expert. Common types of expert witnesses in civil litigation include accounting experts (eg where the amount of damages claimed is complex and disputed), handwriting/computer forensic experts (eg where the validity of documents is disputed), medical experts (eg in personal injury cases) and engineers, builders and architects (eg in construction, building and insurance disputes). In practice, almost anyone with expertise in anything might potentially be called upon to give evidence as an expert witness where the litigation requires a judge to determine something requiring expert knowledge. For example, the New South Wales Court of Appeal decision of *Goode v Angland* concerned the expertise of jockeys considering whether one professional jockey's negligence caused an accident to another jockey. Appeal Justice Leeming (with Beazley P and Meagher JA agreeing) held:

> [149] The *Evidence Act 1995* (NSW), s 79 provides that the rule that opinion evidence is not admissible does not apply to opinion evidence that is wholly or substantially based on a person's training, study or experience. The 'opinion' of each of the experts was based on his experience as a jockey and/or a steward which had involved viewing videos of horse races and having to make various determinations as to what had occurred in a given race. In the absence of an appeal ground and more fundamentally in the absence of any challenge at trial, it is not available to the appellant to now raise a forensic challenge to Mr Burnett's evidence based on *Dasreef v Hawchar*.
>
> [150] But in any event, I do not consider that the appellant has made good that complaint. Each expert was experienced in analysing what had occurred in a particular race by reference to such evidence. Their expertise was directed, having regard to what they considered was depicted on the video and photographic evidence, to how the accident had occurred and to whether there had been a breach of the rules of racing.

38 See Chapter 2.3.1 for analysis of the balancing efficiency and due process theme.
39 UEL s 79 as interpreted by the courts. See, eg, *ELB Pty Ltd v Lumina BPO Pty Ltd* [2021] NSWCA 91 at [52]–[54].
40 See Chapter 14.6.4 below for more detail of the admissibility requirements for opinion evidence.
41 *Goode v Angland* (2017) 96 NSWLR 503, [149]–[151].
42 *Bell Group Ltd (in liq) v Westpac Banking Corporation (No 9)* (2008) 39 WAR 1.

> [151] In particular, the respondent pointed out that it was not suggested in the court below that Mr Burnett did not have the expertise to enable him to interpret the videos or the photographic evidence, nor was he was cross-examined to that effect. The respondent also noted that Mr Burnett had experience judging horse racing videos from his time on the Thoroughbred Racing Appeal Board in Tasmania.[41]

Goode v Angland demonstrates how the content of expertise can be tailored to the specific facts of a case and indicates some of the factors courts may consider when determining who qualifies as an expert witness.

Natural disasters lead to insurance claims and disputes with government agencies which require expertise in flooding, bushfires, earthquakes and tsunamis. Intellectual property and technology cases may require experts in those fields and cases concerning injury or infection may require scientific or medical expertise. For example, if there is a dispute as to whether a particular symptom suffered by a plaintiff is caused by a particular disease, a judge, who does not possess the relevant scientific or medical expertise, cannot be expected to be able to properly understand the disease or the symptoms, let alone to assess the medical and scientific evidence presented without assistance from someone with that expertise. An expert provides the necessary explanation and the assessment of the evidence for the judge who may then rely on the expert opinion in coming to his or her judgment.

Where the plaintiff has retained an expert who has provided a report favourable to the plaintiff, however, it is likely the defendant will then retain an expert who disagrees with the opinion of the plaintiff's expert and is more favourable to the defendant. The complexity of the task faced by judges in utilising expert evidence may be glimpsed from the judgment of Owen J in *Bell Group Ltd (in liq) v Westpac Banking Corporation (No 9)*[42] litigation in the Supreme Court of Western Australia. The Bell litigation, which has run for several decades, concerned a claim by the liquidators of Bell Group, on behalf of all its creditors, against a group of banks, including Westpac, who loaned Bell Group significant funds shortly before its collapse in the late 1980s in exchange for obtaining high level security which would protect all the funds of those banks in the event of liquidation. The legality of the banks' deal was dependent upon whether the Bell Group was solvent at the time of the deal. Justice Owen made numerous complex findings which constituted at least a partial loss for the defendants. In relation to interpreting expert reports, Owen J describes the limitations of the expert's role and the significance of the Court's role in determining the facts of the case:

> [1219] I think the correct approach is to concentrate on the substance of each of the disputed cash flow items rather than on differences of methodology used by expert witnesses. In the end it is the trier of fact, not the experts, who must reach a conclusion. Questions of judgments must be brought to bear as there are no absolutes. What the experts say about individual items, the method they employed in reaching conclusions and the conclusions themselves must all be considered. But these things cannot take on a character other than that of evidence. They are not binding on the court.[43]

---

43 *Bell Group Ltd (in liq) v Westpac Banking Corporation (No 9)* (2008) 225 FLR 1, 147 [1219] (note that the 39 WAR 1 report of this case referred to elsewhere, excludes paragraph [1219]). It should also be noted that the 2008 decision was appealed to the Western Australian Court of Appeal and then to the High Court where it settled subject to numerous ongoing disputes as to costs and related matters. See *Westpac Banking Corporation v Bell Group Ltd (in liq) (No 3)* (2012) 44 WAR 1; *Westpac Banking Corporation v Bell Group Ltd* [2013] HCATrans 85; *Bell Group NV (in liq) v Insurance Commission of Western Australia* [2017] WASCA 229.

14.5.2 Controversy surrounding expert witnesses

The debate in relation to expert witnessing relates to how the experts should be selected and paid and how many there should be. Historically, the party required to prove a matter which required expert knowledge, located and paid a suitable expert to provide the necessary evidence to the court. In many cases, however, the opinion of the expert hired by the first party was not one universally held and the party who disputed the matter would then hire a second expert to provide a contrary opinion. The judge would then be required to assess the experts and determine which opinion to accept (or whether to choose an interpretation somewhere between the two expert opinions).

This has led to concern that many expert witnesses are not independent or objective as they should be to best assist the court. Attempted solutions have included "hot tubbing", in which the experts meet before the trial to work through the issues and determine as many points of commonality as possible to reduce the matters with contested expert evidence. Another alternative is court-appointed experts or jointly-appointed experts, but it can be difficult for parties to agree jointly on an expert and parties may be unwilling to pay for the services of a court-appointed expert.

14.5.3 Rules for expert witnesses

The most important aspect of expert evidence is that it invariably involves opinion evidence. Evidence of an opinion is excluded from admissibility, pursuant to s 76 of the UEL, unless it complies with the s 79 exception to that exclusion which requires expertise. Expert evidence falls within that exception to the opinion rule, both at common law and pursuant to s 79 of the UEL. Accordingly, expert evidence must comply with the requirements of the limited exception to the opinion rule,[44] as well as the other requirements for admissibility.[45] Civil procedure rules also contain provisions governing procedures for witness evidence, particularly expert witness reports.[46]

14.6 Rules of evidence

When preparing an affidavit or witness statement, lawyers should ensure that the contents of the affidavit will be admissible in court in accordance with the rules of evidence. This is important for both lay and expert witnesses' affidavits. Provided an affidavit is in admissible form, the party who filed the affidavit may seek to have it admitted at trial as part (or all) of that party's evidence-in-chief. This process saves court resources and reduces hearing time, but does so without any significant cost to due process. Avoiding court time in evidence-in-chief is, therefore, a procedural step which enables efficiency without procedural cost and is thus an optimiser of CDR.

For the Commonwealth, the Australian Capital Territory, New South Wales, Tasmania, Victoria and the Northern Territory (the UEL jurisdictions), the admissibility of evidence

44 See Chapter 14.6.4.
45 See Chapter 14.6.
46 See Chapter 14.3. See, eg, *Uniform Civil Rules 2020* (SA) r 74; *Uniform Civil Procedure Rules 2005* (NSW) pt 31 div 2 rr 31.17–31.54.

is governed by each state or territory's enactment of legislation mirroring the UEL. In the remaining jurisdictions of Queensland, South Australia and Western Australia, the rules as to admissibility of evidence are mostly governed by the common law, supplemented by state-based *Evidence Acts*. In the following sections, the analysis will be based on the UEL which applies to the vast bulk of Australian litigation, as federal, New South Wales and Victorian disputes make up the large majority of Australian civil disputes.

Evidence law is complex and can be time-consuming. However, evidence law is essential for fair process. Lower courts will not always apply the rules of evidence, particularly for small claims where litigants are unrepresented. These "short cuts" in due process are inevitably made to reduce the costs of litigation to make it more affordable for litigants. They exemplify shifting the balance between efficiency and due process.[47] Evidence law applies to criminal as well as civil disputes and many of the leading authorities on the admissibility of evidence are criminal law cases. Accordingly, there are some criminal law cases necessarily referenced below, although civil authorities have been used where possible.

14.6.1 Rules of evidence and how they interact

The essential rules of evidence and their interaction are set out in the introduction to ch 3 of the UEL extracted from the *Evidence Act 1995* (Cth) below:

> **Chapter 3—Admissibility of evidence**
>
> **INTRODUCTORY NOTE**
>
> **Outline of this Chapter**
>
> This Chapter is about whether evidence adduced in a proceeding is admissible.
>
> Part 3.1 sets out the general inclusionary rule that relevant evidence is admissible.
> Part 3.2 is about the exclusion of hearsay evidence, and exceptions to the hearsay rule.
> Part 3.3 is about exclusion of opinion evidence, and exceptions to the opinion rule.
> Part 3.4 is about admissions and the extent to which they are admissible as exceptions to the hearsay rule and the opinion rule.
> Part 3.5 is about exclusion of certain evidence of judgments and convictions.
> Part 3.6 is about exclusion of evidence of tendency or coincidence, and exceptions to the tendency rule and the coincidence rule.
> Part 3.7 is about exclusion of evidence relevant only to credibility, and exceptions to the credibility rule.
> Part 3.8 is about character evidence and the extent to which it is admissible as exceptions to the hearsay rule, the opinion rule, the tendency rule and the credibility rule.
> Part 3.9 is about the requirements that must be satisfied before identification evidence is admissible.
> Part 3.10 is about the various categories of privilege that may prevent evidence being adduced.
> Part 3.11 provides for the discretionary and mandatory exclusion of evidence even if it would otherwise be admissible.

47 See Chapter 2.3.1 for analysis of this key CDR theme.

Figure 14.1 shows how this chapter applies to particular evidence:[48]

Figure 14.1 Admissible and inadmissible evidence

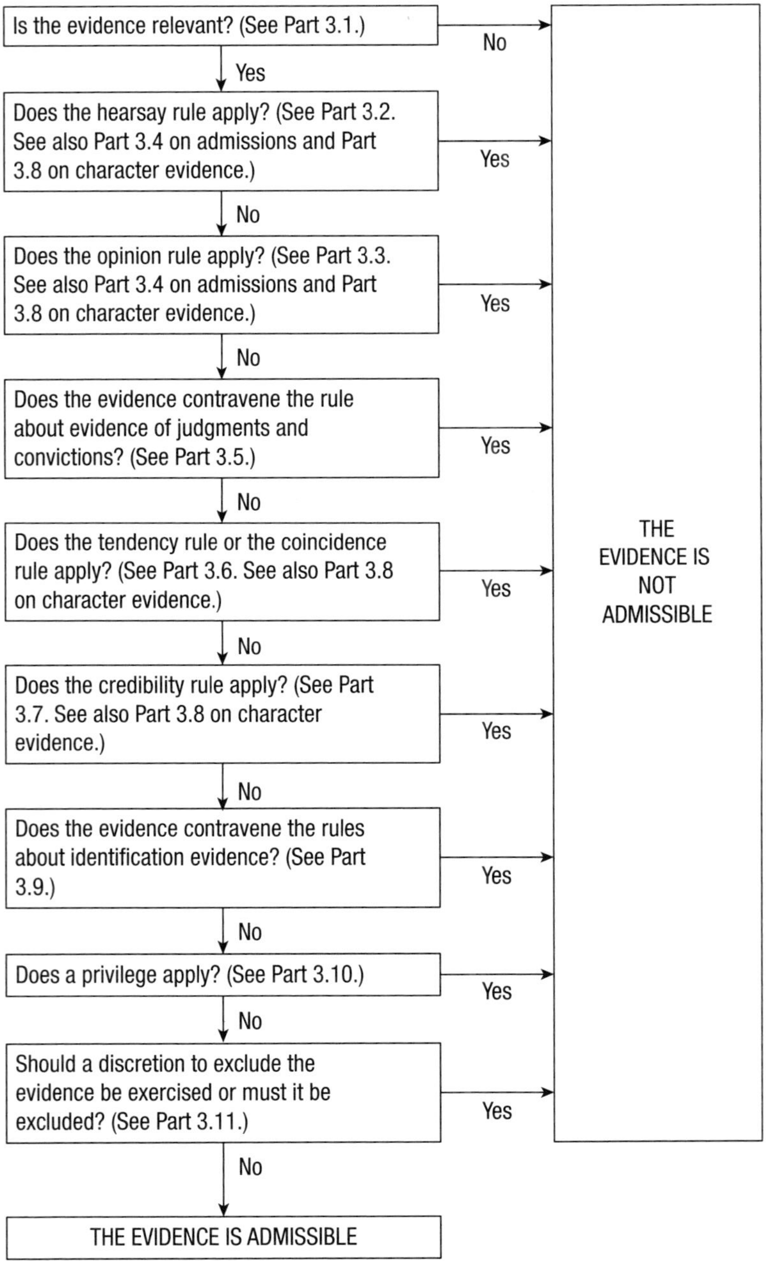

Source: *Evidence Act 1995* (Cth)

48 Uniform Evidence Law as set out in *Evidence Act 1995* (Cth).

Figure 14.1 applies to federal, New South Wales, Victoria, Tasmania, Northern Territory and the Australian Capital Territory courts. In addition, the rules set out in Figure 14.1 and their interactions evolved from the common law which preceded the UEL. Accordingly, many elements of Figure 14.1 apply similarly in the common law jurisdictions of Queensland, South Australia and Western Australia. While Figure 14.1 is useful, exclusions from admissibility need not be considered in the order they are set out in the UEL (as reflected in Figure 14.1). Relevance (pt 3.1) must always be considered first as a fundamental requirement of admissibility but the other considerations do not have an obvious hierarchy. Evidence can always be excluded due to privilege (pt 3.10) or the general exclusions (pt 3.11). The other exclusions to admissibility can be considered in any order.[49] The remaining elements of admissibility will be discussed briefly below.

For a more detailed understanding of admissibility of evidence, readers may consider the Law Reform Commission reports on evidence, including the combined *Uniform Evidence Law Report*[50] of the Australian Law Reform Commission, New South Wales Law Reform Commission and the Victorian Law Reform Commission in 2005 which sets out in detail the admissibility rules in the UEL, how those differ from the common law, and the growing understanding of human psychological tendencies which have led to the need to restrict admission of certain types of evidence to protect parties, particularly criminal defendants, from prejudicial treatment.

14.6.2 Relevance of evidence

Part 3.1 of the UEL (ss 55, 56) set out the default rule for admissibility of evidence. Section 55 sets out the test for relevance being evidence which "could rationally affect (directly or indirectly) the assessment of the probability of the existence of a fact in issue in the proceeding"[51] and confirms that evidence on credibility, admissibility and failures are not expressly excluded from relevance.[52]

Section 56 provides that any relevant evidence may be admitted, subject to other specific provisions of the Act, while evidence irrelevant to the proceedings may not be admitted.

The requirement that evidence be relevant is fundamental and should be addressed first by parties as was reiterated by the High Court in *Smith v The Queen*:

> As is always the case with any issue about the reception of evidence, … the first question is whether the evidence is relevant. … If the evidence is not relevant, no further question arises about its admissibility. Irrelevant evidence may not be received.[53]

49 See Chapter 13 for the application of privilege, pt 3.10 of the UEL, and the exclusion of evidence pursuant to pt 3.11. of the UEL.

50 Australian Law Reform Commission, *Uniform Evidence Law* (Report No 102, December 2005).

51 UEL s 55(1).

52 UEL s 55(2). UEL is mirrored in the following federal and state-based Acts: *Evidence Act 1995* (Cth); *Evidence Act 2011* (ACT); *Evidence Act 1995* (NSW); *Evidence (National Uniform Legislation) Act 2011* (NT); *Evidence Act 2001* (Tas); *Evidence Act 2008* (Vic).

53 *Smith v The Queen* (2001) 206 CLR 650, [6] (Gleeson CJ, Gaudron, Gummow and Hayne JJ).

The High Court explained the importance of the rationality requirement in the s 55 test for relevance in the admissibility of evidence in *IMM v The Queen*:

> [38] By s 55, evidence is relevant if it 'could rationally affect (directly or indirectly) the assessment of the probability of the existence of a fact in issue in the proceeding.' There can be no doubt that the reference to the effect that the evidence 'could' have on proof of a fact is a reference to the capability of the evidence to do so. The reference to its 'rational' effect does not invite consideration of its veracity or the weight which might be accorded to it when findings come to be made by the ultimate finder of fact.
>
> [39] The question as to the capability of the evidence to rationally affect the assessment of the probability of the existence of a fact in issue is to be determined by a trial judge on the assumption that the jury will accept the evidence. This follows from the words 'if it were accepted', which are expressed to qualify the assessment of the relevance of the evidence. This assumption necessarily denies to the trial judge any consideration as to whether the evidence is credible. Nor will it be necessary for a trial judge to determine whether the evidence is reliable, because the only question is whether it has the capability, rationally, to affect findings of fact. There may of course be a limiting case in which the evidence is so inherently incredible, fanciful or preposterous that it could not be accepted by a rational jury. In such a case its effect on the probability of the existence of a fact in issue would be nil and it would not meet the criterion of relevance.[54]

14.6.3 Hearsay evidence

In order to protect the reliability of the evidence allowed in court by preventing the admission of baseless gossip, there are complex rules in the UEL and at common law to limit the admission of hearsay evidence. "Hearsay" might be described as where someone attests to something having been said by someone else as proof that the something is true. For example, person A tells the court that person B told person A that fact X was true. The rule for the exclusion of hearsay says that what person A said is not proof that X is true. It can, however, be evidence of what B told A and/or what A's understanding of X was where such matters are relevant to the proceedings. For an example of where the use of a representation meant it was not excluded as hearsay, refer to *Creata (Australia) Pty Ltd v Faull*.[55] The rules applying to hearsay are complicated and are not entirely settled. As with many rules regarding the admissibility of evidence, hearsay is more commonly a basis for objecting to evidence in criminal trials than civil trials. However, affidavits in civil litigation may be read down or parts excluded if they do not comply with the hearsay rules. Section 59 of the UEL sets out the rule for hearsay. There are numerous exceptions to the hearsay exclusion and, as a result, hearsay evidence is routinely tendered in civil disputes either

54 *IMM v The Queen* (2016) 257 CLR 300, [38]–[39]. While this is a criminal law case, its analysis of relevance of evidence has been cited with approval in civil cases such as *Garston and Yeo (No 2)* [2019] FamCAFC 139, [27]. See also *Ballina Shire Council v Knapp* [2019] NSWCA 146, [23] which discusses the meaning of rationally in s 55 of the *Evidence Act 1995* (NSW) with reference to the High Court decision of *Washer v Western Australia* (2007) 234 CLR 492, [5]; *Demediuk v Demediuk* [2019] VSCA 79.

55 *Creata (Australia) Pty Ltd v Faull* (2017) 125 ACSR 212, [39].

under an exception to s 59 or because its admission is uncontested.[56] Most civil litigation could not proceed without hearsay evidence admitted under an exception.

Arguably the most significant exception to the hearsay rule for civil proceedings is the business records exception in s 69. As demonstrated in Chapters 11 to 13, documents often constitute the most significant aspect of evidence in civil disputes (and those documents are almost invariably hearsay). However, business documents are often a far more objective and reliable form of evidence than oral recollection of events and this is why s 69, and its common law equivalents, allow the tendering of business records as an exception to the hearsay rule.

The New South Wales Court of Appeal case of *Capital Securities XV Pty Ltd v Calleja*, in determining that business documents were admissible as evidence, sets out the history and application of the business records exception to the hearsay rule confirming the high trustworthiness of many business records.[57] In his analysis in *Capital Securities XV v Calleja,* Leeming JA notes the following important points:

- the onus of proving the s 69 exception to the hearsay rule rests with the party seeking to tender the documents into evidence
- there is a distinction between a "document" and a "representation" (made in a document) which is demonstrated through the wording of s 69
- courts may draw inferences from the nature of the information contained in the business record as well as the form of the document, the nature of the document and any other matters from which inferences can properly be drawn.[58]

The New South Wales Court of Appeal case of *Averkin v Insurance Australia Ltd* [2016] NSWCA 122 provides a useful example of the complexity of the interplay between s 59 (the hearsay rule) and s 69 (the business records exception to the hearsay rule), as well as discussing the added complexity of which party bears the burden of proof in relation to the inclusion and exclusion of evidence.[59] *Averkin* concerned a successful appeal by an insured on an insurance claim following a car fire and debated the inclusion of police reports under the business records exception to the hearsay rule. The interplay of the rules might be summarised as follows:

- Relevant evidence should be admitted to assist the court (therefore evidence admitted)
- *Except* that hearsay evidence should be excluded due to the potential unreliability of hearsay representations (therefore evidence is excluded under s 59)
- *Except* that business records are often reliable despite being hearsay and therefore should be an exception to the hearsay exclusion (therefore evidence is admitted under s 69(2))
- *Except* that representations in business documents made for the purposes of criminal investigations may be self-serving and, therefore, should be an exception to the business records exception to the hearsay exclusion (therefore evidence is excluded under s 69(3)(b)).

56 The *Evidence Act 1995* (NSW) includes notes to s 59 summarising the exceptions to the hearsay rule including ss 60, 63, 64, 65, 66, 66A, 69, 70, 71, 72, 73, 74, 75, 81, 87(2), 92(3), 110, 111.

57 *Capital Securities XV Pty Ltd v Calleja* [2018] NSWCA 26, [83]–[110] (Leeming JA with Basten and Gleeson JJA agreeing). See also *Maaz v Fullerton Property Pty Ltd* [2021] NSWCA 79 at [22–23].

58 *Capital Securities XV Pty Ltd v Calleja* [2018] NSWCA 26, [85]–[91].

59 *Averkin v Insurance Australia Ltd* (2016) 92 NSWLR 68 (Leeming JA with Basten JA agreeing with the outcome but offering different reasoning and McColl JA agreeing with Leeming JA).

It is also worth mentioning the exceptions to the hearsay exclusion contained in ss 63 and 64 of the UEL, which cover circumstances such as where the person who made the original statement is unavailable, for example, due to death. The Victorian Supreme Court of Appeal case of *CSR Ltd v Amaca Pty Ltd* concerned the right to contribution of Amaca (formerly James Hardy) from CSR in relation settlements paid to sufferers of asbestos-related diseases connected with their employment.[60] The sufferers were all dead at the time of the litigation and, therefore, unable to lead direct evidence but Amaca held doctors notes from appointments with the sufferers which it sought to admit even though the doctors no longer recalled the meetings which had resulted in the notes. The Court held the documents were admissible, first-hand hearsay pursuant to s 63 of the *Evidence Act 2008* (Vic) and through s 32 of the *Evidence Act 2008* (Vic) which allows a witness to read aloud a document as part of his or her evidence in limited circumstances.[61] In the Victorian Supreme Court of Appeal case of *Cook v Karden Disability Support Foundation*,[62] the Court held that the hearsay rule had no application to exclude a claim form completed by the applicant, given the applicant was present and gave evidence and, therefore the s 64(3) exception resulted in the hearsay rule having no application.[63]

Another exception to the hearsay exclusion of evidence relevant to civil disputes is the *Evidence Act 1995* (NSW) s 75 exception for interlocutory proceedings. Section 75 applies to affidavits prepared by solicitors in interlocutory disputes.[64] For example, in the New South Wales Supreme Court of Appeal case of *New South Wales v Nash*, the State appealed against a damages award in favour of Mr Nash for the tort of wrongful imprisonment and both parties filed notices of motion both of which were partially successful. In relation to the use of an unsworn statement as evidence, the Court held:

> The objection to this document is a hearsay objection pursuant to s 59 of the *Evidence Act*; however, counsel for the respondent acknowledge that the exception in s 75 applies (the hearing by me of the motions being an interlocutory proceeding), provided that the appellant in adducing the evidence also adduces evidence of its source. Evidence of the source is given in the affidavit of Ms Michalk who arranged for the employee to prepare the statement and received it after employer had signed it. The condition for the operation of s 75 (which, of course, disapplies the hearsay rule of its own force and without any exercise of judicial discretion) is therefore satisfied. In any event, the statement of the employee was not tendered upon the hearing before me to prove the truth of the statements made in it by the club employee but, rather, to prove that there exists a person who, if and when events concerning preparation and supply of CCTV footage are put in issue, may be expected to give the evidence set out in the statement. The representation of willingness is, in its own right, a hearsay representation but a much narrower one. Because s 75 disapplies the hearsay rule in relation to the statement of the Club employee, the hearsay objection cannot be upheld.[65]

For Queensland, Western Australia and South Australia, which retain the common law, the common law test of hearsay resembles its UEL equivalent as evident from the Full Federal

60 *CSR Ltd v Amaca Pty Ltd* (2016) 62 VR 359, [33]–[87] (Maxwell P, Beach and Kaye JJA).
61 Ibid [86]–[87].
62 *Cook v Karden Disability Support Foundation* [2016] VSCA 263.
63 Ibid [50].
64 See *Capital Securities XV Pty Ltd v Calleja* [2018] NSWCA 26. See Chapter 14.2.5.
65 *New South Wales v Nash* [2016] NSWCA 98, [36].

Court decision (in an appeal from the South Australian Industrial Relations court) in *Qube Ports Pty Ltd v Maritime Union of Australia*:

> [110]. The common law rule against hearsay operates (relevantly) to preclude a witness giving evidence of a statement made by another as proof of the fact asserted. The classic statement of this aspect of the rule is that given by the Privy Council in *Subramaniam v Public Prosecutor* [1956] 1 WLR 965 at 970:
>
> > Evidence of a statement made to a witness by a person who is not himself called as a witness may or may not be hearsay. It is hearsay and inadmissible when the object of the evidence is to establish the truth of what is contained in the statement. It is not hearsay and is admissible when it is proposed to establish by the evidence, not the truth of the statement, but the fact that it was made.[66]

14.6.4 Opinion evidence

The s 76 UEL opinion rule prevents the admission of opinions as proof of facts; for example, Witness X believing event P happened is not admissible as evidence that event P did, in fact, happen. This does not mean that Witness X's belief is necessarily inadmissible evidence because what X believes, or believed at a particular time, about event P may, itself, be an issue in the proceedings. It simply means that Witness X's evidence cannot be used to prove that event P happened. There are several exceptions to the opinion rule. The expert opinion exception in s 79 of the UEL, often arises in civil litigation. The UEL provides for the opinion evidence rule in pt 3.3 ss 76–80, with s 76 providing the general rule excluding evidence of an opinion from being admissible evidence, and s 79(1) providing an exception to the exclusion for specialist knowledge opinions, thereby allowing for admission of expert evidence.[67]

The opinion evidence rule, and its expert evidence exception, are critical to admitting expert evidence in court. When selecting an appropriate expert and instructing expert witnesses on the preparation of an expert report, it is important to ensure compliance with the principles set out by the High Court of Australia in *Dasreef Pty Ltd v Hawchar* concerning need to rule on objections concerning admissibility of evidence. The joint judgment of French CJ, Gummow, Hayne, Crennan, Kiefel And Bell JJ stated (with Heydon J in dissent) stated:

> 37. It should be unnecessary, but it is nonetheless important, to emphasise that what was said by Gleeson CJ in HG (and later by Heydon JA in the Court of Appeal in *Makita (Australia) Pty Ltd v Sprowles*) is to be read with one basic proposition at the forefront of consideration. The admissibility of opinion evidence is to be determined by application of the requirements of the *Evidence Act* rather than by any attempt to parse and analyse particular statements in decided cases divorced from the context in which those statements were made. Accepting that to be so, it remains useful to record that it is ordinarily the case, as Heydon JA said in Makita, that 'the expert's evidence must explain how the field of "specialised knowledge" in which the witness is expert by reason of "training, study or experience", and on which the opinion is "wholly or substantially based", applies to the facts assumed or observed so as to produce

66 *Qube Ports Pty Ltd v Maritime Union of Australia* [2018] FCAFC 72, [110] (White J with Mortimer and Bromwich JJ agreeing).

67 UEL s 76 which also lists exceptions including s 79.

> the opinion propounded'. The way in which s 79(1) is drafted necessarily makes the description of these requirements very long. But that is not to say that the requirements cannot be met in many, perhaps most, cases very quickly and easily. That a specialist medical practitioner expressing a diagnostic opinion in his or her relevant field of specialisation is applying 'specialised knowledge' based on his or her 'training, study or experience', being an opinion 'wholly or substantially based' on that 'specialised knowledge', will require little explicit articulation or amplification once the witness has described his or her qualifications and experience, and has identified the subject matter about which the opinion is proffered.[68]

Common difficulties in the admission of expert opinion evidence involve the extent of the witness's expertise and the nature and content of the opinion expressed, which must be wholly or substantially based on the expertise. In addition, the expert must be objective and, therefore, cannot be seen to be an advocate for either party. The Federal Court case of *BTQ16 v Minister for Immigration, Citizenship, Migrant Services and Multicultural Affairs*[69] concerned the rejection of an affidavit concerning translation errors by someone who was not a certified translator and whose independence was questionable. Justice Griffiths explained:

> [26]. Whilst in most cases a witness seeking to express a 'specialised knowledge' based on his or her 'training, study or experience', being an opinion 'wholly or substantially based' on that 'specialised knowledge' will require 'little explicit articulation or amplification once the witness has described his or her qualifications and experience, and has identified the subject matter about which the opinion is proffered' (*Dasreef Pty Ltd v Hawchar* [2011] HCA 21; (2011) 243 CLR 588, [37]), the Rostomashvili affidavit was entirely deficient in this respect. The appellant asserted only very late during the hearing on 12 March 2019 that Ms Rostomashvili was an 'expert', and sought leave (which was refused) apparently to have her solicitor give evidence on this point. The appellant had principally advanced that Ms Rostomashvili sought to give a lay opinion within the exception in s 78 of the *Evidence Act*. It is unclear what evidence the solicitor could possibly have given on the question of the expertise of Ms Rostomashvili. On the basis of the evidence, the primary judge was correct to conclude that the witness was not an 'expert': FCCA reasons at [82]. The primary judge was supported in this finding by the fact that on the basis of the proposed affidavit evidence from the witness, her evidence as to translation errors was to be given in order to support the appellant's contention before the Court that such errors had been made. However, an expert witness is not an advocate for a party, and has an overriding duty to assist the Court: see r 15.07 of the *Federal Circuit Court Rules 2001* (Cth) and the Federal Court of Australia Practice Note: Expert Evidence Practice Note (GPM-EXPT).[70]

The New South Wales Supreme Court of Appeal decision in *Fuller v Avichem Pty Ltd* demonstrates how undisputed experts may still have aspects of their evidence challenged as being beyond their expertise.[71] In *Fuller v Avichem Pty Ltd,* the entire Court accepted

68 *Dasreef Pty Ltd v Hawchar* (2011) 243 CLR 588, [37]. *Dasreef* is commonly cited: see, eg, *South Western Sydney Local Health District v Gould* (2019) 97 NSWLR 513, [44]; *Metro North Hospital and Health Service v Pierce* [2018] NSWCA 11, [151]; *ELB Pty Ltd v Lumina BPO Pty Ltd* [2021] NSWCA 91. [53].

69 *BTQ16 v Minister for Immigration, Citizenship, Migrant Servvices and Multicultural Affairs* [2020] FCA 72.

70 Ibid [26].

71 *Fuller v Avichem Pty Ltd* [2019] NSWCA 305.

the expertise of a clinical psychologist but her ability to determine the plaintiff's capacity to undertake future work following a workplace injury claim was only accepted by two out of three Court of Appeal judges. The dissenting judge considered that the psychologist did not have sufficient medical expertise to comment on the ability of the injured plaintiff to undertake call centre work. However, the majority of the Court of Appeal accepted her evidence, holding:

> If the assumptions Ms Owen made about the appellant's current work capacity and restrictions were not made good by appropriate medical evidence her report would be of little if any weight. That does not, however, mean that her report was inadmissible. Dasreef made clear that opinion evidence is not to be excluded solely because the factual bases upon which the opinion is proffered is not established by other evidence. Ms Owen made assumptions based on medical reports about the appellant's ability to lift, to carry, to bend, to twist and to sit. Ms Owen demonstrated relevant specialised knowledge in vocational rehabilitation and the safe return to work of injured workers by her training, study or experience in that topic over many years.[72]

Similarly, in the New South Wales Supreme Court of Appeal case of *Hawkesbury Sports Council v Martin*, part of a civil engineer's report in relation to the dangers of a fence which had caused injury, was rejected. The engineer's expertise on fence construction was accepted but not his evidence as to pedestrian visibility of the fence as he had not established expertise in relation to "human visual perception".[73]

In addition to the legislative provisions in the UEL and common law equivalents (see, eg, *Brown v Daniels*),[74] civil procedure rules also often contain rules governing expert witnesses. For example, there is an Expert Witness Code of Conduct at sch 7 of the *Uniform Civil Procedure Rules 2005* (NSW) which sets out the duty of an expert to the court and to parties, including the duty to confer with other expert witnesses and to endeavour to reach agreement and to present a joint report if so directed by the court.[75] The *Federal Court Rules 2011* (Cth) sets out in pt 23 r 13 basic requirements for expert reports. Similar guidelines exist in non-UEL jurisdictions, such as ch 11 pt 5 of the *Uniform Civil Procedure Rules 1999* (Qld) entitled "Expert Evidence" which "declare(s) the duty of an expert witness in relation to the court and the parties" at r 423(a).

14.6.5 Admissions and prior judgments

There are special evidentiary rules which apply to admissions (pt 3.4 UEL) and to findings of fact in prior judgments (pt 3.5 UEL). An admission is a previous representation made outside of the current proceedings which is adverse to the case a party is making. The most serious form of admission is an admission of guilt in criminal proceedings. Admissions must

---

72 Ibid [89] (Payne JA with White JA agreeing at [107] and Macfarlan JA disagreeing at [41]–[43]).

73 *Hawkesbury Sports Council v Martin* [2019] NSWCA 76, [30]–[33].

74 *Brown v Daniels* (2018) 85 MVR 440, [30]–[36] concerned the admissibility of expert evidence in a motor vehicle accident.

75 It should be noted, however, that, in the event of conflict, the opinion provisions of the *Evidence Act 1995* (NSW) override the operation of the *Uniform Civil Procedure Rules 2005* (NSW) such that expert evidence may be admissible even where the sch 7 code was not complied with: *Chen v The Queen* (2018) 97 NSWLR 915, [10]–[45].

be first-hand (s 82 UEL) and will not be excluded because of the hearsay or opinion rules, constituting a further exception to both those rules (s 81 UEL), and can generally only be used against the party making the admission or someone authorised on its behalf (s 87 UEL).[76] As admissions are commonly made without the protection of court procedure, the court must be particularly careful in giving value to them, including being satisfied that they were not obtained under duress (s 84 UEL).[77]

The rule against judgments and convictions in pt 3.5 UEL provides that evidence of decisions of previous courts, their findings and their reasoning, is not admissible in subsequent proceedings to prove the facts at issue in the earlier proceedings. The exclusion is subject to exceptions, such as proof of death in probate cases and proof of conviction for all civil cases, where evidence remain admissible.

14.6.6 Tendency, coincidence, propensity and similar fact evidence

The UEL and the common law have rules restricting the admissibility of evidence of matters which are similar but not directly relevant to the case before the court. The UEL refers to "tendency" and "coincidence" evidence in pt 3.6 ss 94–101, while the common law generally refers to such evidence as "propensity" and "similar fact" evidence.[78] Tendency (propensity) evidence is, essentially, evidence of past events used to show that a particular person has a tendency to act or think in a particular way. Coincidence (similar fact) evidence generally involves use of similar, and apparently unrelated, events to argue that a pattern exists linking those events to a particular person. The restrictions on admission of tendency and coincidence evidence have arisen on the basis that the probative value of such evidence has the potential to be overestimated and it can be unfairly prejudicial. The exclusion of such evidence is critical particularly for criminal law cases where juries may be inclined to assume a defendant committed a crime on the basis that defendant committed similar crimes previously. Sometimes contextual evidence can be admitted to assist comprehension of other admissible evidence but still not be available for its tendency or coincidence purpose because it does not meet the requirements of the tendency or coincidence exceptions.[79]

In the New South Wales Supreme Court of Appeal decision in *White v Johnston*,[80] Leeming JA (with Barrett and Emmett JJA agreeing) upheld an appeal in part because evidence of a tendency had been improperly admitted. The case concerned a dispute by a customer

76 See, eg, the complex affidavit admissions in *Hurd v Zomojo Pty Ltd* [2015] FCAFC 148. See also *Helicopter Resources Pty Ltd v Commonwealth* (2019) 264 FCR 174 which involved employee evidence under s 87 *Evidence Act 1995* (Cth) in a workplace health and safety claim following the death of a helicopter pilot in a hidden Antarctic ice crevasse.

77 See, eg, *Habib v Nationwide News Pty Ltd* (2010) 76 NSWLR 299 for a civil case example of the *Evidence Act 1995* (NSW) s 84.

78 See Royal Commission into International Responses to Child Sexual Abuse, *Background Paper: Similar Fact and Propensity Evidence and Joint Trials in Australian Jurisdictions* (2014) for additional details on this type of evidence and the distinctions between *UEL* and common law jurisdictions.

79 *Unique International College Pty Ltd v Australian Competition and Consumer Commission* (2018) 266 FCR 631.

80 *White v Johnston* (2015) 87 NSWLR 779.

against her dentist for allegedly undertaking work with no therapeutic purpose but the affidavit evidence in dispute indicated a tendency to invoice for work not performed rather than a tendency to undertake work with no therapeutic purpose:

> [139]. If evidence is relevant only for inferential tendency reasoning, then it is inadmissible unless the protections in s 97(1) of notice and significant probative value are satisfied. If evidence is relevant for some other purpose as well as tendency reasoning, then s 95 ensures that unless the protections in s 97(1) are satisfied, the evidence may only be used for the non-tendency purpose. In either case, the need to assess 'significant probative value' makes it necessary to identify with some precision what the tendering party proposes to establish by the evidence: see *Elomar v R* [2014] NSWCCA 303 at [348].
>
> ...
>
> [141]. 'Probative value' is defined in the Dictionary to mean 'the extent to which the evidence could rationally affect the assessment of the probability of the existence of a fact in issue'. But s 97 requires the Court to consider whether the evidence has significant probative value.
>
> ...
>
> [143]. The primary judge erred in admitting the evidence as significantly probative of one 'particular matter' (a tendency to charge for work never performed) and then relying upon the evidence for a different purpose (a tendency to perform wholly unnecessary work with no therapeutic purpose). There was error in using the tendency evidence for a different purpose from that for which it had been adduced, to assist in a finding that none of the work performed had a therapeutic purpose. To do so was contrary to ss 95 and 97, as well as being procedurally unfair (and not only to Ms White; Ms Johnston may have wished to be heard against his Honour taking that course: cf *Farah Constructions Pty Ltd v Say-Dee Pty Ltd* [2007] HCA 22; 230 CLR 89 at [133]).[81]

Civil cases may also require predictions of future behaviour which can lead to faulty tendency and coincidence reasoning. For example, in *Assistant Minister for Immigration and Border Protection v Splendido*,[82] the Full Federal Court upheld the primary judge's decision that the Assistant Minister's decision had been made without the necessary evidence required to make the decision. Mr Splendido had lived in Australia from the age of two, and his parents, spouse and children were all in Australia and he had committed no crimes until his 40s. However, Mr Splendido was then convicted of numerous criminal offences and had his visa automatically cancelled. Mr Splendido sought revocation of the visa cancellation but the Assistant Commissioner refused to revoke the cancellation, concluding Mr Splendido had a high risk of reoffending. The Full Federal Court unanimously agreed that the Assistant Minister's decision should be set aside, with Mortimer J noting:

> [71] The bare descriptive information in the National Police Certificate was not capable of establishing, in and of itself, the qualitative likelihood of Mr Splendido re-offending, or what offences it was likely he might, or might not, commit in the future. Dicta from cases dealing with the question whether inferences can be drawn from a person's record of criminal offences explain the flaws in such a reasoning process, and why more is needed than the bare facts of past offending.
>
> ...

81 Ibid [139], [141], [143] (Leeming JA).

82 *Assistant Minister for Immigration and Border Protection v Splendido* (2019) 271 FCR 595.

[73] In *Hughes v The Queen* [2017] HCA 20; 344 ALR 187 at [70]–[72], Gageler J explained the vice in tendency reasoning:

> Applied to evidence of past conduct, tendency reasoning is no more sophisticated than: he did it before; he has a propensity to do this sort of thing; the likelihood is that he did it again on the occasion in issue ....[83]

14.6.7 Credibility of witnesses

It is important that lawyers, interviewing witnesses to prepare their affidavit evidence, cover all relevant matters, including those likely to arise in cross-examination. An affidavit should not be simply a self-serving document because the credibility of witnesses is important and inconsistency between affidavit evidence and cross-examination will reduce witness credibility.[84]

14.7 Amending affidavits and supplementary affidavits

Sometimes, it is necessary to amend affidavits and it is also common for witnesses to file supplementary affidavits, especially in reply. Affidavits should be amended, if allowed, where they make an incorrect statement or contain a statement in inadmissible form.

Supplementary affidavits (sometimes called "additional affidavits") are additional to, rather than in replacement to, the original affidavit.[85] For example, where further relevant documents come to light after an affidavit is sworn and served, a supplementary affidavit can be prepared and served. Similarly, where a plaintiff serves an affidavit for a witness and the defendant then provides evidence in reply which contradicts the plaintiff evidence, a supplementary affidavit in reply from a plaintiff witness may be necessary to clarify or expand on issues cast into doubt by the defendant's evidence. A supplementary affidavit of a witness should not revisit matters already attested to in the original affidavit of that witness. A supplementary affidavit must be filed on a timely basis and, where filed in an appeal on an issue of law, cannot introduce factual material which post-dates the decision appealed

14.8 Conclusion

Written witness evidence is increasingly important in civil litigation in Australia and is therefore a significant factor differentiating litigation from ADR. Particularly in higher courts, most witnesses will serve affidavits as their primary form of evidence-in-chief. The ascertainment and preparation of witness evidence which occurs in litigation is simultaneously a key advantage and disadvantage of litigation as a form of CDR. There is significant time and cost

83 Ibid [71]–[73] (with Mortimer J noting at [76] that Gageler J being in dissent in *Hughes* did not affect the value of the principles). See also Australian Law Reform Commission, *Uniform Evidence Law 2006* (Report No 102, February 2006).

84 Witness credibility will be discussed in Chapter 15.

85 *Thorpe v Schulz* [2017] WASCA 199.

associated with preparation of witness evidence which increases the barriers to accessing justice through litigation for those with limited means. However, the information revealed through interviewing witnesses and preparing evidence can be critical to achieving justice. As such, witness evidence is an important example of the challenges of balancing efficiency against due process in CDR.[86] Lawyers have a critical role to play in determining who should give lay and expert evidence in support of their client's cases and in assisting with the preparation of such evidence. Lawyers must ensure that evidence given complies with the rules set out in the relevant *Evidence Act* and, for states not adopting UEL, the appropriate common law and statutory rules. This aspect of litigation is expensive and difficult, as the evidentiary rules affecting witness affidavits discussed in this chapter are both complex and legalistic. The selection of expert witnesses is also challenging due to concerns of bias and the changing and controversial role of experts in civil litigation. Preparing advanced written witness evidence is an example of courts increasing party autonomy and relinquishing some control of the dispute resolution process while also protecting limited court resources by allowing much evidence-in-chief to be in writing rather than heard in court.[87]

In preparing written witness evidence, lawyers must remember that poor evidence preparation cannot usually be rectified on appeal and may be difficult to rectify during trial without breaching considerations of procedural fairness. In many respects, therefore, the preparation of written witness evidence in litigation is one of the most important and challenging aspects of CDR.

86 See Chapter 2.3.1.

87 See Chapter 2.3.1 (balancing efficiency with due process) and Chapter 2.3.4 (balancing autonomy with control).

15 TRIAL PREPARATION AND ATTENDANCE

15.1 Introduction

This chapter concerns civil litigation trials. Trials are actually one of the least common means of civil dispute resolution (CDR). In addition to the significant portion of civil disputes which are resolved without any recourse to litigation, the overwhelming majority of civil litigation cases which are commenced never make it to trial. Most cases for which litigation proceedings commence are resolved by ADR[1] or summary disposition.[2] This is because trials are one of the most expensive aspects of litigation, so it is natural for civil disputants and courts to avoid trials wherever possible in the interests of efficiency. However, a full trial is the only way civil disputants are able to put their entire case, with all the evidence, before an independent decision-maker applying full due process and fully exercising their right to be heard. Accordingly, the decision by parties to pursue the trial process is an example of the key CDR theme of balancing efficiency against due process.[3]

In addition, within the trial process itself, there are numerous instances of all the key CDR balancing themes in the trial process. Different state procedure rules and court-based practice notes provide judges with varying degrees of control over processes within trials, and judges must regularly juggle between allowing the parties autonomy to run their case as they choose and limiting the timing of hearings to ensure efficiency and the protection of scarce court resources. These decisions engage with the key themes of balancing efficiency with due process and balancing autonomy with control.[4] The level of discretion allowed to judges in running trials also engages with the key theme of balancing certainty with flexibility.[5]

Trial is one of the most daunting aspects of litigation for disputants which militates in favour of having clearly specified processes to reduce that fear and uncertainty and the risk of apprehensions of judicial bias. On the other hand, trial is also an individual experience, with disputants often appreciating processes personalised to their specific needs. Thus, courts must balance carefully between certainty and flexibility. Finally, trial is the most open aspect of CDR so there can be significant pressure placed on courts by disputants to hear proceedings in closed court, suppress publication, and prevent the admission of evidence.[6] Thus, trial also reflects the key CDR theme of balancing privacy and openness.

The fact that most civil litigation is disposed of prior to trial does not mean that the preparation for trial has been wasted. It is often the processes necessary to prepare for trial which promote settlement or enable summary resolution by the courts. As parties engage in case preparation, they gain a better understanding of the strengths and weaknesses of their case and this significantly increases the potential for settlement. For cases which do proceed to trial, the work done in drafting the pleadings,[7] obtaining and reviewing relevant

1 See Chapters 4 and 5.
2 See Chapter 5.
3 See Chapter 2.3.1 for the key balancing theme of efficiency and due process.
4 See Chapters 2.3.1 and 2.3.4.
5 See Chapter 2.3.2.
6 See Chapter 3.3 for an analysis of open justice.
7 See Chapters 8 and 9.

documents,[8] and preparation of witness affidavits[9] is now converted into the final materials to be put before the court for determination.

Although civil litigation trials are one of the least common means of resolving disputes, they are crucial to the effective operation of all CDR. When parties commence proceedings, they do so with a possible future trial in mind. When parties settle prior to that trial (through any means of ADR), their settlement decision is influenced by their prediction of what a court would order at trial if they did not settle. The nature, cost, and complexity of trials provides a key incentive for parties to engage meaningfully in ADR.

Trials are critical to CDR because they provide a final binding adjudication of a dispute. There are numerous factors in favour of a court resolution, including a full opportunity to be heard and to present evidence to an independent decision-maker.[10] Without the threat of trial and a potential adverse court decision, many defendants and potential defendants would not resolve their disputes through ADR. The existence of determinative trials is also essential for the effectiveness of the costs incentives to settle.[11] In the absence of trials, outcomes of disputes would inevitably favour the powerful, rather than adhering to concepts of justice. However, it should be noted that these underlying benefits of trials also rely on the enforceability of court decisions by the courts and the states.[12]

In order to reach trial, there is a significant amount of work performed by lawyers in the weeks prior to trial, and during trial itself, and it is these procedures and their role in the CDR process which will be explained in this chapter. This chapter will not consider the rules of evidence in any detail and will not set out in detail the rules of professional responsibility which affect solicitors' obligations during trial.[13]

15.2 Legislative framework

The rules of privilege and admissibility of evidence are critical during trial.[14] Court rules and civil procedure rules contain relevant provisions for trial.[15] This means that *Evidence Acts*, *Civil Procedure Acts*, civil procedure and/or court rules and the common law rules which have been referred to in preceding chapters all have relevance during trial. In addition to these, each court will have practice notes with rules or practices relevant to running trials in that court. There are often practice notes for specific types of cases run in particular courts; for example, there may be practice notes for construction cases, admiralty cases, technology cases, property cases, intellectual property cases and commercial cases. Specific practice notes are common where courts maintain separate court lists for different types of proceedings.

8 See Chapters 11, 12 and 13.
9 See Chapter 14.
10 See Chapter 2.6.
11 See Chapter 6.8.
12 See Chapter 16.
13 See Chapter 6 for a consideration of costs. See Chapter 14 for some key rules of evidence.
14 See Chapters 13 and 14 respectively.
15 See Chapters 8 to 12.

15.2.1 Federal jurisdiction

Admissibility of evidence in the Federal Courts (including the High Court) is governed by ch 3 of the *Evidence Act 1995* (Cth) (which is a Uniform Evidence Law (UEL) Act). In addition, Chapter 2 of the *Federal Court Rules 2011* (Cth) contains provisions relevant to the operation of Federal Court trials including, in particular, pt 29 (Evidence) and pt 30 (Hearings).

Other important Commonwealth court rules which govern trials include the *Federal Circuit Court Rules 2001* (Cth) and the *Federal Circuit Court (Bankruptcy) Rules 2016* (Cth)[16] which govern trials in the Federal Circuit Court, and the *Family Court Rules 2004* (Cth) which govern trials in the Family Court. The *High Court Rules 2004* (Cth) include rules in chs 2 and 3 for the court's original jurisdiction, which is very limited.

15.2.2 Australian Capital Territory

Chapter 3 of the *Evidence Act 2011* (ACT) (which is a UEL Act) primarily governs admissibility of evidence in matters heard in Australian Capital Territory courts.

Part 2.13 of the *Court Procedures Rules 2006* (ACT) governs pre-trial procedures while pt 2.15 governs the trial process and includes r 1508 which sets out the order of evidence and addresses providing, among other matters, that the party with the burden of proof should present their case first. The rules also govern the ability of the court to split proceedings into separate questions (div 2.15.3) (eg separating the question of liability from the question of quantum) and to refer matters out to court appointed assessors and referees (div 2.15.4).

15.2.3 Northern Territory

The *Evidence (National Uniform Legislation) Act 2011* (NT) (which is a UEL Act) applies in the Northern Territory, with rules as to admissibility of evidence set out in ch 3 of the UEL.

The *Supreme Court Rules 1987* (NT) provide in ord 48 pt 3 for the setting down for trial. Order 49 of the *Supreme Court Rules 1987* (NT) governs trial procedure, including the order of evidence and addresses. Order 50 provides for special referees, and ords 51 to 55 provide rules for specialist hearings, such as assessments of damages, administration of estates and sale of land by court order.

15.2.4 New South Wales

Admissibility of evidence in New South Wales is covered by ch 3 of the *Evidence Act 1995* (NSW) (which is a UEL Act) and is, therefore, fairly uniform with other UEL states.

As for other jurisdictions, there are also specific New South Wales provisions for a variety of trial-related matters. For example, in relation to witness evidence at trial,[17] in New South Wales, the *Uniform Civil Procedure Rules 2005* (NSW) pt 24 provides for the examination of witnesses outside of trial, and the *Evidence on Commission Act 1995* (NSW) pts 2 and

16 *Federal Circuit Court (Bankruptcy) Rules 2016* (Cth) apply specifically to bankruptcy trials and contain detailed specific provisions such as for the examination of debtors and other examinable people under ss 50 and 81 (respectively) of the *Bankruptcy Act 1966* (Cth).

17 See Chapter 15.6.

3 provide for the examination of witnesses overseas and interstate, respectively. This is one way in which witnesses unable to appear, for example, due to poor health, may give evidence and such evidence may be recorded audio visually pursuant to r 24.13 of the *Uniform Civil Procedure Rules 2005* (NSW). As another example, pt 28 of the *Uniform Civil Procedure Rules 2005* (NSW) empowers the court to divide or consolidate actions before, during or after trial.[18] Part 29 of the *Uniform Civil Procedure Rules 2005* (NSW) governs trial procedure, including use of juries, the order of proceedings, the recording of proceedings, and applications for dismissal or judgment.

15.2.5 Queensland

Queensland has not adopted the UEL. It retains the *Evidence Act 1977* (Qld), with many rules as to admissibility of evidence also partially governed by the common law.[19] The *Evidence Act 1977* (Qld) contains s 92, which specifically enables use of affidavit evidence to establish facts in issue at trial. The *Evidence Act 1977* (Qld) also contains provisions in relation to the taking of audio-visual evidence, including interstate witnesses and expert witnesses, which enables conformity with other Australian states (see pt 3A ss 39A–39Z). Chapter 13 of the *Uniform Civil Procedure Rules 1999* (Qld) governs trials and other hearings (rr 461–526), with ch 14 governing certain specific issues which can arise in certain trials including personal injury matters. Chapter 13 of the *Uniform Civil Procedure Rules 1999* (Qld) also includes provisions regarding setting matters down for trial, separation of trial questions, and special hearings including assessment of damages hearings and special Magistrate Court matters such as employment cases.

15.2.6 South Australia

South Australia has not adopted the UEL and maintains the *Evidence Act 1929* (SA) with the many rules as to admissibility of evidence partially governed by the common law.[20] The *Evidence Act* 1929 (SA) also contains s 34C, specifically enabling the admissibility of affidavit evidence where it constitutes documentary evidence as to facts in issue; s 34KA providing for out of court statements by unavailable witnesses; and s 34J for ill witnesses. Chapter 13 of the *Uniform Civil Rules 2020* (SA) governs preparation of evidence to be adduced at trials, including tender books, experts reports and lay evidence; while ch 14 *Uniform Civil Rules 2020* (SA) provides for the conduct of trials, including issues upon which evidence may be adduced and the use of oral and written witness evidence.[21]

15.2.7 Tasmania

Admissibility of evidence in Tasmania is predominantly governed by ch 3 of the *Evidence Act 2001* (Tas) (which is a UEL Act) and is, therefore, fairly uniform with other UEL states.

18 See Chapter 15.4.3.
19 See Chapter 14.
20 See Chapter 14.
21 *Uniform Civil Rules 2020* (SA) ch 14 r 172.1(1) gives the court complete discretion to make orders for the conduct of trial, with r 172.1(2) listing numerous examples of possible topics for such orders including: the issues upon which evidence may be adduced, the timing of the trial, the numbers of witnesses allowed, and the order in which evidence may be adduced.

The *Supreme Court Civil Procedure Act 1932* (Tas) pt IV ss 26–37G concern trials including transfer of proceeding to inferior courts, use of juries in civil trials, and the referral of issues and matters to assessors and arbitrators (with consent). The *Supreme Court Rules 2000* (Tas), pt 22 (rr 539–587) also regulate trials, including setting down for trial, place and mode of trial, order of evidence, referring out matters, damages assessment, and other trial-related matters.

15.2.8 Victoria

Use of evidence at trial in Victoria is governed by ch 3 of the *Evidence Act 2008* (Vic) (which is a UEL Act) in essential uniformity with other UEL states. In addition to introducing the *Evidence Act 2008* (Vic), Victoria also introduced the *Charter of Human Rights and Responsibilities Act 2006* (Vic). The *Charter* potentially impacts the interpretation of the *Evidence Act 2008* (Vic) through its requirement (in pt 3 div 3 ss 32–3) that Victorian statutes be interpreted compatibly with human rights or be referred to the Supreme Court to make a declaration when compatibility is not possible.

The *Civil Procedure Act 2010* (Vic) and the *Supreme Court (General Civil Procedure) Rules 2015* (Vic) are also of relevance to trials. The *Supreme Court (General Civil Procedure) Rules 2015* (Vic) provide for place and mode of trial (ord 47), setting the date for trial (ord 48), order of evidence and addresses and adjournments (ord 49), referral to referees (ord 50), assessment of damages (ord 51) and subsequent orders governing various particular types of trial.

15.2.9 Western Australia

Western Australia has not adopted the UEL and maintains the *Evidence Act 1906* (WA), with the common law predominantly governing admissibility of evidence. Sections 79B-79F of the *Evidence Act 1906* (WA) contain provisions governing expert evidence and the admissibility of business records and other documentary evidence. The *Rules of the Supreme Court 1971* (WA) set out rules for place and mode of trial in ord 32, proceedings at trial in ord 34, for assessors and referees at ord 35, for admissibility of evidence at ord 36, and expert evidence at ord 36A.

15.3 Preparing for trial

As Chapters 8 to 14 have demonstrated, there is a lot of work involved in preparing a case for trial. In addition to matters such as pleadings, discovery and preparation of witness evidence discussed in Chapters 8 to 14, there is further work often undertaken immediately prior to trial in preparation for trial, including briefing counsel, subpoenaing witnesses, preparing documents and drafting written submissions.

15.3.1 Brief counsel

Traditionally, in the legal system Australia inherited from the British, solicitors performed the preparation for litigation while barristers made all court appearances and solicitors were never heard in court. This demarcation between barristers and solicitors no longer exists and the legal profession has become increasingly fused. New South Wales is the only state which maintains separate admission requirements for barristers, with Queensland having been the last state to fuse its legal profession in 2004. However, all states continue to maintain independent Bar Associations and there are dedicated barristers in all Australian states and territories. Even in New South Wales, solicitors are entitled to appear, and do regularly appear, in court. Some solicitors perform all their own court work and never hire counsel.

Although solicitors can and do appear in court, barristers continue to be briefed to appear in civil litigation. The role of barristers today varies tremendously, with many being "briefed to advise and appear". Large commercial law firms almost invariably brief counsel on large commercial proceedings, and usually retain one or more barristers early in proceedings. Often, barristers will settle (finalise and sign off) initial pleadings and all subsequent steps of large-scale commercial litigation, including appearing at contested interlocutory hearings, sometimes conducting witness interviews, and even assisting with discovery. Similarly, some sole practitioners cover a wide variety of legal practice by hiring specialist counsel to assist with their litigious matters throughout proceedings. In this type of relationship, barristers are also involved early in proceedings and are likely to draft, or settle, pleadings and be intimately involved with the entire litigation process.

However, trial is by far the most common part of litigation for counsel to be involved in assisting solicitors. A barrister who is simply "briefed to appear" will be sent all the relevant documents and materials, together with a brief instructing him or her on the case. The barrister will then make all oral submissions in court and examine, and cross-examine, all relevant witnesses.

There can be many advantages to briefing counsel in civil litigation. They are experts in advocacy, including witness examination and cross-examination, and the preparation of court documents. Also, counsel may be hired due to specialist experience in a particular type of litigation or litigation in a particular jurisdiction, court or tribunal.[22] This may be particularly helpful for rural and suburban solicitors who often have a broad practice area and cannot have the depth of expertise in every area of their practice the way a specialist barrister can.

15.3.2 Subpoena witnesses

It is important to serve a subpoena to appear in court on all witnesses upon whose evidence you wish to rely at trial. In most instances, the witnesses a party calls will appear willingly but there is always a possibility that a witness will be ill or unable to attend due to some crisis or emergency. A subpoenaed witness who does not turn up to court may be found in contempt of court and fined. A subpoenaed witness who is genuinely unable to attend court due to illness or emergency will be excused from attendance and not found in contempt.

In the event a subpoenaed witness does not attend court, for whatever reason, no adverse inference will be drawn against the party intending to call that witness, provided the subpoena was properly served and evidence of this service can be provided to court. Conversely, if a witness is not subpoenaed and fails to appear, the court may infer that the

22 See Chapter 7 for further detail specialist courts and tribunals.

evidence of that witness would not have assisted the party which would have been expected to call the witness. This is the *Jones v Dunkel* inference.[23]

15.3.3 Prepare documents

Most civil litigation involves documents and, often, large numbers of documents (see Chapters 11–13). One of the most important steps in preparing for trial is determining which documents are likely to be relevant during the trial. This is usually a relatively small subset of the total documents involved in the matter. There are often at least two bundles of document which a lawyer should prepare for trial. The most important bundle contains the documents the lawyer knows will be referred to during the trial, including all the documents the lawyer intends to rely on during the trial. The second bundle of documents contains additional documents which the lawyer considers may arise in trial. The bundle of documents to be used at trial is often tendered to the court and agreed with the other party in advance of the trial and is referred to as the "tender bundle" or the "court book".[24] Usually, the tender bundle or court book will contain all documents which might possibly be referred to in the trial. Some cases will have both a court book and a tender bundle, in which cases the court book will contain pleadings, submissions and other documents prepared by lawyers, while the tender bundle will contain the documents necessary to prove the case (usually a subset of the discovered and subpoenaed documents discussed in Chapters 11 and 12).[25] Parties must ensure that they tender in court all documents necessary to prove their case.

Increasingly, the documents used in trials are electronic and all parties and the judge have access to an agreed bundle of documents. In such cases, it is still important to build electronic databases containing virtual bundles as referred to above.[26] If the documents are not electronic, it is important that there be numerous copies of the first bundle and a significant number of the second bundle. There should be enough copies of documents to provide copies to the judge, the other side, possible witnesses and your own legal team (which may include several barristers). When bundles are electronic, the complicating factor is providing secure access to ensure that documents are only available to those who require them, and that documents which are not made public through the trial itself remain confidential.[27]

23 *Jones v Dunkel* (1959) 101 CLR 298, discussed in Chapter 15.6.4.

24 See *Re Day* (2017) 340 ALR 368, [8], [33]. [251]–[252] which featured a revised tender bundle because further relevant facts had come to light after service of the original tender bundle. See *North East Solution Pty Ltd v Masters Home Improvement Australia Pty Ltd* [2016] VSC 1, [270] and following for an example of use of a court book where submissions refer to numerous documents with supporting court book references footnoted.

25 The old requirement for original documents to be used in court was abolished in UEL jurisdictions pursuant to s 51 of the UEL. The means of adducing documents are now quite broad pursuant to s 48 and the definition of a document in the UEL Dictionary such that most parties will provide the court with copies. The common law traditionally required authentication of documents in order to adduce them in court but this requirement has been overruled for UEL jurisdictions: *Gregg v The Queen* [2020] NSWCCA 245, [365]–[368].

26 See David Robertson, 'Paperless Trials' (2018) (Spring) *Bar News: Journal of the New South Wales Bar Association* 64.

27 See Chapters 13.11 and 13.12.

15.3.4 Prepare written submissions

Judges will sometimes make directions for parties to serve written opening submissions upon the court and each other. Submissions should outline the relevant facts and the applicable law, including both the legal principles and the supporting legislation and cases. Submissions help each party to understand the case to be met and help the judge to understand the remaining issues in contention. Well-written submissions may save considerable court time.

It is also common for some courts (particularly higher-level courts) to direct parties to file written submissions at the close of a hearing summarising the final position for each party. Written submissions are usually made electronically, and some judges will use excerpts from a party's written submissions in their final judgments, particularly the submissions of the party who is ultimately successful in the case.

15.4 How trials actually proceed

This following analysis indicates why trial procedure is complex, why it varies so much, and how trials actually proceed. How trials proceed varies enormously from court to court and matter to matter, as well as between different jurisdictions within Australia. Some of the factors which affect trial procedure are set out below. A possible trial structure for a simple trial is also set out below.

15.4.1 Typical trial steps

Civil procedure rules and practice notes, as referred to in Chapter 15.2, usually provide some guidance as to the conduct of trials (see, eg, r 29.6 of the *Uniform Civil Procedure Rules 2005* (NSW)). However, these rules inevitably leave much to the discretion of the court regarding the order of proceedings. When litigants are self-represented, many of the steps below can become problematic. Self-represented litigants are unlikely to understand the structure and requirements of litigation, let alone complex rules of evidentiary examination and cross-examination which they should be following. This reduces both the efficiency and the effectiveness of the trial process and requires judges to frequently intervene to direct the self-represented parties on execution of the steps below. Self-represented litigants create some of the greatest challenges for courts in balancing efficiency with due process, because their lack of knowledge makes them inherently inefficient but they also require careful adherence to due process because of their vulnerability.[28] It should also be noted that an increasing number of the steps below may now be carried out electronically rather than in person.[29]

The basic order for simple proceedings tends to be as follows in most civil litigation:

1. **Plaintiff gives its opening address:** The opening address will set out what matters the plaintiff says must be proved in order for its case to succeed and what evidence it intends to lead to establish those matters in dispute. The opening address may include a review of relevant documentary evidence. While the vast majority of

28 See Chapter 2.3.1. See also Productivity Commission, *Access to Justice Arrangements* (2014) 494–9.
29 See Chapter 8.6.

cases are opened by the plaintiff, this is because the plaintiff, having commenced the proceedings, most commonly bears the onus of proof. However, there are cases where the initial onus of proof rests on the defendant and the defendant presents to the court first. For example, where the defendant disputes the court's jurisdiction to hear a matter, the defendant would have the onus of proof and would, therefore, open the case.

2. **Plaintiff adduces evidence:** The plaintiff will then seek to have its evidence admitted into court, including documentary evidence, real evidence (objects) and witness evidence:
   a) Plaintiff witness called and examined in chief (and/or affidavit admitted as evidence)
   b) Plaintiff witness cross-examined by defence's counsel, if requested
   c) Plaintiff witness re-examined by plaintiff's counsel, if required to clarify matters raised in cross-examination but not to raise matters which should have been raised in examination-in-chief.

   Steps a) to c) are then repeated for each of the plaintiff's witnesses.
3. **Defendant gives its opening address:** The defendant then opens in response to the plaintiff's case, explaining why it considers the plaintiff's case must fail and what evidence it will adduce to establish this. It is not always necessary for a defendant to adduce evidence, particularly if it considers the evidence of the plaintiff, after cross-examination, is inadequate to prove the plaintiff's case.
4. **Defendant adduces evidence**: The defendant then proffers its documentary and witness evidence (where considered necessary):
   a) Defence witness called and examined in chief (and/or affidavit admitted as evidence)
   b) Defence witness cross-examined by plaintiff's counsel, if requested
   c) Defence witness re-examined by defendant's counsel, if required to clarify matters raised in cross-examination.

   Steps a) to c) are then repeated for each of the defendant's witnesses.
5. **Defendant gives a closing address:** This closing address sets out what the defendant considers it has established and how it says the evidence adduced established its case.
6. **Plaintiff gives a closing address:** This closing address sets out what the plaintiff considers it has established and how it says the evidence adduced established its case.
7. **The court adjourns to consider its judgment:** Most cases do not receive an immediate judgment (an *ex tempore* judgment*)*. Judges generally reserve their decision.[30]
8. **Submissions after adjournment:** Sometimes, judges will grant parties leave to make submissions (often in writing) while it is adjourned to consider judgment. Such submissions may concern issues, such as costs or matters on which the parties were

30 See Chapter 16 for a further discussion of judgment.

unable to provide the court with relevant information during the trial. Sometimes, parties will seek to make further submissions or even reopen proceedings.[31]

Sometimes, each party will give its opening address prior to any evidence being called by a party. The above process becomes significantly more complex the more parties are involved and the more complex the claims of those parties are. The following section sets out some of the factors which potentially complicate trial procedure.

15.4.2 Factors affecting trial procedure

Much civil litigation is not as simple as the above example. The way an actual trial proceeds may vary due to a myriad of factors relating to the court, the nature of the proceedings, the size and complexity of the dispute, the practices of the particular judge hearing the matter, and practicalities peculiar to the dispute itself including who bears the onus of proof.

1. **Court rules and practices:** As mentioned above, most courts have, not only civil procedure rules, but Practice Notes which govern how proceedings run. Many courts have practice notes specific to certain court lists or types of litigation. For example, matters in the Commercial List of a Supreme Court may proceed differently to those in the Defamation List or the Common Law List of that same court. Lower courts, such as Local Courts, tend to have less formality, and adhere less strongly to evidentiary rules, than Supreme Courts. Rules and practice notes can govern the order of proceedings, what documents must be lodged and when, how evidence can be adduced, the length and format of written submissions, and other rules governing documentary evidence.
2. **Complexity of the dispute:** A complex dispute requires more complicated hearing procedures. In a matter with 15 plaintiffs, 4 defendants, and multiple cross-claims and cross-defences, the order of proceedings may need to change several times as the trial develops, depending on which issues are raised and how they impact various different aspects of the case.[32] Judges will also try to minimise the length of the hearing and the number of changes in speaker, and so may hear one party on all issues pertaining to that party, regardless of where they fall in the proceedings. It is also common, in complex proceedings, for a witness to give evidence relevant to multiple aspects of a complex claim. In such cases, the witness will generally only be called once and will be examined, and cross-examined, at that time on all matters on which the witness is able to give relevant evidence. This is efficient for the witness but can mean that the lawyers and judge are traversing back and forth through different issues in dispute many times during the course of a hearing. Determining the most efficient way to manage limited resources, while ensuring due process and compliance with the rules of evidence, can be particularly challenging in complex disputes.[33]

31 See Chapter 15.7 for further details.

32 See, eg, the Bell litigation saga discussed in Chapter 2.5.3, including the original trial decision of *Bell Group Ltd (in liq) v Westpac Banking Corporation (No 9)* (2008) 39 WAR 1.

33 See Chapter 2.3.1

3. **The judge:** Different judges have different preferences which relate to how they best understand matters. It is sensible for judges, within reason, to organise their courts to maximise their own ability to comprehend each case quickly and easily. While it is important that most procedures are consistent, for reasons of procedural fairness and so litigants and litigators know how to run their case, there is also room for judge-driven flexibility. For example, if a judge prefers to have exhibits printed rather than viewing them on a screen, or prefers not to hear witness evidence after 4:00pm, it makes sense for parties to accommodate such preferences. Trials require a balancing of what best suits the judge with the need for certain processes and party autonomy.[34]
4. **Practicalities of the case:** Each case is unique and there are often practical matters which affect the course of proceedings. For example, there is flexibility to accommodate witnesses who are only available to appear on limited dates. A judge may agree for a defence witness to be heard on the first or second day of a two-month trial (even if that is during the plaintiff's opening address) where that is the only date the witness is available. A document may become relevant during the course of proceedings and the court may allow admission of that document by a party who has otherwise finished presenting its evidence. Witnesses may be recalled because matters have been raised which were not foreseen.[35]
5. **Onus of proof and standard of proof:** Which party bears the onus of proof and which standard of proof applies are also key factors affecting trial proceedings. Generally, in civil disputes, matters in dispute need only be proved on the balance of probabilities. This means that whichever party's argument is more persuasive will usually win. However, determining evidence on the balance of probabilities and the standard of proof required can be complex depending on the nature of aspects of the evidence as noted by the New South Wales Supreme Court of Appeal in *Nguyen v Tran*[36] in relation to s 140 of the *Evidence Act 1995* (NSW) (a *UEL* Act) which governs the standard of proof in civil proceedings in *UEL* jurisdictions. It is most commonly the plaintiff who bears the onus of proof, as the plaintiff commences proceedings seeking to prove its case. However, particularly where a positive defence such as fraud is pleaded,[37] the defendant may bear the onus of proof in some aspects of the case.

15.4.3 Separation and consolidation of trials

It is sometimes efficient to divide a trial into multiple potential hearings. Such a division, or separation, is different from simply adjourning a trial mid-hearing, which is discussed briefly later in this chapter. Separation of a trial into components can be beneficial from a cost and timing perspective where a failure on one aspect of the trial will render the remainder

34 See Chapter 2.3.2 and Chapter 2.3.4. for analysis of these key themes.
35 See Chapter 15.6 for a further discussion of these matters.
36 *Nguyen v Tran* (2018) 86 MVR 16 [62]–[63] where the Court also referred to the High Court's pre-UEL common law decision in *Neat Holdings Pty Ltd v Karajan Holdings Pty Ltd* (1992) 110 CLR 445.
37 See Chapter 10.2.2.

of the trial unnecessary.[38] The four common divisible aspects of trials are jurisdiction, liability, damages, and costs. Of these four components, jurisdiction and costs are essentially procedural questions, while liability and damages go to the substantive merits of the dispute.

If there is a dispute as to whether the court has jurisdiction to hear a matter, this will be a threshold question for determination by that court. If determined in the negative, the case can proceed no further. Accordingly, courts will generally hear and determine any jurisdictional disputes as early as possible before the parties prepare their evidence to ensure the court has jurisdiction before proceeding any further. Jurisdictional disputes are common in international commercial litigation where there is often a choice of possible forums for hearing the dispute and parties may even attempt to commence proceedings in multiple jurisdictions.[39] For example, if a party from Japan contracts with an Australian vendor to purchase livestock raised in New Zealand for delivery to a factory in China, there are immediately four possible forums for hearing any dispute arising from that contract. Sometimes, however, the contract between the parties will specify that any dispute should be heard in a particular jurisdiction. If a party commences in a different jurisdiction to that specified in the contract, the Court will usually decline jurisdiction of the matter or stay its proceedings pending commencement in the previously agreed forum.[40] Courts may also decline to hear a matter on the basis that the claim is time barred, so a successful time limitation argument is usually a complete defence to a claim. Pleading that a matter is beyond the statutory limitation period will be determinative of the entire dispute where successful and is, therefore, often heard as separate preliminary hearing.[41]

It is also not uncommon for courts to separate hearings on liability and damage in cases where it is likely to be time-consuming and costly to prepare evidence of damage, and such evidence will be irrelevant where liability is not found. This is common in tortious cases where parties often dispute whether damage to property or personal injury to one party (the plaintiff) is caused by the negligence of the other party (the defendant). If the plaintiff does not succeed in proving the defendant's liability, the claim fails. Assessing damage in such cases commonly involves numerous witness statements, expert accounting and medical evidence, and significant documentary evidence in the form of financial accounts, tax returns etc. The time and expense of preparing such evidence can avoided if the liability case is heard separately and the plaintiff's liability claim fails.

The separation of questions need not relate to different aspects of the court's decision, such as liability and damages. Rather, the basis of separation is whether one aspect of the case can be separated and, if determined in one party's favour, would render the remainder of the case unnecessary and, thereby, save considerable hearing costs. For example, in the New South Wales Supreme Court case of *Nichols Constructions Pty Ltd v Elphick*, McCallum

38 See, eg, *Swashplate Pty Ltd v Liberty Mutual Insurance Co* (2020) 141 ACSR 313, [1]–[5] following the separation of liability in an insurance claim for damage to a helicopter during transportation by sea. The separate hearing on liability resolved the dispute because Allsop CJ determined the insurer was not liable.

39 Disputes as to appropriate forum are known as *forum non conveniens* disputes. The leading Australian High Court authority is *Voth v Manildra Flour Mills Pty Ltd* (1990) 171 CLR 538.

40 A recent *forum non conveniens* is *Republica Democratica de Timor Leste v Lighthouse Corporation Ltd* [2019] VSCA 290.

41 See Chapter 9.3.1 for a brief discussion of statutes of limitation.

J decided to split a contractual issue from the other questions to be heard first as, if resolved in the plaintiff's lender's favour, it would render consideration of the remaining issues unnecessary, noting:

> ... there is no perfect course; the mandate of the *Civil Procedure Act* is to seek to achieve the least unhappy course in the face of difficult, competing considerations.[42]

Nichols Constructions Pty Ltd v Elphick provides an excellent demonstration of the complexity of determining efficiency which courts can face. Courts already face a complex task balancing efficiency with the right to be heard.[43] Separation of questions introduces an added complexity that efficiency itself can be difficult to predict, as separating questions will usually result in reduced efficiency where the preliminary question does not resolve the dispute.

The High Court has indicated dislike of the separation of trials in *Tepko Pty Ltd v Water Board*[44] and again in the separate, but not dissenting, judgment of Kirby J in *X v Australian Prudential Regulation Authority* where he explains his concerns with separation of trials, as follows:

> [93]. *Separated questions*: This is yet another case where a great deal of interlocutory litigation has unfolded as a result of the separation of questions, answered in the course of substantive proceedings without finally resolving those proceedings.
>
> [94]. It is not entirely clear, in the present instance, how the primary judge came to separate the two questions, as he did on 13 May 2005. It is recorded that they were separated 'by consent'. In earlier years, I was sympathetic to this procedure in the hope that it sometimes holds out that preliminary determinations of legal questions will resolve fundamental issues and, perhaps, save a great deal of court time in the process. This may still be true in some cases. I do not deny the occasional utility of the procedure. However, the longer I observe litigation over separated questions, the more I am reinforced in the conclusion that the practice is commonly, or at least often, misguided, counter-productive and, ultimately, unduly expensive and burdensome to the courts and the parties alike. It often seems to grow out of an inclination of parties and their advisers to postpone facing up to the irksome necessities of the trial.[45]

The final issue in proceedings commonly heard separately after judgment on the substantive dispute is claims relating to costs.[46] Costs usually follow the cause (ie the loser pays the bulk of the winner's costs, as well as its own). However, interlocutory disputes, offers of settlement, prospects of success and lawyer conduct can all affect awards of costs. Accordingly, courts will often seek written submissions as to costs at the time of handing down their judgment on the merits of the case, making costs a separate determination.

---

42 *Nichols Constructions Pty Ltd v Elphick* [2015] NSWSC 1732, [51]. This case contains a thoughtful analysis of the advantages and disadvantages of separating questions in litigation including a review of many preceding cases. See also *Heavy Plant Leasing v McConnell Dowell Constructors (Australia)* [2018] NSWSC 1006.

43 See Chapter 2.3.1.

44 *Tepko Pty Ltd v Water Board* (2001) 206 CLR 1 (Kirby and Callinan JJ).

45 *X v Australian Prudential Regulation Authority* (2007) 226 CLR 630, [93]–[94].

46 See Chapter 6 regarding the role of costs in dispute resolution.

The converse of courts separating matters into multiple trials is consolidation of multiple trials into a single hearing to increase efficiency.[47] Where parties have commenced multiple proceedings against each other in relation to related matters, courts may choose to consolidate the matters and hear them as a single trial.

Another form of consolidation may occur where there are similar cases against an identical or related defendant by unrelated plaintiffs. Sometimes, where many parties have the same cause of action, representative action (also called "class action") may be taken.[48] Increasingly, Australian courts are facing multiple class actions commenced by different solicitors in relation to the same incident, which raises the further possibility of consolidation of class actions.[49] However, other cases involve only two or three plaintiffs with similar actions against a common defendant and, in such cases, the courts may simply order that the matters be heard together.

15.5 Documentary and other non-witness evidence in trial

Evidence in court is traditionally oral evidence given by witnesses standing before a judge. This is increasingly inconsistent with the level of written documentation (especially electronic communications) prevalent in Australia and other permanent records which may constitute relevant evidence, such as video footage, photographs, maps, diagrams, graphs, computer metadata and audio recordings. Such materials are often crucial to civil litigation.

15.5.1 The tender bundle

As mentioned above,[50] it is common for parties to prepare a tender bundle containing all the documents (and other permanent records) they seek to rely on in trial. Most judges prefer to receive a single agreed tender bundle containing all relevant documents of all parties. If there is a single tender bundle, any objections to any documents by any party should be noted in the index of the tender bundle. If parties are preparing individual tender bundles, they are usually served on the other side, in accordance with court directions, in advance of the trial.

If there are objections as to the admissibility of the documents, these should be raised as soon as possible. Objections as to admissibility usually relate to the relevance, veracity, or provability of the document.[51] In most cases, there will be a number of documents or permanent records for which neither party disputes validity nor relevance. In some cases, the authenticity of documents or their value is disputed. It is preferable for the efficient running of the litigation if all parties are aware as early as possible of the documents likely to be put before the court during the trial, and directions regarding tender bundles are designed to ensure that no party is taken by surprise as to the documents to be discussed before the court.

47 See, eg, *Draoui v Le* [2019] SASCFC 105, [2].
48 See Chapter 8.4.2 regarding representative actions.
49 See, eg, *Perera v GetSwift Ltd* (2018) 263 FCR 1, [84], [88], [106].
50 See Chapter 15.3.
51 *Re Day* (2017) 340 ALR 368 also discussed above. See also Chapter 14.2.3.

15.5.2 Admitting permanent record evidence through witnesses

One of the best forms of evidence is permanent records, such as documents, X-rays, and recordings, created prior to the dispute and explained by a witness. Therefore, a common way to admit documents is through witnesses, including expert witnesses. If a document was relevant to the understanding, actions or decisions of a witness, the document is likely to be referred to by the witness in evidence (including pre-trial affidavit evidence) and is likely to be tendered as evidence when the witness is called at the hearing, if not before.

Expert evidence is likely to rely on documents or other permanent materials. For example, a medical expert in a personal injury case is likely to refer to X-rays, doctors' reports and other materials in the course of giving evidence. Similarly, a town planning expert in a construction case is likely to refer to relevant maps, plans, photographs and reports in the course of giving evidence.[52]

It is also not uncommon to call expert evidence to confirm the veracity of permanent records relevant to a dispute. For example, handwriting experts give evidence as to the identification of signatures, forgery and other aspects of original written documents.[53] Similarly, computer forensic experts give evidence on computer metadata to establish material deleted or records tampered with.[54]

Accordingly, oral and written evidence in civil litigation is often mutually supportive and interrelated.

15.5.3 Admitting business records

Another key form of evidence is permanent records which are business records. Business records constitute an admissible exception to the hearsay rule pursuant to s69 of the uniform *Evidence Act* (applicable at the federal level, and in the Australian Capital Territory, New South Wales, Northern Territory, Tasmania and Victoria) and may, therefore, be admitted as evidence. There are equivalent exceptions to the hearsay rule for business records in non-UEL jurisdictions. Business records are, themselves, still most commonly admitted into evidence through a witness. In most civil disputes, parties do not object to the admission of business records, however led.

There are many documents to which the business records exception to the hearsay rule clearly applies, such as the published financial records of a corporation. There are, however, areas of uncertainty as to what constitutes business records. For example, in *Hillig (in his capacity as official liquidator of ACN 092 745 330 Pty Ltd (in liq)) v Battaglia*, the New South Wales Supreme Court of Appeal determined that documents recording meetings with the ATO constituted business records admissible through the business records exception to the hearsay rule, including confirming that "The admissibility of a previous representation in a business record does not depend on the form of the representation being recorded in

52 *Dasreef Pty Ltd v Hawchar* (2011) 243 CLR 588, [57] and following discusses the wide range of expert evidence and associated issues.

53 *Fennell v The Queen* (2019) 373 ALR 433, [52].

54 *Sullivan v Trilogy Funds Management Ltd* (2017) 255 FCR 503.

direct speech."[55] There are also circumstances where even relevant and admissible business records are excluded due to their prejudicial value.[56]

15.6 Witness evidence in trial

Chapter 14 briefly introduced the rules for admissibility of evidence in the context of witness affidavits served prior to trial. These evidentiary rules are also applicable to evidence led from witnesses at trial, whether by oral examination, cross-examination or the reading of written affidavits. As explained in Chapter 14, the reason why affidavits must be in admissible form is so that they can be admitted during trial as evidence-in-chief.

In addition to the admissibility rules,[57] there are rules in the UEL (which have their genesis in the common law rules applicable in non-UEL jurisdictions) concerning:

- capacity of witnesses to give evidence[58]
- the examination and cross-examination of witnesses at trial[59]
- limitation of attacks on witness credibility.[60]

There are also common law rules based on fairness which arise in relation to witness evidence during trial, including:

- the rule in *Browne v Dunn*[61]
- the rule in *Jones v Dunkel*.[62]

In addition, there are general exclusory provisions in the UEL (and equivalents at common law) which allow courts to exclude evidence that would otherwise be admissible.[63]

15.6.1 Witness capacity

Part 2.1 of the UEL sets out the rules for adducing evidence from witnesses. Part 2.1, div 1 concerns witness capacity to give evidence. The default rule for potential witnesses, in s 12 of the UEL, is that anyone is competent to give evidence and can be compelled to give evidence. This default rule is, however, subject to exceptions, most of which are set out in the remainder of pt 2.1 div 1. One common exception to witness competence is lack of mental capacity, or reduced mental capacity, which can apply to the mentally ill and mentally impaired.

Witness capacity issues rarely arise in civil disputes but, where they do arise, the Court must satisfy itself that the witness can understand the questions asked and give answers

55 *Hillig (in his capacity as official liquidator of ACN 092 745 330 Pty Ltd (in liq)) v Battaglia* (2018) 125 ACSR 171, [72–81] quote from [80]. The Court also held that the documents should not be excluded pursuant to s 135 UEL: see Chapter 15.6.6.
56 See Chapter 15.6.6.
57 See Chapter 14.
58 See Chapter 15.6.1.
59 See Chapter 15.6.2.
60 See Chapter 15.6.3.
61 *Browne v Dunn* [1893] 6 R 67, discussed in Chapter 15.6.5.
62 *Jones v Dunkel* (1959) 101 CLR 298, discussed in Chapter 15.6.4.
63 See Chapter 15.6.6.

that can be understood. Sometimes, an incapacity may be overcome. For example, where a witness does not speak or understand English, provision of a qualified interpreter resolves the incapacity rendering the witness competent.[64] Where the incapacity of a witness cannot be overcome, that witness cannot give evidence at all.

15.6.2 Examination and cross-examination rules

Different rules exist for examination and cross-examination, with lawyers having the ability to object to the questions posed by their opposing counsel to assist the judge in determining what witness questions are acceptable. In Australia, reasons must be given by counsel for objections and the rules concerning examination and cross-examination of witnesses provide a basis for objections to questions. Objections may be raised where questioning leads to the giving of evidence which is inadmissible under the rules discussed in Chapter 14, such as hearsay and opinion evidence, or where the question breaches the restrictions relating to witness capacity (discussed above) or witness credibility (discussed below). The rules for examination and cross-examination are an area where civil disputants will sometimes allow variations in order to improve efficiency. While the evidentiary rules have been carefully designed to ensure procedural fairness, compliance necessarily takes time and incurs costs. Therefore, civil disputants may allow evidence not in proper form (eg hearsay or opinion evidence) where the efficiencies outweigh the procedural cost.[65]

For jurisdictions which have enacted the UEL (Commonwealth, Tasmania, New South Wales, Northern Territory, Victoria and the Australian Capital Territory), div 2.1.3 and div 2.1.4 (in pt 2 ch 2 of the UEL) set out the general rules for giving witness evidence. These rules include a significant discretion for judges to determine how and when witnesses are examined (ss 26 and 29 of the UEL).

One of the most important rules for examination of witnesses is the rule that leading questions cannot be asked, in examination-in-chief or re-examination except for introductory questions, questions with court-granted leave, questions not in dispute, questions not objected to (and all the other parties are represented by lawyers), or relevant hypothetical facts put to an expert in their area of expertise (UEL s 37). Conversely, leading questions can be asked in cross-examination (UEL s 42), subject to court discretion, provided the question is not misleading, confusing and is not unduly annoying, harassing, intimidating, offensive, oppressive, humiliating or repetitive and is not put in a belittling or insulting tone and is not based purely on a stereotyping of the witness (s 41). A leading question is defined in the Dictionary to the UEL as:

> **leading question** means a question asked of a witness that—
> (a) directly or indirectly suggests a particular answer to the question; or
> (b) assumes the existence of a fact the existence of which is in dispute in the proceeding and as to the existence of which the witness has not given evidence before the question is asked.

64 UEL s 30 expressly allows witnesses to give evidence through an interpreter.
65 This is a good example of the balancing of efficiency and due process. See Chapter 2.3.1.

An example of a non-leading question might be:

"And what did you do then?"

or

"What did he say when you said that?"

An example of a leading question might be:

"But you didn't tell him anything did you?"

or

"But you knew exactly what that document was for didn't you?"

There are also rules concerning how, and in what circumstances, documents should be put to witnesses (s 45), the circumstances in which witnesses can or should be directed to prior inconsistent statements (s 43),[66] and to what extent witnesses can or should be made aware of the evidence of others and the submissions which will be made in relation to their evidence (s 44).[67] These rules of evidence influence the process of civil trials through the court system and are matters which have the potential to delay or even derail proceedings if not complied with.

15.6.3 Witness credibility

In many cases, the evidence of witnesses is critical to the judge's determination of the relevant facts of the case. It is common for each side to present witness evidence which is in direct conflict and the judge must decide which evidence to prefer. Thus, determining the facts of a case usually involves an assessment of the credibility of the witnesses, including factors such as apparent honesty, reliability, memory, and knowledge of the relevant facts. Even if witnesses for both sides are honest, they may have conflicting recollections, due to the infirmity of human memory, which the judge must assess in order to determine the truth as best is possible.[68]

Witness credibility is addressed by the UEL in ch 3 pt 3.7 (and at common law for non-UEL jurisdictions) which imposes restrictions on leading evidence going solely to the credibility of a witness.[69] The restrictions on credibility evidence are stronger in criminal trials than civil trials.

The trial judge's finding as to witness credibility is usually final, even where the case is subsequently appealed, so it is a critical aspect of a trial hearing. Appellate courts are

66 A prior inconsistent statement is one made by the witness out of court (eg in a document) which contradicts the evidence given by the witness in court.

67 *UEL* s 44 and the rule in *Browne v Dunn* [1893] 6 R 67, discussed in Chapter 15.6.5.

68 Courts commonly distinguish between the honesty of the witness and whether their evidence is worthy of belief, because honest witnesses may be mistaken in their recall. However, unfortunately, the terminology employed by the courts is not consistent. See, eg, *Carbone v Toyota Motor Corporation Australia Ltd* [2017] VSCA 249, [116] (Priest JA) who uses the term "credit" for honesty and "credibility" for worthiness of belief. However, in the High Court in *IMM v The Queen* (2016) 257 CLR 300, [114] (Nettle and Gordon JJ) use "credibility" to mean honesty and "reliability" to mean worthiness of belief.

69 See, eg, *King v Australian Securities and Investments Commission* (2018) 134 ACSR 105, [218] (Morrison and McMurdo JJA and Applegarth J). Note this decision was overruled in *Australian Securities and Investments Commission v King* (2020) 376 ALR 1, but not in relation to the evidentiary discussion.

extremely reluctant to interfere with findings on witness credibility is due to the advantages the trial judge has through hearing the witness.[70]

15.6.4 The art of drawing inferences: *Jones v Dunkel*

It is the judge's task to interpret the evidence, and this often requires drawing inferences which can be a complex but important task. One important common law inference is known as the *Jones v Dunkel* inference, based on the case of *Jones v Dunkel*.[71] Failing to call an available witness (or even failing to examine a witness on a particular issue) can result in an inference being drawn that, had that witness been called (or fully examined), their evidence would not have been favourable, thus explaining the decision of the party not to call the witness.

There have been two significant High Court cases, in 2011 and 2012, which have clarified the rule in *Jones v Dunkel*: *Kuhl v Zurich Financial Services Australia Ltd* ('*Kuhl*') and *Australian Securities and Investments Commission v Hellicar* ('*Hellicar*').[72] Both *Kuhl* and *Hellicar* have been cited extensively in subsequent recent decisions, including by the Full Federal Court and the New South Wales Supreme Court of Appeal.[73] *Kuhl* concerned injuries sustained by Mr Kuhl while employed as a "reactor rat" (someone who cleaned up reactor grid floors at an iron ore plant) when his left arm was sucked into a vacuum hose which was passed to him while switched on. Heydon, Crennan and Bell JJ (the majority), with French CJ and Gummow J dissenting, allowed the appeal on the basis that the trial judge had drawn an inappropriate inference in relation to the witness evidence of the plaintiff. The majority, in *Kuhl,* gave the following analysis of the trial judge's erroneous inference with reference to the formative cases of *Jones v Dunkel*[74] and *Browne v Dunn*,[75] which explains the rule and demonstrates the complexity of the rule's application in practice:[76]

> [63]. The rule in *Jones v Dunkel* is that the unexplained failure by a party to call a witness may in appropriate circumstances support an inference that the uncalled evidence would not have assisted the party's case. That is particularly so where it is the party which is the uncalled witness. The failure to call a witness may also permit the court to draw, with greater confidence, any inference unfavourable to the party that failed to call the witness, if that uncalled witness appears to be in a position to cast light on whether the inference should be drawn. These principles have been extended from instances where a witness has not been called at all to instances where a witness has been called but not questioned on particular topics. Where counsel for a party has refrained from asking a witness whom that party has called particular questions on

70 *Aldi Foods Pty Ltd v Moroccanoil Israel Ltd* (2018) 261 FCR 301, [3] (Allsop CJ), [46] (Perram J). Chapter 16 considers appeals in more detail.

71 *Jones v Dunkel* (1959) 101 CLR 298 initially referred to in Chapter 14.4.2.

72 *Kuhl v Zurich Financial Services Australia Ltd* (2011) 243 CLR 361; *Australian Securities and Investments Commission v Hellicar* (2012) 247 CLR 345.

73 See, eg, *RHG Mortgage Ltd v Ianni* [2015] NSWCA 56, [76]; *Fair Work Ombudsman v Hu* (2019) 289 IR 240, [52]–[57]; *Ellis v Central Land Council* (2019) 267 FCR 339, [120]–[123]; *Chetcuti v Minister for Immigration and Border Protection* (2019) 165 ALD 236, [90]; *Jagatramka v Wollongong Coal Ltd* [2021] NSWCA 61, [49].

74 *Jones v Dunkel* (1959) 101 CLR 298.

75 *Browne v Dunn* [1893] 6 R 67.

76 See Chapter 15.6.5.

> an issue, the court will be less likely to draw inferences favourable to that party from other evidence in relation to that issue. That problem did not arise here. The plaintiff's counsel did ask the plaintiff relevant questions.
>
> [64]. The rule in *Jones v Dunkel* permits an inference, not that evidence not called by a party would have been adverse to the party, but that it would not have assisted the party. But the conclusion by the trial judge that the plaintiff — a party-witness — deliberately withheld evidence reflected a stronger reaction. It operated as a finding that there had been an admission. It could be inferred that the evidence was withheld, in breach of the witness's duty to tell the whole truth in answer to the question, because the plaintiff was conscious that success in the litigation would be rendered impossible or less likely if the material withheld were revealed. … A litigant has no duty to call particular witnesses or to procure that any witnesses called by that litigant are asked particular questions. A litigant who enters the witness box, on the other hand, is under a positive duty to tell the whole truth in answer to the questions asked.
>
> …
>
> [68]. … The trial judge gave no reasons at all for the view he formed. Nothing on the face of the evidence indicates reluctance. … The absence of reasoning is the more serious in the following circumstances. The plaintiff had left school at 15. He was apprenticed as a panel beater and spray painter, and worked in that and other trades in the 34 years before the accident. On one occasion during his testimony he went 'blank' and could not think. For him the witness box must have been a more than usually uncomfortable place. His supposed 'reluctance' may have resulted from the shock and pain of a terrifying, indeed life-changing, incident. It may have been momentary forgetfulness or inarticulateness. The problem may have been capable of resolution if counsel had paused, or returned to the subject later. To attribute the paucity of his evidence to deliberate suppression without giving reasons for this course excluding all relevant innocent possibilities was an unjustified course.[77]

Hellicar concerned breaches of directors' duties in the publication of false and misleading statements to the Australian Stock Exchange (ASX) by the directors of James Hardy concerning the restructure of the company to separate its operations from asbestos litigation claims. ASIC tendered minutes of a board meeting which referred to the draft ASX announcement being approved but did not call the company solicitor who had responsibility for the drafting of the minutes and who attended the board meeting. The High Court, allowing ASIC's appeal, discussed the facts and endorsed the principal of *Jones v Dunkel* but clarified its limitations did not extend to requiring ASIC to call the company solicitor:

> [167]. This Court's decision in *Jones v Dunkel* is a particular and vivid example of the principles that govern how the demonstration that other evidence could have been called, but was not, may be used. The essential facts of the case, though well known, should be restated. The personal representative of a driver who had died in a collision with another vehicle brought an action for damages on her own behalf and on behalf of the deceased driver's dependants. The plaintiff's case depended upon demonstration that the other driver's negligence was a cause of the accident. The plaintiff sought to demonstrate negligence by having the tribunal of fact (in that case a jury) infer from facts concerning the road and the two vehicles involved that the collision had occurred

77 *Kuhl v Zurich Financial Services Australia Ltd* (2011) 243 CLR 361, [63]–[64], [68].

when the defendant's vehicle was on the wrong side of the road. One of the defendants, the surviving driver, did not give evidence at the trial. The … Court held 'that any inference favourable to the plaintiff for which there was ground in the evidence might be more confidently drawn when a person presumably able to put the true complexion on the facts relied on as the ground for the inference has not been called as a witness by the defendant and the evidence provides no sufficient explanation of his absence'.

[168]. … There was no basis for drawing any inference that Mr Robb would have given evidence adverse to ASIC's case. … He was not 'a person presumably able to put the true complexion on the facts relied on [by ASIC] as the ground' for any inference that ASIC sought to have drawn from the evidence. …

[169]. ASIC had tendered admissible evidence that, if accepted, showed that the draft ASX announcement had been tabled and approved. This was not a case where ASIC's case depended on inference, …. It was the respondents' case that depended upon inference. The inference they sought to have drawn was that the minutes were not accurate evidence of tabling and approval. ASIC not calling Mr Robb did not entail that the inference which the respondents sought to have drawn could be more safely drawn. …[78]

A *Jones v Dunkel* inference is not mandatory, such that a judge may choose not to make an adverse inference from a witness not being called, particularly where such an adverse inference would be counter to view the judge otherwise holds based on other available evidence.[79]

15.6.5 The rule in *Browne v Dunn*

The common law rule in *Browne v Dunn*,[80] preserved by s 9 of the UEL, protects witnesses from being ambushed by unexpected adverse interpretations of their evidence. It should be noted that, for UEL jurisdictions, s 43, concerning prior inconsistent statements, s 44 concerning previous representations of other people and s 46, concerning leave to recall witnesses, are also relevant in ensuring all appropriate matters have been put to each witness.

It is critical that the legal practitioner cross-examining a witness has given the witness the opportunity to provide their perspective. This often makes cross-examination a lengthy process. For example, if a party wishes to assert that a witness is lying or has incorrectly recalled a matter, counsel may say to that witness in cross-examination:

"I put it to you, Mr X, that you lied when you said you had done PQR and S"

or

"Isn't it the case, Mr Y, that you can't really recall what happened on the day you … "

These questions give the witness the opportunity to verify their credentials. For example, a witness who replied:

"Yes, I definitely recall what I did that day. I keep a diary and I have read the entry for that day and I wrote … "

---

78 *Australian Securities and Investments Commission v Hellicar* (2012) 247 CLR 345, [167]–[169] (French CJ, Gummow, Hayne, Crennan, Kiefel and Bell JJ), [145], [232]–[267] (Heydon J also allowing the appeal in a separate judgment and discussed *Jones v Dunkel* (1959) 101 CLR 298).

79 *RHG Mortgage Corporation Ltd v Ianni* [2016] NSWCA 270, [21], [156]. [165].

80 *Browne v Dunn* [1893] 6 R 67.

might establish his or her credibility better than a witness who responded:

> "How dare you suggest I have forgotten something?"
>
> or
>
> "It's true that I really can't recall things from one week to the next."

The rule in *Brown v Dunn* was discussed in the Supreme Court of South Australian Full Court decision of *Macks v Viscariello*.[81] *Macks v Viscariello* concerned a dispute between Mr Viscariello, who was the sole director and effective controller of Bernsteen Pty Ltd, and Newmore Pty Ltd and Macks, as administrator of Bernsteen Pty Ltd and Newmore Pty Ltd. The Court held that Mr Macks had been denied procedural fairness because he was not put on notice of the potential for his evidence to be discounted by the judge. The Court discussed the application of the rule in *Browne v Dunn* and applied it in Mr Macks' favour:

> [461]. The rule in *Browne v Dunn* has been the subject of judicial comment in many cases. The rule is one of practice or procedure based upon general principles of fairness. As observed by Wells J in *Reid v Kerr*
>
>> It has always seemed to me that if some kind of imputation is to be made against a witness, then, at some stage-ultimately-the precise nature of that imputation should be made clear to the witness so that he is given an opportunity to meet it and, if he can, to explain it or destroy it .... I am well aware that there are more ways of taking a fort than by frontal attack, but I also hold it to be a fundamental principle that, when all arts and devices of cross examination have been exhausted for the purpose of testing whether a particular witness merits adverse criticism, then, at some stage, and in some fair manner, he should be given the opportunity of meeting the implication and answering it.
>
> [462]. It was explained by Hunt J in *Allied Pastoral Holdings Pty Ltd v FCT* in the following terms:
>
>> It has in my experience always been a rule of professional practice that, unless notice has already clearly been given of the cross-examined as intention to rely upon such matters, it is necessary to put to an opponent's witness in cross examination the nature of the case upon which it is proposed to rely in contradiction of his evidence, particularly where that case relies upon inferences to be drawn from other evidence in the proceedings. Such a rule of practice is necessary both to give the witness the opportunity to deal with that other evidence, or the inferences to be drawn from it, and to allow the other party the opportunity to call evidence either to corroborate that explanation or to contradict the inference sought to be drawn.
>
> [463]. The rule has two aspects. First, it is a rule of practice designed to achieve fairness to witnesses and a fair trial between the parties. Secondly, it relates to the weight or cogency of the evidence. As a general proposition, evidence which is not inherently incredible and which is unchallenged ought to be accepted. The evidence may, of course, be rejected if it is contradicted by facts otherwise established by the evidence or the particular circumstances point to its rejection.
>
> ...

81 *Macks v Viscariello* (2017) 130 SASR 1.

> [473]. Further, Mr Macks was not put on notice that, despite his evidence that he had accepted and acted on advice from Minter Ellison, his reliance on their advice would or might be 'discounted; by the Primary Judge. No suggestion was made by Mr Viscariello that Minter Ellison were 'in the same camp' as Mr Macks. Procedural fairness required that Mr Macks (and indeed Minter Ellison) be put on notice about such a potential finding.[82]

The High Court decision of *Kuhl*[83] indicates that the judiciary are themselves obliged to ensure a witness has been appropriately questioned before drawing any inference in relation to what was not said. Heydon, Crennan and Bell JJ expressly cited *Browne v Dunn*[84] and criticised the trial judge for breaching the obligations founded in it, as follows:

> [71]. In *Browne v Dunn* Lord Herschell LC said:
>
>> it seems to me to be absolutely essential to the proper conduct of a cause, where it is intended to suggest that a witness is *not speaking the truth* on a particular point, to direct his attention to the fact by some questions put in cross-examination showing that that imputation is intended to be made, and not to take his evidence and pass it by as a matter altogether unchallenged, and then, when it is impossible for him to explain, as perhaps he might have been able to do if such questions had been put to him, the circumstances which it is suggested indicate *that the story he tells ought not to be believed*, to argue that he is a witness unworthy of credit. My Lords, I have always understood that if you intend to impeach a witness you are bound, whilst he is in the box, to give him an opportunity of making any explanation which is open to him; and, as it seems to me, that is not only a rule of professional practice in the conduct of a case, but is essential to fair play and fair dealing with witnesses. (emphasis added)
>
> ...
>
> [75]. There was no point in the trial judge mentioning his conclusion that the plaintiff's evidence was not frank and complete unless it played a role in his decision adverse to the plaintiff. In the absence of any challenge from the cross-examiner to the frankness and completeness of the plaintiff's evidence, it was incumbent on the trial judge, if his conclusion that the plaintiff had not been frank and complete was to play a role in his decision adverse to the plaintiff, to make the challenge himself. Perhaps the criticism in the judgment did not occur to the trial judge until after the plaintiff had left the box, or until after the hearing had concluded and before the judge's reserved judgment was given. It remained necessary either to recall the plaintiff or to have no regard to that aspect of the plaintiff's evidence. ...[85]

15.6.6 Discretionary exclusions of evidence at trial

Part 3.11 of the UEL also contains discretionary exclusory provisions through which otherwise admissible evidence can nonetheless be excluded where a party objects to its admission and

82 Ibid [461]–[463], [473] (Lovell J, Corboy AJ and Slattery AJ). See also *Broughton v B & B Group Investments Pty Ltd* [2017] VSCA 227, [108]–[110].

83 *Kuhl v Zurich Financial Services Australia Ltd* (2011) 243 CLR 361. See Chapter 15.6.4.

84 *Browne v Dunn* [1893] 6 R 67.

85 *Kuhl v Zurich Financial Services Australia Ltd* (2011) 243 CLR 361, [71], [75]. For insight into the complexity of the rule in *Browne v Dunn* [1893] 6 R 67 and the impact of *Kuhl,* see *Broadway Plaza Investments Pty Ltd v Broadway Plaza Pty Ltd* [2020] NSWSC 1778, [798], [804].

the court agrees with the objection. Section 135 of the UEL is the most common discretionary exclusory provision which applies in civil proceedings.[86] Section 135 gives the court a discretion to exclude evidence where the probative value of the evidence is "substantially outweighed" by the danger of unfair prejudice or the danger that the evidence will be misleading or confusing or the danger that the evidence will be an undue waste of time.[87]

Section 135 of the UEL always requires a discretionary balancing act by the court, as the cases below demonstrate. For example, in the Full Federal Court decision of *Mineralogy Pty Ltd v Sino Iron Pty Ltd*, the expert evidence of mineralogist, Mr van der Heyden, was excluded under s 135 on the basis that it would be misleading or confusing given his performance in cross-examination, changes to one of his reports, and lack of concern as to its origin, completeness and whether it was up to date.[88]

By contrast, in the business documents case of *Hillig (in his capacity as official liquidator of ACN 092 745 330 Pty Ltd (in liq)) v Battaglia*, the New South Wales Supreme Court of Appeal declined to apply s135 to exclude evidence, holding:

> [84]. Plainly, the documents sought to be adduced as further evidence on appeal have significant probative value, because the representations or admissions recorded in those documents directly contradict Mr Battaglia's evidence at trial concerning the nature of the Schedule C payments, and by inference the Schedule B payments.
>
> [85]. Other than asserting that the documents were 'confusing and unreliable', the respondents did not point to any matters suggesting a danger that the evidence might give rise to unfair prejudice or was misleading or confusing. Nor did the respondents direct any argument to the balancing exercise required by s 135 concerning whether the probative value of the representations in the documents was 'substantially outweighed' by the dangers listed in the provision.
>
> [86]. In my view, the significant probative value of the representations or admissions in the documents which affect the assessment of Mr Battaglia's credit, is not 'substantially outweighed' by the risk that the evidence might be unfairly prejudicial to the respondents or might be misleading or confusing. Items (1), (2), (3) and (5) should not be excluded under s 135 of the Evidence Act. As indicated, there was no objection to the admissibility of item (6).[89]

In the case of *Capital Securities XV Pty Ltd v Calleja*,[90] the New South Wales Supreme Court of Appeal held that the primary judge's discretion in applying s 135 of the *Evidence Act 1995*

86 The mandatory exclusion provision, s 137, only applies in criminal cases.

87 Probative value is defined as follows in the UEL Dictionary: "probative value of evidence means the extent to which the evidence could rationally affect the assessment of the probability of the existence of a fact in issue". Unfair prejudice is explained in *R v Dickman* (2017) 261 CLR 601, [48] as follows: "Unfair prejudice may be occasioned because evidence has some quality which is thought to give it more weight in the jury's assessment than it warrants or because it is apt to invite the jury to draw an inference about some matter which would ordinarily be excluded from evidence."

88 *Mineralogy Pty Ltd v Sino Iron Pty Ltd* [2017] FCAFC 55, [41]–[50] (Besanko, Mckerracher and Beach JJ). However, note that parties will not always raise s 135 and, in such cases, the Court will not consider it: *Yirga-Denbu v Victorian WorkCover Authority* (2018) 57 VR 545.

89 *Hillig (in his capacity as liquidator of ACN 092 745 330 Pty Ltd (in liq)) v Battaglia* (2018) 125 ACSR 171, [84]–[86].

90 *Capital Securities XV Pty Ltd v Calleja* [2018] NSWCA 26.

(NSW) to exclude business records evidence had miscarried. The Court noted the following in relation to the complexity of the judicial task in determining the application of s 135:

> [115]. Section 135 is a much more complex provision than, say, s 136, which authorises orders limiting the use of evidence merely upon the court being satisfied of a risk of unfair prejudice. In order to apply s 135, it was necessary for the primary judge to consider two further aspects: (a) to make an assessment of the probative value of the evidence and (b) then to assess whether that probative value was 'substantially outweighed' by the danger that the evidence might be unfairly prejudicial. With respect, the reasons do not disclose any process of analysis answering what was required in these second and third steps under s 135. The omission is substantially the same as that identified by this Court in *Australian Securities and Investments Commission v Rich* [2005] NSWCA 152; 218 ALR 764 at [163] and *James Hardie Industries NV v Australian Securities and Investments Commission* [2009] NSWCA 18 at [31]–[32]. Although Ms Obrart contended to the contrary, it is plain on a fair reading of the reasons that this did not occur. In order to have done so, it would have been necessary for the primary judge to have proceeded, contrary to her view, on the basis that the documents were business records containing representations which were not excluded by the hearsay rule, to have identified the probative value of those representations in light of the issues between the parties, and then asked whether that was substantially outweighed by the risk of unfair prejudice.[91]

The other exclusory provisions which can apply in civil cases are ss 136 and 138. Section 136 enables courts to limit the use of evidence which may be prejudicial, misleading or confusing. Section 138 provides for the exclusion of evidence improperly or illegally obtained with a discretion for the courts to allow such evidence in limited circumstances. The discretionary exclusion provisions are important as they can protect parties from damaging evidence which would otherwise be admissible but which the court recognises would do substantially more harm than good.

15.7 Finishing trials

In the vast majority of civil disputes which complete trial, the trial is heard in a single block of court sitting time (even if run over several days, weeks or even months). Once the closing submissions have been made, the trial is finished and the next step is receiving judgment.[92] However, trials may be adjourned in the middle of proceedings, and cases pending judgment may be reopened in limited circumstances.

15.7.1 Adjourning proceedings

Civil trials may be adjourned mid hearing for several reasons. Settlement, or the prospect of settlement, is perhaps the most common reason for trials to be adjourned, particularly at the beginning of trial. As discussed in prior chapters, ADR can occur at any stage of proceedings including the entirety of the trial process and even after completion of trial. Many cases settle on the court steps before the first morning of trial. This does not mean the litigation

91 Ibid [115].
92 See Chapter 16.

procedures were a waste of time. As discussed in Chapter 2, ADR and litigation interact in complex ways. When parties have prepared everything for trial, each party's position is often much clearer, and parties may realise there is far less in dispute than it seemed at the commencement of proceedings. Accordingly, matters which have failed to reach settlement for years can settle within minutes when the parties meet face-to-face before trial commences. In other cases, it may be after several days of witness evidence that it becomes clear where the matter is going and, suddenly, a party who has been resisting settlement sees the sense in settling. Judges will almost invariably agree to a brief adjournment while parties discuss settlement. Such adjournments are often measured in hours rather than days.

Another common reason for adjourning hearings is where the trial has run for allocated days but remains unfinished and the court needs to allocate further time to complete the hearing. Judges are often flexible and may allow hearings to run late into the evening in order to complete within the allocated timeframe. Sometimes, however, it is clear that further hearing days are required, and the allocated judge or counsel may have another case commencing immediately. In such cases, the trial must be adjourned until the next date the judge, lawyers and parties are available for hearing. The more days required to complete the trial, the longer it is likely to be until a big enough gap in the hearing judge's court schedule can be found. In some complex and lengthy cases, there is an adjournment after completion of evidence to allow the parties sufficient time to prepare written and oral closing submissions.

There are other circumstances, which occur more rarely, where cases may be adjourned mid-hearing. For example, if it becomes apparent that, through no fault of any party, further evidence must be obtained, a judge may adjourn the proceedings so that such evidence may be obtained. Cases may also be adjourned mid-hearing due to the unexpected serious illness or incapacity of a key witness or party or other unexpected disaster which prevents a subpoenaed witness from giving evidence.[93]

However, as the High Court made clear in *Aon Risk Services Australia Ltd v Australian National University*, courts will not make the decision to adjourn trials lightly. Courts will not adjourn trials to suit the convenience of parties who have not complied with their efficiency obligations in running their proceedings and courts will consider the finite nature of their resources when adjourning any trial.[94] Determining when to adjourn proceedings is frequently an example of balancing efficiency against due process and, simultaneously, an example of balancing flexibility against certainty of process (because parties are not getting the timing they agreed to but this flexibility may be essential).[95] For example, in the Federal Court case of *Merck Sharp & Dohme Corporation v Pfizer Inc*, an adjournment was granted due to an expert witness for Pfizer ceasing his role due to the sudden unexpected death of his daughter.[96] The Court was required to balance the prejudice to Pfizer if it were forced to continue with the original timetable without the missing expert against the prejudice to

93 See, eg, *Draoui v Le* [2019] SASCFC 105, [9]–[11] where the Full Court of the South Australian Supreme Court discussed an adjournment for the purposes of determining the mental capability of the plaintiff to proceed as a self-represented litigant.

94 *Aon Risk Services Australia Ltd v Australian National University* (2009) 239 CLR 175, [5], [24], [26]–[27], [30], [143]. See Chapter 2.4 for further analysis of *Aon*.

95 See Chapters 2.3.1 and 2.3.4.

96 *Merck Sharp & Dohme Corporation v Pfizer Inc* [2021] FCA 57, [2].

Merck from the delay involved in allowing Pfizer time to find a new witness.[97] This balancing act involved the Court's discretion in weighing efficiency considerations against due process considerations.[98]

15.7.2 Cases awaiting judgment

At the end of a trial, most cases are adjourned for the judge to deliberate. Such cases are considered closed, provided all closing submissions have been made.

In a small number of cases, an *ex tempore* judgment is given and the matter is then finished, subject to appeal.[99]

It is quite common for judges to request parties to file written submissions on a specific issue, such as costs, or to provide closing written submissions at the end of a hearing. A period of time is usually allocated for such submissions to be made. Once such submissions have been received, the case is considered closed, despite the fact that judgment is reserved.

For the reasons set out below in relation to reopening cases, a closed case awaiting judgment is different to a case adjourned mid-hearing.

15.7.3 Reopening proceedings

There are a limited number of circumstances where a party may be allowed to reopen its case, and these commonly involve the discovery of significant new evidence.[100] The relevant factors for judicial discretion in reopening cases were set out in *Movie Network Channels Pty Ltd v Optus Vision Pty Ltd*, as follows:

> [4]. In every case the overriding principle to be applied is whether the interests of justice are better served by allowing or rejecting the application to reopen [*Inspector-General in Bankruptcy v Bradshaw* [2006] FCA 22 at [24]; *Urban Transport Authority of NSW v Nweiser* (1992) 28 NSWLR 471 at 478]. An application to reopen is subject to various degrees of scrutiny depending on the stage of the proceedings when the application is made. The test of what is 'just' at this stage of the proceedings is akin to the considerations applicable where leave to rely on fresh evidence is sought on appeal. That is the evidence must be credible, highly probative and not previously obtainable by reasonable diligence [*Jesseron Holdings Pty Ltd v Middle East Trading Consultants Pty Ltd (No 2)* (1994) 122 ALR 717 at 719 per Young J; Ritchies at [51.51.50]; *Australasian Meat Industry Employees Union* (WA Branch); *ex parte Ferguson (1986)* 67 ALR 491 at 493–494 per Toohey J; *Murray v Figge* (1974) 4 ALR 612; *Betts v Whittingslowe (No 1)* [1944] SAStRp 18; [1944] SASR 163; *Hughes v Hill* [1937] SAStRp 43; [1937] SASR 285; *Watson v Metropolitan (Perth) Passenger Transport Trust* [1965] WAR 88].

97 Ibid [7], [15]–[16].

98 Ibid [20]. The Court found in favour of Pfizer due to the importance of the expert evidence and the fact that the withdrawal was not foreseeable and was no fault of Pfizer's. The Court still ordered Pfizer to pay the costs of the adjournment, including the adjournment application.

99 An *ex tempore* judgment is an oral judgment delivered immediately upon completion of a hearing. Such judgments are common in urgent interlocutory hearings, such as Anton Piller orders, discussed in Chapter 9.2.2, but are uncommon in most civil litigation, particularly in higher courts where judgments may take months to be handed down in complex litigation. See Chapter 16 regarding appeals.

100 See, eg, *Granitgard Pty Ltd v Termicide Pest Control Pty Ltd (No 3)* [2009] FCA 82.

[5]. Naturally the principles which inform the exercise of the discretion to reopen are to be read against the general background of the obvious public interest in the finality of litigation: cf *Autodesk Inc v Dyason (No. 2)* [1993] HCA 6; (1993) 176 CLR 300 per Mason CJ at 302–303.

[6]. In *Inspector-General in Bankruptcy v Bradshaw* [2006] FCA 22 Kenny J identified at [24] certain recognised classes of cases in which a court may grant leave to reopen as including where:

(a) Fresh evidence becomes available [*Granitgard Pty Ltd v Termicide Pest Control Pty Ltd (No 3)* [2009] FCA 82 (evidence from a 'whistle blower' became available after the conclusion of the hearing)];

(b) There is inadvertent error; [*Telecom Vanuatu Ltd v Optus Networks Pty Ltd (No 2)* [2009] NSWSC 33];

(c) There is a mistaken apprehension of the facts [*Urban Transport Authority of NSW v Nweiser* (1992) 28 NSWLR 471; *Autodesk Inc*]; or

(d) There is a mistaken apprehension of the law [*Urban Transport Authority of NSW v Nweiser* (1992) 28 NSWLR 471].

[7] In *Smith v NSW Bar Association* [1992] HCA 36; (1992) 176 CLR 256 at 266 a majority of the High Court found that:

> If an application is made to reopen on the basis that new or additional evidence is available, it will be relevant, at that stage, to inquire why the evidence was not called at the hearing. If there was a deliberate decision not to call it, ordinarily that will tell decisively against the application. [See also: *Barker v Furlong* [1891] 2 Ch 172 at 184; *Hughes v Hill* [1937] SAStRp 43; [1937] SASR 285 at 287; *Multicon Engineering Pty Ltd v Federal Airports Corporation* (NSWSC, Cole J, 10 December 1993, unreported)].

[8] In *ASIC v Rich* [2006] NSWSC 826; (2006) 235 ALR 587 at [18] per Austin J listed the factors that he agreed were relevant to the exercise of the discretion as follows:

i. The nature of the proceeding [See also *Woolworth Ltd v Olson* [2004] NSWSC 871];

ii. Whether the occasion for calling the further evidence ought reasonably to have been foreseen;

iii. The consideration of fairness that the defendant is entitled to know all of the evidence he has to meet in taking forensic decisions as to cross-examination and the nature and extent of the evidence he will himself adduce on the matters in question;

iv. The extent to which the plaintiff has embarked upon calling evidence on the issue in question in its case in chief;

v. The importance of the issue on which the further evidence is sought to be adduced to the pleaded issues in the case;

vi. The degree of relevance and the probative value of the further evidence sought to be adduced and its potential to involve an undue waste of time;

vii. The prejudice to the defendant in terms of delay in the completion of the proceeding and the consequential costs;

viii. The public interest in the conclusion of litigation [See also *Hawthorn Glen Pty Ltd v Aconex Pty Limited (No 1)* [2007] FCA 2010 at [48]]; and
ix. What explanation is offered by the plaintiff for not having called the evidence in chief.[101]

The Full Federal Court in *Rahman v Commissioner of Taxation* employed the key High Court case management decisions of *Aon Risk Services Australia Ltd v Australian National University* and *Expense Reduction Analysts Group Pty Ltd v Armstrong Strategic Management and Marketing Pty Ltd* in determining that Mr Rahman could not reopen his case for unfair employment dismissal by the ATO because he had failed in his s 37M *Federal Court of Australia Act 1976* (Cth) efficiency obligations.[102]

15.8 Conclusion

In some ways, trials are the pinnacle of CDR, particularly if justice is defined as "having your day in court". However, in reality, trials are a relative rarity in CDR, reserved only for test cases and the most intractable of disputes, the most insoluble of problems, or the most adversarial or recalcitrant of litigants. Those trials which do run provide important precedents for future disputants. It is important that trials are run well, and that evidence is carefully prepared in advance and presented as logically as possible during the trial. This requires considerable effort and planning on the part of lawyers to ensure that all the relevant and necessary material is made available and duly admitted into evidence. Although, in most cases, there are avenues for appeal from a trial judge's decision, as will be explained in Chapter 16, the appeal process is generally far more limited than the trial and there is rarely a second opportunity to lead evidence. The availability of a civil trial for disputants is the most obvious demonstration of access to justice and is, therefore, a key requirement of a well-functioning justice.

Trials involve all four of the key balancing themes of CDR and are possibly the area where judges have the most responsibility for optimising each of the competing aspects of CDR.

101 *Movie Network Channels Pty Ltd v Optus Vision Pty Ltd* [2009] NSWSC 132, [4]–[8]. This analysis was recently cited with approval in the New South Wales decisions of *Randren House Pty Ltd v Water Administration Ministerial Corporation (No 4)* [2019] NSWLEC 5 at [87]; *Re Access Elevators Australia Pty Ltd* [2016] NSWSC 739, [119]; *Bi v Minister for Home Affairs* (2019) 269 FCR 1, [69].

102 *Rahman v Commissioner of Taxation* [2018] FCAFC 54, [31]–[34] (Rares, Logan and Charlesworth JJ). See Chapter 2.4 for detailed consideration of *Aon Risk Services Australia Ltd v Australian National University* (2009) 239 CLR 175 and *Expense Reduction Analysis Group Pty Ltd v Armstrong Strategic Management and Marketing Pty Ltd* (2013) 250 CLR 303.

16 JUDGMENT, APPEALS AND ENFORCEMENT

16.1 Introduction

This chapter concerns the procedure for those rare but important civil disputes which proceed through the entire litigation process to judgment and, in some case, beyond. As this book has demonstrated, most cases settle prior to trial, which means that those cases which proceed through trial and on to judgment tend to be the ones with the most adversarial and persistent parties. However, for some cases, even judgment does not bring an end to proceedings. Judgments are considered final and enforceable as soon as they have been delivered, but they may also be incomplete and appealable and further disputes can arise after judgment. Appeals are a critical example of one of the key balancing themes in this book — being the balance between due process and efficiency.[1] Appeals provide an opportunity to concentrate the hearing of the most legally difficult cases before the highest judges, which enables the development of high-level binding precedent by superior courts. However, appellate processes come at a high price for the efficiency aims of civil procedure as they require significant time and money. They can also reduce public faith in the administration of justice where courts regularly overrule each other, creating the impression of lower court incompetence or arbitrary decision-making. Enforcement proceedings demonstrate the power of courts to deliver justice compared to ADR, as ADR enforcement is only possible through the support of the courts. This chapter focuses on the issues associated with judgment, the appeal process, and enforcing the court's determinations.[2]

16.2 Legislative framework

Civil procedure rules generally include provisions governing judgments and appeals, including enforcing and setting aside judgments.

16.2.1 High Court

The *High Court Rules 2004* (Cth) include rules in ch 4, which concerns court filing and serving summaries of argument, the making of written and oral submissions, and the preparation, filing and service of appeal books.

16.2.2 Federal Court

The Federal Court hears appeals from both courts and quasi-judicial bodies, including numerous tribunals and administrative decision-makers.[3] Chapter 4 of the *Federal Court Rules 2011* (Cth) governs the Federal Court's Appellate Jurisdiction. Parts 35 to 38 of the *Federal Court Rules 2011* (Cth) (ch 4) contain provisions on leave to appeal, formal rules of appeal, cross appeals, preparation of appeal books, and other relevant matters. Chapter 3 of the *Federal Court Rules 2011* (Cth) covers appeals from non-court administrative decisions and tribunal decisions, which form part of the Federal Court's original jurisdiction. Appeals

1 See Chapter 2.3.1.
2 See Chapter 6.5 for the post-trial issue of recovery of legal costs.
3 See Chapter 7.

from decisions made pursuant to the *Administrative Decisions (Judicial Review) Act 1977* (Cth) are governed by pt 31 of the *Federal Court Rules 2011* (Cth). The Federal Court also has jurisdiction granted by a variety of Commonwealth legislation to hear appeals from the Australian Taxation Office, the Administrative Appeals Tribunal, the Superannuation Complaints Tribunal and its successor the Australian Financial Complaints Authority (AFCA), and the Native Title Tribunal (governed by pt 33 of the *Federal Court Rules 2011* (Cth)).[4]

16.2.3 Australian Capital Territory

Chapter 5 of the *Court Procedures Rules 2006* (ACT) (rr 5000–5858) sets out the rules for appellate proceedings. Chapter 5 pt 5.3 *Court Procedures Rules 2006* (ACT) provides for appeals to the Supreme Court of the Australian Capital Territory and ch 5 pt 5.4 provides for appeals to the Court of Appeal of the Supreme Court. Part 2.18 (rr 2000–2064) provide for enforcement including through money orders and non-money orders.

16.2.4 Northern Territory

In the Northern Territory, ord 59 of the *Supreme Court Rules 1987* (NT) concerns judgments and orders. Order 65 governs the procedure for applications to the Full Court. Orders 66 to 75 concern enforcement of judgments and orders. Orders 82 to 86 govern appeals and include provisions for appeals from tribunals and from the Supreme Court. While the Northern Territory Supreme Court Rules are broadly uniform with the *Supreme Court (General Civil Procedure) Rules 2015* (Vic), the rules governing appeals differ significantly between the two states.

16.2.5 New South Wales

In New South Wales, judgments and orders are governed by pt 36 of the *Uniform Civil Procedure Rules 2005* (NSW), with pt 37 governing payment by instalments of judgment debts, pt 39 governing enforcement of judgments, and pt 40 providing additional measures for enforcement of Supreme Court and District Court proceedings. Part 50 of the *Uniform Civil Procedure Rules 2005* (NSW) governs appeals to the Court (generally the Supreme or District Court), and pt 51 governs appeals to the New South Wales Court of Appeal, which include detailed provisions on appeal books, written submissions and other procedural requirements.

16.2.6 Queensland

Chapter 18 of *Uniform Civil Procedure Rules 1999* (Qld) (rr 744–792) sets out the rules of appellate procedure in Queensland, including rules for appeal and cross appeal, preparation of appeal books (rr 758–759), appeals from non-court entities (r 784) and setting down for

4 See, eg, *QSuper Board v Australian Financial Complaints Authority Ltd* (2020) 276 FCR 97, [13]-[18] (Moshinsky, Bromwich and Derrington JJ) explaining the genesis of ACFA and held the Authority had not overstepped its power in upholding its decision in favour of a superannuant who had overpaid premiums. The Federal Court's appellate jurisdiction was through s 1057 of the *Corporations Act 2001* (Cth).

appeal hearings. In Queensland, ch 19 of the *Uniform Civil Procedure Rules 1999* (Qld) deals with the enforcement of monetary orders (rr 793–889), and ch 20 with the enforcement of non-monetary orders (rr 890–947), with ch 20A for enforcement of foreign judgments (rr 947–947N).

16.2.7 South Australia

In South Australia, the new *Uniform Civil Rules 2020* (SA) governing legal proceedings in the Magistrates, District and Supreme Courts of South Australia commenced on 18 May 2020. The new rules contain ch 15, on judgments, which contains the power for courts to give relief other than that sought by the applicant,[5] the power to correct errors in judgments,[6] and the power to set aside or vary a judgment.[7] In the new rules, enforcement is covered in ch 17 (rr 205–27), with monetary judgments covered by rr 201–3, and non-monetary judgments covered by r 204. The appellate jurisdiction is considered in ch 18 rr 211–218 of the *Uniform Civil Rules 2020* (SA), including establishing the appellate jurisdiction of the Full Court of the South Australian Supreme Court.[8]

16.2.8 Tasmania

In Tasmania, appeals are governed by pt 27 (rr 655–715) of the *Supreme Court Rules 2000* (Tas), including appeals to the Full Court (div 1), appeals from inferior courts (div 2), and from statutory tribunals (div 4) and referees (div 5). Enforcement is governed by pt 35 (rr 870–929).

16.2.9 Victoria

The *Supreme Court (General Civil Procedure) Rules 2015* (Vic) provide for appeals from inferior courts pursuant to ord 58 and appeals to the Court of Appeal pursuant to ord 64. Order 59 governs judgments and orders by the court. Orders 66–75 cover enforcement.

16.2.10 Western Australia

In Western Australia, ord 42 and ord 43 of the *Rules of the Supreme Court 1971* (WA) govern judgment. Order 65 of the *Rules of the Supreme Court 1971* (WA) governs appeals. Order 46 governs enforcement in conjunction with the *Civil Judgments Enforcement Act 2004* (WA).

16.3 Obtaining judgment

Most civil trials are heard and determined by a single judge. Some decisions are handed down *ex tempore*, and this is more common in lower courts.[9] Most decisions in superior

5 *Uniform Civil Rules 2020* (SA) r 182.1(1).
6 Ibid r 186.1(1).
7 Ibid r 186.1(2).
8 Ibid r 212.3(1).
9 An *ex tempore* decision is one handed down at the time of the hearing. Such decisions are usually oral judgments, although they may be subsequently recorded and reported in written form.

courts are reserved so that the judges may deliberate and prepare considered written reasons for judgment. Judges are constantly under pressure to provide judgments quickly without sacrificing due process, resulting in the need to carefully consider the information from the hearing and deliver a carefully reasoned and well-written judgment as quickly as humanly possible.[10]

16.3.1 Jury trials

Very few civil disputes are decided by a jury. Juries impose a significant expense on the government (in jury salaries and the extra time taken to explain evidentiary considerations to jurors) and an even greater expense on society in the lost time and productivity of the empanelled jurors. Accordingly, juries will only be available for civil trials in extraordinary circumstances where there are important matters for determination that are predominantly factual. This is an example of the key theme of balancing efficiency with due process.[11] The need to be judged by a group of peers is less relevant in most civil trials than their criminal equivalents.[12] Defamation is one area of civil litigation where juries trials remain common, although not all states allow jury trials even for defamation.[13] Defamation cases may involve consideration of the public interest and also involve the public's impression of published material and its likely impact on a person's reputation.[14] The importance of public opinion in defamation cases makes them more suitable for jury determination than judicial interpretation and thus a jury can be seen as a due process benefit which outweighs its cost.[15]

16.3.2 Awaiting judgment and delay

There can be a significant time lag between the hearing of a case and judgment being handed down. The lengthier and more complex the case, the longer judgment is likely to take because the judge must review all the materials presented in court and assess those materials before making a determination. The length of time taken to obtain judgments is monitored closely by the courts and is reported on annually to ensure efficiency.[16] Judges endeavour to hand down judgment as quickly as possible without compromising the quality of their decisions. For complex cases, this process is likely to take months.

10 See Chapter 2.3.1 regarding this key balancing theme. See also Chapter 3.2 regarding access to justice considerations.

11 See Chapter 2.3.1.

12 The government is not a party to most civil disputes, so the potential for perceptions of unfairness or corrupt influence of a party over the judiciary is less than for criminal trials.

13 For example, jury trials are not allowed in any civil proceedings in South Australia: *Aldridge v Johnston* [2020] SASCFC 31, [47] fn 9.

14 *Trkulja v Google LLC* (2018) 263 CLR 149, [39], [61]-[66].

15 See Steven Rares, 'The Jury in Defamation Trials' [2010] *Federal Judicial Scholarship* 10; David Rolph, 'Are Juries Necessary? The Role of Juries in Defamation Trials' (2009) (92) *Precedent* 10 for further analysis of the role of juries in defamation.

16 See, eg, Federal Court of Australia, *Looking Back to the Future: Annual Report 2018–2019* (Report, 2019) 15 which confirms that the Court is close to its target of handing down 85% of judgments within three months of reserving judgment, achieving 80% for trial decisions and 85% for appellate decisions.

It is, however, difficult to monitor and measure the efficiency of the judiciary, particularly given the desirability of maintaining judicial independence. In 1998, the New South Wales parliament took the unusual step of considering removing Supreme Court Justice Vince Bruce following lengthy delays by him in handing down judgments. The parliamentary debate followed a New South Wales Judicial Commission review into chronic delay by Bruce J. The parliamentary debate centred on the judge's undiagnosed depression and whether that illness, subsequently medicated, was the cause of the delay.[17] In the end, the New South Wales parliament did not sack him. Justice Bruce resigned shortly after the parliamentary decision not to sack him.[18] It can be challenging to determine where additional judicial time is necessary to afford due consideration and due process and where it constitutes inefficiency.[19]

16.3.3 Receiving judgment

Ex tempore judgments are received at the time of hearing and are, usually, oral judgments. The time and method of providing judgments is an example of the tension between due process and efficiency with *ex tempore* judgments an obvious example of a speedy resolution with no scope for research or lengthy consideration. When judgment is reserved, the parties return to court to receive judgment at a later date and such a judgment is almost invariably in written form. Handing down judgment may include an oral address from the judge, together with the handing down of a written judgment. The handing down of judgment is usually brief, but the date of judgment can be significant as it is the starting date for compliance which may therefore be relevant for enforcement proceedings where there is non-compliance. The judgment date is also the date from which parties acquire the right to commence an appeal, for which there is generally a very limited period.

16.4 The finality of judgment

In order to protect the finality of judgment, it is important to prevent parties from attempting to relitigate matters which the court has already determined. Relitigating is a practice which is simultaneously inefficient and a breach of due process which provides a strong imperative for its avoidance. The need to protect the finality of judgments from relitigation has resulted in the development of doctrines to protect the finality of judgments. The finality doctrines do not prevent appeals or variations of judgment, but prevent parties from commencing fresh proceedings in any court in attempt to have that court determine matters which have already been finally determined in court.[20]

As McColl J noted in the New South Wales Court of Appeal decision in *Mamo v Surace*:

> [80]. The appellant reminded the Court of Lord Atkin's aphorism that 'finality is a good thing but justice is better': *Ras Behari Lal v King-Emperor* (1933) 50 TLR 1 (at 2).

---

17 Details of the parliamentary debates in relation to Bruce J can be found at <https://www.parliament.nsw.gov.au/search/pages/hansard-results.aspx?k=%22Justice%20bruce%22%20SittingDate%3A1998-01-01..1998-12-31%20>.

18 See John Waugh, 'A Question of Capacity: The Case of Justice Bruce' (2018) 9(4) *Public Law Review* 223.

19 *Clayton v Bant* (2020) 385 ALR 41, [96] (Edelman J).

20 See Chapters 16.5 and 16.6 respectively for variation of judgments and appeals.

> In *Multicon Engineering* (at 647) Mason P observed that 'there comes a time in any litigation where a party has gone so far in one direction that it would be unjust to allow that party to commence a second run at the same target'. His Honour then referred to Lord Atkin's aphorism and added that it 'raises a false dichotomy if finality is not seen as an aspect of justice'.[21]

This demonstrates the importance of applying the finality doctrines with care to ensure they are not preventing cases which are critically different from previous finalised proceedings. The difficult task for the judiciary is determining, in an interlocutory context with limited evidence,[22] which cases should be allowed to continue and which are an improper relitigation of a prior dispute.[23]

16.4.1 *Res judicata,* Anshun estoppel, issue estoppel and abuse of process

Res judicata is a Latin phrase meaning "a thing judged", which reflects the finality of a judgment.[24] Once a court has decided a matter, the decision handed down is final and enforceable and a litigant cannot choose to relitigate it. This importantly prevents litigants bringing the same matter again and again before different judges which would waste everybody's time and money and lead to the possibility of inconsistent judgments. Issue estoppel and Anshun estoppel similarly prevent parties from litigating matters relevant to prior judgments in ways which might result in inconsistent judgments or abuses of process.[25] Where a judgment is founded on or justified by an underlying conclusion, issue estoppel prevents that underlying issue being raised in subsequent litigation. Issue estoppel and *res judicata* are sometimes used interchangeably to describe the inability of parties to relitigate a dispute already determined by a court. Anshun estoppel is an extension of the issue estoppel concept. Where a party fails to raise an issue in litigation which is so closely related to the issues in dispute that it should have been raised during the litigation, Anshun estoppel prevents that overlooked issue from being raised in a subsequent separate court action.[26] Abuse of process can occur in a wide variety of contexts one of which is the improper pursuit of litigation which has already been determined elsewhere.[27]

There has been significant discussion of *res judicata,* issue estoppel, Anshun estoppel and abuse of process in cases related to a transaction entered by Scott Tyne and his related entities, Telesto and the Argot Trust, including the New South Wales Supreme Court decision of Sackar J in *Telesto Investments Ltd v UBS AG,*[28] and the related Federal Court proceedings

21 *Mamo v Surace* (2014) 86 NSWLR 275, [80].
22 See Chapter 8.7.
23 This again requires a balancing of due process and efficiency considerations.
24 See *Effem Foods Pty Ltd v Trawl Industries of Australia Pty Ltd (recrs and mgrs apptd) (in liq)* [1993] FCA 342 for a detailed discussion of the meaning of the term *res judicata.*
25 Anshun estoppel is named after *Port of Melbourne Authority v Anshun Pty Ltd* (1981) 147 CLR 589 where the High Court set out the concept in detail.
26 *Tomlinson v Ramsey Food Processing Pty Ltd* (2015) 256 CLR 507, [22]–[26].
27 *UBS AG v Tyne* (2018) 265 CLR 77, [38]–[40] cited with approval *Coshott v Official Trustee in Bankruptcy* [2019] FCA 401, [48]–[52].
28 *Telesto Investments Ltd v UBS AG* (2013) 94 ACSR 29.

which culminated in the High Court decision of *UBS AG v Tyne*.[29] The Tyne disputes involve complex conflict of law issues as well as the finality doctrines. Tyne, through his Jersey incorporated company Telesto, invested in bonds issued by the Kazakhstan financial institutions to the equivalent of AU$33,401,266.20 using funds borrowed from UBS allegedly on the recommendation of UBS.[30] The Global Financial Crisis in 2008 resulted in margin calls in excess of US$28,000,000 (because the Kazak bonds were essentially worthless) which Telesto defaulted on leading to a "standstill agreement", pausing the actions of UBS to recover the funds from Telesto in exchange for a letter of undertaking from a related Australian company.[31] Telesto planned to commence proceedings in New South Wales but, when it requested an address for service, UBS instead commenced Singapore proceedings. Tyne commenced the intended New South Wales proceedings and several interlocutory disputes followed, in which the parties sought to prevent each other from proceeding in their non-preferred jurisdiction. To avoid conflicting judgments, the New South Wales Court stayed its proceedings in favour of Singapore, but Telesto refused to appear in Singapore because it contested the Singapore Court's jurisdiction. Tyne then commenced proceedings in the Federal Court in relation to limited issues which he had removed, with consent, from the New South Wales proceedings during the stay dispute in relation to the Singapore proceedings because they were not relevant to the Singapore proceedings.

The Federal Court and, on eventual appeal, the High Court (reversing the Full Federal Court), held that Tyne should not have removed those matters from the New South Wales Supreme Court for later hearing and refused to hear the matters in the Federal Court. The High Court decision was decided by four judges against three in favour of UBS. The decision had the unfortunate effect that Tyne was effectively denied the opportunity to ever put his substantive case, as the only substantive hearing was in Singapore where Tyne did not make substantive submissions on his case, as he merely appeared to dispute the Singapore Court's jurisdiction.[32] Essentially, Tyne was outmanoeuvred by UBS in what was always very much strategic litigation on both sides. However, the decisions of the New South Wales Supreme Court, the Federal Court and the High Court not to hear Tyne's case in Australia did ensure that there was no possibility of a conflict between the Singapore proceeding and an Australian judgment. In this regard, the Australian courts complied with the finality doctrines of *res judicata,* issue estoppel and Anshun estoppel by ensuring that Tyne was unable to relitigate any of the matters determined by the Singapore courts.

Subsequent to the High Court's decision, in 2019, the Federal Court of Australia took one step further when Tyne attempted to proceed with an action commenced in 2017 on behalf of his bankrupt wife, Clare Marks, in relation to the dispute. In *Tyne (Trustee of the Argot*

29 *UBS AG v Tyne* (2018) 265 CLR 77. In *Telesto Investments Ltd v UBS AG* (2013) 94 ACSR 29, Sachar J discussed all four doctrines: *res judicata,* issue estoppel, Anshun estoppel and abuse of process in considerable detail. See also *UBS AG v Tyne* (2018) 265 CLR 77.

30 *Telesto Investments Ltd v UBS AG* (2013) 94 ACSR 29, [14].

31 A margin call is made when the amount of a debt secured against an asset is higher than the value of the asset because the asset has devalued. The borrower is called upon to pay the difference between the value of the loan and the value of the asset — the margin — so that the lender is not exposed should it need to sell the underlying asset to recover its loan. A standstill agreement is an agreement between parties to pause their obligations under a contract for a period of time, often to enable negotiations to occur.

32 *Telesto Investments Ltd v UBS AG* (2013) 94 ACSR 29, [50], [55], [67].

Trust) v UBS AG[33], the Federal Court permanently stayed the proceeding and effectively declared Tyne a vexatious litigant in relation to his dispute against UBS in relation to the Kazakhstan bonds and preventing any further Federal Court litigation in relation to the matter, declaring:

> [2]. Pursuant to section 37AO of the *Federal Court of Australia Act 1976* (Cth), Mr Scott Francis Tyne, either in his capacity as trustee of the Argot Trust, or individually, be prohibited from instituting any further proceedings against UBS AG arising from or relating to the same substratum of facts as:
> (a) This proceeding;
> (b) NSW Supreme Court Proceeding 2010/363808; or
> (c) Proceeding QUD10/2014 in the Federal Court.[34]

Tyne (trustee of the Argot Trust) v UBS AG discussed both abuse of process and Anshun estoppel at length, finding there had been abuse of process in bringing the proceedings as the issues should have been raised in earlier proceedings. The Federal Court's analysis reinforced the High Court's inclusion of the obligations of case management and limited court resources as relevant factors in abuse of process and also cited extensively from the High Court decision in *Tomlinson v Ramsey Food Processing Pty Ltd*,[35] noting the reliance of both the doctrines of estoppel and abuse of process on considerations of "finality and fairness."[36]

Res judicata and estoppel were also recently addressed by the High Court in the international family law dispute of *Clayton v Bant*.[37] *Clayton v Bant* concerned whether an Australian citizen residing with her child in Australia, who had divorced her husband, a citizen of the United Arab Emirates (UAE), could continue her proceedings in the Australian Family Court seeking parenting orders, property settlement and spousal maintenance.[38] The husband, Mr Bant, sought to prevent the continuation of the Australian proceedings on the basis of *res judicata* and Anshun estoppel, due to proceedings he had successfully run in Dubai against his Ms Clayton, his wife, under the Personal Status Law of the UAE granting him an irrevocable fault-based divorce.[39] The High Court unanimously upheld Ms Clayton's appeal, thus allowing her to continue her proceedings on the following bases:[40]

1. Strict *res judicata* could not apply because the wife's rights in the Australian proceedings were statutory rights under ss 74 and 79 of the *Family Law Act 1975*

33 *Tyne (Trustee of the Argot Trust) v UBS AG* [2019] FCA 628.
34 Ibid [2] (Logan J).
35 *Tomlinson v Ramsey Food Processing Pty Ltd* (2015) 256 CLR 507, [22]–[26] cited in *Coshott v Official Trustee in Bankruptcy* [2019] FCA 401, [48]–[52] in turn cited in *Tyne (Trustee of the Argot Trust) v UBS AG* [2019] FCA 628, [16].
36 *Tomlinson v Ramsey Food Processing Pty Ltd* (2015) 256 CLR 507, [24].
37 *Clayton v Bant* (2020) 385 ALR 41.
38 Ibid [6].
39 Australian family law has a no-fault-based system of divorce and, where children are involved, property and maintenance claims focus significantly on the best interests of the children.
40 The High Court handed down three separate judgments: a joint judgment by Kiefel CJ, Bell and Gageler JJ: *Clayton v Bant* (2020) 385 ALR 41, [1]-[44] and separate judgments [45–60] (Gordon J), [60]-[86] (Edelman J). The judges unanimously agreed that *res judicata* and estoppel did not apply and that the appeal must be set aside.

(Cth) and the Dubai court had no jurisdiction to make orders under that Act or to extinguish Ms Clayton's rights under the Act.[41]

2. Cause of action estoppel (more aptly described as "claim estoppel")[42] and Anshun estoppel also could not apply because Mr Bant (who had the onus of proof given he was seeking the stay of proceedings) did not prove that the rights asserted by Ms Clayton in the Australian proceedings corresponded to the rights she could have sought in the Dubai proceedings had she appeared in them, nor that her decision not to make such claims in Dubai was unreasonable.[43]
3. The Court acknowledged that: "Founded on the twin policies of ensuring finality in litigation (thereby promoting respect for and efficient use of courts as well as avoiding inconsistent judgments) and of ensuring fairness to litigants (by sparing them the stress and expense of duplicative proceedings, the focus of the common law doctrine of estoppel is on 'substance rather than form'. The doctrine looks not for absolute identity between the sources and incidents of rights asserted or capable of being asserted in consecutive proceedings."[44] However, the Court found that there was not substantial correspondence between the wife's potential rights in Dubai and Australia.[45]

Clayton v Bant confirms that the Australian interpretation of *res judicata* is narrower than some other jurisdictions.[46] The case also demonstrates the potential for rules of procedure to result in substantive injustice, depending on their interpretation. The Full Family Court's decision, if not overruled, would have prevented an Australian citizen and, potentially, her child from any entitlement to financial support from her very wealthy Emirates husband because of the less favourable family law in Dubai. The High Court is, understandably, keen to protect its jurisdiction and its ability to apply its own laws while trying to balance these objectives with respect for foreign jurisdictions and the desire to minimise inconsistent decisions.

16.4.2 Finality is subject to appeals and variations

There are, however, important exceptions to the finality of judgment, including the potential to vary and set aside judgments and the right to appeal a judgment to a higher court.[47] Many judgments allow a limited right to appeal. Most judgments, however, are not appealed, and even judgments subject to appeal may be enforced while the appeal is occurring. In some cases, especially where the judgment requires a party to do something other than (or additional to) handing over money, a court may stay the enforcement of the judgment while the appeal is being heard. So, for example, a decision to allow a real estate development to

41 *Clayton v Bant* (2020) 385 ALR 41, [26].
42 Ibid [28].
43 Ibid [30]-[32].
44 Ibid [34].
45 Ibid [40].
46 Ibid [26].
47 *Construction Forestry Mining and Energy Union v Director of the Fair Work Building Industry Inspectorate* (2016) 153 ALD 399.

proceed would be likely to be stayed while an appeal was heard because the development could not be undone if the decision were reversed on appeal.[48] In limited circumstances, judgments may be varied or even set aside.[49]

16.4.3 Finality is subject to costs

Judges will often make orders regarding payment of costs. The most common costs order is for "costs in the cause". This means that the losing party has to pay the costs of the winning party and its own costs. However, the amount of costs payable is often a hotly disputed issue itself. It would not be fair for a losing party to be required to pay its opponent's costs where those costs were grossly inflated or unreasonable. The difficulty with determining who pays what legal costs has led to an industry of legal costs assessors and to trials and appeals on issues of legal costs. It is not uncommon for legal costs to exceed the amount in dispute.[50]

16.5 Setting aside and varying judgment

Judgment is not always final. Aside from the possibility of an appeal (discussed in detail below), there are also occasions where judgments are set aside or varied without a full appeal process. One of the most common circumstances in which a judgment will be set aside is where that judgment was a default judgment. Default judgments are routinely granted where defendants have failed to comply with their obligations to court. Such judgments are, however, fairly readily set aside to enable all parties to obtain a fair hearing.[51]

It is far less common for judgments or orders to be set aside when they follow a full hearing of a matter. In *Clone Pty Ltd v Players Pty Ltd (in liq)*, the High Court discussed the equitable power of a court to set aside its own perfected judgment[52] based on misconduct not amounting to fraud where the other party failed to exercise due diligence to discover that misconduct.[53] In allowing the appeal and restoring the set aside judgment, the High Court held:

> [1]. The essential questions in these appeals are whether the power of a court to set aside its perfected judgment extends to each of the following circumstances: (i) misconduct by the party who succeeded at trial which does not amount to fraud; and (ii) where the unsuccessful party failed to exercise reasonable diligence to discover the fraud or misconduct during the earlier proceedings.

48 See Chapters 16.6 and 16.7.

49 See Chapter 16.5.

50 See Chapter 6 for a discussion of costs.

51 A default judgment is a decision in favour of the plaintiff where the defendant has failed to defend the case satisfactorily. Often default judgments are obtained by plaintiffs where defendants have failed to appear or file a defence. Default judgments were discussed in Chapter 5.6.

52 *Clone Pty Ltd v Players Pty Ltd (in liq)* (2018) 264 CLR 165. A judgment is considered perfected once it has been entered; see Margaret Allars, 'Perfected Judgments and Inherently Angelical Administrative Decisions: The Powers of Courts and Administrators to Re-Open or Reconsider Their Decisions' (2001) 30 *Australian Institute of Administrative Law Forum* 1.

53 *Clone Pty Ltd v Players Pty Ltd* (2018) 264 CLR 165.

> [2]. The answers to each of these questions are as follows. First, the general power of a court to set aside its perfected judgment requires actual fraud, although there are other discrete grounds to set aside a perfected judgment which were not in issue in these appeals. Secondly, it is not a precondition to the exercise of the power that the party seeking to set aside the judgment exercised reasonable diligence to attempt to discover the fraud during the earlier proceedings.[54]

In the South Australian Supreme Court case of *Viscariello v Tamasauskas (No 3)*, the Court discussed the very limited circumstances in which a court may set aside its own completed judgment:

> [51]. There is some support in the authorities for a jurisdiction to interfere with orders, even after reasons have been published and orders announced (albeit not entered or perfected), outside of cases traditionally falling within the notion of a 'slip' rule (or involving orders not otherwise reflecting the intention of the Court), or involving fraud of the type contemplated by the High Court in *Clone Pty Ltd v Players Pty Ltd*. There is authority, for example, to the effect that a court may set aside its orders and reopen a matter where it is plain the Court has proceeded upon a fundamental misapprehension of the facts, has overlooked a significant matter, or has not given the parties an opportunity to be heard in respect of a significant matter. On the other hand, and in any event, there is also authority to the effect that even this relatively narrow jurisdiction to intervene may not extend to cases where the Court's orders have been entered or perfected.[55]

Variation of judgments is also uncommon. As the New South Wales Supreme Court of Appeal noted in *Penson v Titan National Pty Ltd (No 2)*:

> [14]. The relevant legal principles applicable on an application, such as this, to set aside or vary part or all of a judgment under UCPR r 36.16 are those discussed by Mason CJ in *Autodesk Inc v Dyason* (No 2) [1993] HCA 6; (1993) 176 CLR 300 at 302–303).
>
> [15]. The power to do so is to be exercised with great caution, having regard to the importance of the public interest in the finality of litigation. It is enlivened where a court has 'apparently proceeded according to some misapprehension of the facts or the relevant law' and where that misapprehension cannot be attributed solely to the neglect or default of the party seeking to set aside or vary the judgment (at 303).
>
> [16]. Importantly, for the present application, it is well recognised that the jurisdiction is not to be exercised for the purpose of re-agitating arguments already considered by the court or 'to provide a backdoor method by which unsuccessful litigants can seek to reargue their cases' (at 303. See also *Tobin v Ezekiel (No 2)* [2012] NSWCA 409 at [7]; *Burrell v The Queen* [2008] HCA 34; (2008) 238 CLR 218 at 223 [15]; and *Streetscape Projects (Australia) Pty Ltd v City of Sydney (No 2)* [2013] NSWCA 240).[56]

Judgments may, however, be varied, particularly at the agreement of both parties, where the terms of the original judgment are impossible or unduly onerous to comply with. Particularly where the winning party is a model litigant such as a government body, agreement may be reached

54 Ibid [1]-[2].
55 *Viscariello v Tamasauskas (No 3)* [2019] SASC 79, [51].
56 *Penson v Titan National Pty Ltd (No 2)* [2015] NSWCA 197, [14]–[16].

to vary a judgment which is proving onerous to the losing party.[57] The decision to vary or set aside judgments once again requires a balancing of efficiency and due process considerations.[58]

16.6 Appeals

While most court decisions are final, there are also, for most courts, statutory entitlements to appeal decisions in limited circumstances. Appeals are generally made to a higher court. This may be the "Full" or "Appeal" court of the original decision-making court. For example, an appeal from a single judge decision of the Supreme Court of Western Australia would be made to the Court of Appeal of the Supreme Court of Western Australia. The High Court is the final court of appeal in Australia. There has been no avenue for Australian cases to be appealed outside Australia to the United Kingdom Privy Council since the *Australia Act 1986* (Cth) and its United Kingdom equivalent. The limitations on appellate entitlement must balance the efficiency benefits of decisions being final against the due process benefits of ensuring there is oversight of lower courts and enabling the development of precedent through superior court consideration of the most challenging and vexed legal disputes.[59]

16.6.1 Circumstances of appeals

It is common for at least one party to be dissatisfied with the judgment it receives from court. This does not automatically indicate a basis for appeal. In most cases, there must be an appealable error of law in the judgment for an appeal to lie. Most commonly, appeals occur where the losing party considers the court erred at law in making its decision.

In some cases, all parties are unhappy, which may result in cross-appeals (where two or more parties appeal the same decision). For example, a personal injury case might lead to a judgment that the defendant was negligent and should pay compensation. The defendant might appeal on the basis that there was an error of law and it is not negligent. The plaintiff might then cross-appeal, arguing that the judgment on liability for negligence was correct but the compensation payment ordered was incorrect — being too low, due to an error by the original judge.

Some cases are almost certain to be appealed because they are seeking to overturn previous authority or are determining a new issue of law which will set a precedent, especially where significant amounts of money are at stake. For example, the case of *Aon Risk Services Australia Ltd v Australian National University* required an appeal to the High

57 A model litigant is a litigant who has extra obligations to provide assistance to an opposing party. Model litigants are usually government bodies which have significantly more power, legal knowledge and resources than most of their opponents, who are often unrepresented. The *Legal Services Direction 2017* (Cth) app B sets out the model litigant obligations of the Commonwealth and its agencies. For example, the Department of Home Affairs and the Australian Taxation Office are both required to be model litigants. The Department of Affairs routinely prepares appeal books in High Court and other court applications where it is acting as the respondent to reduce the obligations on the appellant, who is often an unrepresented litigant, for preparing such documents. This assists both the appellant and the court.

58 See Chapter 2.3.1.

59 See Chapter 2.3.1.

Court in order to overturn the case management precedent set earlier by the High Court in *Queensland v JL Holdings*.[60]

There are numerous steps which a party contemplating appeal should take prior to commencing appeal, including:

1. Identify the errors the party considers the primary judge made in the original decision.[61]
2. Consider whether the errors are appealable:
   a) Errors of law are generally appealable but errors of fact generally are not if the decision being appealed is a court decision.[62]
   b) If a primary judge made an incorrect statement of law, this is clearly appealable, however, such errors are relatively uncommon (particularly in cases where parties are represented) because the lawyers acting for the parties should have correctly set out the law for the judge and judicial standards in Australia are very high.
   c) An incorrect application of the law to the facts is appealable.
   d) A novel application of existing law to facts will be appealable.
   e) The acceptance of one witness's testimony over that of another is generally not appealable unless it can be clearly demonstrated that the judge suffered from improper bias or made an impossible finding.
   f) If the primary judge was required to exercise discretion and did so in a way which was open to him or her, this is not usually appealable.[63]
3. Consider the prospects of success. How likely is it that an appeal court will find differently to the primary judge? The more obvious the alleged error, the more likely there will be a different outcome.
4. Consider the financial, time and emotional costs of further litigation and the potential for ADR during the course of any appellate process. Cases do settle during the course of appellate process such as the enormous Bell litigation which ran for decades including ongoing cost disputes but where the substantive claim was settled during the appeal process prior to the High Court appeal hearing.[64]

While trial hearings are usually heard before a single judge, appeals are often heard by multiple judges, generally an uneven number to ensure there is a majority decision. The most common number for an appeal bench is three, but sometimes appeal benches may contain five or even seven (for the full bench of the High Court). It is less common for an

60 *Aon Risk Services Australia Ltd v Australian National University* (2009) 239 CLR 175; *Queensland v JL Holdings Pty Ltd* (1997) 189 CLR 146. See Chapter 2.4 for discussion of both cases.

61 In appellate cases, the judge who gave the original judgment in the trial proceedings is commonly referred to as the "primary judge" or the "trial judge".

62 See Chapter 16.6.4.

63 *House v The Queen* (1936) 55 CLR 499. *House v The Queen* has been cited extensively and subjected to considerable clarification, including other High Court decisions such as *Minister for Immigration and Border Protection v SZVFW* (2018) 264 CLR 541, [38]-[50] (Gageler J); see also Chapter 2.4.4.

64 See, eg, *Westpac Banking Corporation v Bell Group Ltd (in liq) (No 3)* (2012) 44 WAR 1; *Westpac Banking Corporation v Bell Group Ltd* [2013] HCATrans 85; *Bell Group NV (in liq) v Western Australia* [2016] HCATrans 11.

appeal bench to contain an even number of judges, because this increases the possibility of an even split in the decision making. Where there is an even number on the bench and they split evenly, tie-breaker provisions may apply (eg the decision may go the way the Chief Justice decides).

Appeals are very different to trials. There are limitations on the circumstances in which an appeal can be brought, the scope of what the appeal court will consider, and the materials which may be put before the appeal court to assist its deliberations. Appeal courts do not usually see fresh evidence. Appeals are, therefore, much shorter, on average, than trials.

Appeals should not be commenced inappropriately and can be dismissed for lacking merit. For example, *Gunnarsson-Wiener v Iles* was a Tasmanian Supreme Court appeal from a decision of a single judge regarding a claim of apprehended judicial bias by a magistrate.[65] The magistrate had laughed in response to Sven Olaf Gunnarsson-Wiener, a self-represented litigant, responding to the question as to whether he had children with: "Not that I know of, no".[66] This led Mr Gunnarsson-Wiener to conclude that the magistrate was biased against him in relation to the underlying case involving instructions under the *Animal Welfare Act 1993* (Tas) regarding his care of eight goats. The Full Court of the Tasmanian Supreme Court held that:

> [28]. It is also significant that the notice of appeal contains scandalous material. There is an unfounded allegation of actual bias on the part of Wood J, and of an attempt by her to exonerate a legal practitioner of any wrongdoing. Ms Brooks' alleged laughter is described as 'symptomatic of a state public service gone mad'. There is an implicit suggestion that the learned magistrate committed a criminal offence, the details of which are unclear. There is speculation that the learned magistrate might cease to hold office as a result of a private prosecution. There is the unfounded allegation that somebody tampered with the audio recording from the Magistrates Court. There is an allegation that the stifling of the appellant's political communication seemed to have been an underlying motive of the Department of Primary Industries, Parks, Water and Environment. That scandalous material alone warrants the striking out of the notice of appeal. It provides a second reason for the appeal to be dismissed.
>
> [29]. I need not reach a conclusion as to whether the appeal is vexatious, but I observe that the connection between the appellant's contentions and the primary dispute about the quality of his care for his goats in 2017 is tenuous at best. This appeal is a totally unmeritorious piece of 'satellite litigation' that should never have been instituted.
>
> [30]. For these reasons, I would strike out the notice of appeal and dismiss the appeal.[67]

16.6.2 Rules governing appeals

The court rules and legislation for each state and territory detail which court is appropriate for appeals.[68] Often, the Supreme Court is the correct court of appeal from lower court judgments. Supreme Court decisions are usually appealable to the Appeal Court of the

65 *Gunnarsson-Weiner v Iles* [2020] TASFC 1.
66 Ibid [1] (Blow CJ, Brett J and Geason J).
67 Ibid [28]–[30].
68 See Chapter 16.2.

Supreme Court. Federal Court decisions are generally appealable to the Full Federal Court. Decisions of these appeal courts may be further appealed to the High Court (after obtaining special leave from the High Court to appeal).

There are specific rules for drafting appeals in the rules of each appellate jurisdiction. In some respects, commencing an appeal is like commencing a new proceeding. The appealing party must file originating process in the relevant court of appeal. Often, appeals are commenced by filing a notice of appeal.

16.6.3 Obtaining leave to appeal

There are many circumstances where parties may be required to obtain the court's leave to appeal before they can appeal, usually by filing an application for leave to appeal. In some courts, where leave to appeal is required, the application for leave will be heard together with the appeal itself. If it is likely leave will be granted, then it is efficient for the application for leave to be heard with the appeal itself. If, however, there is a high likelihood leave will not be granted, it is more efficient for the application to be heard separately.

In the High Court, applications for leave to appeal (called "special leave applications") are always heard separately. Only if the High Court grants special leave to appeal, does the appealing party commence appeal proceedings. Most High Court applications for leave are rejected and, as such, the Court spends much of its hearing time listening to applications. This is despite the strict 20-minute time limit on High Court special leave applications. A significant percentage of rejected applications are for migration cases brought by self-represented litigants who have no proper basis at law for their claims.

In the recent Full Federal Court Decision of *Federal Commissioner of Taxation v Israel Discount Bank Ltd*,[69] Lee J (with Perram and Gleeson JJ agreeing) denied the Commissioner of Taxation (a non-party to the dispute) the right to appeal an interlocutory decision requiring the Commissioner to produce a redacted document. By the time of the Court's decision, the evidence had all been heard anyway, making it highly unlikely the Commissioner's document would ever be viewed by the Bank originally seeking it. Justice Lee helpfully reiterated his description from an earlier decision of the circumstances in which a court will grant leave to appeal as follows:

> [12]. The applicable principles attendant on an application for leave to appeal are well known and were not in dispute. I summarised them in *Nationwide News Pty Limited v Rush* [2018] FCAFC 70 at [2]–[4] (in terms with which Allsop CJ and Rares J generally agreed) as follows:
>
>> The principles informing the determination of whether to grant leave to appeal from a decision of a single judge of this Court are not novel. The starting point is that in exercising the power to grant leave, regard must be had to the statutory charge in s 3M(3) of the *Federal Court of Australia Act 1976* (Cth) … that the power must be exercised or carried out in the way that best promotes the overarching purpose, being the just resolution of disputes according to law and as quickly, inexpensively and efficiently as possible.
>>
>> Consistently with the facilitation of a just resolution, an applicant must usually show that: (a) in all the circumstances, the decision to be appealed

69 *Federal Commissioner of Taxation v Israel Discount Bank* (2020) 276 FCR 669.

> is attended with sufficient doubt to warrant its reconsideration on appeal; and (b) supposing the decision to be wrong, substantial injustice would result if leave were refused: *Decor Corporation Pty Ltd v Dart Industries Inc* [1991] FCAFC 844; (1991) 33 FCR 397 at 398–399 (Sheppard, Burchett and Heerey JJ). The sufficiency of the doubt in respect of the decision to be appealed and the question of substantial injustice bear upon each other so that the degree of doubt which is sufficient in one case may be different from that required in another. It has also been said that the considerations are cumulative such that leave ought not be granted unless each limb is made out: *Rawson Finances Pty Ltd v Deputy Commissioner of Taxation* [2010] FCAFC 139; (2010) 81 ATR 36 at 38 [5] (Ryan, Stone and Jagot JJ); *Melbourne City Investments Pty Ltd v Treasury Wine Estates Ltd* [2017] FCAFC 98; (2017) 252 FCR 1 at 4 [3] (Jagot, Yates and Murphy JJ).
>
> Additionally, consistent with the facilitation of a quick, inexpensive and efficient resolution is the principle which emerges from the oft-cited warning of Jordan CJ in *In re the Will of F. B. Gilbert (Deceased)* [1946] NSWStRp 24; (1946) 46 SR (NSW) 318 at 323, that if a tight rein is not kept upon the interference with orders of judges at first instance in the exercise of discretion on a point of practice and procedure, the result will be "disastrous to the proper administration of justice".[70]

Leave to appeal is likely to be refused where the underlying appeal has negligible prospects of success.

16.6.4 Errors of law

Appeals are most commonly limited to errors of law by virtue of the underlying statutory right which entitles the party to appeal. For example, s 148 of the *Civil and Administrative Tribunal Act 1998* (Vic), which confines the appellate jurisdiction of the Court to questions of law, was discussed by French CJ, Gummow J and Bell J in the High Court case of *Osland v Secretary, Department of Justice (No 2)*.[71] Some legislation does not allow any appeal even for errors of law, such as the *Building and Construction Industry Security of Payment Act 1999* (NSW) and its interstate equivalent legislation.[72] In *Probuild Constructions (Australia) Pty Ltd v Shade Systems Pty Ltd*,[73] the High Court held that, not only was there no appeal right, but that the *Building and Construction Industry Security of Payment Act 1999* (NSW) excluded the supervisory jurisdiction of the Supreme Court to the extent that it was unable to quash a decision of an adjudicator under the Act even where the adjudication conveyed an error of law on its face. The purpose of the Act is to create a legislative mechanism to

70 Ibid [12]. See also *Ashby v Slipper* (2016) 241 FCR 55, [35]-[73] for a detailed analysis of when leave to appeal is required and the considerations for granting such leave to appeal.

71 *Osland v Secretary, Department of Justice (No 2)* (2010) 241 CLR 320, [19].

72 *Building and Construction Industry Security of Payment Act 2002* (Vic); *Building and Construction Industry Payments Act 2004* (Qld); *Building and Construction Industry (Security of Payment) Act 2009* (ACT); *Building and Construction Industry Security of Payment Act 2009* (SA); *Building and Construction Industry Security of Payment Act 2009* (Tas).

73 *Probuild Constructions (Australia) Pty Ltd v Shade Systems Pty Ltd* (2018) 264 CLR 1.

require builders and building sub-contractors to be paid for work in progress to ensure that such payments were not withheld. Kiefel CJ and Bell, Keane, Nettle and Gordon JJ held that:

> [43]. Fifth, consistent with the objective of providing a 'speedy and effective means of ensuring cash flow to builders from the parties with whom they contract', there are other aspects of the scheme which reinforce the conclusion that an adjudicator's determination is not subject to judicial review for non-jurisdictional error of law. There is no right of appeal from the determination of an adjudicator under the *Security of Payment Act*. And that omission was deliberate. Next, the *Security of Payment Act* provides that an adjudication certificate may be filed by the claimant as a judgment for a debt in a court of competent jurisdiction. If the respondent commences proceedings to have the judgment set aside, the respondent is not entitled to bring any cross-claim against the claimant, to raise any defence in relation to matters arising under the construction contract or to challenge the adjudicator's determination. In addition, the respondent must pay into court as security the unpaid portion of the adjudicated amount pending the final determination of those proceedings.
>
> [44]. Having regard to the above matters, it is right to say that the *Security of Payment Act* creates an entitlement that is 'determined informally, summarily and quickly, and then summarily enforced without prejudice to the common law rights of both parties which can be determined in the normal manner'.[74]

Determining what constitutes an error of law can be a difficult matter for an appellate court. The dividing line between issues of fact and law is not a clear one and lawyers will go to significant effort to characterise errors as legal where this is the only acceptable avenue for appeal. The unanimous High Court decision of *Comptroller-General of Customs v Pharm-A-Care Laboratories Pty Ltd*[75] demonstrates the potential complexity in distinguishing between issues of fact and law. The High Court was required to assess which aspects of the tariff classification of vitamin preparations and garcinia preparations imported from Germany as not being "food supplements" were questions of fact and which of law. The High Court upheld the decision of the Full Federal Court which had, in turn, upheld the Administrative Appeals Tribunal's decision but was critical of both the Court and the Tribunal's reasoning. However, the High Court held that the only errors of law made by the Tribunal were immaterial to its decision.[76] The High Court held:

> [39]. The Tribunal was therefore wrong to construe Note 1(a) to Chapter 30 of Sch 3 to the *Tariff Act* as excluding the vitamin preparations and the garcinia preparations from the coverage of Chapter 30 only if they answered the relevant description of "[f]oods". The Full Court was also wrong to think that the Tribunal's conclusion that the vitamin preparations were not excluded from the coverage of Chapter 30 could be supported by the parenthetic reference to Section IV at the end of the Note on the basis that those goods were not classifiable under either of the headings within Section IV to which the Comptroller-General had argued that they were classifiable.

74 *Probuild Constructions (Australia) Pty Ltd v Shade Systems Pty Ltd* (2018) 264 CLR 1, [43]–[44].

75 *Comptroller-General of Customs v Pharm-A-Care Laboratories Pty Ltd* (2020) 375 ALR 98.

76 Ibid [65]-[66]. Unanimous decision of a five-judge bench comprising Kiefel CJ, Bell, Gageler, Keane and Gordon JJ.

> [40]. However, it does not follow that the Comptroller-General's appeal to the Federal Court from the decision of the Tribunal ought to have succeeded. That is because, for an error of law on the part of the Tribunal identified in an appeal on a question of law to the Federal Court to result in an order setting aside the decision of the Tribunal, the error must be shown to be material to the decision of the Tribunal in the sense that the decision which was in fact made by the Tribunal might have been different if the error of law had not occurred.
>
> ...
>
> [44]. Though there is no error of law merely in making a wrong finding of fact, there is no doubt that a finding of fact can be erroneous in law if the finding is reached through the application of a wrong legal test. There is also no doubt that the Tribunal would have applied a wrong legal test if the Tribunal had found that the preparations fell outside the description of 'food supplements' by asking how those goods would commonly be described. That error of law, if made, would have been elementary. Its making is not lightly to be inferred.[77]

16.6.5 Evidence in appellate process

The appeal process is significantly different to the trial process because appellate courts generally rely on the factual findings of the court below and purely consider the correctness of the legal issues raised by the appeal which are, commonly, a small subset of the issues raised in trial. Accordingly, appellate courts rely on trial judge findings in relation to evidence except in limited circumstances where the appeal is by way of rehearing or the relevant statute allows appeal. For example, in the Full Federal Court case of *Construction, Forestry, Maritime, Mining and Energy Union v One Key Workforce Pty Ltd*,[78] the Court agreed that, even where there was an unconstrained right to receive evidence on appeal, the discretion should be exercised with regard to the considerations which constrain such evidence at common law:

> Section 27 of the *Federal Court of Australia Act 1976* (Cth) provides that the Court may receive further evidence on appeal. In *Reece v Webber* [2011] FCAFC 33; (2011) 192 FCR 254 a Full Court of this Court (Jacobson, Flick and Reeves JJ) observed at [12] that the discretion conferred by s 27 is not constrained by any requirement that special grounds need be made out or that the further evidence need be 'fresh evidence'. Their Honours said that '[t]he discretion is unconstrained by the circumstances in which evidence could be admitted on appeal at common law'. At [13]-[14], after referring to the decision of Gaudron J in *CDJ v VAJ* (1998) 197 CLR 172 at [52], their Honours referred to other authorities which have subsequently considered the exercise of the discretion to admit further evidence on appeal. At [15] the Court concluded:
>
> > The result, it is considered, is that the discretion conferred by s 27 to adduce further evidence is thus unconfined by any express limitations. But the discretion is to be exercised in a statutory context where the appeal being entertained is an appeal by way of rehearing for the purpose of determining the rights of the parties in accordance with lasw. Although not constrained by common law principles, the considerations to which the common law

77 Ibid [39]-[40], [44]

78 *Construction, Forestry, Maritime, Mining and Energy Union v One Key Workforce Pty Ltd* [2020] FCAFC 27.

> had regard remain considerations relevant to the exercise of the discretion conferred by s 27. The exercise of the discretion conferred by s 27 may be informed by reference to these principles but is not to be constrained by them.[79]

Appeal judges will receive an appeal book which contains documents important to the trial and they may also be taken to a transcript of the trial court proceedings that records what was said by a witness. However, none of these documents will generally enable an appeal court to form an opinion as to the truthfulness of a witness. In relation to such matters, the appeal court must generally rely on the findings of the trial judge (or jury) and appellate courts can only question findings as to witness credibility in very limited circumstances.[80]

However, appellate courts still have obligations to carefully consider the evidence before the primary court and to undertake their own analysis of the law. The High Court case of *Lee v Lee*[81] concerned an insurance dispute as to who was the culpable driver in a motor vehicle accident — the injured person or his father. The High Court allowed the appeal by the injured passenger, finding the evidence did not support his having been the driver of the vehicle. Bell, Gageler, Nettle and Edelman JJ described the appellate court obligations as follows:

> [55]. A court of appeal is bound to conduct a 'real review' of the evidence given at first instance and of the judge's reasons for judgment to determine whether the trial judge has erred in fact or law. Appellate restraint with respect to interference with a trial judge's findings unless they are 'glaringly improbable' or 'contrary to compelling inferences' is as to factual findings which are likely to have been affected by impressions about the credibility and reliability of witnesses formed by the trial judge as a result of seeing and hearing them give their evidence. It includes findings of secondary facts which are based on a combination of these impressions and other inferences from primary facts. Thereafter, 'in general an appellate court is in as good a position as the trial judge to decide on the proper inference to be drawn from facts which are undisputed or which, having been disputed, are established by the findings of the trial judge'. Here, the trial judge's findings of primary fact were not disturbed. However, in material respects, the Court of Appeal found that the inferences that his Honour drew from those findings were wrong. Notably, the trial judge's finding that the driver was not wearing the seatbelt not only was contrary to each party's case but, if correct, on the Court of Appeal's analysis, would lead to the conclusion that there was no real prospect that the appellant was the driver. And the trial judge's acceptance of the RACQ's case, that the appellant had been pulled from the driver's seat to the passenger seat immediately behind in something less than 90 seconds, was, in the Court of Appeal's analysis, unlikely.
>
> [56]. Having rejected the essential planks of the trial judge's reasoning, it was not to the point for the Court of Appeal to formulate the question as which of the two hypotheses the trial judge considered to be the more probable. Nor was it to the point to consider whether the trial judge had been unduly influenced by the DNA evidence. It was an error for the Court of Appeal to dismiss the appeals in this 'very closely balanced' case on the footing that the trial judge's decision was neither glaringly

79 Ibid [50] (McKerracher, Farrell and Markovic JJ).

80 See, eg, *Pell v The Queen* (2020) 376 ALR 478, [37]-[38] in the context of criminal jury trials. See also *Rosenberg v Percival* (2001) 205 CLR 434, [37] in the civil dispute resolution context.

81 *Lee v Lee* (2019) 266 CLR 129.

> improbable nor contrary to compelling inferences. It was the duty of the Court of Appeal to decide for itself which of the two hypotheses was the more probable. It was the duty of the Court of Appeal to persist in its task of 'weighing [the] conflicting evidence and drawing its own inferences and conclusions', and, ultimately, to decide for itself which of the two hypotheses was the more probable. It did not. The appellant's second ground is made good.[82]

16.6.6 Rehearing and remissions

In some instances, an appeal court may be empowered to review the decision of the prior court using its original jurisdiction rather than acting as an appeal court. This may enable the court to reconsider evidentiary material, where an appeal court would simply accept the evidentiary findings of the primary judge. The basis upon which the appeal court is considering the prior decision depends on the law empowering the "appeal", which is generally a statutory basis. It is common for courts to be exercising original jurisdiction where the primary decision was that of a tribunal rather than another court.

For example, in *Osland v Secretary, Department of Justice (No 2)*, French CJ, Gummow and Bell JJ stated in relation to the *Civil and Administrative Tribunal Act 1998* (Vic):

> [18]. Section 148 confers 'judicial power to examine for legal error what has been done in an administrative tribunal'. Despite the description of proceedings under the section as an 'appeal', it confers original not appellate jurisdiction; the proceedings are 'in the nature of judicial review'.[83]

Sometimes an appeal will succeed but will not, itself, result in a determination of the dispute. For example, an appeal court may determine that the primary judge took an incorrect approach in calculating damages or failed to consider necessary evidence. In such cases, it is likely the appeal court will remit the case back to the primary court for that court to undertake correctly the actions it failed to carry out correctly in the original trial. This further increases the uncertainty, cost, time and stress associated with appeals, particularly if the rehearing is a complete retrial. It is, however, a necessary approach, as appeal courts are not usually set up to hear primary evidence or assess damages.

In *Nobarani v Mariconte*,[84] the High Court unanimously upheld Nobarani's appeal on a succession dispute and remitted the matter to the Equity Division of the Supreme Court of New South Wales for a new trial due to a denial of procedural fairness to the appellant in the original trial caused by lack of preparation time, because the trial judge changed the nature of the hearing shortly before the trial and denied a request for adjournment. The High Court concluded:

> [42]. The trial judge was correct that the appellant had been told the previous week, on 14 May 2015, to have all his evidence ready for the trial, and that the proceedings needed to be managed in a just, quick, and cheap manner. Speed and frugality are often closely associated. But they must be consistent with justice. The trial judge erred in his statement that the appellant had had sufficient time to prepare because the matter had,

82 Ibid [55]–[56]. Kiefel CJ delivered a separate judgment, agreeing with Bell, Gageler, Nettle and Edelman JJ.
83 *Osland v Secretary, Department of Justice (No 2)* (2010) 241 CLR 320, [18].
84 *Nobarani v Mariconte* (2018) 265 CLR 236.

for some time, been set down for trial. The trial judge did not appreciate, and was not informed, that the dates that had been set down were only to be used for the hearing of the caveat motion and that no directions had been made for the taking of any steps, or filing or service of any documents by the appellant, save for the misconceived indication on 30 March 2015 for a defence, which, under Pt 78 r 42, would have related to an informal testamentary document.

[43]. As Simpson JA correctly observed in the Court of Appeal, it is apparent that the appellant had little appreciation of the appropriate court procedure or rules of evidence and his command of English was not strong. In these circumstances, it is unsurprising that the appellant's case was vague and disordered when he had only three clear business days to: (i) consider the statement of claim in a proceeding to which he had not been joined; (ii) prepare and serve a defence; (iii) issue any subpoenas, with an abbreviated return date before trial; (iv) locate any supplementary witnesses and obtain supplementary evidence from those upon whom he wished to rely; and (v) secure those witnesses for trial.[85]

Nobarani v Mariconte demonstrates two of the key balancing themes in civil dispute resolution (CDR). The High Court's acknowledgment of the litigant's vulnerability and their consequent exercise of discretion to remit the matter for rehearing demonstrates how litigant certainty must give way to judicial flexibility where failing to do so would cause injustice.[86] The vulnerability of the litigant required additional time to enable due process, even though this came at a cost to efficiency, such that the lower court's failure to allow such time caused injustice.[87]

16.7 Enforcement

Unfortunately, receiving judgment — and even appellate judgment — does not always finish a dispute. In addition to the possibility of an appeal, and disputes regarding recovery of legal costs,[88] difficulties arise where the losing party fails to comply with the orders made in the judgment received. Enforcement procedures are particularly important in lower-level courts and decisions involving individuals, especially self-represented individuals, where failure in compliance with court judgments is common. In these cases, the successful party may need to return to court to obtain assistance with enforcing the court's order. Enforcement is a key part of the justice process. As Keane, Nettle and Gordon JJ stated, in the High Court decision of *Australian Building and Construction Commissioner v Construction, Forestry, Mining and Energy Union*:

[131]. There is no point in a court making orders that cannot be enforced, and, if orders do go unenforced, the lack of enforcement is likely to detract from the prestige of the court and, ultimately, the efficacy of its processes.[89]

85 Ibid [42]–[43] (Kiefel CJ, Gageler, Nettle, Gordon and Edelman JJ).

86 See Chapter 2.3.2. for the balancing of certainty and flexibility and Chapter 3.2 regarding access to justice.

87 See Chapter 2.3.1. for the balancing of efficiency and due process.

88 See Chapter 6.

89 *Australian Building and Construction Commissioner v Construction, Forestry, Mining and Energy Union* (2018) 262 CLR 157, [131] (with Kiefel CJ agreeing in a separate judgment and Gageler J dissenting).

Enforcement is also particularly problematic in international disputes where the assets held by the losing party may be in a different jurisdiction to the court awarding judgment.

16.7.1 Significance of enforcement

Enforceability of court judgments is arguably their most critical feature. Just as the existence of litigation provides an incentive for parties to engage meaningfully in ADR, the enforceability of judgments and ADR settlement deeds provides crucial motivation for respecting court orders. Whilst many disputants, particularly corporate parties, are highly likely to meet their court ordered obligations without enforcement procedures, the ability of courts, acting with bailiffs, sheriffs and police to enforce judgments ensures that justice is carried out in practice.

ADR agreements can also be enforced through courts. This is most easily achieved where the dispute resolution is reflected in an executed deed of settlement. Where litigation has been commenced prior to settlement, parties will ordinarily hand up their settlement deed to the court and this will be incorporated into the court's orders, discontinuing the court proceedings which are enforceable orders.[90] Where there are no court proceedings on foot, parties can commence proceedings expressly seeking enforcement of the settlement deed where a party is failing to comply with their obligations under the deed.

16.7.2 Methods of and processes of enforcement

Where losing parties comply with the orders of the court voluntarily, no further steps are required to enforce the court's judgment once it has been handed down. There are, however, exceptions to voluntary compliance and courts have processes to ensure parties in comply with their orders, including, in some instances, criminal sanctions.

The majority of judgments simply require the transfer of money from one party to another. There are also, however, judgments which require parties to undertake actions other than paying money, such as orders to specifically perform a contract, orders to remove, or cease causing, a nuisance, orders to vacate property, and orders to transfer possession of property. Such non-monetary judgments can be more difficult to enforce.

Enforcement usually involves garnisheeing of bank accounts (where available) or warrants or orders for seizure or sale of property which are executed by bailiffs or sheriffs. Essentially, the bailiff or sheriff visits the residence of the judgment debtor and removes sufficient of that debtor's property to repay the debt. Some states have specific legislation governing the enforcement of judgments, such as the *Enforcement of Judgments Act 1991* (SA) and the *Civil Judgments Enforcement Act 2004* (WA). Other states have provisions for enforcement within their civil procedure legislation; for example, s 102 in the *Civil Procedure Act 2005* (NSW); r 66 of the *Supreme Court (General Civil Procedure) Rules 2015* (Vic); and r 66 of the *Supreme Court Rules 1987* (NT). The law of the state of enforcement can be used to enforce federal judgments pursuant to s 53 of the *Federal Court of Australia Act 1976* (Cth).

Where judgment is for a monetary sum (which is the majority of civil litigation cases), methods of enforcement may be available which attach to a future income stream rather than

90 Enforcement becomes more complex in relation to representative actions (class actions) with large numbers of plaintiffs and, sometimes, multiple disputes, but the principles of enforcing settlement deeds can remain critical to such dispute: *Laszczuk v Bendigo and Adelaide Bank Ltd* (2020) 61 VR 1. See also *Dyczynski v Gibson* (2020) 381 ALR 1, [387]–[404].

to existing assets. These enforcement methods are particularly popular with government authorities, such as the Australian Taxation Office, which do not have an urgent need to obtain the entire judgment amount. The most common of these debt payment mechanisms is a garnishee on wages, whereby a certain amount is removed from an employee's wages by his or her employer before payment and paid directly by the employer to the judgment debtor. Wage garnishees are common for court orders requiring ongoing payments, such as family maintenance payments.

The enforcement of judgments need not necessarily be carried out by the same court which awarded the judgment. For example, the High Court will not usually concern itself with contested enforcement proceedings, but should remit these to a state or federal Court " ... lest the High Court be distracted from performance of its ultimate appellate role by what are quintessentially questions of practice and procedure".[91] It is even more important that enforcement can be undertaken by courts, other than the awarding court, for cases where relevant assets from which enforcement is sought are interstate or overseas. Within Australia, civil judgments are enforced upon registration, regardless of which Australian state or territory the decision emanated, from pursuant to s 105 of the *Service and Execution of Process Act 1992* (Cth). Accordingly, a judgment made in one Australian state is entitled to the same enforcement assistance in a different Australian state, provided it has been registered in the enforcing state. This means the nature of Australia's federation, which enables Australian states and territories to operate as different jurisdictions, does not limit the enforcement of domestic judgments.

16.7.3 Enforcing foreign judgments

Obtaining assistance in Australia with enforcing a judgment obtained in a foreign jurisdiction can be more challenging. If judgment is awarded in one country but the assets of the losing party are in another country, the winning party may seek assistance with enforcing the foreign judgment from the courts of the country where the assets are held.

Where the jurisdiction making the judgment is perceived to have a similar legal system to the Australian legal system, enforcement is more routine. This is logical, as courts are more comfortable enforcing foreign judgments which they perceive as most similar to the judgment they would have given had they heard the case.

Foreign judgments from similar jurisdictions are enforced pursuant to the *Foreign Judgments Act 1991* (Cth), which provides extremely limited circumstances by which a party to a decision may resist enforcement.[92] Foreign judgments from less similar jurisdictions fall outside the operation of the *Foreign Judgments Act 1991* (Cth) and must be enforced using

91 *Aristocrat Technologies Australia Pty Ltd v Allam* (2016) 149 ALD 232, [12]. Justice Gageler noted, [11], in relation to a special leave application costs order that the High Court had authority to remit to the Federal Court under s 44(1) and s 77M of the *Judiciary Act 1903* (Cth).

92 See, eg, *Firebird Global Master Fund II Ltd v Republic of Nauru* (2015) 258 CLR 31, where the Court considered the exception of sovereign immunity in relation to the enforcement in Australia of a decision by a Tokyo court against the Nauru Government. The Court also considered the scope of the public policy exception. The Court (French CJ and Kiefel J with Nettle and Gordon JJ agreeing) held that the foreign judgment was registerable in Australia because it concerned a commercial transaction which provided an exception to sovereign immunity. However, the judgment was unenforceable against the Nauru Government's bank accounts in Australia as these were not commercial bank accounts.

common law, which provides greater discretion to the court to refuse enforcement.[93] Common grounds for refusing enforcement include lack of jurisdiction for the court which made the judgment and public policy reasons.[94] It is even more difficult to enforce non-monetary foreign judgments, such as orders for specific performance than monetary awards.[95] In addition, an Australian judgment will not be enforceable overseas where there is any form of stay on the execution of the judgment in Australia. Thus, in the family dispute of *Talacko v Bennett*, Mr Talacko's Australian bankruptcy was held by the High Court to constitute a stay of enforcement in Australia which also prevented enforcement against Mr Talacko's property in the Czech Republic.[96]

16.8 Conclusion

As has been demonstrated throughout this book, CDR is complex and must remain so because of the tensions that exist between its competing objectives. This final chapter has shown that there can be significant, complex and time-consuming procedures ahead for litigants, even after completion of their court trial. The process of obtaining judgment, determining whether to appeal, enforcing judgments and sorting out outstanding issues, such as costs, are not always routine or efficient. Most litigants will continue to require the services of their lawyers for months or even years after completion of their trial. The issues facing litigants after trial engage strongly with key themes of CDR discussed in Chapter 2 and throughout this book, particularly the theme of balancing efficiency with due consideration. The need to avoid conflicting judgments, the need to ensure finality while preserving judicial ability to correct errors and observe procedural fairness result in complex rules governing appeals, finality and judgment.

Many of the procedures discussed in this final chapter appear to be the antithesis of the efficiency aims of CDR and confirm the place of litigation as the last resort in CDR. However, hopefully this chapter has also demonstrated that, even for the most protracted and hard-fought disputes, courts can and should continue to strive for an optimal balance between efficiency and due consideration and aim to reduce the financial and societal costs of CDR. The processes which occur post-trial are essential for a strong, functioning society. A final, binding and enforceable dispute resolution process with sufficient checks and balances to ensure fairness is essential to a well-functioning society.

The second part of this book[97] has focused predominantly on litigation as the last resort for resolving civil disputes. Whilst ADR should always be properly explored in the resolution of civil disputes, it is equally important that there be formal state-sanctioned enforceable means of dispute resolution to which members of society can turn when ADR fails. Although litigation should be considered a last resort for resolving civil disputes, its availability is also

93 See *Centrebet Pty Ltd v Baasland* [2013] NTSC 59, [157]-[163] which contains a discussion of the common law enforcement requirements. See also *Central Petroleum Ltd v Geoscience Resource Recovery LLC* [2018] 2 Qd R 371, [55]-[59].

94 See, eg, *Wong v Jani-King Franchising Inc* [2014] QCA 76 where lack of jurisdiction was successfully argued in an effort to prevent the enforcement in Australia of a USA (Texas) default judgment.

95 There are complex conflict of law issues underlying enforcement of foreign judgments which are outside the scope of this book.

96 *Talacko v Bennett* (2017) 260 CLR 124.

97 See Chapters 8 to 16.

the key motivation which drives the success of ADR. The effectiveness of how courts balance conflicting obligations of efficiency and due process is, inevitably, most tested by adversarial and hard-fought disputes, and these are often the disputes that engage heavily with post-trial procedures, such as appeals, enforcement proceedings and the finality doctrines. Thus, this chapter is a fitting finale for the book, as it demonstrates well the theory of conflicting imperatives which characterise CDR and the need for finely tuned balance to simultaneously optimise efficiency and fairness.

It is hoped that this book has demystified and justified much of the complexity in CDR. This book has aimed to demonstrated that every process of CDR, from the most informal negotiation to the most complex post-trial enforcement proceeding, is motivated by the need to balance one or more of the key competing imperatives of CDR. Whilst the need to balance efficiency with due process[98] is the most obvious and commonly occurring conflict, the need to balance certainty against flexibility,[99] privacy against openness,[100] and autonomy against control[101] are also all key balancing acts which arise in multiple areas of CDR and which add to the necessary complexity of the legal system Australia has developed to resolve civil disputes.

In conclusion, applying the four key themes to CDR results in four important benefits. First, the thematic approach demonstrates that there are few, or no, procedures or rules anywhere in CDR that are pointless or random. When the lens of balancing competing objectives is applied, even the most complex processes make logical sense and their complexity is invariably justified. Second, the analysis of competing themes provides a justification for stakeholders, including disputants, lawyers, judges, arbitrators, mediators, negotiators and legislators, against criticism that Australian dispute resolution is poorly designed or executed. The complex balancing acts required of all stakeholders in navigating the resolution of civil disputes demonstrate that its imperfections are, mostly, a result of the intractable conflicts between competing imperatives, rather than due to failures of key stake holders. This is important because CDR is regularly criticised as inefficient, unfair, costly, time consuming and so it is important to understand the limitations inherent in the system.

However, the fact that many difficulties in CDR are intractable, does not mean that there is no scope for improvement, which is where the third and fourth benefits of the thematic balancing analysis arise. The third benefit of approaching CDR through the balancing themes is that it provides a new means for disputants to assess different means of CDR and to make decisions as to appropriate processes within chosen methods of dispute resolution. Understanding the reasons for complexity in CDR may enable better decision-making and, thereby, more optimal dispute resolution.

The fourth and final benefit of the balancing theme analysis is that it creates a framework for optimal law reform. Recognising the inherent limitations in the system caused by conflicting imperatives, such as efficiency and due process, is critical to ensuring that we continue to work, as a society, towards optimising the processes available. It is more possible to achieve effective reform when the aims of such reform are realistic rather than idealistic. Therefore, balancing themes and theories in CDR can lead to an optimal CDR system.

---

98 See Chapter 2.3.1.
99 See Chapter 2.3.2.
100 See Chapter 2.3.3.
101 See Chapter 2.3.4.

INDEX